THE US INTELLIGENCE COMMUNITY

SIXTH EDITION

THE US INTELLIGENCE COMMUNITY

JEFFREY T. RICHELSON

WESTVIEW PRESS

A Member of the Perseus Books Group

Westview Press was founded in 1975 in Boulder, Colorado, by notable publisher and intellectual Fred Praeger. Westview Press continues to publish scholarly titles and high-quality undergraduate- and graduate-level textbooks in core social science disciplines. With books developed, written, and edited with the needs of serious nonfiction readers, professors, and students in mind, Westview Press honors its long history of publishing books that matter.

Find us on the World Wide Web at www.westviewpress.com.

Every effort has been made to secure required permissions for all text, images, maps, and other art reprinted in this volume.

Westview Press books are available at special discounts for bulk purchases in the United States by corporations, institutions, and other organizations. For more information, please contact the Special Markets Department at the Perseus Books Group, 2300 Chestnut Street, Suite 200, Philadelphia, PA 19103, or call (800) 810-4145, ext. 5000, or e-mail special.markets@perseusbooks.com.

Library of Congress Cataloging-in-Publication Data
Richelson, Jeffrey.
    The U.S. intelligence community / Jeffrey T. Richelson.—6th ed.
        p. cm.
    Includes bibliographical references and index.
    ISBN 978-0-8133-4511-6 (pbk. : alk. paper)—ISBN 978-0-8133-4512-3 (e-book)
1. Intelligence service--United States. I. Title.

JK468.I6R53 2012
327.1273—dc22
                                                                2011016559

10 9 8 7 6 5 4 3 2 1

CONTENTS

TABLES, FIGURES, AND PHOTOS

TABLES

FIGURES

PHOTOS

PREFACE

As with previous editions of this book, I attempt to accomplish in one volume what could be better accomplished in several. I attempt to provide a comprehensive and detailed overview of the U.S. Intelligence Community—a description of its collection and analysis organizations, the activities of those organizations, and the management structure for directing and supervising those organization and activities.

Given the purpose of the book, I do not generally seek to evaluate the community's effectiveness in performing its varied tasks nor do I comment on the acceptability, wisdom, or morality of its activities. In the concluding chapter I examine the very concept of the Intelligence Community, changes in targets and technologies that influence how the community operates, and the extent of intelligence activities outside the Intelligence Community. All have implications of how the community is managed.

The information in this book comes from a variety of sources: interviews; official documents (many of which were obtained under the Freedom of Information Act); books written by former intelligence officers, journalists, and academics; websites; trade and technical publications; and newspapers and magazines. The public literature on intelligence is vast and I have done my best to sort the wheat from the chaff. I have also sought to incorporate the most recent information available at each stage of the production process to minimize the inevitable discrepancies between the situation described and the situation at the time of publication. In addition, I have identified sources to the maximum extent possible, while protecting the identities of those individuals who wish to remain anonymous.

A number of institutions and individuals were instrumental in providing material for this book. There are the Freedom of Information and public affairs officers who responded to my requests. In addition, a number of websites and e-newsletters have made it easy to obtain a large number of valuable documents—specifically, Steve Aftergood's *Secrecy News* as well as the Cryptome and Public Intelligence websites. Individuals who have provided assistance include Matthew Aid, Robert Windrem, and Ted Molczan. I would also like to thank my research assistants at the National Security Archive—Roger Strother, Patrick Hanlon, and Dan Jenkins—for their work in tracking down documents.

Finally, thanks are due to Anthony Wahl, Michelle Welsh-Horst, Christine Arden, and others at Westview who turned my manuscript into a book.

INTELLIGENCE

The United States government includes a substantial number of officials—individuals who make policy as well as those who implement it—who require foreign or domestic security intelligence to perform their duties. Only if those individuals are sufficiently informed about the state of the world and the likely consequences of various policies and actions can they be expected to make sound decisions.

The individuals and institutions with the most prominent need for foreign and domestic security intelligence are those concerned with making and implementing national security policy. Hence, the President and his national security advisor, the vice president, the National Security Council (NSC) and its staff, the Departments of State, Defense, Homeland Security, and Treasury, the Attorney General, the Joint Chiefs of Staff (JCS), the military services, and the generals and admirals who head the nation's unified commands are the most obvious consumers of foreign and domestic security intelligence.

Today, those individuals and institutions have a multitude of concerns, including the capabilities, activities, financing, and plans of al-Qaeda and other terrorist groups, political and military developments in Afghanistan and Iraq, the status of the Iranian and North Korean nuclear and missile programs, and the domestic situations in Iran, Russia, and China, as well as those nations' foreign and military policies. In addition, they have a multitude of concerns involving India, Pakistan, the Middle East, and Latin America.

The attacks of September 11, 2001, and the continued designs of al-Qaeda, the failure of U.S. forces to find stockpiles of weapons of mass destruction in Iraq after the 2003 invasion and the insurgency that followed, the difficulties involved in trying to halt the North Korean and Iranian nuclear weapons programs, and Iranian, North Korean, and other missile launches all illustrate the potential value of good intelligence to U.S. officials as well as the consequences of poor intelligence.

In addition, there are other policymakers who have a need for intelligence—even if they are dealing with concerns that are less pressing. Those who have responsibilities in the areas of international economics, trade and technology transfer, energy, the environment, and public health may require foreign intelligence. The security of foreign energy resources as well as the stability of the dollar can be influenced by the actions of foreign governments and groups. The Environmental Protection Agency (EPA) requires intelligence on environmental accidents, foreign government compliance with international environmental obligations, and the status of environmentally sensitive areas. With respect to compliance, the EPA is interested in the disposal of nuclear wastes, illegal ocean dumping, and the smuggling of prohibited animals and animal products.[1]

The National Aeronautics and Space Administration (NASA) is interested in foreign technology developments and foreign space programs and is also concerned with space debris that might threaten its manned and unmanned spacecraft. The Department of Agriculture has been concerned with foreign government compliance with negotiated agricultural agreements, the development of global trading blocks, agricultural production and supply, and the food requirements of countries with chronic food deficits.[2]

INTELLIGENCE

Foreign intelligence can be defined as the "product resulting from the collection, processing, integration, analysis, evaluation and interpretation of available information concerning foreign [entities]"—entities that may include foreign governments, groups (including terrorist organizations), or areas.[3] Domestic security intelligence can be similarly defined, substituting "domestic security threats" for "foreign entities." Collection can be defined as the purposeful acquisition of any information that might be desired by an analyst, consumer, or operator. Collection activity can take any of several overlapping forms: open source collection, clandestine collection, human source collection and interrogation, and technical collection.

Open source collection includes the acquisition of material in the public domain: radio and television broadcasts, newspapers, magazines, technical and scholarly journals, books, government reports, documents and other material posted on the Internet, and reports by foreign service officers and defense attachés concerning public activities. The extent to which open source collection yields valuable information varies greatly with the nature of the targeted society and the subject involved. The information might be collected by human sources—individuals who buy government publications and journals, observe military parades, or monitor the Internet— or by technical means—such as automated searches of the Internet or recording television and radio programs.

Clandestine collection involves the acquisition of data that are not publicly available. As with open source collection, both human and technical resources may be employed. The traditional human spy may be employed to provide sensitive political, military, or economic information. Alternatively, technical collection systems can be used to obtain images of military installations, intercept a wide variety of communications and electronic signals, and detect the infrared, acoustic, and other signatures of weapons systems or events.

Great secrecy and sensitivity characterize human source clandestine collection. Although much technical collection is unacknowledged, secrecy is not always as vital in many technical collection activities as it is in human collection. Foreign nations are well aware that the United States operates extensive space imagery and signals intelligence (SIGINT) programs. Even those nations capable of tracking the movements of U.S. spacecraft are limited in the denial and deception measures they can employ. As a result, the ability to effectively collect the required data does not always require secrecy with regard to the identity and location of the collection system. In contrast, a human asset whose identity becomes known to the foreign security service of the targeted nation will soon be arrested or become a channel for disinformation.

Analysis involves the integration of collected information—that is, raw intelligence from all sources—into finished intelligence. The finished intelligence product might be a simple statement of facts, an evaluation of the capabilities of another nation's military forces, a projection of the likely course of political events in another nation, or an analysis of the capabilities and objectives of a terrorist group.

Strictly speaking, intelligence activities involve only the collection and analysis of information and its transformation into intelligence; however, counterintelligence (CI) and covert action are intertwined with intelligence activity.

Counterintelligence encompasses all information acquisition and activity designed to assess foreign intelligence and security services (including those of terrorist groups) and neutralize hostile services. These activities involve clandestine and open source collection as well as analysis of information concerning the structure and operations of foreign services. Such collection and analysis, with respect to the technical collection activities of hostile services, can be employed to guide denial and deception operations. Counterintelligence may also involve the direct penetration and disruption of hostile intelligence activities.

Traditionally, covert action included any operation designed to influence foreign governments, persons, or events in support of the sponsoring government's foreign policy objectives, while keeping the sponsoring government's support of the operation secret. Today, terrorist organizations are an even more important target for covert action operations. Generally, the emphasis in clandestine collection has been on keeping the activity secret, whereas the emphasis in covert action has been on keeping the sponsorship secret. Today, however, there may be no need to hide the sponsorship of certain covert action activities—for example, the support of Northern Alliance forces seeking to overthrow the Taliban or the post-9/11 targeted killings of al-Qaeda personnel.

There are several distinct types of covert action: black propaganda (propaganda that purports to emanate from a source other than the true one); gray propaganda (in which true sponsorship is not acknowledged); paramilitary or political actions designed to overthrow, undermine, or support a regime; paramilitary or political actions designed to counteract a regime's attempts to procure or develop advanced weaponry; support (aid, arms, training) of individuals or organizations (government components, opposition forces and political parties, and labor unions); economic operations; disinformation; and targeted killings.

THE INTELLIGENCE CYCLE

It is important to put the collection and analysis activities conducted by various intelligence units into perspective—that is, to relate those activities to the requirements and needs of the decisionmakers and to the use made of the finished intelligence product. That objective is achieved through the concept of the "intelligence cycle." The intelligence cycle is the process by which information is acquired, converted into finished intelligence, and made available to policymakers. Generally, the cycle comprises five steps: planning and direction, collection, processing, analysis and production, and dissemination.[4]

The planning and direction process involves the management of the entire intelligence effort, from the identification of the need for data to the final delivery of an intelligence product to a consumer. The process may be initiated by requests or requirements for intelligence based on the needs of the President, the Departments of State, Defense, Homeland Security, or Treasury, or other consumers. In some cases, the requests and requirements become institutionalized. Thus, the Intelligence Community need not be reminded to collect information on al-Qaeda's activities, nuclear proliferation, Chinese nuclear forces, or developments in Mexico.

Collection, as indicated above, involves the gathering, by a variety of means, of raw data from which finished intelligence is produced. Processing is concerned with the conversion of the vast amount of information coming into the system to a form suitable for the production of finished intelligence. It involves interpretation and measurement of images and signals, language translation, decryption, sorting by subject matter, and data reduction.

The analysis and production process entails the conversion of basic information into finished intelligence. It includes the integration, evaluation, and analysis of all available data and the preparation of various intelligence products. Because the "raw intelligence" that is collected is often fragmentary and at times contradictory, specialists are needed to give it meaning and significance. The final step in the cycle, dissemination, involves the distribution of the finished intelligence to the consumers—the policymakers (and operators) whose needs triggered the process.

Like any model, the outline of the intelligence cycle is a simplification of the real world. As noted above, certain requirements become standing requirements. Similarly, policymakers do not specify, except in rare cases, particular items of information to be collected. Rather, they indicate a desire for reports on, for example, Chinese strategic forces or the political situation in Israel. The collectors are given the responsibility of determining how to obtain the information necessary to prepare such reports. In addition, the collection agencies have certain internal needs to acquire information to provide for their continued operations—information related to counterintelligence and security and information that will be useful in potential future operations. It should also be noted that decisionmakers, particularly in the midst of a crisis, may require only processed intelligence instead of fully analyzed intelligence. Thus, in the midst of the Cuban missile crisis, the most important intelligence was purely factual reporting concerning Soviet activities in Cuba and on the high seas.

TYPES OF INTELLIGENCE

One step in understanding how specific varieties of foreign intelligence can be useful to government officials is to consider the different varieties of intelligence—political, military, scientific and technical, financial, economic, and sociological.

Political intelligence encompasses both foreign and domestic politics. Clearly, the foreign policies of other nations have an impact on the United States. A variety of issues might be involved: support or opposition to U.S. initiatives in dealing with Iran or North Korea as well as other nations' political and economic relations with those countries, attitudes and policies concerning the Middle East or reform of the United Nations, support of terrorist groups, and perceptions of U.S. leadership.

The domestic politics of other nations—whether friendly, neutral, or hostile—are also of significant concern to the United States. A 1997 study by the National Intelligence Council observed that "most conflicts today are internal, not between states. This trend will continue."[5] The resolution of such conflicts—whether by coup, election, or civil war—can affect the orientation of that nation in the world, the regional balance of power, the accessibility of critical resources to the United States, or the continued presence of U.S. military bases. In addition, terrorist organizations have internal conflicts, and the outcome of those conflicts is critically important information for U.S. leaders.

The outcome of elections in other nations can have a dramatic impact on U.S. relations with those nations and the extent to which those nations support or oppose U.S. policies—whether the elections take place in Spain or in the West Bank and Gaza Strip. Likewise, the resolution of the internal conflict in Iran in 1979 deprived the United States of important oil supplies, a military ally, and critical intelligence facilities from which Soviet missile telemetry could be monitored. And developments within China, such as the repression of protesters at Tiananmen Square in June 1989, had a major impact on U.S.-Chinese relations. More recently, domestic unrest in Iran, Egypt, and other Middle Eastern nations has been of significant interest to U.S. national security officials.

Military intelligence is required for a variety of reasons. In order to determine its own military requirements—whether nuclear, conventional, or special operations—the United States must know the capabilities of potential adversaries. That knowledge is particularly important when the United States employs its forces against one of those adversaries. Military intelligence is also required to assess the need and impact of any military aid the United States may be asked to provide. Furthermore, military intelligence is required to assess the balance of power between pairs of nations (e.g.,

India–Pakistan, North Korea–South Korea) whose interactions can affect U.S. interests.

Scientific and technical intelligence includes both civilian- and military-related scientific and technical developments. A nation's ability to employ modern agricultural methods or efficiently extract energy resources may affect that country's stability, which may, in turn, affect the United States. In many cases, technological developments that occur in the civilian sector have military applications. Examples include computer technology, biotechnology, mirrors and optical systems, and lasers. Hence, intelligence concerning a nation's progress or its ability to absorb foreign-produced technology in those areas is relevant to its potential military capability.

One aspect of scientific and technical intelligence that has been of constant concern for more than fifty years is atomic energy intelligence. Whether the announced purpose of a nation's atomic energy activities has been civilian or military, those activities have received a high intelligence priority. In addition to the obvious need to determine whether various foreign nations are developing nuclear weapons, there has been a perceived need to acquire secret intelligence in support of decisionmaking concerning applications for nuclear technology exports. In 1947, the first Director of Central Intelligence (DCI) noted that the United States "cannot rely on information submitted by a licensee" and that it was necessary for the United States to "determine actual use, [to] endeavor to discover secondary diversions."[6]

A nation's scientific and technical expertise relevant to the production of biological or chemical weapons—the "poor man's atom bomb"—has also been a subject of concern to U.S. intelligence throughout the Cold War and into the present era. In addition, the potential of terrorist organizations to make use of weapons of mass destruction is a major worry for those charged with protecting the United States homeland and overseas possessions and facilities.[7]

Financial intelligence focuses on both the individuals and institutions involved in the transfer of funds for the financing of organizations, activities, or facilities of interest—including terrorist groups, the sale of weapons-related technology, and the construction of nuclear facilities—as well as the data or communications involved in funds transfers. Such intelligence is the basis for U.S. designations of individuals or institutions involved in activities that result in sanctions.[8]

Economic intelligence is also of great importance. One component is the strengths and vulnerabilities of national economies. Knowledge of the strengths may be important in understanding their capacity for conflict, whereas knowledge of their vulnerabilities may be important in assessing threats to stability as well as the likelihood that economic sanctions will produce a change in policy.

Another component is the availability and pricing of key resources, from oil to an assortment of metals and minerals. In addition, economic intelligence is concerned with regional and other economic organizations, national fiscal monetary policy, and international payments mechanisms. Economic intelligence also concerns topics such as sanctions busting, money laundering, terrorist financing, bribery and corruption, and economic espionage.[9]

Sociological intelligence concerns group relations within a particular nation. The relations between groups, whether they be ethnic, religious, or political groups, can have a significant impact on a nation's stability as well as on the nature of its foreign policy—as has been demonstrated in recent years by events in Iraq, in the former Yugoslavia, in Africa, and in Russia.

TARGETS

There is an impressive array of intelligence targets for the U.S. Intelligence Community to monitor in the post–Cold War world. These targets can be grouped into three sometimes overlapping categories:

- transnational targets
- regional targets
- national targets

Transnational targets extend across regions and may require approaches different from the traditional ones with respect to the collection and analysis of relevant intelligence, as well as to the manner in which the intelligence effort is organized. Among the most prominent transnational targets are international terrorist groups, proliferation of weapons of mass destruction, illicit arms trafficking, and international crime and narcotics trafficking. Targets also include international organizations—including the United Nations and, at least potentially, non-governmental organizations (NGOs) hostile to the United States and the West.[10]

Although attempts to develop or procure weapons of mass destruction are undertaken by individual governments, the efforts undertaken by Iraq, Iran, Pakistan, and Libya made use of indigenous capabilities as well as a significant international supplier network and the assistance of foreign governments.[11] This contrasts sharply with the largely indigenous manner in which the Soviet Union and China developed their nuclear arsenals.

Iraq received key nuclear-related equipment from corporations in Britain (plutonium), Switzerland (metal casings), France (research reactors), Italy (plutonium separation utility), South America (uranium ore concentrate), Finland (copper coils), Japan (carbon fiber), Africa (uranium ore concentrate), and the United States (power supply units). Pakistan received considerable assistance in its nuclear program from the People's Republic of China.[12]

Terrorist groups, whether located in the Middle East or Asia, have killed, maimed, and destroyed property far from their home nation or region—in New York and Washington, in Madrid and London, in Africa, and in Indonesia. Furthermore, such groups, unlike states, are capable of relocating when a host government decides that their presence is too burdensome or their operations at a particular location become the target of retaliation. Likewise, the tentacles of South American or Asian drug cartels as well as the Russian Mafia extend far beyond the borders of their home territories.[13]

Other transnational concerns include developments in cyber warfare, the state of the environment (including the impact of toxic waste dumping in the oceans), uncontrolled refugee migrations, population growth, communications technology, the spread of diseases such as AIDS or the avian flu, and international economic activity.[14]

The concept of regional targets recognizes that developments in a particular area of the world may be produced not only by distinct choices of individual governments but also as the result of interaction between governments. Clearly, a war in the Middle East, in Southwest Asia, or on the Korean peninsula would represent the most violent of such regional targets. Regional targets, which increase the chance of war, include border clashes, arms races, and cross-national movements of weapons and troops. Thus, the criteria for U.S. arms transfer policy have included the requirement to take into account "consistency with U.S. regional stability interests, especially when considering transfers involving power projection capability or introduction of a system which may foster increased tension or contribute to an arms race."[15]

Regional activity of interest to the U.S. Intelligence Community may extend beyond governmental activities. The Asian financial crisis of 1997 was of concern to U.S. officials, for it had the potential to affect internal political developments, the foreign trade activities of a number of nations, and, ultimately, the U.S. economy. The same could be said of the 2008–2009 crisis.

National targets are the most traditional targets, and they require a significant commitment of resources. All nations whose policies may have a significant impact on the United States, from the friendliest to the most hostile, represent "targets," although the type of information required and the means employed to acquire it vary considerably.

The intelligence requirements for many countries are substantial. Even after the collapse of the Soviet Union and the end of the Cold War, Russia remains a significant nation of concern to U.S. national security officials and hence a target of intelligence activities, ranging from open source collection to human intelligence to various forms of technical collection.

Topics of concern to U.S. officials regarding Russia include Vladimir Putin's health and behavior, the personalities and views of key Russians, the prospects for Russian democracy, the state of the economy, organized crime and corruption, the security of Russian nuclear weapons, the state of its armed forces, the status of its strategic weapons programs, its arms sales and technology transfer activities, its policy toward Iran and North Korea, China, and other entities, and its intelligence activities targeted on the United States.[16]

China is also a major national target, given its impact on international trade, its turbulent domestic situation, its potential as help or hindrance in dealing with Iran or Korea, as well as the ongoing transformation of the People's Liberation Army "from a mass army designed for protracted wars of attrition on its territory to one capable of fighting and winning short-duration conflicts along its periphery against high-tech adversaries."[17] Thus, collection against the Chinese target concerns military doctrine and technology, internal debates over foreign and domestic policy, attitudes toward the Chinese regime, and its international economic policies.

Other significant national targets include, for a variety of reasons, Afghanistan, Iraq, Syria, Iran, North Korea, and Yemen. Items of interest are the nuclear programs of Syria, Iran, and North Korea, graft in Afghanistan as well as the stability of its president, terrorist activity in Yemen, the eventual succession in North Korea, and the stability of the government of Pakistan as well as the security of its nuclear weapons.[18]

Some examples of topics of concern to the U.S. Intelligence Community in 2010, undoubtedly a small subset of the full set of topics of concern, were noted in Director of National Intelligence Dennis Blair's testimony to the congressional intelligence oversight committees. The topics discussed by the national intelligence director included

- the terrorist threat
- the global economy
- proliferation
- developments in Afghanistan, Pakistan, the Middle East, and Latin America
- China's transformation
- the outlook for Russia
- potential flashpoints in the Balkans and Eurasia
- international organized crime
- the impact of climate change
- strategic health challenges and threats
- intelligence threats.[19]

Additional illustrations of the interests of U.S. intelligence can be found among the subjects of the reports that the Director of National Intelligence had prepared for the Democratic and Republican presidential candidates during the 2008 campaign. Those reports assessed the capabilities of al-Qaeda, Taliban inroads into Afghanistan, militant views on the prospects of seizing control of Pakistan, the status of the Iranian nuclear program, the economic and military implications of China's rise, Russian nationalist sentiments, and the North Korean nuclear arsenal.[20]

THE UTILITY OF INTELLIGENCE

The utility of intelligence activity, here narrowly construed to mean collection and analysis, depends on the extent to which it aids national, departmental, and military service decisionmakers. Two questions arise in this regard: In what ways does intelligence aid decisionmakers, and what attributes make intelligence useful? With respect to the first question, intelligence can be useful to national decisionmakers in five distinct areas: policymaking, planning, conflict situations (ranging from negotiations to war), warning, and monitoring treaty compliance.

In their policymaking roles, national decisionmakers set the basic outlines of foreign, defense, and international economic policy and decide specific actions with regard to key issues. Their need for intelligence to make sound decisions is summed up in the report of the Rockefeller Commission:

> Intelligence is information gathered for policymakers which illuminates the range of choices available to them and enables them to exercise judgment. Good intelligence will not necessarily lead to wise policy choices. But without sound intelligence, national policy decisions and actions cannot effectively respond to actual conditions and reflect the best national interests or adequately protect . . . national security.[21]

In addition to its value in policymaking and guiding decisions concerning alternative courses of action, intelligence is vital to planning decisions. Some planning decisions may be concerned with the development and deployment of new weapons systems. It has been noted that "timely, accurate, and detailed intelligence is a vital element in establishing requirements and for planning and initiating RDT&E (Research, Development, Test, and Evaluation) efforts and continues to impact these efforts throughout the development and system life cycle."[22]

One incident illustrating the role of intelligence in weapons development occurred in 1968, when the U.S. Navy monitored a member of the oldest class of Soviet nuclear submarines traveling faster than 34 miles per hour, with apparent power to spare. That speed exceeded previous Central Intelligence Agency (CIA) estimates for the submarine and led the agency to order a full-scale revision of speed estimates for Soviet submarines. The revised estimates also provoked one of the largest construction programs in the history of the U.S. Navy—the construction of the SSN 688-class attack submarine.[23]

At the same time, intelligence can help save substantial sums of money by avoiding unneeded research and development and deployment programs. Several of the CIA's Soviet human assets, including Peter Popov, Adolf G. Tolkachev, and Dmitri Polyakov, provided information that cumulatively saved the United States billions of dollars in research and development costs. The first successful U.S. photographic reconnaissance satellite system, code-named CORONA, produced information that eliminated fears of a missile gap, and thus permitted U.S. deployment of strategic missiles to be capped at a lower level than otherwise would have been possible.[24]

Another set of planning decisions involves the development of war plans. In the months between the Iraqi invasion of Kuwait (August 1990) and the beginning of Operation Desert Storm (January 1991), the United States collected a massive quantity of intelligence about Iraqi nuclear, chemical, and biological weapons programs, electrical power networks, ballistic missiles, air defense systems, ground forces, and air forces. The data collected allowed for development and implementation of a war plan based on the most up-to-date information that could be gathered. The preparations for the invasion of Afghanistan in 2001 and Iraq in 2003 also required intensive intelligence collection efforts.

Other decisions aided by intelligence include the suspension or resumption of foreign aid, the employment of trade sanctions and embargoes, and attempts to block the transfer of commodities related to nuclear or ballistic missile proliferation. Intelligence may be able to inform the decisionmaker(s) of the likely effects of such actions, including the reactions of those nations targeted by the decision. The Carter administration went ahead with the planned sale of planes to Saudi Arabia in part as a result of intelligence indicating that if the United States backed out of the deal, the Saudis would simply buy French planes.[25]

In 1992, the United States, based on intelligence indicating a "suspicious procurement pattern" by Iran, acted to prevent the sale of equipment that could be used to begin manufacturing nuclear weapons. Argentina halted certain sales to Iran after the United States expressed concern that the equipment in question would have allowed Iran to convert natural uranium into precursor forms of highly enriched uranium. Similarly, the United States successfully lobbied the People's Republic of China to halt the sale of a large nuclear reactor that would have included a supply of enriched fuel and would have permitted Iran to conduct research related to the nuclear fuel cycle.[26]

In January 1998, National Security Agency intercepts of communications between a senior Iranian official and mid-level counterparts in Beijing indicated that Iran was negotiating to purchase "a lifelong supply" of a chemical that could be used to transform naturally occurring uranium to the highly enriched form required for nuclear weapons. Senior Chinese officials halted the sale after being contacted by U.S. officials.[27]

During the spring of 2000, U.S. intelligence agencies uncovered plans for the D. V. Efremov Institute in St. Petersburg to provide Iran with a laser facility that could be used for uranium enrichment. Once U.S. officials became aware of the proposed transaction, they urged Russian officials to cancel it because, in the words of one official, there was "no question that the turn-key facility was intended for" Iran's nuclear weapons program. During preparations for the September 2000 meeting between President Bill Clinton and President Vladimir Putin of Russia, the subject was raised again. Russian officials informed White House aides that the contract had been suspended and was under review.[28]

Intelligence is also useful in a variety of conflict situations, most prominently combat. Indeed, "support to military operations"—including combat operations as well as planning and exercise activities—has become a major priority of U.S. intelligence. Regardless of how well developed a war plan is, combat forces require intelligence on the movements and actions of enemy forces and on the impact of air and other attacks against enemy facilities and troops. Thus, even after months of extensive collection prior to Operation Desert Storm, the United States still needed to conduct an intense intelligence collection campaign during the conflict. Similarly, the prolonged combat operations in Iraq and Afghanistan have required an extensive use of intelligence resources.

Preventing terrorist attacks is another potential benefit of intelligence collection and analysis. Good intelligence has been credited with the ability to short-circuit the plot, hatched in Yemen, to destroy two U.S. freight aircraft in flight over the United States.[29]

Conflict situations in which intelligence is of value need not be exclusively of a military nature, however. Any situation where nations have at least partially conflicting interests—such as arms control negotiations, trade negotiations, or international conferences—would qualify. Intelligence can indicate how far the other negotiator can be pushed and the extent to which a position must be modified to be adopted. In 1969 the United States intercepted Japanese communications concerning the negotiations between the United States and Tokyo over the reversion of Okinawa to Japanese control.[30]

Intelligence can also provide warning of upcoming hostile or unfavorable actions, which might include military, terrorist, or other action to be taken against the decisionmaker's nation or against another country that the decisionmaker is interested in protecting. Sufficient advance notice allows defenses to be prepared, responses to be considered and implemented, and preemptive actions (diplomatic or military) to be taken to forestall or negate the action. For example, in 1980, on the basis of intelligence from a human source, President Jimmy Carter warned Soviet General Secretary Leonid Brezhnev of the danger of invading Poland. In March 1991, on the basis of communications intelligence indicating Iraqi intentions to use gas against rebel forces, the United States warned the Iraqis that such an action would not be tolerated.[31]

Intelligence is also necessary to assess whether other nations are in compliance with various international obligations. The United States is concerned, for example, with whether Russia and China are complying with arms control agreements currently in force. Intelligence is also vital in detecting violations of agreements and treaties limiting nuclear proliferation and nuclear testing. In 1993 it was reported that the United States was concerned with China's apparent violation of its pledge not to sell M-11 missiles to Pakistan.[32]

The overall utility of intelligence in regard to military matters was concisely summarized by the Eisenhower administration's Technological Capabilities Panel:

> If intelligence can uncover a new military threat, we may take steps to meet it. If intelligence can reveal an opponent's specific weakness, we may prepare to exploit it. With good intelligence we can avoid wasting our resources by arming for the wrong danger at the wrong time. Beyond this, in the broadest sense, intelligence underlies our estimate of the enemy and thus helps guide our political strategy.[33]

For maximum utility, the intelligence must not only address relevant subjects but also possess the attributes of quality and timeliness. Unless all relevant information is marshaled when assessing intelligence on a subject, the quality of the finished product may suffer. Covertly obtained intelligence should not be assessed in isolation from overtly obtained intelligence. As Professor H. Trevor-Roper observed,

> Secret intelligence is the continuation of open intelligence by other means. So long as governments conceal a part of their activities, other governments, if they wish to base their policy on full and correct information, must seek to penetrate the veil. This inevitably entails varying methods. But, however the means may vary, the end must still be the same. It is to complement the results of what for convenience we may call "public" intelligence: that is, the intelligence derived from the rational study of public or at least available sources. Intelligence is, in fact, indivisible.[34]

In addition to being based on all relevant information, the assessment process must be objective. As former secretary of state Henry Kissinger told the U.S. Senate in 1973, "Anyone concerned with national policy must have a profound interest in making sure that intelligence guides, and does not follow, national policy."[35] Furthermore, intelligence must reach decisionmakers in good time for them to act decisively—either by warning a foreign government before it is irrevocably committed to a particular course of action (whether diplomatic or military) or by ordering actions to undermine or negate such actions.

THE INTELLIGENCE COMMUNITY

The U.S. Intelligence Community officially consists of seventeen organizations: the Office of the Director of National Intelligence, the Central Intelligence Agency, the National Security Agency, the National Reconnaissance Office, the National Geospatial Intelligence Agency, the Defense Intelligence Agency, the Bureau of Intelligence and Research of the State Department, the intelligence elements of the five military services, the Federal Bureau of Investigation, and intelligence components of the Drug Enforcement Administration, the Department of Energy, the Department of the Treasury, and the Department of Homeland Security. Those intelligence elements can be grouped into four categories:

- national intelligence organizations
- Department of Defense intelligence organizations
- military service intelligence organizations
- civilian intelligence organizations

There is also a fifth group of intelligence organizations that play a significant role in the production of intelligence: the intelligence components of the unified commands.

Notes

1. Environmental Protection Agency, "EPA NSR–29 Intelligence Requirements," May 14, 1992.

2. National Aeronautics and Space Administration, "NSR–29 Intelligence Requirements," January 17, 1992; "Space Surveillance Network NASA Support Requirements Matrix," attachment to Daniel S. Goldin, Administrator, NASA to General Howell M. Estes III, August 27, 1997; Department of Agriculture, "NSR–29 Intelligence Requirements," January 15, 1992.

3. Joint Chiefs of Staff, *U.S. Department of Defense Dictionary of Military Terms* (New York: Arco, 1988), p. 183.

4. Central Intelligence Agency, *Intelligence: The Acme of Skill*, n.d., pp. 6–7; Central Intelligence Agency, *Fact Book on Intelligence*, 1993, pp. 10–11.

5. National Intelligence Council, *Global Trends 2010* (Washington, D.C.: NIC, 1997), p. 1.

6. Sidney Souers, "Atomic Energy Intelligence," RG 218 (Joint Chiefs of Staff), File 131, July 1, 1947, Military Reference Branch, National Archives and Records Administration.

7. For example, Central Intelligence Agency, *Chemical and Biological Weapons: The Poor Man's Atomic Bomb*, December 1988; and Central Intelligence Agency, *The Chemical and Biological Weapons Threat*, March 1996.

8. Department of the Treasury, TG-782, "Treasury Targets Taliban and Haqqani Network Leadership: Treasury Designates Three Financiers Operating in Afghanistan and Pakistan," July 22, 2010; Department of the Treasury, TG-838, "Treasury Designates Al-Qai'da Finance Section Leader," August 24, 2010; Peter Fritsch, "Small Bank in Germany Tied to Iran Nuclear Effort," *Wall Street Journal*, July 19, 2010, pp. A1, A14; Chico Harlan, "U.S. official outlines plan targeting firms, banks that help fund North Korea," www.washingtonpost.com, August 3, 2010.

9. U.S. Congress, Senate Select Committee on Intelligence, *Current and Projected National Security Threats to the United States and Its Interests Abroad* (Washington, D.C.: U.S. Government Printing Office, 1997), p. 92; Department of the Treasury, "Treasury Targets Colombian Money Laundering Network Tied to FARC," May 6, 2010, www.treas.gov.

10. For discussions of various transnational threats, see Hans A. Binnendijk and Patrick L. Clawson, eds., *1997 Strategic Assessment: Flashpoints and Force Structure* (Washington, D.C.: National Defense University, 1997), pp. 185–228; Office of the Secretary of Defense, *Proliferation: Threat and Response* (Washington, D.C.: U.S. Government Printing Office, November 1997); U.S. Congress, Senate Select Committee on Intelligence, *Current and Projected National Security Threats to the United States*, pp. 7–11, 22–23; and Ernest Sternberg, "Purifying the World: What the New Radical Ideology Stands For," *Orbis* 54, 1 (Winter 2010): 61–86.

11. See David Albright, *Peddling Peril: How the Secret Nuclear Trade Arms America's Enemies* (New York: Free Press, 2010); and Gordon Corera, *Shopping for Bombs: Nuclear Proliferation, Global Insecurity and the Rise of the A.Q. Khan Network* (New York: Oxford University Press, 2006).

12. R. Jeffrey Smith and Glenn Frankel, "Saddam's Nuclear Weapons Dream," *Washington Post*, October 13, 1991, pp. A1, A44–A45; Michael Wines, "U.S. Is Building Up a Picture of Vast Iraqi Atom Program," *New York Times*, September 22, 1991, p. A8; William E. Burrows and Robert Windrem, *Critical Mass: The Dangerous Race for Superweapons in a Fragmenting World* (New York: Simon & Schuster, 1994), pp. 378–402; 500th MI Brigade, U.S. Army In-

telligence and Security Command, "Pakistani Use of Chinese Nuclear Weapons Test Facilities," June 19, 1991.

13. See Department of State, *Patterns of Global Terrorism 1996* (Washington, D.C.: U.S. Government Printing Office, 1997); U.S. Congress, House Committee on International Relations, *The Threat from Russian Organized Crime* (Washington, D.C.: U.S. Government Printing Office, 1996); and Roger Medd and Frank Goldstein, "International Terrorism on the Eve of a New Millennium," *Studies in Conflict & Terrorism* 20, 3 (July–September 1997): 281–316.

14. Binnendijk and Clawson, eds., *1997 Strategic Assessment: Flashpoints and Force Structure*, pp. 209–228; Richard Smith, "The Intelligence Community and the Environment: Capabilities and Future Missions," *Environmental Change and Security Project Report* 2 (Spring 1996): 103–108.

15. The White House, Office of the Press Secretary, "Criteria for Decisionmaking on U.S. Arms Exports," February 17, 1995, p. 1.

16. Some of these concerns are mentioned in U.S. Congress, Senate Select Committee on Intelligence, *Current and Projected National Security Threats to the United States*, passim; and U.S. Congress, Senate Committee on Governmental Affairs, *Compilation of Hearings on National Security Issues* (Washington, D.C.: U.S. Government Printing Office, 1998), pp. 285–333; Charles Levinson and Jay Solomon, "Syria Gave Scuds to Hezbollah, U.S. Says," *Washington Post*, April 14, 2010, pp. A1, A12.

17. Office of the Secretary of Defense, *Military Power of the People's Republic of China 2008* (Washington, D.C.: Department of Defense, 2009), p. 1; Ken Dilanian, "Quick Strides by China's Military," *Los Angeles Times*, January 7, 2011, pp. A1, A22.

18. Thom Shanker and Eric Schmitt, "U.S. Intelligence Puts New Focus on Afghan Graft," *New York Times*, June 13, 2010, pp. 1, 4; Choe Sang-Hun, North Korean Political Gathering Could Hint at Future Leadership," *New York Times*, September 7, 2010, p. A4; Robert F. Worth, "Yemen Emerges as Base for Qaeda Attacks," *New York Times*, October 30, 2010, p. A6.

19. Dennis C. Blair, Director of National Intelligence, *Annual Threat Assessment of the US Intelligence Community for the Senate Select Committee on Intelligence*, February 2, 2010, passim; Dennis C. Blair, Director of National Intelligence, *Annual Threat Assessment of the US Intelligence Community for the House Permanent Select Committee on Intelligence*, February 3, 2010, passim.

20. David E. Sanger, *The Inheritance: The World Obama Confronts and the Challenges to American Power* (New York: Harmony, 2009), pp. xvii–xviii.

21. Commission on CIA Activities Within the United States, *Report to the President* (Washington, D.C.: U.S. Government Printing Office, 1975), p. 6.

22. HQ USAF, ACS, I INOI 80–1, "The Intelligence Role in Research, Development, Test and Evaluation (RDT&E)," January 18, 1985.

23. Patrick Tyler, "The Rise and Fall of the SSN 688," *Washington Post*, September 21, 1986, pp. A1, A18.

24. On Popov, Polyakov, and Tolkachev, see Jeffrey T. Richelson, *A Century of Spies: Intelligence in the Twentieth Century* (New York: Oxford University Press, 1995), pp. 257–258, 269, 272, 395; David Wise, *Nightmover: How Aldrich Ames Sold the CIA to the KGB for $4.6 Million* (New York: HarperCollins, 1995), pp. 59–66, 105–106, 124, 271, 327; and Barry G. Royden, "Tolkachev, a Worthy Successor to Penkovsky," *Studies in Intelligence* 47, 3 (2003): 5–33. On CORONA, see Dwayne A. Day, John Lodgson, and Brian Latell, eds., *Eye in the*

Sky: The Story of the CORONA Spy Satellites (Washington, D.C.: Smithsonian Institution Press, 1998); and Curtis Peebles, *The CORONA Project* (Annapolis, Md.: Naval Institute Press, 1997).

25. Zbigniew Brzezinski, *Power and Principle: Memoirs of the National Security Adviser, 1977–1981* (New York: Farrar, Straus and Giroux, 1983), p. 248.

26. Steve Coll, "U.S. Halted Nuclear Bid by Iran," *Washington Post*, November 17, 1992, pp. A1, A30.

27. Barton Gellman and John Pomfret, "U.S. Action Stymied China Sale to Iran," *Washington Post*, March 13, 1998, pp. A1, A20.

28. Walter Pincus, "Russia: Laser Deal with Iran Blocked," *Washington Post*, September 20, 2000, p. A25.

29. Mark Mazzetti, Robert F.Worth, and Eric Liptor, "Quick Response to Intelligence Foiled Bombers," *New York Times*, November 1, 2010, pp. A1, A6.

30. Seymour Hersh, *The Price of Power: Kissinger in the Nixon White House* (New York: Summit, 1983), p. 103.

31. Benjamin Weiser, "A Question of Loyalty," *Washington Post Magazine*, December 13, 1992, pp. 9ff.; Benjamin Weiser, *A Secret Life: The Polish Officer, His Covert Mission, and the Price He Paid to Save His Country* (New York: PublicAffairs, 2004); Patrick E. Tyler, "U.S. Said to Plan Bombing of Iraqis If They Gas Rebels," *New York Times*, March 10, 1991, pp. 1, 15.

32. Ann Devroy and R. Jeffrey Smith, "U.S. Evidence 'Suggests' China Breaks Arms Pact," *Washington Post*, May 18, 1993, p. A9; Douglas Jehl, "China Breaking Missile Pledge, U.S. Aides Say," *New York Times*, May 6, 1993, pp. A1, A6; John M. Goshko, "U.S. Warns China of Sanctions of Missile Exports to Pakistan," *Washington Post*, July 26, 1993, p. A10; "Psst . . . Want to Buy a Missile?" *Newsweek*, September 6, 1993, p. 28; R. Jeffrey Smith, "Ukraine Begins to Dismantle Nuclear Missiles Aimed at U.S.," *Washington Post*, July 28, 1993, p. A13.

33. James J. Killian Jr., *Sputnik, Scientists, and Eisenhower: A Memoir of the First Special Assistant to the President for Science and Technology* (Cambridge, Mass.: MIT Press, 1977), p. 80.

34. Hugh Trevor-Roper, *The Philby Affair: Espionage, Treason and Secret Services* (London: Kimber, 1968), p. 66.

35. U.S. Congress, Senate Committee on Foreign Relations, *Nomination of Henry A. Kissinger* (Washington, D.C.: U.S. Government Printing Office, 1973). For evidence that Kissinger did not always follow his own advice, see Hersh, *The Price of Power*, pp. 529–560.

2

NATIONAL INTELLIGENCE ORGANIZATIONS

Over thirty years ago a National Security Council (NSC) study noted that "U.S. intelligence is unique in the world for its state of the art, the scope of its activities, and the extraordinary range and variety of organizations and activities that constitute its consumership."[1] That judgment remains just as valid today.

The United States collects information through the use of reconnaissance satellites, aircraft, ships, signals intercept and seismic ground stations, radar, and undersea surveillance, as well as through the traditional overt and clandestine human sources. It also examines open sources, exploits recovered equipment and documents, and receives data from emplaced sensors. Intelligence Community personnel process and analyze the information collected, using the most advanced computers and a variety of specially developed techniques for extracting a maximum of information from the data. The total cost of the activities funded in the National Intelligence Program and Military Intelligence Program budgets is approximately $80 billion per year.[2]

Given this wide range of activity and the large number of intelligence consumers, it is not surprising that a plethora of organizations are involved in intelligence activities. Of these organizations, four are unambiguously "national" intelligence organizations, in that they perform intelligence functions on behalf of the entire government rather than just a department or military service. Their activities provide intelligence for national-level policymakers, and they are responsive to direction by supra-departmental authority. The four organizations are the Central Intelligence Agency (CIA), the National Security Agency (NSA), the National Reconnaissance Office (NRO), and the National Geospatial-Intelligence Agency (NGA).

CENTRAL INTELLIGENCE AGENCY

World War II resulted in the creation of America's first central intelligence organization—the Office of Strategic Services (OSS). OSS functions included traditional espionage, covert action (ranging from propaganda to sabotage), counterintelligence, and intelligence analysis. The OSS represented a revolution in United

States intelligence not only because of the varied functions performed by a single, national agency but also because of the breadth of its intelligence interests and its use of scholars to produce finished intelligence.[3]

In the aftermath of World War II, the Office of Strategic Services was disbanded, officially closing down on October 1, 1945, as ordered by President Harry S Truman. The X-2 (counterintelligence) and secret intelligence branches were transferred to the War Department to form the Strategic Services Unit, while the Research and Analysis Branch was relocated in the State Department.[4]

At virtually the same time that he ordered the closure of the OSS, Truman authorized studies of the intelligence structure required by the United States in the post–World War II world. The result was the creation of the National Intelligence Authority (NIA) and its operational element, the Central Intelligence Group (CIG). In addition to its initial responsibility for coordinating and synthesizing the reports produced by the military service intelligence agencies and the Federal Bureau of Investigation (FBI), the CIG was soon assigned the task of clandestine intelligence collection.[5]

As part of a general consideration of national security needs, the question of intelligence organization was addressed in the National Security Act of 1947. The act established the Central Intelligence Agency as an independent agency within the Executive Office of the President to replace the CIG. According to the act, the CIA was to have five functions:

1. to advise the National Security Council in matters concerning such intelligence activities of the government departments and agencies as relate to national security
2. to make recommendations to the National Security Council for the coordination of such intelligence activities of the departments and agencies of the government as relate to national security
3. to correlate and evaluate the intelligence relating to national security, and to provide for the appropriate dissemination of such intelligence within the government, using, where appropriate, existing agencies and facilities
4. to perform for the benefit of existing intelligence agencies such additional services of common concern as the National Security Council determines can be more effectively accomplished centrally
5. to perform other such functions and duties related to intelligence affecting the national security as the National Security Council may from time to time direct.[6]

The provisions of the act left considerable scope for interpretation. Thus, the fifth and final provision has been cited as authorization for covert action operations. In fact, the provision was intended only to authorize espionage.[7] The ultimate legal basis for covert action is presidential direction and congressional approval of funds for such programs.

Whatever the intentions of Congress in 1947, the CIA developed in accord with a maximalist interpretation of the act. Thus, the CIA became the primary U.S. government intelligence agency for intelligence analysis, clandestine human intelligence collection, and covert action. It has also played a major role in the development of reconnaissance and other technical collection systems employed for gathering imagery, signals, and measurement and signature intelligence.

Under President Ronald Reagan's Executive Order 12333, which is still partially in effect, the CIA is permitted to secretly collect "significant" foreign intelligence within the United States if the collection effort is not aimed at the domestic activities of U.S. citizens and corporations. The order also gives the CIA authority to conduct, within the United States, "special activities" or covert actions approved by the President that are not intended to influence U.S. political processes, public opinion, or the media.[8]

The CIA's founding legislation established the position of Director of Central Intelligence (DCI), responsible for managing the activities of the entire national Intelligence Community as well as running the CIA. The position of DCI was eliminated by the Intelligence Reform and Terrorism Prevention Act of 2004, which established the new position of Director of National Intelligence (DNI) to oversee and guide the activities of the Intelligence Community. The individual heading the CIA became simply Director, Central Intelligence Agency (D/CIA).

CIA headquarters is in Langley, Virginia, just south of Washington, although the agency has a number of other offices scattered around the Washington area. In 1991, the CIA had approximately 20,000 employees, but post–Cold War reductions in the 1990s and the transfer of the CIA's imagery analysts to the new National Imagery and Mapping Agency (NIMA) probably reduced that number to about 16,000. In the aftermath of 9/11, the CIA expanded and probably passed the 20,000 mark in employees. Its budget probably exceeds $5 billion.[9]

As indicated in Figure 2.1, in addition to the offices and staff elements that report to the DCI, the Deputy DCI (DDCI), and the Associate Deputy Director (which replaced the position of Executive Director), there are four main components: the Directorate of Support, the National Clandestine Service, the Directorate of Science and Technology, and the Directorate of Intelligence.

The Directorate of Support was previously known as the Directorate of Administration; its current components are also shown in Figure 2.1.

Of these components, the one that has been around the longest is the Office of Medical Services. The office has planned and directed the CIA's medical programs. It has been responsible for medical examinations and immunizations for employees and dependents traveling overseas, health education and emergency health care, and psychiatric services. It also helped develop the Psychological Assessment Program—to determine which individuals are best suited for the agency—and was involved in psychiatric and medical intelligence production.[10]

The Office of Security had been split into separate components responsible for personnel security and physical security, but these have been reunited—giving the

FIGURE 2.1   Organization of the Central Intelligence Agency

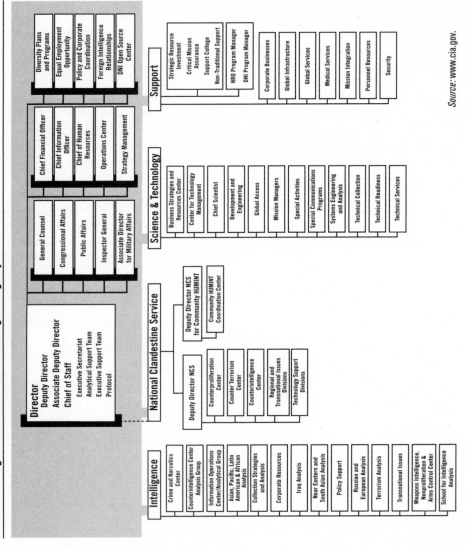

Source: www.cia.gov.

office responsibility for clearing personnel, investigating possible security breaches, and ensuring the security of CIA facilities. The other offices in the directorate provide a variety of functions essential to CIA operations—including facilities for communications between CIA headquarters and overseas personnel, logistics, maintenance of facilities, disbursement of funds for CIA operations, determination of personnel requirements, training and education, and information technology. The directorate operates the CIA training facilities, including the main facility, the Armed Forces Experimental Training Facility at Camp Peary, Virginia.[11]

The National Clandestine Service (NCS) (formerly the Directorate of Operations and before that the Directorate of Plans) is responsible for clandestine collection and covert action (special activities). It is headed by the Director of the National Clandestine Service (D/NCS), who not only is responsible for managing human intelligence and covert action operations of the CIA but also is to "coordinate, deconflict, and assess HUMINT operations throughout the IC." The NCS director has two deputies: one responsible for the daily activities of the CIA's Clandestine Service, and one who focuses on the human intelligence activities across the Intelligence Community. The second Deputy Director—the Deputy Director of the NCS for Community HUMINT (DDNCS/CH)—supervises the Community HUMINT Office, the National HUMINT Requirements Tasking Center, and a center devoted to HUMINT standards and practices.[12] The NCS has more than 5,000 employees. (The functions of the components reporting to the DDNCS/CH are discussed in Chapter 19.)

Figure 2.1 shows the structure of the NCS as presented in the CIA organizational chart. It indicates the existence of a number of "Technology Support Divisions" that probably augment the work of the Directorate of Science and Technology's Office of Technical Service. These divisions, in turn, probably can trace their origins back to Deputy Director of Operations Thomas Twetten's creation, in the early 1980s, of a rival technology group within the operations directorate.[13]

The other components of the directorate comprise eight divisions and five centers.

The National Resources Division (NRD) area of operations is the United States. It is the result of the 1991 merger of the Foreign Resources Division (FRD) and the National Collection Division (NCD), which became branches under the new division. The NRD has offices in about thirty U.S. cities. The FRD was created in 1963 as the Domestic Operations Division and given the responsibility for "clandestine operational activities of the Clandestine Services conducted within the United States against foreign targets."[14]

The present function of the Foreign Resources Branch (FRB) is to locate foreign nationals of special interest who reside in the United States and recruit them to serve as CIA assets when they return home (or to some other foreign location). As a means of identifying such individuals the FRB has relationships with scores of individuals in U.S. academic institutions, including faculty. These individuals do not attempt to recruit students but assist by providing background information and occasionally by brokering introductions.[15]

According to one report, a key element in FRB operations (which constitutes nearly 30 percent of the NRD's activities) is the recruitment, while they are in the United States, of foreign scientists, engineers, and corporate officials to provide telecommunications intelligence or assist the U.S. Intelligence Community in acquiring such intelligence. The program involved is, or was, designated MXSCOPE, according to the report.[16]

The National Collection Branch (NCB), known previously as the Domestic Collection Division and Domestic Contact Service, openly collects intelligence from U.S. residents who have traveled abroad, including scientists, technologists, economists, and energy experts returning from foreign locations of interest. Among those interviewed are academics; in 1982 the Domestic Collection Division was in touch with approximately 900 individuals on 290 campuses in the United States.[17]

The chief of the NRD (and probably the chiefs of the NCB and FRB) can approve the use of individuals who are employees or invitees of an organization within the United States to collect significant foreign intelligence at fairs, workshops, symposia, and similar types of commercial or professional meetings that are open to those individuals in their overt roles but closed to the general public. After 9/11 the division received additional funding, and some offices that had been closed in the 1990s were reopened, bringing the total number of NRD offices to the present complement of about thirty. In 2005, it was reported that the NRD's headquarters would be relocated to Denver, Colorado, "for operational reasons."[18]

One division has worldwide responsibilities. The Special Activities Division (SA) handles paramilitary activities, such as those directed against the Sandinista government in Nicaragua and the Soviet intervention in Afghanistan during the 1980s, as well as those in support of U.S. efforts to capture Osama bin Laden, unseat the Taliban in Afghanistan, and depose Saddam Hussein in Iraq. SA's heritage includes a number of earlier incarnations, including the International Activities Division; Paramilitary, Insurgency, Narcotics Staff; Special Activities Staff; and the Military and Special Programs Division.[19]

The regional divisions, which today apparently consist of the Central Eurasian, Latin American, European, East Asian, Near East, and African divisions, have been the core of the directorate since its inception.[20]

The two centers established as "DCI Centers" and contained within the National Clandestine Service—the Counterterrorist Center (CTC) and the Counterintelligence Center (CIC)—were formed during the tenures of William Casey and William Webster, respectively. The objective was to give heightened status to the counterintelligence and counterterrorism missions as well as to bring together representatives of different Intelligence Community components, including analysts, involved in these missions. In 1997, a Terrorism Warning Group was established within the CTC with the mission of alerting civilian and military leaders to specific terrorist threats. As early as 1996, the CTC established a special unit, with about twenty-five staff members and designated Alec Station, whose mission was tracking Osama bin Laden and his top aides. That unit, which was reported to be understaffed in the fall of 2004, was closed in late 2005, and its analysts were reassigned within the CTC. The CTC itself grew to more than 1,100 analysts and operators after the terrorist attacks of September 11, 2001.[21]

The CIC consolidated the Counterintelligence Staff, the Foreign Intelligence Capabilities Unit (established in 1983 to look for attempts by foreign intelligence agencies to influence the perceptions of U.S. intelligence), elements of the administration directorate's Office of Security, and other Intelligence Community elements. The director of the CIC was given the status of Associate Deputy Director for Operations for Counterintelligence.[22]

The Information Operations Center, established in the very late 1990s, absorbed some of the functions of the Directorate of Science and Technology's Clandestine Information Technology Office (CITO), established in 1996. The office was officially described as being responsible for addressing "collection capabilities within emerging information technologies." A fourth center within the directorate is the National Resettlement Operations Center (NROC), previously known as the Defector Resettlement Center. The center was established to eliminate CIA deficiencies in handling defectors, such as those who played a role in the redefection of Vitaly Yurchenko.[23]

The most recently established center, whose creation was announced in August 2010, is the Counterproliferation Center (CPC). One key element of the center is what used to be the NCS Counterproliferation Division. The Counterproliferation Division (CPD) was established in the mid-1990s, in recognition of the transnational character of the proliferation of weapons of mass destruction. Creation of the CPD was intended to facilitate the CIA's ability to collect information regarding proliferation activities, or to neutralize proliferation activities, that involve multiple regions of the world—such as those involving A. Q. Khan—without having to operate through several divisions. Along with the CPD the new center, which will be headed by an undercover NCS officer with deputies for operations and analysis, will include elements of the Directorate of Intelligence's Weapons Intelligence, Nonproliferation, and Arms Control Center (WINPAC).[24]

The complete organization chart of the NCS probably looks like the one shown in Figure 2.2.

The Directorate of Science and Technology (DS&T), with over 5,000 employees, was created in 1962 as the Directorate of Research and assumed responsibility for the CIA's efforts in developing and operating technical collection systems, particularly the U-2 and A-12 (OXCART) skyplanes and the CORONA reconnaissance satellite. In 1963, it became the Directorate of Science and Technology.[25]

The DS&T has undergone several reorganizations and has gained and lost responsibilities in the forty-three years since it was created. Both the Directorate of Intelligence (DI) and the Directorate of Operations (the predecessor of today's National Clandestine Service) have at times disputed actual or planned DS&T control

FIGURE 2.2 Probable Organization of the National Clandestine Service

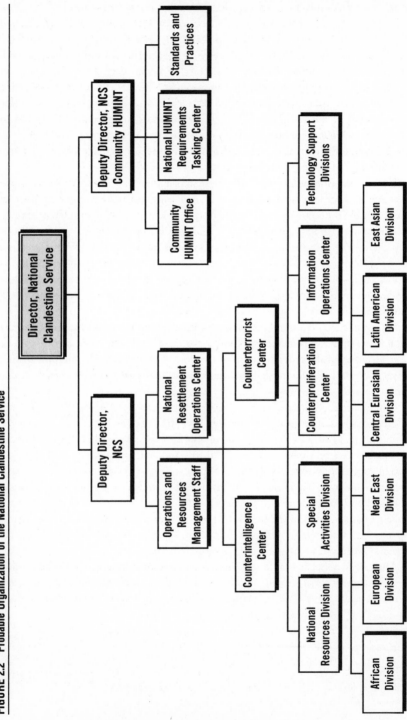

of various offices and divisions. In 1963, the DS&T assumed control of the Office of Scientific Intelligence, which had been in the Directorate of Intelligence. In 1976, all scientific and technical intelligence analysis functions were transferred back to the DI. In 1996, the National Photographic Intelligence Center (NPIC), which had been transferred to the DS&T in 1973, was merged into the newly created National Imagery and Mapping Agency (NIMA). In 2005, the responsibility for open source collection, including the activities of the Foreign Broadcast Information Service, was transferred from the DS&T to the Office of the Director of National Intelligence, although it is administered by the Director of the CIA.[26]

The components of the DS&T, shown in Figure 2.1, include offices that have long lineage and those established within the last decade.

The Office of Development and Engineering (OD&E), as it has been known since 1973, is the successor to several CIA components involved in overhead reconnaissance, including the Development Project Staff (established in 1954 to manage the U-2 program), the Office of Special Activities, and the Office of Special Projects. It has been involved in the development of major technical collection systems, such as the KH-11 imaging satellite. The office "provide[d] total systems development for major systems—from requirements definition through design engineering, and testing and evaluation, to implementation, operation and even support logistics and maintenance." Specific areas of research in developing such systems included laser communications, digital imagery processing, real-time data collection and processing, electro-optics, advanced signal collection, and advanced antenna design.[27] Today, as a result of the reorganization of the National Reconnaissance Office (NRO), discussed below, OD&E's mission is to provide personnel to the NRO rather than conduct its own research and development of satellite systems.

The Office of Technical Collection (OTC) was created by merging the Office of SIGINT Operations (OSO) and the Office of Special Projects. The OSO "develop[ed], operat[ed] and maintain[ed] sophisticated equipment required to perform collection and analysis tasks." Through the Special Collection Service, operated in conjunction with the National Security Agency (NSA), the OSO operated a large number of covert listening posts in U.S. embassies, placing "sophisticated eavesdropping equipment—from bugs to parabolic antennas—in difficult to reach places."* It was involved in the construction of signals intelligence (SIGINT) facilities operated by foreign nations such as China and Norway, in the training of their personnel, and in the maintenance of equipment at the site.[28]

The Office of Special Projects, in its last incarnation, was involved in the development and operational support of systems, including emplaced sensor systems, that collected measurement and signatures intelligence (MASINT), signals intelligence,

---

*The OSO itself was established in 1978, bringing together the Office of Electronic Intelligence and Division D (formerly Staff D) of the Directorate of Operations. Staff D had originally been the funnel for COMINT into the CIA, had operated against foreign cipher personnel, and had conducted embassy-based COMINT collection.

and nuclear intelligence. According to a CIA document, the office "develop[ed] collection systems tailored to specific targets."[29]

One component of the OTC is the Clandestine MASINT Operations Center, which likely monitors the operations of emplaced MASINT systems. The Office of Technical Service (OTS) was previously the Technical Services Division (TSD) of the Directorate of Operations. The TSD was transferred to the DS&T in 1973, as part of a series of moves by DCI William Colby to break down barriers between the operations directorate and the rest of the agency. The technical services provided by OTS include secret writing methods, bugging equipment, hidden cameras, coding and decoding devices, video and image enhancement, and chemical imagery. Prior to the April 1980 attempted mission to rescue U.S. hostages in Iran, OTS devised battery-powered landing lights that could be emplaced easily and switched on remotely from the air. After the September 1988 explosion of Pan Am 103 over Lockerbie, Scotland, the OTS matched the timing device that was to be used in a planned Libyan terrorist operation with a part of the timing device that survived the Pan Am 103 explosion. In the early 1990s the service implanted a beacon in a walking stick provided to Osman Ato, an arms importer and financial supporter of Somali warlord Gen. Mohammed Farah Aideed. The beacon allowed Delta Force personnel to capture Ato as he drove through Mogadishu. In late 2001, a six-member ordnance team from the DS&T arrived in Kandahar, Afghanistan, to help dismantle explosive devices that the first CIA teams deployed to the country after 9/11 were encountering. The team discovered a 2,500-pound Improvised Explosive Device (IED) and disarmed it shortly before it was to explode.[30]

The Systems Engineering Acquisition Office, created in 2002, was established by DCI George J. Tenet to provide a more independent CIA capability in the field of reconnaissance satellite development in response to concerns that the NRO had become much less imaginative and innovative than it had been in the past.[31]

The Office of Global Access, established in 2003, supports technical collection and operations against priority intelligence requirements. Established in the same year was the Office of Special Activities, which provides technical, engineering, research, and analytical expertise to tactical and strategic operations. The Office of Technical Readiness, also created in 2003, provides support to DS&T technical personnel and facilities overseas—including the construction, operation, and maintenance of directorate facilities. In addition, it works on the concealment of CIA devices and capabilities, as an aid to tradecraft. All three offices were created out of already existing directorate components.[32]

Also established in 2003, although not out of an existing component, was the Office of Special Communications Programs, which serves an advocate for programs in the CIA and the wider national security community that are used to provide the continuous worldwide transfer of data in support of intelligence activities outside the United States.[33]

In the fall of 2009, the CIA established the Center on Climate Change and National Security, within the Directorate of Science and Technology. The center has been charged with examining the impact of desertification, rising sea levels, population shifts, and increased competition for natural resources. It will "provide support to American policymakers as they negotiate, implement, and verify international agreements on environmental issues." It will also assume responsibility for coordinating with other elements of the Intelligence Community with respect to the review and declassification of imagery and other data that scientists can use in climate-related research.[34]

The In-Q-Tel Interface Center serves as a liaison between individuals and organizations inside and outside the intelligence agency. The CIA created In-Q-Tel in late 1999 as an in-house nonprofit venture-capital firm and appropriated $28.5 million in agency funds for its support. In 2000, In-Q-Tel received proposals from about 500 private vendors for technologies that could potentially benefit the agency. Of those, twelve projects were funded for development.[35]

One project funded by In-Q-Tel involved a commercial search engine, named NetOwl, that uses natural-language processing in place of key words to locate information. In-Q-Tel funding was also vital in developing the Presidential Intelligence Briefing System (PIBS), which is used to produce the President's Daily Brief (PDB). Rather than having intelligence analysts sort through hundreds of cables, PIBS places the cables in a Lotus Notes database, performs a variety of search and analysis functions, and then places the brief on a notebook computer. A third project involved enhancing a piece of software called Triangle Boy, which allows users to examine websites anonymously. Recently, In-Q-Tel has provided support to a company developing microbatteries, which could potentially be useful in electronic intelligence collection operations.[36]

The Directorate of Intelligence has also undergone extensive reorganization in the post–Cold War years. A 1996 reorganization, the directorate's first major reorganization since 1981, reduced the number of directorate offices from nine to six. Today, the directorate consists of four offices that focus on regions of the world, two that deal with transnational issues, two centers (established as DCI centers), analytical groups linked to the National Clandestine Service, an office of policy support, and an office for collection strategies and analysis. Figure 2.1 shows the present structure.

The four offices within the directorate that focus on regions or nations are the Office of Russian and European Analysis, the Office of Near Eastern and South Asian Analysis, the Office of Asian Pacific, Latin American, and African Analysis, and the Office of Iraq Analysis. The Russia/Europe office was formed by merging the Office of Russian and Eurasian Analysis and the Office of European Analysis. The other two regional offices represent the rearrangement of the responsibilities of three former offices—those for Near Eastern and South Asian Analysis, East Asian Analysis, and African and Latin American Analysis. [37]

The Office of Iraq Analysis was created in 2003. In addition to producing analytical reports of the situation in Iraq, it holds annual conferences, which in the past have included analytical presentations such as "Iraq's Insurgency in Historical Comparative Perspective" and "After Saddam: Democracy, Insurgency, and Reconstruction in the

New Iraq." In 2006 it completed a study, *Misreading Intentions: Iraq's Reaction to Inspections Created Picture of Deception.*[38]

A new Office of Transnational Issues (OTI) was formed from the merger of the Office of Weapons, Technology, and Proliferation (OWTP) and the Office of Transnational Security and Technology Issues (OTSTI). OWTP was the successor to the Office of Scientific and Weapons Research, which itself was formed from the late 1970s merger of the Office of Weapons Intelligence (OWI) and the Office of Scientific Intelligence (OSI), both of which had been transferred to the Directorate of Intelligence from the Directorate of Science and Technology in 1976. OTSTI was first established in 1981 as the Office of Global Issues and was designated the Office of Resources, Trade and Technology (ORTT) in 1990.[39]

The Office of Transnational Issues (OTI) examines developments in international energy, trade, and finance, as well as topics such as refuge flows, food security, and border tensions. OTI analysts also focus on money laundering, illicit finance, corruption, and sanctions violations. Other office analysts analyze foreign denial and deception efforts as well as attempts to manipulate U.S perceptions. Within OTI is the Medical and Psychological Analysis Center (MPAC), which produces assessments on global health issues (such as disease outbreaks) and the health of foreign leaders.[40]

The Office of Terrorism Analysis (OTA) is the analytic component of the NCS Counterterrorist Center. Its analysts track terrorists and states that sponsor terrorism and assess terrorist vulnerabilities—analyzing their ideology, goals, capabilities, associates, and locations. They also examine worldwide terrorist threat information and look for patterns that would allow them to warn of planned terrorist activity. In addition, they seek to identify emerging and nontraditional terrorist groups and possible collusion among terrorist groups. Finally, the office is involved in "identifying, disrupting, and preventing international financial transactions that support terrorist networks and operations." In December 2006, the office conducted a simulation of the impact of the Iraq war on the global jihadist movement, involving seventy-five CIA analysts and outside experts. The directorate also houses the Analysis Group of the NCS Counterterrorist Center.[41]

The DCI's Crime and Narcotics Center (CNC) is staffed by analysts and operators from the CIA, the Federal Bureau of Investigation, the Defense Department, the National Security Agency, the State Department, and the Treasury Department, who monitor, analyze, and disseminate intelligence on narcotics trafficking and international organized crime. They analyze the impact of the drug trade and of organized crime on U.S. national security, follow trafficking methods and routes, and monitor cooperation between organized criminal groups, traffickers, and terrorists. In addition, they seek to identify key individuals, organizations, and trends in criminal organizations. The CNC was established in 1989 as the DCI Counternarcotics Center. Its mission and name were changed in 1994 to include international organized crime intelligence.[42]

Also housed in the Directorate of Intelligence is the Weapons Intelligence, Nonproliferation, and Arms Control Center (WINPAC). The core of WINPAC was established in September 1991 as the DCI Nonproliferation Center (NPC) after disclosures about Iraq's capabilities to produce nuclear and other weapons of mass destruction indicated that the Intelligence Community had underestimated both the diversity and progress of the program. By 1999, the NPC consisted of about 200 intelligence analysts and clandestine operators, about a quarter to a third of whom had come from agencies other than the CIA. The center monitored the worldwide development and acquisition of production technology, designs, components, or entire military systems in the area of nuclear, chemical, and biological weapons, as well as advanced conventional weapons. The NPC's Transfer Network Groups analyzed and identified international suppliers of technologies and the trade mechanisms used to transfer goods.[43]

To improve operational effectiveness, the NPC developed strategic plans to help guide the U.S. government's response to the proliferation problem and provided support to collection and law-enforcement organizations. It also worked on collection platform development and produced a "gaps" study that identified deficiencies in proliferation-related collection activities. Furthermore, the NPC was authorized to review the Intelligence Community's performance on proliferation activities and to make relevant budget recommendations.[44]

WINPAC was created in March 2001 from the merger of the NPC, the DCI's Arms Control Intelligence Staff (ACIS), and the Weapons Intelligence Staff of the Office of Transnational Issues. The creation of ACIS stemmed from the establishment in the mid-1970s of a four-person staff within the Directorate of Intelligence to coordinate CIA arms control–related activities and positions on pivotal verification and monitoring issues. The staff grew in the 1980s, in concert with negotiations on intermediate nuclear forces, strategic arms reduction, and the verification protocols of the Peaceful Nuclear Explosions Treaty and the Threshold Test Ban Treaty. In 1989 the ACIS was further expanded when it absorbed the DCI's Treaty Monitoring Center and the conventional forces component of the Office of Soviet Analysis. At that time the ACIS was transferred from the Directorate of Intelligence to the office of the DCI.[45]

Today, WINPAC is responsible for (1) "studying the development of the entire spectrum of threats, from weapons of mass destruction . . . to advanced conventional weapons like lasers, advanced explosives, and armor, as well as all types of missiles"; (2) monitoring strategic arms control agreements; and (3) supporting military and diplomatic operations. It was an analyst associated with WINPAC who played a pivotal role in solidifying the Intelligence Community's position that Iraq's attempt to acquire aluminum tubes was motivated by a desire to use them in centrifuges for the purpose of uranium enrichment.[46]

The Information Operations Center's Analytical Group evaluates foreign threats, from both state and nonstate organizations, to U.S. computer systems, particularly those that support critical infrastructures. It explores the intentions, plans, and capabilities of those organizations. The Counterintelligence Center's Analysis Group focuses on two specific types of counterintelligence threats. One type is transnational threats, including the counterintelligence component of terrorism or the threats posed by emerging or changing technologies to the U.S. government and its information systems, and intelligence operations. The second type pertains to the threats posed by foreign intelligence services.[47]

The Office of Policy Support provides on-site intelligence support to a number of departments and agencies in Washington, sanitizes and delivers analysis to CIA foreign liaison partners, acts as the intelligence directorate's "focal point" for the tasking and dissemination of profiles of foreign leaders, and produces graphics, maps, and multimedia products for the Directorate of Intelligence. Prior to the creation of the office of the Director of National Intelligence, it also prepared the President's Daily Brief.[48]

The Office of Collection Strategies and Analysis assists the Directorate of Intelligence and its analysts in making use of current collection systems and in providing guidance for the development of future systems. Specifically, its functions include informing the President and other senior policymakers on U.S. collection capabilities and intelligence-gathering issues, running special collection efforts, evaluating the use of and value of current collection capabilities and guiding the development of future collection programs, and providing 24-hour collection support to the CIA's Operations Center.[49]

The CIA's latest strategic plan, *CIA 2015*, envisions four priorities for the agency in the coming years. Counterterrorism, it states, "will be the center of CIA's collection, analytic, and operational efforts." Second on the list is counterproliferation, "the focus of hundreds of CIA clandestine officers, scientists, engineers, and weapons analysts." Also among the top priorities are cyber threats, which represent, according to the agency plan, "the confluence of . . . counterintelligence and counterterrorism." Fourth on the list is "global reach."[50]

As indicated in Figure 2.1, other directorate components include the Office of Corporate Resources and the School for Intelligence Analysis.

NATIONAL SECURITY AGENCY

The National Security Agency (NSA) is one of the most secretive members of the U.S. Intelligence Community. The predecessor of NSA, the Armed Forces Security Agency (AFSA), was established within the Department of Defense, under the command of the Joint Chiefs of Staff, on May 20, 1949, when Secretary of Defense Louis Johnson signed JCS Directive 2010. In theory, the AFSA was to direct the communications intelligence activities of the military service signals intelligence units (at the time consisting of the Army Security Agency, Naval Security Group, and Air Force Security Service). In practice, the AFSA had little power, since its functions were defined in terms of activities not performed by the service units.[51]

On October 24, 1952, President Harry S Truman sent a Top Secret, eight-page (now declassified) memorandum, titled "Communications Intelligence Activities," to the Secretary of State and the Secretary of Defense; the memorandum abolished the AFSA and transferred its personnel to the newly created National Security

Agency, which was established that day by draft National Security Council Intelligence Directive No. 9. (The draft was formally approved in December.)[52]

The creation of the NSA had its origins in a December 10, 1951, memo sent by Walter Bedell Smith to National Security Council Executive Secretary James B. Lay, which stated that "control over, and coordination of, the collection and processing of Communications Intelligence had proved ineffective" and recommended a survey of communications intelligence activities. The proposal was approved on December 13, 1951, and the study was authorized on December 28, 1951. The resulting report, generally known as the "Brownell Committee Report," after committee chairman Herbert Brownell, was completed within six months, and it surveyed the history of U.S. communications intelligence activities. Its primary finding identified the need for a much greater degree of coordination and direction at the national level. As the change in the security agency's name indicated, the role of the NSA was to extend beyond the armed forces; hence, the NSA is considered to be "within but not part of DOD [Department of Defense]."[53]

Although the agency was created in 1952, it was not until 1957 that its existence was officially acknowledged in the U.S. Government Organization Manual as a "separately organized agency within the Department of Defense" that "performs highly specialized technical and coordinating functions relating to national security." Despite the lack of official acknowledgment, the NSA's existence was a matter of public knowledge from at least early 1954, when Washington newspapers ran several stories concerning the construction of the NSA's new headquarters at Fort George G. Meade, Maryland. In late 1954 the NSA was again in the news when an NSA employee was caught taking secret documents home.[54]

The charter for NSA is National Security Council Intelligence Directive (NSCID) 6. In its most recent version, NSCID 6, "Signals Intelligence," of January 17, 1972, directs NSA to produce SIGINT "in accordance with the objectives, requirements and priorities established by the Director of Central Intelligence Board." The directive also authorizes the Director of NSA (DIRNSA) "to issue direct to any operating elements engaged in SIGINT operations such instructions and assignments as are required" and states that "all instructions issued by the Director under the authority provided in this paragraph shall be mandatory, subject only to appeal to the Secretary of Defense."[55]

NSCID 6 defined SIGINT activities as consisting of Communications Intelligence (COMINT) and Electronic Intelligence (ELINT). The directive states that

> COMINT activities shall be construed to mean those activities which produce COMINT by interception and processing of foreign communications by radio, wire, or other electronic means, with specific exception stated below and by the processing of foreign encrypted communications, however transmitted. Interception comprises range estimation, transmitter operator identification, signal analysis, traffic analysis, cryptanalysis, decryption, study of plain text, the fusion of those processes, and the reporting of the results.

COMINT and COMINT activities as defined herein shall not include (a) any intercept and processing of unencrypted written communications, press and propaganda broadcasts, or (b) censorship.

When the NSA was established it did not have authority over ELINT operations, which remained the responsibility of the military services, but this authority was assigned to the agency in 1958. NSIC 6 defined ELINT activities as

the collection (observation and recording) and the processing for subsequent intelligence purposes, of information derived from foreign non-communications, electro-magnetic radiation emanating from other than atomic detonation or radioactive sources. ELINT is the technical and intelligence product of ELINT activities.[56]

From its inception, ELINT was primarily associated with the interception of emanations from radar systems. Telemetry Intelligence (TELINT), the interception and exploitation of signals from foreign missile tests, was originally a branch of ELINT but became a separate "INT" in 1971. Subsequently, it became part of a new third component of SIGINT—Foreign Instrumentation Signals Intelligence (FISINT)—that included telemetry, missile and satellite command signals, beacons, and computer-based data.

The SIGINT responsibilities of NSA and its director are specified by DOD Directive S-5100.20, "The National Security Agency and the Central Security Service":

- Collect (including through clandestine means), process, analyze, produce, and disseminate SIGINT information and data for foreign intelligence and counterintelligence purposes to support national and departmental missions. . . .
- Provide SIGINT support for the conduct of military operations, pursuant to tasking, priorities, and standards of timeliness assigned by the Secretary of Defense.
- Establish and operate an effective, unified organization for SIGINT activities, including executing any SIGINT-related functions the Secretary of Defense so directs.
- Develop rules, regulations, and standards governing the classification and declassification of SIGINT. . . .
- Exercise SIGINT operational control and establish policies and procedures for departments and agencies to follow when appropriately performing SIGINT activities. . . . [57]

The NSA has a second major mission, originally known as Communications Security (COMSEC), which became Information Security (INFOSEC) in the 1980s, and which is currently known as Information Assurance (IA). In its Information Assurance role, NSA creates, reviews, and authorizes the communications procedures

FIGURE 2.3   Organization of the National Security Agency

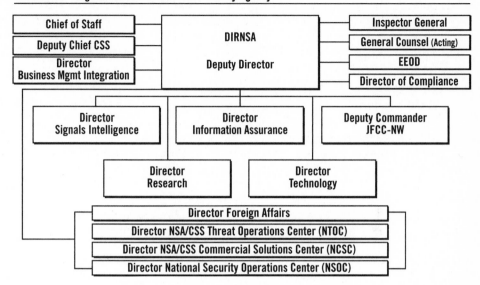

and codes of a variety of government agencies, including the State Department, the DOD, the CIA, and the FBI. This role includes development of secure data and voice transmission links on such satellite systems as the Defense Satellite Communications System (DSCS). Likewise, for sensitive communications, FBI agents use a special scrambler telephone that requires a different code from NSA each day. The NSA's IA responsibilities also include ensuring communications security for strategic weapons systems, so as to prevent unauthorized intrusion, interference, or jamming. In addition, the NSA is responsible for developing the codes by which the President must identify himself in order to authorize the release of nuclear weapons.[58] As part of its IA mission the NSA is also responsible for protecting national security data banks and computers from unauthorized access by individuals or governments.

NSA headquarters at Fort George G. Meade, Maryland, houses between 20,000 and 24,000 employees in three buildings. The NSA budget is probably over $15 billion. As indicated in Figure 2.3, it is divided into two directorates, Signals Intelligence and Information Assurance, and a number of additional components, as the result of a reorganization in 2000 initiated by the new director, Michael Hayden.[59]

Within the Signals Intelligence Directorate (formerly the Directorate of Operations), whose organization chart is shown as Figure 2.4, are three directorates, which highlight the three key elements of the mission of the directorate: collecting signals intelligence (the Directorate for Data Acquisition), analyzing the data and producing reports (the Directorate for Analysis and Production), and providing those reports to the appropriate individuals in NSA or in other government agencies (the

FIGURE 2.4   Organization of the NSA Signals Intelligence Directorate

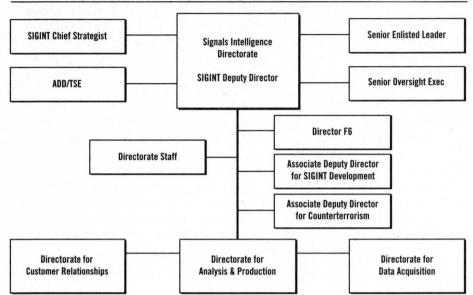

Directorate for Customer Relationships). An NSA office probably located in the Directorate for Data Acquisition is the Office of Unconventional Programs, which is involved in "unconventional signals intelligence operations to penetrate targets which cannot be accessed via conventional means."[60]

A key element of the Directorate of Analysis and Production is the Defense Special Missile and Aerospace (formerly Astronautics) Center (DEFSMAC), which was established as a joint operation of the NSA and Defense Intelligence Agency (DIA) by Department of Defense Directive S-5100.43, "Defense Special Missile and Astronautics Center," of April 27, 1964. Its current charter is Department of Defense Instruction S-5100.43 of September 24, 2008. DEFSMAC was reported to have a staff of more than 230 in 2001.[61]

According to a history of DEFSMAC, its mission is

> to accomplish 24 hour surveillance of foreign missile and space activities; alert and exercise technical control of DOD intelligence collection systems directed against foreign missile and space events; provide technical support, including tip-off, to all DOD missile and space intelligence collection activities to enable mission accomplishment; and, perform all source current analysis and reporting of all detected foreign missile and space events based on initial site reporting of all detected foreign missile and space events received up to 72 hours after the event.[62]

A former deputy director of the NSA has commented that "DEFSMAC is a combination of the DIA with its military components and the NSA. It has all the inputs from all the assets and is a warning activity. They probably have a better 'feel' for any worldwide threat to this country from missiles, aircraft or overt military activities, better and more timely, at instant fingertip availability than any group in the United States. So DEFSMAC is an input to NSA, but it also [is] an input to DIA and the CIA and the White House Situation Room and everybody else."[63]

DEFSMAC receives data related to Iranian, North Korean, Russian, Chinese, and other nations' space and missile launches. In turn, it notifies those who task or operate collection assets—from satellites to aircraft to ground stations—that a launch is imminent, so that they can prepare to monitor the event and obtain the maximum intelligence available.[64]

An allied center in the Directorate for Analysis and Production is the National Telemetry Processing Center, which receives the telemetry signals from foreign missiles that have been intercepted by NRO and NSA collection assets and seeks to determine which channels of telemetry relate to which particular functions of the missile and what the intercepted data mean in terms of missile performance.[65]

The mission of the Information Assurance Directorate "involves detecting, reporting, and responding to cyber threats; making encryption codes to securely pass information between systems; and embedding IA measures directly into the emerging Global Information Grid. It includes building secure audio and video communications equipment, making tamper protection products, and providing trusted microelectronics solutions." In addition, its mission "entails testing the security of customers' systems, providing OPSEC [operations security] assistance, and evaluating commercial software and hardware against nationally set standards, to better meet our nation's IA needs."[66]

Two key centers outside of the Signals Intelligence and Information Assurance Directorates are the National Security Operations Center (NSOC) and the NSA/CSS Threat Operations Center (NTOC). The National Security Operations Center used to be the National SIGINT Operations Center, and it was responsible for overseeing and directing the SIGINT coverage of any crisis event. It operated around the clock and was in instantaneous touch with every major NSA facility in the world. In the event that a facility intercepted signals that it believed to be significant, the facility personnel filed a CRITIC intelligence report with NSOC, which could immediately pass the message on to the Director of NSA. If NSOC authorities felt that the event lacked sufficient importance, they could revoke the report's CRITIC status. As a result of the increased emphasis on information warfare, NSOC was rechristened the National Security Operations Center. It continues to perform its previous missions but now operates an Information Protect Cell (IPC) and has a Defensive Information Operations Staff.[67]

The NSA/CSS Threat Operations Center is staffed by representatives of both the Signals Intelligence and Information Assurance Directorates. NTOC personnel attempt to identify cyber threats from foreign nations or terrorist groups to NSA, Defense Department, and military service computer systems.

In addition to directing the activities at NSA headquarters and NSA installations overseas, the Director of NSA is responsible for supervising the SIGINT activities of the Service Cryptologic Elements (SCEs). In this role, the director serves as the head of the Central Security Service (CSS). The CSS function of the NSA, with the DIRNSA serving simultaneously as Chief of the CSS, was established in 1971 in order "to provide a unified, more economical and more effective structure for executing cryptologic and related operations presently conducted under the Military Departments." There is, however, no separate CSS staff.[68]

NATIONAL RECONNAISSANCE OFFICE

In its May 2, 1946, report, *Preliminary Design for an Experimental World-Circling Spaceship*, the Douglas Aircraft Corporation examined the potential value of satellites for scientific and military purposes. Possible military uses included missile guidance, weapons delivery, weather reconnaissance, communications, attack assessment, and "observation."[69]

A little less than nine years later, on March 16, 1955, the Air Force issued General Operational Requirement No. 80, officially establishing a high-level requirement for an advanced reconnaissance satellite. Over the next five years the U.S. reconnaissance satellite program evolved in a variety of ways. The Air Force program was first designated the Advanced Reconnaissance System (ARS), then SENTRY, and finally SAMOS. Management responsibility for SAMOS was transferred from the Air Force to the Advanced Research Projects Agency (ARPA), established on February 7, 1958, and then back to the Air Force in 1959.[70]

Concern about the length of time it would take to achieve the primary objective of the SAMOS program—a satellite that could return its imagery electronically—led to President Dwight Eisenhower's approval, in early February 1958, of a CIA program to develop a reconnaissance satellite. That program, designated CORONA, focused on development of a satellite that would physically return its images in a canister, an objective that had been a subsidiary portion of the SAMOS program.[71]

By June 1960 the continued problems with the SAMOS program led the President to order a review of various aspects of the program. The urgency of attaining an operational satellite reconnaissance program had increased with the Soviet downing of Francis Gary Powers and his U-2 spy plane on May 1. The review culminated in an August 25, 1960, meeting in which a streamlined form of management for the SAMOS program was recommended and accepted by Eisenhower. Under the new arrangement, there would be a direct line of authority from the Secretary of the Air Force to the SAMOS project director, eliminating intervening levels of bureaucracy, including the Air Staff.[72]

On August 31, Secretary of the Air Force Dudley C. Sharp signed Secretary of the Air Force Order 115.1, establishing the Office of Missile and Satellite Systems within his own office. The office's director was to assist the Secretary "in discharging his responsibility for the direction, supervision and control of the Samos project." He was also made responsible for "maintaining liaison with the Office, Secretary of Defense and other interested Governmental agencies on matters relative to his assigned responsibilities."[73]

With Order 116.1, Sharp designated Brig. Gen. Robert E. Greer, Assistant Chief of Staff for Guided Missiles, as director of the SAMOS project. Greer was to organize a project office at the California headquarters of the Air Force Ballistic Missile Division, as a field extension of the Office of the Secretary of the Air Force, and to carry out development of the satellite. The order specifically stated, "The Director is responsible to and will report directly to the Secretary of the Air Force."[74]

The decisions of August and September 1960 gave a new structure to the Air Force program but did not affect the management arrangements for the CIA's secret CORONA program. However, a number of events and individuals would lead to the creation of a new office to manage overhead reconnaissance. Among them were James Killian and Edwin Land, two key presidential scientific advisors. Looking at the successful Air Force–CIA partnerships that had existed with respect to the U-2, OXCART, and CORONA programs, they pushed for permanent and institutionalized collaboration between the two organizations.[75]

Subsequent to John F. Kennedy's assumption of the presidency, Under Secretary of the Air Force Joseph Charyk drafted a proposal, at Killian and Land's request, for the establishment of a national coordinating agency for satellite reconnaissance. They were sufficiently persuasive, for sometime after the middle of July, Secretary of Defense Robert McNamara asked Charyk to draft the specific documents that would put the proposal into effect.[76]

On September 6, 1961, an agreement signed by the acting DCI, Gen. Charles Pearre Cabell, and Deputy Secretary of Defense Roswell Gilpatric established the National Reconnaissance Office (NRO) as a joint CIA–Air Force operation.[77] For the next thirty-one years the NRO's existence was classified SECRET. Outside of the Department of Defense directive that served as a charter, its name or initials could not be used in any government document that did not carry a special security classification.

From its inception the NRO's core responsibilities have included overseeing and funding the research and development of reconnaissance spacecraft and their sensors, procuring the space systems and their associated ground stations, determining launch vehicle requirements, operating spacecraft after they attain orbit, and disseminating the data collected.

According to the 1964 Department of Defense directive on the NRO, the Director of the NRO "will establish the security procedures to be followed for all matters of the (TS) National Reconnaissance Program . . . to protect all elements of the (S) National Reconnaissance Office."[78] Those security procedures—which constituted the BYEMAN Control System—concerned both the criteria for granting personnel access to information about NRO programs and the requirements concerning the physical security of documents relating to those programs.

NRO representatives also served on policy review committees and conducted studies dealing with topics related to satellite security and secrecy, such as the NSAM [National Security Action Memorandum] 156 committee, established in 1962 to review the political aspects of U.S. policy on space reconnaissance.[79]

The NRO's involvement in aerial reconnaissance issues has varied over the years. During the Cuban missile crisis it was involved in developing overflight plans for the U-2 and other aerial reconnaissance platforms. In 1974, it undertook a review of remotely piloted vehicles to "establish the evolution of present vehicles in the inventory, R&D that has been undertaken, and current requirements that exist for which they may be utilized."[80]

By 1989, the Director of the National Reconnaissance Office (DNRO) had assumed responsibility for managing the Airborne Reconnaissance Support Program (ARSP). NRO also was assigned responsibility for developing a highly secret, unmanned follow-on to the SR-71, ultimately designated QUARTZ and referred to in unclassified congressional hearings as the Advanced Airborne Reconnaissance System (AARS). (The program was canceled in 1993 for budgetary reasons.)[81]

NRO's structure, from shortly after its creation to 1992, reflected the fact that it was not a unified organization but rather a federation of intelligence and military organizations that maintained their separate identities while being part of the NRO and conducting space reconnaissance programs. Yet, there was a central headquarters; the NRO staff used the already existing Office of Missile and Satellite Systems (renamed the Office of Space Systems at the time of NRO's creation) as a cover, with the director of this office, an Air Force general, serving as NRO staff director.[82]

However, rather than establishing an organization fully subordinate to its director and divided among different aerospace reconnaissance functions—imagery, signals intelligence, ocean surveillance—the new organization became an umbrella organization for the ongoing reconnaissance efforts of the Air Force, the CIA, and the Navy. The early years of the arrangement would see a number of fierce battles between the CIA and the director of the NRO over the extent of the director's control. Throughout the 1960s and 1970s, at the very least, the CIA and the Air Force competed over which organization was responsible for new collection systems.[83]

The Air Force Office of Special Projects, as the SAMOS project office had been renamed, retained that unclassified designation and its California headquarters but also became the NRO's Program A. The CIA effort—which included aspects of CORONA, the A-12 reconnaissance aircraft, and its U-2 fleet—became Program B. The Navy was also brought into the NRO on the basis of the signals intelligence satellite system it was operating, ostensibly as the Galactic Radiation and Background (GRAB) experiment. That effort, initially funded through the Naval Research Laboratory, became Program C. Although the Air Force and Navy elements were fully subordinate to the director of the NRO, the CIA element, coming from an organization outside the Defense Department, was not.[84]

In early 1963, a second Air Force element, Program D, was established. The program initially encompassed what was then designated the R-12, and which subsequently became known as the RF-12 and then the SR-71—the Air Force version of the CIA's A-12/OXCART. Program D also assumed responsibility for the TAG-BOARD/D-21 reconnaissance drone and a non-reconnaissance project—the interceptor version of the R-12, variously designated the AF-12, XF-12, and YF-12.[85]

Program D continued as a major component of the NRO until the responsibility for the SR-71 was turned over to the Strategic Air Command in 1969, although as early as the summer of 1963, elements of the Air Force were seeking to assume control of the programs it managed. Program D was formally dissolved in 1970 or 1971.[86]

The NRO operated through the 1960s, the 1970s, and the 1980s with the same basic structure, excluding Program D, with the cover arrangements that had been established in the 1961–1963 period. But in the 1990s, a wide-ranging restructuring of the NRO was prompted by congressional pressure, the recommendations of a review group, and post–Cold War budget constraints.[87]

In April 1992 DCI Robert Gates announced before a joint public hearing of the Senate and House intelligence oversight committees that there would be "a far-reaching internal restructuring of the Intelligence Community organization responsible for designing, building, and operating our overhead reconnaissance assets."[88]

That restructuring, which replaced the Air Force, CIA, and Navy program offices with a functional structure, resulted in the creation of three major directorates: the IMINT Systems Acquisition and Operations Directorate, the SIGINT Systems Acquisition and Operations Directorate, and the Communications Systems Acquisition and Operations Directorate. Each directorate was responsible for both acquiring and supervising contractor research and development as well as for purchasing and operating the relevant spacecraft and ground stations.[89]

In March 1997, in response to the recommendation of a review panel, the Office of Systems Applications (OSA), which was established to investigate the feasibility of small satellites for reconnaissance, was upgraded to become NRO's fourth directorate: the Advanced Systems and Technology Directorate. The directorate's mission is to investigate and conduct research and development for systems that would be significantly different from those operated by the other three acquisition and operations directorates.[90]

On October 15, 2006, the office of the Deputy Director for Systems Engineering was replaced by a fifth directorate: the Directorate of Systems Integration and Engineering. The new directorate was created to establish standards for systems engineering, to develop and coordinate with the other NRO directorates a high-level NRO architectural description, and to "review all major trade-off analyses [and] architectural alternatives . . . prior to their presentation outside of NRO."[91] Today, it is known as the Systems Engineering Directorate.

In recent years the number of NRO directorates has expanded dramatically, as shown in Figure 2.5. The Imagery and SIGINT directorates (although not the Communications directorate) were stripped of their operational responsibilities, becoming the Imagery Intelligence Systems Acquisition Directorate and the Signals

Intelligence Systems Acquisition Directorate. Operation of imagery and signals intelligence systems in orbit became the responsibility of the Mission Operations Directorate—in an attempt to allow customers to have a single point of contact for space intelligence data, regardless of the collection system that obtained it. Responsibility for the operations of the ground stations was also transferred from the imagery and SIGINT directorates to a newly established Ground Enterprise Directorate, with the expectation that greater attention would be devoted to the ground component of the NRO effort.[92]

The three other directorates are Business Plans & Operations, Management Services & Operations, and Mission Support. The latter directorate's history began in April 1990 when the position of Deputy Director for Military Support (DDMS) was established to facilitate the provision of NRO support to military commanders. In late 1996 the position of Deputy Director for National Support (DDNS) was established to balance the DDMS position. According to the DDNS mission statement, the new official was to "maintain close coordination with senior officials in all national-level departments and agencies who can represent their respective current and future space-based reconnaissance needs." The position was created in response to a frequently expressed concern about the extent of focus on supporting military operations. In 2006, the two positions were merged into the single position of Deputy Director for Mission Support (DDMS). Subsequently, the Deputy Director position was eliminated and the functions placed into a directorate.[93]

Among the offices constituting the NRO Corporate Staff is the Office of Security and Counterintelligence. In June 1992 the NRO established a Counterintelligence Staff to "increase the awareness of foreign intelligence threats to NRO programs, facilities and personnel, . . . communicating that information to NRO CI activities." Its primary functions included research and analysis; coordination within the NRO, the CI community, and investigative agencies; and operations support. In March 2006, the director of the NRO announced that the Counterintelligence Staff would be realigned within the office of the Director of Security, whose position would become Director of NRO Security and Counterintelligence. The Director of Security and Counterintelligence reports to the Principal Deputy Director, as do the directors of Human Resources and Management Services and Operations. Four other officials report directly to the Director of the NRO: the General Counsel, the Inspector General, the Chief Information Officer, and the director of the Equal Employment Opportunity Office.[94]

NRO's budget is probably in the vicinity of $10 billion. As of late 1997, it had 2,753 government employees. As has always been the case, NRO employees are assigned to the reconnaissance office from their parent organizations. In 1997, the 2,753 NRO employees consisted of representatives from the Air Force (1,456, or 53 percent), the CIA (649, or 24 percent), the NSA (412, or 15 percent), the Navy (214, or 8 percent), and other agencies such as DIA and the Army (22, or <1 percent). In March 2006, the Government Accountability Office estimated that Air Force personnel made up approximately 57 percent of NRO employees.[95]

FIGURE 2.5 Organization of the National Reconnaissance Office

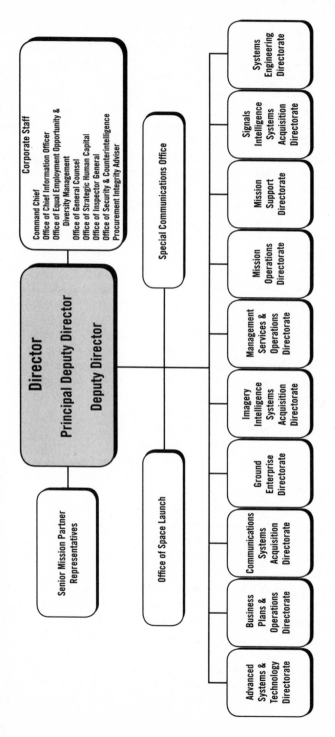

Source: www.nro.gov.

In 2009, the Intelligence Authorization Act for Fiscal Year 2010 mandated that the Director of National Intelligence and Secretary of Defense produce a new charter for the NRO, updating the 1965 charter. That charter has not yet been finalized.[96]

NATIONAL GEOSPATIAL-INTELLIGENCE AGENCY

In his April 1992 testimony before the House and Senate intelligence committees, DCI Robert Gates noted that the Imagery Task Force he had established upon becoming DCI had recommended the creation of a National Imagery Agency (NIA), which would absorb the CIA's National Photographic Interpretation Center as well as the Defense Mapping Agency (DMA).[97]

The task force's vision for an NIA was not as broad as that which had been recommended by some in congressional hearings and written into proposed legislation by both the House and Senate intelligence committees. The broader vision would have created an NIA responsible for virtually the entire range of imagery functions—decisions on spacecraft and aircraft capabilities, research and development to support those decisions, tasking, collection operations, and analysis.[98]

During his testimony Gates rejected the recommendations of both his task force and the congressional committees—in part because Chairman of the Joint Chiefs of Staff Colin Powell wanted to maintain DOD control of the Defense Mapping Agency. However, Gates and Secretary of Defense Richard Cheney agreed to a less dramatic fix, and the next month a Central Imagery Office was established within the Department of Defense. Its creation was due to some of the same factors that produced suggestions for the establishment of an NIA, including congressional frustration with a lack of coherent imagery management, imagery collection and dissemination problems that surfaced during the Persian Gulf War, budgetary constraints, and changing requirements for the support of military operations. Thus, the Central Imagery Office (CIO) was established on May 6, 1992, chartered by both a Department of Defense Directive (5105.56) and a Director of Central Intelligence Directive (2/9) as a DOD Combat Support Agency.[99]

In contrast to the alternative national imagery agencies that had been proposed, the CIO was not designed to absorb existing agencies or take on their collection and analysis functions. Rather, the mission of the CIO included tasking of national imagery systems (assuming that mission in place of the DCI Committee on Imagery Requirements and Exploitation) to ensure responsive imagery support to the Department of Defense, combat commanders, the CIA, and other agencies; advising the Secretary of Defense and the DCI regarding future imagery requirements; and evaluating the performance of imagery components. Pursuant to the provision of imagery support, the CIO was assigned the role of systems development—specifically, establishing imagery architectures and standards for interoperability of imagery dissemination systems, and supporting and conducting research and development.[100]

Establishing the CIO delayed, but did not prevent, creation of a national imagery and mapping agency. In April 1995, DCI-designate John Deutch told the Senate Select Committee on Intelligence that, if confirmed, he would "move immediately to consolidate the management of all imagery collection, analysis, and distribution." He went on to argue that "both effectiveness and economy can be improved by managing imagery in a manner similar to the National Security Agency's organization for signals intelligence."[101]

After his confirmation, Deutch established a National Imagery Agency Steering Group, which in turn chartered an NIA Task Force. The task force produced eleven different options for an NIA, ranging from a strengthened CIO to a highly centralized NIA, with program, budget, and management authority for all aspects of imagery.[102]

In late November 1995 Deutch and Secretary of Defense William Perry sent a joint letter to congressional leaders and relevant committees on their joint plan to establish a National Imagery and Mapping Agency as a combat support agency within the Department of Defense on October 1, 1996. Their letter noted that the proposed agency would be formed by consolidating the Defense Mapping Agency, Central Imagery Office, National Photographic Interpretation Center, the imagery exploitation element of the Defense Intelligence Agency, and portions of the Defense Airborne Reconnaissance Office and National Reconnaissance Office that were involved in imagery exploitation and dissemination.[103]

The planned agency would have left the acquisition and operation of space systems and their ground stations to the NRO, and it would also have left the imagery exploitation activities of the service intelligence organizations untouched. According to the letter, the task force recommended the proposed consolidation for three basic reasons:

1. A single, streamlined and focused agency could best serve the imagery and mapping needs of a growing and diverse customer base across government;
2. the current dispersion of imagery and mapping responsibilities does not allow one agency to exploit the tremendous potential of enhanced collection systems, digital processing technology and the prospective expansion in commercial imagery; and
3. the revolution in information technology makes possible a symbiosis of imagery intelligence and mapping which can best be realized through more central management.[104]

The wisdom of the plan was questioned by both former intelligence (particularly CIA) officials and many within Congress—particularly the vice chairman of the Senate Select Committee on Intelligence, Robert Kerrey (D–Neb.), and the House Permanent Select Committee on Intelligence. The primary concern was that, as a result of the transfer of NPIC personnel from the CIA to the Defense Department, imagery support to national policymakers would suffer in order to support the requirements of military commanders. However, although the opposition was unable to block the creation of the new agency, the Senate Select Committee on Intelligence did persuade the Senate Armed Services Committee to amend the legislation creating the National Imagery and Mapping Agency (NIMA). Thus, the final legislation stipulated that the

DCI would retain tasking authority over national imagery systems and that the Secretary of Defense needed to obtain the DCI's concurrence before appointing the NIMA director, or note the DCI's lack of concurrence before recommending a candidate to the President. In addition, the Senate Armed Services Committee agreed to the modification of the National Security Act, so that it would explicitly state NIMA's responsibility to provide intelligence for national policymakers.[105]

NIMA came into being as projected on October 1, 1996. It incorporated all the elements mentioned in the late November statement as well as the Office of Imagery Analysis of the CIA's Directorate of Intelligence and the Defense Dissemination Program Office. It would also eventually absorb some activities of the CIA's Office of Development and Engineering. The consolidation thus created an agency with about 9,000 personnel—about 2,000 from the imagery interpretation activities and about 7,000 from the Defense Mapping Agency (DMA).[106]

To emphasize the fact that the organization "merges imagery, maps, charts and environmental data to produce . . . 'geospatial intelligence' [GEOINT]—the exploitation and analysis of imagery and geospatial information to describe, assess, and visually depict physical features and geographically referenced activities of the earth," Director James Clapper sought to change NIMA's name to the National Geospatial-Intelligence Agency (NGA), a change that was authorized by the 2004 Defense Authorization Bill and took effect when President George W. Bush signed the bill on November 24, 2003.[107]

As with the CIO, NIMA was chartered by both a DOD directive—(5105.60 of October 11, 1996, "National Imagery and Mapping Agency (NIMA)"—and a DCI directive. The most recent DOD Directive to govern the activities of NGA was issued on July 29, 2009.

The directive specifies NGA's mission, organization and management, and the responsibilities and functions of the Director of NGA. It specifies the director's forty-two responsibilities with regard to the production of GEOINT, GEOINT architecture and standards, GEOINT Systems, GEOINT Training and Education, GEOINT Functional Management and Program Management, and GEOINT International Engagement. Those responsibilities include the responsibility to

- provide responsive GEOINT products, support, services, and information.
- manage GEOINT planning, collection, operations, analysis, production, and dissemination.
- establish and/or consolidate DOD geospatial data collection requirements and, as appropriate, task or coordinate collection with the DOD components to collect and provide these data.
- monitor and evaluate the performance of the DOD components having GEOINT planning, programming, tasking, collection, processing, production, exploitation, dissemination, and retention functions in meeting national and military GEOINT requirements—and monitor, to the extent authorized by

the DNI, the performance of other U.S. government departments having GEOINT functions.

- serve as the DOD lead for GEOINT standards and prescribe, mandate, and enforce standards and architectures related to GEOINT and GEOINT tasking, collection, processing, exploitation, and international geospatial information.
- establish end-to-end and system architectures related to GEOINT in compliance with National and Defense Infrastructure guidance and standards.
- develop, acquire, and field GEOINT-related systems.
- serve as the Program Manager for the National Geospatial Intelligence Program within the National Intelligence Program.
- establish and maintain international GEOINT agreements and arrangements with foreign governments and international organizations.[108]

The core of NGA's organizational structure is composed of the five directorates shown in Figure 2.6. The Analysis and Production Directorate is the home for imagery interpreters focused on particular nations and regions as well as on specific topics such as warning, global navigation, and counterproliferation. They "provide geospatial intelligence and services to policy makers, military decisionmakers, and tailored support to civilian federal agencies and international organizations."[109]

The Acquisition Directorate, as its title indicates, is responsible for the procurement of systems, such as processing equipment used by NGA in receiving imagery from satellites and aircraft, and computers used by NGA personnel analyzing the data received. It conducts pre-acquisition studies, acquisition program engineering, and systems engineering work. According to NGA, the InnoVision Directorate "forecasts future environments, defines future needs, [and] establishes plans to align resources."[110]

The key function of the Source Operations & Management Directorate is carried out by its Source Operations Group. The group is responsible, as was the Central Imagery Office's Central Imagery Tasking Office and the Committee on Imagery Requirements and Exploitation (COMIREX) in earlier years, for the tasking of U.S. imagery satellites—sorting through requests for imagery coverage of targets from government military and civilian organizations, determining which satellites should be employed against specific targets, and selecting the altitude and angle from which imagery is to be obtained.[111]

Beyond being renamed and reorganized since it was established in 1996, the agency has also evolved in a number of ways. The development of high-resolution commercial imagery satellites has made it possible for NGA to procure significant quantities of imagery through commercial channels that in the past could be obtained only from NRO's classified systems. As a result, NGA has become a significant factor in the financial health of commercial imagery firms.[112]

The terrorist attacks of 9/11 led to NGA assuming a homeland security role through the provision of detailed maps and imagery to federal, state, and local agen-

FIGURE 2.6 Organization of the National Geospatial-Intelligence Agency

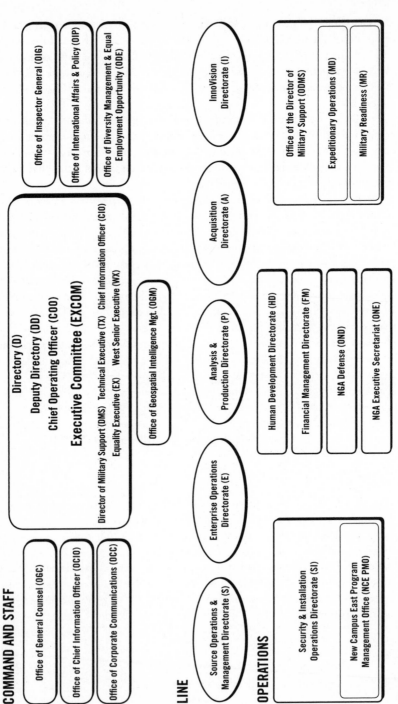

COMMAND AND STAFF

Office of General Counsel (OGC)

Office of Chief Information Officer (OCIO)

Office of Corporate Communications (OCC)

Directory (D)
Deputy Directory (DD)
Chief Operating Officer (COO)

Executive Committee (EXCOM)

Director of Military Support (DMS) Technical Executive (TX) Chief Information Officer (CIO)
Equality Executive (EX)   West Senior Executive (WX)

Office of Geospatial Intelligence Mgt. (OGM)

Office of Inspector General (OIG)

Office of International Affairs & Policy (OIP)

Office of Diversity Management & Equal Employment Opportunity (ODE)

InnoVision Directorate (I)

Office of the Director of Military Support (ODMS)

Expeditionary Operations (MD)

Military Readiness (MR)

Acquisition Directorate (A)

Analysis & Production Directorate (P)

Human Development Directorate (HD)

Financial Management Directorate (FM)

NGA Defense (OND)

NGA Executive Secretariat (ONE)

LINE

Enterprise Operations Directorate (E)

Source Operations & Management Directorate (S)

OPERATIONS

Security & Installation Operations Directorate (SI)

New Campus East Program Management Office (NCE PMO)

Source: www.nga.mil.

cies, including the Department of Homeland Security, involved in securing facilities and protecting domestic activities. NGA products have also been employed in disaster relief operations in the United States and abroad, including operations dealing with the devastation of Hurricane Katrina in the southeastern United States, the 2004 Asian tsunami, the 2006 earthquake in Pakistan, and the 2010 oil spill in the Gulf of Mexico.[113]

In 2006, legislation added ground-based photography—including still photographs and video—to the set of overhead imagery products (from satellites and aircraft) in NGA's library. One objective was to provide information to soldiers on what facilities looked like from their perspective on the ground rather than just aerial views.[114]

Because of the geographical distance between the agencies absorbed by NGA, significant portions of NGA are not found at its northern Virginia headquarters but are located instead at the Washington Navy Yard (former NPIC); in Washington, D.C. (various offices of the DIA); in Bethesda, Maryland (headquarters and DMA hydrographic production); in St. Louis, Missouri (DMA aerospace production); and in Fort Belvoir, Virginia (the main ground station for NRO's electro-optical satellites). NGA began moving into its new headquarters facility at Fort Belvoir, Virginia, in January 2011. When it was established, NIMA had about 9,000 employees, but there were plans to reduce that number to 7,500. Today, there are 16,000 NGA employees, 8,500 of whom will work at the Ft. Belvoir facility when it is completed. [115]

Notes

1. National Security Council, *Report on Presidential Review Memorandum/NSC 11: Intelligence Structure and Mission*, 1977, p. 1.

2. Office of the Director of National Intelligence, ODNI Press Release No. 21-10, "DNI Releases Budget Figure for 2010 National Intelligence Program," October 28, 2010. The figure for the NIP budget was $53.1 billion. Subsequently the Defense Department released the figure for the Military Intelligence Program budget—$27 billion.

3. See R. Harris Smith, *OSS: The Secret History of America's First Central Intelligence Agency* (Berkeley: University of California Press, 1981); and Bradley F. Smith, *The Shadow Warriors: O.S.S. and the Origins of the C.I.A.* (New York: Basic Books, 1983).

4. Harry S. Truman, "Executive Order 9621: Termination of the Office of Strategic Services and Disposition of Its Functions," September 20, 1945, in *Emergence of the Intelligence Establishment*, ed. C. Thomas Thorne Jr. and David S. Patterson (Washington, D.C.: U.S. Government Printing Office, 1996), pp. 44–46.

5. Thomas F. Troy, *Donovan and the CIA: A History of the Establishment of the Central Intelligence Agency* (Frederick, Md.: University Publications of America, 1981), pp. 325–349.

6. U.S. Congress, House Permanent Select Committee on Intelligence, *Compilation of Intelligence Laws and Executive Orders* (Washington, D.C.: U.S. Government Printing Office, 1983), p. 7.

7. Lawrence Houston, Memorandum for the Director, Subject: CIA Authority to Perform Propaganda and Commando Type Functions, September 25, 1947.

8. Ronald Reagan, "Executive Order 12333: United States Intelligence Activities," December 4, 1981, in *Federal Register* 46, no. 235 (December 8, 1981): 59941–59954, at 59950.

9. Ronald Kessler, *Inside the CIA: Revealing the Secrets of the World's Most Powerful Spy Agency* (New York: Pocket Books, 1992), pp. xxvii, 144; Walter Pincus, "CIA Struggles to Find Identity in a New World," *Washington Post*, May 9, 1994, pp. A1, A9; U.S. Congress, House Committee on Appropriations, *Department of Defense Appropriations for 1995, Part 3* (Washington, D.C.: U.S. Government Printing Office, 1994), p. 784.

10. Victor Marchetti and John Marks, *The CIA and the Cult of Intelligence* (New York: Knopf, 1974), pp. 73–74; Commission on CIA Activities in the United States, *Report to the President* (Washington, D.C.: U.S. Government Printing Office, 1975), p. 91; Directorate of Administration, Central Intelligence Agency (Washington, D.C.: CIA, n.d), unpaginated; David Atlee Phillips, *Careers in Secret Operations: How to Be a Federal Intelligence Officer* (Frederick, Md.: University Publications of America, 1984), p. 27.

11. Marchetti and Marks, *The CIA and the Cult of Intelligence*, pp. 73–74; Phillips, *Careers in Secret Operations*, pp. 26–28; Jeffrey Lenorovitz, "CIA Satellite Data Link Study Revealed," *Aviation Week & Space Technology*, May 2, 1997, pp. 25–26; Arnaud de Borchgrave, "Space-Age Spies," *Newsweek*, March 6, 1978, p. 37; Commission on CIA Activities in the United States, *Report to the President*, pp. 91–92; *Directorate of Administration, Central Intelligence Agency*, unpaginated; R. James Woolsey, "National Security and the Future Direction of the Central Intelligence Agency," address to the Center for Strategic and International Studies, Washington, D.C., July 18, 1994, p. 12.

12. Central Intelligence Agency, "DNI and D/CIA Announce Establishment of the National Clandestine Service," October 13, 2005, and Central Intelligence Agency, "Fact Sheet: Creation of the National HUMINT Manager," October 13, 2005 (both available at http://www.cia.gov); Central Intelligence Agency, "Transcript of Interview of Major General Michael E. Ennis, USMC, Deputy Director of the National Clandestine Service for Community HUMINT, by WTOP Radio's J.J. Green, February 28, 2007," March 7, 2007, http://cia.gov.

13. Jeffrey T. Richelson, *The Wizards of Langley: Inside the CIA's Directorate of Science and Technology* (Boulder, Colo.: Westview, 2001), pp. 223–224, 224 n.

14. Kessler, *Inside the CIA*, p. 18; David Wise, *Nightmover: How Aldrich Ames Sold the CIA to the KGB for $4.6 Million* (New York: HarperCollins, 1995), p. 77 n.; David Wise, *The American Police State* (New York: Vintage, 1976), p. 188; Robert Dreyfuss, "Left Out in the Cold," *Mother Jones*, January/February 1998, pp. 52–84; Vernon Loeb, "Gathering Intelligence Nuggets One by One," *Washington Post*, April 19, 1999, p. A17; Massimo Calabresi, "When the CIA Calls," *Time*, June 6, 2001, http://www.time.com.

15. U.S. Congress, Senate Select Committee to Study Governmental Operations with Respect to Intelligence Activities, *Final Report, Book I: Foreign and Military Intelligence* (Washington, D.C.: U.S. Government Printing Office, 1976), p. 439; Ralph E. Cook, "The CIA and Academe," *Studies in Intelligence* (Winter 1983): 33–42 at 38–39; Kessler, *Inside the CIA*, p. 18.

16. Dreyfuss, "Left Out in the Cold."

17. U.S. Congress, Senate Select Committee to Study Governmental Operations with Respect to Intelligence Activities, *Final Report, Book I: Foreign and Military Intelligence*, p. 439; Cook, "The CIA and Academe," p. 38; Wise, *The American Police State*, p. 189.

18. Central Intelligence Agency, *Appendices to Guidance for CIA Activities Within the United States and Outside the United States*, November 30, 1982, p. 20; Dana Priest, "CIA Is Expanding Domestic Operations," *Washington Post*, October 23, 2002, p. A2; Dana Priest, "CIA Plans to Shift Work to Denver," *Washington Post*, May 6, 2005, p. A21.

19. Robert Parry, "CIA Manual Producers Say They're Scapegoats," *Washington Post*, November 15, 1984, p. A28; "Aides Disciplined by CIA Are Irked," *New York Times*, November 15, 1984, pp. A1, A8; Duane R. Clarridge, *A Spy for All Seasons: My Life in the CIA* (New York: Scribner, 1997), p. 190; Barton Gellman, "Broad Effort Launched After '98 Attacks," *Washington Post*, December 19, 2001, pp. A1, A26; Bob Woodward, "Secret CIA Units Playing a Central Combat Role," *Washington Post*, November 18, 2001, pp. A1, A16; Andrew Koch, "Covert Warriors," *Jane's Defence Weekly*, March 29, 2003, pp. 22–27; Gary Bernsten and Ralph Pezzullo, *Jawbreaker: The Attack on Bin Laden and Al Qaeda: A Personal Account by the CIA's Key Field Commander* (New York: Crown, 2005), pp. 82–83, 191, 211, 236, 268, 275–276.

20. "The CIA's Darkest Secrets," *U.S. News & World Report*, July 4, 1994, pp. 34–37; Clarridge, *A Spy for All Seasons*, pp. 8, 49, 180, 193; Walter Pincus, "Justice Asked to Investigate Leaks by CIA Ex-Officials," *Washington Post*, July 19, 1997, p. A16.

21. Loch Johnson, "Smart Intelligence," *Foreign Policy* (Winter 1992–1993): 53–69; Clarridge, *A Spy for All Seasons*, pp. 322–329; Roberto Suro, "2 Terrorist Groups Set Up U.S. Cells, Senate Panel Is Told," *Washington Post*, May 14, 1997, p. A4; Vernon Loeb, "Where the CIA Wages Its New World War," *Washington Post*, September 9, 1998, p. A17; James Risen, "C.I.A. Unit on bin Laden Is Understaffed, a Senior Official Tells Lawmakers," *New York Times*, September 15, 2004, p. A18; Mark Mazzetti, "CIA Closes Unit Focused on Capture of bin Laden," *New York Times*, July 4, 2006, p. A4; "DCI Counterterrorist Center," http://www.cia.gov/terrorism/ctc.html, accessed October 5, 2001; Douglas Waller, "At the Crossroads of Terror," *Time*, June 30, 2002, http://www.time.com. Whether the centers were considered truly interagency centers was a matter of perspective. See Douglas E. Garthoff, *Directors of Central Intelligence as Leaders of the U.S. Intelligence Community, 1946–2005* (Washington, D.C.: Center for the Study of Intelligence, 2005), pp. 188–189.

22. Johnson, "Smart Intelligence"; David Wise, *Molehunt: The Secret Search for Traitors That Shattered the CIA* (New York: Random House, 1992), pp. 298–299; Angelo Codevilla, *Informing Statecraft: Intelligence for a New Century* (New York: Free Press, 1992), p. 155.

23. Central Intelligence Agency, "Restructuring in the DS&T," June 1996; Jeffrey T. Richelson, "CIA's Science and Technology Gurus Get New Look, Roles," *Defense Week*, August 19, 1996, p. 6; "The CIA's Darkest Secrets"; Barry G. Royden, "CIA and National HUMINT: Preparing for the 21st Century," *Defense Intelligence Journal* 6, 1 (Spring 1997): 15–22. On the CIA's handling of Yurchenko, see Ronald Kessler, *Escape from the CIA: How the CIA Won and Lost the Most Important KGB Spy Ever to Defect to the U.S.* (New York: Pocket Books, 1991).

24. George Tenet with Bill Harlow, *At the Center of the Storm: My Life at the CIA* (New York: HarperCollins, 2007), pp. 283, 453; Central Intelligence Agency, "CIA Launches New Counterproliferation Center," August 18, 2010, www.cia.gov. For more on the CPD, see Valerie Plame Wilson, *Fair Game: How a Top CIA Agent Was Betrayed by Her Own Government* (New York: Simon & Schuster, 2008), pp. 60–62, 352–354. ("Afterword" by Laura Rozen.)

25. Richelson, *The Wizards of Langley*, pp. 39–73.

26. Ibid., pp. 72–73, 195–196, 271–276; Central Intelligence Agency, "DNI and D/CIA Announce Establishment of DNI Open Source Center," November 8, 2005, http://www.cia.gov.

27. U.S. Congress, House Select Committee on Intelligence, *U.S. Intelligence Agencies and Activities: Intelligence Costs and Fiscal Procedures* (Washington, D.C.: U.S. Government Printing Office, 1975), pp. 537–544; *Directorate of Science and Technology, Central Intelligence Agency* (Washington, D.C.: CIA, n.d.), unpaginated.

28. *Office of SIGINT Operations* (Washington, D.C.: CIA, n.d.), unpaginated; Desmond Ball, *A Suitable Piece of Real Estate: American Installations in Australia* (Sydney: Hale & Ire-monger, 1980), p. 73; Bob Woodward, *Veil: The Secret Wars of the CIA, 1981–1987* (New York: Simon & Schuster, 1987), pp. 313–314; James Bamford, *Body of Secrets: Anatomy of the Ultra-Secret National Security Agency* (New York: Doubleday, 2001), p. 477.

29. CIA document fragment, released under the FOIA; Kessler, *Inside the CIA*, p. 168.

30. *Directorate of Science and Technology, Central Intelligence Agency*; Thomas Powers, *The Man Who Kept the Secrets: Richard Helms and the CIA* (New York: Knopf, 1979), p. 340 n. 38; U.S. Congress, Senate Select Committee to Study Governmental Operations with Respect to Intelligence Activities, *Final Report, Book IV*, p. 101; William Colby with Peter Forbath, *Honorable Men: My Life in the CIA* (New York: Simon & Schuster, 1978), p. 336; Robert Gates, *From the Shadows: The Ultimate Insider's Story of Five Presidents and How They Won the Cold War* (New York: Simon & Schuster, 1996), p. 154; Ronald Kessler, *The CIA at War: Inside the Secret Campaign Against Terror* (New York: St. Martin's Press, 2003), p. 137; Vernon Loeb, "After-Action Report," *Washington Post Magazine*, February 27, 2000, pp. 7ff; Central Intelligence Agency, *Devotion to Duty: Responding to the Terrorist Attacks of September 11, 2010*, pp. 37–39.

31. Central Intelligence Agency, "DS&T Realignment Overview," n.d.; private information.

32. Private information.

33. Ibid.

34. Central Intelligence Agency, "CIA Opens Center on Climate Change and National Security," September 25, 2009, www.cia.gov. In early 2011 it was reported that the center faced an "uncertain future." See Jeff Stein, "CIA's unit on climate change faces uncertain future," *Spy Talk* (www.washingtonpost.com), January 11, 2011.

35. Gary H. Anthes, "Cloak & Dagger IT," http://www.computerworld.com, accessed February 6, 2001; Rick E. Yannuzzi, "In-Q-Tel: A New Partnership Between the CIA and the Private Sector," *Defense Intelligence Journal* 9, 1 (Winter 2000); Daniel G. Dupont, "The Company's Company," *Scientific American*, August 2001, pp. 26–27; Anne Laurent, "Raising the Ante," *Government Executive*, June 2002, pp. 34–44.

36. Anthes, "Cloak & Dagger IT"; Neil King Jr., "Small Start-Up Helps the CIA to Mask Its Moves on the Web," *Wall Street Journal*, February 12, 2001, pp. B1, B6; "Battery Startup Gains CIA Funding," http://www.eetimes.com, November 13, 2006.

37. Central Intelligence Agency, *Fact Book on Intelligence, 50th Anniversary Edition*, p. 8; "Directorate of Intelligence Organizational Components," http://www.odci.gov/cia/di/mission/components.html; Rochelle McConkie, "U Alumni Return for CIA Recruitment," http://www.dailyutahchronicle.com, October 3, 2006.

38. Naval Postgraduate School, NPS-09–06–005, *Summary of Research 2004*, 2005, p. 85; Texas Tech University, *College of Arts & Sciences Annual Report & Plan*, July 2005, p. 54; U.S. Congress, Senate Select Committee on Intelligence, *Postwar Findings About Iraq's WMD Pro-*

grams and Links to Terrorism and How They Compare with Pre-War Assessments Together with Additional Views, September 8, 2006, p. 127.

39. Information provided by the CIA Public Affairs Staff; Richelson, *The Wizards of Langley,* pp. 195–196; CIA, A *Consumer's Guide to Intelligence,* p. 17; John J. Gentry, *Lost Promise: How CIA Analysis Misserves the Country* (Lanham, Md.: University Press of America, 1993), pp. 8, 10.

40. "The Office of Transnational Issues (OTI)," http://www.cia.gov/cia/di/organizationt_oti_page.html, accessed June 1, 2006; Jonathan D. Clemente, "CIA's Medical and Psychological Analysis Center (MPAC) and the Health of Foreign Leaders," *International Journal of Intelligence and Counterintelligence* 19, 3 (Fall 2006): 385–427; Jonathan D. Clemente, "In Sickness and In Health," *Bulletin of the Atomic Scientists,* March–April 2007, pp. 38–44, 66.

41. "The Office of Terrorism Analysis (OTA)," http://www.cia.gov/cia/di/organizationt_ota_page.html, accessed June 1, 2006; Rowan Scarborough, "CIA Exercise Reveals Consequences of Defeat," http://www.washingtontimes.com, December 21, 2006.

42. Robin Wright and Ronald J. Ostrow, "Webster Unites Rival Agencies to Fight Drugs," *Los Angeles Times,* August 24, 1989, pp. 1, 27; Michael Isikoff, "CIA Creates Narcotics Unit to Help in Drug Fight," *Washington Post,* May 28, 1989, p. A12; Central Intelligence Agency, *A Consumer's Guide to Intelligence* (1993), p. 18; "The DCI Crime and Narcotics Center (CNC)," http://www.cia.gov/cia/di/organizationt_cnc_page.html, accessed June 1, 2006.

43. "Bush Approved Covert Action by CIA to Halt Spread of Arms," *Los Angeles Times,* June 21, 1992, p. A20; Bill Gertz, "CIA Creates Center to Monitor Arms," *Washington Times,* December 3, 1991, p. A5; "Intelligence Will Be Key Tool in Proliferation Battle," *Defense Week,* December 9, 1991, p. 3; Johnson, "Smart Intelligence"; Paula L. Scalingi, "Intelligence Community Cooperation: The Arms Control Model," *International Journal of Intelligence and Counterintelligence* 5, 4 (Winter 1991–1992): 402–403; Barbara Starr, "Woolsey Tackles Proliferation as the Problem Gets Worse," *Jane's Defence Weekly,* November 13, 1993, p. 23; Central Intelligence Agency, *A Consumer's Guide to Intelligence* (1995), p. 18.

44. U.S. Congress, House Permanent Select Committee on Intelligence, *Intelligence Authorization Act for Fiscal Year 1998, Report 105–135, Part 1* (Washington, D.C.: U.S. Government Printing Office, 1997), p. 25.

45. Vernon Loeb, "CIA Is Stepping Up Attempts to Monitor Spread of Weapons," *Washington Post,* March 21, 2001, p. A15; Scalingi, "Intelligence Community Cooperation," pp. 405–406; Garthoff, *Directors of Central Intelligence as Leaders of the U.S. Intelligence Community, 1946–2005,* p. 189.

46. "The DCI Center for Weapons Intelligence, Nonproliferation, and Arms Control (WINPAC)," http://www.cia.gov/cia/di/organizationt_winpac_page.html, accessed June 1, 2006; Jeffrey T. Richelson, *Spying on the Bomb: American Nuclear Intelligence from Nazi Germany to Iran and North Korea* (New York: W. W. Norton, 2006), pp. 477–480.

47. The Information Operations Center's Analysis Group (IOC/AG)," http://www.cia.gov/cia/di/organizationt_ioc_page.html, accessed June 1, 2006; "The Counterintelligence Center Analysis Group (CIC/AG)," http://www.cia.gov/cia/di/organizationt_cic_page.html, accessed June 1, 2006.

48. "The Office of Policy Support," http://www.cia.gov/cia/di/organizationt_ops_page.html, accessed June 1, 2006.

49. "The Office of Collection Strategies and Analysis (CSAA)," http://www.cia.gov/cia/di/organizationt_csaa_page.html, accessed June 1, 2006.

50. Central Intelligence Agency, *CIA 2015*, n.d. Also see Siobhan Gorman, "Technology Is Central to CIA's Strategic Plan," *Wall Street Journal*, April 27, 2010, p. A7.

51. *Report to the Secretary of State and the Secretary of Defense by a Special Committee Appointed Pursuant to Letter of 28 December 1951 to Survey Communications Intelligence Activities of the Government*, June 13, 1952, pp. 47–48, 119; RG 457, SR–123, Military Reference Branch, NARA; The National Cryptologic School, *On Watch: Profiles from the National Security Agency's Past 40 Years* (Fort Meade, Md.: NCS, 1986), p. 17.

52. Harry S Truman, "Memorandum for: The Secretary of State and the Secretary of Defense, Subject: Communications Intelligence Activities," October 24, 1952; Center for Cryptologic History, *The Origins of NSA* (Fort Meade, Md.: NSA, n.d.), p. 4.

53. Walter Bedell Smith, "Proposed Survey of Communications Intelligence Activities," December 10, 1951; *Report to the Secretary of State and the Secretary of Defense by a Special Committee*, p. 118; U.S. Congress, Senate Select Committee to Study Governmental Operations with Respect to Intelligence Activities, *Final Report, Book III: Foreign and Military Intelligence* (Washington, D.C.: U.S. Government Printing Office, 1976), p. 736; National Security Agency/Central Security Service, *NSA/CSS Manual 22–1* (Fort Meade, Md.: NSA, 1986), p. 1.

54. *United States Government Organization Manual* (Washington D.C.: U.S. Government Printing Office, 1957), p. 137; "Washington Firm Will Install Ft. Meade Utilities," *Washington Post*, January 7, 1954, p. 7; "U.S. Security Aide Accused of Taking Secret Documents," *New York Times*, October 10, 1954, pp. 1, 33.

55. NSCID No. 6, "Signals Intelligence," February 17, 1972; Department of Justice, *Report on CIA-Related Electronic Surveillance Activities* (Washington, D.C.: Department of Justice, 1976), pp. 77–78.

56. NSCID No. 6, "Signals Intelligence."

57. Department of Defense Directive S-5100.20, "The National Security Agency and the Central Security Service," January 26, 2010.

58. U.S. Congress, Senate Select Committee to Study Governmental Activities with Respect to Intelligence Activities, *Final Report, Book I*, p. 354; U.S. Congress, House Committee on Appropriations, *Department of Defense Appropriations for 1983, Part 3* (Washington, D.C.: U.S. Government Printing Office, 1981), pp. 824–829; Leslie Maitland, "FBI Says New York Is a 'Hub' of Spying in U.S.," *New York Times*, November 14, 1981, p. 12; Patrick E. Tyler and Bob Woodward, "FBI Held War Code of Reagan," *Washington Post*, December 13, 1981, pp. 1, 27.

59. Vernon Loeb, "Back Channels: The Intelligence Community," *Washington Post*, December 19, 2000, p. A31.

60. Department of Defense, "DOD Distinguished Civilian Service Awards Presented," November 4, 1999, http://www.pentagon.mil/releases/1999.

61. Department of Defense, "Defense Special Missile and Astronautics Center: Organization, Mission, and Concept of Operations," September 27, 1982, p. 1; NSA, "FOIA J9347–98," June 15, 1998; Bamford, *Body of Secrets*, p. 503; Department of Defense Instruction S-5100.43, "Defense Special Missile and Aerospace Center (DEFSMAC)," September 24, 2008.

62. [Deleted], DEFSMAC, *DEFSMAC—A Community Asset* (1964–1989), n.d., p. 2.

63. Raymond Tate, "Worldwide C³I and Telecommunications," Harvard University Center for Information Policy Resources, Seminar on C³I, 1980, p. 30.

64. Bamford, *Body of Secrets*, pp. 503–504.

65. Ibid., p. 504.

66. "Information Assurance," http://www.nsa.gov/ia/index.cfm, accessed July 19, 2006; *JASON Global Grid Study* (Arlington, Va.: MITRE Corporation, 1992).

67. Seymour Hersh, *"The Target Is Destroyed": What Really Happened to Flight 007 and What America Knew About It* (New York: Random House, 1986), pp. 52–53, 67–69; "NSOC Opens New Information Protect Cell (IPC)," *NSA Newsletter*, July 1997, p. 7.

68. James Bamford, *The Puzzle Palace: A Report on NSA, America's Most Secret Agency* (Boston: Houghton Mifflin, 1982), p. 157; Melvin Laird, National Security Strategy of Realistic Deterrence: Secretary of Defense Melvin Laird's Annual Defense Department Report, FY 1973 (Washington, D.C.: U.S. Government Printing Office, 1972), p. 135.

69. Douglas Aircraft Corporation, *Preliminary Design of an Experimental World-Circling Spaceship* (Santa Monica, Calif.: DAC, 1946).

70. Robert L. Perry, *Origins of the USAF Space Program, 1945–1956* (Washington, D.C.: Air Force Systems Command, June 1962), pp. 42–43; Jeffrey T. Richelson, *America's Secret Eyes in Space: The U.S. KEYHOLE Spy Satellite Program* (New York: Harper & Row, 1990), pp. 31–64.

71. Richelson, *America's Secret Eyes in Space*, p. 27; Richard M. Bissell Jr. with Jonathan E. Lewis and Frances T. Pudlo, *Reflections of a Cold Warrior* (New Haven, Conn.: Yale University Press, 1996), p. 135.

72. Jeffrey T. Richelson, "Undercover in Outer Space: The Creation and Evolution of the NRO, 1960–1963," *International Journal of Intelligence and Counterintelligence* 13, 3 (Fall 2000): 301–344.

73. Carl Berger, *The Air Force in Space: Fiscal Year 1961* (Washington, D.C.: Air Force Historical Liaison Office, 1966), pp. 41–42; Secretary of the Air Force Order 115.1, "Organization and Functions of the Office of Missile and Satellite Systems," August 31, 1960.

74. Berger, *The Air Force in Space: Fiscal Year 1961*, p. 42; Secretary of the Air Force Order 116.1, "The Director of the SAMOS Project," August 31, 1960.

75. Richard M. Bissell Jr. to Allen W. Dulles, August 8, 1961; Donald Welzenbach, "Science and Technology: Birth of a Directorate," *Studies in Intelligence* 30 (Summer 1986): 13–26; Albert Wheelon, "CORONA: A Triumph of American Technology," in *Eye in the Sky: The Story of the CORONA Reconnaissance Satellite*, ed. Dwayne Day, John S. Logsdon, and Brian Latell (Washington, D.C.: Smithsonian Institution Press, 1998), pp. 29–47.

76. Richelson, "Undercover in Outer Space."

77. Frederic C. E. Oder, James C. Fitzpatrick, and Paul E. Worthman, *The CORONA Story* (Washington, D.C.: NRO, 1987), p. 69.

78. DOD Directive TS 5105.23, "(S) National Reconnaissance Office," March 27, 1964, p. 4.

79. Raymond Garthoff, "Banning the Bomb in Outer Space," *International Security* 5 (1980/1981): 25–40.

80. John McCone, Memorandum of Mongoose Meeting Held on Thursday, October 4, 1962; Office of the Deputy Director, NRO Memorandum for Colonel [deleted] The Inspector General, USAF, Subject: RPVs, February 26, 1974.

81. Letter from William H. Webster, Director of Central Intelligence, and Richard B. Cheney, Secretary of Defense, to David L. Boren, Chairman, Select Committee on Intelligence, U.S. Senate, February 26, 1990; U.S. Congress, Senate Armed Services Committee, *Department*

of Defense Authorization for Appropriations for Fiscal Year 1994 and the Future Years Defense Program (Washington, D.C.: U.S. Government Printing Office, 1993), p. 477; interview.

82. Secretary of the Air Force/Public Affairs, "Biography: Major General John L. Martin Jr.," November 1, 1969.

83. See Richelson, *America's Secret Eyes in Space*, pp. 87–143.

84. Interview; *GRAB: Galactic Radiation and Background, First Reconnaissance Satellite* (Washington, D.C.: Naval Research Laboratory, 1998), p. 2.

85. "Procurement and Security Provisions for the R-12 Program," attachment to letter, Eugene Zuckert to General Schriever, April 5, 1963; NRO, "Analysis of 'A $1.5 Billion Secret in Sky,'" *Washington Post*, December 9, 1973,'" n.d., p. 2.

86. Interview; B. A. Schriever, General USAF, Commander, AFSC, to Honorable Eugene M. Zuckert, July 11, 1963; Brockway MacMillan, Director, NRO, Memorandum for Deputy Chief of Staff, Research and Development, October 30, 1964; Headquarters, Air Force Systems Command, Andrews Air Force Base, Air Force Aeronautical Systems Operations, Operations Order (Draft), March 26, 1964.

87. See Jeffrey T. Richelson, "Restructuring the NRO: From the Cold War's End to the 21st Century," *International Journal of Intelligence and Counterintelligence* 15, 4 (Winter 2002–2003): 496–539.

88. U.S. Congress, Senate Select Committee on Intelligence and House Permanent Select Committee on Intelligence, *S. 2198 and S. 421 to Reorganize the United States Intelligence Community* (Washington, D.C.: U.S. Government Printing Office, 1993), p. 18.

89. NRO, http://www.nro.gov.

90. Admiral David Jeremiah et al., *Report to the Director, National Reconnaissance Office: Defining the Future of the NRO for the 21st Century, Executive Summary*, August 26, 1996, p. 24.

91. NRO, Director's Note 2006–03, "National Reconnaissance Office Enterprise System Engineering," January 26, 2006.

92. National Reconnaissance Office, "Transforming the NRO Enterprise," April 2008, www.nro.gov.

93. National Reconnaissance Office, "Deputy Director for National Support (DDNS)," n.d.

94. Mission Statement, NRO, http://www.nro.gov, June 14, 1996; NRO, Director's Note 2006–07, "Organizational Announcement," March 17, 2006.

95. Commission on Roles and Capabilities of the United States Intelligence Community, *Preparing for the 21st Century: An Appraisal of U.S. Intelligence* (Washington, D.C.: U.S. Government Printing Office, 1996), p. 132; "NRO Organization," Briefing Slide for Presentation of Frank Strickland, NRO, to National Military Intelligence Association, November 19, 1997; Government Accountability Office, *Defense Space Activities: Management Actions Are Needed to Better Identify, Track, and Train Air Force Space Personnel*, September 2006, p. 9.

96. U.S. Congress, House of Representatives, Report 14–186, *Intelligence Authorization Act for Fiscal Year 2010*, June 26, 2009, p. 36.

97. Robert M. Gates, Director of Central Intelligence, *Statement on Change in CIA and the Intelligence Community*, April 1, 1992, p. 28; Imagery Blue Ribbon Task Force, *Restructuring the Imagery Community: Recommendations of the Blue Ribbon Task Force*, 1992, p. 14.

98. H.R. 4165, "National Security Act of 1992," 1992; S. 2198, "Intelligence Reorganization Act of 1992," 1992.

99. Garthoff, *DCIs as Leaders of the U.S. Intelligence Community*, 1947–2005, p. 209; Department of Defense Directive 5105.26, "Central Imagery Office," May 6, 1992; Central Imagery Office, Briefing Slides, pp. 2–3; Director of Central Intelligence Directive 2/9, "Management of National Imagery Intelligence," June 1, 1992.

100. Central Imagery Office, Briefing Slides, p. 2.

101. Statement of John Deutch Before Senate Select Committee on Intelligence, April 26, 1995, pp. 8–9.

102. "DCI Plans a National Imagery Agency," *Communiqué*, August 1995, pp. 1, 8.

103. Central Intelligence Agency, "National Imagery and Mapping Agency Proposed to Congress," November 28, 1995.

104. Ibid.

105. U.S. Congress, Senate Select Committee on Intelligence, *Special Report of the Senate Select Committee on Intelligence, United States Senate, January 4, 1995 to October 3, 1996* (Washington, D.C.: U.S. Government Printing Office, 1997), pp. 7–8. There was also some concern about the proposed merger from Defense Mapping Agency officials, who feared that their formal inclusion in the Intelligence Community might have a negative impact on their relationship with foreign nations that provided mapping information.

106. NIMA, "National Imagery and Mapping Agency Established," October 1, 1996; William S. Cohen and George J. Tenet, Memorandum of Agreement Between the Secretary of Defense and the Director of Central Intelligence on the National Imagery and Mapping Agency, October 16, 1998.

107. "NGA History," http://www.nga.mil, accessed July 14, 2006; James R. Clapper Jr., *NGA Today*, n.d.

108. DOD Directive 5105.60, " National Geospatial-Intelligence Agency (NGA)," July 29, 2009, pp. 1–7.

109. "The National Geospatial-Intelligence Agency (NGA): Major Organizations," http://www.nga.mil, accessed July 17, 2006.; National Geospatial Intelligence Agency, "How We Are Organized," www.nga.mil, accessed March 4, 2010.

110. "The National Geospatial-Intelligence Agency (NGA): Major Organizations," http://www.nga.mil, accessed July 17, 2006.; National Geospatial Intelligence Agency, "How We Are Organized."

111. Richelson, *America's Secret Eyes in Space*, pp. 252–256. On the directorate's other functions, see Gene Reich, "Source Directorate Expands," *Pathfinder*, May–June 2006, pp. 9–10; and National Geospatial Intelligence Agency, "How We Are Organized."

112. Rick Akers, "NextView Will Provide the Vision and Solutions for New U.S. Policy on Commercial Imagery," *Pathfinder*, July/August 2003, pp. 8–9; Frank Morring Jr., "NIMA Sets Big Jump in Commercial Imagery Buy," *Aviation Week & Space Technology*, September 9, 2002, pp. 30–31.

113. Robert Wall, "Homeland Security Demands Strain NIMA's Resources," *Aviation Week & Space Technology*, February 3, 2003, p. 37; Warren Ferster, "NGA Embraces Disaster Relief Role, Collaboration," *Space News*, November 7, 2005, p. 17; Katherine S. Whitaker, "NGA Supports Gulf of Mexico Spill Remediation Efforts," *Pathfinder*, July/August 2010, pp. 12–13.

114. Missy Frederick, "Bill Allows NGA to Provide Ground-based Photography," *Space News*, June 19, 2006, p. 11; Walter Pincus, "Senators Seek Better Defense Imagery," *Washington Post*, June 6, 2006, p. A13.

115. Clapper Jr., *NGA Today*, p. 5; Missy Frederick, "Murrett Striving for Right Balance at NGA," *Space News*, November 20, 2006, p. 12; Marjorie Censer, "Letitia A. Long becomes first female director of NGA," www.washingtonpost.com, August 10, 2010; "NGA Staff Begin Moving into Massive New Headquarters," *Space News*, January 24, 2011, p. 9.

3

DEFENSE DEPARTMENT INTELLIGENCE

THE DEFENSE INTELLIGENCE AGENCY

In addition to the national intelligence organizations within the Department of Defense—the National Security Agency (NSA), the National Reconnaissance Office (NRO), and the National Geospatial-Intelligence Agency (NGA)—the department has its own agency, the Defense Intelligence Agency (DIA), which operates in support of the Secretary of Defense, the Joint Chiefs of Staff, and military commanders, and participates in the production of national intelligence. DIA contains within it organizations for the collection of human intelligence, for technical collection, and for intelligence production.

HISTORY AND CURRENT CHARTER

The Defense Intelligence Agency was one manifestation of the trend toward centralization that began in the Eisenhower administration and reached its peak in the Kennedy administration. The Eisenhower administration concluded in the late 1950s that a consolidation of the military services' general (that is, all non-SIGINT, non-overhead, nonorganic) intelligence activities was needed. This belief was, according to one analyst, a by-product of the missile gap controversy of the time: "Faced with the disparate estimates of Soviet missile strength from each of the armed services which translated into what have been called self-serving budget requests for weapons of defense, the United States Intelligence Board created a Joint Study Group in 1959 to study the intelligence producing agencies."[1]

The Joint Study Group, chaired by the CIA's Lyman Kirkpatrick, concluded that there was considerable overlap and duplication in defense intelligence activities and a resulting maldistribution of resources. The consequence was that the "overall direction and management of DOD's total intelligence effort becomes a very difficult if not impossible task. Indeed, the fragmentation of effort creates 'barriers' to the free and complete interchange of intelligence information among the several components of the Department of Defense." The study group recommended that the Secretary of

Defense "bring the military intelligence organization within the Department of Defense into full consonance with the concept of the Defense Reorganization Act of 1958."[2]

How to do this was a subject of controversy. The study group's report noted that it had been suggested that a single intelligence service be established for the entire Defense Department, reporting directly to the Secretary of Defense. The study group concluded, however, that "on balance it would be unwise to attempt such an integration of intelligence activities so long as there are three military services having specialized skills and knowledge."[3]

Despite the study group's conclusions, in a February 8, 1961, memorandum to the Joint Chiefs of Staff, Defense Secretary Robert McNamara observed, "It appears that the most effective means to accomplish the recommendations of the Joint Study Group would be the establishment of a Defense Intelligence Agency which may include the existing National Security Agency, the intelligence and counterintelligence functions now handled by the military departments, and the responsibilities of the Office of the Assistant Secretary, Special Operations."[4]

McNamara requested that the JCS provide, within thirty days, a concept for a defense intelligence agency, a draft DOD directive that would establish such an agency, and a time-phased implementation schedule. He also provided some preliminary guidelines for developing a plan that included the complete integration of all defense intelligence requirements and the elimination of duplication in intelligence collection and production. On February 9, the Joint Staff suggested that the JCS direct the staff to develop a concept for the DIA that would be consistent with McNamara's memo and would place the new agency under the control of the JCS.[5]

On March 2, 1961, the Joint Chiefs sent McNamara their recommendations, including an organizational concept for the establishment of a Military Intelligence Agency (MIA) under the JCS. On April 3, McNamara requested advice on several basic issues concerning the proposed agency, including its proposed placement under the JCS and its specific functions. Ten days later the JCS approved a Joint Staff draft memorandum for the Secretary of Defense. The memo justified placing a DIA/MIA under the JCS on the grounds that the DOD Reorganization Act of 1958 specifically assigned the Joint Chiefs the responsibility of strategic planning and operational direction of the armed forces, and the fulfillment of such responsibilities required control of appropriate intelligence assets. In contrast, placing the DIA/MIA in the Office of the Secretary of Defense (OSD) would "concentrate military intelligence assets at a level above, and isolated from, the organization charged with strategic planning and operational direction of the armed forces."[6]

The Joint Staff memo also suggested placing NSA under the authority of the JCS. In addition, it argued that total integration of all military intelligence activities might not be a sound concept. It also recommended that if any intelligence activities were left with the services, the DIA/MIA director should be charged with closely monitoring them and that the director be authorized to eliminate duplication, review all service intelligence programs and budgets, and assign priorities to military intelligence collection requirements.[7]

The agency that resulted was a compromise, but it was close to the JCS viewpoint. On July 5, 1961, McNamara decided to establish a DIA reporting to the Secretary of Defense through the JCS. On August 1, he did so through DOD Directive 5105.21 and made DIA responsible for (1) organization, direction, management, and control over all DOD intelligence resources assigned to or included within the DIA; (2) review and coordination of those DOD intelligence functions retained by or assigned to the military departments; (3) supervision over the execution of all approved plans, programs, policies, and procedures for intelligence functions not assigned to the DIA; (4) exercise of maximum economy and efficiency in allocation and management of DOD intelligence resources; (5) response to priority requests by the United States Intelligence Board; and (6) fulfillment of intelligence requirements of major DOD components.[8] As a result of the DIA's creation, the Joint Staff Director for Intelligence (J-2) was abolished, as was the Office of Special Operations, the small intelligence arm of the Secretary of Defense.

On December 16, 1976, the Secretary of Defense issued a new charter for the DIA (i.e., a new version of DOD 5105.21), limiting the operational control of the JCS over the DIA to (1) obtaining the intelligence support required to perform their statutory function and assigned responsibilities, and (2) ensuring that adequate, timely, and reliable intelligence support was available to the unified and specified commands. In all other matters, the Director of the DIA would report to the Secretary of Defense through the Assistant Secretary of Defense for Intelligence (ASDI). The mission of the DIA was also stated more concisely as being "to satisfy, or to ensure the satisfaction of, the foreign intelligence requirements of the Secretary of Defense, the Joint Chiefs of Staff, DOD components and other authorized recipients, and to provide the military intelligence contribution to national intelligence."[9]

About five months later, on May 19, 1977, the Secretary of Defense signed a new version of DOD Directive 5105.21 that slightly altered the organization and administration of the agency. Under the revised charter, the director would report to the Secretary of Defense and the chairman of the JCS. In addition, the Director of the DIA would be under the operational control of the JCS for purposes of (1) obtaining intelligence support required to perform the statutory and assigned responsibilities of the JCS, and (2) ensuring adequate, timely, and reliable intelligence support for the unified and specified commands. Staff supervision of the DIA would be exercised by the Assistant Secretary of Defense for Command, Control, Communications, and Intelligence (C³I) with respect to resources and by the ASD for International Security Affairs with respect to policy.[10]

In February 1990, the ASD (C³I) established a steering group of senior officers in DOD intelligence organizations to review the readiness of the defense intelligence system in the face of the changing international security environment. The effort, which would be labeled "Defense Intelligence in the 1990s," was intended to identify the potential issues, risks, and opportunities expected to emerge in the 1990s. In June 1990, the group prepared a fairly brief TOP SECRET/CODEWORD draft interim executive summary of issues that had been raised by the participants in the effort and appended a listing of "issues" suggesting alternative ways of addressing individual topics.[11]

The draft summary was intended to be a forerunner of the final review. However, because of a shift in thinking at the senior level of the DOD, no final review study was completed, although the results of the study were presented to the Secretary of Defense, Deputy Secretary of Defense, and other senior defense officials in the September–December 1990 period. On December 14, 1990, Under Secretary of Defense Donald J. Atwood issued a memorandum titled "Strengthening Defense Intelligence Functions," which noted that senior-level DOD officials had reviewed the department's intelligence activities and requested from the memo's addressees detailed plans to achieve a variety of objectives, including strengthening "the role and performance of the Defense Intelligence Agency in the intelligence requirements, production, and management processes."[12]

The memo resulted in the March 15, 1991, ASD (C³I) *Plan for Restructuring Defense Intelligence*. With respect to the DIA, the plan called for the following:

- strengthening the role of DIA as a Combat Support Agency;
- improving the quality of the Defense Intelligence product through streamlining and reconfiguring DIA to improve its estimative capability with emphasis on quality analysis and reporting strategically important intelligence;
- strengthening DIA's management of intelligence production and analysis;
- assigning DIA responsibility to perform/oversee basic encyclopedic data production;
- establishing within DIA a capability to validate threat information to ensure an independent intelligence input to the acquisition process;
- establishing within DIA a Policy Issues Office to improve support to the Office of the Secretary of Defense.[13]

Much of the effort to implement these and other aspects of the plan took place in the administration of Lt. Gen. James R. Clapper, who became DIA director in November 1991. Nearly six years after the March 1991 plan was laid out, a new DIA directive, reflecting many of the DIA's new responsibilities, was finally issued. The directive itself was produced only after several years of effort, which was partially reflected in organizational changes. DOD Directive 5105.21, "Defense Intelligence Agency," of February 18, 1997, replaced the 1977 directive, which had been only slightly modified in 1978. That directive was, in turn, replaced by the March 18, 2008, version of 5105.21.[14]

The new directive or charter specified over seventy specific responsibilities and functions for the Director of the DIA, within the agency's twelve areas of responsibility and functions. Among the director's responsibilities and functions are

- All-Source Intelligence Analysis: providing all-source intelligence to joint task force and Combatant Commanders, as well as to Defense planners and national security policymakers.
- Human Intelligence: centrally managing the DOD-wide HUMINT enterprise as well as conducting DIA HUMINT collection activities worldwide.
- Joint Staff Intelligence: operating the Joint Staff Intelligence Directorate (J-2) to respond to the direct intelligence support requirements of the Chairman of the Joint Chiefs of Staff and the Secretary of Defense.
- Technical Collection: conducting integrated planning, coordination, and execution of DOD Measurement and Signature Intelligence (MASINT) and designated technical collection management activities.
- Counterintelligence (CI) and Security: performing assigned CI functions as well as Sensitive Compartmented Information (SCI) policy implementation, security clearance adjudication, and facility accreditation.
- International Engagement: entering into military and military-related intelligence agreements and arrangements with foreign governments and other entities.
- Resource Management: developing and managing the DIA Military Intelligence Program (MIP) resources and capabilities, the General Defense Intelligence Program (GDIP), and the DIA portion of the Foreign Counterintelligence Program (FCIP) as an element of the National Intelligence Program (NIP).
- Defense Intelligence Operations Coordination Center (DIOCC): operating the DIOCC to plan, prepare, integrate, direct, synchronize, and manage continuous Defense Intelligence operations and other functions in accordance with Secretary of Defense guidance.[15]

ORGANIZATIONAL OVERVIEW

The main headquarters for the DIA is the Defense Intelligence Analysis Center (DIAC) at Bolling Air Force Base, in Washington, D.C. The DIA is also building a Joint-Use Intelligence Facility near Charlottesville, Virginia, that will be managed by a DIA Field Support Activity–Rivanna Station. The activity's chief "will serve as the focal point for DIA interactions with the National Ground Intelligence Center (NGIC), the University of Virginia, and the greater Charlottesville community." Eight hundred DIA employees will be relocated to the facility by September 2011. The DIA employs more than 16,000 people (including more than 3,000 overseas) and has a budget that easily exceeds $1 billion.[16]

The DIA underwent several extensive reorganizations during the 1960s and 1970s, and although occasional changes were made to DIA's organizational structure in subsequent years, they were not as significant as the earlier changes. However, from 1991 to 1993, the DIA underwent two extensive reorganizations designed to improve performance, deal with mandated personnel and budget reductions, adapt to changing international realities, and better coordinate military intelligence activities—as intended by the March 1991 *Plan for Restructuring Defense Intelligence*. The primary result of the latter reorganization was the creation of three DIA centers: the National Military Intelligence Collection Center, the National Military Intelligence Production Center, and the National Military Intelligence Systems Center. These centers were renamed after Clapper, who had established them, retired as DIA director.

In February 2003, DIA director Vice Admiral Lowell E. Jacoby approved yet another significant reorganization, which created the Director's Special Staff and seven primary operating elements: directorates for human intelligence, MASINT and technical collection, analysis, information management, external relations, intelligence support for the Joint Staff, and administration.[17] Subsequent organizational changes, including the creation of a human intelligence and counterintelligence center and the Defense Intelligence Operations Coordination Center, have produced the structure shown in Figure 3.1. In early January 2011, remarks by Secretary of Defense Robert Gates indicated that DIA would assume some of the responsibilities that had been assigned to some of the unified combatant commands—responsibilities that would be exercised by two new task forces.[18]

DEFENSE COUNTERINTELLIGENCE AND HUMINT CENTER

The Defense Counterintelligence and HUMINT Center (DCHC) was established by a July 22, 2008, memorandum from the Deputy Secretary of Defense that simultaneously disestablished the Pentagon's Counterintelligence Field Activity (CIFA) and transferred its non-law enforcement counterintelligence functions to DIA. That memo was subsequently superseded by a DOD Instruction, which serves as the center's charter.[19] As shown in Figure 3.2, the DCHC consists of five major components—the CI/HUMINT Enterprise Management Office, the Counterintelligence Directorate, the HUMINT Directorate, the Defense Cover Office, and D2X.

The CI/HUMINT Management Office is responsible for "managing commonalities" across the counterintelligence and human intelligence disciplines. The office oversees Defense Department counterintelligence and HUMINT long-range planning; policy, doctrine, training, and professional development; resource and performance management; and the development of technology.[20]

The Directorate for Counterintelligence combines the functions performed by CIFA—operational counterintelligence support, management of operations and investigations, adversarial situation awareness, and force protection support to Defense Department components—with those that had been the responsibility of DIA. The agency's counterintelligence activities had included strategic analysis and production, management of counterintelligence requirements, counterintelligence support to the Joint Staff, and support and oversight of counterintelligence staff officers at the combatant commands.[21]

The Directorate for Human Intelligence plans and conducts Defense Department HUMINT operations and "centrally direct[s] and manage[s]" DIA HUMINT

FIGURE 3.1 Organization of the Defense Intelligence Agency

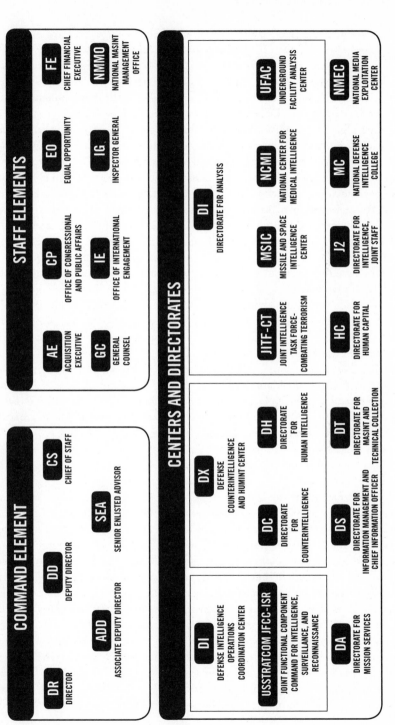

Source: www.dia.mil.

personnel—including the Defense Attaché System, DIA overt and clandestine collection field personnel, and document exploitation.[22]

The key elements of the Directorate for Human Intelligence are (1) the divisions that were components of what had been known as the Defense HUMINT Service (DHS) and the Defense Attaché Service (DAS), and (2) the clandestine collection officers who work for the DHS. The origins of the DHS can be traced to the early years of the Reagan administration, when Deputy Under Secretary of Defense (Policy) Richard Stillwell sought to establish a DOD HUMINT agency. His effort, code-named MONARCH EAGLE, partially resulted from DOD and military service dissatisfaction with CIA collection priorities. The project was vetoed by Congress, however, on the grounds that it would overlap with CIA HUMINT collection efforts and make control of sensitive operations more difficult.[23]

In December 1992, DOD Directive 5200.37, "Centralized Management of DOD Human Intelligence (HUMINT) Operations," centralized HUMINT decisionmaking under a DOD HUMINT manager, established the concept of HUMINT support elements at combatant commands, and required consolidation of HUMINT support services. In June 1993, in response to discussions with DCI James Woolsey during the annual Joint Review of Intelligence Programs, Deputy Secretary of Defense William J. Perry requested that the ASD (C³I) develop a plan to consolidate the separate human intelligence components of the Defense Department into a single organization.[24]

The *Plan for Consolidation of Defense HUMINT* was approved by Perry in a November 2, 1993, memorandum. It specified that the ASD (C³I) effect the consolidation of the service HUMINT operations by fiscal year 1997 to establish a Defense HUMINT Service (DHS). The plan also called for the Director of the DIA to activate the DHS as a provisional organization, "using existing DOD GDIP HUMINT resources and structures within FY 1994," and "to establish a headquarters structure . . . followed by support, clandestine, and overt elements in accordance with [a] time-phased schedule."[25]

Thus, the plan made the Director of the DIA responsible for consolidating the DIA's human intelligence activities with those of the Army, Navy, and Air Force. The DIA's HUMINT operations included the activities of its 100-plus openly acknowledged attaché offices throughout the world. The mission of the attachés is to observe and report military and politico-military information, represent the Department of Defense and the military services, administer military assistance programs and foreign military sales, and advise the U.S. ambassador on military and politico-military matters. The DIA also maintained a small contingent of clandestine case officers responsible for recruiting agents.[26]

Of the military services, the most significant contribution in forming the DHS came from the Army, specifically the Intelligence and Security Command's Foreign Intelligence Activity. The Army had maintained a significant clandestine HUMINT effort throughout the Cold War. Not surprisingly, significant opposition to creation of the DHS emanated from Army intelligence officials.[27]

FIGURE 3.2 Organization of the Defense Counterintelligence and Human Intelligence Center

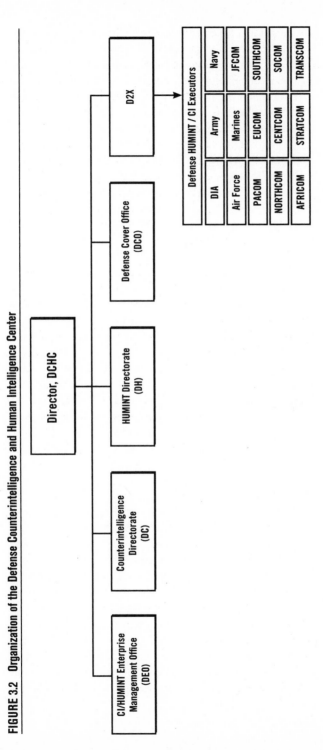

Source: "CI and HUMINT—Partners in the HUMAN Domain," *Communiqué,* November/December 2008, pp. 19–22.

In 1966, the Navy established an organization—first known as the Naval Field Operations Support Group and then as Task Force 157—to conduct clandestine and overt collection operations. That organization was disestablished in 1977. At the same time, Task Force 168 was assigned the task of overt collection. The Navy's contribution to the DHS came from the turnover of much of 168's assets, which were absorbed by the Office of Naval Intelligence in 1993, as well as the contingent of clandestine case officers (intended to reach a maximum of 100) that the Navy began recruiting around 1993.[28]

The Air Force contribution to the DHS came from the transfer of personnel from the former Air Force Intelligence Command's 696th Intelligence Group. The group, which conducted clandestine collection activities and debriefed defectors, was previously known as the Air Force Special Activities Center, the 7612th Air Intelligence Group, and the 1127th Field Activities Group. The 1127th was described as "an oddball unit, a composite of special intelligence groups who 'conducted worldwide operations to collect intelligence from human sources.' The men of the 1127th were con artists. Their job was to get people to talk—Russian defectors, North Vietnamese soldiers taken prisoner."[29]

In the late 1990s, key components of the DHS's collection operations outside of the Washington area were the HUMINT Support Elements (HSE) stationed at the headquarters of the commanders in chief of the Atlantic, Southern, Pacific, European, and Central Commands and at the headquarters of the sub-unified commands in order to "improve support to warfighters." The HSEs helped "commands develop and process HUMINT collection requirements and facilitate planning and coordination of DOD HUMINT support to operational commands." The HSEs also "develop[ed] exercise scenarios and Command contingency plans to ensure HUMINT support is planned, practiced, and available for deployment."[30]

Other DHS elements overseas included a large number of operating bases. The largest of the bases outside the United States at the turn of the century was Operations Base Stuttgart (OBST), with fifteen separate operating locations. It served as "the primary resource for DIA personnel deploying in support of Operations Joint Endeavor." Thus, by October 1995, when the DHS was declared to have achieved its initial operational capability, it had "over 2,000 personnel in over 100 locations including Washington, D.C." The 2003 reorganization of DIA created a separate Directorate for Human Intelligence out of the human intelligence activities that had been contained in the Directorate for Intelligence Operations.[31]

Subsequent to Jacoby's reorganization of DIA, a Strategic Support Branch was established within DHS. Similar to the service's Human Support Elements, the branch's Strategic Support Teams (SSTs), originally known as HUMINT Augmentation Teams, are deployed into the field to support the intelligence requirements of combatant commanders. In contrast to the representatives of the HSE in the field, the SSTs are engaged in a variety of collection missions in conjunction with members of U.S. special forces units, including prisoner interrogation, recruitment of foreign assets, and direct intelligence collection.[32]

The Defense Cover Office was previously an element of the HUMINT Directorate. Now, as a distinct component of DCHC, it executes defense cover programs on behalf of the entire Defense Department. The D2X office, which is composed of the Operations Management Division and the Operations Support Division, is responsible for coordinating, de-conflicting, and synchronizing Defense Department counterintelligence and HUMINT activities. Its responsibilities include, but are not limited to, "situational awareness, requirements tasking, technical support, source registration and de-confliction, intelligence planning, and leading the development of integrated precision targeting strategies for hard targets."[33]

DIRECTORATE FOR MASINT AND TECHNICAL COLLECTION

The Directorate of MASINT and Technical Collection was created in 2003 through the merger of the Central MASINT Office and the Defense Collection Group—both of which had been located in DIA's Directorate of Intelligence Operations. The DIA director's message to agency personnel stated that the directorate's primary mission would be "providing DOD and larger Intelligence Community with invigorated MASINT support and the DOD with expert collection management and specialized collection."[34]

The Central MASINT Office (CMO) was established in 1993 and had about forty employees in 1999. It was described as a "joint combat support directorate, [which] serves a dual role as the Director of Central Intelligence's Executive Agent for MASINT and as the DOD MASINT Manager." Hence, its responsibilities were enumerated in both a DCI directive (DCID 2/11 of December 1992) and a DOD directive.[35]

More recently, the DIA's MASINT and technical collection responsibilities were specified in the March 18, 2008, DOD directive concerning DIA. This directive specified that DIA and thus the Directorate of MASINT and Technical Collection were to

- Manage and implement Secretary of Defense and DNI plans and policies on designated technical collection matters.
- Develop and implement standards, architectures, and procedures providing for integrated MASINT capabilities.
- Develop, coordinate, and advocate Defense Intelligence positions on technical collection needs, capabilities, and strategies; collection management applications; and future collection systems and architectures.
- Conduct research, development, testing, and evaluation activities to enhance technical collection.
- Define and present consolidated DOD positions on technical intelligence collection issues to the USD (I) and Chairman of the Joint Chiefs of Staff, and chair and operate a board or panel to support these processes.
- Execute the tasking of DOD MASINT collection platforms to meet national level collection requirements with the exception of those activities assigned to

the National Geospatial-Intelligence Agency (NGA), and conduct end-to-end oversight of tasked collection, processing, exploitation, reporting, and customer satisfaction.

- Provide MASINT services of common concern for the IC on behalf of, and as assigned by, the DNI in coordination with the USD (I).
- Plan, enable, and conduct MASINT and technical intelligence collection training and operations in support of military operations, counterterrorism, counterinsurgency operations, and Homeland Defense. Employ air-, ground-, and sea-based systems for close-access collection and persistent surveillance capabilities in support of the COCOMs.
- Lead the DOD Special Communications Enterprise Office and manage the National Signatures Program.
- Manage and implement technical identity management and biometrics plans and policies consistent with DOD, interagency, and international information sharing activities.[36]

The CMO produced or participated in the production of documents such as the *U.S. Spectral Plan*, the *CMO MASINT Plan*, and *MASINT 2010: Planning the U.S. MASINT System for the 21st Century*.[37]

As a result of the reorganization of the directorate, the CMO became the directorate's MASINT Group. One element of the group is the MASINT Operations Coordination Center (MOCC), formed in October 2000. The center is an around-the-clock unit that "provides continuous access to MASINT products, visibility of MASINT activities and the ability to optimally task sensors in time-sensitive situations to a diverse list of customers." The MOCC has produced a Daily MASINT Summary (DMS) that "provides critical intelligence to senior leadership and analysts alike," including current information on MASINT collections and the status of MASINT resources.[38]

The Collection Management Group (known as the Defense Collection Group prior to the 2003 reorganization) supported military forces and policymakers through levying intelligence requirements on collection agencies and resources, monitoring collection responses, and evaluating collection efforts in terms of reliability, efficiency, and cost. It also operated the twenty-four-hour Defense Collection Coordination Center (DCCC). During the Persian Gulf War, the DCCC acted as the executive agent for all national imagery in support of Desert Storm operations. All overhead imagery supporting the war effort was planned and developed at the coordination center. Other elements of the directorate have included the Collection Operations Group, the Science and Technology Group, the National Signatures Program, the Overhead Non-Imaging Infrared Group, and the Financial Management Office.[39]

DIRECTORATE FOR ANALYSIS

The Directorate for Analysis was created by merging the Directorate for Analysis and Production with most of the elements of the Directorate for Policy Support.

The analysis and production directorate contained five key production elements, including three groups and two centers. The Regional Military Assessments Group consisted of six offices—Asia, Europe, Infrastructure, Latin America, Middle East/Africa, Russia/NIS. The Technology Assessment Group produced assessments through six offices: Acquisition Threat Support, DODFIP (DOD Futures Intelligence Program), Advanced Conventional Weapons, Foreign Materiel Program, Advanced Technology/Technology Transfer, and Modeling and Simulation. The Transnational Warfare Group (TWG) had five offices: Counterterrorism Analysis, Counter-drug, Information Warfare Support, Joint Warfare Support, and Counterproliferation and NBC Assessment.[40]

The Information Warfare Support Office (and its Special Activities, Intelligence Preparation of the Battlespace, Threat Analysis and Foreign Denial and Deception divisions) produced studies on computer and cybernetic warfare, electronic warfare, psychological operations, deception, and physical destruction of information systems. The Joint Warfare Support Office was responsible for providing all-source intelligence, including intelligence to U.S. special forces, with regard to the operational environment, physical vulnerability, geospatial analysis, denial and deception, and POW/MIA affairs.[41]

The Office of Counterterrorism Analysis consisted of two divisions—the Terrorism Analysis Division (TAD) and the Terrorism Warning Division (TWD). The TAD was the primary producer of terrorism assessments and studies for the Defense Department intelligence community. It produced and maintained the DOD terrorism database, which contained more than 20,000 finished intelligence products on terrorist threats, groups, incidents, facilities, and personalities. It also reviewed the terrorist threat to hundreds of Defense Department exercises and deployment operations each year. The TWD was responsible for terrorism-related indications and warning and crisis support and staffed the National Military Command Center Support Division Terrorism Desk. In addition, the TWD produced the daily *Defense Intelligence Terrorism Summary* (DITSUM), which "serves as the primary source of terrorism-related analysis and threat information for senior policymakers as well as commanders, security officers, and planners."[42]

The Office for Counter-drug Analysis produced the *Interagency Assessment of Cocaine Movement,* and its Colombia Division deployed five all-source analysts to assist the Colombian government in its counter-drug operations. Working with the FBI in Project DOMINANT CHRONICLE, the office translated and exploited over 160,000 documents. It has also provided intelligence support to counternarcotics operations in Southeast and Southwest Asia.[43]

The Directorate for Policy Support provided direct intelligence support for the Office of the Secretary of Defense and other national-level policymakers through the DIA's Defense Intelligence Officers—senior analysts who are now part of the analysis directorate. It also managed selected special access programs.[44]

Today, the directorate's offices focus on similar topics, although the office segment of the directorate's structure has changed in recent years. As of 2008, those offices included the Military Forces Analysis Office as well as three regional offices: Asia/Pacific; Middle East/North Africa; and Latin America, Europe/Eurasia, and Africa. The personnel in those offices are some of the 2,500 personnel in the directorate.[45]

Other directorate personnel work for three centers—the Missile and Space Intelligence Center (MSIC), the National Center for Medical Intelligence (NCMI), and the Underground Facilities Analysis Center (UFAC)—and one task force, the Joint Intelligence Task Force–Combating Terrorism.

In its 1991 report, *Intelligence Authorization Act, Fiscal Year 1992*, the House Permanent Select Committee on Intelligence strongly recommended that "the Armed Forces Medical Intelligence Center [and] the [Army] Missile and Space Intelligence Center . . . be transferred in their entirety to DIA and become designated Field Production Activities of DIA." By early 1992 the DIA had developed a plan for transfer of the centers to its control, and the transfer orders were issued.[46]

The Missile and Space Intelligence Center has several hundred employees and is located at Redstone Arsenal, near Huntsville, Alabama. In June 1956, the Special Security Office of the Army Ballistic Missile Agency (ABMA) was established to procure missile and space intelligence data for the commander of the ABMA. To analyze the data, a Technical Intelligence Division (TID) was established. This division was subordinate to the ABMA's Assistant Chief of Staff for Research and Development. Subsequent to the March 1958 consolidation of all Army activities at Redstone Arsenal into the Army Ordnance Missile Command (AOMC), the fifty-person TID was redesignated the Office of the Assistant Chief of Staff for Missile Intelligence (OACSMI). When the AOMC was absorbed in 1962 by the Army Missile Command (itself subordinate to the U.S. Army Materiel Command), the OACSMI was redesignated the Directorate of Missile Intelligence, and in September 1970 it became the Missile Intelligence Agency. On August 1, 1985, it was redesignated the U.S. Army Missile and Space Intelligence Center (AMSIC) with the mission to "produce worldwide scientific and technical intelligence (S&TI) on surface-to-air missiles, ballistic missile defense systems (both strategic and tactical), antitank guided missiles, antisatellite missiles, directed energy weapons, and relevant space programs/systems and command, control, communications, and computers."[47]

In recent years, MSIC has enhanced its analytical capabilities with the addition of the Joint Research Analysis and Assessment Center (JRAAC) and the Integrated Sensor Data Analysis Facility (ISDAF). JRAAC is a modeling and simulation facility that is employed to evaluate capabilities, limitations, and vulnerabilities of threat systems in simulated one-on-one and force-on-force scenarios. ISDAF allows weapons system and data analysts to directly communicate with other Intelligence Community agencies as well as with collection sites around the world. ISDAF analysts "can also access sensor data collected on recent missile tests of high interest."[48]

In July 2008 the Armed Forces Medical Intelligence Center (AFMIC) was renamed the National Center for Medical Intelligence, which remains headquartered at Fort Detrick, Maryland. AFMIC had been established in 1982, replacing the Army's Medical Intelligence and Information Agency (MIIA), which provided medical intelligence for the entire defense community. AFMIC's formation was possibly the result of unhappiness with the medical intelligence efforts of the MIIA. Discussions of Defense Audit Service personnel with the Director of the General Defense Intelligence Program Staff in 1981 indicated Intelligence Community concern about a lack of adequate medical intelligence in Southwest Asian and Third World countries, "where casualties from unusual diseases and environmental conditions could occur."[49]

Medical intelligence is particularly vital in planning for combat operations, particularly in areas significantly different from the United States in terms of environment and prevalence of disease. One aspect of AFMIC's activities consisted of producing general medical intelligence on health and sanitation, epidemiology, environmental factors, and military and civilian medical care capabilities, as in AFMIC's *Medical Capabilities Study, Democratic People's Republic of Korea, Asia: Health Impacts from Indonesian Earthquake and Tsunami,* and *Poisonous Snakes of Europe.* A second aspect of its work involved the production of medical, scientific, and technical intelligence concerning all basic and applied biomedical phenomena of military importance, including biological, chemical, psychological, and biophysical information. The AFMIC report titled *Medical Effects of Non-Ionizing Electromagnetic Radiation-LASER* represents one example of the effort.[50]

More recent AFMIC activities, beginning in the fall of 2005, included production of a weekly situation report for operational forces and policymakers that assessed the risk from avian flu as well as the authoring of nine articles for the *President's Daily Brief.* In addition, AFMIC analysts supported the Northern Command's Joint Task Force–Katrina as well as Joint Task Force–Burma. (The latter was established after Cyclone Nargis hit Burma in May 2008.) Center analysts also evaluated the threat from chlorine-enhanced improvised explosive devices in Iraq and the military implications of human performance modification.[51]

NCMI is also responsible for assessing foreign biomedical R&D and its impact on the physiological effectiveness of medical forces, as well as assessing the exploitation of foreign medical materiel obtained under the DOD Foreign Materiel Exploitation Program (FMEP).[52]

A 2009 DOD directive on NCMI described it as "the DOD lead activity for the production of medical intelligence" and stated that it "will prepare and coordinate integrated, all-source intelligence for the Department of Defense and other government and international organizations on foreign health and other medical issues to protect U.S. interests worldwide." The new name and the directive's language reflects the increased responsibility assigned to the organization—specifically, its homeland health protection mission. That additional responsibility dated back to 2006, when NCMI was instructed, by the Secretary of Defense, to include assessment on foreign human health threats to the homeland and began expanding its contacts with other agencies.[53]

About 150 people work for NCMI. Its divisions include, but are not necessarily limited to, an Environmental Health Division, Medical Capabilities Division, and an Infectious Disease Division. The Environmental Health Division's products include industrial hazard assessments, industrial facility risk assessments, and chemical and radiological hazard areas models. The Medical Capabilities Division locates medical facilities and assesses health care infrastructures. And the Infectious Disease Division seeks to forecast, track, and analyze the occurrence of infectious diseases with pandemic potential—such as avian flu, West Nile virus, anthrax, and plague. Recent NCMI products include *Baseline Infectious Disease Risk Assessment: Haiti* (2009), *Worldwide: New 2009–H1N1 Influenza Virus Poses Potential Threat to U.S. Forces* (2009), and *Haiti: Health Risks and Health System Impacts Associated with Large-Scale Earthquake* (2010).[54]

The Underground Facilities Analysis Center (UFAC), established in 1997, is dedicated to "detecting, identifying, characterizing and assessing for defeat adversarial underground facilities or Hardened and Deeply Buried Targets." More specifically, it seeks to provide intelligence and related data to national policymakers, weapons developers, and military forces concerned about the nature of underground facilities or means to destroy them.[55]

Whereas the UFAC is located in the DIA Directorate for Analysis, the center is an interagency effort. Agencies with personnel working at the center include the CIA, DIA (particularly from the Directorate for MASINT and Technical Collection), the Defense Threat Reduction Agency, the National Security Agency, the U.S. Geological Survey, and the U.S. Strategic Command Joint Intelligence Operations Center. In addition, personnel from the Air Force Technical Applications Center probably work at the center.[56]

The Joint Intelligence Task Force–Combating Terrorism consolidates national-level all-source terrorism-related intelligence and serves as senior Defense Department representative within the Intelligence Community for threat warning—proposing and coordinating warnings to Defense Department organizations and combatant commands. Its analysts produce daily assessments of possible terrorist threats to Defense Department personnel and facilities. The task force also provides analytical support to interrogations, debriefings, HUMINT collection, and law enforcement—including to operations seeking to disrupt terrorist travel. Its Exploitation Branch has produced guidelines for personnel involved in interrogations and debriefing activities.[57]

DIRECTORATE FOR INTELLIGENCE, J2

The Directorate for Intelligence, J2, serves as the Joint Chiefs of Staff intelligence directorate. Its components include an Executive Support Division, the National Military Command Center Support Division, and the Targeting Division.[58]

The Executive Support Division provides current and warning intelligence to the Secretary of Defense, the chairman of the JCS, and other DOD officials. It assesses, coordinates, produces, and integrates all-source current and indications and warning intelligence; provides daily briefings on current intelligence to the Secretary of Defense, the chairman of the JCS, and other DOD officials; produces a Morning Summary, daily Defense Intelligence Notices, and intelligence appraisals; and contributes to the Senior Executive Intelligence Brief.[59]

The National Military Command Center Support Division, which operates under the supervision of the J2 directorate, is an indications and warning center that "operates 24 hours a day and is responsible for providing time-sensitive intelligence to the National Military Command Center, the Secretary of Defense, the Joint Chiefs of Staff, military commands, and military services."[60]

NATIONAL MEDIA EXPLOITATION CENTER

The National Media Exploitation Center (NMEC) was established by Director of Central Intelligence George J. Tenet in October 2002, with DIA becoming responsible for managing the center in January 2003. In 2005, DIA director Lt. Gen. Michael Maples placed the Directorate for Human Intelligence Document Exploitation (DOCEX) and Translation Services Element, the Joint Document Exploitation centers, and the Combined Media Processing Center–Qatar under the organization and management of NMEC—thus combining both headquarters and field elements in one organization. In October 2008, NMEC became an independent center/directorate reporting directly to the DIA command element.[61]

As its name indicates, the center is responsible for extracting intelligence from both paper documents as well as electronic and visual media—particularly in support of military commanders and forces (such as the Joint Improvised Explosive Device Defeat Organization), but also in support of the Intelligence Community, law enforcement, and the Department of Homeland Security. In November 2005, NMEC received 1.2 terabytes (TB) of data for exploitation. By June 2008, the monthly average exceeded 25 TB. The NMEC reporting element produces more than 1,000 intelligence information reports a year, while the center's collection management element oversees the response to homeland security and Intelligence Community requirements. [62]

DEFENSE INTELLIGENCE OPERATIONS COORDINATION CENTER

The Defense Intelligence Operations Coordination Center (DIOCC) was established by order of the Secretary of Defense in October 2007 to integrate into a single organization the functions of the DIA's Defense Joint Intelligence Operations Center (DJIOC) and the U.S. Strategic Command's Joint Functional Component Command–Intelligence, Surveillance, and Reconnaissance (JFCC-ISR), which was headed by the DIA Director.[63]

The creation of the DJIOC was the result of two initiatives undertaken by the Office of the Under Secretary of Defense for Intelligence in 2003, which were merged into the Remodeling Defense Intelligence (RDI) initiative. One consequence of the initiative was the creation of the DJIOC, with the objective of "more tightly [coupling] intelligence with traditional operations and plans." Specifically, the DJIOC was created to "plan, prepare, integrate, direct, synchronize, and manage continuous full-spectrum Defense Intelligence operations in support of the [combatant commands]." The DJIOC achieved initial operational capability in April 2006 and was expected to achieve full operational capability by December 31, 2007.[64]

The JFCC-ISR, which was established in March 2005, is responsible for conducting planning for the employment of international, national (NRO, NSA, NGA), and Department of Defense ISR resources to satisfy national, departmental, and combatant commands intelligence requirements.[65]

Notes

1. U.S. Congress, Senate Select Committee to Study Governmental Operations with Respect to Intelligence Activities, *Final Report, Book I: Foreign and Military Intelligence* (Washington, D.C.: U.S. Government Printing Office, 1976), p. 325; U.S. Congress, Senate Select Committee to Study Governmental Operations with Respect to Intelligence Activities, *Final Report, Book VI: Supplementary Reports on Intelligence Activities* (Washington, D.C.: U.S. Government Printing Office, 1976), p. 266.

2. Secretary of Defense Robert S. McNamara, Memorandum for the President, Subject: The Establishment of a Defense Intelligence Agency, July 6, 1961, Declassified Document Reference System (DDRS), 1986–000085; Joint Study Group, *The Joint Study Group Report on Foreign Intelligence Activities of the United States Government*, December 15, 1960, p. 31.

3. Joint Study Group, *The Joint Study Group Report on Foreign Intelligence Activities of the United States Government*, p. 23.

4. Robert McNamara, Memorandum for the Chairman, Joint Chiefs of Staff, Subject: Establishment of a Defense Intelligence Agency, February 8, 1961, National Archives and Record Administration (NARA), Record Group (RG) 218, CCS 2010 (Collection of Intelligence), 1960 Box, Dec. 20, 1960 Folder, p. 1127.

5. Ibid., p. 1129; Joint Staff, DJSM–156–61, Memorandum for General Lemnitzer et al., Subject: Establishment of a Defense Intelligence Agency, February 8, 1961, NARA, RG 218, CCS 2010 (Collection of Intelligence), 1960 Box, Dec. 20, 1960 Folder.

6. JCS 2031/166, Joint Chiefs of Staff Decision on JCS 2031/166, Memorandum by the Director, Joint Staff, on Establishment of a Defense Intelligence Agency, April 13, 1961; JCS 2031/166, Memorandum by the Director, Joint Staff for the Joint Chiefs of Staff on Establishment of a Defense Intelligence Agency, April 7, 1961, with Enclosure (Revised Draft Memorandum [April 12, 1961] for the Secretary of Defense, Subject: Establishment of a Defense Intelligence Agency [DIA], both in NARA, RG 218, CCS 2010 [Collection of Intelligence]), 1960 Box, Dec. 20, 1960 Folder.

7. Revised Draft Memorandum for the Secretary of Defense, Subject: Establishment of a Defense Intelligence Agency (DIA).

8. Historical Division, Joint Secretariat, Joint Chiefs of Staff, *Development of the Defense Agencies*, November 3, 1978, p. B-1.

9. Ibid., p. B-2, citing Department of Defense Directive 5105.21, "Defense Intelligence Agency," December 16, 1976.

10. Historical Division, Joint Secretariat, Joint Chiefs of Staff, *Development of Defense Agencies*, pp. B-2 to B-3.

11. William K. O'Donnell, Memorandum for W. M. MacDonald, Director, Freedom of Information and Security Review OASD (PA), Subject: Freedom of Information Act (FOIA) Appeal—Jeffrey T. Richelson, July 31, 1991.

12. Ibid.; Assistant Secretary of Defense (Command, Control, Communications, and Intelligence), *Plan for Restructuring Defense Intelligence*, March 15, 1991, p. 1; Donald J. Atwood, Memorandum for Secretaries of the Military Departments et al., Subject: Strengthening Defense Intelligence Functions, December 14, 1990.

13. Assistant Secretary of Defense (Command, Control, Communications, and Intelligence), Plan for Restructuring Defense Intelligence, p. 3.

14. Department of Defense Directive 5105.21, "Defense Intelligence Agency," March 18, 2008.

15. Ibid.

16. Vernon Loeb, "Intelligence Priorities Set for Modern Battlefield," *Washington Post*, September 14, 2000, p. A33; Defense Intelligence Agency, DIA Release 10–04–02, "Phillip Roberts Selected to Head DIA Activity at Rivanna Station," April 22, 2010.

17. Memorandum, VADM Lowell E. Jacoby, Subject: Agency Restructuring, February 11, 2003.

18. Chris Strohm, "Gates moves to overhaul, boost military intelligence," www.govexec.com, January 7, 2011.

19. Gordon England, Subject: Directive-Type Memorandum (DTM) 08–032–Establishment of the Defense Counterintelligence and Human Intelligence Center (DCHC), July 22, 2008; Office of the Assistant Secretary of Defense (Public Affairs), News Release No. 651–08, "DOD Activates Defense Counterintelligence and Human Intelligence Center," August 4, 2008; "Defense Counterintelligence and Human Intelligence Center Established," *Communiqué*, March 2009, pp. 2–3; DOD Instruction O-5100.93, "Defense Counterintelligence (CI) and Human Intelligence Center," August 13, 2010. On CIFA's history, see Michael J. Woods and William King, "An Assessment of the Evolution and Oversight of Defense Counterintelligence Activities," *Journal of National Security Law & Policy* 3, 1 (2009): 169–219; and Jeffrey T. Richelson (ed.), National Security Archive Electronic Briefing Book No. 230, *The Pentagon's Counterspies*, September 17, 2007, available at www.nsarchive.org.

20. "CI & HUMINT—Partners in the HUMAN DOMAIN," *Communiqué*, November/December 2008, pp. 19–22; "Defense CI & HUMINT Enterprise Management Office," *Communiqué*, May/June 2009, pp. 31–32.

21. "CI & HUMINT—Partners in the HUMAN DOMAIN."

22. Ibid.

23. Raymond Bonner, "Secret Pentagon Intelligence Unit Is Disclosed," *New York Times*, May 11, 1983, p. A13; Robert C. Toth, "U.S. Spying: Partnership Re-emerges," *Los Angeles Times*, November 14, 1983, pp. 1, 12; Robert M. Lisch, *Implementing the DHS: Views from the Leadership* (Washington, D.C.: Joint Military Intelligence College, 1995), p. 9; Margaret H. Livingstone, "Directorate for Intelligence Operations Renews Its Focus on the Fifth Thrust," *Communiqué*, June–July 2001, pp. 12–14; "Professional Profiles: David L. Church," *Communiqué*, March/April 2008, pp. 39–40.

24. Office of the Assistant Secretary of Defense (Command, Control, Communications, and Intelligence), Plan for the Consolidation of Defense HUMINT, 1993, p. 1. For an account of

the formation of the Defense HUMINT Service, see Jeffrey T. Richelson, "From MONARCH EAGLE to MODERN AGE: The Consolidation of U.S. Defense HUMINT," *International Journal of Intelligence and Counterintelligence* 10, 2 (Summer 1997): 131–164.

25. William J. Perry, Memorandum for Secretaries of the Military Departments et al., Subject: Consolidation of Defense HUMINT, November 2, 1993; Office of the Assistant Secretary of Defense (Command, Control, Communications, and Intelligence), *Plan for the Consolidation of Defense HUMINT*, p. 7.

26. Private information.

27. Richelson, "From MONARCH EAGLE to MODERN AGE: The Consolidation of U.S. Defense HUMINT"; private information.

28. Jeffrey T. Richelson, "Task Force 157: The U.S. Navy's Secret Intelligence Service, 1966–1977," *Intelligence and National Security* 11, 1 (January 1996): 106–145; Office of Naval Intelligence, "ONI–65 Mission Statement," n.d.

29. Benjamin Schemmer, *The Raid* (New York: Harper & Row, 1975), pp. 26–27.

30. Barbara Starr, "Military Network Now Handles DOD HUMINT," *Jane's Defence Weekly*, March 11, 1995, p. 13; Les Aspin, *Secretary of Defense Annual Report to the President and the Congress* (Washington, D.C.: U.S. Government Printing Office, 1995), p. 240; Nick Eftimiades, "DHS Stands Up," *Communiqué*, October 1995, pp. 1, 10; Howard E. Locke, "HUMINT Support Element Synchronizes Full-Spectrum Intelligence," *Communiqué*, July/August 2006, pp. 24–25.

31. Starr, "Military Network Now Handles DOD HUMINT"; Aspin, *Secretary of Defense Annual Report to the President and the Congress*, p. 240; Eftimiades, "DHS Stands Up"; "Director Visits DHS Element," *Communiqué*, September 1996, p. 35.

32. Barton Gellman, "Secret Unit Expands Rumsfeld's Domain," http://www.washington post.com, January 23, 2005; Josh White and Barton Gellman, "Defense Espionage Unit to Work with CIA," http://washingtonpost.com, January 25, 2005, p. A3; Barton Gellman, "Controversial Pentagon Espionage Unit Loses Its Leader," *Washington Post*, February 13, 2005, p. A8; "DOD Background Briefing on Strategic Support Teams," http://www.dod.mil; VADM Lowell E. Jacoby, Subject: Message to the Workforce—DH Strategic Support Teams, January 27, 2005.

33. "CI & HUMINT—Partners in the HUMAN DOMAIN"; "D2X: The Crossroads for CI and HUMINT," *Communiqué*, May/June 2009, pp. 26–27.

34. Memorandum, Jacoby, Subject: Agency Restructuring.

35. Defense Intelligence Agency, "Mission Description" (Central MASINT Office), n.d.; CMO, "Script for CMO Brief to the 8th Annual Defense Intelligence Status Symposium," November 1996, p. 1.

36. DOD Directive 5105.21, "Defense Intelligence Agency," March 18, 2008.

37. CMO, "Script for CMO Brief . . . ," pp. 1–2.

38. Mike Elliott, "MASINT's 24/7 Watch," *Communiqué*, February 2004, p. 12.

39. William B. Huntington, "DIA's Collection Group," *Communiqué*, November-December 1996, p. 18; Laura L. Sifuentes, "Attention! DT-101 Is Here!," *Communiqué*, July-August 2005, p. 9.

40. *Department of Defense Telephone Directory*, December 1997, p. O-22; Defense Intelligence Agency, *Vector 21: A Strategic Plan for the Defense Intelligence Agency*, 1996, p. 13.

41. John Y. Yurechko, "On Guard Against Information Warfare," *Communiqué*, April–May 1997, p. 37; "Joint Warfare Support Office Gets New Chief," *Communiqué*, May 2003, p. 10.

42. Maj. Chip Cutler and Jeff Rote, "Terrorism: Threat and Response," *Communiqué*, March 1997, pp. 15–17; "Interview with the Director for Intelligence, J2," *Communiqué*, May–June 2006, pp. 21–23.

43. Rex Mills, "The Office of Counterdrug Analysis," *Communiqué*, June–July 1997, p. 17; Tony M. Tomlinson, "The Circle of Life: The Evolution of Counterdrug Analysis," *Communiqué*, May–June 2006, pp. 4–6.

44. Defense Intelligence Agency, *Vector 21*, p. 13.

45. "Professional Profiles: Col. Dawn T. Jones," *Communiqué*, May/June 2008, pp. 42–43; "Interview with the Deputy Director for Analysis," *Communiqué*, May/June 2008, pp. 22–26.

46. U.S. Congress, House Permanent Select Committee on Intelligence, Report 102–65, *Intelligence Authorization Act, Fiscal Year 1992, Part 1* (Washington, D.C.: U.S. Government Printing Office, 1991), p. 8; Letter, John W. Shannon, Acting Secretary of the Army, to Lt. Gen. James R. Clapper, Jr. Director, Defense Intelligence Agency, February 4, 1992; Defense Intelligence Agency, *Plan for the Transfer of the Armed Forces Medical Intelligence Center to the Defense Intelligence Agency*, n.d.

47. *Organization, Mission and Functions: U.S. Army Missile and Space Intelligence Center, Redstone Arsenal, Alabama* (Redstone Arsenal, Ala.: AMSIC, n.d.), pp. 4–6; Missile and Space Intelligence Center, "Missile and Space Intelligence Center (MSIC)," 1996.

48. "MSIC Expands Capabilities," *Communiqué*, March 2009, p. 19.

49. Defense Audit Service, *Semiannual Audit Plan, First Half, Fiscal Year 1982* (Washington, D.C.: DAS, 1981), p. 32. On the evolution of post–World War II medical intelligence, see Jonathan D. Clemente, "The Fate of an Orphan: The Hawley Board and the Debates over the Post-War Organization of Medical Intelligence," *Intelligence and National Security* 20, 2 (June 2005): 264–287.

50. Armed Forces Medical Intelligence Center, *Organization and Functions of the Armed Forces Medical Intelligence Center* (Fort Detrick, Md.: AFMIC, April 1986), p. vi; Defense Audit Service, *Semiannual Audit Plan, First Half, Fiscal Year 1982*, p. 32; Defense Intelligence Agency, Poisonous Snakes of Europe, September 1986; DOD Directive 6420.1, "Armed Forces Medical Intelligence Center," October 9, 2004; Lynn A. McNamee, "AFMIC Responds to Tsunami Disaster," *Communiqué*, January 2005, pp. 10–11.

51. "AFMIC Transitions to a National Center," Communiqué, March 2009, p. 10.

52. Defense Audit Service, *Semiannual Audit Plan, First Half, Fiscal Year 1982*, p. 32; DOD Directive 6420.1, "Armed Forces Medical Intelligence Center."

53. DOD Instruction 6240.01, "National Center for Medical Intelligence," March 20, 2009; "AFMIC Transitions to a National Center."

54. Damien K., "Medical Intelligence Relies on Teamwork," *Pathfinder*, March/April 2010, pp. 10–11; "Center for medical intelligence expanding," www.boston.com, July 2, 2008; Anthony L. Kimery, "National Medical Intelligence Capabilities Expanded," *Homeland Security Today* (at http://hstoday.us), July 7, 2008; Jonathan Bor, "Fort Detrick unit to track diseases that affect U.S.," www.baltimoresun.com, July 3, 2008; Defense Intelligence Agency, "U.S. Dedicates National Center for Medical Intelligence; Pentagon Facility Expands into National Mission," July 2, 2008; Defense Intelligence Agency, *Baseline Infectious Disease Risk Assessment: Haiti*, 2009; Defense Intelligence Agency, *Haiti: Health Risks and Health System Impacts Associated with Large-Scale Earthquake*, January 13, 2010; Defense Intelligence Agency, Defense Intelligence Assessment, *Worldwide: New 2009–H1N1 Influenza Virus Poses Potential Threat to U.S. Forces*," May 1, 2009.

55. Maj. Mark Esterbrook, "'Unearthing' the Truth in Defense of Our Nation," *Pathfinder*, January–February 2005, pp. 19–21.

56. Ibid.

57. David Eisenberg, Center for Defense Information, "Multitude of Data Bases Complicates Information Sharing," October 29, 2002, www.cdi.org; JITF-CT, Exploitation Branch, *Guidelines for Personnel Supporting Interrogations and Debriefing Activities*, August 2004; National Counterterrorism Center, *National Strategy to Combat Terrorist Travel*, May 2, 2006, p. 10.

58. "Interview with the Director for Intelligence, J2."

59. Ibid.; Defense Intelligence Agency, *Organization, Mission, and Key Personnel*, 1984, pp. 43–46.

60. "Interview with the Director for Intelligence, J2"; Central Intelligence Agency, *A Consumer's Guide to Intelligence*, 1993, p. 42.

61. "NMEC Matures Under LTG Maples," *Communiqué*, March 2009, p. 11.

62. Ibid; Roy I. Apseloff, "National Media Exploitation Center—WAY AHEAD," *Communiqué*, May/June 2009, p. 29–31; Roy I. Apseloff, "NMEC Strives for 'Legendary' CUSTOMER SERVICE," *Communiqué*, November/December 2008, pp. 32–33.

63. Defense Intelligence Agency, "DIA Update: Defense Intelligence Operations Coordination Center," October 3, 2007, www.dia.mil; "Emergence of the Defense Intelligence Enterprise," *Communiqué*, March 2009, p. 4.

64. Department of Defense, "Remodeling Defense Intelligence (RDI) Initiative Fact Sheet," March 22, 2006; Department of Defense, "Joint Intelligence Operations Center (JIOC) Fact Sheet," March 22, 2006; Defense Intelligence Agency, *Defense Joint Intelligence Operations Center (DJIOC)*, April 12, 2006; Barry Harris, "DJIOC Integrates and Synchronizes Military and National Intelligence Capabilities," *Communiqué*, July/August 2006, pp. 10–12.

65. U.S. Strategic Command, Fact Sheet, "Joint Functional Component Command for Intelligence, Surveillance, and Reconnaissance, www.stratcom.mil/factsheets/isr, accessed July 9, 2010.

4

MILITARY SERVICE INTELLIGENCE ORGANIZATIONS

Unlike the United Kingdom and Canada, which abolished their military service intelligence organizations in favor of a unified defense intelligence organization, or Australia and France, whose service intelligence organizations are restricted to tactical intelligence production, the United States has maintained elaborate Army, Navy, and Air Force intelligence organizations. The other two military services, the Marines and the Coast Guard, maintain intelligence organizations as well.

The continued major role of U.S. service intelligence organizations is partly a function of bureaucratic politics, partly a function of law (Title 10), and partly the result of the structure and requirements of the U.S. military. A military force with large service components, and major combat commands distributed across the globe, may be better served in terms of intelligence support by organizations that are not too detached from the service components and commands.

Until the early 1990s, it could be said that each of the major services maintained an intelligence community of its own—a number of distinct, often geographically separated, intelligence organizations directed by the service's intelligence chief. However, in 1991 a significant process of disestablishment and/or consolidation of formerly separate intelligence organizations began in each of the major services. The factors producing the changes included budget and personnel cuts taking place in the aftermath of the Cold War and pressure exerted by congressional oversight committees. In a 1990 report, the Senate Select Committee on Intelligence observed,

> While new requirements and the increasing cost of collection systems have driven a share of the increase in intelligence, the cost of maintaining large numbers of intelligence organizations internal to the Department of Defense has also contributed. Every echelon from the Office of the Secretary of Defense, to the Service Departments, to the CINCs [Commanders in Chief of the unified commands] and below have their own organic intelligence arms. For each organization, we

need separate buildings, separate administration, separate security, separate communications, and separate support services.

Over the years, numerous individuals and reports . . . have criticized the Defense Department for significant duplication of effort; insufficient integration and sharing of information; uneven security measures and regulations; pursuit of parochial service, CINC, [and] other interests rather than joint intelligence interests; and gaps in intelligence support and coverage, despite the number of intelligence organizations.[1]

As a result, the committee, along with the Senate Armed Services Committee, directed the Secretary of Defense to review all of the Defense Department's intelligence activities and "to the maximum degree possible, consolidate or begin consolidating all disparate or redundant functions, programs, and entities."[2]

The following year, on March 15, the Assistant Secretary of Defense (C³I) issued his *Plan for Restructuring Defense Intelligence*. The plan instructed each military service to "consolidate all existing intelligence commands, agencies, and elements into a single intelligence command within each Service."[3] Although that objective has never been completely met, each of the major services instituted significant consolidations of their intelligence activities.

ARMY INTELLIGENCE ORGANIZATIONS

U.S. Army intelligence collection and production operations are the ultimate responsibility of the Deputy Chief of Staff, G-2. Those operations are carried out by the U.S. Army Intelligence and Security Command (INSCOM), which conducts imagery, MASINT, and SIGINT operations, and the National Ground Intelligence Center (NGIC), which produces scientific and technical, as well as general, military intelligence. NGIC is formally subordinate to INSCOM.

The Deputy Chief of Staff, G-2, determines Army intelligence policy, supervises the activities of INSCOM and NGIC, and represents the Army in military and national intelligence fora. The deputy chief of staff's office consists of seven directorates—Foreign Liaison, Operations, and Plans; Counterintelligence; Human Intelligence; Security and Disclosure; Resource & Integration; Intelligence Community Information Management; and Foreign Intelligence—as well as two offices (the Army Intelligence Master Plan Office and the Intelligence Personnel Management Office) and two groups (the Command Group and the Initiatives Group).[4] The organizational structure of the office is shown in Figure 4.1.

The Foreign Intelligence Directorate, which has three components (the Analysis Division, the Weapons Systems Support Division, and the Intelligence Watch) is responsible for estimative support to the Army, the Defense Department, and the national intelligence community; current intelligence support to the Army Operations Center; and threat support to acquisition programs. The CI/HUMINT Counterintelligence/Foreign Disclosure and Security Directorate is responsible for policy for-

FIGURE 4.1   Organization of the Deputy Chief of Staff, G-2

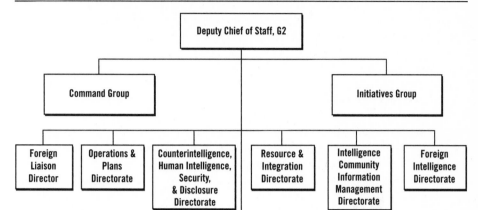

mulation, planning, programming, oversight, and representation for counterintelligence, human intelligence, and security countermeasures.[5]

On January 1, 1977, the U.S. Army Security Agency (ASA) was redesignated as the U.S. Army Intelligence and Security Command and absorbed the U.S. Army Intelligence Agency (AIA), the Forces Command Intelligence Group, the Intelligence Threat Analysis Detachment, and the Imagery Interpretation Center. The latter three organizations had been field-operating activities of the Assistant Chief of Staff for Intelligence.[6]

The commanding general of INSCOM is therefore responsible both to the Army's Intelligence Chief and to the Chief of the Central Security Service (i.e., the Director of the NSA). INSCOM personnel staff SIGINT collection facilities at numerous overseas bases. In addition, INSCOM conducts MASINT and imagery collection operations as well as offensive counterintelligence operations (OFCO). In 1992, it was assigned responsibility for supervising the intelligence production activities of the Foreign Science and Technology Center (FSTC) and the Intelligence and Threat Analysis Center (ITAC). The two organizations were subsequently merged to form NGIC. Today, INSCOM, headquartered at Ft. Belvoir, Virginia, has approximately 15,000 personnel and a $2.1 billion budget.[7]

Within INSCOM a number of Assistant Chiefs of Staff are responsible for different areas of activity. There are assistant chiefs of staff for Personnel (G1), Security (G2), Operations (G3), Logistics (G4), and Information Management (CIO/G6).

Subordinate to the ACS for Operations, who is responsible for overseeing human and technical collection as well as production, are six divisions (Operations and Training, IOC, Intelligence Information Services, Force Management, Aviation and Air Services, and Plans) and two offices (the Army Cryptologic Office and the Contract Linguist Support Office).[8]

However, the key activities conducted by INSCOM are those not at headquarters but those in the units that are deployed in the United States and overseas. Those units fall into five basic groups: the theater military intelligence brigades, the SIGINT units, the counterintelligence and human intelligence elements, the functional brigades, and the National Ground Intelligence Center (NGIC).

INSCOM's five theater brigades are the 66th, 470th, 500th, 501st, and 513th Military Intelligence Brigades. The brigades consist of five battalions: Operations, Collection, Aerial Exploitation, Strategic SIGINT, and Theater Support. The 66th MIB, with over 1,100 personnel, provides intelligence support to the European Command. Its personnel have supported Operations Enduring Freedom, Iraqi Freedom, Enduring Freedom Trans-Sahara, Georgia Humanitarian Assistance, and counterterrorist activities. The 470th MIB, also with over 1,100 personnel, is headquartered at Ft. Bliss, Texas, and supports the U.S. Army South, Southern Command (SOUTHCOM), Pacific Command, and national intelligence efforts. Its 204th MI Battalion conducts airborne SIGINT operations in support of SOUTHCOM, while its 314th MI Battalion provides signals intelligence support to "deployed U.S. forces." Its Operations Battalion, at Fort Sam Houston, Texas, "provides tailored counterintelligence and analytical support to worldwide contingency operations."[9]

The 500th MIB, headquartered at Schofield Barracks, Hawaii, and with almost 1,300 personnel, supports U.S. Pacific Command (PACOM) operations. Its 15th MI Battalion (aerial exploitation), which has provided support to operations in Iraq and Afghanistan, is based at Fort Hood, Texas, and is part of the Army's aerial intelligence, surveillance, and reconnaissance fleet, gathering both aerial imagery and signals intelligence. The brigade's 205th MI Battalion, at Fort Shafter, Hawaii, is responsible for all-source analysis; it deployed to Iraq in 2005. The 301st MI Battalion, headquartered in Phoenix, Arizona, is a theater support component that deploys "theater collection teams to support operations and exercises in the theater." The 441st MI Battalion (Provisional), located at Camp Zama, Japan, is to become a forward collection battalion in the 2012 fiscal year—conducting open source, counterintelligence, and human intelligence operations throughout the Pacific area of responsibility. Finally, the brigade's 732nd MI Battalion, also at Schofield Barracks, conducts strategic signals intelligence operations at NSA/Hawaii (Kunia) under the control of the NSA/CSS.[10]

The 501st MI Brigade at Seoul, South Korea, with over 1,300 personnel, provides support to U.S. Forces Korea. It conducts imagery, SIGINT, MASINT, and HUMINT activities. Its 524th Battalion conducts human intelligence and counterintelligence collection operations as well as open source intelligence and document exploitation activities. Another of its battalions, the 3rd MI Battalion, employs RC-12 Guardrail and RC-7 Airborne Reconnaissance Low aircraft to gather intelligence.[11]

The 513th MI Brigade, with almost 1,200 personnel, is headquartered at Ft. Gordon, Georgia, and consists of four battalions and a task force. The brigade's 202nd MI Battalion, also headquartered at Ft. Gordon, is responsible for counterintelligence and human intelligence support in the United States and the Central Command's area of responsibility. The 224th MI Battalion, located at Hunter Army Airfield, Georgia, conducts imagery and signals intelligence operations. The brigade's 297th MI Battalion, whose soldiers have deployed to Iraq, Kuwait, and Afghanistan, "provides tailored, deployable intelligence support" to CENTCOM operations, while the 345th MI Battalion (Army Reserves) "mobilizes and deploys individuals and teams to conduct multi-discipline intelligence operations in support of the brigade." The brigade's Task Force Lightning was originally its 201st MI Battalion. Its personnel have been deployed to Kuwait, Saudi Arabia, Somalia, Haiti, Ecuador, Colombia, Chile, Mexico, Qatar, Australia, Singapore, Korea, Bosnia, and Kosovo.[12]

INSCOM's two MI brigades specifically dedicated to SIGINT collection are the 704th and the 706. The 704th is headquartered at Fort George G. Meade, Maryland, and has subordinate battalions at Ft. Meade as well as at Buckley Air Force Base, Colorado. Additional elements are assigned to support a variety of Army and joint commands, which include the CENTCOM, the Army Special Operations Command, and the Army Forces Command. The brigade's 741st MI Battalion provides personnel for "information superiority" operations within the National Security Agency and other U.S. agencies. The 742nd MI Battalion contributes analysis and reporting via the Army Technical Control and Analysis Element. And the 743rd MI Battalion, located at Buckley AFB, the ground station for a number of reconnaissance satellites, "provides advanced geospatial intelligence . . . in support of Operation Enduring Freedom.[13]

The 706th MI Group, at Ft. Gordon, Georgia, is the host to NSA/CSS Georgia, providing personnel, intelligence assets, and technical support to conduct signals intelligence operations in support of commanders and decisionmakers involved in ongoing military operations.[14]

INSCOM's counterintelligence unit is the 902nd Military Intelligence Group. Located at Ft. George G. Meade, it provides direct and general counterintelligence support to Army activities and major commands. It also provides support to other military department counterintelligence and intelligence elements, unified commands, defense agencies, and national agency counterintelligence and security activities and organizations. Its 308th MI Battalion "conducts counterintelligence operations and investigations throughout the continental United States to detect, identify, neutralize and defeat the foreign intelligence services and international terrorism threats" to U.S. Army and selected Defense Department forces, technologies, and infrastructure.[15]

The group's 310th MI Battalion conducts worldwide counterintelligence operations, technical counterintelligence operations, surveillance (physical and technical) operations, and investigations in support of INSCOM and the Army.

Another element of the 902nd is the U.S. Army Foreign Counterintelligence Activity (FCA), which is "a multi-function, strategic counterintelligence activity that supports U.S. Army and national counterintelligence and counterterrorist objectives by detecting, identifying and providing a unique operational 'window' into foreign intelligence organizations."[16]

Another key INSCOM activity is the Army Operations Activity, established in March 2003 on a provisional basis and located at Fort George G. Meade, Maryland. Its mission, according to INSCOM, is to "conduct human intelligence operations and provide expertise in support of ground component priority intelligence requirements using a full spectrum of human intelligence collection methods." Its tactical and strategic collection activities support military commanders involved in operations in Iraq, Afghanistan, and elsewhere. Its creation, and the plans for it to expand both in terms of mission and organization, are a reflection of the regrowth of service HUMINT, which was to have been restricted to low-level overt HUMINT following the creation of the Defense HUMINT Service.[17]

Analytical work on foreign ground forces is the responsibility of INSCOM's National Ground Intelligence Center; located in Charlottesville, Virginia, it was established in 1962 as the Foreign Science and Technology Center (FSTC) by consolidating the intelligence offices of the individual Army technical services— among them Signal, Ordnance, Quartermaster, Engineering, and Chemical services. It was redesignated as NGIC in 1994 and absorbed the Intelligence and Threat Analysis Center in 1995.[18]

NGIC functions include

- Developing and maintaining a database of ground forces intelligence
- Producing ground intelligence in support of research, development, and acquisition programs of the Department of the Army, United States Marine Corps, warfighting commanders, the Army force modernization community, the Defense Intelligence Agency, Department of Defense and national policymakers
- Discovering S&T [Science and Technology] threats to the security of U.S. ground forces
- Forecasting foreign military trends and developments through study of worldwide S&T and GMI [General Military Intelligence] accomplishments
- Identifying significant foreign improvements that may be incorporated into U.S. weapon and equipment systems
- Pinpointing deficiencies in foreign developments to assist in evolving U.S. countermeasures for exploitation
- Managing the U.S. Army program for the acquisition and exploitation of foreign materiel
- Providing support to the U.S. Army S&T intelligence collection effort.[19]

The specific areas that NGIC focuses on include close combat, fire support, air combat, maneuver support, battlefield reconnaissance, battlefield electronics, chemical warfare and biotechnology, advanced military applications, military technologies, acquisition strategies, signatures, imagery exploitation, and foreign materiel exploitation.[20]

NGIC has approximately 900 employees, over three-quarters of whom are located at the Charlottesville headquarters, with the remainder at NGIC facilities at Fort Meade, Maryland, the Aberdeen Proving Ground, and the Washington Navy Yard.[21]

NAVY INTELLIGENCE ORGANIZATIONS

Of all the military services, the Navy experienced the most dramatic changes in its intelligence structure in the early 1990s. On September 30, 1991, the Navy had seven distinct intelligence organizations. On January 1, 1993, it had two—the Office of Naval Intelligence (ONI) and the Naval Security Group Command (NSGC). In December 2005, the NSGC was disestablished, and its signals intelligence responsibilities were transferred to the control of a command with broader responsibilities.

The seven naval intelligence organizations that existed on September 30, 1991, were the Office of Naval Intelligence, the Naval Intelligence Command, Task Force 168, the Naval Technical Intelligence Center, the Navy Operational Intelligence Center, the Naval Intelligence Activity, and the Naval Security Group Command.

The Office of Naval Intelligence represented the apex of the naval intelligence community and was responsible for management and direction and some intelligence production. The Naval Intelligence Command (NIC), a second-echelon command, performed a variety of management functions. The remaining organizations, with the exception of the Naval Security Group Command, were third-echelon commands and reported to the NIC. Task Force 168 engaged in overt human source collection and provided support to fleet technical collection operations. The Naval Technical Intelligence Center (NTIC) was the Navy's scientific and technical intelligence organization, its primary focus being the Soviet navy. The Navy Operational Intelligence Center (NOIC) monitored naval movements, relying heavily on signals intelligence acquired by national and Navy collection systems. The Naval Intelligence Activity (NIA) was responsible for providing automatic data processing support to naval intelligence organizations. Finally, the Naval Security Group Command (NSGC) performed SIGINT and COMSEC (Communications Security) missions.

On October 1, 1991, Task Force 168, NOIC, and NTIC were disestablished as separate organizations, and their functions and personnel were assigned to a newly created Naval Maritime Intelligence Center (NAVMIC). Under the new arrangement the analytical functions previously performed by NTIC and NOIC were integrated into NAVMIC's Intelligence Directorate.[22]

The consolidation was designed to achieve several objectives, including satisfying congressional and Secretary of Defense instructions to consolidate and reorganize the service intelligence structures and adjusting "to current and anticipated future changes in the threat to maritime forces and to an expected redefinition of requirements levied upon naval intelligence."[23]

On January 1, 1993, an even more drastic consolidation took place. The Naval Intelligence Command, Naval Maritime Intelligence Center, and Naval Intelligence Activity were all disestablished, and their functions and most of their personnel were absorbed by the Office of Naval Intelligence.[24]

Although plans had been in place in the fall of 1991 to merge the NSGC with the Naval Intelligence Command, no such merger took place.[25] Thus, the Navy remains the only major service that has not merged its Service Cryptologic Element (SCE) with one or more of its other intelligence components. However, the Navy consolidation represented, overall, the most complete consolidation among the services. All other intelligence functions were assigned to the new ONI, with no subordinate commands, and all activities were consolidated at a single location—the National Maritime Intelligence Center complex at Suitland, Maryland.

Today's ONI has over 3,000 employees worldwide—made up of civilian, military, reservist, and contractor personnel. Its customers include "fleet commanders, operators and analysts, war fighters, the Navy acquisition community, other intelligence community organizations, the Department of Homeland Security, foreign and coalition partners, and law enforcement agencies."[26]

ONI produces analysis concerning

- Worldwide scientific and technical developments
- Military research, development, test and evaluation
- Military production and proliferation
- Military systems characteristics and performance
- Foreign naval forces leadership, organization, strategy, doctrine, tactics, techniques, procedures and readiness
- Identification and tracking of merchant shipping.[27]

In February 2009, ONI was reorganized into four centers, a number of offices, and one directorate, as indicated in Figure 4.2. Its Hopper Information Services Center "provides information services that support intelligence operations," while the Kennedy Irregular Warfare Center provides intelligence support to Naval Special Warfare forces as well as those of the Navy Expeditionary Combat Command. The Center's Deployed Forces Department prepares analytical personnel for deployments in support of military operations, while its Global Analysis Department "provides all-source operational intelligence" and can be accessed around the clock by deployed forces.[28]

ONI's two main intelligence-producing units are the Nimitz Operational Intelligence Center (NOIC) and Farragut Technical Analysis Center (FTAC). With approximately 560 personnel, the NOIC has four cells that provide operational intelligence support to the Pacific Fleet, U.S. Naval Forces Europe, U.S. Naval

FIGURE 4.2   Organization of the Office of Naval Intelligence

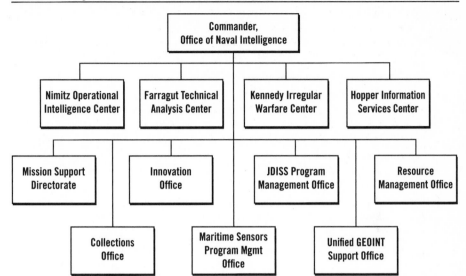

Forces Central, and the Fleet Forces Command/U.S. Naval Forces South, respectively. The center also includes a Navy Intelligence Task Force—Maritime Security, which focuses on illicit networks, intelligence support to counterterrorism, counternarcotics, counterproliferation, and counterpiracy operations.[29]

The Nimitz center also contains the Global Maritime Watch, which serves at the NORAD/NORTHCOM Maritime Fusion Center and, in conjunction with the Coast Guard Intelligence Coordination Center Coast Watch, constitutes the National Maritime Intelligence Watch. The Global Maritime Watch is responsible for "worldwide situational awareness on high-interest white shipping" and "generates the civil maritime feed to the worldwide common operating picture and monitors worldwide naval activity." As of January 2009, the NCIS Multiple Threat Alert Center (MTAC) was to be colocated with the Global Maritime Watch to bring "an antiterrorism I&W focus to ONI's mission."[30]

The center also contains three warfare analysis components. The Submarine Warfare Operations Research Division (SWORD) is responsible for producing analysis of submarine and anti-submarine capabilities, operations, and tactics. The Strike Project and Anti-Air Warfare Research Division (SPEAR) produces operational threat assessment of selected nation's near-term military capabilities. And the Surface Branch for Evaluation and Reporting (SABER) is responsible for providing "tailored operational threat assessments to operational commanders and mission planners."[31]

The technical analysis center is responsible for producing analysis on the following topics: foreign navies, platforms, and weapons; strategic assessments of foreign

FIGURE 4.3   Organization of the Farragut Technical Analysis Center

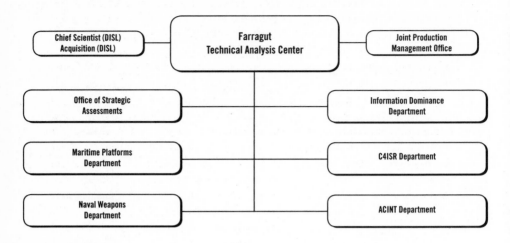

future naval capabilities; geophysical signature measurements, modeling, and projections; acoustic and non-acoustic sensor capabilities; technical ELINT analysis; command, control, communications, computers, intelligence, surveillance, and reconnaissance (C⁴ISR) assessments; foreign materiel exploitation; foreign weapons system and engineering assessments, modeling, and projections; counterintelligence assessments; critical information and infrastructure projection threat assessments, collection planning and analysis; and acoustic intelligence.[32]

With a total of approximately 519 individuals, the Farragut Technical Analysis Center is divided into the Office of Strategic Assessments and five departments, as shown in Figure 4.3: Maritime Platforms, Naval Weapons, Information Dominance, C⁴ISR, and ACINT. The strategic assessments office is responsible for "projecting the future environment in which the U.S. Navy will operate, and characterize foreign efforts that could put U.S. naval forces at risk." The Maritime Platforms Department is responsible for the study of all surface ships, submarines, aircraft, unmanned vehicles, and merchant ships. The Naval Weapons Department, which includes a Foreign Materiel Laboratory, covers torpedoes, mines, naval guns, cruise and ballistic missiles, surface-to-air missiles, and directed energy weapons.[33]

The C⁴ISR Department, which includes a SIGINT Laboratory, analyzes foreign naval sensors—including fire control, sonars, and target acquisition. In addition, the department studies components of command, control, communications, and computers—devices, networks, procedures—as well as intelligence, surveillance, and reconnaissance capabilities. The Information Dominance Department is responsible for identifying, analyzing, and warning of cyber threats to the Navy, both on land and on sea, including cyber threats to Navy acquisition programs. The department's effort involves both defensive and offensive elements. Department components include a Counterintelligence Technical Cell and a Deep Penetration Solutions element. As its name indicates, the ACINT Department, which includes the ACINT Laboratory, is responsible for the analysis of acoustic intelligence—such as that collected by the Navy's Sound Surveillance System (discussed in Chapter 9).[34]

The ONI Collections Office, with a staff of about 100, and the Technical Collections, Requirements Management, Foreign Materiel, and Knowledge Center components are "responsible for articulating and implementing all-source intelligence collection strategies to satisfy . . . gaps in information as identified by Naval Intelligence analysts." Until sometime in 2009 it also contained a Navy HUMINT Department, whose mission was transferred to the Naval Criminal Investigative Service (NCIS). This transfer was predicated on the premise that it would be beneficial to place the Navy's counterintelligence and HUMINT activities in the same organization.[35]

From the early days of the Cold War until late 2005, the Navy's signals intelligence collection operations were conducted by the Naval Security Group Command (NSGC). The command was the descendant of the Communications Security Group (OP-20-G) within the Office of Naval Communications, which was established in March 1935. After World War II it was renamed the Communications Supplementary Activities, and in 1950 it became the Naval Security Group. In 1968, it was redesignated the Naval Security Group Command.[36]

For over two decades the NSGC was responsible for signals intelligence and communications security. As a result, NSGC personnel staffed land-based HF-DF collection sites, installed and operated SIGINT and COMSEC equipment on ships and submarines, manned the downlinks for the Navy's ocean surveillance satellite systems, and conducted COMSEC monitoring operations. On September 30, 2005, the Navy disestablished the NSGC and merged all its Information Operations capabilities under one authority. NSGC became the Information Operations Directorate (IOD) of the Naval Network Warfare Command (NETWARCOM).[37]

The most important IOD units are the Navy Information Operations Commands (NOICs) and Navy Information Operations Detachments (NIODs) distributed across the world, which had previously been known as Naval Security Group Activities and Detachments. Over the course of 2011 these units may change names as a result of realignment of the parent Navy Information Operations Command at Suitland from being subordinate to the Naval Network Warfare Command to Navy Cyber Forces. Thus, the NIOC-Suitland has become the Navy Cyber Warfare Development Group.[38] The locations of these units are listed in Table 4.1.

AIR FORCE INTELLIGENCE ORGANIZATIONS

Two Air Force organizations perform departmental intelligence functions: the Office of the Deputy Chief of Staff of the Air Force, Intelligence, Surveillance, and Reconnaissance (DCS,ISR), and the Air Force Intelligence, Surveillance, and Reconnaissance Agency (AFISRA).

TABLE 4.1   Location of Navy Information Operations Commands and Detachments

NAVY INFORMATION OPERATIONS DETACHMENTS

Name	Location
NIOD San Antonio	San Antonio, Texas
NIOD Chesapeake	Chesapeake, Virginia
NIOD Dam Neck	Virginia Beach, Virginia
NIOD Jacksonville	Jacksonville, Florida
NIOD Groton	Groton, Connecticut
NIOD Kaneohe Bay	MCB, Kaneohe Bay, Hawaii
NIOD Digby	Digby, United Kingdom
NIOD Alice Springs	Alice Springs, Australia
NIOD Seoul	Seoul, Korea

NAVY INFORMATION OPERATIONS COMMANDS

Name	Location
NIOC Suitland	Washington, D.C.
NIOC Maryland	Fort George G. Meade, Maryland
NIOC Sugar Grove	Sugar Grove, West Virginia
NIOC Norfolk	Norfolk, Virginia
NIOC Pensacola	Pensacola, Florida
NIOC Colorado	Aurora, Colorado
NIOC Georgia	Fort Gordon, Georgia
NIOC Texas	San Antonio, Texas
NIOC Whidbey Island	Oak Harbor, Washington
NIOC Hawaii	Schofield Barracks, Hawaii
NIOC San Diego	San Diego, California
NIOC Menwith Hill	Menwith Hill, United Kingdom
NIOC Bahrain	Bahrain
NIOC Yokosuka	Yokosuka, Japan
NIOC Misawa	Misawa, Japan

SOURCE: "Section 2: Shore Activities by Command," at http://doni.daps.dla.mil/sndl.aspx, accessed March 15, 2010.

In early 1997, the Air Force disbanded the Office of the Assistant Chief of Staff, Intelligence (OACSI) and assigned the tasks previously performed by the OACSI to the Directorate of Intelligence, Surveillance, and Reconnaissance within the office of the Deputy Chief of Staff for Air and Space Operations. In 2005, the Air Force reestablished the ACSI position, which was subsequently upgraded to a Deputy Chief of Staff, Intelligence (DCSI), a position that subsequently was retitled Deputy Chief of Staff of the Air Force, Intelligence, Surveillance, and Reconnaissance.[39]

FIGURE 4.4   Organization of the Office of the Deputy Chief of Staff for Intelligence, Surveillance, and Reconnaissance (AF/A2)

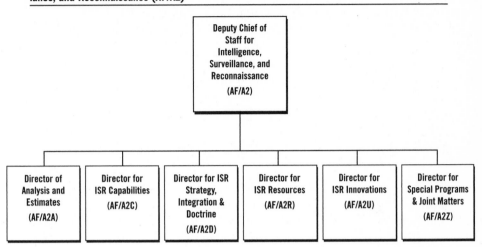

The deputy chief of staff is responsible for the supervision of all matters pertaining to Air Force intelligence, surveillance, and reconnaissance capabilities. As shown in Figure 4.4, subordinate to the deputy chief of staff are six directorates. The Directorate of Analysis and Estimates directs and manages all overhead imagery requirements and collection for the Air Force. It also provides intelligence products for mission support and indications and warning intelligence to senior Air Force officials, as well as representing the Air Force in the national intelligence estimates process. The Directorate of Special Programs is responsible for the "management, oversight, and integration of operational, research and development, and limited access programs within the intelligence community."[40]

The remaining four directorates—the Directorate of ISR Capabilities; the Directorate of ISR Strategy, Integration, and Doctrine; the Directorate of ISR Resources; and the Directorate of ISR Innovations—all involve some aspect of intelligence, surveillance, and reconnaissance. The ISR Capabilities directorate monitors the performance and effectiveness of operational ISR assets as well as directing the implementation of plans and procedures to improve the collection, processing, exploitation, and dissemination of ISR data.

The ISR Resources directorate represents the Air Force with regard to policy, manpower, funding, and requirements issues in Intelligence Community and Defense Department committees and boards. The ISR Innovations directorate manages the rapid insertion of advanced technology to Air Force operations in peacetime and during combat. It is also responsible for quick response deployment of off-the-shelf imagery and geospatial capabilities. The ISR Strategy, Integration, and Doctrine directorate develops Air Force ISR strategy plans in support of national security and military strategy.[41]

The AFISRA is the ultimate product of a 1971 directive issued by the Secretary of the Air Force mandating reassignment of Air Staff operating and support functions to other organizations. In response to the directive, the Air Force Intelligence Service (AFIS) was established on June 27, 1972.[42] In 1988, AFIS's status was upgraded, and it became the Air Force Intelligence Agency (AFIA). On October 1, 1991, as part of a reorganization of Air Force intelligence activities, it became the Air Force Intelligence Support Agency (AFISA).

A second part of the 1991 reorganization involved the establishment of the Air Force Intelligence Command (AFIC) by merging the Electronic Security Command,* the Foreign Technology Division (FTD) of the Air Force Systems Command, the Air Force Special Activities Center (AFSAC), and other elements of the AFIA. The result was the creation of an Air Force equivalent of INSCOM that combined SIGINT operations with intelligence production and HUMINT functions in the same organization. And, like INSCOM, AFIC had a center located a significant distance from headquarters that had its own identity and produced S&T intelligence.

In addition to fulfilling the ASD (C³I)'s mandate for consolidation and satisfying congressional oversight committees, AFIC was intended to provide "enhanced intelligence support to theater commanders in the conduct of their warfighting responsibilities" by establishing a "single focal point across intelligence disciplines to satisfy intelligence requirements to support operations." The new command was also intended to improve Air Force support to national agencies.[43]

On October 1, 1993, yet another reorganization occurred. Under the new plan, mandated by the June 15, 1993, HQ USAF Program Action Directive 93–8, "Restructuring Air Force Intelligence," and detailed in HQ AFIC Programming Plan 93–01, Establishment of the Air Force Intelligence Field Operating Agency, the Air Force Intelligence Command (AFIC) became the Air Intelligence Agency (AIA). Non-tactical HUMINT operations were transferred to the Defense HUMINT Service. In addition, an internal restructuring of the remaining AFIC elements was undertaken. On February 1, 2001, AIA was "realigned under Air Combat Command as a primary subordinate unit."[44]

---

*The Electronic Security Command (ESC) was first established informally as the Air Force Security Group (AFSG) in May 1948 and then formally on July 1, 1948, under the same title. In October 1948 it became the Air Force Security Service (AFSS), headquartered at Arlington Hall Station, Arlington, Virginia. The AFSG of May 1948 consisted of eleven officers and some enlisted clerical personnel on loan from the Army Security Agency. See Gabriel Marshall, "FOA Becomes Fact," Spokesman, November 1993, p. 8; and Electronic Security Command: Master of the Electronic Battlefield (San Antonio, Tex.: ESC, n.d.), p. 1.

In August 1997, AIA had over 16,000 military and civilian employees distributed among 95 locations, with headquarters at Kelly Air Force Base, Texas. By early 2006, the number of AIA personnel had been reduced to 12,000 and the number of locations to 70. Then, on June 15, 2007, AIA became the Air Force Intelligence, Surveillance, and Reconnaissance Agency (AFISRA). Beyond the title there were two additional differences between the new agency and the AIA. AFISRA was to be transformed from a SIGINT-centric agency to one in which there was greater emphasis on geospatial intelligence, imagery, human intelligence, and MASINT. In addition, rather than be subordinate to the Air Combat Command, as AIA was, the new agency reported to the Deputy Chief of Staff of the Air Force for Intelligence, Surveillance, and Reconnaissance.[45]

AFISRA's various collection and analytical activities are distributed across the United States and the rest of the world, as indicated in Figure 4.5. The agency employs almost 17,000 individuals, who work at approximately 72 locations worldwide.[46] Key components are the 70th Intelligence, Surveillance, and Reconnaissance Wing, the 480th Intelligence, Surveillance, and Reconnaissance Wing, the National Air and Space Intelligence Center (NASIC), and the Air Force Technical Applications Center (AFTAC).

The 70th ISR Wing, headquartered at Ft. Meade, Maryland, "conducts worldwide real-time SIGINT and information assurance missions for ongoing air, space and cyberspace operations" and includes five key operational intelligence groups located in the continental United States, the Pacific, and Europe.[47]

The 70th ISR Wing's 373 ISR Group, headquartered at Misawa AB, Japan, has intelligence squadrons at Misawa and at Elmendorf Air Force Base, Alaska. The group is the host service organization and support provider for the Misawa Security Operations Center and the Alaska Mission Operations Center. The two centers "provide time-critical combat intelligence to U.S. theater battle commanders, unified and specified commands, as well as a national and Department of Defense leadership."[48]

The 543rd Intelligence, Surveillance, and Reconnaissance Group, with headquarters at Lackland Air Force Base, Texas, provides personnel for national SIGINT operations and is the AFISRA's primary SIGINT component to the Department of Homeland Security. The group also provides air, space, and cyberspace SIGINT analysts for NSA/CSS Texas as well as providing national SIGINT in support of the operations centers of the Air Force components of the Southern and Northern Commands. Group operating locations include those at Peterson AFB, Colorado; Key West Naval Air Station, Florida; and Miami, Florida.[49]

The 544th Intelligence, Surveillance, and Reconnaissance Group, with headquarters at Peterson AFB, Colorado, manages units that engage in SIGINT collection, including SIGINT collection targeted on foreign space operations. Its key components are three detachments—at Alice Springs, Australia (Detachment 2), Sugar Grove, West Virginia (Detachment 3), and the Pentagon (Detachment 5)—and the 18th Intelligence Squadron at Vandenberg Air Force Base, with detachments at

94

FIGURE 4.5   Organization of the Air Force Intelligence, Surveillance, and Reconnaissance Agency

Source: Air Force Intelligence, Surveillance, and Reconnaissance Agency.

361 ISRG HURLBURT FLD AB FL
- 19 IS POPE AFB NC
- 25 IS HURLBURT FLD AB FL
  - OL-A (FTU) HURLBURT FLD AB FL
  - DET 1 CANNON AFB NM
  - DET 2 MILDENHALL UK
  - DET 3 KADENA AB JA

NASIC W-PATT AFB OH
- OL-UK LONDON UK

AIR & CYBERSPACE ANALY GP W-PATT AFB OH
- ACFT ANALY SQ W-PATT AFB OH
- CYBER ANALY SQ LACKLAND AFB TX
- ELECT ANALY SQ W-PATT AFB OH
- ENGRG ANALY SQ W-PATT AFB OH
- IADS ANALY SQ W-PATT AFB OH

DATA ANALY GP W-PATT AFB OH
- OL-CZ CAMP ZAMA JA
- OL-DE PENTAGON VA
- FOREI MAT EXPL SQ W-PATT AFB OH
- GEOINT/MASINT ANALY SQ W-PATT AFB OH
- IMAGY ANLY SQ W-PATT AFB OH
- INFO EXPLOIT SQ W-PATT AFB OH
- SIG ANLY SQ W-PATT AFB OH

GLOBAL THREAT ANALY GP W-PATT AFB OH
- DET 1 W-PATT AFB OH
  - OL-HA ANDREWS AFB MD
- C4/IO ANALY SQ W-PATT AFB OH
- FUTR THREATS ANALY SQ W-PATT AFB OH
- REGN THREATS ANALY SQ W-PATT AFB OH

SPACE & MISSILE ANALY GP W-PATT AFB OH
- BALLISTIC MISSILES ANALY SQ W-PATT AFB OH
- COUNTERSPACE ANALY SQ W-PATT AFB OH
- SPACE ANALY SQ W-PATT AFB OH
- SPECIAL ANALY SQ W-PATT AFB OH

AFTAC PATRICK AFB FL
- OL-EH PENTAGON VA
- OL-GT CHEYENNE MT CO
- OL-MC MACDILL AFB FL
- OL-PG PATRICK AFB FL
- DET 1 OFFUTT AFB NE
- DET 45 BUCKLEY AFB CO
- DET 46 SCHRIEVER AFB CO
- DET 319 RAMSTEIN AB GE
- DET 402 YOKOTA AB JA
- DET 415 CHIANG MAI TH
  - OL-CW BANGKOK TH
- DET 421 ALICE SPRINGS AUS
- DET 452 WONJU KO
- DET 460 EIELSON AFB AK

Agency-Gained ARC Units

MA ANG
- 102 IG OTIS ANGB MA
- 101 IS OTIS ANGB MA
- 102 ISS OTIS ANGB MA
- 102 OSS OTIS ANGB MA

AFRC
- 50 IS BEALE AFB CA*

AL ANG
- 117 IS BIRMINGHAM AL

AR ANG
- 123 IS LITTLE ROCK AR

GA ANG
- 139 IS FT. GORDON GA*

NV ANG 152 IS RENO NV

IN ANG
- 181 IG TERRE HAUTE IN
- 137 IS TERRE HAUTE IN
- 181 ISS TERRE HAUTE IN
- 181 OSS TERRE HAUTE IN

KS ANG
- 184 IG MCCONNELL AFB KS
- 161 IS MCCONNELL AFB KS
- 184 ISS MCCONNELL AFB KS
- 184 OSS MCCONNELL AFB KS

VA ANG
- 192 IS LANGLEY AFB VA*

HI ANG
- 201 IS HICKAM AFB HI*

CA ANG
- 234 IS BEALE AFB CA*
- 222 ISS BEALE AFB CA
- 222 OSS BEALE AFB CA

*Classic Association Units

NOTE: ARC units are gained by AF ISR Agency upon mobilization

Wright-Patterson Air Force Base, Ohio (Detachment 1); Osan, Air Base, Korea (Detachment 2); and Feltwell, U.K. (Detachment 3).[50]

The 691st Intelligence, Surveillance, and Reconnaissance Group is headquartered at Menwith Hill Station, United Kingdom. With an intelligence squadron at Menwith Hill and a detachment at Digby, U.K., it trains U.S. and British personnel in SIGINT collection and security operations.[51]

A much smaller component of the AFISRA—originally consisting of 9 individuals, with a projected strength of 28 and squadron status—was established in November 2007, when the agency's Detachment 6 was activated at Wright-Patterson Air Force Base. The detachment was created to assume the HUMINT operation mission that had been the responsibility of Operating Location Dayton. The AFISRA commander noted that the event signified "another step forward in re-establishing HUMINT in the Air Force."[52]

Also subordinate to AFISRA is the National Air and Space Intelligence Center (NASIC) at Wright-Patterson Air Force Base, Ohio. It has about 2,700 employees, consisting of military, civilian, reserve, and contractor personnel. Its budget in 2008 was reported to be $302 million, 93 percent of which was provided by other intelligence agencies and 7 percent by the U.S. Air Force.[53]

NASIC is, in one sense, the latest version of what began in 1917 as the Foreign Data Section of the Airplane Engineering Department. Shortly after its creation it was transferred from Washington, D.C., to Dayton, Ohio. Its subsequent redesignations include Technical Data Section (1927), the Technical Data Laboratory (1942), and T-2 (Intelligence) of the Air Technical Service Command (1945). In 1947 all non-intelligence functions were removed from T-2's mission statement. In 1951, T-2 became the Air Technical Intelligence Center (ATIC) and, in 1961, the Foreign Technology Division (FTD) of the Air Force Systems Command (AFSC).[54] The FTD's intelligence activities were directed at avoiding technological surprise, advancing U.S. technology by use of foreign technology, identifying weaknesses in foreign weapons systems, and using certain design traits of foreign weapons systems as indicators of strategic intent. Under the October 1, 1991, restructuring of Air Force intelligence, the FTD was removed from control of the AFSC, renamed the Foreign Technology Center (FTC), and placed under the AFIC. In 1992, it was renamed again, becoming the Foreign Aerospace Science and Technology Center (FASTC).[55]

The National Air Intelligence Center (NAIC) was established on October 1, 1993, as part of the restructuring that produced the AIA, by the organizational (but not geographic) consolidation of FASTC with the 480th Intelligence Group, which was subsequently moved out of the center and subordinated to AIA. On February 15, 2003, it became the National Air and Space Intelligence Center (NASIC), reflecting its role in the production of intelligence concerning foreign space systems.[56]

With respect to air and space forces, NASIC is the national and Department of Defense executive agent for the processing, exploitation, and dissemination of MASINT data collected from radar, electro-optical, and infrared sensors. It prepares spectral, spatial, and temporal signatures of potential targets; it is the sole organization involved in interpreting the imagery obtained under the Open Skies Treaty; and it also is responsible for the exploitation of signals collected during RC-135 RIVET JOINT and COMBAT SENT missions.[57]

As shown in Figure 4.6, NASIC is organized into four directorates (Human Resources, Logistics, Communications and Information, and Plans & Programs) and four groups, which are responsible for generating the center's analytical products. The Air and Cyberspace Analysis Group "produces integrated intelligence defining present and future air and defense systems" in support of military operations, force planning, and policymaking. A squadron from the group that is located at Lackland AFB, Texas, "provides critical foreign network intelligence." The Global Threat Analysis Group produces estimates on integrated capabilities "across the air, space and information domains."[58]

The Data Analysis Group processes and analyzes data on foreign weapons systems, subsystems, technologies, and forces—with squadrons focusing on what can be determined from foreign materiel exploitation; geospatial, measurement, and signature intelligence; and signals intelligence. The Space and Missile Systems Analysis Group produces approximately 90 percent of the nation's assessments and estimates concerning foreign space, counterspace, and ballistic missile all-source scientific and technical intelligence.[59]

The Air Force Technical Applications Center (AFTAC) was originally an independent organization and then an "AIA-supported" organization; now it is a subordinate unit of the AFISRA. AFTAC was first established in 1948 as the Special Weapons Squadron and subsequently became known as AFOAT-1 (Air Force Office of Atomic Energy, Section 1). It received its present name in July 1959. Until the 1970s its mission was classified, and it was described in sanitized congressional hearings only as "Project CLEAR SKY."[60]

With about 800 Defense Department personnel, and headquartered at Patrick Air Force Base, Florida, AFTAC operates the U.S. Atomic Energy Detection System (AEDS). AEDS is a worldwide system that employs space-based, aerial, ground, and hydroacoustic sensors to detect indications of nuclear detonations and accidents, collect information relevant to the discrimination between earthquakes and nuclear detonations, and detect signs of nuclear weapons research and development and production. AFTAC's operations and the analysis, by AFTAC and other organizations, of the data collected are relevant to the monitoring of a variety of treaties: the Limited Test Ban Treaty, the Non-Proliferation Treaty, the Threshold Test Ban Treaty (which limits the yield of underground tests to 150 kilotons), the Peaceful Nuclear Explosions Treaty, the Intermediate Range Nuclear Forces (INF) Agreement, the Strategic Arms Reduction Treaty (START), and the Comprehensive Test Ban Treaty (CTBT). AFTAC was also responsible for tracking debris from the Chernobyl disaster of 1986. In addition, today's operations are particularly directed at collecting data on the nuclear activities of nations such as North Korea, Pakistan, India, and Iran.

FIGURE 4.6 Organization of the National Air and Space Intelligence Center

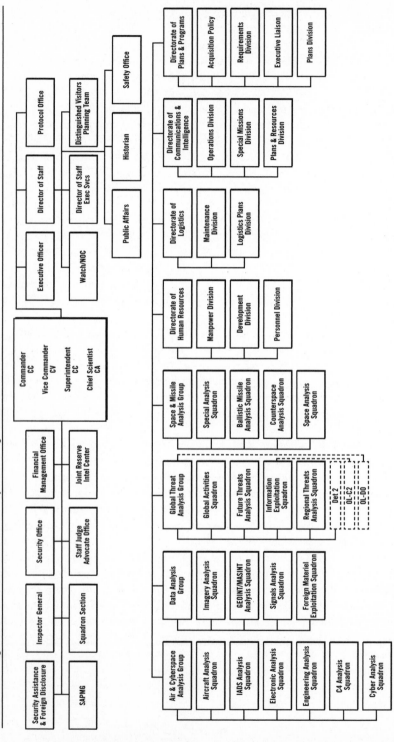

Source: National Air and Space Intelligence Center.

FIGURE 4.7   Organization of the Air Force Technical Applications Center

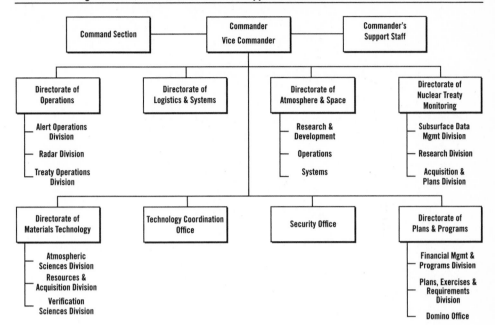

Furthermore, AFTAC collection and analysis activities are directed at monitoring chemical and biological warfare programs—both for intelligence and treaty verification purposes.[61]

AFTAC worldwide operations are managed through its headquarters organizational components, which are shown in Figure 4.7, and carried out by its detachments and operating locations, which are discussed in Chapter 9.

AFTAC's Directorate of Operations (with its Alert Operations, Radar, and Treaty Operations divisions—the latter division with Airborne Operations and Ground Operations branches) is responsible for planning, coordinating, operating, and reporting the product of the U.S. Atomic Energy Detection System (USAEDS) data collection effort.[62]

The Directorate of Materials Technology (with Nuclear Sciences, Atmospheric Sciences, Verification Sciences, Sciences Support, and Resources and Acquisition divisions) is responsible for laboratory analysis, evaluation, and reporting of the various materials obtained from collection operations. The Directorate of Nuclear Treaty Monitoring (with Research, Subsurface Data Management, and Acquisition and Plans divisions) plans, manages, and coordinates research.[63]

Despite its history of relying overwhelmingly on high-technology collection and analysis techniques, AFTAC did, in the 1970s, join other intelligence agencies such as CIA and DIA, in attempting to use "remote viewers" to gather intelligence. A more recent departure from high-tech collection and analysis of weapons of mass destruction data is AFTAC's deployment of personnel to the National Archives in College Park, Maryland, to secretly review and reclassify documents that had been in the Archives' holdings.[64]

MARINE CORPS INTELLIGENCE ORGANIZATIONS

Management of Marine Corps intelligence activities is the responsibility of the Corps' Director of Intelligence, who heads its Intelligence Department, which was established by the Commandant of the Marine Corps in April 2000 in order to enhance Marine Corps intelligence capabilities. The director represents the Marine Corps within the national Intelligence Community and manages the Intelligence Department's collection and analysis activities. As indicated in Figure 4.8, that department includes the Intelligence Plans/Policy Division, whose primary focus is on technical collection and analysis activities such as geospatial and signals intelligence, and the Intelligence Operations Division. The operations division includes components for counterintelligence/HUMINT plans and policy and intelligence estimates. The intelligence estimates branch participates in the formulation of JCS papers containing current and estimative intelligence. It also conducts liaison with the JCS, DIA, NSA, CIA, the Department of State, and other intelligence organizations in matters pertaining to intelligence estimates.[65]

Also subordinate to the Director of Intelligence is the Marine Corps Intelligence Activity (MCIA), whose organization is shown as part of Figure 4.8. Located at the National Maritime Intelligence Center (NMIC) complex at Suitland, Maryland, and the Marine Corps facility at Quantico, Virginia, MCIA was originally created as the Marine Corps Intelligence Center (MCIC), as the result of a 1987 study on Marine Corps intelligence requirements. On January 1, 1993, the center was redesignated as the MCIA. In mid-1995 it had a staff of 82 analysts. Its overall workforce in early 1997 was 130. It had grown to 250 by 2002, when a further restructuring of Marine Corps intelligence quadrupled its size to more than 1,000 Marines, civilian Marines, and contractors.[66]

The Marine Cryptologic Support Battalion, headquartered at Fort Meade, Maryland, provided for Marine Corps participation in Naval Security Group Command activities, with lettered companies assigned to NIOC field sites throughout the world.* The CI/HUMINT Support Company was established to provide administrative control of Marines serving in the Defense HUMINT Service and in positions funded by the Foreign Counterintelligence Program.[67]

---

*The lettered companies are: A (Denver, Colorado), B (Fort Meade, Maryland), D (Fort Gordon, Georgia), G (Menworth Hill, U.K.), H (Meclina, San Antonio, Texas), I (Kunia, Hawaii), and L (Suitland, Maryland). See Marine Corps, *Marine Corps 2005–2015, ISR Roadmap, Version 1.1*, October 2, 2006, p. 46.

FIGURE 4.8   Organization of the Marine Corps Intelligence Department

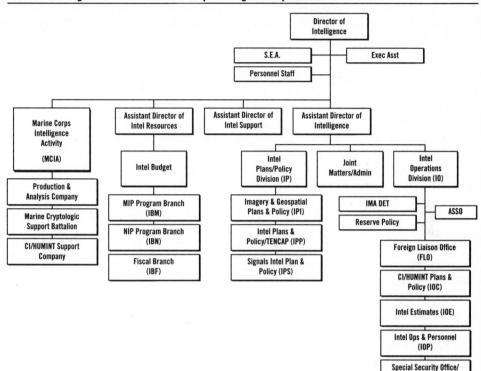

The Production and Analysis Company functions include the following:

- providing tailored intelligence analysis and estimates to the Commandant of the Marine Corps in his role as Marine Corps member of the JCS;
- producing tailored general military intelligence and scientific and technical intelligence;
- providing support to the Marine Corps Combat Development Command;
- serving as the Service Threat Validator for threats, assessments, and estimates used in the Service concepts, plans, and scenarios;
- providing tailored mid-range and long-range threat analysis, assessments, and estimates supporting the development of expeditionary, naval, joint, and combined concepts, plans, and doctrine;
- preparing threat portions of Marine Corps plans, including the Marine Corps Long-Range Plan.[68]

COAST GUARD INTELLIGENCE ORGANIZATIONS

The U.S. Coast Guard, the nation's fifth military service, was placed within the Department of Transportation after that department was established in October 1966, and then, on December 28, 2001, it became a member of the Department of Homeland Security. Coast Guard missions include three missions that are classified as homeland security missions—ports, waterways, and coastal security; defense readiness; and migrant interdiction—as well as non-homeland security missions. The first of these missions involves conducting harbor patrols, vulnerability assessments, intelligence gathering and analysis, and other activities "to prevent terrorist attacks and minimize the damage from attacks that occur." Additional homeland security missions include defense readiness (which includes deploying cutters and other boats in and around harbors to protect Department of Defense force mobilization operations) and migrant interdiction using cutters and aircraft. Non-homeland security missions include drug interdiction, aids to navigation, search and rescue, enforcing fishing laws, marine safety, ice operations, and marine environmental protection.[69]

On the same day that the Coast Guard became an element of the DHS, Coast Guard intelligence (which traces it origins to the appointment of a Coast Guard Chief Intelligence Officer in 1915) became a member of the U.S. Intelligence Community when President George W. Bush signed an amendment to the 1947 National Security Act. Membership extends to all Coast Guard intelligence elements. From 2002 to 2004, the number of active-duty Coast Guard personnel working on intelligence matters increased from 194 to 437. By August 2005 it stood at 800.[70]

Those elements are headed by the Assistant Commandant for Intelligence and Criminal Investigations, who is responsible for the Coast Guard Intelligence Coordination Center (CGICC) (which is co-located with the Office of Naval Intelligence), Field Intelligence Support Teams, and several Maritime Intelligence Fusion Centers (MIFCs)[71]—all of which are part of the Coast Guard Intelligence Program.[72]

The CGICC, whose organization chart is shown as Figure 4.9, produces and disseminates intelligence derived from human and technical sources to support Coast Guard planning and operations. It is also responsible for ensuring "the adequacy of Coast Guard intelligence support to other government agencies." It validates requests from Coast Guard elements for tasking of national collection systems, such as reconnaissance satellites, and inserts validated requirements into the national collection systems' requirements and tasking processes. It is also the Coast Guard representative on interagency assessments as well as the designated center for the exploitation of imagery to support maritime interdiction and detection and monitoring operations.[73]

The CGICC's COASTWATCH program gathers and analyzes information based on the ship's 96-hour Notice of Arrival (NOA) report on vessels and people approaching U.S. ports. According to congressional testimony by the Coast Guard's intelligence chief, the "COASTWATCH mission has detected and provided advance

FIGURE 4.9   Organization of the Coast Guard Intelligence Coordination Center

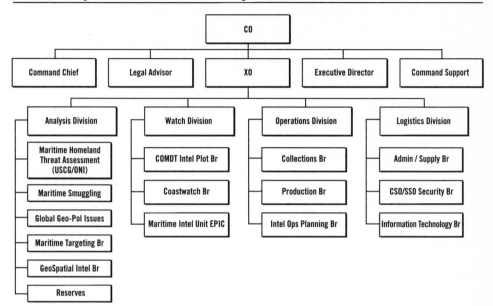

warning about numerous arriving individuals identified in federal law enforcement and immigration databases as criminal or security concerns."[74]

In 1999, the CGICC produced, along with the Office of Naval Intelligence, *Threats and Challenges to Maritime Security 2020*. In December 2005, the center's Intelligence Analysis Division produced an analysis of the proposed transfer of port operations from the London-based Peninsular & Oriental Stream Navigation Company to the Dubai-based DP World. The report stated, "There are many intelligence gaps, concerning the potential for DPW or P&O assets to support terrorist operations, that preclude an overall threat assessment of the potential merger." More recently, the coordination center produced an unclassified report titled "Yemen: Internal Situation Report for October 2009."[75]

Beginning in September 2003, the Coast Guard established two facilities—the Maritime Intelligence Fusion Center, Atlantic (MIFC, Atlantic) at Dam Neck, Virginia, and the Pacific Area Maritime Intelligence Fusion Center (PAMIFC) at Alameda, California—to provide around-the-clock monitoring of maritime traffic and developments. The centers monitor areas of interest, track events, follow vessels of interest, produce analysis, and evaluate trends. In the Atlantic center's watch office, Coast Guard members survey individual computers while a large monitor displays tracking maps, station locators, radar, and several other news networks. The

Atlantic center produces daily intelligence briefings and teleconferences for each of the five Coast Guard districts in the Atlantic region. The centers' reporting is also sent to the DHS Office of Intelligence and Analysis and to national intelligence agencies and is posted on the classified Intelink computer network. [76]

Notes

1. U.S. Congress, Senate Select Committee on Intelligence, *Report 101–358: Authorizing Appropriations for Fiscal Year 1991 for the Intelligence Activities of the U.S. Government, the Intelligence Community Staff, the Central Intelligence Agency Retirement and Disability System, and for Other Purposes* (Washington, D.C.: U.S. Government Printing Office, 1990), pp. 4–5.

2. Ibid., p. 5.

3. Assistant Secretary of Defense (Command, Control, Communications, and Intelligence), *Plan for Restructuring Defense Intelligence*, March 15, 1991, p. 7.

4. "Deputy Chief of Staff, G-2," www.dami.army.pentagon.mil, accessed December 11, 2010.

5. Ibid.

6. U.S. Army, Memorandum to Correspondents, n.d.; James L. Gilbert, "In '77, Command Created New Identity," *INSCOM Journal*, Summer 2002, pp. 14–16.

7. Letter, Paul D. Sutton, INSCOM, to the author, November 20, 1992; INSCOM Permanent Order 41–1, "United States Army Intelligence and Security Command, Intelligence Production Management Activity (Provisional), Falls Church, Virginia, 22041," April 9, 1992; INSCOM Permanent Order 41–2, "United States Army Foreign Science and Technology Center (WOKPAA), Charlottesville, Virginia, 22901, United States Intelligence and Threat Analysis Center (W3YDAA), Washington, D.C. 20370," April 9, 1992.

8. U.S. Army Intelligence and Security Command, INSCOM Regulation 10–2, *Organization and Functions: United States Army Intelligence and Security Command*, October 15, 2009, pp. 38, 49, 66, 80, 98.

9. U.S. Army Intelligence and Security Command, "INSCOM Today: Overview Briefing," n.d.; "66th Brigade," *INSCOM Journal*, Almanac 2009, p. 15; "470th Military Intelligence Brigade," www.inscom.army.mil, accessed March 23, 2010.

10. U.S. Army Intelligence and Security Command, "INSCOM Today: Overview Briefing"; "500th MI Brigade," *INSCOM Journal*, Almanac 2009, p. 18; "500th Military Intelligence Brigade," www.inscom.army.mil, accessed March 23, 2010.

11. "501st MI Brigade," *INSCOM Journal*, Almanac 2006, p. 16; "66th MI Group," *INSCOM Journal*, Almanac 2006, p. 11; "513th MI Brigade," *INSCOM Journal*, Almanac 2006, p. 17; "Command Briefing"; "501st Military Intelligence Brigade," *INSCOM Journal*, Almanac 2009, p. 19; "501st Military Intelligence Brigade," www.inscom.army.mil, accessed March 23, 2010.

12. U.S. Army Intelligence and Security Command, "INSCOM Today: Overview Briefing"; "513th Military Intelligence Brigade," *INSCOM Journal*, Almanac 2009, p. 20; "513th Military Intelligence Brigade," www.inscom.army.mil, accessed March 23, 2010.

13. U.S. Army Intelligence and Security Command, "INSCOM Today: Overview Briefing";"704th Military Intelligence Brigade," *INSCOM Journal*, Almanac 2009, p. 21; "704th Military Intelligence Brigade," www.inscom.army.mil, accessed March 23, 2010.

14. U.S. Army Intelligence and Security Command, "INSCOM Today: Overview Briefing";"706th MI Group," *INSCOM Journal*, Almanac 2009, p. 22; "706th Military Intelligence Brigade," www.inscom.army.mil, accessed March 23, 2010.

15. U.S. Army Intelligence and Security Command, "INSCOM Today: Overview Briefing";"902nd MI Group," *INSCOM Journal*, Almanac 2009, p. 23; "902nd Military Intelligence Group," www.army.inscom.mil, accessed March 23, 2010.

16. U.S. Army Intelligence and Security Command, "INSCOM Today: Overview Briefing";"902nd MI Group"; "902nd Military Intelligence Group."

17. "AOA," *INSCOM Journal*, Almanac 2006, p. 23; "AOA," *INSCOM Journal*, Almanac 2009, p. 27; "Army Operations Activity," www.inscom.army.mil, accessed March 23, 2010.

18. *U.S. Army Foreign Science and Technology Center Unit History, FY 63–77* (Charlottesville, Va.: FSTC, n.d.), p. 3; Paul E. Menoher, "INSCOM Thrives Despite Changes," *INSCOM Journal*, September 1994, p. 1; NGIC, "Lineage of the NGIC," n.d.

19. NGIC, " . . . About the National Ground Intelligence Center," 1998; "NGIC," *INSCOM Journal*, Almanac 2006, p. 20.

20. NGIC, " . . . About the National Ground Intelligence Center," 1998.

21. "Army Intelligence Site Lifts Secrecy Veil," *Washington Post*, January 5, 1997, p. A10; Walter Pincus, "Intelligence Center, Contractor MZM on Cozy Terms," *Washington Post*, July 7, 2005, p. A7.

22. R. M. Walsh, Assistant Vice Chief of Naval Operations, Memorandum for the Secretary of the Navy, Subject: Disestablishment and Establishment of Certain Naval Intelligence Command Shore Activities, July 31, 1991; OPNAV Notice 5450, Subject: Disestablishment and Establishment of Commander, Naval Intelligence Command Shore Activities, and Modification of Detachments, September 13, 1991; Naval Intelligence Command, Organization, Mission, and Key Personnel: Naval Intelligence Command, HQ, Naval Maritime Intelligence Center, Naval Intelligence Activity, October 1991, pp. 59–80.

23. "Fact and Justification Sheet: COMNAVINTCOM Claimancy Reorganization," attachment to R. M. Walsh, Assistant Vice Chief of Naval Operations, Memorandum for the Secretary of the Navy.

24. Memorandum for the Secretary of the Navy, Subject: Disestablishment of Three Shore Activities and Establishment of One Consolidated Shore Command, December 1, 1992; Office of Naval Intelligence, *Consolidating the Naval Intelligence Command, Naval Maritime Intelligence Center, Naval Intelligence Activity* (Suitland, Md.: ONI, January 7, 1993).

25. Maj. Herbert M. Strauss, *Status Report: Strengthening Defense Intelligence* (Washington, D.C.: OASD [C³I], 1991), p. 4.

26. Office of Naval Intelligence, "Office of Naval Intelligence Fact Sheet," n.d.

27. Ibid.

28. Office of Naval Intelligence, "Hopper Information Services Center Fact Sheet," n.d.; Office of Naval Intelligence, "Kennedy Irregular Warfare Center Fact Sheet," n.d.; Chief of Naval Operations, OPNAV Notice 5400, Subject: Establishment of Nimitz Operational Intelligence Center, Washington, D.C., Farragut Technical Analysis Center, Washington, D.C., Kennedy Irregular Warfare Center, Washington, D.C., and Hopper Information Services Center, Washington, D.C., January 14, 2009.

29. Office of Naval Intelligence, "Nimitz Operational Intelligence Center Fact Sheet," n.d.; Office of Naval Intelligence, *Transforming for the 21st Century*, January 2009, pp. 14–17.

30. Office of Naval Intelligence, *Transforming for the 21st Century*, p. 18.

31. Ibid., p. 19.

32. Office of Naval Intelligence, "Farragut Technical Analysis Center Fact Sheet," n.d.

33. Office of Naval Intelligence, *Transforming for the 21st Century*, p. 21.

34. Ibid., pp. 23, 24.

35. Ibid., pp. 6, 27; Letter, Jeana D. Watson, to author, November 19, 2009; Deputy Command, Office of Naval Intelligence, To: All ONI-36 Employees, Subject: Civilian ONI-36 Employees Notice of ONI-36 Transfer of Function and Request for Decision to Exercise Transfer Rights, January 22, 2009.

36. HQNSGINST 5450.2G CH–1, *Headquarters, Naval Security Group Command* Organizational Manual, August 17, 1995, pp. I-1 to I-2.

37. Ibid.; Joseph Grunder, "Naval Security Group Aligns with NETWARCOM," October 5, 2005, http://www.news.navy.mil; "IOD—Information Operations Directorate," http://ekm.netwarcom.navy.mil, August 1, 2006.

38. OPNAV Notice 5450, Subj: Disestablish Commander, Naval Security Group Command (COMNAVSECGRU), Fort George G. Meade, MD; Rename and Realign All Subordinate NAVSECGRU Commands and Detachments, December 29, 2005; Chief of Naval Operations, OPNAV Notice 5400, Subj: Rename Navy Information Operations Command Suitland, Disestablish Navy Operations Detachment Chesapeake, and Realign Navy Information Operations Detachment Dam Neck, February 28, 2011.

39. Jeffrey Richelson, "New Look for Air Force Intelligence," *Defense Week*, March 31, 1997, p. 6; Office of the Director of National Intelligence, *An Overview of the United States Intelligence Community*, 2007, p. 22.

40. HAF Mission Directive 1–33, "Deputy Chief of Staff of the Air Force, Intelligence, Surveillance & Reconnaissance," September 4, 2009.

41. Ibid.

42. "Air Force Intelligence Service," *Air Force Magazine*, May 1982, p. 126.

43. Department of the Air Force, "Air Force Creates New Intelligence Command," June 6, 1991.

44. HQ USAF, "Basic Plan to HQ USAF Program Action Directive (PAD) 93–8, Restructuring Air Force Intelligence," June 15, 1993; Headquarters, Air Force Intelligence Command, HQ AFIC Programming Plan 93–01, Establishment of the Air Force Intelligence Field Operating Agency, August 17, 1993; "Air Intelligence Agency," http://www.af.mil/factsheets, accessed February 12, 2006.

45. United States Air Force Office of Public Affairs, "Air Intelligence Agency," Fact Sheet 95–10, September 1995, p. 1; "About the Agency," Air Intelligence Agency Almanac, August 1997, pp. 12–13; "Air Intelligence Agency," http://www.af.mil/factsheets, accessed February 12, 2006; Theresa Shannon, "AFISR Agency," *Spokesman*, July 2007, p. 4; "Air Force Aligns Intelligence Agency under Intelligence Directorate," *Spokesman*, June 2007, p. 4.

46. U.S. Air Force, Fact Sheet, "Air Force ISR Agency," May 2009.

47. U.S. Air Force, Fact Sheet, "Air Force ISR Agency," May 2009; U.S. Air Force, Fact Sheet, "70th Intelligence, Surveillance and Reconnaissance Wing," January 2009; AFISRA Organization Chart, 2010.

48. U.S. Air Force, Fact Sheet, "70th Intelligence, Surveillance and Reconnaissance Wing," January 2009; AFISRA Organization Chart.

49. U.S. Air Force, Fact Sheet, "70th Intelligence, Surveillance and Reconnaissance Wing," January 2009; AFISRA Organization Chart.

50. U.S. Air Force, Fact Sheet, "70th Intelligence, Surveillance and Reconnaissance Wing," January 2009; AFISRA Organization Chart.

51. U.S. Air Force, Fact Sheet, "70th Intelligence, Surveillance and Reconnaissance Wing," January 2009; AFISRA Organization Chart.

52. Juliet L. Montalvo, Chief, Manpower, Org and Resources Division, Special Order GC-14, November 16, 2007; Air Force Intelligence, Surveillance, and Reconnaissance Agency, "Justification Activation of Detachment 6," n.d.; Organization Chart, "Detachment 6 (Current), n.d.; "Detachment 6 (Proposed)"; Michelle Lai, "Air Force stands up HUMINT detachment, " August 21, 2008,www.afsir.af.mil/news/story_print.asp?id=123111883.

53. U.S. Air Force, Fact Sheet, "National Air and Space Intelligence Center," June 23, 2008; Jeremy Singer, "A History of Providing Intelligence Products to the Policymaker," *Space News*, January 21, 2008, p. 14.

54. "Unit Designations and Assignments," http://www.wpafb.af.mil/naic/history7.html, accessed February 12, 2006; FTD 1917–1967 (Dayton, Ohio: FTD, 1967), pp. 8, 10, 12, 22, 26; Col. Robert B. Kalisch, "Air Technical Intelligence," *Air University Review* 12 (July–August 1971): 2–11 at 7, 9; "National Air Intelligence Center," *Air Intelligence Agency Almanac 1997*, pp. 14–15. For a short history of FTD, see "F-T-D," http://www.wpafb .af.mil/naic/history4.html; and Mike Turner, "Air, Space Center Vital to U.S," http://www.timesgazette.com, January 23, 2007.

55. Kalisch, "Air Technical Intelligence"; Bruce Ashcroft, "National Air Intelligence Center Emerges from FASTC, 480th IG," *Spokesman*, November 1993, p. 12; Rob Young, "National Air Intelligence Center," *Spokesman*, September 1996, pp. 4–5.

56. "Units Designations and Assignments"; "National Air Intelligence Center Emerges from FASTC, 480th IG"; United States Air Force Office of Public Affairs, Fact Sheet 95–10, "Air Intelligence Agency," p. 1.

57. "National Air Intelligence Center."

58. U.S. Air Force, Fact Sheet, "National Air and Space Intelligence Center," June 23, 2008, "National Air and Space Intelligence Center, Organization Chart," July 1, 2010.

59. U.S. Air Force, Fact Sheet, "National Air and Space Intelligence Center.

60. U.S. Congress, Senate Committee on Appropriations, *Department of Defense Appropriations, FY 1973, Part 4* (Washington, D.C.: U.S. Government Printing Office, 1972), pp. 364–365; "Air Force Technical Applications Center," *Air Force Magazine*, May 2006, pp. 123–124; Mary Welch, "AFTAC Celebrates 50 Years of Long Range Detection," AFTAC *Monitor*, October 1997, pp. 8–32; Science Applications International Corp., *Fifty Year Commemorative History of Long Range Detection: The Creation, Development, and Operation of the United States Atomic Energy Detection System* (Patrick AFB, Fla.: AFTAC, 1997), pp. 4–5.

61. "Air Force Technical Applications Center," *Air Force Magazine*, May 1997, p. 126; Air Force Technical Applications Center, Center Instruction 38–101, *Organization and Functions Chart Book*, June 2, 2003, p. 4; U.S. Air Force, Fact Sheet, "Air Force Technical Applications Center," June 2007.

62. "Air Force Technical Applications Center, Staff Directory," March 11, 2010; "Air Force Technical Applications Center Staff Directory," January 6, 2006; Air Force Technical Applications Center, Center Instruction 38–101, *Organization and Functions Chart Book*, pp. 8, 9–12.

63. "Air Force Technical Applications Center Staff Directory"; Air Force Technical Applications Center, Center Instruction 38–101, *Organization and Functions Chart Book*, pp. 13, 16.

64. *Report of the GRILL FLAME Scientific Evaluation Committee* (Washington, D.C.: Defense Intelligence Agency, 1980), p. 10; Michael J. Kutz, Assistant Archivist, and William A. Davidson, Administrative Assistant to the Secretary of the Air Force, Memoran-

dum of Understanding (MOU) Between the National Archives and Records Administration and the United States Air Force, March 8, 2002; National Archives and Records Administration, Performance and Accountability Report, FY 2005 (Washington, D.C.: NARA, 2005), p. 149; "National Archives Agreed to Documents Coverup," *Washington Post*, April 12, 2006, p. A13.The performance and accountability report notes that "Patrick Air Force Base employees [where AFTAC has its headquarters] are working at NARA on declassification of records." NARA officials confirmed that those employees were from AFTAC.

65. "Headquarters, U.S. Marine Corps Intelligence Department: Mission & Functions," http://hqinet.001.hqmc.usmc.mil/DirInt/mission.html, accessed February 12, 2006; "Headquarters, U.S. Marine Corps Intelligence Department: Organization," http://hqinet001hqmc .usmc.mil/DirInt/organizational_chart.html, accessed February 12, 2006; MCO P5400.45, Headquarters Marine Corps Organization Manual (HQMCORGMAN), May 15, 1989, pp. 7-47, 7-51 to 7-55; CMC to ALMAR, Subj: Establishment of an Intelligence Department (Code I) at HQMC, April 27, 2000.

66. Neil Munro, "Center Will Spearhead Marines' Data Analysis," *Defense News*, January 20, 1992, p. 12; "Director Visits MCIA," *Communiqué*, January–February 1997, p. 30; Robert W. Livingston, "Marine Corps Intelligence Activity—Excellence in Expeditionary Intelligence," *American Intelligence Journal* 17, 1 and 2 (1996): 29–33; CMC, Subject: Reorganization of the Marine Corps Intelligence Activity (MCIA), July 31, 2002.

67. "Marine Corps Intelligence," Military Intelligence, July–September 1983, pp. 121ff.; CMC, Subject: Reorganization of the Marine Corps Intelligence Activity (MCIA).

68. "MCIA Mission," n.d., provided by Marine Corps in response to Freedom of Information Act request.

69. Government Accountability Office, GAO-10–411T, Statement of Stephen L. Caldwell, Coast Guard: Observations on the Requested Fiscal Year 2011 Budget, Past Performance, and Current Challenges, February 25, 2010, pp. 26–27. An examination of how the Coast Guard became an Intelligence Community can be found in Kevin E. Wirth, *The Coast Guard Intelligence Program Enters the Intelligence Community: A Case Study of Congressional Influence on Intelligence Community Evolution* (Washington, D.C.: National Defense Intelligence College, 2007).

70. "Missions," http://www.uscg.mil, accessed August 11, 2006; "US Coast Guard Intelligence," http://www.intelligence.gov/1-members_coastguard.shtml, accessed August 11, 2006.

71. "U.S. Coast Guard Intelligence"; "Coast Guard Intelligence/CGI," http://www.uscg .mil/history/faqs/CGI.html, accessed August 11, 2006; U.S. Congress, *Intelligence Authorization Act for Fiscal Year 2007* (Washington, D.C.: U.S. Government Printing Office, 2007), p. 34; Patricia Kime, "Maritime 'Fusion' Centers Expand Coast Guard Intelligence Capabilities," *Sea Power*, May 2004, http://www.findarticles.com; Sue A. Lackey, "More Clout," *Sea Power*, August 2005, http://www.military.com.

72. ComdtNote 1524, Subj: People—Solicitation for the 2004 CG-210 Intelligence Unit Award, March 1, 2004, http://www.uscg.mil; James F. Sloan, "Coast Guard Expands Intelligence Efforts," *Proceedings*, May 2005, p. 98; Asst Comdt for Intelligence and Criminal Investigations (CG-2) United States Coast Guard, and Mike Payne, Chief, Office of ISR Systems & Technology (CG-26), *Coast Guard Intelligence and Criminal Investigations (CG-2)*, Presentation to AFCEA, June 20, 2006; James F. Sloan, Assistant Commandant for Intelligence and Criminal Investigations U.S. Coast Guard, "Intelligence Support to Border Security," State-

ment to the House Committee on Homeland Security, June 28, 2006, p. 4; Office of the Director of National Intelligence, *An Overview of the United States Intelligence Community,* p. 26.

73. Office of National Drug Control Policy, General Counterdrug Intelligence Plan, February 2000, p. A-14.

74. Sloan, Assistant Commandant for Intelligence and Criminal Investigations, U.S. Coast Guard, "Intelligence Support to Border Security," p. 5.

75. Commander Jim Howe, *The Fifth Side of the Pentagon: Moving the Coast Guard to the Department of Defense* (Quantico, Va.: Marine Corps War College, 2002), p. 29; Liz Sidoti, "Paper: Coast Guard Has Port Co. Intel Gaps," February 27, 2006, http://www.comcast.net; Carl Hulse and David E. Sanger, "Coast Guard Had Concerns About Ports Deal," *New York Times,* February 28, 2006, p. A15; U.S. Coast Guard, Intelligence Coordination Center, "Yemen: Internal Situation Report for October 2009," October 22, 2009.

76. Kime, "Maritime 'Fusion' Centers Expand Coast Guard Intelligence Capabilities"; Admiral Thomas H. Collins, "Transportation Security," Statement Before the Senate Committee on Commerce, Science, and Transportation, September 9, 2003, p. 3; Lackey, "More Clout."

5

UNIFIED COMMAND INTELLIGENCE ORGANIZATIONS

In addition to the intelligence functions performed by organizations reporting to the headquarters of the Department of Defense and military services, a substantial intelligence capability is maintained within the unified military commands. The missions, functions, forces, and geographic areas of responsibilities of those commands are detailed in the Unified Command Plan (UCP), drawn up by the Joint Chiefs of Staff and approved by the President. The most recent version was approved on December 17, 2008.[1]

As with other parts of the national security establishment, the terrorist attacks of September 11, 2001, have had a significant impact on the UCP. Within a month of the attacks, it was reported that consideration was being given to creation of a new "Americas Command" for defense of the Western Hemisphere, as well as expanding the powers of the U.S. Special Operations Command, so that it could carry out operations rather than simply provide forces to regional commanders. In addition, "the most radical and controversial change" contemplated was one that would have moved away from the structure that divided the world among four regional commanders.[2]

The commanders, each formerly known as a Commander-in-Chief (CINC), of those regional commands were responsible for directing the conduct of military operations in their area of responsibility, employing the military forces in the component commands assigned to them.* Technically, the chain of command runs from the President to the Secretary of Defense directly to the commander of each of the unified commands, bypassing the Joint Chiefs of Staff, although the chairman of the JCS may be a conduit for orders from the secretary.[3]

Although the regional commands survived, since early 2002 one command has been created; another was transformed and, in 2010, designated for extinction; and a third was abolished and absorbed by another command. Today there are six re-

---

*A component command of a unified command is a particular service command. Thus, for example, the Pacific Fleet is a component command of the Pacific Command.

gional commands: Africa Command, Central Command, European Command, Northern Command, Pacific Command, and Southern Command. The geographic responsibilities of the relevant unified commands are shown in Figure 5.1. Three commands have worldwide responsibilities: the U.S. Special Operations Command, the U.S. Strategic Command, and the U.S. Transportation Command. There is also a Joint Forces Command, the successor to the Atlantic Command, which has geographical and functional responsibilities.

The intelligence responsibilities of the unified commands have included intelligence analysis—for both the command and higher authorities—as well as supervision of national reconnaissance and other sensitive collection operations conducted within the command's theater. Until 1991, intelligence analytical functions were often distributed across several unified and component command organizations. However, in the *Plan for Restructuring Defense Intelligence,* the ASD(C^3I) specifically required that the analysis centers of the Atlantic, Pacific, and European commands and their components be consolidated into joint intelligence centers that would be under the control of the unified command's commander in chief. That other commands would be expected to follow this lead was clear. It was believed that such action would "not only yield resource savings through elimination of duplicative efforts but . . . strengthen support to the CINC and components through improved efficiency." The Joint Chiefs of Staff's *National Military Strategy* describes the joint intelligence center as "the principal element for ensuring effective intelligence to combat commanders in chief and theater forces."[4]

The formation of the joint intelligence centers resulted in the disestablishment of organizations such as the Fleet Intelligence Center, Pacific (FICPAC); the European Defense Analysis Center (EUDAC); and the Fleet Intelligence Center, Europe and Atlantic (FICEURLANT); their responsibilities and personnel were assigned to new joint intelligence organizations. In Hawaii, five major intelligence organizations under the Pacific Command or its component commands, including FICPAC, were combined into the Joint Intelligence Center Pacific (JICPAC).[5]

The plan allowed for the retention of intelligence staffs in the form of J-2/Intelligence Directorates at both the unified and component command levels in order to "support planning for and conduct of current military operations and to provide focused intelligence requirements statements."[6]

In November 1997, there were approximately 4,000 individuals working in the various joint intelligence centers, at which time it was announced that there would be a 10 percent reduction in personnel, a reduction that was probably reversed in recent years. On April 3, 2006, Secretary of Defense Donald Rumsfeld issued a directive to establish a Joint Intelligence Operations Center at DIA as well as at each unified command, in order to provide better intelligence support to combatant commanders.[7]

In October 2007, the process of converting employees of the unified command intelligence directorates (including joint intelligence centers) into employees of DIA began—as a consequence of the Joint Intelligence Centers/Joint Analysis Center Military Intelligence Program Implementation Study (JMIS). Even before

FIGURE 5.1 Geographic Responsibilities of the Unified Commands

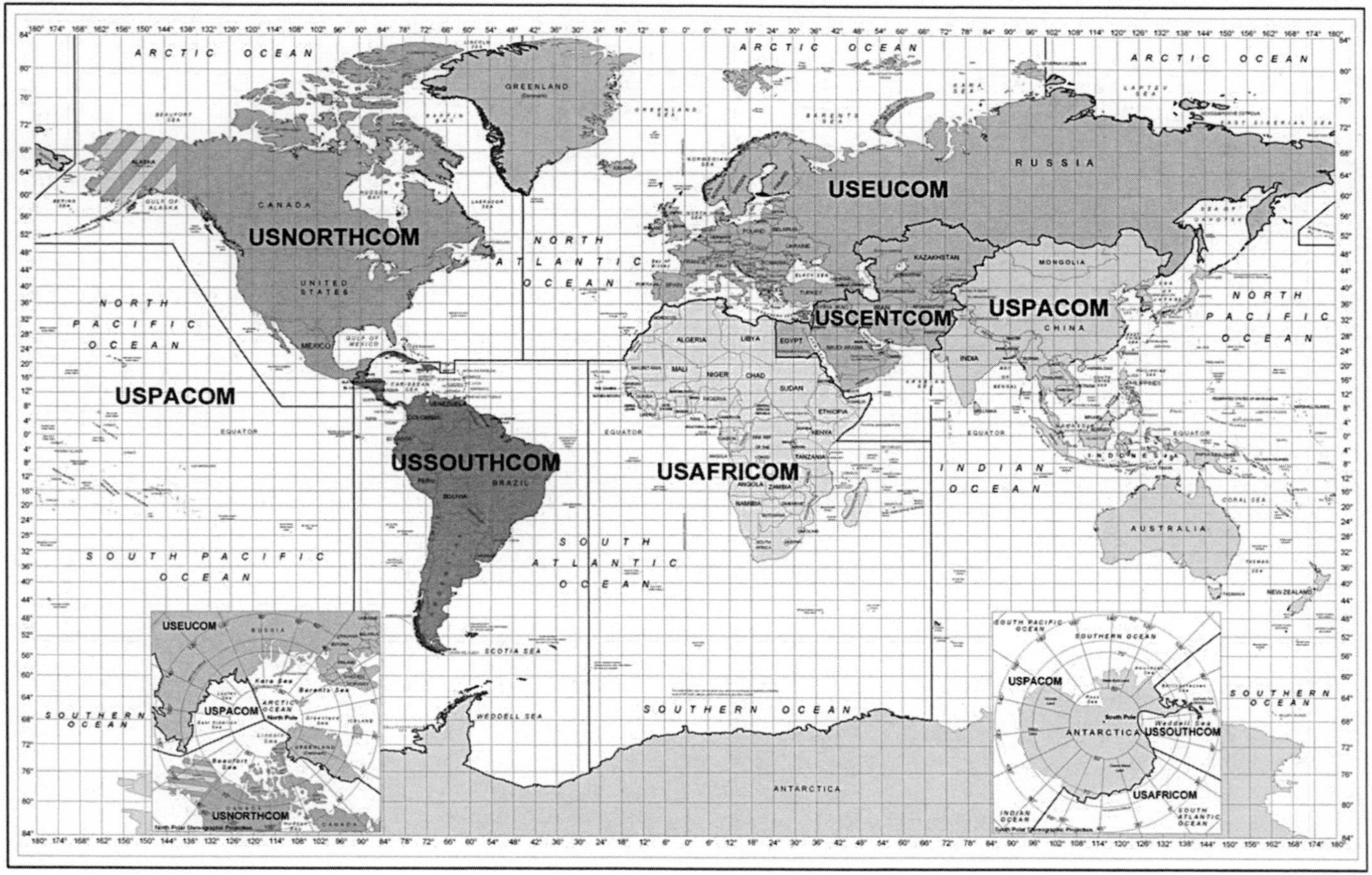

Source: Unified Command Plan, 2008.

the process was complete, over 4,000 personnel and $2 billion in funds had been transferred to DIA.[8]

AFRICA COMMAND

On February 6, 2007, President George W. Bush announced plans to establish a Unified Combatant Command with responsibility for the African continent (except for Egypt, which remains the responsibility of the Central Command). The new Africa Command (AFRICOM), according to a Congressional Research Service study, "evolved in part out of concerns about DOD's division of responsibilities for Africa among three geographic commands, which reportedly posed coordination challenges." In addition, the wars in Iraq and Afghanistan reportedly overstretched the demands on the European and Central Commands.[9]

AFRICOM began as sub-unified command on October 1, 2007, under the European Command (EUCOM) and became a fully operational command on October 1, 2008. Its current mission statement asserts that the command, "in concert with other U.S. government agencies and international partners, conducts sustained security engagement through military-to-military programs, military sponsored activities, and other military operations as directed to promote a stable and secure African environment in support of U.S. foreign policy." Thus, it "is expected to oversee military operations, when directed to deter aggression and respond to crises."[10]

Currently, AFRICOM headquarters are located in Stuttgart, Germany. Since EUCOM previously was responsible for most of the nations now in AFRICOM's area of responsibility and thus most of the personnel working on Africa issues were located in Stuttgart, and since African leaders were not receptive to establishing the command headquarters in Africa, a decision was made to establish AFRICOM's initial headquarters there. AFRICOM's four component commands are U.S. Army, Africa; U.S. Naval Forces, Africa; U.S. Marine Forces, Africa; and U.S. Air Forces, Africa/17th Air Force. Their respective locations are Vicenza, Italy; Naples, Italy; Stuttgart, Germany; and Ramstein, Germany. Africa Command also has a joint theater special operations command—Special Operations Command, Africa, which is located in Stuttgart. Permanent headquarters are expected to be selected in 2012.[11]

Among AFRICOM's headquarters components is its Directorate for Intelligence & Knowledge Development, whose organization chart is shown as Figure 5.2.

In addition to AFRICOM headquarters, intelligence personnel are deployed to contingents in Molesworth, United Kingdom, and Tampa, Florida. Approximately 300 Africa Command personnel are deployed to the U.S. Africa Command Intelligence Knowledge Development–Molesworth team, located in the same compound as the U.S. European Command's joint intelligence center.[12] The Intelligence Knowledge Development–Tampa team apparently works in concert with the U.S. Special Operations Command intelligence center.

FIGURE 5.2   Organization of the AFRICOM Directorate for Intelligence and Knowledge Development

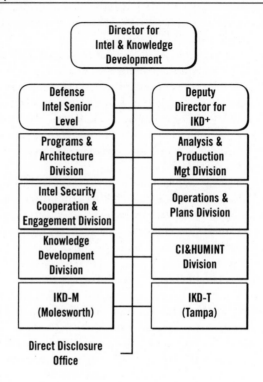

CENTRAL COMMAND

The U.S. Central Command (CENTCOM) was formed on January 1, 1983, as a successor to the Rapid Deployment Force. Headquartered at MacDill Air Force Base in Tampa, Florida, it assumed responsibility for the nations of the Middle East and the Persian Gulf area (including Iran, Iraq, Jordan, Saudi Arabia, Syria, Lebanon, Yemen, Oman, and Kuwait), Northeast Africa (Egypt, Somalia, Kenya, Ethiopia, and Sudan), and Southwest Asia (Pakistan and Afghanistan). With the demise of the Soviet Union it also became responsible for Turkmenistan, Uzbekistan, Kyrgyzstan, Tajikistan, and Kazakhstan.[13] The Intelligence Directorate (J-2) of the Central Command "provides threat warning, targeting intelligence, and assessments" to the Commander, U.S. Central Command, component commands, U.S. embassy country teams, and the President and Secretary of Defense through "the conduct of all-source collection, analysis, fusion, targeting, production, and dissemination." Among the elements subordinate to the J-2 is the Joint Intelligence Center, Central (JICCENT).[14]

JICCENT's mission is to provide all-source intelligence and warning, operational intelligence, and assessments capability to the CENTCOM commander to meet wartime and peacetime needs, provide mission-oriented intelligence support to component commanders, serve as the theater collection manager, and produce and disseminate finished intelligence. The two divisions of the center, which grew out of Operation Desert Storm and have about 550 employees, are Analysis and Operations.[15] The organization of the center is shown in Figure 5.3.

Among the Analysis Division's key elements are those responsible for producing intelligence on Iraq, Iran, and Terrorism. The Iraq section has components focusing on different regions in Iraq (north, central, south) as well as on issues relating to Iraqi security forces and governance. The Terrorism section includes an element that monitors foreign fighters. The Iran unit is divided into three elements: Military Forces, Political, and Inspired Nomad.[16]

The Operations Division has four sections: Indications & Warning, Production, Geospatial Intelligence, and Targeting. Its responsibilities include the production of finished intelligence, including imagery and geospatial intelligence; targeting intelligence; assessments of current and future military capabilities; and the evaluation of ongoing military operations.[17]

EUROPEAN COMMAND

The European Command (EUCOM) was responsible for a geographic area that includes fifty-one countries. As noted above, the creation of AFRICOM eliminated the EUCOM's responsibility for the nations of the African continent. In the aftermath of the Soviet Union's collapse, EUCOM assumed responsibility for Georgia, Armenia, and Azerbaijan. It is also responsible for Israel.[18]

The European Command's Intelligence Directorate, as indicated in Figure 5.4, contains divisions for Plans and Requirements, HUMINT/CI, Intelligence Engagement, and the Foreign Disclosure Office. The HUMINT/CI Division "provides staff supervision (policy, planning, direction, and oversight) of all Theater and component human resources intelligence . . . and counterintelligence . . . operations supporting USEUCOM."[19]

Reporting to the EUCOM J2 are two key centers, as also shown in Figure 5.4. One is the Intelligence Mission Operations Center, responsible for managing collection activities under EUCOM control, whether human or technical. The other is the Joint Intelligence Operations Center–Europe Analytical Center (JAC)— formerly the Joint Analysis Center. Both centers, along with the intelligence directorate, are located at RAF Molesworth.[20]

The functions of the JAC include the following:

- theater-wide, all-source analyses and assessments;
- collection management;
- multisource processing/exploitation/dissemination;

FIGURE 5.3 Organization of the Joint Intelligence Center, Central (JICCENT)

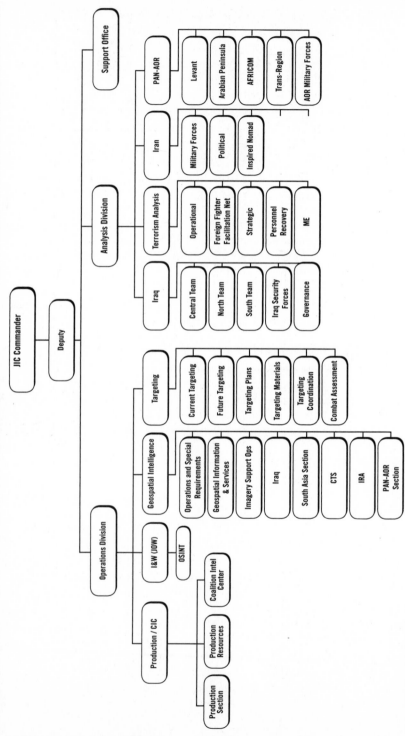

Source: U.S. Central Command.

FIGURE 5.4 Organization of the EUCOM Intelligence Directorate

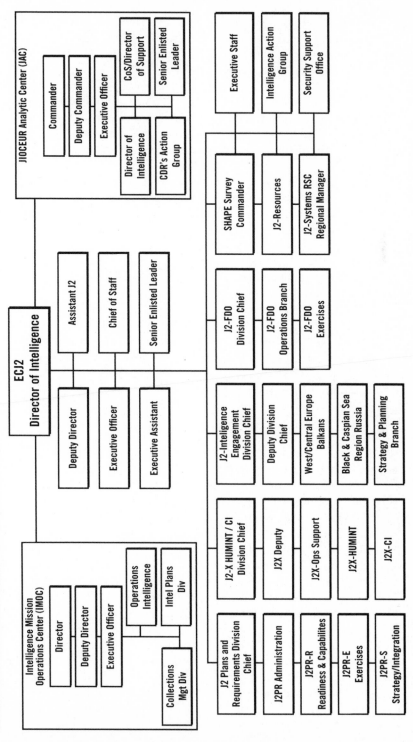

Source: U.S. European Command.

- indications and warning (I&W) support;
- target intelligence support;
- support to NATO multinational forces and U.S. joint task forces;
- distribution of intelligence production.[21]

The JAC's products include theater current intelligence summaries; theater regional assessments; theater threat assessments; electronic, air, defensive missile, and ground orders of battle; topical reports; indications and warning reports; counterterrorism, counterintelligence, and counternarcotics events reports; and exercise analyses and support.[22]

In March 2005, the EUCOM commander, Gen. James L. Jones, told a congressional committee that JAC "has provided support for peacekeeping operations in the Balkans, U.S. policymakers in the Caucasus, and supported crises response and counterterrorism operations in Africa." In addition, Jones stated that the JAC "supports the GWOT [Global War on Terrorism] with counter-terrorism analysis and has almost a quarter of its analysts temporarily deployed to Iraq and Afghanistan."[23]

The JAC operations directorate contains teams with responsibilities for analysis of specific regions (Eurasia, Middle East), for analysis of transnational issues (including terrorism and counterintelligence issues), for the production of strategic estimates, for geospatial intelligence, for electronic intelligence support, and for target assessment.[24]

In addition to the JAC employees at Molesworth, the center's work is augmented by military reservists at five different locations in the United States, which operate twenty-four hours a day, seven days a week. Included among the five units are those at Fort Sheridan, Illinois, and at Wright-Patterson Air Force Base, Ohio.[25]

JOINT FORCES COMMAND

The U.S. Atlantic Command (USACOM), established in 1993, was the successor to the Atlantic Command (LANTCOM), established in 1947, and the U.S. Atlantic Command (USLANTCOM), established in 1983. USLANTCOM had geographic responsibility for the Atlantic Ocean, the Caribbean, and other areas. In 1993, the Unified Command Plan was revised to further expand the responsibilities of USLANTCOM, transforming it into USACOM. The new command was assigned the responsibility of conducting joint training of most U.S.-based forces and staffs assigned to joint task forces and of providing joint trained and ready forces for worldwide employment. It assumed command of the Army's Forces Command (FORSCOM), the Air Force's Air Combat Command (ACC), the Marine Corps's Forces Command (MARFORLANT), and the Navy's Atlantic Fleet (LANTFLT). As a result of a 1995 review, some parts of USACOM's responsibilities were transferred to the U.S. Southern Command, as discussed below.[26]

In October 1999, the Atlantic Command became the U.S. Joint Forces Command (USJFCOM) in order to emphasize the command's "functional mandate to lead [the] transformation of U.S. military joint warfighting into the 21st Century," in contrast to its regional responsibility. The command's geographical responsibility was also revised to more closely mirror the area of responsibility of the NATO Allied Command Atlantic. The command was also charged with supporting terrorist response operations in the continental United States. In 2010, Secretary of Defense Robert Gates announced plans to disestablish the command.[27]

The command's Intelligence Directorate, which includes two key directorates—Plans, Policy, and Programs as well as Intelligence Operations—"provides military intelligence to warfighters and force planners in the [command] to support force provision, joint training, experimentation, and integration initiatives." The command's intelligence center is the Joint Transformation Command–Intelligence (JTC-I). Its organizational structure is shown in Figure 5.5.[28]

The JTC-I, like the command as a whole, is primarily concerned with transformation rather than intelligence production, which is the focus in other commands. It is responsible for the following:

- providing an experimental environment, the Joint Intelligence Lab (JIL), where intelligence concepts, processes, technology, and prototype initiatives can be tested;
- creating a joint intelligence environment for experimentation, training, and operations;
- exploring and evaluating new intelligence analysis concepts, techniques, and networks;
- serving as the test site for intelligence products and tools;
- operationalizing lessons learned, including those from counterterrorism operations, and operations in Afghanistan and Iraq.[29]

As of 2010, the JTC-I had 354 personnel, divided among military (146), civilian (100), and contractor (108) personnel.[30]

NORTHERN COMMAND

The most dramatic change in the unified command structure that resulted from the terrorist attacks of September 11, 2001, was the creation of the Northern Command—an idea that emerged not long after the attacks and was favored by the nation's top military officials. Before the command could be established a number of questions needed to be resolved, including whether the command would be assigned its own forces or would rely on forces supplied by other military commands, and whether there were legal restrictions on the use of military forces for law enforcement purposes. Such a command had been proposed during the Clinton administration, but the idea was dropped after protests from both civil libertarians and, reportedly, right-wing militia groups.[31]

On April 17, 2002, the Department of Defense announced the creation of the U.S. Northern Command (NORTHCOM) to bring together in a single military

120

FIGURE 5.5 Organization of the Joint Transformation Command–Intelligence

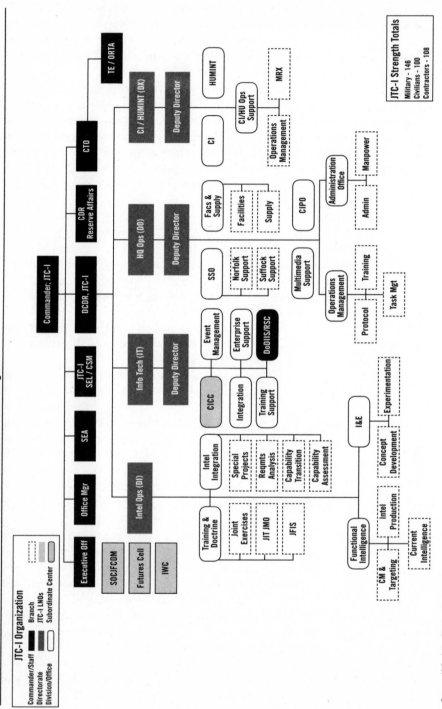

Source: U.S. Joint Forces Command.

command the homeland defense and civil support missions that were being performed by other military organizations. The command, which is colocated with the headquarters of the North American Aerospace Defense Command (NORAD) at Peterson Air Force Base in Colorado, reached initial operational capability on October 1, 2002.[32]

The U.S. Northern Command has two primary missions:

- Conducting operations to deter, prevent, and defeat threats and aggression aimed at the United States, its territories and interests within its assigned area of responsibility, which includes the air, land, and sea approaches to the continental United States, Alaska, and the surrounding water out to approximately 500 nautical miles. Areas also included are the Gulf of Mexico, Puerto Rico, and the U.S. Virgin Islands.
- Providing defense support of civil authorities, including consequence management, at the direction of the President or Secretary of Defense.[33]

In carrying out its missions NORTHCOM "conducts maritime operations to deter terrorist operations and prevent attacks on the United States and its allies." With regard to land operations, the command "postures and positions forces to deter and prevent attacks." During the 2004 election period, NORTHCOM provided assistance for border security, conducted airport vulnerability assessments, and deployed forces, at the request of the Department of Homeland Security, trained for radiological detection.[34]

The command's headquarters staff had grown to about 640 by August 2005. The military services have established component commands for NORTHCOM. In addition to Army North, Air Force North, and Marine Forces North, the Commander, Fleet Forces Command at Norfolk, Virginia, is designated as the Navy's Supporting Commander to NORTHCOM. The command's defense support to civil authorities is carried out primarily through task forces in Virginia, Washington, D.C., Alaska, and Texas. The command has few forces permanently assigned to it but is rather assigned forces as needed to execute its missions. Thus, fighter aircraft from the Air Combat Command and NORAD fly irregular air patrols to identify and intercept suspect aircraft in support of NORTHCOM's mission.[35]

The NORTHCOM Intelligence Directorate (J2), which is simultaneously the Joint Intelligence Operations Center–North, is composed of five divisions, as shown in Figure 5.6. Its mission is to provide "predictive and actionable threat estimates and timely warning of worldwide threats against North America using fused all-source intelligence and law enforcement information."[36]

As its organization chart indicates, this directorate/center is concerned with threats emanating both from foreign governments and from terrorist or other non-state groups. The chart also indicates the directorate/center's role in producing or collating intelligence relevant to support of NORTHCOM's role in domestic disaster relief, counterterrorism, or emergency response operations. The Intelligence

FIGURE 5.6   Organization of the NORTHCOM Intelligence Directorate/Joint Intelligence Operations Center–North

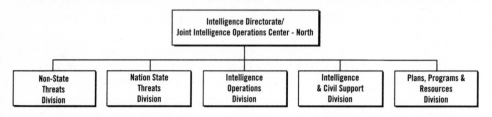

Operations Division is responsible for planning, coordinating, and executing NORTHCOM counterintelligence and HUMINT operations.[37]

The NORTHCOM JIOC replaced the Combined Intelligence and Fusion Center (which was "not a JIC," according to NORTHCOM briefing slides) and was relieved of "delegated production" (that is, production responsibilities assigned by DIA). The Fusion Center collated intelligence from NSA, CIA, the FBI, and other agencies as well as from open source intelligence. Ideally, the center would "connect the dots, [and] make a picture out of disparate information and intelligence," according to NORTHCOM's first commander.[38]

The CIFC's specific functions included

- indications and warning (against terrorist organizations, foreign intelligence, and strategic threats such as missiles and aircraft);
- current intelligence;
- intelligence summaries and assessments;
- long-term threat and vulnerability assessments for specific events/areas;
- tailored support to NORTHCOM plans and operations directorates;
- targeting tips to law enforcement;
- requirements management.[39]

PACIFIC COMMAND

The geographic area of responsibility for the Pacific Command (PACOM) includes the Indian and Pacific Oceans; Japan, China, Mongolia, North and South Korea, the countries of Southeast Asia, the southern Asian landmass to the western border of India, Australia, New Zealand, Hawaii, and Guam.[40]

As noted above, PACOM was one of three commands specifically ordered to establish a joint intelligence center. On July 3, 1991, the JICPAC was commissioned. It absorbed the Intelligence Center, Pacific (IPAC), the 548th Reconnaissance Technical Group, Task Force 168's Forward Area Support Team, Pacific (PACFAST), the Fleet Intelligence Center, Pacific (FICPAC), and the Fleet Ocean Surveillance Information Center (FOSIC)—creating a single organization with more than 1,200 personnel.[41]

Those organizations had been responsible for intelligence concerning the nations within PACOM's area of responsibility (IPAC), imagery interpretation (the 548th), technical support to fleet collection operations (PACFAST), intelligence on foreign naval capabilities and issues (FICPAC), and the monitoring of maritime movements (FOSIC).

JICPAC produced port directories, employed multispectral imagery in support of amphibious and special operations, produced target materials in support of conventional and special operations actions, analyzed target systems, and produced battle damage assessments. The center was also responsible for indications and warning, operational intelligence concerning maritime movements, first-phase imagery analysis, and the production of current intelligence products. In addition, it produced political and military analysis, general military intelligence, and order of battle products for the Russian Far East, both Koreas, as well as China, Taiwan, Japan, Mongolia, Macau, and Hong Kong. The South Asia Department performed similar tasks for more than twenty nations—from Indonesia, Vietnam, and India to Bhutan, the Comoros, and Réunion.[42]

The center also produced intelligence on air defense systems throughout the North and South Asia regions, conducted penetration and attrition analysis, and provided current intelligence support. Components of JICPAC also produced counterterrorism and counterintelligence products, including force protection analytical products, counterintelligence and counterterrorism support to operations, and assessments of the terrorist threat against U.S. interests.[43]

As part of the transformation of Joint Intelligence Centers, the JICPAC was replaced by the PACOM Joint Intelligence Operations Center, whose two key directorates are Operations and Strategies & Outcomes.[44]

The JIOC's mission has been to

- conduct intelligence operations (defined as comprehensive, end-to-end unilateral, bilateral, and combined intelligence actions and functions [planning, analysis, production, dissemination, exploitation, collection]);
- develop and carry out strategic concepts (defined as activities focused on the creation and preservation of capabilities, long-range plans for the intelligence enterprise);
- direct intelligence activities of all Defense Intelligence components within the Pacific theater so that they are aligned with the PACOM commander's priorities.[45]

The JIOC itself is subordinate to the PACOM Intelligence Directorate, headed by the command's Director of Intelligence.[46]

SOUTHERN COMMAND

The U.S. Southern Command (SOUTHCOM) has been responsible for U.S. military activities in Central and South America since 1946, when it was established as the Caribbean Command (CARIBCOM). As a result of a 1995 review of the unified command structure, USACOM's responsibility for the Gulf of Mexico, the Caribbean Sea and the nations within it, and adjoining waters around Central and South America was transferred to SOUTHCOM. With its creation NORTHCOM was assigned responsibility for Mexico, as well as parts of the Caribbean. It was also announced that NORTHCOM would eventually replace SOUTHCOM as the command responsible for Cuba. Today, without responsibility for Cuba, SOUTH-COM's area of responsibility is the landmass of Latin America south of Mexico; the waters adjacent to Central and South America; the Caribbean Sea, its twelve island nations and European territories; the Gulf of Mexico; and a portion of the Atlantic Ocean.[47]

The SOUTHCOM Security and Intelligence Directorate was established as part of a 2008 reorganization. Examples of directorate activities include (1) direct planning and execution for operations and exercises, (2) conducting operations and intelligence support related to counterterrorism operations, (3) production and dissemination of intelligence products, and (4) managing decision support activities.[48]

U.S. SPECIAL OPERATIONS COMMAND

On April 16, 1987, pursuant to Public Law 99–661 of November 1986, the U.S. Special Operations Command (USSOCOM) was established by Secretary of Defense Caspar Weinberger, on instructions from President Ronald Reagan, to exert supervision over the activities of the military services special operations units, which became component commands of the USSOCOM.[49]

USSOCOM consists of the organizations shown in Figure 5.7: the Army Special Operations Command, the Naval Special Warfare Command, the Air Force Special Operations Command, the Marine Special Operations Command, and the Joint Special Operations Command (JSOC).[50]

Whereas USSOCOM is based in Tampa, Florida, JSOC headquarters is located at Fort Bragg, North Carolina. JSOC consists of a variety of "special mission units," some of whose existence is classified or near-classified, including Delta Force (also known as the Combat Applications Group), the Naval Special Warfare Development Group (formerly Seal Team 6), the 75th Ranger Regiment, the 160th Special Operations Aviation Regiment, the 24th Special Tactics Squadron, and, probably, the U.S. Army Security Coordination Detachment.[51]

In 1997, USSOCOM had a budget of approximately $3 billion and 47,000 personnel—30,000 on active duty, 14,000 reservists and National Guard members, and 3,000 civilians. At that time, according to a General Accounting Office study, during an average week between 2,000 and 3,000 USSOCOM personnel would be deployed on 150 missions in sixty to seventy countries (where they operated under the command of the theater commander-in-chief). In 2007, the command budget was approximately $8 billion and its personnel numbered around 53,000.[52]

FIGURE 5.7   Organization of the USSOCOM Intelligence Directorate

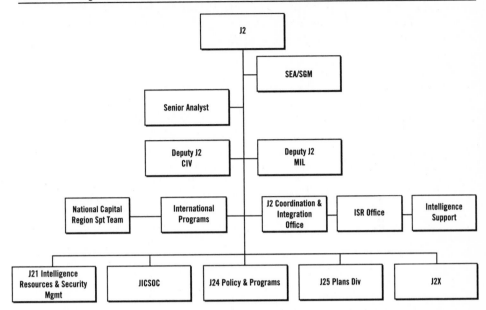

In June 2010, it was reported that the command had grown in numbers and budget, with command personnel operating in seventy-five countries, up from sixty a year earlier—although 9,000 of the 13,000 deployed overseas were split (almost evenly) between Iraq and Afghanistan. In addition to teams that had spent years in countries such as Colombia and the Philippines, there were teams operating in Yemen and other Middle East nations, Africa, and Central Asia—with plans for increased use in Somalia, where a special operations forces attack in 2009 had resulted in the death of the alleged head of al-Qaeda's East Africa branch.[53]

Originally, ten missions were specified for USSOCOM: direct action, strategic reconnaissance, unconventional warfare, foreign internal defense, counterterrorism, civil affairs, psychological operations, humanitarian assistance, theater search and rescue, and other activities as specified by the President or the Secretary of Defense. In May 1995, at the direction of the President and the Secretary of Defense, counterproliferation was added to the list. In 1999, the six key missions were counterproliferation, foreign internal defense, special reconnaissance, counterterrorism, unconventional warfare, and direct action.[54] A description of those activities is provided in Table 5.1.

In the wake of 9/11, counterterrorism became the primary mission of U.S. special operations forces—particularly the special mission units of JSOC. Under the

TABLE 5.1 Description of Activities Assigned to U.S. Special Operations Command

Activity	Description
Direct Action	Short-duration strikes and other small-scale offensive actions undertaken to seize, destroy, capture, recover, or inflict damage on designated personnel or materials.
Strategic Reconnaissance	Reconnaissance and surveillance actions conducted to obtain or verify, by visual observation or other collection methods, information concerning the capabilities, intentions, and activities of an actual or potential enemy or to secure data concerning the meteorological, hydrographic, or geographic characteristics of a particular area.
Unconventional Warfare	A broad spectrum of military and paramilitary operations, normally of long duration, predominately conducted by indigenous or surrogate forces that are organized, trained, equipped, supported, and directed in varying degrees by an external source.
Foreign Internal Defense	Participation by civilian and military agencies of a government in any of the action programs taken by another government to free and protect its society from subversion, lawlessness, and insurgency.
Civil Affairs	Operations that establish, maintain, influence, or exploit relations between military forces, government and nongovernment civilian organizations and authorities, and the civilian populace in friendly, neutral, or hostile areas of operations in order to facilitate military operations and consolidate and achieve U.S. national objectives.
Psychological Operations	Planned operations to convey selected information and indicators to foreign audiences to influence their emotions, motives, objective reasoning, and ultimately the behavior of foreign governments, organizations, groups, and individuals.
Counterterrorism	Offensive measures taken to prevent, deter, and respond to terrorism.
Humanitarian Assistance	Programs conducted to relieve or reduce the results of natural or man-made disasters or other endemic conditions such as hunger pain, disease, hunger, or deprivation that might present a serious threat to life or loss of property. This assistance supplements or complements the efforts of host national civil authorities or agencies that may have the primary responsibility for providing this assistance.
Theater Search and Rescue	Actions performed to recover distressed personnel during wartime or contingency operations.
Other Activities	Specified by the President or the Secretary of Defense.

Unified Command Plan signed by President Bush, the USSOC "leads, plans, synchronizes, and as directed, executes global operations against terrorist networks." Ad hoc, numbered task forces have searched for al-Qaeda in Afghanistan and Pakistan, searched for Iraqi weapons of mass destruction, and pursued Abu Musab al-Zarqawi and Saddam Hussein in Iraq.[55]

In addition, special mission unit personnel were given broader responsibilities in the collection of intelligence outside of combat areas. In early 2006 it was reported that small groups, sometimes just one or two at a time, had been deployed to more than a dozen embassies in Africa, Southeast Asia, and South America as "Military Liaison Elements." However, in 2010 the command retreated from a plan that would have given it the authority to carry out secret counterterrorist missions on its own.[56]

Intelligence production responsibilities in the U.S. Special Operations Command are located in the Intelligence Directorate (J-2) and the USSOCOM Joint Intelligence Operations Center (a subordinate element of the directorate). The Intelligence Directorate's mission is to provide all-source intelligence "to support the Global War on Terrorism." The joint intelligence center mission has been described as providing "intelligence to the [Commander, USSOCOM], Center for Special Operations (CSO), SOCOM Staff, Component Commands, and Subordinate Units; advocate for SOF intelligence requirements; interface with national/theater intelligence agencies; and [monitor/integrate] enhanced intelligence capabilities to support SOF."[57]

A special unit, known for many years as the Intelligence Support Activity (ISA), was first established as the Foreign Operating Group in 1980 in response to the Iran hostage crisis, conducts clandestine human and signals intelligence collection and other operations in support of special operations forces—particularly JSOC units. Since its creation, ISA, which is also designated by changing code names—among the most recent being CENTRA SPIKE and GREY FOX—has engaged in at least nine different types of activities: (1) intelligence collection, (2) pathfinder missions, (3) foreign leadership protection, (4) security and intelligence assessment, (5) prestrike reconnaissance, (6) operational support, (7) training of foreign personnel, (8) hostage rescue, and (9) acquisition of foreign weapons systems. GREY FOX personnel, as part of Task Force 20, were among those pursuing Saddam Hussein. A recent designation for the unit—which may have replaced ISA as its official title, or might simply be a cover name—is U.S. Army Security Coordination Detachment.[58]

The organization charts for the J-2 and JICSOC organizations are shown as Figures 5.7 and 5.8. The chart for the JICSOC, specifically the boxes that begin "SOC," illustrate a key fact about deployed USSOCOM elements—that they operate under the control of the theater commander (e.g., CENTOM commander, EUCOM commander) and not the commander of USSOCOM.

Also appearing on the JICSOC chart are boxes for the Global Mission Support Center and the Strategic Analysis Division. The latter focuses on producing an assessment of the strategic environment in which operations take place—rather than on threats from terrorist organizations or WMD suppliers.[59]

FIGURE 5.8   Organization of the Joint Intelligence Center: Special Operations Command

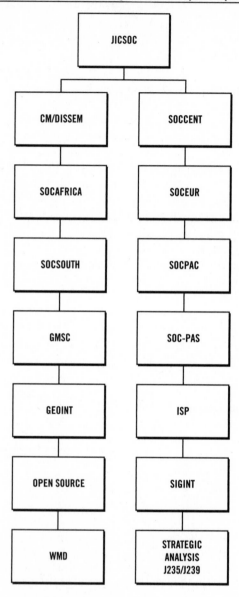

Source: Department of Defense.

U.S. STRATEGIC COMMAND

On September 27, 1991, President George H. W. Bush announced plans to disestablish the Strategic Air Command (SAC) and to create two new commands to take over SAC's functions. Operation of SAC aircraft would be assigned to the Air Combat Command, and nuclear strategic planning would be assigned to the new U.S. Strategic Command (STRATCOM). Like SAC, it is located at Offutt AFB in Omaha, Nebraska.[60]

In late June 2002, Secretary of Defense Donald Rumsfeld announced his intention to transform the Strategic Command by having it absorb another unified command—the U.S. Space Command, which had been established in 1985 to provide overall direction of U.S. military (other than reconnaissance) space activities. That action had been considered in previous Unified Command Plan reviews, as both commands had global missions that supported regional commanders. The merger took effect, as scheduled, on October 1, 2002.[61]

A Defense Department press release explained that "the missions of SPACECOM [the command of military space operations, information operations, computer network operations and space campaign planning] and STRATCOM [command and control of nuclear forces] have evolved to the point where merging the two into a single entity will eliminate redundancies in the command structure and streamline the decisionmaking process."[62]

STRATCOM's Senior Intelligence Officer is the Director of Intelligence, who manages the Intelligence Directorate. The directorate itself has three key components: the Security, Training, Resources & Systems Staff; the Strategic Planning division; and the Strategic Joint Intelligence Operations Center.

STRACOM's Strategic Joint Intelligence Center (SJIOC) consists of five divisions, as shown in Figure 5.9: Analysis, Production, Current Intelligence; Intelligence Plans; Intelligence Requirements and Capabilities; Targeting; and HUMINT/CI. The Analysis division has four key components. One is divided between regional and functional analysts (who work on space, WMD, and strategic communications issues), another produces current intelligence, a third is concerned with strategic cyber operations and analysis, and the fourth is the missile analysis unit.[63]

An element of STRATCOM, established in September 2006, is the Joint Functional Component Command–Intelligence, Surveillance, and Reconnaissance (JFCC-ISR). The command is located in Washington, D.C., and is headed by the Director, DIA. JFCC-ISR is responsible for "coordinating global intelligence collection to address DOD worldwide operations and national intelligence requirements. It will serve as the focal point for the planning, execution, and assessments of the military's global, intelligence, surveillance, and reconnaissance operations."[64]

The JFCC-ISR is responsible for assigning Defense Department ISR assets based on priorities set by DIA's DJIOC. With respect to national collection assets, it works with the Office of the Director of National Intelligence, CIA, NSA, NRO, and NGA "to apply national assets to DOD problems and vice versa."[65]

FIGURE 5.9   Organization of the Strategic Joint Intelligence Center

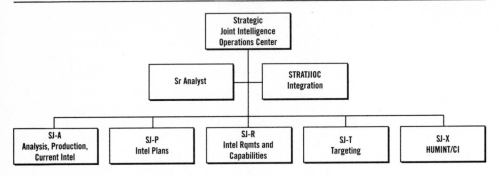

TRANSPORTATION COMMAND

On February 28, 1986, the Blue Ribbon Commission on Defense Management, appointed by President Ronald Reagan, recommended the creation of a single unified command to integrate global air, land, and sea transportation for the military. On April 1, Reagan signed National Security Decision Directive 219, "Implementation of the Recommendations of the President's Commission on Defense Management," which included the direction to the Secretary of Defense to "take those steps necessary to establish a single Unified Command to provide global air, land, and sea transportation," once legislation prohibiting such a command was repealed.[66]

Later in 1986, the Department of Defense Reorganization Act ordered the Secretary of Defense to consider creation of a Unified Transportation Command (UTC) and repealed the law that blocked such action. On October 1, 1987, the U.S. Transportation Command (TRANSCOM), as the UTC had been renamed, was activated at Scott Air Force Base, Illinois, with a staff of fifty. TRANSCOM is responsible for consolidating all U.S. strategic air, sea, and transportation during war or buildup to war and for exercising centralized control. TRANSCOM components include the Navy's Military Sealift Command, the Army's Military Traffic Management Command, and the Air Force Military Airlift Command.[67]

The Transportation Command's Intelligence Directorate is simultaneously the USTRANSCOM Joint Intelligence Operations Center (JIOC-TRANS). As indicated in Figure 5.10, it has four major divisions: Current Intelligence, Intelligence Plans & Programs, Intelligence Operations, and CI/HUMINT. The Current Intelligence Division has two main functions, providing executive support and operating the watch branch. Executive support involves producing the Daily Executive Read Book, current intelligence highlights, and commander intelligence updates as well as responding to requests for information. The watch branch produces the daily current intelligence briefing and is, inter alia, responsible for indications and warning.[68]

FIGURE 5.10 Organization of the USTRANSCOM Joint Intelligence Operations Center (JIOC-TRANS)

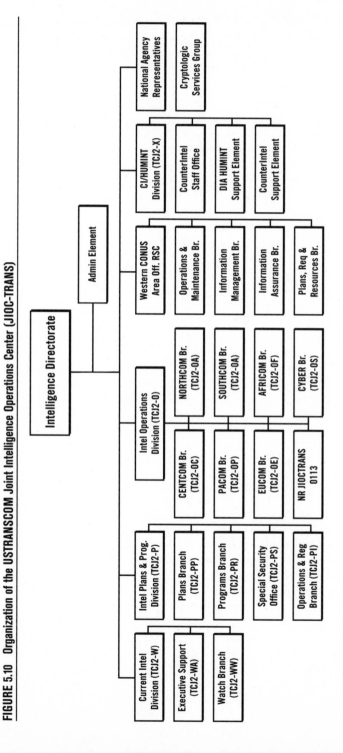

Source: U.S. Transportation Command.

The Plans and Programs Division reviews and coordinates the intelligence input to all command policy documents and joint publications, including memoranda of agreement with other combatant commands' intelligence staffs and national agencies. It also is responsible for programming sufficient resources to carry out the Command's intelligence responsibilities.[69]

The center produces an Executive Intelligence Summary (EXINTSUM) for TRANSCOM and component command decisionmakers and planners; a modernized integrated database on commercial seaports and approaches, which is part of the Intelligence Community's consolidated database; port directories in support of U.S. Navy operations, which provide navigational, berthing, services, and tourism information for ports around the world; current intelligence analysis and briefings; and indications and warning of threats to TRANSCOM operations and the Defense Transportation System.[70]

Another center product is the Transportation Intelligence Digital Environment (TIDE), which allows the center's analysts to "create comprehensive transportation intelligence products directly on the Internet"—permitting the products to be transmitted to decisionmakers and planners faster than other methods allow. Analysts can combine graphics, text, video, photos, and audio files into comprehensive briefings or reports.[71]

Notes

1. General Accounting Office, GAO/NSIAD-97-41-BR, *Unified Command Plan: Atlantic and Southern Command Participation in 1995 Review* (Washington, D.C.: GAO, December 1996), p. 9; George Bush, Memorandum for the Secretary of Defense, Subject: Unified Command Plan 2008, December 17, 2008.

2. Thomas E. Ricks, "Military Overhaul Considered," *Washington Post*, October 11, 2001, pp. A1, A18.

3. Eric Schmitt, "Pentagon Revamping Command Structure," *New York Times*, April 17, 2002, p. A19. For an account of the status and power of the CINCs when they were so designated and a discussion of the decision to eliminate the designation, see Dana Priest, "A Four-Star Foreign Policy?" *Washington Post*, September 28, 2000, pp. A1, A18–A19; and Vernon Loeb, "One 'Chief' Commands; Others Are Out of CINC," *Washington Post*, October 29, 2002, p. A19.

4. Assistant Secretary of Defense (Command, Control, Communications, and Intelligence), *Plan for Restructuring Defense Intelligence*, March 15, 1991, p. 4; "Joint Intelligence Center JICPAC–USPACOM," http://131.84.1.218/about/jicpac.shtml, accessed February 23, 2006. For the history of earlier joint intelligence centers, see James D. Marchio, "The Evolution and Relevance of Joint Intelligence Centers," *Studies in Intelligence* 49, 1 (Spring 2005), http:// www.cia.gov/csi/studies.

5. Arthur D. Baker III, "Farewell to the FICs," *Naval Intelligence Professionals Quarterly* (Winter 1992): 7–9; Capt. J. R. Reddig, "The Creation of JICPAC," *Naval Intelligence Professionals Quarterly* (Fall 2001): 18–21.

6. Assistant Secretary of Defense (Command, Control, Communications, and Intelligence), *Plan for Restructuring Defense Intelligence*, p. 4. William S. Cohen, *Defense Initiative Reform Report* (Washington, D.C.: U.S. Government Printing Office, November 1997), p. 76.

7. "DOD to Set Up Joint Intelligence Operations Center Worldwide," http://intelligence-summit.blogspot.com, April 18, 2006.

8. "JMIS and the Enterprise: A Retrospective Look," *Communiqué*, March 2009, pp. 6–7.

9. Lauren Ploch, Congressional Research Service, *Africa Command: U.S. Strategic Interests and the Role of the U.S. Military in Africa,* April 3, 2010, pp. 1–2. On the creation of AFRICOM, also see Carmel Davis, "AFRICOM's Relationship to Oil, Terrorism and China," *Orbis,* Winter 2009, pp. 122–136; and George W. Bush, The White House, *Unified Command Plan*, December 17, 2008.

10. Ploch, *Africa Command*, p. 1; U.S. Africa Command, "Fact Sheet: United States Africa Command," www.africom.mil, accessed March 1, 2010. For a list of sixteen different responsibilities, see George W. Bush, The White House, *Unified Command Plan*, pp. 5–7.

11. Ploch, *Africa Command*, pp. 10, 12 n. 3; Craig Whitlock, "Pentagon hunting for a home for Africom," www.washingtonpost.com, November 27, 2010.

12. E-mail, Vincent M. Crawley, AFRICOM to author, March 31, 2010; Melony C. Angelilli, "General Ward Visits Intelligence and Knowledge Development Molesworth," January 7, 2010, www.africom.mil.

13. U.S. Congress, *House Committee on Armed Services, Hearings on HR 1816* (Washington, D.C.: U.S. Government Printing Office, 1983), p. 955. Also see Thomas E. Ricks, "A War That's Commanded at a Distance," *Washington Post,* December 27, 2001, p. A16; Thomas E. Ricks, "Un-Central Command Criticized," *Washington Post,* June 3, 2002, pp. A1, A4; and George W. Bush, The White House, *Unified Command Plan*, p. 8.

14. U.S. Central Command, "J2 Mission: Intelligence Director's Mission Statement," n.d.

15. U.S. Central Command, "The CENTCOM Perspective: CENTCOM/SOCOM Joint Intelligence Support Concept," 1992; Richard Lardner, "Behind CentCom's Closed Doors," http://www.tampatrib.com, March 15, 2004; "Joint Intelligence Center Central (JICCENT)" (Organization Chart), December 10, 2009.

16. "Joint Intelligence Center Central (JICCENT)" (Organization Chart).

17. Ibid.

18. "501st Combat Support Wing," www.501.csw.usafe.af.mil/units/molesworth/index.asp, accessed April 1, 2010; U.S. Congress, House National Security Committee, *Hearings on National Defense Authorization Act for Fiscal Year 1997–H.R. 3230 and Oversight of Previously Authorized Programs, Authorization and Oversight* (Washington, D.C.: U.S. Government Printing Office, 1997), p. 734; United States European Command, ED 40–1, "Intelligence Mission and Responsibilities," May 24, 1996; George W. Bush, The White House, *Unified Command Plan*, p. 10.

19. EUCOM Directive 20–1, *Headquarters United States European Command Organization and Functions*, November 1, 2004, pp. S-9 to S-10. The 2004 manual was still in force as of early 2010.

20. "501st Combat Support Wing."

21. European Command, "USEUCOM Plan for Theater Intelligence," July 1, 1991, pp. 2–3.

22. Ibid., pp. 2–4.

23. General James L. Jones, USMC, Commander, United States European Command, "Statement Before the Senate Armed Services Committee," March 1, 2005, pp. 10–11, www.eucom.mil.

24. EUCOM Directive 20–1, *Headquarters United States European Command Organization and Functions*, pp. S-55 to S-62.

25. "501st Combat Support Wing"; Tim Hodges, "Fort Sheridan CELEBRATES 10th Anniversary as JRIC," *Communiqué*, January/February 2008, pp. 8–9.

26. General Accounting Office, *Unified Command Plan*, pp. 9–10; U.S. Congress, House National Security Committee, *Hearings on National Defense Authorization Act for Fiscal Year 1997—H.R. 3230 and Oversight of Previously Authorized Programs, Authorization and Oversight*, p. 862; "USJFCOM: History," Section 8, http://www.jfcom.mil/about/History, accessed February 23, 2006.

27. "USJFCOM: History," Section 11; Bradley Graham, "Teamwork as Military Task," *Washington Post*, October 12, 1999, p. A17; David Hughes, "The Future of Joint Warfighting," *Aviation Week & Space Technology*, May 26, 2003, pp. 76–77; Walter Pincus, "Joint Forces Command, which relies on contractors, is tempting target for Gates," www.washingtonpost.com, August 18, 2010.

28. United States Joint Forces Command, "Intelligence Directorate," http://www.jfcom.mil/about/abt_j2.htm, accessed July 7, 2006; United States Joint Forces Command, "Joint Transformation Command for Intelligence (JTC-I)," http://www.jfcom.mil/about/fact_jtci.htm, accessed July 7, 2006.

29. United States Joint Forces Command, "Joint Transformation Command for Intelligence (JTC-I)."

30. "Joint Transformation Command–Intelligence, Organization Chart," 2010.

31. Yochi J. Dreazen and David S. Cloud, "Pentagon, White House Consider New Command Against U.S. Attacks," *Wall Street Journal*, November 21, 2001, p. A8; Bradley Graham, "Military Favors a Homeland Command," *Washington Post*, November 21, 2001, pp. A1, A6.

32. "U.S. Northern Command: A History," http://www.northcom.mil/about_us/history.htm, accessed February 23, 2006; Department of Defense, "Unified Command Plan," News Release 188–02, April 17, 2002, http://www.defenselink.com; Jim Garamone, American Forces Press Service, "Unified Command Plan Changes Transparent, But Important," May 22, 2002, http://www.defenselink.com.

33. "U.S. Northern Command," http://www.northcom.mil/about_us/about_us.htm, accessed February 23, 2006. Other responsibilities are listed in George W. Bush, The White House, *Unified Command Plan*, pp. 12–14.

34. "Statement of Lieutenant General Joseph R. Inge, USA, Deputy Commander United States Northern Command Before the Senate Armed Services Committee Subcommittee on Emerging Threats and Capabilities," March 10, 2006, p. 2.

35. Ibid., pp. 3–4; "U.S. Northern Command"; Bradley Graham, "War Plans Drafted to Counter Terror Attacks in U.S.," *Washington Post*, August 8, 2005, pp. A1, A7.

36. "HQ NORAD-USNORTHCOM Directorate of Intelligence Mission Statement," provided by NORTHCOM in response to author FOIA request; U.S. Northern Command, NNCMAN38–153, *NORTHCOM Organization and Functions Manual* (August 1, 2007), ch. 5, p. 1.

37. U.S. Northern Command, NNCMAN38–153, *NORTHCOM Organization and Functions Manual*, ch. 5, p. 7.

38. William B. Scott, "Northern Command Adds Teeth to Homeland Defense, Security," *Aviation Week & Space Technology*, October 7, 2002, pp. 29–30; CIFC Commander, *Welcome to the NORAD/USNORTHCOM Combined Intelligence Fusion Center*, n.d., p. 7.

39. CIFC Commander, *Welcome to the NORAD/USNORTHCOM Combined Intelligence Fusion Center*, n.d., p. 7.

40. George W. Bush, The White House, *Unified Command Plan*, p. 16.

41. Letter from K. Kibota, Chief, Administrative Support Division, Joint Secretariat, U.S. Pacific Command to author, October 8, 1991; "The New Boy on the Block," *Naval Intelligence Professionals Quarterly* (Spring 1992), p. 2; "West Coast Intelligence Consolidations," *Naval Intelligence Bulletin* (Fall/Winter 1990), pp. 22–23.

42. Joint Intelligence Center, Pacific, *JICPAC Quick Reference Office and Function Guide* (Pearl Harbor, Hawaii: JICPAC, June 1996), pp. 11–15.

43. Ibid., pp. 15–16.

44. "USPACOM Intelligence Directorate," www.pacom.mil, accessed March 1, 2010.

45. U.S. Pacific Command, "PACOM JIOC Mission."

46. "USPACOM Intelligence Directorate."

47. General Accounting Office, *Unified Command Plan*, pp. 9–10; Garamone, "Unified Command Plan Changes Transparent, But Important"; "Area of Responsibility (AOR)," http://www.southcom.mil/pa/Facts/AOR.htm, accessed February 23, 2006.

48. Government Accountability Office, GAO-10-801, *U.S. Southern Command Demonstrates Interagency Collaboration, But Its Haiti Disaster Response Revealed Challenges Conducting a Large Military Operation*, July 2010, p. 21; "Directorate of Security and Intelligence," www.southcom.mil, accessed March 8, 2010.

49. Ronald Reagan, Memorandum for the Honorable Caspar W. Weinberger, Secretary of Defense, Subject: Establishment of Combatant Commands, April 13, 1987; Caspar Weinberger, Memorandum for the President, Subject: Establishment of the U.S. Special Operations Command, and the Specified Forces Command, April 16, 1987; General Accounting Office, GAO/NSIAD-97-85, *Special Operations Forces: Opportunities to Preclude Overuse and Misuse*, May 1997, p. 1.

50. Andrew Feickert, Congressional Research Service, *U.S. Special Operations Forces (SOF): Background Issues for Congress*," January 25, 2008, pp. 2–4.

51. Andrew Feickert, Congressional Research Service, *U.S. Special Forces (SOF): Background and Issues for Congress*, April 17, 2006, pp. 2–4; Sean D. Naylor, "JSOC to Become Three-Star Command," http://www.airforcetimes.com, February 13, 2006.

52. General Accounting Office, *Special Operations Forces*, p. 2; Ann Scott Tyson, "New Plans Foresee Fighting Terrorism Beyond War Zones," www.washingtonpost.com, April 23, 2006.

53. Karen De Young and Greg Jaffe, "U.S. 'secret war' expands globally as special operations forces take larger role," www.washingtonpost.com, June 4, 2010.

54. General Accounting Office, *Special Operations Forces*, pp. 6–7, 22.

55. Thom Shanker, "Study Is Said to Find Overlap in U.S. Counterterror Effort," *New York Times*, March 18, 2006, p. A5; Dana Priest and Thomas E. Ricks, "U.S. Units Attacking Al Qaeda in Pakistan," *Washington Post*, April 25, 2002, pp. A1, A8; Rowan Scarborough, "Elite U.S. Unit Keeps Heat on Terrorists," *Washington Post*, July 12, 2002, pp. A1, A10; William M. Arkin, "Zarqawi's Death and Task Force 145," http://www.washingtonpost.com (Early Warning Blog), June 9, 2006; Barton Gellman, "Covert Unit Hunted for Iraqi Arms," *Washington Post*, June 13, 2003, pp. A8, A14–A15.

56. Thomas Shanker and Scott Shane, "Elite Troops Get Expanded Role on Intelligence," *New York Times*, March 8, 2006, pp. A1, A6; Thom Shanker, "Wider Antiterrorism Role for Elite Forces Is Rejected," *New York Times*, May 27, 2008, p. A10.

57. "J2 Mission," briefing slide provided by USSOCOM in response to author's FOIA request; "J23 (JIC) Mission," n.d., provided to author in response to FOIA request.

58. See Jeffrey T. Richelson, "'Truth Conquers All Chains': The U.S. Army Intelligence Support Activity, 1981–1989," *International Journal of Intelligence and Counterintelligence* 12, 2 (Summer 1999): 168–200; Peter Beaumont, "'Grey Fox' Closes In on Prize Scalp: Saddam," http://observer.guardian.co.uk, June 22, 2003; and Michael Smith, *The Killer Elite: The Inside Story of America's Most Secret Special Operations Team* (London: Weidenfeld & Nicolson, 2006), pp. 254–256. The U.S. Army Security Coordination Detachment was shown on a 2008 organizational chart of the U.S. Army Intelligence and Security Command as a subordinate element of INSCOM, but it was not mentioned as an INSCOM element in the most recent *INSCOM Today* almanac.

59. Kathy L. Weyenberg, "Strategic APPRECIATION Focus for SOCOM Intelligence Support," *Communiqué*, May/June 2009, pp. 16–17.

60. "Intelligence Community Notes," *Defense Intelligence Journal* 1 (1992): 105–112.

61. Department of Defense, "DOD Announces Merger of U.S. Space and Strategic Commands," Release No. 331–02, June 26, 2002, http://www.defenselink.mil; William B. Scott, "'Stratcom' to Be All-New Command," *Aviation Week & Space Technology*, July 29, 2002, p. 48; Sonja Chambers, "Strategic, Space Commands Merge," October 1, 2002, http://www.defenselink.mil; William B. Scott, "'New' Strategic Command Could Assume Broader Roles," *Aviation Week & Space Technology*, October 14, 2002, p. 63; George W. Bush, The White House, *Unified Command Plan*, p. 27.

62. Department of Defense, "DOD Announces Merger of U.S. Space and Strategic Commands."

63. Strategic Command, "SJ-A—Analysis, Production, and Current Intelligence Division" (Organization Chart), March 22, 2010; Strategic Command, "SJ-A12–Functional Analysis Section" (Organization Chart), March 22, 2010.

64. Government Accountability Office, *Military Transformation: Additional Action Needed by U.S. Strategic Command to Strengthen Implementation of Its Many Missions and New Organizations*, September 2006, p. 59; Defense Intelligence Agency, "STRATCOM's Joint Functional Component Command for Intelligence, Surveillance and Reconnaissance Formally Opens for Business," September 13, 2006, http://www.dia.mil/publicaffairs/Press15.htm.

65. Jim Garamone, Armed Forces Press Service, "DOD Cuts Ribbon on Joint Intelligence Resource Center," September 21, 2006, http://www.stratcom.mil/News/ISR%20opens.html.

66. United States Transportation Command, *United States Transportation Command: 10 Years of Excellence, 1987–1997*, n.d. p. 9; Ronald Reagan, National Security Decision Directive 219, "Implementation of the Recommendations of the President's Commission on Defense Management," April 1, 1986.

67. United States Transportation Command, *United States Transportation Command*, pp. 9–10; James W. Canan, "Can TRANSCOM Deliver?" *Air Force Magazine*, October 1987, pp. 40–46.

68. "Current Intelligence Division," www.transcom.mil/j2/j2w.cfm, accessed March 8, 2010.

69. "Plans and Programs Division," www.transcom.mil/j2/j2p.cfm, accessed March 15, 2010.

70. United States Transportation Command, USTRANSCOM Pamphlet 14–7, *Joint Intelligence Center–Transportation (JICTRANS)*, November 2004; "Statement of Gen. Norton A. Schwartz, Commander, United States Transportation Command Before the House Armed Services Committee on the State of the Command," March 2, 2006, p. 21.

71. Gary Henry, "USTRANSCOM creates effective intelligence tool," www.imake news.com, January 22, 2003.

6

CIVILIAN INTELLIGENCE ORGANIZATIONS

The bulk of U.S. intelligence resources, whether in terms of personnel or dollars, lies in the hands of the national intelligence organizations, the Defense Department, and the military services. However, intelligence activities are also carried out by branches of the Departments of State, Energy, Homeland Security, Justice (the Federal Bureau of Investigation and the Drug Enforcement Administration), which collect and/or analyze intelligence on terrorist activities, foreign policies, military forces, economic affairs, and narcotics trafficking. In some cases, they serve their departments as well as contributing to the national intelligence effort.

DEPARTMENT OF STATE INTELLIGENCE

With the dissolution of the Office of Strategic Services (OSS) after World War II, its research and analysis functions were transferred to the State Department and placed in the Interim Research and Intelligence Service (IRIS). Two subsequent name changes followed until the service became the Bureau of Intelligence and Research (INR) in 1957. INR now employs between 315 and 330 individuals. Its budget is approximately $60 million dollars.[1]

The bureau does not engage in clandestine collection, although it receives reports through normal diplomatic channels and conducts open source collection. It does perform several functions concerning operational matters, serving as a liaison between the Department of State and the Intelligence Community to ensure that the actions of other intelligence agencies are in accord with U.S. foreign policy.[2]

In terms of production, INR faces in two directions—or, as the INR director stated in 2009, "as a State Department bureau and element of the IC, INR has 'two masters.'" One direction is outward, where it is involved in interagency intelligence production efforts such as National Intelligence Estimates (NIEs) and Special Estimates (SEs). The second direction is inward—toward the State Department's internal organization. In this role INR prepares a variety of intelligence products. The Secretary of State's *Morning Intelligence Summary* is designed to inform the Secretary and his or her principal deputies of current events and current intelligence.

INR also prepares a variety of regional and functional summaries as well as single-subject reports.[3]

INR's analytical reach has been described as ranging "from pirates in Somalia and North Korean missile launches, to narco-violence in Mexico, new cyber threats, and infectious diseases."[4]

The Director of INR is simultaneously the Assistant Secretary of State for Intelligence and Research. As shown in Figure 6.1, the Assistant Secretary is assisted by the Principal Deputy Assistant Secretary, the Deputy Assistant Secretary for Analysis, and the Deputy Assistant Secretary for Intelligence Policy and Coordination. The Principal Deputy Assistant Secretary for Intelligence and Research is the second-ranking individual in the bureau and directly supervises the Office of the Executive Director, the Office of Publications, and INR Watch.[5]

The Deputy Assistant Secretary for Analysis supervises offices of analysis for six geographic regions: Africa, East Asia and the Pacific, Western Hemisphere, the Near East and South Asia, Russia and Eurasia, and Europe. These offices primarily produce analyses of developments and issues that are, or will be, of concern to policymakers. The offices are also responsible for preparing regional and other special summaries and for contributing to Intelligence Community estimates and assessments. An analyst for the Office of Analysis for Europe might be asked to examine the domestic situation in Germany, the likely results of upcoming French elections, the impact of Islam on the future of democracy in Turkey, or the situation in Cyprus. An East Asia and Pacific analyst might be concerned with the role of the Chinese People's Liberation Army in domestic politics.[6]

The Deputy Assistant Secretary for Analysis is also responsible for the bureau's long-range analytical studies. He or she supervises the Office of Economic Analysis, the Office of the Geographer and Global Issues, the Office of Analysis for Strategic, Proliferation, and Military Issues, and the Office of Analysis for Terrorism, Narcotics, and Crime.[7]

The Office of Economic Analysis produces reports for policymakers on current and long-range issues involving international economic concerns such as foreign economic policies, business cycles, trade, financial affairs, food, population and energy, and the economic relations between the industrialized countries and the developing nations. The Office of the Geographer and Global Issues prepares studies of policy issues associated with physical, cultural, economic, and political geography, U.S. maritime issues, international boundaries, and jurisdictional problems. It also contains a division dedicated to the study of war crimes and atrocities and a unit for the provision of support to humanitarian efforts.[8]

The Office of Strategic, Proliferation, and Military Issues focuses on the strategic forces of the acknowledged nuclear states (Russia, China, Britain, France, Pakistan, India, and North Korea), the nuclear/ballistic missile activities of unacknowledged and aspiring nuclear nations, military technologies, proliferation, and regional military forces. The Office of Analysis for Terrorism, Narcotics, and Crime examines the structure, operations, and linkages of terrorist groups and drug cartels.[9]

FIGURE 6.1 Organization of the Bureau of Intelligence and Research (INR)

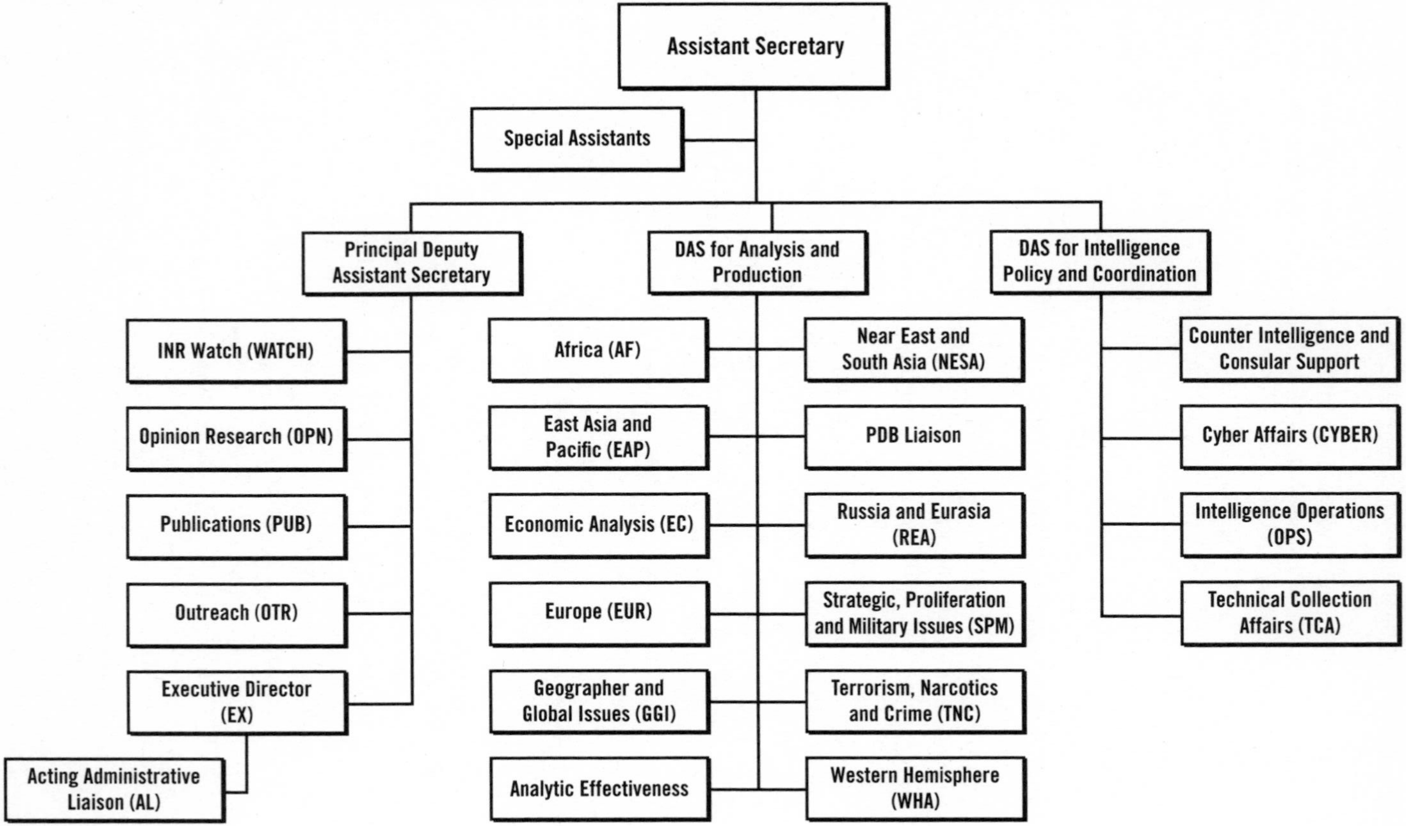

Source: Department of State.

Two newly created offices under the Deputy Assistant Secretary for Analysis are the Office of Cyber Affairs and the Office of Opinion Research. The Cyber Affairs office "analyzes cyber developments for State policymakers, facilitates State Department cyber-related activities, and contributes to cyber-related Intelligence Community products." And the Office of Opinion Research, which has 40 members, more than any other INR office, "directly supports public diplomacy through its analysis of public opinion polls and foreign media commentary." According to the 2009 nominee for the INR director's position such analysis "can assist public diplomacy officials to align strategic goals and programmatic activities with what we know about the attitudes, aspirations, and need of foreign publics."[10]

The Deputy Assistant Secretary for Intelligence Policy and Coordination supervises the Office of Intelligence Operations and the Office of Technical Collection Affairs.

The Office of Intelligence Operations handles requests for biographic information and foreign maps, while the Office of Technical Collection Affairs has assumed some of the responsibilities of the former Office of Intelligence Resources (OIR). The Technical Collection Affairs office works with other Intelligence Community agencies and other branches of the department and overseas missions in planning, tasking, deploying, and evaluating technical collection activities. It also advises department offices on the use of intelligence produced by major technical collection systems and includes a unit for the support of diplomatic operations. In 1992, the Director of the OIR advised the National Reconnaissance Office on how to handle the forthcoming declassification of its existence.[11]

DEPARTMENT OF ENERGY INTELLIGENCE

The Department of Energy's intelligence role can be traced to July 1946, when the National Intelligence Authority decided that the Atomic Energy Commission (AEC) had an appropriate foreign intelligence role and authorized AEC representation on the Intelligence Advisory Board. On December 12, 1947, the AEC's intelligence role was affirmed by National Security Council Intelligence Directive No. 1.[12]

The Energy Reorganization Act of 1974 transferred the AEC's intelligence operations to the Energy Research and Development Administration, and the Department of Energy Organization Act of 1977 transferred them to the newly created Department of Energy. In April 1990, the Energy Department consolidated its intelligence functions by establishing an Office of Intelligence to bring under one roof the Offices of Foreign Intelligence, Threat Assessment, and Counterintelligence. A 1994 reorganization resulted in the redesignation of the office as the Office of Energy Intelligence (OEI) within the Office of Nonproliferation and National Security, with the Office of Threat Assessment moved outside the new intelligence office.[13] A 1998 reorganization, in response to concerns about the effectiveness of Energy Department security and Presidential Decision Directive 61 ("U.S. Department of Energy Counterintelligence Program," February 11, 1998), split the OEI into two offices: the Office of Intelligence and the Office of Counterintelligence. The new offices reported directly to the Secretary and Deputy Secretary of Energy. In the spring of 2006, the intelligence and counterintelligence offices were renamed directorates and resubordinated to a joint office—the Office of Intelligence and Counterintelligence. A year before the merger, the Office of Intelligence had 33 analysts, 19 of whom were focused on weapons of mass destruction issues.[14]

As shown in Figure 6.2, the Intelligence Directorate has five subordinate components: the Collection Management Staff, the Nuclear Division, the Counterterrorism Division, the Energy Security Division, and the S&T Division.

The Nuclear Division studies and reports on foreign nuclear weapons programs for intelligence, military planning, diplomatic, and treaty-monitoring purposes. During Operations Desert Shield and Desert Storm, the division provided the Joint Chiefs of Staff and DIA with assessments of the Iraqi nuclear weapons program and its capabilities. It has also been concerned with issues such as the command, control, and security of tactical and strategic nuclear weapons in Russia and other former Soviet states, the dismantlement of nuclear weapons in the former Soviet Union, the disposition of the nuclear materials removed from those weapons, and the proliferation potential (through a "brain drain") of the former Soviet republics.[15]

The Energy Security Division focuses on international developments that could affect the overall U.S. energy posture and the Strategic Petroleum Reserve. Special studies conducted by the office examined the prospects for disruption of energy supplies due to worldwide political, economic, and social instabilities. In addition, the division analyzed overall energy balances within Russia and other nations, focusing on total energy needs that might influence supply and demand. It also examined energy technologies that may have dual uses (civil and military) in support of foreign availability studies related to the Energy Department's Military Critical Technologies List.[16]

The Counterterrorism Division is responsible for monitoring and analyzing developments related to the ability of terrorist groups to obtain or produce nuclear or radiation dispersal devices, including scientific publications, the security at Russian and other nuclear installations, and attempts to acquire fissile material. The S&T Division examines developments in science and technology that affect the ability of nations or groups to produce nuclear weapons.

The Counterintelligence Directorate conducts counterintelligence risk assessments, including assessments of the Energy Department's susceptibility to economic espionage. Energy Department counterintelligence products have included *Statistical Analysis of Foreign Visits to DOE Facilities* (September 1993) and *Information Brokers* (August 1994). Counterintelligence newsletters and bulletins cover such topics as "Targeting of DOE Travelers."[17]

A geographically separated, subordinate unit of the office is the Nevada Intelligence Center. It represents the Energy Department with respect to intelligence and intelligence-related activities at the Nevada Test Site (NTS), where nuclear tests and/or related experiments have been conducted) and with respect to DOE-sponsored activities at the Tonopah Test Range (TTR). Specific functions include intelligence oversight, intelligence collection management (coordinating Intelligence

FIGURE 6.4 Organization of the DHS Office of Intelligence and Analysis (I&A)

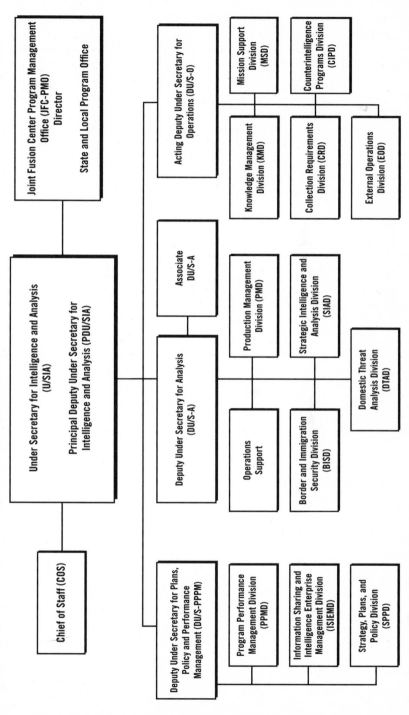

Source: Department of Homeland Security.

Border and Immigration Security, Strategic Intelligence and Analysis, and Domestic Threat Analysis.[28]

Reporting directly to the Under Secretary and Deputy Under Secretary is the Joint Fusion Center Program Management Office, which supports information sharing between state, local, tribal, and federal law enforcement partners—including seventy-two fusion centers—and coordinates support from all elements of the DHS.[29]

Both the number of individuals employed by the office and the office's budget are classified. As of March 2010, 63 percent of the office workforce consisted of contractor personnel.[30]

In the fall of 2005, Richard Ben-Veniste, a member of the 9/11 Commission, told a joint hearing of subcommittees of the House Committee on Homeland Security and the House Permanent Select Committee on Intelligence that "nearly all now agree that IA [Intelligence and Analysis] had not fulfilled that mandate" to be the primary intelligence shop within DHS. Among the problems was that DHS did not have a centralized, integrated database of its own intelligence. To try to remedy the situation, senior Intelligence Community official Charles Allen, who had served as National Intelligence Officer for Warning and Assistant Director of Central Intelligence for Collection, was appointed as the department's chief intelligence officer. Allen subsequently established a Homeland Security Intelligence Council (HSIC), consisting of the heads of the intelligence elements within the department.[31]

DEPARTMENT OF TREASURY INTELLIGENCE

The Department of the Treasury's intelligence apparatus is another organization that has undergone radical revision since 9/11. Prior to that time, Treasury's intelligence organization was the Office of Intelligence Support (OIS), headed by the Special Assistant to the Secretary (National Security), who reported to the Secretary and Deputy Secretary. It was established in 1977, succeeding the Office of National Security, which had been created in 1961. The office began representing the Treasury with the Intelligence Community as a result of a 1971 presidential memorandum and became a member of the National Foreign Intelligence Board in 1972.[32]

The office overtly collected foreign economic, financial, and monetary data in co-operation with the Department of State. Its three primary functions were providing intelligence related to U.S. economic policy to the Secretary of the Treasury and other Treasury officials, representing the Treasury on Intelligence Community committees and maintaining liaison with other elements of the Intelligence Community, and reviewing all proposed support relationships between the Intelligence Community and any Treasury office or bureau. As part of its participation on Intelligence Community committees and of its liaison role, the OIS developed intelligence requirements for the Treasury Department and disseminated them to the relevant intelligence agencies.[33]

Today, the Treasury Department's senior intelligence official is the Under Secretary of the Treasury for Terrorism and Financial Intelligence, who heads the Office

FIGURE 6.5   Organization of the Office of Terrorism and Financial Intelligence

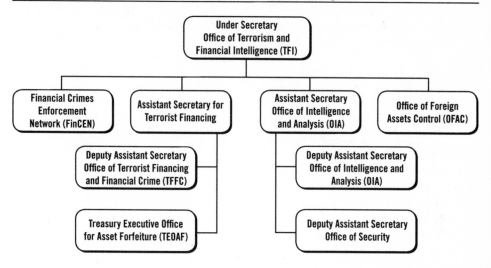

of Terrorism and Financial Intelligence (OTFI), which was created in 2004. The OTFI, according to the Treasury Department, "marshals the department's intelligence and enforcement with the twin aims of safeguarding the financial system against illicit use and combating rogue nations, terrorist facilitators, weapons of mass destruction (WMD) proliferators, money launderers, drug kingpins, and other national security threats."[34]

As shown in Figure 6.5, there are two assistant secretaries who report to the Under Secretary. One heads the Office of Intelligence and Analysis (OIA), which was established in 2004 by the *Intelligence Authorization Act for Fiscal Year 2004* to replace the OIS. OIA, rather than OTFI, is designated a formal member of the U.S. Intelligence Community and represents the Treasury Department on Intelligence Community boards and committees. The other assistant secretary is responsible for assorted control and enforcement measures related to terrorist financing.[35]

The *Intelligence Authorization Act* mandated that OIA would be responsible for the receipt, analysis, collation, and dissemination of foreign intelligence and foreign counterintelligence information related to the operation and responsibilities of the Department of the Treasury. Specifically, OIA's mission is to provide "analysis and intelligence production on financial and other support networks for terrorist groups, proliferators, and other key national security threats," as well as intelligence support on economic, political, and security issues. It is also responsible for coordinating intelligence analysis within the Treasury Department.[36]

In June 2005, the nominee for the position of Assistant Secretary for Intelligence and Analysis explained that the office was "divided up organizationally in terms of both al-Qa'ida and its affiliates, Iraq, Syria, Iran. We have transnational threats. We have East Asia and Central Eurasia."[37]

The Assistant Secretary (Terrorist Financing) supervises the Office of Terrorist Financing and Financial Crime as well as the Executive Office for Asset Forfeiture. Two other offices—the Office of Foreign Assets Control (OFAC) and the Financial Crimes Enforcement Network (FINCEN)—report to the Under Secretary and OTFI. FINCEN, which was created in April 1990, is, according to its strategic plan, the "nation's financial intelligence unit" and is responsible for "managing, analyzing, safeguarding, and appropriately sharing financial transaction information collected under the Bank Secrecy Act."[38] In the aftermath of the September 11 terrorist attacks, the Treasury Department developed the Terrorist Finance Tracking Program "to identify, track, and pursue suspected foreign terrorists . . . and their financial supporters." As part of the program, the Office of Foreign Assets Control has issued subpoenas to financial institutions to provide records on international financial transactions. One of these institutions was the Belgian-based Society for Worldwide Interbank Financial Telecommunication (SWIFT), which has offices in the United States and operates an international messaging system used to transmit bank transaction information.[39]

FEDERAL BUREAU OF INVESTIGATION

The responsibilities of the Federal Bureau of Investigation (FBI) are predominantly in the areas of criminal law enforcement, domestic counterterrorism, and domestic counterintelligence.

The FBI was one of the organizations whose internal structure was significantly affected by the events of September 11, 2001. In the investigation that followed the terrorist attacks, it was found that FBI headquarters had not followed up on warnings from the Minneapolis and Phoenix field offices that might have uncovered the 9/11 plot. Even prior to the attacks there had existed long-standing concerns about the effectiveness of an organization whose culture was far more rooted in law enforcement and the prompt arrest of criminals than in the patient monitoring of spies and terrorists. In the wake of 9/11 there were calls not only for the reorganization of the FBI's national security efforts but for the creation of an entirely new agency for counterterrorism and counterintelligence—an agency along the lines of the British Security Service, the Australian Security Intelligence Organization, and the Canadian Security Intelligence Service.[40]

A less radical alternative was recommended by the National Commission on Terrorist Attacks Upon the United States, which was concerned that creating a new domestic intelligence agency would divert the attention of officials responsible for counterterrorism efforts at a time when the threat remained high. Instead, the commission suggested that "a specialized and integrated national security workforce should be established at the FBI consisting of agents, analysts, linguists, and surveillance specialists who are recruited, trained, rewarded, and retained to ensure the development of an institutional culture imbued with a deep expertise in intelligence and national security."[41]

The following spring, in March 2005, the Commission on the Intelligence Capabilities of the United States Regarding Weapons of Mass Destruction recommended the creation of a new National Security Service within the FBI under a single Executive Assistant Director to ensure that the FBI's intelligence elements were responsive to the Director of National Intelligence and "to capitalize on the FBI's progress." The commission also recommended that the new service include the FBI's counterterrorism and counterintelligence divisions and its Directorate of Intelligence. The Directorate of Intelligence had originally been established as the Office of Intelligence in the wake of 9/11 to implement FBI intelligence strategies and to supervise FBI intelligence collection, sharing, analyst recruitment, and training. Later, the *Intelligence Reform and Terrorist Prevention Act of 2004* directed that the Office of Intelligence become the Directorate of Intelligence and awarded its director the responsibility for the "supervision of all national intelligence program projects and activities in the Bureau."[42]

On June 29, 2005, in a memorandum to several officials with national security responsibilities, including the Attorney General, President George W. Bush ordered the creation of such a service—one that would "combine the missions, capabilities, and resources of the counterterrorism, counterintelligence, and intelligence elements of the FBI. . . ." The memo also drew from the language of the 9/11 Commission report, directing the Attorney General to "establish programs to build an FBI National Security Service workforce. . . ."[43]

In response, on September 12, 2005, the FBI officially established a National Security Branch (NSB), headed by an Executive Assistant Director responsible for the counterterrorism and counterintelligence divisions as well as the Directorate of Intelligence. The directorate, which is responsible for all FBI intelligence functions, operates via FBI headquarters, and each field division operates through Field Intelligence Groups (FIGs). On July 26, 2006, a Weapons of Mass Destruction (WMD) Directorate was added to the NSB, one of a number of changes to the FBI organization. According to FBI Director Robert Muller, the new directorate would "study the consequences of a WMD attack, increase our level of preparedness, and coordinate the Government's response in the event of a WMD attack." In 2007, the bureau reorganized the Counterterrorism Division by merging its two international terrorism units—the one for al-Qaeda and the one for more established groups such as Hezbollah—and began to funnel raw intelligence and threat information through desk officers who were experts on specific world regions and terrorist groups.[44]

In addition to the four directorates, the NSB also includes the Terrorist Screening Center. The center's mission is to consolidate the federal government's approach to terrorist screening and create a single comprehensive watchlist of known or suspected terrorists. It is also responsible for ensuring that local, state, and federal screeners "have ready access to information and expertise."[45]

The organizational structure of the NSB is shown in Figure 6.6.

FIGURE 6.6   Organization of the FBI National Security Branch

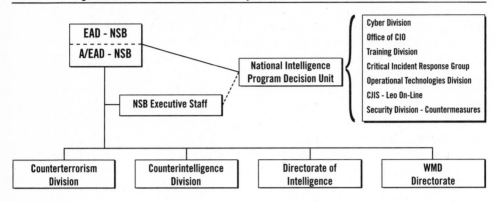

In 1939, President Franklin D. Roosevelt gave the FBI responsibility for the collection of intelligence in the Western Hemisphere and created a Special Intelligence Service (SIS) for this function. The SIS had approximately 360 agents, mostly in Mexico, Argentina, and Brazil. Despite J. Edgar Hoover's proposal, made shortly after the end of World War II, that the SIS's mandate be extended to the rest of the world, the Bureau was stripped of its foreign intelligence role, which was assumed by the Strategic Services Unit and then the CIG and CIA.[46] The Bureau did maintain representatives as legal attachés in ten embassies as of 1970. The attachés' official function was to be a liaison with national police forces on matters of common concern and to deal with Americans who found themselves in trouble with the law. In 1970 the Bureau increased from ten to twenty the number of embassies with FBI representation and instructed agents to collect foreign intelligence, with particularly interesting intelligence being identified as HILEV (High Level) by overseas agents. Some material was distributed to high officials—for example, Henry Kissinger—outside normal channels. In the aftermath of J. Edgar Hoover's death and FBI revelations, the program was terminated, and FBI representation abroad was reduced to fifteen embassies.[47]

At least two instances of FBI attempts to engage in foreign clandestine collection have come to light. During the investigation of the murder of former Chilean Defense Minister Orlando Letelier, the FBI operated an undercover agent in Chile. The agent told the FBI that the right-wing Partia y Libertad had contracted with Chilean narcotics traffickers to murder Letelier. The FBI agent, however, turned out to be a DEA informant who had been terminated and blacklisted years earlier for deception and moral turpitude. A more successful operation involved the FBI placement of a young woman informant in one of the first groups of U.S. leftists to visit China in the 1970s.[48]

The FBI does maintain a presence overseas, in the form of legal attachés. The program has been expanding from the mid-1990s' 23 offices and 70 agents overseas.

In 1996, there were plans to add another 23 offices and 59 additional agents over the following four years. By mid-1998, new offices had been opened in Tel Aviv, Cairo, Riyadh, Buenos Aires, Pretoria, Tallinn, Warsaw, and Kiev, with others in the planning stage or under consideration. The expansion was intended to permit closer liaison with foreign counterpart organizations, with respect to the investigation of international terrorism, narcotics trafficking, and organized crime.[49]

In March 2004, the FBI maintained "LEGAT" offices in 46 countries, staffed by about 119 special agents and 75 support personnel. In October 2007, it had 60 fully operational LEGAT offices and 15 sub-offices, with 165 agents and 103 support personnel. As of August 2010 the program, which was under the purview of the bureau's Office of International Operations and LEGATs, remained at 60 offices. The investigative priorities of these offices "mirror those of the FBI as a whole," according to a Department of Justice audit. Tier One for the Bureau and the attaché offices includes "foreign intelligence, terrorist, and criminal activities that directly threaten the national or economic security of the United States."[50]

Table 6.1 lists the location of the offices and their areas of responsibility.

Even when those offices were not authorized to gather foreign intelligence, the FBI has been involved in domestic activities that generate foreign intelligence. Executive Order 12333 allows the FBI to "conduct within the United States, when requested by the officials of the intelligence community designated by the President, activities undertaken to collect foreign intelligence or support foreign intelligence collection requirements of other agencies within the intelligence community."[51]

Thus, in September 1980, two FBI officials were briefed by the Joint Staff on intelligence requirements in support of a possible second attempt to rescue U.S. hostages in Iran. One of the officials was the Deputy Assistant Director for Intelligence, who was responsible for coordinating the use of non-U.S. persons in the United States for intelligence purposes. The Joint Staff asked FBI officials for their assistance in developing information relevant to the rescue mission, instructing them to "seek any potential Iranian leads that they may spot for exploitation in the conduct of their programs."[52]

In 2009, FBI agents investigating a domestic case learned of plans to attack targets in India and Pakistan, mostly at locations frequented by Americans, Israelis, and other Westerners, including hotels and synagogues. India's National Defense College and other government buildings were also scouted as possible targets.[53]

In the past, FBI foreign intelligence–related activities have also included wiretapping and break-ins. The FBI has operated wiretaps against numerous foreign embassies in Washington. FBI agents regularly monitored the phones in the offices of all communist governments represented in Washington. The phones in the offices of noncommunist governments were also tapped, especially when those nations were engaged in negotiations with the United States or when significant developments were taking place in those countries. At one point, the FBI tapped the phones of an ally's trade mission in San Francisco. In addition, the FBI has conducted break-ins at foreign embassies to obtain cryptanalytic material and other foreign intelligence.[54]

TABLE 6.1   Main Legal Attaché Offices and Areas of Responsibility

Location	Area of Responsibility
Abu Dhabi, UAE	Oman, United Arab Emirates
Amman, Jordan	Jordan, Lebanon, Syria
Baghdad, Iraq	Iraq
Doha, Qatar	Qatar
Islamabad, Pakistan	Pakistan
Kabul, Afghanistan	Afghanistan
Riydah, Saudi Arabia	Bahrain, Kuwait, and Saudi Arabia
Sanaa, Yemen	Djibouti, Eritrea, Ethiopia, Yemen
Tel Aviv, Israel	Israel, Palestinian National Authority
Berlin, Germany	Germany
Bern, Switzerland	Liechtenstein, Switzerland
Brussels, Belgium	Belgium, Luxembourg, The Netherlands, US Mission to European Union, US Mission to NATO and Europol
Copenhagen, Denmark	Denmark, Finland, Greenland, Iceland, Norway, Sweden
London, England	United Kingdom, Republic of Ireland, Channel Islands
Madrid, Spain	Andorra, Gibraltar, Portugal, Spain
Paris, France	France, Monaco
Rome Italy	Italy, Malta
Vienna, Austria	Austria, Hungary, Slovenia
Astana, Kazakhstan	Kazakhstan, Kyrgyzstan, Tajikistan, Turkmenistan, Uzbekistan
Ankara, Turkey	Turkey
Athens, Greece	Greece, Cyprus
Bucharest, Romania	Hungary, Moldova, Romania
Kyiv, Ukraine	Belarus, Ukraine
Moscow, Russia	Russia
Prague, Czech Republic	Czech Republic, Slovakia
Sarajevo, Bosnia-Herzegovina	Bosnia-Herzegovina, Croatia, Serbia, Montenegro, Kosovo
Sofia, Bulgaria	Albania, Bulgaria, Macedonia
Tallinn, Estonia	Estonia, Latvia, Lithuania
Tbilisi, Georgia	Armenia, Azerbaijan, Georgia
Warsaw, Poland	Poland
Bangkok, Thailand	Burma, Laos, Thailand
Beijing, China	Mongolia, People's Republic of China
Canberra, Australia	Australia, New Zealand, and South Pacific islands

Location	Area of Responsibility
Hong Kong, China	Hong Kong, Macau, Taiwan
Jakarta, Indonesia	Indonesia, Timor Leste (East Timor)
Kuala Lumpur, Malaysia	Malaysia
Manila, Philippines	Philippines
New Delhi, India	India
Phnom Penh, Cambodia	Cambodia, Vietnam
Seoul, South Korea	Republic of Korea
Singapore, Singapore	Brunei, Diego Garcia, Singapore
Tokyo, Japan	Japan
Cairo, Egypt	Egypt, Libya, Sudan
Dakar, Sengal	Burkino Faso, Cape Verde, Central African Republic, Cote D'Ivoire, Democratic Republic of Congo, Gabon, Gambia, Guinea, Guinea Bissau, Republic of Congo, Senegal
Freetown, Sierra Leone	Liberia, Sierra Leone
Lagos, Nigeria	Benin, Cameroon, Equatorial Guinea, Ghana, Nigeria, Sao Tomé and Principe, Togo
Nairobi, Kenya	Burundi, Kenya, Rwanda, Somalia, Tanzania, Uganda
Pretoria, South Africa	Botswana, Angola, Comoros, Lesotho, Madagascar, Malawi, Mayotte, Mauritius, Mozambique, Namibia, Reunion Islands, Seychelles, South Africa, Swaziland, Zambia, Zimbabwe
Rabat, Morocco	Chad, Mali, Mauritania, Morocco/Western Sahara, Niger, Tunisia
Bogota, Colombia	Colombia, Ecuador
Brasilia, Brazil	Brazil
Bridgetown, Barbados	Caribbean Islands
Buenos Aires, Argentina	Argentina, Paraguay, Uruguay
Caracas, Venezuela	French Guiana, Guyana, Suriname, Trinidad, Tobago, Venezuela
Mexico City, Mexico	Mexico
Ottawa, Canada	Canada
Panama City, Panama	Panama, Costa Rica, Nicaragua
Santiago, Chile	Bolivia, Chile, Peru
Santo Domingo, Dominican Republic	Dominican Republic, Haiti, Jamaica
San Salvador, El Salvador	Belize, El Salvador, Guatemala, Honduras

DRUG ENFORCEMENT ADMINISTRATION INTELLIGENCE

The Drug Enforcement Administration (DEA)—which, like the Federal Bureau of Investigation (FBI), is part of the Department of Justice—operates in the United States and abroad. It has 5,235 special agents, a budget of more than $2.3 billion, 87 offices in 63 countries, and about 680 analysts around the world. DEA intelligence operations are the responsibility of the Chief of Intelligence, who heads the DEA Intelligence Division.[55] The division is responsible for

- providing technical and operational intelligence products and services that identify the structure and members of international and domestic drug trafficking organizations and exploitable areas for enforcement operations;
- preparing strategic intelligence assessments, estimates, and probes focusing on trafficking patterns, source country production, and domestic production and consumption trends;
- developing intelligence that focuses on the financial aspects of drug investigations such as money-laundering techniques, drug-related asset discovery and forfeiture, and macroeconomic impact assessments of the illegal drug trade;
- providing interagency intelligence support to other federal, state, and local law enforcement organizations and a variety of state and foreign drug intelligence clearinghouses and participating in the National Narcotics Interdiction System.[56]

As Figure 6.7 illustrates, the DEA Intelligence Division consists of five offices and two centers. The Office of National Security Intelligence (ONSI), part of the Office of Strategic Intelligence, was established in early 2006, as a result of the desire of DEA's leadership to have the DEA "rejoin" the Intelligence Community, an idea that had been proposed by individuals in Congress, the Intelligence Community, academia, and the executive branch. Except for a brief time between the executive orders signed by President Jimmy Carter and President Ronald Reagan, DEA intelligence was not formally considered part of the Intelligence Community. With the signing of Executive Order 12333 by President Reagan in 1981, DEA remained on the law enforcement side of the imaginary wall between intelligence and law enforcement. A February 2006 memorandum signed by the DNI and Attorney General designated ONSI as a member of the Intelligence Community.[57]

ONSI is responsible for providing drug-related information relevant to Intelligence Community requirements. The office is responsible for establishing and managing a centralized tasking system of requests and for analyzing national security information obtained in the course of DEA's drug enforcement activities. ONSI also manages requests from the Intelligence Community for information either held by DEA or obtained for the community through existing DEA assets operating pursuant to the DEA's law enforcement missions.[58]

The relationship between DEA and the Intelligence Community and the rationale for establishing ONSI have been explained as follows:

FIGURE 6.7   Organization of the DEA Intelligence Division

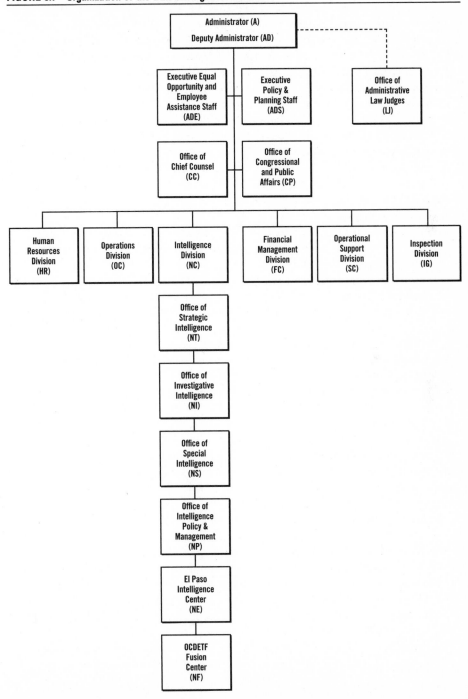

The DEA and the IC have a history of partnering for purposes of identifying and disrupting illegal drug trafficking. This partnership has been successful in facilitating the exchange of vital information and the leveraging of expertise. [ONSI's] membership in the Community helps optimize the overall US government counter-narcotics interdiction and security effort and furthers creative collaboration between the many organizations involved in countering the threats from narcotics trafficking, human smuggling/trafficking, immigration crimes, and global terrorism.

It is at the nexus of these transnational threats that some of the most serious threats to national security exist. Having DEA as a member of the IC permits greater exploitation of its intelligence capabilities against . . . transnational targets.[59]

In its 2010 Congressional Budget submission, the DEA requested $758,000 in support of Special Field Intelligence Programs (SFIPs) to respond to National Foreign Intelligence priorities, explaining that "part of DEA's Office of National Security Intelligence . . . mission is to proactively provide reports of foreign intelligence value to the Intelligence Community." The submission further elaborated, stating that the SFIPs are intended to "achieve results such as

- Identifying emerging drug trafficking organizations and their modus operandi.
- Determin[ing] relationships of the drug trade or drug trafficking organizations with terrorists or other insurgent groups to include human smuggling organizations.
- Identify[ing] all aspects of money laundering, including bulk cash movement and the use of drug proceeds.
- Determin[ing] if illicit drugs are financing terrorist or insurgent activities.
- Develop[ing] Cooperating Individuals (CIs) to satisfy requirements levied on DEA field offices to collect information as requested by DEA Headquarters."[60]

The Office of Strategic Intelligence produces strategic intelligence assessments, studies, reports, and estimates from both foreign and domestic sources. It assesses the drug situation in Europe, Asia and Africa, and Latin America, including drug production capability and activity, transportation systems, makeup of trafficking groups, effectiveness of traffic interdiction, and local political attitudes regarding drug trafficking.[61]

The Office of Investigative Intelligence is responsible for planning, organizing, coordinating, and implementing the DEA's investigative intelligence programs. The cocaine and heroin investigative units of the office's Investigative Intelligence Section are responsible for identifying major traffickers and organizations engaged in cultivation, production, transportation, and distribution as well as in the laundering of drug proceeds.[62]

The El Paso Intelligence Center (EPIC) was established in 1974 as the result of a Department of Justice study, which focused on drug and border enforcement strategies and programs and proposed the creation of a Southwest Border intelligence service to be staffed by representatives of the Immigration and Naturalization Service, the U.S. Customs Service, and DEA. Today, EPIC still concentrates primarily on drug movement and immigration violations, although its geographic area of responsibility has expanded to include all of the Western Hemisphere "where drug and alien movements are directed toward the United States." EPIC coordinates a staff of more than 300 analysts, agents, and support personnel from fifteen federal agencies, the Texas Department of Public Safety, and the Texas Air National Guard.[63]

Notes

1. U.S. Congress, Senate Select Committee to Study Governmental Operations with Respect to Intelligence Activities, *Final Report, Book VI: Supplementary Reports on Intelligence Activities* (Washington, D.C.: U.S. Government Printing Office, 1976), pp. 271–276; "DC&P—Bureau of Intelligence and Research," www.state.gov/documents/organizations/123571.pdf, accessed August 11, 2010.

2. U.S. Congress, House Committee on Foreign Affairs, *The Role of Intelligence in the Foreign Policy Process* (Washington, D.C.: U.S. Government Printing Office, 1980), p. 57; "State INR and Its Role in the Intelligence Community," summary of presentation by Dr. Thomas Fingar on April 6, 2005, at MIT Security Studies Seminar, http://www.mit.edu.

3. *INR* (Washington, D.C.: Department of State, n.d.), pp. 2, 4; Philip S. Goldberg, "Prehearing Questions for Ambassador Philip S. Goldberg upon His Nomination to Be Assistant Secretary, Bureau of Intelligence & Research, Department of State," 2009, p. 3, available at www.senate.gov/intelligence.

4. "DC&P—Bureau of Intelligence and Research."

5. *INR*, pp. 9–10; *United States Department of State Telephone Directory*, www.state.gov, accessed March 22, 2010, pp. OD-30 to OD-31; Department of State, "Bureau of Intelligence and Research (INR) Organization Chart," September 22, 2006.

6. *INR*, p. 10; U.S. Congress, House Committee on Appropriations, *Departments of Commerce, Justice and State, the Judiciary and Related Agencies Appropriations for FY 1987, Part 6* (Washington, D.C.; U.S. Government Printing Office, 1986), p. 351; *United States Department of State Telephone Directory*, pp. OD-30 to OD-31; Department of State, "Bureau of Intelligence and Research (INR) Organization Chart."

7. Department of State, "Bureau of Intelligence and Research (INR) Organization Chart"; *United States Department of State Telephone Directory*, pp. OD-30 to OD-31.

8. *INR* (Washington, D.C.: Department of State, 1983), pp. 12–13; U.S. Congress, House Committee on Appropriations, *Departments of Commerce, Justice and State, the Judiciary and Related Agencies Appropriations for FY 1987, Part 6*, p. 351; *INR*, p. 4; United States Department of State, *Foreign Affairs Manual 1—Organization and Function*, 1999, Section 430, pp. 3–4.

9. *INR* (1983), pp. 12–13; *INR*, p. 10.

10. *United States Department of State Telephone Directory*, pp. OD-30 to OD-31; Goldberg, "Prehearing Questions for Ambassador Philip S. Goldberg upon His Nomination to Be Assistant Secretary, Bureau of Intelligence & Research, Department of State," pp. 9–11.

11. *INR*, pp. 8–9; Jeffrey T. Richelson, "Out of the Black: The Disclosure and Declassification of the National Reconnaissance Office," *International Journal of Intelligence and Counterintelligence* 11, 1 (Spring 1988): 1–25; *United States Department of State Telephone Directory*,

pp. OD-30 to OD-31; United States Department of State, *Foreign Affairs Manual Volume 1—Organization and Functions*, 1999, Section 430, p. 6.

12. Statement by Robert W. Daniel Jr., Director, Office of Intelligence, Department of Energy, in U.S. Congress, House Committee on Appropriations, *Energy and Water Development Appropriations for 1992, Part 6* (Washington, D.C.: U.S. Government Printing Office, 1991), pp. 819–836 at p. 820.

13. Ibid.; "Watkins Reorganizes DOE's Intelligence Work," *Washington Post*, April 18, 1990, p. A25; U.S. Congress, Senate Committee on Armed Services, *Department of Defense Authorization for Appropriations for Fiscal Years 1992 and 1993, Part 1* (Washington, D.C.: U.S. Government Printing Office, 1991), p. 657; Department of Energy, *National Telephone Directory* (Washington, D.C.: U.S. Government Printing Office, 1994), p. 46.

14. "Secretary Peña Strengthens DOE Intelligence Programs," *DOE News*, February 10, 1998; Department of Energy Chart, "Office of Intelligence and Counterintelligence," July 28, 2006; Alfred Cumming, Congressional Research Service, *Intelligence Reform at the Department of Energy: Policy Issues and Organizational Alternatives*, September 25, 2009, p. 2; President's Foreign Intelligence Advisory Board, *Science at Its Best/Security at Its Worst*, June 1999; John A. Russack, Director, Office of Intelligence to Hon. Laurence H. Silberman, n.d., w/enclosure: Question for the Record, Commission on the Intelligence Capabilities of the United States Regarding Weapons of Mass Destruction.

15. U.S. Congress, Senate Committee on Armed Services, *Department of Defense Authorization for Fiscal Years 1992 and 1993, Part 1* (Washington, D.C.: U.S. Government Printing Office, 1991), p. 657; Daniel, in U.S. Congress, House Committee on Appropriations, *Energy and Water Development Appropriations for 1992, Part 6*, p. 823; Statement of Robert W. Daniel Jr., Director, Office of Intelligence, Department of Energy, in U.S. Congress, House Committee on Appropriations, *Energy and Water Appropriations for 1993, Part 6* (Washington, D.C.: U.S. Government Printing Office, 1992), p. 2081.

16. Daniel, in U.S. Congress, House Committee on Appropriations, *Energy and Water Development Appropriations for 1992, Part 6*, p. 823; Daniel, in U.S. Congress, House Committee on Appropriations, *Energy and Water Development Appropriations for 1993, Part 6*, p. 2195.

17. U.S. Congress, House Committee on Appropriations, *Energy and Water Development Hearings for 1997, Part 4* (Washington, D.C.: U.S. Government Printing Office, 1996), p. 441; Department of Energy, Office of Intelligence, Office of Counterintelligence, *Statistical Analysis of Foreign Visits to DOE Facilities*, September 1993; Department of Energy, Office of Intelligence, Office of Counterintelligence, *Information Brokers*, August 1994; Department of Energy, Office of Counterintelligence, OCI Bulletin Number 93–007, "Targeting of DOE Travelers," 1993.

18. "Nevada Intelligence Center Awarded for Training Program," *Site Lines* 120 (October 2006): 1–2; Department of Energy, *National Nuclear Security Administration, Functions, Responsibilities, and Authorities Manual*, February 3, 2004, pp. II-16 through II-17; Frederick T. Martin To: ICAHST Council Members, Subject: Feedback from 14 April 2009 ICAHST Meeting, April 15, 2009.

19. Lawrence Livermore National Laboratory, "Nonproliferation, Arms Control, and International Security," n.d.; Lawrence Livermore National Laboratory, "Nonproliferation, Homeland and International Security," http://www.llnl.gov/llnl/organization/nai.jsp, accessed August 7, 2006; W. F. Raborn, Director of Central Intelligence, and Glenn T. Seaborg, Chairman, Atomic Energy Commission, "Memorandum of Understanding Between the Atomic

Energy Commission and the Central Intelligence Agency Concerning Work to Be Performed at the Lawrence Radiation Laboratory," August 3, 1965; "Jobs at LLNL," http:/jobs.llnl.gov, accessed May 23, 2006; Stephen Wampler, "NAI Realigns to Changing Security Environment," *LLNL Newsline*, March 31, 2006, p. 2; "Z Program," https://www-gs.llnl.gov/zprogram.html, accessed March 24, 2010.

20. U.S. Congress, House Committee on Armed Services, *Department of Energy: National Security and Military Applications of Nuclear Energy Authorization Act of 1984* (Washington, D.C.: U.S. Government Printing Office, 1983), p. 394.

21. Michael R. Anastasio, "Establishment of the Department of Homeland Security," Statement Before the U.S. Senate Energy and Natural Resources Committee, July 10, 2002, p. 8.

22. "National Security Directorate," www.pnl.gov, accessed August 12, 2010; "Global Security Directorate Organization Chart," www.lanl.gov, accessed August 12, 2010.

23. Department of Homeland Security, *Securing Our Homeland: U.S. Department of Homeland Security Strategic Plan,* 2004, p. 6; "History: Who Will Become Part of the Department?," http://www.dhs.gov, accessed August 9, 2006; "Department of Homeland Security Organization Chart," November 7, 2005.

24. President George W. Bush, The White House, *The Department of Homeland Security,* 2002, pp. 3, 14–15.

25. *Statement of Bart R. Johnson, Acting Under Secretary for Intelligence and Analysis, Before the Subcommittee on Intelligence, Information Sharing, and Terrorism Risk Assessment, Committee on Homeland Security, U.S. House of Representatives,* September 24, 2009, p. 8.

26. *Testimony of Under Secretary Caryn Wagner Before the House Subcommittee on Homeland Security on the President's Fiscal Year 2011 Budget Request for the Department's Office of Intelligence Analysis,* March 4, 2010, pp. 3–4, www.dhs.gov.

27. "Office of Intelligence and Analysis (I&A) Organization Chart"; Department of Homeland Security, *"Preserve, Protect, Secure,"* March 2006, p. 8; Department of Homeland Security, Office of Information Analysis, *Priority Intelligence/Information Requirements, January 2005–July 2005,* January 7, 2005; William Arkin, "The Department of Homeland Security's Unlimited Priorities," *Early Warning Blog,* http://www.washingtonpostcom, July 13, 2006; "Prepared Statement of Charles E. Allen," U.S. Congress, House Committee on Homeland Security, *A Report Card on Homeland Security Information Sharing* (Washington, D.C.: U.S. Government Printing Office, 2009), pp. 49–57 at p. 56.

28. "Office of Intelligence and Analysis (I&A) Organization Chart."

29. Ibid.; *Testimony of Under Secretary Caryn Wagner Before the House Subcommittee on Homeland Security on the President's Fiscal Year 2011 Budget Request for the Department's Office of Intelligence Analysis,* pp. 2, 5.

30. U.S. Congress, Senate Select Committee on Intelligence, *Prehearing Questions for Caryn Wagner upon Nomination to Be Under Secretary for Intelligence and Analysis, Department of Homeland Security,* March 2010, p. 18.

31. Richard Ben-Veniste, "Intelligence and Information Analysis Within the Department of Homeland Security," Statement Before the Subcommittee on Intelligence, Information Sharing, and Terrorism Risk Assessment, House Committee on Homeland Security and the Subcommittee on Terrorism, Human Intelligence, Analysis, and Counterintelligence, House Permanent Select Committee on Intelligence, October 19, 2005; "Share the Wealth," *Aviation Week & Space Technology,* October 24, 2005, p. 23; "Allen Leaves CIA to Lead Homeland Security Intelligence Shakeup," http://www.bloomberg.com, March 15, 2006; "Allen: Chief

Intelligence Officer," http://www.washingtonpost.com, January 11, 2006; Jeff Stein, "Allen's Wrench at Work on Homeland Security," http://www.cqcom, November 23, 2005; Robert Block, "Homeland Security Attracts More Scrutiny," *Wall Street Journal*, February 5, 2007, p. A7; Eric Lipton, "C.I.A. Veteran Races Time to Rescue Fledgling Agency," *New York Times*, February 10, 2007, p. A16; Office of the Director of National Intelligence, *An Overview of the United States Intelligence Community*, 2007, p. 11.

32. Office of the Director of Central Intelligence, "Treasury Department—Office of Intelligence Support," n.d.

33. Ronald Reagan, "Executive Order 12333: United States Intelligence Activities," December 4, 1981, in *Federal Register* 46, no. 235 (December 8, 1981): 59941–59954 at 59946; "Foreign Intelligence—It's More Than the CIA," *U.S. News and World Report*, May 1, 1981, pp. 35–37; Department of the Treasury Order 100–3, "Functions of the Executive Secretariat," January 13, 1987, p. 2; Department of the Treasury, "Office of Intelligence Support," 1997.

34. Department of the Treasury, "Terrorism and Financial Intelligence," www.ustreasgov/offices/enforcements, accessed March 24, 2010. Also see U.S. Treasury, "Under Secretary for Terrorism and Financial Intelligence Stuart Levey, Testimony Before Senate Committee on Finance," April 1, 2008.

35. "Department of the Treasury: Office of Intelligence and Analysis," www.intelligence.gov/1-members_treasury.shtml, accessed February 12, 2006; U.S. Congress, Senate Select Committee on Intelligence, *Nomination of Janice B. Gardner to Be Assistant Secretary of the Treasury for Intelligence and Analysis* (Washington, D.C.: U.S. Government Printing Office, 2006), p. 1; Office of the Director of National Intelligence, *An Overview of the United States Intelligence Community*, p. 13.

36. "Department of the Treasury: Office of Intelligence Analysis"; U.S. Congress, Senate Select Committee on Intelligence, *Nomination of Janice B. Gardner to Be Assistant Secretary of the Treasury for Intelligence and Analysis*, p. 4.

37. U.S. Congress, Senate Select Committee on Intelligence, *Nomination of Janice B. Gardner to Be Assistant Secretary of the Treasury for Intelligence and Analysis*, p. 13.

38. Ibid.; Financial Crimes Enforcement Network, *Strategic Plan FY 2006–2008: Safeguarding the Financial System from the Abuse of Financial Crime*, February 2005, p. 3, http://www.ustreas.gov.

39. Department of the Treasury, "Terrorist Finance Tracking Program Fact Sheet," June 23, 2006, http://www.treasury.gov; Barton Gellman, Paul Blustein, and Dafna Linzer, "Bank Records Secretly Tapped," http://www.washingtonpost.com, June 23, 2006. Also see Eric Lichtblau and James Risen, "Bank Data Sifted in Secret by U.S. to Block Terror," *New York Times*, June 23, 2006, pp. A1, A10; Glenn R. Simpson, "Treasury Tracks Financial Data in Secret Program," *Wall Street Journal*, June 23, 2006, pp. A1, A2; Josh Meyer and Greg Miller, "U.S. Secretly Tracks Global Bank Data," *Los Angeles Times*, June 23, 2006, pp. A1, A18–A19; Greg Miller, "Officials Defend Bank Data Tracking," *Los Angeles Times*, June 24, 2006, pp. A1, A12; Karen DeYoung, "Officials Defend Financial Searches," http://www.washingtonpost.com, June 24, 2006; Jennifer K. Elsea and M. Maureen Murphy, Congressional Research Service, *Treasury's Terrorist Finance Program's Access to Information Held by the Society for Worldwide Interbank Financial Telecommunication (SWIFT)*, July 7, 2006; National Commission on Terrorist Attacks Upon the United States, *Monograph on Terrorist Financing*, 2004; Kim Murphy, "Keeping an Eye on Bank Data," *Los Angeles Times*, August 24, 2006, p. A6; Martin Rudner, "Using Financial Intelligence Against the Funding of

Terrorism," *International Journal of Intelligence and Counterintelligence* 19, 1 (Spring 2006): 32–58; and Thomas Winston, "Intelligence Challenges in Tracking Terrorist Internet Fund Transfer Activities," *International Journal of Intelligence and Counterintelligence* 20, 2 (Summer 2007): 327–343.

40. National Commission on Terrorist Attacks Upon the United States, *The 9/11 Commission Report: Final Report of the National Commission on Terrorist Attacks Upon the United States* (New York: W. W. Norton, 2004); Richard A. Posner, *Uncertain Shield: The U.S. Intelligence System in the Throes of Reform* (Lanham, Md.: Rowman & Littlefield, 2006), pp. 87–140.

41. National Commission on Terrorist Attacks Upon the United States, *The 9/11 Commission Report: Final Report of the National Commission on Terrorist Attacks Upon the United States,* pp. 424–426.

42. Commission on the Intelligence Capabilities of the United States Regarding Weapons of Mass Destruction, *Report to the President* (Washington, D.C.: U.S. Government Printing Office, 2005), p. 495; Federal Bureau of Investigation, "FBI Creates Structure to Support Intelligence Mission," April 3, 2003; Alfred Cumming and Todd Masse, Congressional Research Service, *Intelligence Reform Implementation at the Federal Bureau of Investigation: Issues and Options for Congress*, August 16, 2005, p. 10.

43. President George W. Bush, Memorandum for the Vice President, Secretary of State, Secretary of Defense, Attorney General, Secretary of Homeland Security, Director of OMB, Director of National Intelligence, Assistant to the President for National Security Affairs, Assistant to the President for Homeland Security and Counterterrorism, Subject: Strengthening the Ability of the Department of Justice to Meet Challenges to the Security of the Nation, June 29, 2005.

44. Federal Bureau of Investigation, *The National Security Branch of the Federal Bureau of Investigation*, n.d.; Federal Bureau of Investigation, "FBI National Security Branch" (Organization Chart), January 9, 2006; Federal Bureau of Investigation, *National Security Branch Overview*, n.d., www.fbi.gov/hq/nsb/whitepaper.htm, accessed December 13, 2006, pp. 7–8; Office of the Director of National Intelligence, *An Overview of the United States Intelligence Community*, pp. 15–16; Federal Bureau of Investigation, "FBI Announces Restructuring," July 26, 2006, www.fbi.gov; Dan Eggen, "New FBI Division to Probe Weapons Terrorists May Use," www.washingtonpost.com, July 27, 2006; John Solomon, "FBI Reorganizes Effort to Uncover Terror Groups' Global Ties," www.washingtonpost.com, September 26, 2007; Federal Bureau of Investigation, *The National Security Branch of the Federal Bureau of Investigation: Integrating Intelligence and Operations to Protect America*, n.d., www.fbi.gov, accessed August 17, 2010.

45. Federal Bureau of Investigation, *The National Security Branch of the Federal Bureau of Investigation*, p. 3.

46. G. Gregg Webb, "The FBI and Foreign Intelligence: New Insights into J. Edgar Hoover's Role," *Studies in Intelligence* 48, 1 (Spring 2004): 45–58; Sanford J. Ungar, *The FBI* (Boston: Little, Brown, 1976), pp. 225–226, 242.

47. Ungar, *The FBI*, pp. 225–226, 242.

48. Ibid., pp. 240–241; Taylor Branch and Eugene M. Proper, *Labyrinth* (New York: Viking, 1982), pp. 231, 350, 358.

49. R. Jeffrey Smith and Thomas W. Lippman, "FBI Plans to Expand Overseas," *Washington Post*, August 20, 1996, pp. A1, A14; telephone conversation with Michael Kortan, FBI, March 27, 1998; Alan G. Ringgold, "The FBI's Legal Attaché Program," *The Investigator*, June 1997, p. 1.

50. Todd Masse and William Krouse, Congressional Research Service, *The FBI: Past, Present, and Future*, October 2, 2003, p. 46; Office of the Inspector General, Department of Justice, *Federal Bureau of Investigation Legal Attaché Program*, March 2004, pp. i, iii; Thomas V. Fuentes, Assistant Director, Office of International Operations, Federal Bureau of Investigation, "Statement Before the Subcommittee on Border, Maritime, and Global Counterterrorism House Homeland Security Committee," October 4, 2007, p. 1.

51. Reagan, "Executive Order 12333: United States Intelligence Activities," Section 1.14, Provision C, p. 59949.

52. JCS Joint Staff, Memorandum for the Record, Subject: Briefing of FBI Representatives, September 25, 1980.

53. Josh Meyer, "On U.S. Man's Tips, FBI Rushes to Avert Terror," *Los Angeles Times*, December 13, 2009, pp. A1, A28.

54. Victor Marchetti and John Marks, *The CIA and the Cult of Intelligence* (New York: Knopf, 1974), p. 204; "Mole Tunnels Under a Soviet Consulate," *Newsweek*, August 15, 1983, p. 21; Douglas Watson, "Huston Says NSA Urged Break-Ins," *Washington Post*, March 3, 1975, pp. 1, 6.

55. "Drug Enforcement Administration: Office of National Security Intelligence," http://ww.intelligence.gov/1-members_dea.shtml, accessed August 11, 2006; "Intelligence," http://www.usdoj.gov/dea/programs/intelligencep.htm, accessed February 21, 2006; "DEA History," wwwjusticegov/dea/history.htm, accessed March 24, 2010.

56. Drug Enforcement Administration, *Annual Report, Fiscal Year 1986* (Washington, D.C.: DEA, 1986), pp. 9–10.

57. "Inside the DEA, Organizational Chart," http://www.dea.gov, accessed March 24, 2010; Barry A. Zulauf, "The DEA and the IC: Back to the Future," *Naval Intelligence Professionals Quarterly* (Summer 2006): 24–26; Office of the Director of National Intelligence, ODNI News Release No. 6–06, "Drug Enforcement Administration Element Becomes 16th Intelligence Community Member," February 17, 2006, http://www.odni.gov; John D. Negroponte, "To My Intelligence Community Colleagues," February 7, 2006; John Negroponte and Alberto Gonzales (signators), "Joint Designation of an Element of the Drug Enforcement Administration Intelligence Division as a Member of the Intelligence Community," February 6, 2006.

58. "Drug Enforcement Administration: Office of National Security Intelligence."

59. Ibid.

60. Drug Enforcement Administration, *FY 2010 Performance Budget, Drug Enforcement Administration, U.S. Department of Justice—Congressional Budget Submission,* www.usdoj.gov/jmd/2010justification, accessed December 12, 2010.

61. Memorandum from Thomas A. Constantine, Administrator, to Paul V. Daly, Assistant Administrator, Intelligence Division, Subject: Reorganization of the Intelligence Division, June 7, 1996, pp. 18–19, 21–23.

62. Ibid., pp. 3–7.

63. "El Paso Intelligence Center," http://www.dea.gov/programs/epicp.htm, accessed February 21, 2006.

Central Intelligence Agency headquarters, Langley, Virginia. Photo credit: Central Intelligence Agency.

National Security Agency headquarters, Fort George G. Meade, Maryland. Photo credit: Department of Defense.

The headquarters of the National Reconnaissance Office in Chantilly, Virginia.
Photo credit: National Reconnaissance Office.

DIA's Defense Intelligence Analysis Center, Bolling Air Force Base, Washington, D.C.
Photo credit: Department of Defense.

The National Maritime Intelligence Center (NMIC) in Suitland, Maryland. The NMIC houses the Office of Naval Intelligence (which absorbed the Naval Technical Intelligence Center, Task Force 168, and the Navy Operational Intelligence Center in 1993) along with Coast Guard and Marine Corps intelligence organizations. Photo credit: U.S. Navy.

Headquarters, U.S. Army National Ground Intelligence Center (NGIC), Charlottesville, Virginia. NGIC was formed in 1995 with the merger of the Army Foreign Service and Technology Center and the Army Intelligence Threat Analysis Center. Photo credit: FSTC.

7

IMAGERY COLLECTION, PROCESSING, EXPLOITATION, AND DISSEMINATION

The modern use of overhead platforms to observe events on the ground can be traced to the French Revolution, when France organized a company of aerostiers, or balloonists, in April 1794.* One balloon is reported to have been kept in the air for nine hours while the group's commander made continuous observations during the Battle of Fleurus in Belgium.[1]

The United States made similar use of balloons during the Civil War, although little intelligence of value was obtained. By the latter part of the nineteenth century, Britain was conducting experiments using balloons as platforms from which to obtain "overhead photography." In January 1911, the San Diego waterfront became the first target of cameras carried aboard an airplane. That same year the U.S. Army Signal Corps put aerial photography into the curriculum at its flight training school. From 1913 to 1915, visual and photographic reconnaissance missions were flown by the U.S. Army in the Philippines and along the Mexican border.[2] During World War II the United States made extensive use of airplane photography using remodeled B-17 (Flying Fortress) and B-24 (Liberator) aircraft. The remodeled B-24, known as the F-7, carried six cameras internally—all triggered via remote control by an operator over the sealed rear bomb-bay doors. After the war, with the emergence of a hostile relationship with the Soviet Union, the United States began conducting photographic missions along the Soviet periphery, but the aircraft cameras could capture images of territory within only a few miles of the flight path.[3]

---

*"Geospatial intelligence"—involving not only imagery but imagery with geolocation—has replaced imagery as the counterpart discipline to SIGINT and MASINT. As indicated by the title, this chapter will focus only on the imagery component of geospatial intelligence. Processing, Exploitation (i.e., interpretation), and Dissemination represent the final three segments of what is abbreviated as TPED. The Tasking segment is discussed in the Managing Satellite Imaging section of Chapter 19.

On some missions, aircraft actually flew into Soviet airspace, but even those missions could not provide the necessary coverage of the vast Soviet interior. As a result, in the early 1950s the United States began seriously exploring more advanced methods for obtaining images of targets across the Soviet Union. The result was the development, production, and employment of a variety of aircraft and spacecraft that permitted the U.S. Intelligence Community to closely monitor developments in the Soviet Union and other nations through overhead imagery.[4]

In the years since the United States began operating such systems, their capabilities have improved in numerous ways. Satellites now have longer lifetimes, produce more detailed images, and transmit their imagery almost instantaneously (i.e., in "near-real-time"). Aircraft are also able to relay their imagery as soon as it has been obtained, and unmanned aerial vehicles are capable of providing full-motion imagery of events being monitored.

In addition, the capabilities of spacecraft and aircraft evolved from being limited to black-and-white visible-light photography to producing images using different parts of the electromagnetic spectrum, which is illustrated in Figure 7.1. As a result, imagery can often be obtained under circumstances (darkness, cloud cover) where standard visible-light photography is not feasible. In addition, employment of different portions of the electromagnetic spectrum, individually or simultaneously, has expanded the information that can be produced concerning a target. Photographic equipment can be film-based or electro-optical. A conventional camera captures a scene on film by recording the varying light levels reflected from all of the separate objects in the scene. In contrast, an electro-optical camera converts the varying light levels into electrical signals. A numerical value is assigned to each of the signals, which are called picture elements, or pixels. The process transforms a picture (analog) image to a digital image that can be transmitted electronically to distant points. The signal can then be reconstructed from the digital to the analog format. The analog signal can be displayed on a video screen or transformed into a photograph.[5]

In addition to the visible-light portion of the electromagnetic spectrum, the near-infrared portion, which is invisible to the human eye, can be employed to produce images. Near-infrared imagery, like visible-light imagery, depends on objects reflecting solar radiation rather than on their emission of radiation. As a result, such imagery can be produced only in daylight and in the absence of substantial cloud cover.[6]

Thermal infrared imagery, obtained from the mid- and far-infrared portions of the electromagnetic spectrum, provides imagery purely by detecting the heat emitted by objects. Thus, a thermal infrared system can detect buried structures, such as missile silos or underground construction, as a result of the heat they generate. Since thermal infrared imagery does not require visible light, it can be obtained under conditions of darkness—if the sky is free of cloud cover.[7]

Imagery can be obtained during day or night in the presence of cloud cover by employing an imaging radar (an acronym for radio detection and ranging). Radar imagery is produced by bouncing radio waves off an area or an object and using the reflected returns to produce an image of the target. Since radio waves are not attenu-

FIGURE 7.1   The Electromagnetic Spectrum

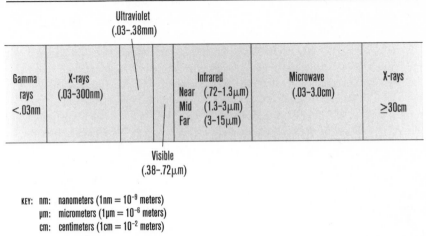

KEY: nm: nanometers (1nm = 10^{-9} meters)
     μm: micrometers (1μm = 10^{-6} meters)
     cm: centimeters (1cm = 10^{-2} meters)

SOURCE: James B. Campbell, *Introduction to Remote Sensing* (New York: Guilford), p. 24.

ated by the water vapor in the atmosphere, they are able to penetrate cloud cover.[8] Two types of imagery also important to intelligence analysts and military planners are multispectral imagery (MSI) and hyperspectral imagery (HSI). MSI is defined as "multiple discrete bands of digital electro-optical imagery collected simultaneously in different spectral regions that can be easily registered and exploited synergistically."[9] Hyperspectral imagery employs at least sixty narrow (less than 10 nm), contiguous spectral bands, including the visible light, infrared, thermal infrared, ultraviolet, and radio wave portions of the electromagnetic spectrum. The data produced by examination of those bands allow analysts to detect an object's shape, density, temperature, movement, and chemical composition.[10]

The six primary missions that hyperspectral imagery can contribute to are support to military operations; nonproliferation; counternarcotics; mapping, charting, and geodesy; technical intelligence; and civil applications. Specific applications are expected to include determination of beach composition; location of amphibious obstacles; production of hydrography and bathymetry data; battle damage assessment; support of special operations; counter-camouflage, concealment, and deception (CC&D); terrain analysis and mapping; trafficability analysis; vegetative cover and stress determination; and combat identification.[11]

COLLECTION

Space systems are the most important means employed by the U.S. Intelligence Community for producing imagery—due to the volume they can produce and the access they provide to even the most denied territories. There are three key operators of the current fleet of imaging spacecraft employed in support of U.S. national security users—the National Reconnaissance Office (NRO), commercial firms, and the Pentagon's Operationally Responsive Space (ORS) Office.

At one time, the only spacecraft producing significant imagery intelligence (for the United States) were those operated by the NRO. A variety of such spacecraft has been employed since the first successful reconnaissance satellite was launched in 1960. Some, such as the KH-8 (KEYHOLE-8), took highly detailed pictures of specific targets. In contrast, the KH-9 produced images of broader areas, allowing photo interpreters to examine a large area and select targets for closer inspection. In December 1976, the KH-8 and KH-9 systems were joined by the KH-11,* which became the sole type of intelligence imaging satellite operated by the United States between October 18, 1984 (when the last KH-9 mission concluded), and December 2, 1988.[12]

The KH-11 represented a quantum leap in imagery capabilities because, in contrast to the KH-8 and KH-9, it could return its imagery in near-real-time. That is, rather than record images on film, with film canisters being deorbited once a reel of film was fully exposed, the KH-11 was an electro-optical system. First employing light-sensitive silicone diodes and then charged couple devices (CCDs), the KH-11's optical system converted images into electronic signals that were transmitted to elliptically orbiting relay satellites and back to a ground station for near-instantaneous reconstruction.[13]

The origins of the KH-11, which was also known by the BYEMAN code names KENNAN and CRYSTAL, go back to the early days of the U.S. satellite reconnaissance program. Intelligence and defense officials had always recognized that it would be desirable, particularly for indications and warning purposes, to have imagery data returned in near-real-time. However, it was not until the late 1960s that technological developments made such a system a realistic possibility.[14] In 1969, a study conducted by the DCI's Committee on Imagery Requirements and Exploitation (COMIREX)—*Implications of Near Real Time Imagery on Intelligence Production and Processes*—examined the potential utility of a near-real-time system. The study examined how such data could have been used during the Cuban missile crisis, the Six Day War, and the Soviet invasion of Czechoslovakia. The ultimate result was a presidential decision to authorize development of the near-real-time system proposed by the Central Intelligence Agency.[15]

---

*The KH designation with respect to satellites actually referred to the *optical* system carried by the satellite, although it is often used to designate the satellite itself. NRO satellite programs have also been designated by code names—GAMBIT in the case of both the KH-7 and KH-8, and HEXAGON in the case of the KH-9. The use of KH designations was terminated in 1987 because of repeated press disclosures of those designations.

On December 19, 1976, the first KH-11, known by the numerical designation 5501,* was launched from Vandenberg Air Force Base into an orbit of 164 by 329 miles. Another four of the first-generation KH-11s were subsequently launched successfully, the last on November 17, 1982, by which time the satellite program's code name had been changed to CRYSTAL. The satellites were about 64 feet long and weighed about 30,000 pounds. Primarily as a result of employing an optical system that did not rely on a finite supply of film, KH-11 lifetimes far exceeded those of its film-return predecessors. Lifetimes of the KH-11 satellites grew from approximately 25 months for the first satellite to between 32 and 38 months for the first generation's remaining four.[16] The satellites flew lengthwise, with the axis of the optical system parallel to the earth.

The inclination of the satellites, approximately 97 degrees, meant that they flew in a sun-synchronous orbit, so that the sun angle was the same each time the satellite was over a target. In the front was a downward-looking mirror that could be flipped from side to side, allowing the area under observation to be changed from moment to moment. Two benefits resulted from that capability. One was that the menu of targets included not only areas under the spacecraft but areas to the sides and for hundreds of miles in front. In addition to expanding the Intelligence Community's ability to monitor a given target, the mirror complicated foreign denial and deception activities. In addition, it permitted the production of stereoscopic images.

In late 1978 President Carter approved an improved version of the KH-11, which was known, at least at first, as Improved KENNAN. The first of the three "IK" satellites was launched on December 1984 and was the first to carry charged couple devices in place of light-sensing diodes. The last of these three was orbited on October 26, 1987, and it remained operational for more than seven years.[17]

Today there are three or four descendants of the original KENNAN program in orbit. One or two come from the series of four satellites launched between November 1988 and December 1996. The second of these satellites—known as Improved Metric CRYSTAL—was the first to carry a thermal infrared imagery system, code-named DRAGON, permitting nighttime imagery. The satellites also carry the Improved CRYSTAL Metric System (ICMS), which places the necessary markings on returned imagery to permit full geolocation for mapping purposes. The third and fourth, which also carried the DRAGON system along with their electro-optical imaging system, were launched on December 5, 1995, and December 20, 1996—the latter into a 155-by-620-mile orbit with an inclination of 97.9 degrees. All were launched from Vandenberg Air Force Base, employing Titan IV boosters. As of mid-2006 both remained in orbit and were apparently operational, at least to some extent. In November 2008, the satellite launched in 1995 was deorbited.[18]

---

*The designation consisted of two components. The 5500 portion of the designation indicated that the satellite was a KH-11, while the 01 portion indicated it was the first KH-11 mission.

The latest generation of descendants, the Enhanced CRYSTAL System (ECS), has been referred to in press accounts and congressional testimony as the Enhanced Imaging System, or "8X"—the latter designation due to the new system's reputed ability to capture eight times as much territory, or 800 to 1,000 square miles, in an image as the previous generation of KENNAN descendants could. This enhanced capability was developed after the Persian Gulf War of 1991, when the U.S. inability to simultaneously monitor significant parts of the battlefield posed significant problems. According to a DIA official, only the enemy's "large static defense strategy allowed us to track his numbers and disposition with acceptable accuracy." The lack of broad, synoptic, or near-simultaneous coverage made it difficult to fix the table of organization of some Iraqi units, led to an overestimate of Iraqi troop numbers, and contributed to the problems NATO countries confronted in trying to completely eliminate the mobile Scuds.[19]

ECS-1 and ECS-2 were launched on October 5, 2001, and October 19, 2005, respectively—the latter into an initial 109-by-632-mile orbit, although it was reported that the perigee would be raised to 171 miles. In addition to carrying the DRAGON infrared system along with the electro-optical system, the satellites are capable of longer dwell time over targets and more rapid data transmission. A third Enhanced CRYSTAL System (ECS-3) was under construction in 2006, using spare parts, due to delays in the Future Imagery Architecture program.[20] It was launched from Vandenberg AFB into a polar orbit on a Delta IV Heavy launch vehicle on January 20, 2011.

In addition to the two generations of KENNAN descendants in orbit in 2006, there were another two types of NRO imagery satellites in orbit. One was the product of a program first designated MISTY. The first was placed into orbit by the space shuttle Atlantis, which was launched from Cape Canaveral on February 28, 1990. Contrary to initial reports, the satellite did not break up; it was located later that year by civilian space observers, orbiting with a perigee of 494 miles and an apogee of 503 miles at a 65-degree inclination. That satellite was replaced by a similar one on May 22, 1999, using a Titan IVB rocket launched from Vandenberg Air Force Base. Its orbit ranged from 434 to 558 miles above the earth, with a 63-degree inclination, similar to the first MISTY.[21]

Like the later generations of KENNAN descendants, MISTY carried both an electro-optical imaging system and the DRAGON thermal infrared imagery sensor. However, unlike those satellites, MISTY was designed to be a stealth satellite that would be difficult for foreign space surveillance systems to detect. It was also designed to yield intelligence that more easily detected satellites in predictable sun-synchronous orbits could not. The technology that MISTY employed to evade detection is not known, although it may involve one or more of the technologies described in patent applications filed over the past several decades. Those include an anti-radar screen for controlling and suppressing a satellite's radar cross section, which may make the satellite appear to be a decoy, or a satellite signature suppression shield to prevent detection altogether. A plan to purchase a new MISTY satellite, at the cost of $10.5 billion, was canceled by DNI John McConnell in 2007, so the program will produce no further imagery once the 1999 satellite expires.[22]

The third component of the U.S. space imaging fleet comprises satellites developed and deployed under a program first known as INDIGO, then as LACROSSE, and most recently as ONYX. Rather than employing an electro-optical system, they carry an imaging radar. The first two satellites that were deployed were known by the numerical designations 3101 and 3102, respectively.[23]

These satellites closed a major gap in U.S. capabilities by allowing the U.S. Intelligence Community to obtain imagery even when targets were covered by clouds. The first LACROSSE/ONYX spacecraft was launched on December 2, 1988, from the space shuttle orbiter Atlantis. A second was orbited on March 8, 1991, from Vandenberg Air Force Base on a Titan IV. The satellites operated in orbits of approximately 400 miles and at inclinations of 57 and 68 degrees, respectively. Satellite 3101 was deorbited in early 1997, and a replacement for it was scheduled to be launched in July 1997. Although a faulty control valve led to a brief postponement, it was successfully launched into orbit from Vandenberg on October 24, 1997. The fourth and fifth LACROSSE/ONYX satellites were launched on August 17, 2000, and August 21, 2005.[24]

The fourth LACROSSE/ONYX, estimated to weigh about 30,000 pounds, was launched from Vandenberg, whereas the fifth was orbited from Cape Canaveral Air Force Base in Florida. That satellite was placed in a 57-degree, 445-mile circular orbit, and it is expected to be operational until 2012. The LACROSSE/ONYX satellite that was launched in October 1997 may have been one of a new generation of radar imagery satellites with greater resolution. The fifth was reported to have a resolution of 2–3 feet, an improvement from the 3–5 feet of the first LACROSSE, which was reportedly sufficient to allow discrimination between tanks and armored personnel carriers and identification of bomb craters of 6 to 10 feet in diameter.[25]

The primary purpose envisioned for the satellite was monitoring Soviet and Warsaw Pact armor, but the LACROSSE/ONYX satellites have been very useful in a broad range of missions: providing imagery for bomb damage assessments of Navy Tomahawk missile attacks on Iraqi air defense installations in September 1996; monitoring Iraqi weapons storage sites; and tracking Iraqi troop movements, such as the dispersal of the Republican Guard when they were threatened with U.S. attack in early 1998. The satellites may also have been used to determine whether submarines operating underwater could be located and tracked via radar imagery. More recently, they may have been used in attempts to track vehicles in the mountainous terrain of Afghanistan and Pakistan, to detect attempts at camouflage, and to identify efforts at underground construction.[26]

In the past several years, U.S. imagery satellites have been used to monitor a large number of activities and facilities around the world. As indicated in Table 7.1, they have imaged various targets in Russia; nuclear facilities in Iran, Iraq, Algeria, and

TABLE 7.1 Targets of U.S. Imagery Satellites, 1990–2010

Country	Target	Year
Afghanistan	Garmabak Ghar terrorist training camp	2001
	Qandahar Surface-to-Air Missile Site	2001
	Herat Airfield	2001
Algeria	Nuclear reactor	1991
Bosnia	Air-dropped air bundles	1993
China	M-11 canisters	1995
	Fighter/refueling aircraft	1995/1996
	Nuclear test preparations	1996
	Aircraft/missile plants	1996
	IRBM Complexes	1996
Croatia	Aircraft/arms shipment	1994
Cuba	Russian Lourdes SIGINT facility	1990
	Russian freighter	1992
India	Pokaran nuclear test site	1995/1998
	Missile movements	1997
Iran	Bushehr nuclear facility	2002
	Loading activity at airport	2010
Iraq	Compliance evasion activities	1991
	Attack on Shiite dissidents	1991
	Work on CBW facilities	1992
	Scud bunkers	1992
	Presidential palaces	1994
	Reconstruction operations	1995
	Al Furat Manufacturing Facility	1998
	Abu Ghurayb presidential grounds	1999
	MEK Headquarters Complex	2000
	Basrah Petroleum Facility	2000
	BW related facility, Taji	2002
	Amiryah Serum and Vaccine Institute	2002
	Special Security Offices, Baghdad	2003
Israel	West Bank settlements	1992
	Patriot missile batteries	1992
	Ramat David/Tel Nof air bases	1992
Laos	Military/narcotics convoy	1991
Lebanon	Hizballah Janta Camp	1992
Libya	Rabat chemical weapons facility	1990/1991
	Tarhuna chemical weapons facility	1996/1997

Country	Target	Year
North Korea	Ballistic missiles	1990/1991
	Nuclear facility	1991
	Tunnel construction	1991
	Nuclear waste storage facility	1992
	Taepo-Dong IRBM Mock-ups	1994
	Artillery deployments/DMZ	1995
	Nodong mobile launchers	1996/1997
	Yongbyon nuclear facility	2003
	Kilju nuclear test tunnel	2005
	Nuclear test site	2010
Pakistan	M-11 canisters/Sargodha Air Base	1994
	M-11 production plant	1997
	Chagai Hills nuclear test site	1998
	Nuclear reactor	2010
Russia	Military exercise	1992
	Train with SA-12 canisters	1996
	Urals underground military complex	1996
	Second Urals underground military complex	1997
	Novaya Zemlya nuclear test site	1997
Rwanda	Refugee movements	1995
Serbia	Nis Airfield	1999
	Pristina Army Garrison	1999
	Belgrade Internal Security Institute	1999
	Leskovac Army Barracks & Ammo Depot	1999
Ukraine	Aircraft carrier	1996
United States	Murrah Federal Building, Oklahoma City	1996
Yugoslavia	Vinca Institute of Nuclear Science	1999

North Korea; two Libyan chemical warfare facilities during early stages of construction; Israeli–South African missile development activities; Israeli West Bank settlement construction; and drug production facilities.[27]

The targets and uses of satellite imagery can be further illustrated by some additional details:

- In 1996 a satellite image obtained while over central China showed one of five Chinese B-6D bombers that had been converted into air-refueling tankers. According to the Defense Intelligence Agency, the tankers allow Chinese planes to fly well into the South China Sea.[28]
- Satellite photos of a military complex of China's Nachang Aircraft Company showed that equipment sold to China in 1994 for civilian purposes had been diverted to military use.[29]
- In late 1995, U.S. imagery satellites detected "a flurry of activity at (India's) Pokaran test site in the Rajasthan desert," causing concern that India was planning to test a nuclear device.[30]
- The Clinton administration showed satellite images to foreign leaders to demonstrate that Iraq had been rebuilding factories that could produce chemical weapons or missiles and armored vehicles.[31]
- In late May 1992, imagery satellites were used to monitor activity at Israel's Ramat David air base, in anticipation of a possible Israeli airstrike on Hezbollah facilities. Satellites then monitored the aftermath of the Israeli strike of May 31 on the Hezbollah Janta Camp in Lebanon.[32]
- In July 1996, satellite photographs showed that North Korea was adding more powerful, longer-range artillery along the demilitarized zone (DMZ) separating the two Koreas.[33]
- Satellite photographs showed that the layout of a plant in the suburbs of Rawalpindi, Pakistan, was similar to a M-11 rocket facility in Hubei province in central China.[34]
- U.S. imagery satellites monitored Russian construction of a huge underground military complex inside Yamanatau mountain in the Ural Mountains as well as a second underground facility at the same location.[35]
- In February 1998, it was reported that recent satellite photographs showed Iraqi forces—both Republican Guard and regular army units—throughout the country were increasing their warfighting readiness within garrisons.[36]
- In October 1999, U.S. spy satellites imaged construction at a PLA missile base at Yanang, about 275 miles from Taiwan.[37]
- In May 1999, NRO satellites imaged elements of the main offensive strike force of the Indian army loading tanks, artillery, and other heavy equipment onto flatbed railcars.[38]
- In early 2001, U.S. spy satellites imaged a trainload of Chinese short-range CSS-7 ballistic missiles outside a factory in Yuanan.[39]

- In May 2002, it was reported that U.S. imaging satellites had detected that Iranian military forces had moved additional air defense missiles to the vicinity of the Bushehr nuclear reactor.[40]
- In July 2002, NRO satellites detected activity at an Iraqi factory near Taji associated with Iraq's biological weapons program.[41]
- It was reported in January 2003 that American satellites had spotted trucks at the Yongbyon nuclear facility in North Korea that appeared to be moving 8,000 nuclear fuel rods out of storage.[42]
- In April 2005, NRO satellites detected the digging of a tunnel—similar to the one used by Pakistan in its 1998 nuclear tests—in the northern Kilju region of North Korea, which was considered a possible nuclear test site.[43]
- In August 2006, a U.S. reconnaissance satellite detected the loading of crates, believed to be of C-802 anti-ship missiles, onto a Iranian transport aircraft near Tehran.[44]
- In January 2010, NRO satellites spotted wisps of steam emanating from the cooling towers of a new Pakistani nuclear reactor.[45]
- In October 2010, a U.S. spy satellite was reported to have detected "continual movements of personnel and vehicles at North Korea's main nuclear test site."[46]

Of course, U.S. imaging satellites were used extensively against targets before and during military conflicts in the Balkans, Afghanistan, and Iraq. Post-strike images obtained during the conflict in the Balkans included army garrisons, a radar facility, an explosive storage facility, a petroleum products storage facility, a communications site, a surface-to-air missile site, security headquarters, a repair base, and a highway bridge. Among the targets imaged in Iraq were presidential palaces; VIP facilities; weapons of mass destruction sites; military sites such as military headquarters, command, control, and communication sites; security and intelligence facilities; and civilian sites such as mosques and petroleum refineries.[47]

The next generation of NRO's electro-optical and radar imagery satellites was to be the Future Imagery Architecture (FIA). However, delays in the FIA schedule, which originally envisioned a process that did not include full-scale testing, impeded the discovery of problems. Furthermore, as a result of the post-9/11 Global War on Terrorism, another requirement was added: improving FIA's ability to track moving targets.[48]

However, delays in the FIA schedule, which envisioned a first launch in 2003, began even before Boeing was awarded the contract. Subsequently, FIA—particularly the electro-optical portion—was plagued with additional delays and projected substantial cost increases, possibly because of the initial attempt to develop satellites that were considerably smaller than KENNAN and its descendants while matching or surpassing their capabilities. Ultimately, Director of National Intelligence John Negroponte decided to cancel the electro-optical portion of the contract and to award Lockheed Martin a contract to build ECS-3, while leaving the radar imagery segment with Boeing. In April 2009, President Obama agreed to a plan for the next generation of electro-optical satellites that would include both the procurement of satellites by the NRO and increased use of commercial imagery.[49]

In addition to NRO imagery systems, there are systems that have been developed or are under development by military organizations to provide tactical imagery support to military forces. The Pentagon's Operationally Responsive Space Office built the ORS-1 satellite, carrying a U-2 camera adapted for space operations, to provide imagery to the Central Command. Launch is planned for 2011. The Army is paying to have a satellite, designated NanoEye, developed to provide "rapid access to imagery over a specific location and launch within hours of call-up." The satellite is being designed to operate at an altitude as low as 100 miles, although the optimal altitude would be 125 to 186 miles—from which it could produce images with 20- to 28-inch resolution.[50]

The United States has also obtained significant quantities of imagery from commercial imagery systems. In past years, the only such systems were very low-resolution systems such as LANDSAT (which did have the virtue of a multispectral imagery capability) and France's SPOT satellites, with resolutions of about 33 feet for black-and-white imagery. The most recent version of LANDSAT can produce multispectral imagery with a resolution of about 16 feet, while SPOT satellites have a resolution of 33 feet. Both were used for a variety of purposes in the 1991 Persian Gulf War, including identifying disturbances in the terrain (indicating possible passage of Iraqi forces) and detecting wet areas that might slow down an advance.[51]

However, for over a decade, fueled by government interest, a relaxation of government restrictions on the resolution of commercial satellites, and technological capability, commercial firms have been launching satellites with resolutions that can produce imagery of significant intelligence value. Digital Globe's Quickbird satellite, which was launched in October 2001, operates in a sun-synchronous 280-mile orbit and produces black-and-white images with a maximum 23-inch resolution. Its Worldview-1 satellite, launched in September 2007, provides black-and-white imagery with a 19.5 inch resolution at nadir. The company's Worldview-2 satellite, launched in October 2009, which operates in 477-mile orbit, also produces black-and-white images—with a resolution of 18 inches at nadir. Worldview-2 is able to cover over 10,000 square kilometers in a single pass and has a rapid retargeting capability.[52]

GeoEye operates three satellites that produce imagery of intelligence value. Ikonos, launched in September 1999, orbits at 422 miles and returns images with about 2.7 foot resolution. And GeoEye-1, launched in September 6, 2008, orbits at the same altitude as Ikonos and returns panochromatic images with 16-inch resolution. GeoEye-2, with a resolution of 13 inches, is scheduled for launch by late 2012.[53]

The National Geospatial-Intelligence Agency is also augmenting the product from NRO radar imaging satellites with the product of foreign commercial satellites. In December 2009 the agency awarded three contracts for commercial synthetic radar imagery data products and downlink services. The satellites involved in providing the imagery are the Italian COSMO-SkyMed satellites (three of which were launched between June 2007 and October 2008); Canada's RADARSAT-2, launched in December 2007; and the German TerraSAR-X, with accuracy of 1 meter or better. The Southern Command has also obtained radar imagery from Israel's TecSAR satellite to obtain additional intelligence on narcotics activities in South America.[54]

A different type of space system that could well be employed for reconnaissance is the Air Force Rapid Capabilities Office's unmanned X-37B space plane, which is about one-fourth the size of the space shuttle. Launched on April 22, 2010, it returned to Earth on December 3, after circling the planet for 225 days in a test run. All details of the mission were classified, but it is capable of carrying a payload of hundreds of pounds, which certainly might include imagery or other intelligence collection sensors in the future. A second vehicle was launched in early March 2011.[55]

Aside from the use of satellites, the United States employs a variety of aerial reconnaissance systems—manned and unmanned—to obtain overhead imagery. Aerial systems can supplement the coverage of satellites, provide a quick reaction capability, and produce imagery that can be more widely distributed than satellite imagery under present security policy. In addition, aircraft can fly a route that focuses on a particular region or track, whereas satellite coverage is limited to the territory rotating under the satellite's orbit.

The most important aerial system employed to collect imagery is the U-2. The CIA and Lockheed began development of the aircraft in 1954, with the support of the Eisenhower administration's Technological Capabilities Panel. The aircraft became operational in 1956 and began overflying the Soviet Union in July of that year. The U-2 proceeded to return significant imagery of airfields, missile testing and training facilities, nuclear weapons storage sites, submarine production, and atomic facilities. Overflights of the Soviet Union ended after a U-2 was shot down on May 1, 1960, over the Soviet Union.[56]

Even in the 1950s, the U-2 was employed against a variety of other targets. A U-2 mission was flown over Israel, Egypt, Jordan, Lebanon, and Syria in August 1956, and later in the decade, a U-2 detected the site in the Negev Desert where Israel's nuclear weapons production facility was under construction. In subsequent years, U-2s flew missions over, or along the borders of, Nicaragua, Cuba, the People's Republic of China, North Vietnam, North Korea, and Iraq. In the 1980s, U-2s regularly took pictures of military construction and arms depots in Nicaragua in order to document the buildup of forces there. During Operations Desert Shield and Desert Storm, U-2s flew more than 800 missions over the Persian Gulf region, enabling U.S. personnel to track Iraqi troop and armor buildups, assess bomb damage, survey Iraq for nuclear, chemical, and biological weapons sites, and monitor a massive Persian Gulf oil spill. On two occasions, U-2s provided warning of incoming Scud missiles. In 2009, U-2s flew more than 300 missions over Iraq and almost 600 flights over Afghanistan. In January 2010, a U-2 collected wide-area images of the damage from the earthquake in Haiti.[57]

Today, there are thirty-three U-2s (including five two-seat trainers and two ER-2s operated by NASA). In 1992, all U-2s were designated as U-2Rs—both the planes originally produced under the TR-1 designation and the U-2Rs that began flying in

1967. Upgrades to the airframe, sensors, and engines have resulted in the redesignation of all the aircraft as U-2S. They have a wingspan of 105 feet and are 16 feet high and 63 feet long. Their standard speed is over 410 miles per hour, their range is over 7,000 miles, and they can fly at altitude of over 70,000 miles.[58] The planes can carry three imagery sensors, although not all at once. A U-2 can carry the SENIOR YEAR Electro-Optical Reconnaissance System (SYERS). In June 2008, flight testing of the SYERS-3 sensor, an upgraded version of the SYERS-2 sensor then being carried on the planes, was to begin shortly. Planes equipped with the SYERS-2 have an ability to provide precise geolocation of targets as well as improved measurement and signature intelligence processing tools. They are also able to collect data in three visible bands and as well as three infrared bands—a capability that has proven useful in detecting improvised explosive devices.[59]

The SYERS can transmit its images in near-real-time, if it is within 220 miles of its ground station. If it is outside that range, it can store the imagery and transmit it when it comes back within line of sight of the station. The station, designated SENIOR BLADE, controls the SYERS, in addition to processing, exploiting, and reporting the imagery received. The Advanced Synthetic Aperture Radar System IIA (ASARS-IIA) is an all-weather, day-night, standoff imaging system designed to detect, locate, classify, and, in some cases, identify enemy ground targets. ASARS was designed to collect and process radar imagery in near-real-time at a 10-foot resolution. The ASARS-IIA has provided an improved moving target indicator (MTI) capability. It can also detect disturbed ground in areas where mines or explosive devices have been installed. U-2 aircraft equipped with the SENIOR SPUR system can transmit ASARS-II imagery through the Tracking and Data Relay Satellite (TDRS) system.[60]

The third imagery sensor available for placement on a U-2S is the Optical Bar Camera (OBC). The camera is a 30-inch, focal-length panoramic camera capable of providing black-and-white images with 6-inch resolution. The images created can be miles long. Since the images are recorded on film, it can take three to seven days for users to receive the images after the plane returns from its mission.[61]

All U-2 operations are directed by the 9th Reconnaissance Wing at Beale Air Force Base in California, which is subordinate to the Air Combat Command, and are tasked by theater commanders. Located at Beale are the 99th Reconnaissance Squadron for operational deployments and the 1st Reconnaissance Squadron for six-month qualification training. Overseas units include the 5th Reconnaissance Squadron (5RS) at Osan, Korea; Detachment 4 at Al Dhafra Air Base in the United Arab Emirates, from which planes have flown over Afghanistan and other parts of the Middle East; and the 99th Expeditionary Reconnaissance Squadron/Detachment 1 at RAF Akrotiri on Cyprus.[62]

Missions flown from RAF Akrotiri include those that monitored the 1973 Arab-Israeli peace accord. The 5th RS at Osan was the first U-2 unit to receive the MTI-equipped U-2S, to ease the task of monitoring the movement of missiles and heavy mortars that are moved in and out of North Korean mountain caves. On April 5, 2003, four days before U.S. forces consolidated their control in Baghdad, a U-2, flying from the United Arab Emirates, spotted thirty Iraqi artillery pieces as well as three tanks north of the city. An analyst alerted the operations center, which directed planes to attack the target, which they were able to do within ten minutes. During Operation Iraqi Freedom, fifteen U-2s flew from three bases (Al Dharfa, Akrotiri, and Al Kharj in Saudi Arabia) and completed 169 missions. During the last fourteen days of major combat operations at least one U-2 was always airborne, searching for Scud mobile missiles in western Iraq. [63]

U-2s based at Osan focus on North Korea and the Chinese border. Those flying out of the base near Iraq collect intelligence targets there as well as along the Iranian and Syrian borders and over Afghanistan. Cyprus-based U-2s focus on the Middle East and conduct treaty-monitoring flights.[64]

In 2006, the decision was made to retire the entire U-2 fleet by 2011. However, Congress instructed the Air Force to refrain from retiring any U-2s until "the capabilities provided by the aircraft no longer contribute to mitigating gaps in ISR identified in the 2006 Quadrennial Defense Review." It appears that any phased retirement of the U-2 will not begin until at least 2013.[65]

With the collapse of the Soviet Union, the mission of the Navy's P-3C ORION aircraft, originally employed and equipped to detect and monitor Soviet submarines, has been employed on overland imagery missions. The P-3C is the third-generation P-3. The first model, the P-3A, was produced by shortening the airframe of an Electra airliner by 12 feet, equipping it with weapons, and giving it an increased fuel capacity.[66]

There are presently about 130 P-3Cs in the Navy's inventory, based at twelve locations. Squadron designations (VP-) and locations are listed in Table 7.2. The P-3C, according to one account, had "become a crucial photographic reconnaissance tool for operations to monitor peacekeeping in Bosnia and to track the new crisis in Albania." In a fourteen-month period in 1996 and 1997, P-3Cs were employed in 324 missions and examined 2,425 targets. More recently, P-3 crews attempted to detect leaders of the Taliban and al-Qaeda who attempted to escape the U.S. 2001 attacks on Afghan targets by fleeing to Pakistan or Iran. The planes also monitored coastal freighters used by smugglers that might have been carrying escaping leaders to Lebanon, Syria, Somalia, or Yemen. Flying over the Philippines, the planes supported the campaign against the Abu Sayyaf group. They have also flown over Baghdad, Basra, and Fallujah.[67]

P-3Cs have carried standard cameras under the base of the plane as well as an infrared camera (the Infrared Detection System) and synthetic aperture radar. But P-3Cs are also capable of providing full-motion video, which is sometimes used to monitor activity 50 nautical miles ahead of a convoy. In 2007 it was reported that the video often showed insurgents digging holes to emplace improvised explosive devices. A smaller set of P-3Cs, designated Eagle Archer, carry the Littoral Surveillance Radar System (LSRS), which has proven useful in hunting insurgents in Iraq and Afghanistan. The radar can track vehicles as well as smaller objects—presumably including people.[68]

TABLE 7.2   Location of VP Squadrons

Squadron	Location
VP-1	NAS Whidbey Island, Washington
VP-4	Marine Corps Base, Kaneohe Bay, Hawaii
VP-5	NAS Jacksonville, Florida
VP-8	NAS Jacksonville, Florida
VP-9	Marine Corps Base, Kaneohe Bay, Hawaii
VP-10	NAS Jacksonville, Florida
VP-16	NAS Jacksonville, Florida
VP-26	NAS Jacksonville, Florida
VP-40	NAS Whidbey Island, Washington
VP-45	NAS Jacksonville, Florida
VP-46	NAS Whidbey Island, Washington
VP-47	Marine Corps Base, Kaneohe Bay, Hawaii

SOURCE: "Patrol Squadrons," www.gonavy.jp/NavalSqn06.html, accessed November 22, 2010.

Current plans are to replace the P-3 fleet with a fleet of about 117 P-8A Poseidon Multimission Maritime Aircraft (MMA), with some of the P-3's current imagery functions reassigned to the Broad Area Maritime Surveillance (BAMS) system—to be made up of Predator-B Mariner or Global Hawk unmanned aerial vehicles. The BAMS may carry a version of the SENIOR YEAR Electro-Optical System as well as an advanced version of the LSRS carried by the Eagle Archer P-3Cs.[69]

A recent addition to the U.S. aerial reconnaissance fleet is the MC-12W Liberty, a medium-to low-altitude twin-engine turboprop aircraft. The MC-12W Liberty is a military version of the Hawker Beechcraft Super King Air 350 and the Super King 350Extended Range (ER). Its primary mission is to provide intelligence, surveillance, and reconnaissance support directly to ground forces. The operational system includes the aircraft with sensors along with a ground exploitation cell.[70]

The MC-12W has a wingspan of almost 58 feet and is over 46 feet long and just over 14 feet high. Its ceiling is 35,000 feet, and it has a range of 1,500 nautical miles or 2,400 nautical miles, depending on whether the modified plane was a 350 or 350 ER, respectively. The plane carries an electro-optical infrared sensor "and other sensors as the mission requires." It is capable of providing full-motion video.[71]

The first of twenty-four MC-12Ws earmarked for Afghanistan was scheduled to arrive in December, with the remainder to be in the air by September 2010. That month, the thirty-seventh and final M-12W Liberty was delivered to the Air Force. Of the thirty-seven, seven are Block 1 aircraft, based on the King Air 350, while the remaining thirty are Block 2, based on the King Air 350ER.[72]

During the Persian Gulf War, the United States relied on unmanned aerial vehicles (UAVs)/remote piloted vehicles (RPVs) in addition to manned reconnaissance aircraft. Subsequently, UAVs came to represent a significant element in projected U.S. intelligence capabilities—extending beyond their use for purely tactical purposes. In February 1994, the CIA deployed a UAV unit to an Albanian base on the northern Adriatic coast to operate two specially modified General Atomics (GNAT) 750 UAVs. A primary mission of the unmanned reconnaissance craft was the monitoring of Serbian artillery emplacements in Bosnia.[73]

Today, there are several key UAV programs in operation. The GNAT 750–45, better known as the Predator, is an advanced version of the UAVs flown over Bosnia by the CIA in 1994. The original version of the Predator, the RQ-1, had an approximate range of 450 miles and a maximum altitude of 25,000 feet. It carried electro-optical and infrared imagery systems as well as synthetic aperture radar. In the aftermath of 9/11, the Air Force and CIA armed Predators with Hellfire missiles, an effort first code-named NIGHT FIST and then POSITIVE PILOT, so as to eliminate the delay between detecting a target and attempting to destroy the target.* Since the armed version of the Predator was a multimission aircraft, its designation was changed to the MQ-1 in 2002.[74]

Prior to its transformation to the MQ-1, the Predator performed a variety of intelligence collection missions in Eastern Europe. Three of the vehicles were deployed to Gjader, Albania, from July to November 1995. Another three were deployed to Taszar, Hungary, in 1996. During the late summer and early fall of 1996, the Predators based at Taszar monitored mass grave sites near Sarajevo. In September 1996, the UAVs also monitored election activities in Bosnia, and in October they monitored the deployment of peacekeeping forces. Imagery could be simultaneously transmitted to ground commanders in Europe and to officials in the United States, employing Joint Broadcast Satellites. In October 1998, Predators were designated for surveillance duty over Kosovo.[75]

The current version, the MQ-1B, "is a medium-altitude, long-endurance" vehicle—with an endurance of 22 hours. It carries the Multi-Spectral Targeting System (MTS-A), which integrates an infrared sensor, a color/monochrome daylight TV camera, an image-intensified TV camera, a laser designator, and a laser illuminator into a single sensor package. The full-motion video from each video sensor can be viewed as individual video streams or fused together. Squadrons operating the Predator are the 15th and 17th Reconnaissance Squadrons at Creech Air Force Base, Nevada. The active force consist of 130 MQ-1Bs.[76]

The MQ-9 Reaper is also a "medium-altitude, long-endurance" craft that can reach 50,000 feet. It carries the MTS-B, which has essentially the same capabilities as the MTS system carried on the Predator. As with the Predator, full-motion video from the sensors can be viewed separately or fused together. The Reapers are operated by the 17th Reconnaissance Squadron as well as the 42nd Attack Squadron,

---

*The use of armed Predators as part of CIA covert action and paramilitary operations is discussed in Chapter 8.

both at Creech Air Force Base, Nevada, and by the 29th Attack Squadron at Holloman AFB, New Mexico. The active force currently consists of forty-nine MQ-9s.

An upgraded sensor pod, Gorgon Stare, was scheduled to begin being installed on MQ-9s in spring 2010 but had not been deployed as of early 2011. The pod uses five electro-optical and four infrared cameras to obtain pictures from assorted angles to produce a larger image. The first three will be able to provide ten video images to ten different recipients simultaneously, while the following six will be able to provide thirty video images to thirty different operations. But a December 30, 2010, draft report by the 53rd Wing of the Air Combat Command stated that the surveillance system was "not operationally effective" and had "significant limitations that degrade its operational utility," which included an inability to monitor people on the ground in real-time and delays in transmitting real-time images to the ground. The report recommended that the system not be deployed until the problems were fixed, although the Air Force asserted in late January 2011 that some of the problems had already been resolved.[77]

The RQ-170 Sentinel, a tailless flying wing known in the trade press as the "Beast of Kandahar," is a low-observable UAV operated by two units—the Air Combat Command's 432nd Wing at Creech Air Force Base, Nevada, and the 30th Reconnaissance Squadron at Tonopah Test Range, Nevada. The RQ-170 Sentinel appeared in Afghanistan as early as 2007.[78]

Continuing missions in unarmed intelligence collection and reconnaissance are the more advanced GLOBAL HAWKs—the RQ-4A and RQ-4B—operated by the 12th Reconnaissance Squadron at Beale Air Force Base. The squadron is subordinate to the 9th Reconnaissance Wing at Beale. The RQ-4A can carry a 2,000-pound payload, while the RQ-4B can carry up to 3,000 pounds of payload. The sensors carried in the payloads include electro-optical, synthetic aperture radar as well as medium-wave infrared sensors. The RQ-4A has a range of 9,500 nautical miles, while the RQ-4B range ends at 8,700 nautical miles. Eventually, one version will carry the Radar Technology Insertion Program active electronically scanned array radar. The GLOBAL HAWKs are able to stay on station for twenty-four hours (if flown to maximum radius) at an altitude of 60,000 feet. In that time, they can obtain 1,900 2-kilometer-square images, covering an area of 40,000 nautical square miles. Data can be transmitted to ground stations below or to satellites for relay to the United States or other locations.[79]

Three GLOBAL HAWK test platforms were pressed into service after the terrorist attacks of 9/11. By December 2002, GLOBAL HAWK vehicles, flying from a base in Al Dharfa in the United Arab Emirates, had flown more than fifty missions and provided 15,000 images in support of U.S. and Allied operations in Afghanistan (Operation Enduring Freedom). In Operation Iraqi Freedom, in March and April 2003, a GLOBAL HAWK provided continuous, real-time images of Republican Guard tanks, troops, and artillery to the Combined Air Operations Center (CAOC) at Prince Sultan Air Base, Saudi Arabia. In addition, the UAV's radar allowed the detection of Iraqi movements through some large sandstorms. By late February 2006,

GLOBAL HAWKs had performed more than 260 missions over Iraq and Afghanistan, totaling more than 5,400 hours.[80]

In Iraq, GLOBAL HAWK vehicles have been used to patrol the borders since the U.S. invasion of March 2003 and to collect imagery over central Iraq. For example, they obtained electro-optical imagery of a weapons cache compound during a January 18, 2007, mission, and after an improvised explosive device detonated west of Baghdad, synthetic aperture radar images of the bomb crater were used to determine where personnel scattered after the explosion.[81]

Four Global Hawks, three belonging to the Air Force (Block 10) and one to the Navy, provide intelligence on Afghanistan, Iraq, the Horn of Africa, and the Strait of Hormuz—flying from Al Dharfa Air Base in the United Arab Emirates. Several improved versions are in development—Block 20 (with the Battlefield Airborne Communications payload), Block 30 (which will carry the Airborne Signals Intelligence payload as well as electro-optical, infrared, and synthetic aperture radar sensors), and Block 40 (with the Multi-Platform Radar Technology Insertion Program).[82]

As of 2010, there are seven RQ-4A and three RQ-4B vehicles in the inventory and plans to procure another forty-four RQ-4B vehicles.[83]

A new/old type of aerial intelligence platform that the Department of Defense hopes to field in the future is the airship or blimp—a far more mobile version of the tethered version being used in Iraq and Afghanistan to obtain full-motion video employed to detect insurgents. Flying at 65,000 feet, it would be 450 feet long and able to fly to any spot and stay airborne for ten years. Targets of its built-in radar system would include urban areas, forested areas, high- and low-altitude aerial movements, and deep- and shallow-water ocean activities. It would be able to conduct surveillance out to 375 miles. In 2009, the Air Force signed an agreement with the Defense Advanced Research Project Agency to develop a 150-foot-long demonstration dirigible by 2012.[84]

The Army is also exploring the feasibility of developing a similar surveillance platform, designated the Long Endurance Multi-Intelligence Vehicle. The Army's envisioned version would be 250 feet long and fly for more than three weeks over the target area at an altitude of 20,000 feet, which would give it a view of 173 miles. It would carry 2,500 pounds of imagery and signals intelligence equipment.[85]

PROCESSING AND EXPLOITATION

As noted above, imagery can be obtained by relying on single portions of the electromagnetic spectrum (visible light, infrared, radio) or by combining a number of bands into a single image (multispectral, hyperspectral, or ultraspectral imagery). However the imagery is obtained, it requires processing and interpretation to convert it into intelligence data.

Computers can be employed to improve the quantity and quality of the information extracted. Obviously, digital electro-optical imagery arrives in a form that facilitates such operations, but even analog imagery obtained by a conventional camera can be converted into digital signals. In any case, a computer disassembles a picture into millions of electronic pulses and then uses mathematical formulas to manipulate the color, contrast, and intensity of each spot. Each image can be reassembled in various ways to highlight special features and objects that were hidden in the original image.[86] Computer processing allows interpreters to

- build multicolored single images out of several pictures taken in different bands of the spectrum, making the patterns more obvious;
- restore the shapes of objects by adjusting for the angle of view and lens distortion;
- change the amount of contrast between objects and backgrounds;
- sharpen out-of-focus images;
- restore ground details largely obscured by clouds;
- conduct electronic optical subtraction, in which earlier pictures are subtracted from later ones, making unchanged buildings in a scene disappear while new objects, such as missile silos under construction, remain;
- enhance shadows;
- suppress glint.[87]

Computer processing plays a crucial role in easing the burden on photogrammetrists and imagery interpreters. Photogrammetrists are responsible for determining the size and dimensions of objects from overhead photographs, using, along with other data, the shadows cast by the objects. Photo interpreters are trained to provide information about the nature of the objects in the photographs, based on information as to what type of crates carry MiG-29s, for instance, or what an IRBM site or fiber-optics factory looks like from 150 miles in space. Such information is provided in interpretation keys such as those listed in Table 7.3. Thus, an interpreter might see a picture with excavations, mine headframes, derricks, piles of waste, conveyor belts, bulldozers, and power shovels, but with just a few buildings. His key would suggest that this is a mine. Special kinds of equipment, the tone or color of the waste piles and the ore piles, as well as knowledge of local geology, could further indicate that this is a uranium mine.[88]

The ultimate utility of any electro-optical, infrared, or radar imaging system is a function of several factors—the most prominent being spatial resolution. A simple measure of spatial resolution is the minimum size an object must be in order to be measurable and detectable by photo analysts. The "higher" the resolution, the greater the detail that can be extracted from an image. It should also be noted that resolution is a product of several factors, including the optical or imaging system, atmospheric conditions, and orbital parameters. The degree of resolution required depends on the specificity of the intelligence desired.[89]

Five different interpretation tasks have been differentiated. Detection involves locating a class of units or objects or an activity of interest. General identification involves determining a general target type, and precise identification involves

TABLE 7.3   Joint Imagery Interpretation Keys

World Tanks and Self-Propelled Artillery	Major Surface Combatants
World Towed Artillery	Minor Surface Combatants
General Transportation Equipment	Mine Warfare Types
World Tactical Vehicles	Amphibious Warfare Types
Combat Engineer Equipment	Naval Auxiliaries
World Mobile Gap and River Crossing Equipment	Intelligence Research Vehicles
Coke, Iron, and Steel Industries	Shipborne Electronics
Chemical Industries	Shipborne Weapons
World Electronics	Airfield Installation
World Missiles and Rockets	Petroleum Industries
Military Aircraft of the World	Atomic Energy Facilities
Submarines	

SOURCE: Defense Intelligence Agency Regulation 0-2. "Index of DIA Administrative Publications," December 10, 1982, pp. 35–36.

discrimination within target type of known types. Description involves specifying the size-dimension, configuration-layout, components-construction, and number of units. Technical intelligence involves determining the specific characteristics and performance capabilities of weapons and equipment.[90] Table 7.4 gives estimates of the resolution required for interpretation tasks.

Factors other than resolution that are considered significant in evaluating the utility of an imaging system include coverage speed, readout speed, analysis speed, reliability, and enhancement capability. Coverage speed is the area that can be surveyed in a given amount of time; readout speed is the speed with which the information is processed into a form that is meaningful to imagery interpreters; and reliability is the fraction of time in which the system produces useful data. Enhancement capability refers to whether the initial images can be enhanced to draw out more useful data.

Digital satellite imagery can also be employed for purposes that go beyond intelligence on a target facility or activity. Such data, when combined with elevation data, can be used to produce a three-dimensional image of the landscape of an area of interest—whether it be Serbia or south Beirut. The capability, first developed at the Jet Propulsion Laboratory, can be used to familiarize individuals—from national leaders to military personnel to clandestine intelligence personnel—with a particular geographical area.

In the spring of 1994, the CIA acquired an additional capability. Once a three-dimensional view of an area has been created, an individual can use a joystick to wander around the area as well as inside the three-dimensional buildings. Such an orientation experience is particularly useful to inspectors and intelligence officers,

TABLE 7.4 Resolution Required for Different Levels of Interpretation

Target	Detection	General Identification	Precise Identification	Description	Technical Intelligence
Bridge	20 ft.	15 ft.	5 ft.	3 ft.	1 ft.
Communications radar/radio	10 ft./10 ft.	3 ft./5 ft.	1 ft./1 ft.	6 in./6 in.	1.5 in./6 in.
Supply dump	5 ft.	2 ft.	1 ft.	1 in.	1 in.
Troop units (bivouac, road)	20 ft.	7 ft.	4 ft.	1 ft.	3 in.
Airfield facilities	20 ft.	15 ft.	10 ft.	1 ft.	6 in.
Rockets and artillery	3 ft.	2 ft.	6 in.	2 in.	.4 in.
Aircraft	15 ft.	5 ft.	3 ft.	6 in.	1 in.
Command and control HQ	10 ft.	5 ft.	3 ft.	6 in.	1 in.
Missile sites (SSM/SAM)	10 ft.	5 ft.	2 ft.	1 ft.	3 in.
Surface ships	25 ft.	15 ft.	2 ft.	1 ft.	3 in.
Nuclear weapons components	8 ft.	5 ft.	1 ft.	1 in.	.4 in.
Vehicles	5 ft.	2 ft.	1 ft.	2 in.	1 in.
Land minefields	30 ft.	20 ft.	3 ft.	1 in.	—
Ports and harbors	100 ft.	50 ft.	20 ft.	10 ft.	1 ft.
Coasts and landing beaches	100 ft.	15 ft.	10 ft.	5 ft.	3 in.
Railroad yards and shops	100 ft.	50 ft.	20 ft.	5 ft.	2 ft.
Roads	30 ft.	20 ft.	6 ft.	2 ft.	6 in.
Urban area	200 ft.	100 ft.	10 ft.	10 ft.	1 ft.
Terrain	—	300 ft.	15 ft.	5 ft.	6 in.
Surfaced submarines	100 ft.	20 ft.	5 ft.	3 ft.	1 in.

SOURCES: Adapted from U.S. Congress, Senate Committee on Commerce, Science, and Transportation, *NASA Authorization for Fiscal Year 1978, Part 3* (Washington, D.C.: U.S. Government Printing Office, 1977), pp. 1642–1643; and Bhupendra Jasani, ed., *Outer Space—A New Dimension in the Arms Race* (Cambridge, Mass.: Oelgeschlager, Gunn & Hain, 1982), p. 47.

who benefit from the experience of being able to preview a building or area before actually entering it.

In 2009, it was reported that the CIA was investing in technology intended to allow satellite and aerial imagery to be merged with maps so that thousands of data sources could be mined for information about points of interest that appear in the images. The expectation is that when the project is completed CIA personnel will be able to click on a building or other facility shown in the video and a variety of information will pop up, including the identity of tenants and their phone numbers, company records, links to company and organization websites, news reports concerning tenants or incidents at the location, and property records.[91]

The availability of full-motion video from UAVs has led to research and development work on systems that can more efficiently exploit that imagery. For example, as of June 2010, the U.S. military's archive contained 400,000 hours of video gathered by Predator UAVs, although the archive was of little utility because analysts had no means of searching for information. It was also reported that the Air Force and other reconnaissance experts were working with experts from the television industry to adapt the methods used in NFL and other sports broadcasts to quickly find and show replays as well as annotate the images.[92]

Other work in the area has been funded by other agencies. In September 2008, Kitware, a small software company, along with nineteen partners, won the initial phase of a DARPA contract to create the capability to monitor live video feeds as well as search large volumes of archived videos for activities of interest. And in August 2009, the Defense Information Systems Agency, on behalf of the Joint Forces Command and the National Security Agency, launched an initiative designated Valiant Angel. The initiative involved hiring Lockheed Martin and Harris Broadcasting "to deliver a military version of Harris software that manages and displays videos for sportscasters and newscasters." The objective is to give intelligence users the ability to retrieve videos through the use of keywords, location, or time.[93]

DISSEMINATION

At one time, when imagery was obtained solely by film-based cameras, there was a simple dissemination sequence. Imagery was returned from satellites in capsules or on aircraft when they returned from a mission. The film was then transported to the relevant national (e.g., NPIC), departmental (DIA), service (FTD), or command (PACOM) imagery interpreters. The imagery interpretation reports produced, as well as the reports incorporating the imagery-derived intelligence, were then disseminated to the appropriate groups and individuals. For much of the history of the satellite reconnaissance program, this was a very restrictive set of individuals, in part because film-return systems were not terribly useful in the heat of battle, with the long delays between the imaging of a target and the intelligence reaching military commanders.

The advent of real-time digital imagery dramatically increased the potential value of the imagery obtained from national systems for military commanders and combatants, as the technology made it possible to provide military commanders with a very current view of enemy forces and movements. Even before the first KH-11 was placed into orbit in December 1976, the Intelligence Community began studying how the system might be used to support forces in the field. For example, in January 1976, one of a series of Tactical-National Intelligence Interface Studies—*Report on the Pilot Study on National Intelligence Support to Field Commanders*—was completed well in advance of the KH-11 launch.[94]

The dissemination sequence for digital imagery begins, of course, with the downlinking of the imagery data from a spacecraft or aircraft to a ground station. In some cases, the downlink may be direct; in others, the process may require a relay because the ground station is not in the line of sight of the satellite.

For the Improved Metric CRYSTAL, ECS, and MISTY satellites, the primary ground station is the Aerospace Data Facility–East at Fort Belvoir, Virginia, about 20 miles south of Washington, D.C. It is a large, windowless, two-story concrete building officially known as the Defense Communications Electronics Evaluation and Testing Activity (DCEETA), also known as Area 58. Although initially the Fort Belvoir site was the only downlink for the KH-11, additional sites were subsequently added, apparently in Hawaii and Europe.[95]

The signals arriving at the Mission Ground Site are relayed from more than one type of relay satellite, which receive the electronic signals from an imagery satellite and then forward them to a ground station. At first there was only one type of relay satellite employed—the elliptically orbiting Satellite Data System (SDS) satellites. The initial SDS was orbited into a 240-by-24,000-mile, 63-degree inclined, highly elliptical orbit in June 1976. Additional launches followed in August 1976, August 1978, and in the 1980s and 1990s—all into highly elliptical orbits. In addition, the geosynchronous Defense Satellite Communications System (DSCS) satellites may have been used to relay advanced KH-11 data.[96]

Because SDS satellites had a number of additional, non-NRO-related functions—including relaying communications between the central hub of the Air Force Satellite Control Facility and its ground stations around the world, as well as hosting nuclear detonation detectors—they were originally operated by the Air Force. But after several instances of the satellites not being in appropriate positions to relay KH-11 imagery, the CIA component of the NRO (Program B) assumed responsibility in 1983. Eventually, the relay satellite program was designated QUASAR, and it has come to involve satellites in both highly elliptical and geosynchronous orbits.[97]

Since 1998 there have apparently been five QUASAR satellites placed into orbit: two spacecraft launched—on January 21, 1998, and on August 31, 2004—into highly elliptical orbits and up to three—including one launched on March 11, 2011—placed in geosynchronous orbit. All were acknowledged to be NRO spacecraft and relied on one version or another of the Atlas booster to get them into orbit.

In contrast, the signals from the LACROSSE/ONYX system are relayed via NASA's Tracking and Data Relay Satellites (TDRS), of which there are six in geosynchronous orbit, and three of which are available at any time. The others provide backup in the event of the failure of an operational spacecraft. The signals are transmitted to a ground station at White Sands, New Mexico. In the future, a joint military-civilian National Space Communications System may handle relay of intelligence, military, and civilian communications.[98]

Primary transmission systems link Washington (or other locations in the United States) to military command headquarters or facilities in the United States and overseas. The first node in these systems has been either the Defense Satellite Communications System (DSCS) or the now-defunct Fleet Satellite Communications System (FLTSATCOM). In 1990, one primary transmission system was the Digital Imagery Transmission System (DITS), which linked Washington with the U.S. Central Command headquarters at MacDill Air Force Base, Florida.[99]

Secondary transmission systems allow military commands that have received imagery from primary distribution systems or other means to relay such data to subordinate units. Secondary imagery transmission systems have included the Central Command Imagery Transmission System (CITS). Among its components was the Portable Receive and Transmit System (PORTS). The U.S. Central Command's PORTS reached initial operational capability in 1987.[100]

A secondary transmission system also exists within the European Command. In 1989, the EUCOM Secondary Imagery Transmission System (EUCOMSITS) network consisted of five SITS nets composed of Air Force ICON (Image Communications and Operations Node), Fleet Imagery Support Terminals (FISTs), PORTS Imagery Processing Systems, ancillary devices, and interconnecting communications circuits.[101]

In addition to receiving data via primary and secondary dissemination systems, U.S. forces deployed overseas may receive data directly from certain collection systems. The successors to the FLTSATCOM system, the Navy's UHF Follow-On (UFO) spacecraft, have been employed as part of a Global Broadcast Service (GBS). GBS provides a near-global capability to forward NRO imagery to a wider spectrum of users than in the past. NRO helped set up a "GBS Phase 1" demonstration, which involved the transmission of imagery and other data to U.S. forces in Bosnia. The first GBS Phase 2 satellite (UFO F8) was launched in March 1998, the first satellite in what would become a three-satellite constellation. Imagery can be uplinked to the satellites from ground stations in Hawaii, Virginia, and Europe. Among those receiving data via GBS terminals were U.S. forces participating in Operation Enduring Freedom in Afghanistan.[102]

U.S. forces operating at sea and in the air have also been beneficiaries of improved dissemination capabilities that have been developed over the past decade or more. By the early 1990s, the Fleet Imagery Support Terminals (FISTs) on U.S. aircraft carriers, which could transmit imagery from shore locations and transmit imagery from ship to shore, from ship to ship, or from shore to shore, could also receive data directly from space systems. In 2001, there were newly developed (by NRO) Rapid Targeting System data receivers in place on key Navy ships and in forward-deployed ground command centers in Afghanistan. In 2002, in an experiment designated RADIANT

ETHER, a system for the receipt of national intelligence data was tested on the USS *Theodore Roosevelt.*[103]

The Marines also have access to a secondary imagery dissemination system—the MAGTF (Marine Air-Ground Task Force) Secondary Imagery Dissemination System (MSIDS). It is described in a budget document as "Family of System (FoS) that provides organic and tactical digital imagery collection, transmission, and receiving capability to the MAGTF Commander." Funding for the program in the 2007 fiscal year allowed procurement of multiple suites for the Marine Special Operations Command, Light Armed Reconnaissance, Reconnaissance, and Infantry Battalion Sniper units.[104]

Throughout the 1990s, systems were tested to allow the transmission of imagery and signals intelligence directly to aircraft cockpits. Under a program designated TALON SWORD, tests conducted in April 1993 used intelligence data to directly cue missiles fired at simulated enemy radars by F-16 and EA-6B aircraft. Another phase of TALON SWORD involved transmitting satellite intelligence into F-15E cockpits for targeting enemy positions with smart bombs.[105]

Another program, TALON LANCE, was directed at equipping aircraft with a computer package that would allow high-speed processing of space intelligence data. TALON LANCE–equipped aircraft would be able to locate and identify an enemy on the ground or in the air. The aircraft crew could then decide whether to attack or avoid contact long before the aircraft's normal onboard sensors could detect the enemy. TALON SHOOTER encompassed a number of programs, including Project STRIKE, to provide threat, target, and weather information to the cockpit, "to make space a reality for operational aircraft." In July 1995, the program was tested on B-1B and F-15E aircraft.[106]

In Kosovo in 1999, the Joint Targeting Work Station was successfully tested. The station allowed field operators to select a target and provide precise coordinates based on satellite data. The data could then be relayed directly to the cockpits of attack aircraft within minutes.[107]

The U-2, Global Hawk, Predator, and Reaper systems can all downlink their data to the Air Force Distributed Common Ground System (DCGS), operated by the Air Force Intelligence, Surveillance, and Reconnaissance Agency's 480th ISR Wing Operations Center. Composed of twenty separate but networked sites, the DCGS is the successor to the Deployable Ground Station-1, which began operations in July 1994. In addition to the Air Force system there is the Distributed Common Ground System–Army (DCGS-A), which receives data from Army-operated aerial surveillance assets.[108]

Notes

1. William E. Burrows, *Deep Black: Space Espionage and National Security* (New York: Random House, 1986), p. 28.

2. Ibid., p. 32.

3. See Jeffrey T. Richelson, *American Espionage and the Soviet Target* (New York: William Morrow, 1987), p. 16.

4. Donald E. Welzenbach, "From the U-2 to Corona and Those Who Searched for Invisibility," in *CORONA: Between the Sun and the Earth—The First NRO Reconnaissance Eye in Space*, ed. Robert A. McDonald (Baltimore, Md.: American Society for Photogrammetry and Remote Sensing, 1997), pp. 135–140.

5. Farouk el-Baz, "EO Imaging Will Replace Film in Reconnaissance," *Defense Systems Review* (October 1983): 48–52.

6. Richard D. Hudson Jr. and Jacqueline W. Hudson, "The Military Applications of Remote Sensing by Infrared," *Proceedings of the IEEE* 63, 1 (1975): 104–128; James B. Campbell, *Introduction to Remote Sensing* (New York: Guilford, 1987), p. 26.

7. Hudson and Hudson, "The Military Applications of Remote Sensing by Infrared"; Bruce G. Blair and Garry D. Brewer, "Verifying SALT," in *Verification and SALT: The Challenge of Strategic Deception*, ed. William Potter (Boulder, Colo.: Westview, 1980), pp. 7–48; Campbell, *Introduction to Remote Sensing*, p. 26.

8. Homer Jensen, L. C. Graham, Leonard J. Porcello, and Emmet N. Leith, "Side-Looking Airborne Radar," *Scientific American*, October 1977, pp. 84–95.

9. Defense Intelligence Agency, *Multispectral Applications—A Significant New Resource for Warfighting Planning and Execution, The Final Report on the Joint DIA–OSAF/DSPO Merit Program for Evaluating Landsat, SPOT and Aircraft Multispectral Imagery* (Washington, D.C.: DIA, 1988), p. 1-1.

10. Curtiss O. Davis, Naval Research Laboratory, *Hyperspectral Imaging: Utility for Military, Science, and Commercial Applications*, October 15, 1996.

11. Ibid.

12. The KH-10, which was the camera system for the Manned Orbiting Laboratory (MOL), never became operational, since the MOL program was canceled before the first flight. For a history of the KEYHOLE program, see Jeffrey T. Richelson, *America's Secret Eyes in Space: The U.S. KEYHOLE Spy Satellite Program* (New York: Harper & Row, 1990); and Jeffrey T. Richelson, *The Wizards of Langley: Inside the CIA's Directorate of Science and Technology* (Boulder, Colo.: Westview, 2001).

13. Richelson, *America's Secret Eyes in Space*, pp. 128–131.

14. Ibid.

15. Ibid., p. 126; private information. The CIA's Imagery Analysis Service did its own study of the impact, completed in December 1969: *Impact of a Near Real Time Collection System on CIA's Imagery Analysis Needs*—the declassified portion of which is available from CREST database at NARA, College Park.

16. Richelson, *America's Secret Eyes in Space*, p. 362; interview.

17. Richard A. Stubbing, "Improving the Output of Intelligence," in *National Insecurity: U.S. Intelligence After the Cold War*, ed. Craig Eisendrath (Philadelphia: Temple University Press, 2000), pp. 172–189 at pp. 177–178; interview.

18. Richelson, *America's Secret Eyes in Space*, p. 362; Craig Covault, "Advanced KH-11 Broadens U.S. Recon Capability," *Aviation Week & Space Technology*, January 6, 1997, p. 24; Craig Covault, "Fade to Black," *Aviation Week & Space Technology*, May 15, 2006, pp. 24–26; e-mail from Ted Molczan, September 10, 2010; interviews.

19. R. Jeffrey Smith, "Senators, CIA Fight over $1 Billion," *Washington Post*, July 16, 1993, p. A4; David A. Fulghum, "Key Military Officials Criticize Intelligence Handling in Gulf

War," *Aviation Week & Space Technology*, June 24, 1991, p. 83; Roger Guillematte, "Titan 4B to Launch Classified Payload from California," http://www.space.com, September 29, 2001.

20. "New Recon Satellite Poised for Liftoff," *Aviation Week & Space Technology*, August 7, 2000, p. 66; Craig Covault, "Titan, Adieu," *Aviation Week & Space Technology*, October 24, 2005, pp. 28–29; National Reconnaissance Office, Release # 02–11, "NRO Satellite Successfully Launched Aboard Delta IV Heavy, January 20, 2011; interview.

21. Douglas Isbell and Vincent Kiernan, "Long-Delayed Atlantis Flight Orbits Military Spy Satellite," *Space News*, March 5–11, 1990, p. 12; Patrick E. Tyler, "Satellite Fails," *Washington Post*, March 17, 1990, pp. A1, A11; "U.S. Spy Satellite Spotted by Europeans," *Washington Times*, November 1, 1990, p. A6; "NRO's Unusual Mission," *Aviation Week & Space Technology*, July 5, 1999, p. A17; communications from Ted Molczan, January 11, 2000, and May 28, 2002.

22. Jeffrey T. Richelson, "A Satellite in the Shadows," *Bulletin of the Atomic Scientists*, May–June 2005, pp. 26–33; Mark Mazetti, "Spy Director Ends Program on Satellites," *New York Times*, June 22, 2007, p. A16.

23. Bob Woodward, *Veil: The Secret Wars of the CIA, 1981–1987* (New York: Simon & Schuster, 1987), p. 221; private information.

24. "Space Reconnaissance Dwindles," *Aviation Week & Space Technology*, October 6, 1980, pp. 18–20; "Navy Will Develop All-Weather Ocean Monitor Satellite," *Aviation Week & Space Technology*, August 28, 1978, p. 50; Craig Covault, "USAF, NASA Discuss Shuttle Use for Satellite Maintenance," *Aviation Week & Space Technology*, December 17, 1984, pp. 14–16; "Washington Roundup," *Aviation Week & Space Technology*, June 4, 1979, p. 11; Robert C. Toth, "Anaheim Firm May Have Sought Spy Satellite Data," *Los Angeles Times*, October 10, 1982, pp. 1, 32; Bill Gertz, "New Spy Satellite, Needed to Monitor Treaty, Sits on Ground," *Washington Times*, October 20, 1987, p. A5; Woodward, *Veil*, p. 221; Bill Gertz, "Senate Panel Asks for Radar Funds," *Washington Times*, April 5, 1988, p. A4; Craig Covault, "Atlantis' Radar Satellite Payload Opens New Reconnaissance Era," *Aviation Week & Space Technology*, December 12, 1988, pp. 26–28; "Valve Work Delays Another Titan Flight," *Space News*, August 18–31, 1997, p. 2; Vincent Kiernan, "Satellite Buffs Conclude That Titan Launch Carried Lacrosse," *Space News*, April 8–14, 1991, p. 22; Philip S. Clark, "Satellite Digest," *Spaceflight* 40, January 1998, pp. 35–36; "World News Roundup," *Aviation Week & Space Technology*, August 21, 2000, p. 24; National Reconnaissance Office, "Reconnaissance Office Satellite Successfully Launched," October 23, 1997; Craig Covault, "Secret Mission Surge," *Aviation Week & Space Technology*, May 9, 2005, pp. 24–25.

25. David Fulghum and Craig Covault, "U.S. Set to Launch Upgraded Lacrosse," *Aviation Week & Space Technology*, September 20, 1996, p. 34; Covault, "Secret Mission Surge"; Gertz, "New Spy Satellite, Needed to Monitor Treaty, Sits on Ground."

26. Gertz, "New Spy Satellite, Needed to Monitor Treaty, Sits on Ground"; Covault, "Atlantis' Radar Satellite Payload Opens New Reconnaissance Era"; "Radar Satellite Assesses Raids," *Aviation Week & Space Technology*, September 16, 1996, p. 26; David Fulghum and Craig Covault, "U.S. Set to Launch Upgraded Lacrosse," *Aviation Week & Space Technology*, September 20, 1996, p. 34; William Claiborne, "Taiwan-Born Scientist Passed Defense Data," *Washington Post*, December 12, 1997, p. A23; Craig Covault, "Secret Relay, Lacrosse NRO Spacecraft Revealed," *Aviation Week & Space Technology*, March 23, 1998, pp. 26–28.

27. Craig Covault, "Recon Satellites Lead Allied Intelligence Effort," *Aviation Week & Space Technology*, February 4, 1991, pp. 25–26; Bill Gertz, "S. Africa to Test Ballistic Missile,"

Washington Times, May 3, 1991, p. A3; Bill Gertz, "Laotian Military Smuggling Drugs," *Washington Times*, April 25, 1991, p. A11; Bill Gertz, "Soviets Testing Rail-Mobile Rocket," *Washington Times*, April 12, 1991, p. A5; Bill Gertz, "China Helps Algeria Develop Nuclear Weapons," *Washington Times*, April 11, 1991, p. A3; David E. Sanger, "Furor in Seoul over North Korea's Atomic Plant," *New York Times*, April 16, 1991, p. A3; Bill Gertz, "Satellites Spot Poison Bomb Plant in Libya," *Washington Post*, March 5, 1991, p. 3; "International," *Military Space*, January 27, 1992, p. 6; Covault, "Secret Mission Surge."

28. Bill Gertz, "Beijing Creates Military Monster," *Washington Times*, April 10, 1997, pp. A1, A10.

29. Jeff Gerth, "Officials Say China Illegally Sent U.S. Equipment to Military Plant," *New York Times*, April 23, 1997, pp. A1, A9.

30. Tim Weiner, "U.S. Suspects India Prepares for Nuclear Test," *New York Times*, December 15, 1995, p. A6.

31. Elaine Sciolino, "U.S. Says It's Won Votes to Maintain Sanctions on Iraq," *New York Times*, March 5, 1995, pp. 1, 9.

32. Boerfink MHE to 26 IW et al., Subj: TFC Southern Region Disum (SORD) NR 146–92, May 26, 1992, pp. 3–4; Boerfink MHE to 26 IW et al., Subj: TFC Southern Region Disum (SORD) NR 211–92, July 30, 1992.

33. Bill Gertz, "N. Korea Masses Artillery at Border," *Washington Times*, July 25, 1996, pp. A1, A9.

34. Douglas Waller, "The Secret Missile Deal," Time, June 30, 1997, p. 58.

35. Michael R. Gordon, "Despite Cold War's End, Russia Keeps Building a Secret Complex," *New York Times*, April 16, 1996, pp. A1, A6; Bill Gertz, "Moscow Builds Bunkers Against Nuclear Attack," *Washington Times,* April 1, 1997, pp. A1, A16; Bill Gertz, "Russian Nuke Shelters Don't Concern Pentagon," *Washington Times*, April 2, 1997, p. A6.

36. Bill Gertz, "Hidden Iraqi Scuds Threaten Israel, Gulf Countries," *Washington Times*, February 11, 1998, pp. A1, A12.

37. Bill Gertz, "China Points More Missiles at Taiwan," *Washington Times*, November 22, 1999, pp. A1, A9.

38. John Lancaster, "Kashmir Crisis Was Defused on Brink of War," *Washington Post*, July 26, 1999, pp. A1, A15.

39. Bill Gertz and Rowan Scarborough, "Inside the Ring," *Washington Times*, April 6, 2001, p. A7.

40. Bill Gertz and Rowan Scarborough, "Inside the Ring," *Washington Times*, May 10, 2002, p. A10.

41. Bill Gertz, "Iraqis 'Moving Stuff' at Germ Plant," *Washington Times*, August 14, 2002, pp. A1, A18.

42. David E. Sanger and Eric Schmitt, "Satellites Said to See Activity at North Korean Nuclear Site," *New York Times*, January 31, 2003, pp. A1, A10.

43. David E. Sanger and William J. Broad, "U.S. Cites Signs of Korean Steps to Nuclear Test," *New York Times*, May 6, 2005, pp. A1, A6.

44. John Diamond, "Trained eye can see right through box of weapons," www.usatoday.com, August 17, 2006.

45. David E. Sanger and William J. Broad, "Agenda of Nuclear Talks Leaves Out a New Threat," *New York Times*, April 12, 2010, pp. A1, A8.

46. Hyung-Jin Kim, "S Korea denies N Korea is preparing nuclear test," www.washington post.com, October 21, 2010.

47. See Jeffrey T. Richelson, ed., National Security Archive Electronic Briefing Book #13, *U.S. Satellite Imagery, 1960–1999*, April 14, 1999, and Jeffrey T. Richelson, ed., National Security Archive Electronic Briefing Book #88, *Eyes on Saddam*, April 30, 2003, both at www.nsarchive.org.

48. Jeremy Singer, "Air Force Satellite Program Faces Delay, Higher Cost," *Space News*, July 8, 2002, p. 8; Annie Marie Squeo, "Officials Say Space Programs, Facing Delays, Are 'in Trouble,'" *Wall Street Journal*, December 4, 2002, pp. A1, A3; Joseph C. Anselmo and Amy Butler, "Beyond Repair?," *Aviation Week & Space Technology*, September 5, 2005, pp. 23–24; Douglas Jehl, "Boeing Lags in Building Spy Satellites," *New York Times*, December 4, 2003, pp. C1, C8.

49. Office of the Director of National Intelligence, ODNI News Release No. 12–09, "DNI Blair Announces Plan for the Next Generation of Electro-Optical Satellites," April 7, 2009.

50. "ORS-1 Sensor Damaged, But Satellite Is on Schedule," *Space News*, March 22, 2010, p. 3; "ORS-1 Satellite Now Set for April Launch," *Space News*, December 13, 2010, p. 3; Peter Grier, "Making Space Responsive," *Air Force Magazine*, December 2010, pp. 58–61; Turner Brinton, "Microcosm Designing Low-Cost Imagery Satellite for Army, Working on Launch Vehicle," *Space News*, March 15, 2010, p. 20.

51. Campbell, *Introduction to Remote Sensing*, pp. 137–138, 149–153; HQ United States Space Command, *Command History, January 1990–December 1991*, pp. 83–84, 307; 309–310; "Spot-4 Images Released," *Aviation Week & Space Technology*, April 13, 1998, p. 75.

52. "Quickbird," www.digitalglobe.com, accessed November 22, 2010; "Worldview-1," www.digitalglobe.com," accessed November 22, 2010; "Worldview-2," www.digitalglobe.com, accessed November 22, 2010; Chuck Herring, "At the Tipping Point: How Digital Globe's Latest Satellite Launch Is Breaking Down Barriers," *Imaging Notes* 25, 1 (Winter 2010): 24–28.

53. "Imagery Sources," www.geoeye.com, accessed November 22, 2010; Stephen Clark, "Government imaging contract will hasten new satellites," www.spaceflight.now, August 10, 2010.

54. Thomas A., "NGA Employs Emerging Commercial Space Radars," *Pathfinder*, September/October 2010, pp. 8–9; Amy Butler, "New Image," *Aviation Week & Space Technology*, April 12, 2010, pp. 50–51.

55. Tariq Malik, "X-37B Wraps Up 7-Month Mission Shrouded in Secrecy," *Space News*, December 6, 2010, p. 17; William J. Broad, "Surveillance Is Suspected as Main Role of Spacecraft," *New York Times*, May 23, 2010, pp 1, 18; Stephen Clark, "Inspections have begun on Air Force space plane," www.spaceflightnow.com, December 12, 2010; Stephen Clark, "Air Force's Second Robotic Space Shuttle Circling Earth," *Space Flight Now* (www.spaceflightnow.com), March 5, 2011.

56. Chris Pocock, *Dragon Lady: The History of the U-2 Spyplane* (Shrewsbury, England: Airlife, 1989), pp. 18–32.

57. Seymour Hersh, *The Samson Option: Israel's Nuclear Arsenal and Foreign Policy* (New York: Random House, 1991), pp. 52–54; Dino Brugioni, *Eyeball to Eyeball: The Inside Story of the Cuban Missile Crisis* (New York: Random House, 1991), p. 33; Pocock, *Dragon Lady*, pp. 90–106, 143–163; Howard Silber, "SAC U-2s Provided Nicaraguan Pictures," *Omaha World Herald*, March 10, 1982, p. 2; Frank Oliveri, "The U-2 Comes in from the Cold," *Air Force Magazine*, September 1994, pp. 45–50; Christopher Drew, "U-2 Spy Plan Evades the Day of Retirement," *New York Times*, March 22, 2010, pp. A1, A6; Amy Butler, "Devil in the Details," *Aviation Week & Space Technology*, July 12, 2010, pp. 26–27.

58. U.S. Air Force, Fact Sheet, "U-2S/TU-2S," November 2009, www.af.mil/information/factsheets.

59. Amy Butler, "More, More, More," *Aviation Week & Space Technology*, June 16, 2008, pp. 26–27; Amy Butler and David A. Fulghum, "Dragon Lady in Korea," *Aviation Week & Space Technology*, September 1, 2008, pp. 50–51.

60. Michael A. Dornheim, "U-2 Runs at Frenzied Pace in New World Order," *Aviation Week & Space Technology*, April 29, 1996, pp. 55–56; Coy F. Cross, *The Dragon Lady Meets the Challenge: The U-2 in Desert Storm* (Beale AFB, Calif.: 9th Strategic Reconnaissance Wing, 1995), p. 15; Chris Pocock, "U-2: The Second Generation," *World Airpower Journal* 28 (Spring 1997): 50–99; Chris Pocock, *50 Years of the U-2: The Complete Illustrated History of the "Dragon Lady"* (Atglen, Pa.: Schiffer Military History, 2005), p. 325.

61. Dave Majumdar, "High altitude, high stakes," www.c4isrjournal.com, September 9, 2010.

62. U.S. Air Force, Fact Sheet, "U-2S/TU-2S"; David A. Fulghum, "Searching for Clues," *Aviation Week & Space Technology*, September 1, 2008, pp. 51–52; Ross Tweten, "U-2 squadron continues to fly high," *Air Force Print News Today*, March 12, 2008 (at www.af.mil); Pocock, *50 Years of the U-2*, pp. 327, 239; Kevin Whitelaw, "No Rest for a Cold Warrior," www.usnews.com, September 20, 2007.

63. "News Breaks," *Aviation Week & Space Technology*, November 21, 1994, p. 23; "More Eyes"; Eric Schmitt, "6,300 Miles from Iraq, Experts Guide Raids," *New York Times*, June 24, 2003, p. A13; Pocock, *50 Years of the U-2*, pp. 330–331.

64. Amy Butler, "Going Global," *Aviation Week & Space Technology*, March 12, 2007, pp. 60–61.

65. Pamela Hess, "Pentagon to Retire U2 Spy Plane," www.spacewar.com, January 5, 2006; Chris Pocock, "Resisting Retirement," *C4ISR Journal*, January–February 2007, pp. 22–23; U.S. Congress, House Permanent Select Committee on Intelligence, Report 109–411, *Intelligence Authorization Act for Fiscal Year 2007*, p. 12; Christopher Drew, "U-2 Spy Plane Evades the Day of Retirement," *New York Times*, March 22, 2010, pp. A1, A6.

66. David Miller, *An Illustrated Guide to Modern Sub Hunters* (New York: ARCO, 1984), p. 125; George A. Wilmoth, "Lockheed's Antisubmarine Warfare Aircraft: Watching the Threat," *Defense Systems Review* 3, 6 (1985): 18–25.

67. "Upgrades for P-3s to Begin in 1998," *Aviation Week & Space Technology*, March 31, 1997, p. 33; Robert Wall, "Navy to Link UAVs Manned Aircraft Units," *Aviation Week & Space Technology*, April 29, 2002, pp. 58–59; David A. Fulghum, "MMA = P-8A," *Aviation Week & Space Technology*, March 28, 2005, p. 36; David A. Fulghum, "Air Patrols Watch for Fleeing Leaders," *Aviation Week & Space Technology*, March 4, 2002, p. 62; David A. Fulghum, "P-3 Tactical Value Increases with Age," *Aviation Week & Space Technology*, March 4, 2002, p. 65; Robert Wall, "Patrol's Partner," *Aviation Week & Space Technology*, April 30, 2007, pp. 51–52; United States Navy, Fact File, "P-3C *Orion* long range ASW aircraft," February 18, 2009, www.navy.mil/navydata.

68. Wall, "Patrol's Partner"; David A. Fulghum and Amy Butler, "Budget Changes," *Aviation Week & Space Technology*, September 21, 2009, pp. 23–25; Keith Button, "Revealing Radar," *C4ISR Journal*, January/February 2009, pp. 20–21; *P-3C Orion Weapon System Update* (Burbank, Calif.: Lockheed, n.d.), p. 18; David A. Fulghum, "Navy Exploits P-3 in Overland Recce Role," *Aviation Week & Space Technology*, March 4, 2002, pp. 60–62.

69. Laura L. Myers, "Time to Fly," *C4ISR Journal*, November/December 2009, pp. 22–25; Government Accountability Office, GAO-09–326SP, *Defense Acquisitions: Assessments of Selected Weapon Programs*, March 2009, p. 130; Robert Wall, Andy Nativi, and Guy Norris,

"Priming Poseidon," *Aviation Week & Space Technology*, June 23, 2008, p. 44; Amy Butler, "Intelligence Choices," *Aviation Week & Space Technology*, September 13, 2010, pp. 44–49.

70. U.S. Air Force, Fact Sheet, "MC-12," www.af.mil/information/factsheets.

71. Ibid.; Ben Iannotta and Mike Hoffman, "Pentagon Tries to Get Liberty ISR Planes Back on Track," *C4ISR Journal*, July 2009, p. 8.

72. Michael Hoffman, "First Liberty Planes to Arrive in Afghanistan Shortly," *C4ISR Journal*, October 2009, p. 12; Bryant Jordan, "L-3 Aims for Army 'Liberty,'" www.dodbuzz.com, September 14, 2010; Lt. Col. Cook, A2, "Bullet Background Paper on MC-12W Project Liberty," December 15, 2009.

73. David A. Fulghum, "CIA to Deploy UAVs in Albania," *Aviation Week & Space Technology*, January 31, 1994, pp 20–22; "Gnats Weathered Out," *Aviation Week & Space Technology*, February 14, 1994, p. 19.

74. James Risen, "Eyes (Arms) in the Sky," *New York Times*, November 10, 2002, Section 4, p. 5; Karen DeYoung and Thomas E. Ricks, "Iraqis Down Reconnaissance Drone," *Washington Post*, December 24, 2002, p. A11; U.S. Air Force, Fact Sheet, "MQ-1B," wwwaf.mil/information/factsheets, accessed December 16, 2010; Chitra Ragavan, "Clinton, Bush, and the Hunt for bin Laden," http://www.usnews.com, September 29, 2006.

75. Kenneth Israel, *NMIA Defense Intelligence Status '96 Supporting the Warfighter*, p. 21; Defense Airborne Reconnaissance Office, *UAV Annual Report FY 1996*, November 6, 1996, pp. 7, 9, 18, 21; "World News Roundup," *Aviation Week & Space Technology*, June 15, 1998, p. 41.

76. U.S. Air Force, Fact Sheet, "MQ-1B"; March V. Schanz, "The Indispensable Weapon," *Air Force Magazine*, February 2010, pp. 32–36.

77. U.S. Air Force, Fact Sheet, "MQ-9 REAPER," www.af.mil/information/factsheets, accessed December 16, 2010; Julian E. Barnes, "Military Refines a 'Constant Stare Against Our Enemy,'" *Los Angeles Times*, November 2, 2009, pp. A1, A14; Colin Clark, "Many-Headed Dragon Heads to Af-Pak," www.dodbuzz.com, December 16, 2009. As of March 2009, another nineteen were to be procured. See Government Accountability Office, *Defense Acquisitions: Assessments of Selected Weapons Programs*, March 2009, p. 117; 53WG/CC, Memorandum for: USAFWC/CC, ACC/AS, Subject: MQ-9 Gorgon Stare (GS) Fielding Recommendation, December 30, 2010 (DRAFT); Ellen Nakashima, "New drone sensors not working as hoped," www.washingtonpost.com, January 25, 2011, p. A2; Colin Clark, "AF: Some Gorgon Stare Probs Fixed," www.dodbuzz.com, January 25, 2011.

78. U.S. Air Force Fact Sheet, "RQ-170 SENTINEL," www.af.mil/information/factsheets, accessed December 16, 2010; David A. Fulghum and Bill Sweetman, "Stealth Over Afghanistan," *Aviation Week & Space Technology*, December 14, 2009, pp. 26–31.

79. David A. Fulghum, "Global Hawk UAVs to Remain Unarmed," *Aviation Week & Space Technology*, April 15, 2002, pp. 20–21; Israel, *NMIA Defense Intelligence Status '96, Supporting the Warfighter*, p. 21; Defense Airborne Reconnaissance Office, *UAV Annual Report FY 1996*, pp. 13, 31; Michael A. Dornheim, "Global Hawk Begins Flight Test Program," *Aviation Week & Space Technology*, March 9, 1998, pp. 22–23; Defense Airborne Reconnaissance Office, *UAV Annual Report FY 1997*, 1997, p. 32; "First Global Hawk Squadron in Place," *C4ISR Journal*, January–February 2005, p. 10; "Global Hawk Camera Range Will Double," *C4ISR Journal*, January–February 2005, p. 6; U.S. Air Force, Fact Sheet, "Global Hawk," www.af.mil/information/factsheets, accessed December 16, 2010.

80. "UAVs to UAE," *Aviation Week & Space Technology*, March 3, 2003, p. 61; Rowan Scarborough, "Hovering Spy Plane Helps Rout Iraqis," *Aviation Week & Space Technology*,

April 3, 2003, pp. A1, A12; "Loss Leaders," *Aviation Week & Space Technology*, April 7, 2003, p. 21; "Production Global Hawks Enter War on Terrorism," *Space News*, January 30, 2006, p. 8. On GLOBAL HAWK's contributions to Operation Iraqi Freedom, also see David A. Fulghum, "War from 60,000 Ft.," *Aviation Week & Space Technology*, September 8, 2003, pp. 54–57; and Northrop Grumman, "Photo Release—Global Hawk Unmanned Aerial Vehicle Returns After More Than 4,800 Flight Hours in Fight Against Terrorism," February 21, 2006.

81. Amy Butler, "Constantly Watching," *Aviation Week & Space Technology*, March 12, 2007, pp. 56–59.

82. Amy Butler, "Sweet and Sour," *Aviation Week & Space Technology*, June 28, 2010, pp. 42–43; "U.S. Air Force Orders Five Global Hawks from Northrup," *Aviation Week & Space Technology*, November 30, 2009, p. 8.

83. U.S. Air Force, Fact Sheet, "RQ-4 Global Hawk"; Government Accountability Office, *Defense Acquisitions: Assessments of Select Weapons Programs*, March 2010, pp. 71–72.

84. Julian E. Barnes, "Taking Spying to New Heights," *Los Angeles Times*, March 13, 2009, p. A18; Graham Warwick, "Persistence Pays Off," *Aviation Week & Space Technology*, May 18, 2009, pp. 54–55; Walter Pincus, "Military seeks an intelligence-gathering airship," www.washingtonpost.com, February 16, 2010.

85. Pincus, "Military seeks an intelligence-gathering airship."

86. Paul Bennett, *Strategic Surveillance* (Cambridge, Ma.: Union of Concerned Scientists, 1979), p. 5.

87. Richard A. Scribner, Theodore J. Ralston, and William D. Mertz, *The Verification Challenge: Problems of Strategic Nuclear Arms Control Verification* (Boston: Birkhauser, 1985), p. 70; John F. Ebersole and James C. Wyant, "Real-Time Optical Subtraction on Photographic Imagery for Difference Detection," *Applied Optics* 15, 4 (1976): 871–876.

88. Scribner, Ralston, and Mertz, *The Verification Challenge*, p. 69.

89. Campbell, *Introduction to Remote Sensing*, p. 226; James Fusca, "Space Surveillance," *Space/Aeronautics* (June 1964): 92–103.

90. U.S. Congress, Senate Committee on Commerce, Science and Transportation, *NASA Authorization for Fiscal Year 1978, Part 3* (Washington, D.C.: U.S. Government Printing Office, 1977), pp. 1642–1643.

91. William Matthews, "Firm Adapting Civilian Geospatial Tool for Intel Applications," *Space News*, May 4, 2009, p. 16.

92. Julian E. Barnes, "U.S. Military Borrows from NFL," *Los Angeles Times*, June 8, 2010, pp. A1, A11. One system that has been deployed is the Multi-Int Analysis and Archive System (MAAS). See Turner Brinton, "New Video Exploitation Tools Geared Toward Tactical Users," *Space News*, November 1, 2010, p. 12.

93. Walter Pincus, "DARPA Contract Description Hints at Advanced Video Spying," www.washingtonpost.com, October 20, 2008; Ben Iannotta, "Playing Catch-Up," *C4ISR Journal*, October 2009, pp. 26, 28; Turner Brinton, "NGA Pushes Full-Motion Video Analysis," *Space News*, October 19, 2009, p. 12.

94. *Report on the Pilot Study on National Intelligence Support to Field Commanders*, January 12, 1976, CREST. The study was prepared by an interagency working group.

95. James Bamford, "America's Supersecret Eyes in Space," *New York Times*, January 13, 1985, pp. 39ff; Paul Stares, *Space and National Security* (Washington, D.C.: Brookings Institution, 1987), p. 18; Scott F. Large, memorandum for: the Honorable Daniel K. Inoye and the Honorable Thad Cochran, Subject: Declassification of the "Fact of" National Reconnaissance

Mission Ground Stations and Presence Overseas, September 24, 2008. It is notable that the uplinks for the NRO Global Broadcast System are located in Hawaii, Europe, and Virginia.

96. Dwayne Day, "Relay in the Sky: The Satellite Data System," *Journal of the British Interplanetary Society* 51, Supplement 1 (2006); 56–62; Bamford, "America's Supersecret Eyes in Space"; Stares, *Space and National Security*, p. 18.

97. Day, "Relay in the Sky"; interviews.

98. Robert C. Toth, "Anaheim Firm May Have Sought Spy Satellite Data," *Los Angeles Times*, October 10, 1982, pp. 1, 32; Warren Ferster, "NRO Studies Relay Satellites," *Space News,* September 1–7, 1997, pp. 1, 19; National Space Science Data Center, "NASA's Tracking and Data Relay Satellites (TDRS)," http://nssdc.gsfc.nasa.gov, accessed September 15, 2006.

99. Central Command, *United States Central Command 1987 Command History*, March 27, 1990, p. II-26.

100. Ibid., p. II-36.

101. Space Applications Corporation, *European Command Secondary Imagery Transmission System (EUCOMSITS)* (Vienna, Va.: Space Applications Corporation, June 1989).

102. Craig Covault, "'Info War' Advanced by Navy GBS Satcom," *Aviation Week & Space Technology*, March 23, 1988, p. 28; Jeremy Singer, "U.S. Air Force Pays Raytheon Millions to Fix GBS System," *Space News*, August 14, 2000, p. 6; Jeremy Singer, "U.S. Air Force Maps Out Plans for Lighter GBS Ground Terminals," *Space News*, September 9, 2002, p. 22; Stew Magnuson, "Satellite Data Distribution Lagged, Improved in Afghanistan," *Space News*, September 2, 2002, p. 6.

103. U.S. Congress, House Appropriations Committee, *Department of Defense Appropriations for 1992, Part 6* (Washington, D.C.: U.S. Government Printing Office, 1991), p. 470; Craig Covault, "NRO KH-11 Readied for Afghan Recon," *Aviation Week & Space Technology*, October 8, 2001, pp. 68–69; Jason Stahl, "Bringing National Space System Capabilities to the Fleet," *Domain*, Fall 2002, pp. 17–18.

104. Department of Defense, *FY 2008 Budget Justification Book, Military Intelligence Program, Volume I, Summary*, 2007, p. 67.

105. "AF Would Send Real-Time Recce Satellite Images to Tactical Planes," *Aerospace Daily*, January 8, 1993, p. 1: James R. Asker, "F-16, EA-6B to Fire Missiles Cued by Intelligence Satellites" *Aviation Week & Space Technology*, April 19, 1993, p. 25; Ben Iannotta, "Space to Play Bosnian Role," *Space News*, May 10–16, 1993, pp. 1, 2; Tony Capaccio," Air Force Pushes 'In Your Face from Outer Space,'" *Defense Week*, July 12, 1993, pp. 1,8.

106. David A. Fulghum, "Talon Lance Gives Aircrews Timely Intelligence from Space," *Aviation Week & Space Technology*, August 23, 1993, p. 71; Capt. Michelle Dietrich, "Talon Lance Supports Warfighters," *Guardian*, August 1993, pp. 6–7; Col. Jack Fry, Air Force Space Command Space Warfare Center, *AF TENCAP Programs—AF TENCAP Briefing to AFSAB New World Vistas Space Applications Panel*, March 15, 1995; William B. Scott, "USAF to Broadcast Mission Data to Cockpit," *Aviation Week & Space Technology*, June 5, 1995, p. 23.

107. "Eye Spy," *Aviation Week & Space Technology*, July 12, 1999, p. 21.

108. U.S. Air Force, Fact Sheet, "Air Force Distributed Common Ground System," www.af.mil/information/factsheets, accessed December 9, 2010; Northrup Grumman, "Distributed Common Ground System–Army (DCGS–A)," www.es.northrupgrumman.com, accessed December 9, 2010.

8

SIGNALS INTELLIGENCE

Signals intelligence (SIGINT) is generally considered to be one of the most important and sensitive forms of intelligence. The interception of the signals of foreign governments or organizations can provide data on diplomatic, military, scientific, and economic capabilities and plans of nations, the capabilities and plans of terrorist groups, and the characteristics of radars, spacecraft, and weapons systems.

Signals intelligence is defined in the most recent DOD Instruction on the subject as "intelligence comprising, either individually or in combination, all communications intelligence, electronic intelligence, and foreign instrumentation signal intelligence, however transmitted."[1]

As its name and the above definition indicate, communications intelligence (COMINT) is intelligence obtained through the interception, processing, and analysis of the electronic communications of foreign government or organizations. Those communications have traditionally, and often explicitly, excluded radio and television broadcasts (and presumably today excludes government postings on any social media sites). The communications may take a variety of forms—voice (transmitted via telephone, standard cell-phone, Blackberry, satellite telephone, radio-telephone, walkie-talkie), the Internet, Morse code, facsimile—and may be either encrypted or transmitted in the clear.

The targets of COMINT operations are varied. The most traditional COMINT target is diplomatic communications—the communications from each nation's capital to its diplomatic establishments around the world. The United States has intercepted and deciphered the diplomatic and intelligence communications of a variety of nations—for example, Britain's communications during the 1956 Suez Crisis, Iraq's communications to its embassy in Japan in the 1970s, and Libya's communications to its East Berlin People's Bureau prior to the bombing of a West Berlin nightclub in 1985. In early 2003, the United States stepped up its effort at targeting the diplomatic communications of UN Security Council members, as the council debated whether to approve the use of military force against Iraq.[2]

The United States also targets communications between different components of a large number of governments and organizations; on some occasions both components are located within the country being monitored, but on others at least one is located outside national boundaries. Frequently targeted communications include those between government and/or ministry officials; a ministry or agency and its subordinate units throughout the country and abroad; weapons production facilities and various military or government officials; military units, especially during exercises and operations, and higher authorities; and police and security forces and their headquarters.

Thus, the United States COMINT effort has targeted communications between the Chinese Ministry of Defense and subordinate military units, the Russian government and its military units, the Pakistani Atomic Energy Commission and Pakistani nuclear facilities, the President of Egypt and his subordinates (including when Egypt was holding the hijackers of the *Achille Lauro*), and Israeli officials in Tel Aviv and Israeli representatives on the West Bank. In recent years, the United States intercepted and deciphered the communications of the Iranian intelligence service.[3]

In 1968, intercepted voice communications in the Beijing Military Region indicated a field exercise involving the 4th Armored Division. In 1980, U.S. intercepts of Soviet communications led to a fear that the Soviets were about to invade Iran. COMINT played a significant role in preparing a 1982 study on Indian heavy-water shortages. Intercepts allowed the United States to piece together the details concerning the sinking of a Soviet submarine in the North Pacific in 1983, and in 1988 intercepted Iraqi military communications led U.S. officials to conclude that Iraq had used chemical weapons in its war with Iran. After the Iraqi invasion of Kuwait in August 1990, COMINT and other intelligence reports indicated that some Saudi leaders were considering an attempt to pay off Saddam Hussein. In September 1994, the United States intercepted communications from Haitian dictator Raoul Cedras, in which he said he would determine his response to President Clinton's demands based on the reaction of the American public to the President's forthcoming speech on U.S. policy toward Haiti.[4]

Intercepts of Chinese diplomatic communications in 1996 and thereafter raised the question of whether the PRC had attempted to funnel money to American politicians are in their campaigns. A January 1997 intercept of Israeli diplomatic communications led to an FBI investigation of possible Israeli penetration of the U.S. government. In 1998, intercepts revealed that the Russian foreign intelligence service had facilitated the sale of Russian missile technology to Iran. The following year, COMINT showed that high-ranking Yugoslav officials had ordered an attack on the village of Racak in Kosovo, resulting in the massacre of forty-five unarmed Albanian civilians.[5]

The communications of terrorist groups, particularly al-Qaeda, have been an important target of the U.S. COMINT effort. By 2001, NSA was listening to the unencrypted calls from Osama bin Laden, which he made on his portable INMARSAT phone. That effort failed to provide warning of the September 11 attacks, but it did provide convincing evidence that al-Qaeda was involved in those attacks as well as earlier ones in Nairobi, Kenya, and Dar es Salaam, Tanzania. In 2002, an intercepted satellite telephone conversation allowed the apprehension of Abu Musab al-Zarqawi's deputy.[6]

As noted above, governmental communications do not exhaust the set of COMINT targets. The communications of political parties and corporations involved in the sale of technology related to advanced weapons developments may also be targeted. In addition, the communications of terrorist groups are targeted—both to permit understanding of how the group functions and of the personalities of its leaders and to allow prediction of where and how it will attempt to strike next.

Another major set of COMINT targets is associated with economic activity (of both the legal and illegal variety), such as the communications of international banking firms and narcotics traffickers. In 1970, the predecessor of the Drug Enforcement Administration informed the NSA that it had "a requirement for any and all COMINT information which reflects illicit traffic in narcotics and dangerous drugs." Specific areas of interest included organizations and individuals engaged in such activities, the distribution of narcotics, cultivation and production centers, efforts to control the traffic in narcotics, and all violations of U.S. laws concerning narcotics and dangerous drugs.[7]

Electronic intercept operations are intended to produce electronic intelligence (ELINT) by collecting the noncommunication signals from military and civilian hardware, excluding those from atomic detonations. Under the NSA's Project KILTING, all ELINT signals are (or were) stored in computerized reference files containing the most up-to-date technical information about the signals.

The earliest of the ELINT targets were World War II air defense systems. The objective was to gather sufficient information to identify the location and operating characteristics of the radars and then to circumvent and neutralize them during bombing raids (through direct attack or electronic countermeasures). The information desired included frequencies, signal strengths, pulse duration, pulse repetition, and other specifications. Since that time, missile detection, space tracking, and ballistic missile early warning radars have joined the list of ELINT targets.

In the early 1950s, the primary targets were Soviet Bloc (including   ) radars; Russian radars remain a target, although a less critical one. Mon   Russian radars also had an arms control verification aspect, since the 1972 Anti-   ic Missile (ABM) Treaty restricted the use of radars in an "ABM" mode. To   , Iranian, North Korean, Syrian, and PRC radars are among the prime targets.

While logically a subcategory of ELINT, Foreign Instrumentation Signals Intelligence (FISINT) was, several years ago, decreed to be a component of the SIGINT enterprise co-equal with COMINT and the other elements of ELINT. Foreign instrumentation signals are electromagnetic emissions associated with the testing and operation of aerospace, surface, and subsurface systems that have military or civilian applications. Such signals include but are not limited to those from telemetry, beaconing, electronic interrogation, tracking/fusing/aiming command systems, and video data links.[8]

A subcategory of FISINT is Telemetry Intelligence (TELINT). Telemetry is the set of signals by which a missile or missile component sends back data about its performance during a test flight. The data relate to structural stress, rocket motor thrust, fuel consumption, guidance system performance, and the physical conditions of the ambient environment. Intercepted telemetry can provide data used to estimate the number of warheads carried by a given missile, its payload and throwweight, the probable size of its warheads, and the accuracy with which the warheads are guided from the missile's post-boost vehicles to their targets.[9]

The ease with which communications or electronic signals can be intercepted and understood depends on three factors: the method of transmission, the frequencies employed, and the encipherment (or lack thereof) used to conceal the signals' meanings from unauthorized personnel.

The most secure method of transmission is by cable, via either landlines or ocean cables. Communications or other signals transmitted in this manner cannot be snatched out of the air and do not leak out into space. Interception of cable traffic has involved physically tapping into the cables or the use of "induction" devices placed in the proximity of the cables and maintenance of the equipment at the point of access. This option might be impossible in the case of hardened and protected internal landlines—the type that carry much high-priority secret command and control communications.

Over the last several decades a tremendous volume of communications has been sent via satellite systems—although the "market share" for communications satellites had significantly declined in recent years due to ever-growing use of fiber-optic cables for communications transmission. But the use of satellite systems for both domestic and international communications led the United States and other nations to establish major programs for the interception of communications transmitted via satellite. By placing satellite dishes at the proper locations, technicians can intercept an enormous volume of traffic. Whereas ground station antennas can direct signals to a satellite with great accuracy, satellite antennas are smaller and the signals they send down to Earth are less narrowly focused—perhaps covering several thousand square miles.[10]

Often communications are transmitted partly by satellite and partly via microwave towers. In other cases—particularly in the case of telephone calls within a country, as in Canada—microwave towers have served as the only means of transmission and reception. Likewise, the vast expanse of the Soviet Union and Russia has caused it to rely heavily on microwave communications. As one observer has written with regard to microwave relay towers: "With modern communications, 'target' messages travel not simply over individually tappable wires . . . but as part of entire message streams . . . and have voice, telegram, telex and high-speed data bunched together."[11]

Microwave signals can be intercepted by two means: (1) ground stations near the invisible line connecting the two microwave towers, and (2) space collection systems, if the area of transmission is within the footprint of the system.

Radio is the most traditional means for the transmission of signals, including communications, missile telemetry, and foreign instrumentation signals. The accessibility of radio signals to interception often depends on the frequencies upon which the signal is transmitted and the signal's geographic location. Messages transmitted at lower frequencies (ELF, VLF, LF, HF) travel for long distances since they bounce off the atmosphere and will come down in locations far from the transmitting and intended receiving locations.

In contrast, data sent at higher frequencies will "leak" through the atmosphere and out into space. To intercept such signals, intercept stations must be within line of sight of the radio communications. The curvature of the earth can therefore make monitoring from ground-based sites impossible. Several years ago, former CIA Deputy Director for Intelligence Sayre Stevens wrote of the Soviet ballistic missile defense test center at Sary Shagan: "It lies deeply enough within the USSR to make it difficult to monitor from peripheral intelligence gathering sites along the border. Because flight operations at Sary Shagan can be conducted well below the radio-horizon from such external monitoring locations, the Soviet Union has been able to conceal the details of its activities at Sary Shagan for many years."[12] Under such conditions, either emplaced intercept systems close to the site or geosynchronous satellites over 20,000 miles away maybe the only alternatives to gather the signals.

Three other traditional methods of communication that are targets of interception operations are walkie-talkie, radio-telephone communications, and fascimile transmissions. Walkie-talkie communications are employed during military exercises and during emergency situations, such as the explosion at the Chernobyl nuclear power plant in 1986. Radio-telephone communications have been employed by government officials—including the highest-ranking Soviet officials—as they traveled in their limousines. And fax transmissions have long been the target of U.S. intercept operations, going back to the 1950s.

Satellite telephone, computer, cell-phone, and Blackberry traffic also constitute major targets for COMINT collection systems. (In addition to the traffic between computers, cell-phones, and Blackberry devices, the data stored in them—"data at rest" such as files, databases, address books, calendars, and saved e-mails—are targets of intelligence operations, including cyber operations conduced by NSA or other intelligence organizations.)

Once intercepted, signals have to be processed. For communications sent without encipherment or scrambling, the only processing necessary will be translation. Communications may be sent in the clear either because they are considered to be of too little importance to justify the time and expense involved in protecting them or because the method of transmission is believed to be immune to interception.

Electronic signals sent in the clear still need to be interpreted, however. In such instances, telemetry signals on all channels may be transmitted as numbers. The variables being measured and the units of measurement must be inferred by correlating data on missile maneuvers with intercepted telemetry. For example, measurement may be made concerning different types of events: one-time events (e.g., the firing of explosive bolts or the separation of reentry vehicles (RVs) from the post-boost bus), discontinuous events (e.g., adjustments to the guidance system during flight), and continuous events (e.g., fuel flow, motor burn, or acceleration of the missile during the boost phase). These events can be expressed in terms of absolute values, arbitrary values (on a one-to-ten scale), relative values (percentages), or inferential values. Which particular characteristic an intercepted reading refers to, or the particular values being used, will not necessarily be evident. A fuel tank reading may be given as a "30," which may refer to a tank that is either 30 percent full or 30 percent empty. The temperature in the rocket combustion chamber can be measured from the temperature of another part known to have a specific temperature relative to that in the chamber.[13]

Communications or electronic signals may be either encrypted or scrambled, thus complicating the process of turning the intercepted signals into intelligence. Diplomatic communications are traditionally enciphered. The sophistication of the encipherment and the quality of the operators determine whether the encipherment can be broken. Conversations via radio and radio-telephone are frequently scrambled. Soviet leaders started having their radio-telephone conversations scrambled after they became aware of a U.S. operation to intercept those conversations. Noncommunications signals may also be encrypted, as were a large portion of Soviet missile telemetry signals.

The U.S. SIGINT effort is a massive one and employs space and airborne collectors, ground stations, covert listening posts, surface ships, and submarines.

SPACE COLLECTION

The United States operates signals intelligence satellites in three different types of orbit—low-earth, geosynchronous, and highly elliptical ("Molniya"). In June 1960, the Navy orbited the first electronic intelligence satellite—known as GRAB (for Galactic Radiation and Background) and eventually DYNO (its NRO code name). Another four missions followed through 1962, one of which was successful. GRAB's primary targets were Soviet radar systems. A follow-on to GRAB, designated POPPY, was first orbited in 1962.[14]

Also in 1962, the Air Force began operating low-earth orbiting satellites designed to intercept signals emitted by Soviet, Chinese, and other nations' air defense, ABM, and early-warning radars. The first of these heavy ferret satellites was launched by a Thor-Agena-B on February 21, 1962. Between the first launch and July 16, 1971, sixteen of these satellites were launched, about one to three satellites per year, with inclinations ranging from 75 to 82 degrees. The sixteen satellites involved three different generations—three successful launches in the first generation, nine in the second generation (with a first launch in January 1963 and the final launch in January 1968), and four in the third generation.[15]

A second class of ferrets was put into operation beginning in August 1963. Whereas each satellite in the first class had been launched as a primary payload, the satellites in the second class were piggybacked on launch vehicles carrying imaging satellites. The orbits of both classes evolved in a similar fashion—with initial orbits of approximately 180 by 250 miles giving way to near-circular orbits of around 300 miles. The ferrets were usually arranged in constellations of four to maximize their utility for direction-finding.[16]

From 1972 to 1988, all ferret satellites were launched as secondary payloads. One set of ferret satellites, designated 989, was launched along with KH-9 imagery satellites (which were launched from 1971 to 1984) as well as with a class of SIGINT satellites designated JUMPSEAT (discussed below).

On September 5, 1988, the first satellite of what was intended to be a new four-satellite constellation of ferrets was launched. The new-generation ferret was the primary payload on a Titan II launched from Vandenberg Air Force Base. It was placed into an 85-degree inclined, 500-mile circular orbit. This launch was followed by similar Titan II launches on September 5, 1989, and April 25, 1992. However, in 1993, three Titan II boosters that had been designated for a "classified user" were reassigned to the Strategic Defense Initiative Organization (now the Missile Defense Agency).[17]

That action apparently reflected a decision noted in a draft version of the Joint Chiefs of Staff "Roles and Missions" report that the missions being performed by two existing national satellite systems would be performed in the future by a single new system. That system would be a follow-on to the advanced version of the PARCAE ELINT ocean surveillance satellite. PARCAE (as well as the advanced PARCAE satellite constellation), first launched in 1976, and its associated ground sites had, for many years, the unclassified designation CLASSIC WIZARD. It is apparently now known as ICEbox, with "ICE" being an acronym for Improved Collection Equipment.[18]

The CLASSIC WIZARD Global Surveillance System, as it was referred to in one Naval Security Group Command Instruction, had its origins in U.S. Navy studies started in 1968 to investigate the feasibility of a dedicated ocean surveillance satellite system. In 1970, the Chief of Naval Operations ordered a study of overall ocean surveillance requirements. This project resulted in a five-volume *Naval Research Laboratory Ocean Surveillance Requirements Study*. In turn, the study produced Program 749, a study that focused on the development of high-resolution, phased-array radars that would allow all-weather ocean surveillance monitoring as well as detection of low-trajectory, sea-launched missiles.[19]

Despite the emphasis of these initial studies, the ocean surveillance satellite that resulted, PARCAE, lacked radar capability. Rather, it was a passive interceptor, equipped with a passive infrared scanner and millimeter wave radiometers, as well as with radio-frequency antennas capable of monitoring radio communications and radar emissions from submarines and ships. It used passive interferometry techniques (the use of interference phenomena) to determine the location of ships; that is, the craft could compute a ship's position from data on radar or radio signals provided by several antennas.[20]

The PARCAE system consisted of a mother ship and three subsatellites tethered to the mother ship. The basic techniques involved in using multiple spacecraft to eavesdrop on and detect Soviet surface vessels and submarines were first demonstrated using three Naval Research Laboratory spacecraft launched on December 14, 1971. The subsatellites were relatively small, each measuring approximately 3 by 8 by 1 feet. The largest surface area on one side was covered by solar cells, and four spherical objects on the end of the metal booms were believed to be sensors.[21]

PARCAE satellites were launched from Vandenberg Air Force Base into a near-circular, 63-degree inclined orbit with an altitude of approximately 700 miles. At that altitude, the spacecraft could receive signals from surface vessels more than 2,000 miles away. Given that there was a displacement of approximately 1,866 miles between passes, PARCAE could provide overlapping coverage on successive passes.[22]

There were eight operational clusters put into orbit from 1976 to May 15, 1987. An increased rate in the 1980s led the Navy to request and receive funds for antenna upgrades at all CLASSIC WIZARD ground stations. Those stations, colocated with Navy Regional Reporting Centers, were situated in Diego Garcia, British Indian Ocean Territory; Guam; Adak, Alaska; Winter Harbor, Maine; and Edzell, Scotland. Information received at the stations could be quickly transmitted to regional ocean surveillance centers and via satellite to a main downlink in the Washington area. In recent years, all of the sites have been closed, beginning with the Adak and Edzell sites, and Army and Air Force SIGINT personnel were colocated with Navy SIGINT personnel at other sites, further indicating that the CLASSIC WIZARD system focuses on more than naval targets. Army participation began in the mid-1980s under a program known as TRUE BLUE (which also involved Army participation at other sites). In 1995, Detachment 1 of the Air Intelligence Agency's 692nd Intelligence Group was established on Guam to participate in the CLASSIC WIZARD program, described in an Air Intelligence Agency publication as a "joint global surveillance reporting system."[23]

The first advanced PARCAE system was deployed during a June 1990 shuttle mission, launched from Cape Canaveral. The second advanced PARCAE was carried into orbit by a Titan IV, launched in November 1991 from Vandenberg Air Force Base. In both cases, the satellites were deployed in orbits similar to those of the earlier PARCAE satellites. However, it appears that there is no mother ship attached to the triplets. An August 1993 launch from Vandenberg produced an explosion shortly after takeoff that destroyed the booster and the spacecraft. A successful advanced PARCAE launch followed, although not until May 12, 1996.[24]

Shortly after the explosion it was reported that the NRO and the Navy planned to develop a new generation of spacecraft with improved detection capabilities. The new generation is apparently even more of a dual system—employed against land- and sea-based targets—than the advanced PARCAE. The first launch took place on

September 8, 2001, and was followed by launches on December 2, 2003; February 3, 2005; June 15, 2007; and April 14, 2011. Unlike the previous generation of ELINT-ocean surveillance satellites, the new generation has been launched into orbit on Atlas launch vehicles. And rather than using three objects in orbit, the new generation uses only a pair. As with earlier generations, the satellites orbit with a 63-degree inclination and at about 700 miles above the earth.[25]

Operational control of the satellites is the responsibility of the Program Operations Coordination Group at NSA. However, all the original ground stations associated with CLASSIC WIZARD have now been closed. Apparently data are downlinked to two overseas sites—one at Misawa Air Base, Japan, and the other at Griesheim in Germany.[26]

Customers of CLASSIC WIZARD/ICEbox data, such as commanders of U.S. fleets, can specify, through an automated system, particular data they require with respect to area of interest, signals of interest, and units of interest. Among the major targets of the new generation are the thousands of civilian and merchant ships, particularly those suspected of transporting weapons or weapons-related materiel for terrorist groups and rogue regimes. According to one report, information from the satellites that was passed to the Spanish government allowed commandos to stop a North Korean ship carrying Scud missiles to Yemen.[27]

In the late 1960s and early 1970s, the NRO began orbiting two geosynchronous systems, CANYON and RHYOLITE (subsequently renamed AQUACADE), developed under the auspices of the Air Force Office of Special Projects and the CIA, respectively. The first CANYON was launched in August 1968 from Cape Canaveral into orbit with a perigee of 19,641 miles, an apogee of 22,853 miles, and a 9.9-degree inclination. Controlled from a ground station at Bad Aibling, Germany, the satellite was America's first high-altitude SIGINT system and first dedicated COMINT satellite. Six additional launches would follow, concluding with a 1977 launch.[28]

In 1970, the first of four RHYOLITE spacecraft were placed into geosynchronous orbit, although it was closer to achieving a pure geostationary orbit (0-degree inclination, 22,300 miles for both perigee and apogee) than CANYON. Rather than focusing on communications intelligence, RHYOLITE's primary function was intercepting the telemetry signals from Soviet and Chinese offensive and defensive missile tests, ASAT tests, and space launches. One satellite was apparently located somewhere above the Horn of Africa, at 69 degrees east, to receive telemetry signals transmitted from liquid-fueled Intercontinental Ballistic Missiles (ICBMs) launched from Tyuratam in a northeasterly direction toward the Kamchatka Peninsula impact zone. Another station was over Borneo, at 115 degrees east, to monitor Soviet solid-propellant missiles, such as the SS-16 ICBM and SS-20 IRBM, launched from Plesetsk.[29]

In addition to intercepting the telemetry signals from Soviet and Chinese missile tests, the RHYOLITE satellites had a significant COMINT capability. Their use for COMINT purposes was dramatically increased on orders from President Nixon and

Henry Kissinger, once they were made aware of the capability. The satellites apparently were used to intercept Soviet and Chinese telephone and radio communications across the UHF, VHF, and microwave frequency bands. Walkie-talkie communications generated by Soviet military exercises, which fell in the VHF/UHF range, also were regularly monitored by RHYOLITE satellites. Beyond the Soviet Union, RHYOLITE satellites, whose footprints collectively covered virtually the entire world outside of the Western Hemisphere, intercepted communications from China, Vietnam, Indonesia, Pakistan, and Lebanon.[30]

The CANYON and RHYOLITE/AQUACADE programs led, eventually, to follow-on programs originally code-named CHALET and MAGNUM, respectively. On June 10, 1978, the first CHALET satellite was placed into an orbit similar to those inhabited by the CANYON satellites. Subsequently, after disclosure of the program in the press in 1979, it was renamed VORTEX. In 1987, its name was again changed to MERCURY after another disclosure.[31]

CHALET's original mission was strictly COMINT. However, after the loss of ground stations in Iran and the discovery that information on RHYOLITE had been sold to the KGB, CHALET was modified to allow it to intercept Soviet telemetry. The first modified CHALET was launched on October 1, 1979 (by which time it was known as VORTEX). Subsequent launches, not all successful, occurred on October 1, 1981; January 31, 1984; September 2, 1988; May 10, 1989; and September 4, 1989. The final MERCURY satellite was destroyed as a result of a 1998 launch failure.[32]

The primary targets of VORTEX, for most of the program's existence, were in the Soviet Union. In particular, they included the communications of Soviet missile and nuclear RDT&E sites, defense-related ministries, and defense industries. At the height of the VORTEX operations, there were at least three operating VORTEX satellites—one covering Eastern Europe and the western USSR, another the central USSR, and the third the eastern portion of the USSR.[33]

Each also covered non-Soviet targets in its footprint, including Israel, Iran, and other Middle Eastern countries. Thus, the VORTEX ground station at Menwith Hill in the United Kingdom was heavily involved in supporting Operations Desert Shield and Desert Storm. In 1989, it received a Joint Meritorious Unit Award from Secretary of Defense Dick Cheney for "meritorious achievement from May 1987 to 1 September 1988"—a period that matches U.S. naval operations in the Persian Gulf.[34]

On January 25, 1985, the first satellite developed under the MAGNUM program was launched from the space shuttle Discovery into a geosynchronous orbit. By the time of launch, the program had been redesignated ORION. The second and final MAGNUM/ORION spacecraft was placed into orbit on November 22, 1989, also from a space shuttle orbiter. The satellites were reported to weigh about 6,000 pounds and to have two huge parabolic antennas. One is intended to intercept communications and telemetry signals, the other to relay the intercepted material to

Earth. The first ORION may have been stationed over Borneo, the second over the Horn of Africa.[35]

One or more of the satellites that were launched in the 1980s may still be operating—although certainly not at full capacity—as indicated by comments of a senior NRO official. The core of the U.S. geosynchronous SIGINT constellation consists of the new generations of SIGINT satellites that the NRO began launching in 1994. Titan IV boosters placed the new SIGINT satellites into orbit on August 25, 1994; May 14, 1995; April 24, 1996; May 8, 1998; and September 9, 2003. One or more SIGINT satellites may be among those launched on Atlas IIA vehicles on December 6, 2000, and October 10, 2001. Additional geosynchronous SIGINT satellites, possibly upgraded ORIONs, were apparently launched on Delta IV boosters in January 2009 and November 2010.[36]

It appears that the launches involve three distinct programs, with the first and third launches being from the same program, whose unclassified designation is RAMROD. The system associated with RAMROD has been described as providing "near real time reporting of highly sensitive, perishable data to national and tactical commanders." It consists of two "strings," each with a "specific geographic reporting area," suggesting that it is an ORION follow-on. The second, fourth, and fifth launches appear to be satellites in the follow-on program to MERCURY, whose unclassified designation is RUTLEY.[37]

In 1993, a SIGINT satellite system, designated INTRUDER, was reported to be under development. Whether that satellite proceeded from development to becoming an operational spacecraft is not clear. However, in 1999, a new generation of geosynchronous SIGINT satellites, with the unclassified designation RANGER, was scheduled to become operational in the near future, and it is likely that at least one or two of the post-2000 high-altitude SIGINT launches carried a RANGER satellite, which has both COMINT and ELINT (and probably TELINT) functions.[38]

Unlike VORTEX, ORION, and its successors, a third class of SIGINT satellites did not operate in geosynchronous orbit. Rather, the first generation of this class—designated JUMPSEAT—was launched into a 63-degree, highly inclined, elliptical orbit (200 by 24,000 miles) from Vandenberg Air Force Base. Approximately six JUMPSEATs were launched after the initial launch on March 20, 1971, with a final launch in 1987. In its highly elliptical orbit, JUMPSEAT "hovered" over the Soviet Union for eight to nine hours at a time, intercepting communications and electronic signals from the northern Soviet Union as well as from Molniya communications satellites that operated in the same orbit. When paired with 989 ferret satellites, the combination was first designated YIELD and then (from 1982 on) WILLOW.[39]

A far more advanced version of JUMPSEAT, code-named TRUMPET, was launched on May 3, 1994. That launch culminated a ten-year effort to orbit the new satellite, including a three-year wait from the time it first reached its launchpad at Cape Canaveral. A second launch followed on July 10, 1995. The satellites weigh about 10,000 pounds. Like JUMPSEAT, TRUMPET operates in a highly inclined, elliptical orbit, but it has a more extensive mission. Although the Intelligence Community wished to leave the satellites in storage, feeling that the cost of operation and maintenance exceeded the benefit in the post–Cold War world, congressional overseers directed otherwise. The program was eventually canceled in favor of a less expensive alternative, but not until after three successful launches had taken place (in 1994, 1995, and 1997), and therefore data should be available from at least some of the satellites for several more years.[40]

The first launch in a follow-on program to TRUMPET may have taken place on June 27, 2006, when a Delta rocket launched from Vandenberg Air Force Base in California placed an NRO satellite into a Molniya-type orbit. Initial parameters associated with the launch indicate that the satellite had a 62.4-degree inclination and an orbit of 690 by 23,785 miles. It was reported that it may also have been carrying an experimental infrared sensor to be used in the Space-Based Infrared System (SBIRS). A subsequent launch carrying a TRUMPET follow-on along with a SBIRS payload was launched on March 13, 2008, from Vandenberg Air Force Base on a Atlas V booster.[41]

SIGINT satellite operations are supported by several specialized ground stations, located at Buckley Air National Guard Base, Colorado; Menwith Hill, United Kingdom; and Pine Gap, Australia.

The Buckley site serves as a ground station for four satellite programs—ORION, TRUMPET, and the systems whose unclassified designations are RAMROD and RANGER.* Although Buckley has been one of three stations associated with the ORION program, it is apparently the sole ground station for TRUMPET, whose orbit permits it to operate in view of the Buckley station when it is over the Northern Hemisphere. It is the most important of the two ground stations associated with RAMROD, "providing 75% of all information reported by the RAMROD system worldwide."[42]

From 1972 to 1974, NSA began augmenting its listening post at Menwith Hill (which it took over from the Army in 1966), a tri-service station located eight miles west of Harrogate in Yorkshire. The station encompasses 562 acres and consists of a large array of satellite-tracking aerials. One objective was to make Menwith Hill the primary ground station for the forthcoming CHALET system. Information received at Menwith Hill from the remaining operational VORTEX satellites can be transmitted directly to Fort Meade via the Defense Satellite Communications System (DSCS). In addition, Menwith Hill serves as the ground station for the new generation of RUTLEY SIGINT satellites launched in May 1995. Responsibility for the operation of Menwith Hill was transferred to the Army Intelligence and Security Command in 1994 and 1995, although representatives of the other services' SIG-

---

*SIGINT satellites are given unclassified designations (whose meaning is classified) that begin with R. The unclassified designations for various SIGINT satellites have included RAINFALL (RHYOLITE), RUNWAY (VORTEX), ROSTER (MAGNUM), and RUFFER (JUMPSEAT/TRUMPET). The designations allow reference to the satellites in unclassified publications or settings.

INT organizations are also involved in operation of the facility, including the Air Intelligence Agency's 451st Information Operations Squadron.[43]

The Joint Defence Space Research Facility at Pine Gap, Australia, was established to serve as the ground control station and downlink for the RHYOLITE satellite located over Borneo and subsequently was assigned the same mission for the ORION satellite over Borneo. It may have assumed a similar mission for one of the satellites associated with the RAMROD system. The facility consists of at least seven large radomes, a huge computer room, and about twenty other support buildings. The radomes (the first of which were built in 1968 and which resemble gigantic golf balls with a slice off the bottom) are made of Perspex and mounted on a concrete structure. They were intended to protect the enclosed antennas against dust, wind, and rain and to hide some of the operational elements of the antennas from Soviet reconnaissance satellites.[44]

The computer room is divided into three principal sections. The Station-Keeping Section is responsible for maintaining the satellites in geosynchronous orbit and for correctly aligning them toward targets of interest. The Signals Processing Office receives the signals transmitted from the satellite and transforms them into a form that can be used by the analysts in the Signals Analysis Section. In 1996, plans to upgrade Pine Gap were announced by the U.S. and Australian governments.[45]

Day-to-day tasking of the satellites is the responsibility of an NSA element at Fort George G. Meade—the Overhead Collection Management Center (OCMC). The SIGINT Overhead Mission Management System is a hardware and software tool "that provides the OCMC the capability to allocate SIGINT satellites against intelligence targets in accordance with priorities and guidance established by the [National SIGINT Collection Subcommittee]."[46]

AIRBORNE COLLECTION

Each of the three major military services operates aircraft for the collection of strategic and tactical signals intelligence. The 55th Wing of the Air Combat Command (ACC), headquartered at Offutt Air Force Base, Nebraska, is responsible for the operations of the Air Force's RC-135 fleet. Personnel to operate the sensors, analyze the data, and disseminate it are provided by AFISR Agency Intelligence Squadrons and Air Combat Command Reconnaissance Squadrons. Tasking is the responsibility of both the AFISR Agency and the National Security Agency.

There have been twelve versions of the aircraft. The first RC-135, an RC-135B, joined the Strategic Air Command's reconnaissance fleet in December 1965. This step began the process of replacing thirty obsolescent RB-47Hs and ERB-47Hs that were then "performing the ELINT portion of the Global Peacetime Airborne Reconnaissance Program."[47]

The RC-135 fleet stands at twenty-one aircraft, seventeen of which are RC-135V/W RIVET JOINT planes. These models have an overall length of 135 feet, a wingspan of 131 feet, and an overall height of 42 feet. At an operational altitude of

34, 990 feet, they can fly at over 500 miles per hour. They can be refueled in the air, which they require after ten hours, and can stay aloft for thirty hours. Their unrefueled range is 3,900 miles.[48]

The RIVET JOINT aircraft fly missions, designated BURNING WIND, that intercept both communications and electronic signals. One system carried by the plane is the Automatic Electronic Emitter Locating System (AEELS), which scans each side of the aircraft to identify and locate emitters of interest. It can reportedly locate, analyze, and identify a radar within seconds, although not with sufficient precision to permit targeting of smart weapons. The data can then be transmitted via a secure voice link—the Tactical Information Broadcast Service (TIBS) or the Tactical Digital Information Link (TACDIL). The Multiple Communications Emitter Location System (MUCELS) carried on earlier versions has been replaced by plain blade antennas.[49]

The RIVET JOINT aircraft operate from five primary locations: Offutt Air Force Base, Nebraska; RAF Mildenhall, United Kingdom; Souda Bay, Crete; Kadena Air Base, Okinawa, Japan; and Al Kharj, Saudi Arabia (the 763rd Expeditionary Reconnaissance Squadron [ERS]).[50]

With the end of the Cold War, the targets of RIVET JOINT missions changed considerably. During 1995 and 1996, 79 percent of those missions were conducted in support of joint task force operations in the Middle East (Iraq) and Bosnia. On February 22, 1995, a RIVET JOINT aircraft flew the 1,000th mission in support of Operation Southern Watch, the enforcement of United Nations sanctions against Iraq. In October 1996, a RIVET JOINT from Mildenhall flew the 1,000th Adriatic mission, four years after the beginning of those missions in support of Operation Provide Promise. Another 19 percent were targeted on Cuba, the Mediterranean (particularly Libya), and the Pacific (including North Korea, China, and Vietnam). The remaining 2 percent of flights involved training and exercises. RC-135s have "become a key tool in the electronic attack of enemy air defenses that rely on rapid exchanges of data about location of attacking enemy aircraft." In the last decade RIVET JOINT aircraft have flown missions in support of Operation Iraqi Freedom and Operation Enduring Freedom (Afghanistan). According to an Air Force fact sheet, "RC-135s have maintained a constant presence in Southwest Asia since the early 1990s." In 2008 the 763rd ERS surpassed the 50,000 flight-hour mark during a mission over Afghanistan.[51]

According to one account, today the RC-135 is employed primarily to locate and monitor the movements of enemy forces. The plane delivers combat advisory broadcast and warnings of imminent threats to aircraft or ground units.[52]

A RIVET JOINT aircraft was also used in a series of electronic attack experiments at Nellis AFB, Nevada. An EC-130 COMPASS CALL electronic attack aircraft fired a data stream into an integrated air defense network's antennas, while a RC-135W monitored changes in the network's emissions.[53]

Two RC-135s are RC-135U versions, which bear the designation COMBAT SENT and have flown missions designated HAVE TERRA and HAVE UNION.

The planes fly at the same speed and altitude as the RIVET JOINT's, although with a different mission—the location and identification of foreign military land, naval, and airborne radar signals. Specifically, the missions are intended to provide "signal parametrics used for the development of radar warning receivers, EW [electronic warfare] systems, threat system simulators, [and] mission planning." The signal parametrics include power, pulse, and polarization data. The primary sensor carried on the COMBAT SENT aircraft is the Precision Power Measurement System, which determines the absolute power, power pattern, and polarization of selected target emitters. In addition, a high-resolution camera and television and radar sensors are in the tail and are used when the occasion permits. One COMBAT SENT plane is equipped with the COMPASS ERA system, which contains infrared thermal imaging, interferometer-spectrometer, and spectral radiometer sensors. Among the targets of the COMBAT SENT planes that flew during the Cold War along the periphery of the Soviet Union and other Warsaw Pact countries were the ODD PAIR, SIDE NET, and TOP STEER radar systems.[54]

The COMBAT SENT also carries the Automatic Electronic Emitter Locating System. The crew includes two pilots, two navigators, two airborne systems engineers, a minimum of ten electronic warfare officers, and six or more electronic, technical, and area specialists. The aircraft are manned by Air Combat Command crews from the 45th Reconnaissance Squadron and the AFISR Agency's 97th Intelligence Squadron.[55]

The final component of the RC-135 fleet is the RC-135S model, designated COBRA BALL, whose missions have been designated BURNING STAR. There are three such aircraft. The COBRA BALL aircraft had been based at Eielson Air Force Base, Alaska, until late 1991, and often operated from Shemya, when the COBRA BALL mission was transferred to Offutt Air Force Base.[56]

COBRA BALL missions, which numbered about 100 per year in the mid-1990s, were directed at obtaining intelligence on the missile tests of Russia, China, India, and Israel. Thus, in January1994, a COBRA BALL was deployed of the Bay of Bengal, from its base on Diego Garcia, to monitor an imminent Indian test. Aircraft stationed at Souda Bay, Greece, can be employed to monitor Israeli and Iranian missile tests. In 1996, COBRA BALL aircraft monitored Chinese tests near Taiwan, Indian tests, and several Russian tests. In May 1997, a COBRA BALL monitored the test of a North Korean anti-ship missile. In early March 2003, North Korean fighter jets intercepted a COBRA BALL about 150 miles off the North Korean coast and ordered it to land in North Korea—instructions that were ignored by U.S. pilots.[57]

Among the systems carried by the RC-135S aircraft is the Advanced Telemetry System (ATS), which automatically searches a portion of the frequency band and makes a digital record of all signals present.* The operator of the ATS system allocates its collection resources to reentry vehicle links and records all telemetry detected.[58]

---

*The MASINT sensors on COBRA BALL are discussed in Chapter 9.

The Navy's counterpart SIGINT fleet is made of EP-3E ARIES II aircraft. In 1999, the fleet of twelve was evenly divided between Fleet Air Reconnaissance Squadron One (VQ-1), the "World Watchers," located at Naval Air Station Whidbey Island, Washington, and Fleet Air Reconnaissance Squadron Two (VQ-2) located at Rota, Spain. VQ-1's area of responsibility stretched from the west coast of the United States to the east coast of Africa and the Arabian Gulf. Its detachments were located at Bahrain, UAE; Misawa, Japan; Kadena, Japan; and Osan, Republic of Korea.[59]

In September 2005, VQ-2 and its aircraft and 450 personnel were relocated from Rota, Spain, to NAS Whidbey Island, such that both VQ-1 and VQ-2 are now headquartered there. The move, according to the Navy, was "in keeping with the Navy's ongoing transformation of forces in Europe" and would give the squadrons the ability to "surge worldwide." Currently, there are eleven aircraft in the combined EP-3 fleet. Current plans are to retire the fleet, with the last planes being retired around 2017.[60]

The EP-3Es are 116-foot, four-engine turboprops that fly at altitudes just over 28,000 feet, at 466 miles per hour, for up to twelve hours, and have a range of 2,738 miles. The plane is distinguished from the P-3C by a flat circular radome under the fuselage, and it lacks the long, thin Magnetic Anomaly Detector boom at the tail. The planes are manned by a five-man flight crew, with another eighteen individuals working on system operations. These include a Secure Communications Operator/trainee, a Story Book Operator, a Laboratory Operator, a Big Look Electronic Warfare Operator, a Tactical Evaluator, a Senior Evaluator, a Communication Evaluator, a Petty Officer–in–Charge, four Special Operators, a Special Operator/Electronic Warfare Operator/Scientific and Technical Operator, a relief crewman/trainee, an In-Flight Technician, and two relief crew members/trainees.[61]

The Story Book system is an integrated communications intelligence signal acquisition, data processing, and data fusion capability, which is reported to provide tactical assessment and a real-time transmission capability. Six operators (the Petty Officer–in–Charge, the four Special Operators, and the Special Operator/Electronic Warfare Operator/Scientific and Technical Operator) operate the Story Classic system, which provides an upgraded search and acquisition capability for low band signals. The Senior, Communication, and Tactical Evaluators have access at their work stations to data collected by the EP-3E as well as other U.S. intelligence assets (the latter through the Tactical Related Applications, Tactical Digital Information Exchange Systems, Tactical Information Broadcast System, and other links), which allows them to integrate the data collected by the plane with other data to provide a comprehensive assessment of their target's activity and to disseminate their conclusions.[62]

VQ-1 targets have included foreign surface and submarine activity (in support of Carrier Battle Groups) as well as land-based radars and UHF/VHF communications systems. By 1993, VQ-1 operations targeted on the PRC became its highest priority in the Western Pacific. It flew "nationally and fleet-tasked collection efforts against the PRC and also provided I&W [Indications and Warning] of PRC military activity to several transiting battle groups." During 1993, VQ-1 operations were also directed at collecting information on the changes in the Russian military in the wake of the collapse of the Soviet Union.[63]

In 1996, VQ-1 flew 1,319 sorties, involving "both nationally and fleet-tasked SRO [Sensitive Reconnaissance Operations] and I&W missions, in support of DESERT STRIKE, SOUTHERN WATCH, VIGILANT WARRIOR, and VIGILANT SENTINEL." Its operating areas included the "North Arabian Sea, Gulf of Oman, Arabian Gulf, Overland Saudi Arabia, Sea of Japan, Sea of Okhotsk, Indian Ocean, South China Sea, East China Sea, Luzon Strait, Gulf of Thailand, Overland Korea, and the Western Pacific." As a result of operations in those areas VQ-1 "intercepted and processed 2,911 signals of tactical significance from target-country naval, airborne, and land-based emitters" and located seventy-two nonfriendly submarines.[64]

In 2001, VQ-1 operated five EP-3Es (and three P-3s), whose area of operations included the Persian Gulf, South America, Indian Ocean, Korea, Thailand, Afghanistan, the Bay of Bengal, Gulf of Oman, North Arabian Sea, Kuwait, Sea of Japan, Pakistan, East China Sea, Gulf of Thailand, Saudi Arabia, South China Sea, and Western Pacific. On April 1, 2001, an EP-3E, while conducting operations over international waters off the coast of Hainan Island, was disabled in a midair collision with a shadowing Chinese F-8 interceptor and was forced to land on Hainan. The crew spent eleven and a half days in detainment before they were released.[65]

Not long after the terrorist attacks of September 11, VQ-1 began operations in Southwest Asia, in support of Operation Enduring Freedom. It also conducted intercept operations in support of Operation Southern Watch and Plan Columbia. According to its annual history, VQ-1 collected 6,113 signals of tactical significance in 2001. In 2005, VQ-1 detachments included those located at Manama, Bahrain, and Kadena Air Base, Okinawa, Japan. Subsequently, the Bahrain detachment was relocated to Qatar. In 2008, VQ-1 EP-3s participated in Operations Iraqi Freedom, NOMAD SHADOW (a European Command Counterterrorist effort involving Turkey and Iraq), WILLING SPIRIT (the recovery of three Americans held hostage by Colombia's FARC), and INCA GOLD (a Southern Command counter-narcotics operation).[66]

In the summer of 1990, VQ-2 provided electronic reconnaissance support during the evacuation of 2,000 noncombatant personnel from Liberia in Operation Sharp Edge. From August 1990 to April 1991, the squadron provided combat reconnaissance during Operations Desert Storm, Desert Shield, Proven Force, and Provide Comfort. A 1997 Mediterranean mission might involve eavesdropping on military, government, and police communications in North Africa, primarily Algeria and Libya. In 1997, EP-3Es from the Souda Bay detachment conducted missions to monitor the crisis in Albania.[67]

VQ-2 is currently assigned five EP-3Es (and four PC-3Cs). From 2001 to 2005, EP-3E detachments were located at Naval Support Activity Souda Bay, Crete; Incirlik Air Base, Turkey; Naval Air Station Roosevelt Road, Puerto Rico; Manama, Bahrain; Mildenhall, U.K.; Curaçao, Netherlands Antilles; RAF Akrotiri, Cyprus; Jacksonville, Florida; and Kadena Air Base, Okinawa, Japan. During that period, VQ-2 flew missions in support of Operations Enduring Freedom (Afghanistan), Joint Forge (Yugoslavia), Inca Gold (Latin America), Joint Guardian (Adriatic Sea), Northern Watch (Iraq), Southern Watch (Iraq), Iraqi Freedom (Iraq), Mountain Lion (Afghanistan), Mountain Sweep (Afghanistan), Dolphin Eagle (Latin America), Caribbean Shield, Atlas Shield (SOUTHCOM), and Secure Tomorrow (EUCOM), as well as Maritime Intercept Operations and JCS Sensitive Reconnaissance Operations. In addition, VQ-2's 2001 operations in support of SOUTHCOM contributed to the seizure of 54.1 metric tons of cocaine and 2.6 metric tons of marijuana.[68]

Current plans are to replace the EP-3 (as well as the VPU planes, discussed in Chapter 9) with the EP-X. The planes are expected to carry not only passive signals intercept equipment but a radar system and possibly other intelligence collection sensors as well. The plane may also carry "expendable systems"—possibly stealthy vehicles small enough to fly into enemy air defenses (which could induce the systems to be turned on).[69]

In addition to their imagery capabilities, U-2 aircraft can be equipped with SIGINT sensors. SENIOR RUBY is a near-real-time ELINT collection, processing, and reporting system that provides information (including type and location) on radar emitters within line of sight of the U-2. It can handle a large number of emitters simultaneously and sends its data to a Ground Control Processor colocated with the COMINT Transportable Ground Intercept Facility (TGIF).[70]

SENIOR SPEAR is a near-real-time COMINT collection, processing, and reporting system that provides line-of-sight collection capability—out to 300 nautical miles—from the aircraft. When flown together, the SENIOR RUBY and SENIOR SPEAR systems constitute SENIOR GLASS. Data collected by the U-2 SIGINT systems can be transmitted to a satellite via the SENIOR SPAN data link, carried in a dorsal fairing on the top of the aircraft.[71]

U-2 missions have been flown from several bases against a variety of targets. From Patrick Air Force Base, Florida, U-2Rs have flown collection missions against Cuba. The main targets are Cuban army, air force, and navy communications, with the intercepts being transmitted to Key West Naval Air Station, Florida. U-2Rs have flown from RAF Akrotiri (Operating Location OLIVE HARVEST) to intercept signals from Syria, Egypt, and Israel. The data are then uplinked to a DSCS satellite for transmission to the Remote Operations Facility, Airborne (ROFA). From Osan Air Base, South Korea, SENIOR SPEAR U-2s fly OLYMPIC GAME missions to intercept Chinese and North Korean communications, with the intercepted communications being downlinked to an Air Force ISR Agency unit at Osan.[72]

The SIGINT capability of the U-2s will be improved, as they are slated to receive the Advanced Signals Intelligence Platform (ASIP) pod for high- and low-band signals intelligence collection. Developmental testing began in late 2006 and was reported to be nearing the end of development in March 2010.[73]

Two further airborne SIGINT systems are operated by the Army: the RC-12 GUARDRAIL and the RC-7B/Airborne Reconnaissance Low–Multifunction (ARL-M). The RC-12s are two-engine turboprops that can fly as low as 20,000 or as high as 32,000 feet, at 130 knots, and operate for up to five hours. The planes come in a variety of models—the RC-12H, RC-12K, RC-12N, RC-12P, and RC-12Q. They carry remotely controlled, ground-based intercept and direction-finding systems to exploit HF, VHF, and UHF voice communications. They also carry Global Positioning System receivers, which permit location of data to within 60 feet. An adjunct to the RC-12 is the Remote Relay System (RRS). Intercepted SIGINT data are downlinked to the RRS, where they can automatically be relayed by satellite to any location where the appropriate receiving equipment can be set up.[74]

RC-12s are deployed in four groups of twelve. One group is located in Korea; another is assigned to the 205th MI Brigade in Germany and has been employed to support Operation Joint Endeavor. The third group is assigned to the 525th MI Brigade at Fort Bragg, North Carolina.[75]

The RC-7B/ARL-M is a four-engine turboprop that flies at altitudes between 6,000 and 20,000 feet at 220 knots and has a ten-hour endurance. The ARL-M is a modification of the ARL aircraft that were dedicated to either imagery or SIGINT missions exclusively. It carries HF, VHF, and UHF receivers. Originally designed to satisfy SOUTHCOM intelligence requirements, its mission was to "provide low profile signals intelligence and imagery collection support for counter-narcotics." Of the Army's five ARL-Ms, three are assigned to Korea. In addition to SIGINT equipment, they carry a variety of imagery sensors—SAR, MTI, infrared, and electro-optical. The planes' mission includes watching military and civilian movements near the demilitarized zone in Korea.[76]

In addition to aerial SIGINT missions flown by NSA and the service cryptologic elements, other missions have been flown for more than two decades by the Army's Intelligence Support Activity (aka Security Coordination Detachment). In the 1980s, Beechcraft and King Air aircraft were procured for ISA and equipped with a variety of communications intercept equipment, which was used to intercept communications involving the Sandinistas in Nicaragua as well as leftist Salvadoran and Honduran rebels. In the early 1990s, ISA airborne SIGINT missions helped in tracking Colombian drug lord Pablo Escobar and, in late 2001, were intercepting communications of fleeing Taliban and al-Qaeda leaders.[77]

UAVs are also expected to provide an overhead signals intelligence capability. In 2008, the Air Force requested Northrop Grumman to develop the ASIP for use of the Predator and Reaper drones. In March 2010, it was reported that the payload would also be carried on Global Hawk aircraft.[78]

GROUND STATIONS

Starting in the late 1940s, the United States began establishing ground stations from which to monitor the Soviet Union and Eastern Europe. This network changed composition over the years and grew to include stations targeted on China, Vietnam, North Korea, the Middle East, Central America, and other areas. As the Cold War ended and the Soviet Union collapsed, dramatic cutbacks were made in the overseas network operated by NSA and the service cryptological elements, particularly in Europe, as the fear of a large-scale European war disappeared. As a result, major U.S. SIGINT facilities in Italy (San Vito), Germany (Field Station, Berlin; Field Station, Augsburg; and a number of lesser tactical stations), the United Kingdom (RAF Chicksands), and Turkey (Field Station, Sinop) were closed or turned over to local governments.[79]

At the same time, the NSA established three Regional SIGINT Operations Centers (RSOCs) to receive data from manned and unmanned SIGINT sites in particular regions. These sites are manned by personnel from each of the three major service cryptological elements: the Army Intelligence and Security Command (INSCOM), the Navy Information Operations Command (NIOC), and the Air Force Intelligence, Surveillance, and Reconnaissance Agency (AFISR Agency). NSA and Marine Support Battalion personnel may also be present.

The three regional centers are located in Texas, Hawaii, and Georgia. NSA/CSS Texas, originally known as the Medina Regional SIGINT Operations Center (MRSOC), is located at Medina Annex, Lackland, Texas. It focuses on Central and South America as well as the Caribbean. The units present as NSA/CSS Texas come from INSCOM, the AFISR Agency, the Navy, and the Marine Corps (Marine Support Battalion, Company H).[80]

NSA/CSS Hawaii (formerly the Hawaii Regional Security Operations Center and, before that, the Kunia Regional SIGINT Operations Center) at Kunia, Hawaii, is focused on Asia. It is staffed by representatives from INSCOM, the Navy, and the AFISR Agency. The third regional SIGINT center is NSA/CSS Georgia (formerly the Georgia Regional SIGINT Operations Center and, prior to that, the Gordon Regional SIGINT Operations Center) at Fort Gordon, Georgia, which focuses on Europe and the Middle East. It hosts INSCOM and Air Force ISR Agency personnel as well as the Ft. Gordon NIOC and Company D, Marine Support Battalion.[81]

Among the remaining stations in the SIGINT ground station network are those in Alaska, Japan, the United Kingdom, Germany, Thailand, and Korea. Shemya Island, Alaska (also the home of the COBRA DANE radar), which is approximately 400 miles across the Bering Sea from the Russian eastern seaboard, was for many years, and may still be, the home of the Anders Facility. Run by the Bendix Field Engineering Corporation (which became Allied Signal in 1992) for the NSA, the facility's Pusher antenna monitored Russian communications in the Far East.[82]

Elmendorf Air Force Base, located in Anchorage, is the home of an AN/FLR-9 "Elephant Cage" antenna. The AN/FLR-9 consists of three circular arrays, each made up of antenna elements around a circular reflecting screen. In the middle of the triple array is a central building containing the electronic equipment used to form directional beams for monitoring and direction-finding. The entire system is about 900 feet in diameter. The Air Force contingent has monitored Far Eastern military activity through voice, Morse, and printer intercepts and probably continues to do so.[83]

The collection equipment at Misawa Air Base in Japan has also been targeted on the Russian Far East, and probably on North Korea and China as well. Four miles northwest of Misawa is the "Hill," on which a 100-foot AN/FLR-9 antenna is situated. The base and its antenna lie at the northern tip of Honshu Island, about 500 miles west of Vladivostok and 400 miles south of Sakhalin Island. Misawa is a major base and employs representatives of all four services' cryptological elements. At one time (in the mid-1980s), there were over 1,800 personnel from those elements— 900 from the Air Force, 700 from the Navy, 200 from the Army, and 80 from the Marines.[84]

Two stations in Asia are unmanned—those at Khon Kean, Thailand, and Taegu, South Korea—with the intercepted data being transmitted to NSA/CSS Hawaii. The Khon Kean facility was apparently set up in the fall of 1979 to correct a short-fall of intelligence during the China-Vietnam war earlier that year. The Taegu facility is equipped with a Pusher HF antenna and targeted against communications in China, North Korea, and Vietnam.[85]

Located at Pyong-Taek, South Korea, is the 719th Military Intelligence Battalion (formerly U.S. Army Field Station Korea), a 304-person contingent with three detachments at various operating locations: Detachment J (at Koryo-San Mountain on the island of Kangwna), Detachment K (at Kani-San Mountain, 6 miles from the Demilitarized Zone [DMZ]), and Detachment L (on Yawol-San Mountain, within 1,500 meters of the DMZ). Collectively, the installations have a variety of North Korean COMINT and ELINT targets.[86]

Latin America, and particularly Central America, became a target of increased importance during the Reagan administration. Although Central America is no longer a priority, Cuba still is a significant target. At Lackland Air Force Base, Medina Annex, San Antonio, are Army and Air Force SIGINT contingents. SIGINT sites in Florida used to include a Naval Security Group Activity at Homestead Air Force Base, which monitored Cuban HF military communications. Although Homestead has closed, the antennas operated by the 749th Military Intelligence Company and the NIOC unit at Pensacola, Florida, still target Cuba and the Caribbean.[87]

There is also a collection of ground stations dedicated to the interception of INTELSAT and other civilian communications satellites. One station involved in the effort, at Sabana Seca, Puerto Rico—where the equipment was operated by Detachment 2 of the Air Intelligence Agency's 544th Information Operations Group (headquartered at Falcon AFB, Colorado Springs) and the mission designated CORALINE—was closed several years ago. Other detachments of the 544th involved in similar SATCOM intercept operations are Detachment 2 at Alice Springs,

Australia; Detachment 3 at Sugar Grove, West Virginia; and Detachment 4 at Yakima Research Station, Washington. The Yakima site has targeted the Pacific IN-TELSAT/COMSAT satellite and probably the INMARSAT-2 mobile communications satellite. The intelligence it produces is (or was) designated COWBOY. The NSA facility at Sugar Grove, with 30-, 60-, 105-, and 150-foot satellite antennas, intercepts the signals sent by the INTELSAT/COMSAT satellite over the Atlantic and intended for the INTELSAT/COMSAT ground station at Etam, West Virginia. Its mission, designated TIMBERLINE, is officially described as directing "satellite communications equipment supporting research and development for multi-service national missions."[88]

The stations are part of what has been referred to in the press as ECHELON—a term that actually refers to computer software at such stations that allows the sorting of intercepts (particularly printed material such as faxes) by key words. A latter addition to the ECHELON network is the satellite intercept equipment at Misawa Air Base. Previously, Misawa was the site of Project LADYLOVE, which involved the interception of communications transmitted via several Russian satellite systems, including Molniya, Raduga, and Gorizont. By the mid-1990s, NSA was considering converting Misawa to an ECHELON site, which it did subsequently.[89]

During the final years of the Cold War, intercept equipment at Menwith Hill intercepted a variety of Russian satellite communications under Project MOON-PENNY. Whether the satellite communications intercept equipment there is still targeting Russian satellites or has been retasked to focus on civilian communications satellites is not clear.[90]

Various Naval Information Operations Command activities operate land-based SIGINT stations that conduct HF/DF monitoring of naval activity. Those operations support national and naval intelligence collection objectives, general ocean surveillance, and search-and-rescue operations. The stations generally use the AN/FRD-10 antenna array, which has a nominal range of 3,000 nautical miles. The network, originally known as CLASSIC BULLSEYE, underwent a multiyear modernization program in the early 1990s, designated CLASSIC CENTERBOARD. The modifications resulted in the renaming of the network as CROSSHAIR as well as in the reduction of net control stations from three (Atlantic, Pacific, Naval Forces Europe) to one, located at NSGA Northwest, Virginia.[91]

The present network includes the NIOC at Sugar Grove, West Virginia, as well as the NIOC-operated AN/FRD-10 at Wahiawa, Hawaii, which is employed to monitor naval traffic around the Hawaiian Islands. At Imperial Beach, California, sixty members of the NIOC from San Diego operate an AN/FRD-10.[92]

EMBASSY AND CONSULAR INTERCEPT SITES

In addition to the ground-based listening posts such as those described above, which use large tracts of land, there is a set of posts that are located within and on top of

U.S. embassies and consulates. Such listening posts allow the United States to target the internal military, political, police, and economic communications of the nation in which the embassy or consulate is located. The listening posts, known as Special Collection Elements, are operated by a joint CIA-NSA organization—the Special Collection Service (SCS)—which was established as such in the late 1970s. Over forty U.S. embassies and consulates host such elements.[93]

The best known of the embassy listening posts is the one located in Moscow. In the late 1960s and early 1970s, this post intercepted the radio-telephone conversations of Soviet Politburo members—including General Secretary Leonid Brezhnev, President Nikolai Podgorny, and Premier Alexei Kosygin—as they drove around Moscow. Traffic from the interception operation was transmitted to a special CIA facility a few miles from the agency's Langley, Virginia headquarters.[94]

Originally, the conversations simply needed to be translated, since no attempt had been made to scramble or encipher the conversation. After a 1971 disclosure in the press concerning the operation, which was code-named BROADSIDE, the Soviets began enciphering their limousine telephone calls. Despite that effort, the United States was able to intercept and decode a conversation between General Secretary Brezhnev and Minister of Defense A. A. Grechko that took place shortly before the signing of the SALT I treaty. Grechko assured Brezhnev that the heavy Soviet SS-19 missiles under construction would fit inside the launch tubes of lighter SS-11 missiles, making the missiles permissible under the SALT treaty.[95]

In general, however, the intelligence obtained, code-named GAMMA GUPY, was less than earthshaking. According to a former intelligence official involved in the operation, the CIA "didn't find out about, say, the invasion of Czechoslovakia. It was very gossipy—Brezhnev's health and maybe Podgorny's sex life." At the same time, the official said that the operation "gave us extremely valuable information on the personalities of top Soviet leaders."[96]

Undoubtedly, during the abortive coup of August 1991, the listening post was part of the effort to eavesdrop on the communications of those attempting to replace the Gorbachev government and those resisting the coup. Among the communications monitored by the United States were those from the Chairman of the KGB and the Minister of Defense, both coup plotters.[97]

Other covert listening posts are or have been located in the U.S. embassies in Beijing, Tel Aviv, Buenos Aires, Santiago, Tegucigalpa, Brasilia, and Karachi. The Tel Aviv outpost has been targeted on Israeli military and national police communications. Thus, the United States has closely followed police activities directed at the Palestinians. The presence of a U.S. eavesdropping site has not gone unnoticed by Israeli officials, as a large number of antennas are visible on the roof of the Tel Aviv embassy.[98]

In Tegucigalpa, the SCS monitored the communications of the police and military as well as some of the forces fighting the government. The Buenos Aires post was used to target the communications of the Argentine General Staff during the

1982 Falklands crisis—information that was quickly passed to the British. The eavesdropping operation in the Karachi consulate yielded intelligence on drug trafficking, terrorist networks, and the Pakistani nuclear program. In 1996, an SCS unit at the U.S. embassy in Nairobi began intercepting telephone and fax messages entering and leaving five telephone numbers in the city, which were believed to belong to members of al-Qaeda.[99]

SURFACE SHIPS

The United States has employed surface ships for the collection of signals intelligence against both land-based and sea-based targets. In the 1950s, destroyers and destroyers' escorts were employed in intercept operations against land-based targets. In 1961 and 1965, respectively, two new types of ships were deployed—Auxiliary General Technical Research (AGTR) and Auxiliary General Environmental Research (AGER) ships. Transfer of the SIGINT mission to those ships was a response to fears of some Navy officials that stationing a destroyer off a foreign shore, especially that of a hostile nation, would be a provocation. However, the bombing of the AGTR USS *Liberty* by the Israelis during the 1967 Six Day War and the seizure of the USS *Pueblo* by North Korea in 1969 led to the eventual termination of the AGTR and AGER programs.[100]

In the 1980s, the United States began employing *Spruance*-class destroyers and frigates to collect intelligence concerning Nicaragua and El Salvador. The 7,800-ton destroyer *Deyo* and its sister ship, *Caron*, were stationed in the Gulf of Fonseca. The ships could monitor suspected shipping, intercept communications, and probe the shore surveillance and defense capabilities of other nations. Both ships remain in operation.[101]

A *Ticonderoga*-class cutter, the USS *Yorktown*, operated in the Black Sea, and was outfitted with electronic equipment that could monitor voice communications and radar signals. Such systems were used during a 1986 mission into the Black Sea to determine whether new radars had been deployed onshore and to check the readiness of Soviet forces. In a previous expedition, the *Yorktown*'s equipment was used in part to monitor aircraft movements within the Soviet Union.[102]

Two now-retired Navy frigates that were stationed in the Pacific—the *Blakely* and the *Julius A. Furei*—were used against targets in Nicaragua, El Salvador, and Honduras in the 1980s. The missions involved homing in on and recording voice and signal communications, locating transmitting stations, logging ships' movements, and studying their waterlines to help determine whether they were riding low in the water when entering port and high when exiting—indicating the unloading of cargo.[103]

Frigates were also used for monitoring telemetry from missile tests. It was reported in 1979 that "American ships equipped with sensitive listening gear . . . patrol the North Atlantic, where they collect telemetry broadcast by the new Soviet submarine-launched missiles tested in the White Sea, northeast of Finland." Likewise, on the night of August 31, 1983, when the United States was expecting the Soviet Union to test an SS-X-24 missile, the frigate *Badger* was stationed in the Sea of Okhotsk.[104]

Ship-based ocean surveillance operations employ equipment that allows the detection, classification, and location of hostile ships, aircraft, and submarines by exploiting their command-and-control communications. The data collected are analyzed on board and transmitted to Net Control Centers for correlation.[105]

During the 1980s and early 1990s, the intercept equipment operated on Navy cruisers and destroyers was code-named CLASSIC OUTBOARD. In the 1990s, the Navy began installing the COMBAT DF system on frigates and the newest cruisers and destroyers. COMBAT DF relies on a gigantic antenna built into the hull of a ship to intercept signals and determine the location of long-range, high-frequency radios.[106]

UNDERSEAS COLLECTION

The use of submarines for intelligence-gathering purposes had its genesis in the later years of the Eisenhower administration. Known by a variety of code names, the best known of which is HOLYSTONE, the program has been one of the most sensitive intelligence operations of the United States. The program is directed by a still-classified CIA-Navy office, the National Underwater Reconnaissance Office.[107]

HOLYSTONE, which has also been known as BINACLE and BOLLARD, and more recently as BARNACLE, began in 1959 and has involved the use of specially equipped electronic submarines to collect electronic communications and photographic intelligence. The primary target through 1991 was the former Soviet Union, but at times, countries such as Vietnam and China have been targets of the operations, which occasionally involved penetration of Soviet, Chinese, and Vietnamese 3-mile territorial limits.[108]

It was reported in 1975 that each mission lasted about ninety days. Missions conducted through 1975 apparently provided vital information on the Soviet submarine fleet, including its configuration, capabilities, noise patterns, missiles, and missile-firing capabilities. One mission involved obtaining the "voice autographs" of Soviet submarines. Using detailed tape recordings of noise made by submarine engines and other equipment, naval intelligence analysts were able to develop a methodology for the identification of individual Soviet submarines, even those tracked at long range under the ocean. The analysts could then follow the submarine from its initial operations to its decommissioning.[109]

HOLYSTONE operations also provided information about theater and strategic sea-based missiles. Some Soviet sea-based missiles were tested against inland targets to reduce U.S. monitoring. On occasion, HOLYSTONE submarines would penetrate close enough to Soviet territory to observe the missile launchings, providing information on the early stages of the flight. According to one government official, the most significant information provided by the missions was a readout of the computer calculations and signals put into effect by Soviet technicians before launching the missiles. Beyond that, the U.S. submarines provided intelligence by tracking the flight and eventual landing of the missiles and relaying continuous information on guidance and electronic systems.[110]

The submarines were also able to bring back valuable photographs, many of which were taken through the submarine's periscope. In the mid-1960s, photographs were taken of the underside of an E-class submarine that appeared to be taken inside Vladivostok harbor.[111]

More recent operations have employed, at various times, some of the thirty-eight nuclear-powered *Sturgeon*-class submarines. The submarines have dimensions of 292 by 31.7 by 26 feet and carry SUBROC and antisubmarine torpedoes as well as Harpoon and Tomahawk missiles. With their 107-person complement (12 officers and 95 enlisted personnel), the ships can travel at speeds of greater than 20 knots when surfaced and at more than 30 knots underwater and can reach a depth of 1,320 feet. Their standard electronic equipment includes a search radar and both active and passive sonar systems.[112]

Other operations have employed submarines from the more modern *Los Angeles*-class attack submarines. The subs are 362 by 33 by 32. 3 feet and carry Tomahawk cruise missiles and from four to twenty-one torpedoes. They travel at 32 knots and carry 133 personnel, including 13 officers.[113]

The special equipment placed on submarines on HOLYSTONE/BARNACLE missions has included the WLR-6 Waterboy Signals Intelligence System. In the 1980s, the WLR-6 was replaced by a more advanced system known as SEA NYMPH, described in one document as an "advanced automatic, modular signals exploitation system designed for continuous acquisition, identification, recording, analysis and exploitation of electromagnetic signals." All the *Sturgeon*-class submarines carry a basic skeletal system that can be upgraded to full capacity when authorized.[114]

There is evidence that HOLYSTONE/BARNACLE operations continued through the early 1990s. In February 1992, the USS *Baton Rouge*, a *Los Angeles*-class attack submarine, collided with a Russian submarine near the Kola Peninsula. It was reported that the *Baton Rouge* was on an intelligence-gathering mission targeted on the Russian port of Murmansk.[115]

Another collision occurred on March 20, 1993, when the *Sturgeon*-class USS *Grayling* bumped into a Russian Delta-III class ballistic missile submarine in the Barents Sea about 100 miles north of Murmansk. During a summit with Russian President Boris Yeltsin the following month, President Clinton apologized for the incident. He also ordered a review of the submarine reconnaissance operations.[116]

Although such operations may have been temporarily curtailed with respect to Russia, they apparently did not cease altogether. In early December 1997, a Russian Typhoon submarine launched twenty submarine-launched ballistic missiles (SLBMs) as part of the destruction routine under the START I treaty. Subsequently, the Russians charged that a submerged *Los Angeles*-class submarine monitored the event, although Navy officials indicated that it was not an American sub (leaving open the possibility that it was British).[117]

In any case, there are other targets. The still-operational *Los Angeles*-class subs USS *Topeka* and USS *Louisville* arrived in the Persian Gulf in November 1992 and January 1993, respectively. Their mission was to keep watch on Iran's new submarine fleet. When U.S. pilot Scott O'Grady was shot down over Bosnia in 1995, submarines intercepted communications among Bosnian Serbs hoping to capture the pilot. That same year, a submarine assigned to counternarcotics work in the eastern Pacific intercepted transmissions from a suspicious trawler, which helped the U.S. Coast Guard seize eleven tons of cocaine. In a more recent development, the USS *Virginia*, the first of a new class of nuclear attack submarines, measuring 377 feet long, was sent to the Caribbean and South Atlantic in August 2005 to intercept communications.[118]

Other submarines have been used as part of the SIGINT collection effort to place taps on underseas cables. In an operation designated IVY BELLS, the Navy placed induction devices on a Soviet military communications cable under the Sea of Okhotsk in the late 1970s and contemplated placing one on a similar cable in the Barents Sea. More recently, a new submarine, the USS *Jimmy Carter*, has been modified so that it can be employed in operations to tap into targeted fiber-optic cables. The submarine is a replacement for another submarine specially equipped for intelligence collection—the USS *Parche*. The USS *Jimmy Carter* is the third and last of the *Seawolf* class. This 18,130-ton submarine is 453 feet long and is capable of traveling at more than 25 knots an hour when submerged.[119]

Notes

1. DOD Instruction O-3115.07, "Signals Intelligence," September 15, 2008, p. 19.

2. Bill Gertz, "U.S. Intercepts from Libya Play Role in Berlin Bomb Trial," *Washington Times*, November 19, 1997, p. A13; Scott Shane and Ariel Sabar, "Alleged NSA Memo Details U.S. Eavesdropping at U.N.," *Baltimore Sun*, March 4, 2003, www.sunspot.net.

3. James Risen and David Johnston, "Chalabi Reportedly Told Iran That U.S. Had Code," *New York Times*, June 2, 2004, pp. A1, A11.

4. Defense Intelligence Agency, *Soviet and People's Republic of China Nuclear Weapons Employment Policy and Strategy*, March 1972, p. II-B-5; [deleted], "Indian Heavy Water Shortage" (from an undetermined NSA publication), October 1982; George C. Wilson, "Soviet Nuclear Sub Reported Sunk," *Washington Post*, August 11, 1983, p. A9; David B. Ottaway, "Iraq Said to Have Expelled High-Level US Diplomat," *Washington Post*, November 17, 1988, p. A33; George J. Church, "Destination Haiti," *Time*, September 26, 1994, pp. 21–26.

5. Christopher Andrew, *For the President's Eyes Only* (New York: HarperCollins, 1995), p. 520; David Johnston, "U.S. Agency Secretly Monitored Chinese in '96 on Political Gifts," *New York Times*, March 13, 1997, pp. A1, A25; Nora Boustany and Brian Duffy, "A Top U.S. Official May Have Given Sensitive Data to Israel," *Washington Post*, May 7, 1997, pp. A1, A28; Russell Watson and John Barry, "Our Target Was Terror," *Newsweek*, August 31, 1998, pp. 24–29; Matthew M. Aid, "The Time of Troubles: The US National Security Agency in the Twenty-First Century," *Intelligence and National Security* 15, 3 (Autumn 2000): 1–32;

Matthew M. Aid, "All Glory Is Fleeting: Sigint and the Fight Against International Terrorism," *Intelligence and National Security* 18, 4 (Winter 2003): 72–120.

6. Aid, "All Glory Is Fleeting"; Patrick E. Tyler, "British Detail Bin Laden's Link to U.S. Attacks," *New York Times*, October 5, 2001, pp. A1, B4; James Bamford, *Body of Secrets: Anatomy of the Ultra-Secret National Security Agency, from the Cold War Through the Dawn of a New Century* (New York: Doubleday, 2001), p. 410; Patrick E. Tyler, "Intelligence Break Led U.S. to Tie Envoy Killing to Iraq Qaeda Cell," *New York Times*, February 6, 2003, pp. A1, A12.

7. John E. Ingersoll, "Request for COMINT of Interest to Bureau of Narcotics and Dangerous Drugs," in U.S. Congress, Senate Select Committee to Study Governmental Operations with Respect to Intelligence Activities," *The National Security Agency and Fourth Amendment Rights* (Washington, D.C.: U.S. Government Printing Office, 1976), pp. 152–155.

8. U.S. Congress, House Permanent Select Committee on Intelligence, *Annual Report* (Washington, D.C.: U.S. Government Printing Office, 1978), p. 38.

9. John Prados, *The Soviet Estimate: U.S. Intelligence Analysis and Russian Military Strength* (New York: Dial, 1982), p. 203; Farooq Hussain, *The Future of Arms Control, Part 4, The Impact of Weapons Test Restrictions* (London: International Institute for Strategic Studies, 1980), pp. 44; Robert Kaiser, "Verification of SALT II: Art and Science," *Washington Post*, June 15, 1979 p. 1.

10. Deborah Shapley, "Who's Listening? How NSA Tunes In on America's Overseas Calls and Messages," *Washington Post*, October 7, 1977, pp. C1, C4.

11. Ibid.

12. Sayre Stevens, "The Soviet BMD Program," in *Ballistic Missile Defense*, ed. Ashton B. Carter and David N. Schwartz (Washington, D.C.: Brookings Institution, 1984), pp. 182–221 at p. 192.

13. David S. Brandwein, "Telemetry Analysis," *Studies in Intelligence* (Fall 1964): 21–29; Hussain, *The Future of Arms Control*, p. 46.

14. Robert A. McDonald and Sharon K. Moreno, *Grab and Poppy: America's Early ELINT Satellites* (Chantilly, Va.: National Reconnaissance Office, 2005); Dwayne Day, "Listening from Above: The First Signals Intelligence Satellite," *Spaceflight* 41, 8 (August 1999): 339–347.

15. Private information; Anthony Kenden, "U.S. Reconnaissance Satellite Programs," *Spaceflight* 20, 7 (1978): 243 ff.; Philip Klass, *Secret Sentries in Space* (New York: Random House, 1971), p. 194.

16. Kenden, "U.S. Reconnaissance Satellite Programs"; Klass, *Secret Sentries in Space*, p. 194.

17. "Refurbished Titan Missile Orbits Secret Payload," *Washington Post*, September 6, 1988, p. A2; William J. Broad, "Military Launches First New Rocket for Orbital Loads," *New York Times*, September 6, 1988, pp. A1, B7; "New Military Satellites," *Aviation Week & Space Technology*, May 25, 1992, p. 13; "Mission Control," *Military Space*, June 15, 1992, p. 1; John Lancaster, "The Shroud of Secrecy—Torn," *Washington Post*, June 5, 1992, p. A29; "Navy Uses Space to Spot Stealth Fighter," *Military Space*, April 23, 1980, p. 1.

18. ITT Industries, *Authorized Federal Supply Schedule Price List Professional Engineering Services* (Arlington, Va.: ITT Industries, n.d.), p. 20.

19. NAVSECGRU Instruction 5450.9A, "Mission, Functions and Tasks of Naval Security Group Command Detachment (NAVSECGRU Det.) Potomac, Washington, D.C.," February 7, 1994; Kenden, "U.S. Reconnaissance Satellite Programs"; Janko Jackson, "A Methodology for Ocean Surveillance Anaylsis," *Naval War College Review* 27, 2 (September–October

1974): 71–89; "Navy Plans Ocean Surveillance Satellites," *Aviation Week & Space Technology*, August 30, 1971, p. 13; "Industry Observer," *Aviation Week & Space Technology*, February 28, 1972, p. 9.

20. "Navy Ocean Surveillance Satellite Depicted," *Aviation Week & Space Technology*, May 24, 1976, p. 22; "Expanded Ocean Surveillance Effort Set," *Aviation Week & Space Technology*, June 10, 1978, pp. 22–23; Mark Hewlish, "Satellites Show Their Warlike Face," *New Scientist*, October 1, 1981, pp. 36–40.

21. "Expanded Ocean Surveillance Effort Set"; Hewlish, "Satellites Show Their Warlike Face."

22. "Expanded Ocean Surveillance Effort Set"; Hewlish, "Satellites Show Their Warlike Face." For further details on PARCAE, see Maj. A. Andronov, "Komischeskaya Sistema Radiotecknicheskoy Razvedki VMS Ssha 'Vayt Klaud,'" *Zarubezhnoye Voyennoye Obozreniyo (Foreign Military Review)* 7 (1993): 57–60.

23. Paul Stares, *Space and National Security* (Washington, D.C.: Brookings Institution, 1987), p. 188; United States Military Communications–Electronics Board USMCEB Publication No. 6, *Message Address Directory* (Washington, D.C.: U.S. Government Printing Office, July 25, 1986), p. 48; U.S. Army Intelligence and Security Command, "Analysis of Project TRUE BLUE–INFORMATION DF," May 28, 1986; Dan Marcella, "Det. 1 Builds upon Operational Missions," *Spokesman*, October 1995, p. 20.

24. "U.S. Defense and Intelligence Space Programs," *Aviation Week & Space Technology*, March 19, 1990, p. 37; Edward H. Kolcum, "Second Titan 4 Carries Secret Surveillance Satellite into Orbit," *Aviation Week & Space Technology*, June 18, 1990, p. 27; "Sky Peepers Learn Titan Secrets," *Space News*, January 13–26, 1992, p. 2; "Air Force Launches Second Titan 4 from Vandenberg," *Aviation Week & Space Technology*, November 18, 1991, p. 20; Bruce Van Voorst, "Billion Dollar Blowup," *Time*, August 16, 1993, p. 41.

25. R. Jeffrey Smith and John Mintz, "Pentagon Plans Multibillion-Dollar Sea Spy Satellite System," *Washington Post*, August 7, 1993, p. A5; John R. Cushman Jr., "Pentagon Found to Have Ignored Congress in Buying Spy Satellite," *New York Times*, September 24, 1993, p. A14; Theresa Hitchens and Neil Munro, "Pentagon Review Might Terminate Nuclear Spy Plans," *Defense News*, October 18–24, 1993, p. 3; Ralph Vartabedian, "TRW Loses Key Military Jobs to Archrival," *Los Angeles Times*, July 26, 1994, pp. A1, A6; John Mintz, "Martin Gets Big Contract for Satellites," *Washington Post*, July 26, 1994, pp. D1, D5; "World News Roundup," *Aviation Week & Space Technology*, September 17, 2001, p. 30; "In Orbit," *Aviation Week & Space Technology*, December 8, 2003, p. 17; "World News Roundup," *Aviation Week & Space Technology*, February 7, 2005, p. 20; Justin Ray, "Atlas 3B Launch Successful," www.spaceflightnow.com, February 3, 2005; Craig Covault, "Sea Recon Readied," *Aviation Week & Space Technology*, December 3, 2003, pp. 30, 32; e-mail from Ted Molczan, Subj: Observation of Atlas 2AS Mission, September 10, 2001; Craig Covault, "Secret Maneuvers," *Aviation Week & Space Technology*, July 23, 2007, pp. 38–39.

26. Aid, "The Time of Troubles," pp. 14–15.

27. CINCPACFLT Instruction S3251.1D, "Classic Wizard Reporting System," September 23, 1991; "In Orbit"; Niles Latham, "Spy Satellites Set Up Commando's Daring Sea Raid," www.nypost.com, December 12, 2002.

28. Christopher Anson Pike, "CANYON, RHYOLITE and AQUACADE: U.S. Signals Intelligence Satellites in the 1970s," *Spaceflight* 37, 11 (November 1995): 381–382; private information.

29. Philip Klass, "U.S. Monitoring Capability Impaired," *Aviation Week & Space Technology*, May 14, 1979, p. 18; Victor Marchetti in *Allies* (a Grand Bay film directed by Marian Wilkinson and produced by Sylvia Le Clezio, Sydney, 1983).

30. Robert Lindsey, *The Falcon and the Snowman: A True Story of Friendship and Espionage* (New York: Simon & Schuster, 1979), p. 111; Desmond Ball, *Pine Gap: Australia and the US Geostationary Signals Intelligence Satellite Program* (Sydney: Allen & Unwin Australia, 1988), pp. 14–15.

31. The first planned follow-on program to RHYOLITE, ARGUS, was canceled in the late 1970s. Richard Burt, "U.S. Plans New Way to Check Soviet Missile Tests," *New York Times*, June 29, 1979, p. A3; William Burrows, *Deep Black: Space Espionage and National Security* (New York: Random House, 1986), p. 192.

32. Hussain, *The Future of Arms Control, Part 4*, p. 42; Ball, *Pine Gap*, pp. 14–15; "U.S. Spy Satellite Falls Short on Orbit and Expectations," *New York Times*, September 4, 1988, p. 22; Edward H. Kolcum, "Titan 34D Upper Stage Failure Sets Back Pentagon Intelligence Strategy," *Aviation Week & Space Technology*, June 5, 1989, p. 32; "Last Titan 3 Rocket Lofts a Secret Military Satellite," *Washington Post*, September 5, p. A2; Edward H. Kolcum, "Last Titan 34D, Transtage Launches Classified Military Spacecraft," *Aviation Week & Space Technology*, September 11, 1989, p. 41; Craig Covault and Joseph C. Anselmo, "Titan Explosion Destroys Secret 'Mercury' Sigint," *Aviation Week & Space Technology*, August 17, 1998, pp. 28–30.

33. Private information.

34. Dick Cheney, Joint Meritorious Unit Award, June 23, 1989.

35. James Gerstenzang, "Shuttle Lifts Off with Spy Cargo," *Los Angeles Times*, January 25, 1985, pp. 1, 11; "Final Launch Preparations Under Way for Signals Intelligence Satellite Mission," *Aviation Week & Space Technology*, November 6, 1989, p. 24.

36. Dennis Fitzgerald, "Observations on 'The Decline of the NRO,'" *National Reconnaissance: Journal of the Discipline and Practice* (2005-U1): 59–66; Steve Weber, "Third Straight Titan 4 Launch Success Buoys Martin," *Space News*, September 5–11, 1994, pp. 3, 21; James T. McKenna, "Martin, USAF Speed Titan 4 Processing," *Aviation Week & Space Technology*, September 12, 1994, pp. 54–55; James T. McKenna, "Titan 4 Lofts Classified Payload," *Aviation Week & Space Technology*, May 22, 1995; "DOD Titan 4 Launched," *Aviation Week & Space Technology*, April 29, 1996, p. 28; "Titan on Defense Mission," *Aviation Week & Space Technology*, May 6, 1996, p. 16; Craig Covault, "Eavesdropping Satellite Parked over Crisis Zone," *Aviation Week & Space Technology*, May 18, 1998, pp. 30–31; "World News Roundup," *Aviation Week & Space Technology*, September 15, 2003, p. 21; Craig Covault, "Launch Surge Begins for Secret NRO Missions," *Aviation Week & Space Technology*, September 10, 2001, p. 43; National Reconnaissance Office, "National Reconnaissance Office Accomplishes Third Successful Launch in 33 Days," October 12, 2001; Craig Covault, "Intel Operations Delayed as Iraq, Al Qaeda Loom," *Aviation Week & Space Technology*, September 21, 2002, pp. 34–35; Craig Covault, "Night Fright," *Aviation Week & Space Technology*, December 8, 2008, pp. 26–28; National Reconnaissance Office, "NRO satellite successfully launched aboard Delta IV Heavy," January 17, 2009, www.nro.gov; National Reconnaissance Office, Release #02–10, "NRO Satellite Successfully Launched Aboard Delta IV Heavy," November 22, 2010; William Harwood, "Delta 4 Rocket blasts off with classified NRO satellite," *Spaceflight Now* (www.spaceflightnow.com), November 21, 2010.

37. Naval Security Group Activity, Denver, Subject: Annual Command History Report for 1996, March 5, 1997, pp. 3–4; R. Jeffrey Smith, "As Woolsey Struggles, CIA Suffers," *Washington Post*, May 10, 1994, pp. A1, A7.

38. Commanding Officer, Naval Security Group Activity, Denver, Subject: Annual Command History Report for 1999, March 23, 2000, p. 3; Commander, Naval Security Group Activity, Denver, Subject: Annual Command History for 1998, February 12, 1999, Enclosure 2; *History of the Air Intelligence Agency, 1 January–31 December 1994, Volume I* (San Antonio, Tex.: AIA, n.d.); résumé, Michael K. Buckingham, accessed September 19, 2006.

39. Seymour Hersh, *"The Target Is Destroyed": What Really Happened to Flight 007 and What America Knew About It* (New York: Random House, 1986), p. 4; Burrows, *Deep Black*, p. 223; Philip J. Klass, "NSA 'Jumpseat' Program Winds Down as Soviets Shift to Newer Satellites," *Aviation Week & Space Technology*, April 2, 1990, pp. 46–47; private information.

40. James T. McKenna, "Titan 4/Centaur Orbits Classified Payload," *Aviation Week & Space* Technology, May 9, 1994, p. 24; "Titan/Centaur Lofts Classified Payload," *Aviation Week & Space Technology*, July 17, 1995, p. 29; Tom Bowman and Scott Shane, "Battling High-Tech Warriors," *Baltimore Sun*, December 15, 1995, pp. 1, 15; "News Breaks," *Aviation Week &* Space Technology, November 17, 1997, p. 27; private information.

41. Michael Mecham, "A Re-Creation," *Aviation Week & Space Technology*, June 26, 2006, pp. 43–44; Justin Ray, "New Era of Rocket Launches Begins at California Base," *Spaceflight Now,* June 27, 2006, wwwspaceflightnow.com; Fitzgerald, "Observations on 'The Decline of the NRO'"; Steve Weber, "Third Straight Titan 4 Launch Success Buoys Martin," *Space News*, September 5–11, 1994, pp. 3, 21; James T. McKenna, "Martin, USAF Speed Titan 4 Processing," *Aviation Week & Space Technology*, September 12, 1994, pp. 54–55; James T. McKenna, "Titan 4 Lofts Classified Payload," *Aviation Week & Space Technology*, May 22, 1995; "DOD Titan 4 Launched," *Aviation Week & Space Technology*, April 29, 1996, p. 28; "Titan on Defense Mission," *Aviation Week & Space Technology*, May 6, 1996, p. 16; Craig Covault, "Eavesdropping Satellite Parked over Crisis Zone," *Aviation Week & Space Technology*, May 18, 1998, pp. 30–31; "World News Roundup," *Aviation Week & Space Technology*, September 15, 2003, p. 21; Craig Covault, "Launch Surge Begins for Secret NRO Missions," *Aviation Week & Space Technology*, September 10, 2001, p. 43; National Reconnaissance Office, "National Reconnaissance Office Accomplishes Third Successful Launch in 33 Days," October 12, 2001; Craig Covault, "Intel Operations Delayed as Iraq, Al Qaeda Loom," *Aviation Week & Space Technology*, September 21, 2002, pp. 34–35; "Atlas V Debuts at Vandenberg," *Aviation Week & Space Technology*, March 17, 2008, p. 22.

42. Naval Security Group Activity, Denver, *Annual Command History Report for 1996*, p. 4.

43. Ball, *Pine Gap*, pp. 27–28; private information; Air Intelligence Agency, Mission Directive 1517: 451st Intelligence Squadron, March 14, 1997.

44. Desmond Ball, *A Suitable Piece of Real Estate: American Installations in Australia* (Sydney: Hale & Iremonger, 1980), p. 59.

45. Ball, *Pine Gap*, pp. 67, 80; Dan Greenglees, "Pine Gap Upgrades Aim to Enhance US Alliance," *The Australian*, July 22, 1996, p. 5.

46. Matthew Aid, "The Time of Troubles: The US National Security Agency in the Twenty-First Century," *Intelligence and National Security* 15, 3 (Autumn 2000): 1–32; National Reconnaissance Office, *FY 2006–2007 Congressional Budget Justification, Volume IV: National Reconnaissance Program*, February 2005, p. 200.

47. ACC Regulation 23–1, Volume 15, "Headquarters Air Combat Command Organization and Functions, Summary of Changes," October 23, 1992, p. 4; Untitled memo, Declas-

sified 'Documents Reference System (DDRS), 1982–001538; David Willis, "An Extended Family," *Air Enthusiast*, July/August 2007, pp. 23–42.

48. U.S. Air Force, Fact Sheet, "RC-135V/W RIVET JOINT," March 2009, www.af.mil/information/factsheets.

49. "Specialized Equipment Key to Rivet Joint," *Aviation Week & Space Technology*, June 24, 1996, p. 59; David A. Fulghum, "Rivet Joint Carves Out New Combat Roles," *Aviation Week & Space Technology*, June 24, 1996, pp. 52–53; "Rivet Joint Hits 6,000 Days Deployed in Southwest Asia," *Spokesman*, February 2007, p. 4; Jon Lake, "Elite ELINT," *Combat Aircraft* 9, 4 (August-September 2008): 38–47.

50. David A. Fulghum, "Large, Diverse Crews Make RC-135 a Heavy Hitter," *Aviation Week & Space Technology*, June 24, 1996, pp. 61–62; Karina Jennings, "RJ Adriatic Operations," *Spokesman*, December 1996, pp. 11–12; Air Combat Command, ACCMD 23–108, "Reconnaissance Squadrons," June 25, 1993; Karina Jennings, "Vice Chief of Staff Visits Mildenhall; Flies Aboard RC-135 Rivet Joint," *Spokesman*, June 1996, pp. 24–25.

51. Fulghum, "Large, Diverse Crews Make RC-135 a Heavy Hitter"; Michael Harris, "Rivet Joint Flies 700th Adriatic Mission," *Spokesman*, November 1995, p. 27; "RC-135 Takes to the Sky," *Spokesman*, April 1995, p. 7; Jennings, "RJ Adriatic Operations"; David A. Fulghum, "Storied Rivet Joint Adds New Missions," *Aviation Week & Space Technology*, November 25, 2002, pp. 54–55; U.S. Air Force, Fact Sheet, "RC-135V/W RIVET JOINT"; Tania Bryan, "RC-135 surpasses 50,000 flying-hour," *Air Force Print News Today* (www.af.mil/news/story), April 1, 2008.

52. Lake, "Elite ELINT."

53. David A. Fulghum, "Stealthy and Subtle," *Aviation Week & Space Technology*, November 9, 2009, pp. 76–77.

54. Defense Airborne Reconnaissance Office, *Manned Airborne Reconnaissance Division*, 1995, p. 19; Capt. Paul Issler, "97th IS Participates in Recce Expo '96," *Spokesman*, September 1996, p. 15; U.S. Air Force, Fact Sheet, "RC-135U COMBAT SENT," September 2007, www.af.mil/information/factsheets.

55. U.S. Air Force, Fact Sheet, "RC-135U COMBAT SENT."

56. Martin Streetly, "U.S. Airborne ELINT Systems, Part 3, The Boeing RC-135 Family," *Jane's Defence Weekly*, March 16, 1985, pp. 460–465; "6985th Deactivates," *Spokesman*, July 1992, p. 10.

57. Jeffrey Richelson, "Cold War Recon Planes Find New Missions," *Defense Week*, September 5, 1995, pp. 6–7; "Recon Wing Famed for Skill, Endurance," *Aviation Week & Space Technology*, August 14, 1997, p. 53; Bill Gertz, "N. Korea Fires New Cruise Missile," *Washington Times*, June 30, 1997, pp. A1, A8; Eric Schmitt, "North Korea MIG's Intercept U.S. Jet on Spying Mission," *New York Times*, March 4, 2003, pp. A1, A5; Eric Schmitt, "North Korean Fliers Said to Have Sought Hostages," *New York Times*, March 8, 2003, pp. A1, A11; David A. Fulghum, "Risky Business," *Aviation Week & Space Technology*, March 10, 2003, p. 38.

58. . Defense Intelligence Agency, *Capabilities Handbook, Annex A, to the Department of Defense Plan for Intelligence Support to Operational Commanders,* March 1983, p. 220.

59. Fleet Air Reconnaissance Squadron One, *1994 VQ-1 Command History*, March 23, 1995, pp. 2, 5; Fleet Air Reconnaissance Squadron One, Naval Air Station Whidbey Island, Washington, *Command Composition and Organization,* 1996, p. 1; Maj. Gen. Kenneth R. Israel, Director, DARO, *DARO: Supporting the Warfighter, NMIA Defense Intelligence Status '96,* November 19, 1996, p. 20; "VQ-1 Command History," www.naswi.navy.mil/vq-1/history.htm, accessed March 1, 2006.

60. David A. Fulghum and Robert Wall, "Mixed Signals," *Aviation Week & Space Technology*, April 10, 2006, pp. 22–23.

61. Martin Streetly, "Secretive Orioin: EP-3E ARIES II," *Air International*, September 2004, pp. 31–38; "Flexibility, Endurance Are Valued EP-3 Assets," *Aviation Week & Space Technology*, May 5, 1997, pp. 50, 52; Defense Airborne Reconnaissance Office, *Manned Airborne Reconnaissance Division*, p. 11; Fleet Air Reconnaissance Squadron One, Naval Air Station, Whidbey Island, Washington, *Command Composition and Organization*, p. 1; Dick Van der Art, *Aerial Espionage: Secret Intelligence Flights by East and West* (New York: Arco/Prentice Hall, 1986), pp. 53–54; private information; United States Navy, Fact File, "EP-3E (ARIES II) Signals Intelligence Reconnaissance Aircraft," www.navy.mil/navydata, accessed April 10, 2010.

62. Streetly, "Secretive Orion."

63. Fleet Air Reconnaissance Squadron One, Naval Air Station, Whidbey Island, Washington, *Common Composition and Organization*, p. 1; Van der Art, *Aerial Espionage*, pp. 53–54; Fleet Air Reconnaissance Squadron One, *1993 Command History*, April 8, 1994, p. 4.

64. Fleet Air Reconnaissance Squadron One, Naval Air Station, Whidbey Island, Washington, *Command Composition and Organization*, p. 4.

65. Fleet Air Reconnaissance Squadron One, Naval Air Station Whidbey Island, Washington, *2001 Command Composition and Organization*, n.d., p. 2.

66. Ibid., pp. 2–3; Fleet Air Reconnaissance Squadron Two, *Command Operations Report*, May 17, 2006; Fleet Air Reconnaissance Squadron One, *Command Operations Report*, 2009, pp. 3, 6; MARADMIN Notice 654/08, Subject: Expansion of the Area of Eligibility (AOE) for the Global War on Terrorism Expeditionary Medal (GWOTEM), November 20, 2008, www.marines.mil/news/messages; U.S. Southern Command, *U.S. Southern Command 2009 Posture Statement*, 2009, p. 26.

67. "Flexibility, Endurance Are Valued EP-3 Assets"; Fleet Air Reconnaissance Squadron Two, *Fleet Air Reconnaissance Squadron Two History*, n.d.

68. Fleet Air Reconnaissance Squadron Two, *Command History 2001*, n.d., pp. 3, 7, Department Highlights (Enclosure 5), p. 2; Fleet Air Reconnaissance Squadron Two, *Command History 2002*, June 8, 2004, pp. 2, 5; Fleet Air Reconnaissance Squadron Two, *Command History 2003*, June 8, 2004, pp. 2, 6; Fleet Air Reconnaissance Squadron Two, *Command History 2004*, March 15, 2005; pp. 2, 5–6; Fleet Air Reconnaissance Squadron Two, *Command Operations Report*, p. 1; "VQ-2 Scheduled for Homeport Change," www.news.navy.mil, June 8, 2005; Commander, Naval Forces Europe/Commander, U.S. 6th Fleet, "VQ-2 Scheduled for Homeport Change," www.eucom.mil, June 15, 2005; OPNAV Notice 3111, "Relocation of Fleet Air Reconnaissance Squadron Two (VQ-2)," June 9, 2005; Fleet Air Reconnaissance Squadron Two, *Command History 2001*, p. 10.

69. David A. Fulghum, "The Value of X," *Aviation Week & Space Technology*, February 25, 2008, pp. 28–30; Andrzej Jeziorski, "SIGINT plus," *C4ISR Journal*, July 2008, pp. 22–24; David A. Fulghum, "AESA for EP-X," *Aviation Week & Space Technology*, April 13, 2009, pp. 52–53.

70. Chris Pocock, "U-2: The Second Generation," *World Airpower Journal* 28, (Spring 1997): 50–99; Defense Intelligence Agency, *Capabilities Handbook, Annex A to the Department of Defense Plan for Intelligence Support to Operational Commanders*, pp. 254–262; U.S. Air Force, Fact Sheet, "U-2S/TU-2S," www.af.mil/information/factsheets, accessed December 19, 2010.

71. Pocock, "U-2: The Second Generation"; Jim Coulter, "Senior Spear Maintenance Facility," *Spokesman*, January 1992, p. 10.

72. Private information.

73. Amy Butler, "Bermuda Triangle," *Aviation Week & Space Technology*, April 17, 2006, pp. 34–35; Government Accountability Office, *Defense Acquisitions: Assessments of Selected Weapon Programs*, March 2010, pp. 31–32.

74. Defense Airborne Reconnaissance Office, *Manned Airborne Reconnaissance Division*, p. 18; Israel, *DARO: Supporting the Warfighter*, p. 20; private information; "News in Brief," *Jane's Defence Weekly*, July 22, 1989, p. 110; James W. Rawles, "Guardrail Common Sensor Comes on Line," *Defense Electronics*, October 1990, pp. 33–41.

75. Dennis Buley, *The US Army's Fleet of Special Electronic Mission Aircraft (SEMA), Version of March 14, 1997*, www.jncps.com/dbuley; Col. Ronald W. Wilson, "Eyes in the Sky: Aerial Systems," *Military Intelligence* (July–September 1996): 16–18; William M. Arkin, Joshua M. Handler, Julia A. Morrissey, and Jacquelyn M. Walsh, *Encyclopedia of the U.S. Military* (New York: Harper & Row, 1990), p. 183.

76. Defense Airborne Reconnaissance Office, *Manned Airborne Reconnaissance Division*, p. 18; Israel, *DARO: Supporting the Warfighter*, p. 20; Wilson, "Eyes in the Sky"; Stacey Evers, "US Army Deploys Third Patrol Aircraft to Korea," *Jane's Defence Weekly*, August 20, 1987, p. 6; David A. Fulghum, "Army Spy Aircraft Watch North Korea," *Aviation Week & Space Technology*, November 24, 1997, pp. 58–59; David A. Fulghum, "Multisensor Observations Key to Army's RC-7," *Aviation Week & Space Technology*, November 24, 1997, pp. 60–61.

77. Jeffrey T. Richelson, " 'Truth Conquers All Chains': The U.S. Army Intelligence Support Activity," *International Journal of Intelligence and Counterintelligence* 12, 2 (Summer 1999): 168–200; Mark Bowden, *Killing Pablo: The Hunt for the World's Greatest Outlaw* (New York: Atlantic Monthly Press, 2001), p. 204; Michael Smith, *The Killer Elite: The Inside Story of America's Most Secret Special Operations Team* (London: Weidenfeld and Nicolson, 2006), p. 224.

78. "Predator, Reaper to get SigInt Sensors," *C4ISR Journal*, June 2008, p. 8; Government Accountability Office, *Defense Acquisitions: Assessments of Select Weapon Programs*, pp. 31–32.

79. Susan Dowdee, "Farewell to the Last Outpost of Freedom," *INSCOM Journal*, April 1992, pp. 10–11; "6917th Bids San Vito Arrivederci," *Spokesman*, July 1993, pp. 14–15; T. K. Gilmore, "The 701st MI Brigade and Field Station Augsburg's Discontinuance and Farewell Ceremony," *INSCOM Journal*, March 1993, pp. 8–9.

80. NAVSECGRU Instruction 5450.6A, "Mission, Functions and Tasks of Naval Security Group Activity (NAVSECGRUACT) Medina, Texas, April 8, 1996; Gabriel Marshall, "Medina Offers Multi-Service Intelligence," *Spokesman*, July 1995, p. 15.

81. Richard J. Fisher, "GRSOC," *INSCOM Journal*, July–August 1996, pp. 35–36; NAVSECGRU Instruction 5450.66, "Mission, Functions, and Tasks of Naval Security Group Activity (NAVSECGRUACT)," Fort Gordon, Georgia, April 26, 1996; NSA/CSS, *FY 2007 Military Construction Program: Fort Gordon, Georgia*, February 2006; NSA/CSS, *FY 2007 Military Construction Program: Naval Security Group Activity, Kunia, Wahiawa, Hawaii*, February 2006; United States Army Intelligence and Security Command, Fort Gordon, Georgia, "Vigilant Knights," June 20, 2006, www.gordon.army.mil/513mi.

82. Private information; "Bendix Fielding Engineering Corporation," www.bfec.us, accessed December 18, 2010.

83. Duncan Campbell, *The Unsinkable Aircraft Carrier: American Military Power in Britain* (London: Michael Joseph, 1984), p. 155; "British MP Accuses U.S. of Electronic Spying," *New Scientist*, August 5, 1976, p. 268; Department of the Army, Field Manual 34–40–12, *Morse Code Intercept Operations*, August 26, 1991, p. 4-4; "Northern Lights of Freedom," *Insight*, Spring 1991, pp. 16–18; private information.

84. Hersh, *"The Target Is Destroyed,"* p. 47; "Company E, Marine Support Battalion," www.misawa.af.mil/orgs/coe.history.htm.

85. Private information; Brian Toohey and Marian Wilkinson, *The Book of Leaks: Exposés in Defence of the Public's Right to Know* (North Ryde, Australia: Angus & Robertson, 1987), p. 135.

86. U.S. Army Field Station Korea, *Fiscal Year 1986, Annual Historical Report*, 1987, p. 2; private information; History Office, U.S. Army Intelligence and Security Command, *Annual Historical Review: U.S. Army Intelligence and Security Command Fiscal Year 1988*, 1989, p. 105; Jason Merrell, "501st MI Soldiers Maintain Excellence," *INSCOM Journal*, Spring 2004, pp. 14–16.

87. Private information; History Office, U.S. Army Intelligence and Security Command, *Annual Historical Review: U.S. Army Intelligence and Security Command Fiscal Year 1988*, p. 105; NAVSECGRU Instruction 5450.58 B, "Mission, Functions and Tasks of Naval Security Group Activity (NAVSECGRUACT), Pensacola, Florida," October 15, 1966.

88. "New Commander Takes Over Det. 4, 544th IG," *Spokesman*, March 1997, p. 27; 554th Intelligence Group, untitled, undated briefing; James Bamford, *The Puzzle Palace: A Report on NSA, America's Most Secret Agency* (Boston: Houghton Mifflin, 1982), pp. 172–173; Nicky Hager, *Secret Power: New Zealand's Role in the International Spy Network* (Nelson, N.Z.: Craig Potton, 1996), p. 166; Air Intelligence Agency, *Air Intelligence Agency Almanac*, August 1997, pp. 30–32; U.S. Naval Security Group Activity Sabana Seca, *U.S. Naval Security Group Activity, Sabana Seca, Puerto Rico Command History for 1996*, February 28, 1997, p. 5; Naval Security Group Detachment Sugar Grove, *Naval Security Group Detachment, Sugar Grove History for 1991*, February 26, 1992; private information.

89. Hersh, *"The Target Is Destroyed,"* p. 49; U.S. Congress, House Committee on Appropriations, *Military Construction Appropriations for 1981, Part 2* (Washington, D.C.: U.S. Government Printing Office, 1980), p. 875; Jeffrey Richelson, "Desperately Seeking Signals," *Bulletin of the Atomic Scientists*, March–April 2000, pp. 47–51.

90. David Morison, "Sites Unseen," *National Journal*, June 4, 1998, pp. 1468–1472; Duncan Campbell and Linda Melvern, "America's Big Ear on Europe," *New Statesman*, July 18, 1980, pp. 10–14.

91. NSG Instruction C3270.2, "Bullseye Concept of Operations," June 30, 1989; NAVSECRU Instruction C5450.27D, "Mission, Functions, and Tasks of U.S. Naval Security Group Activity (NAVSECGRUACT) Hanza, Japan," September 5, 1995; private information.

92. Private information; U.S. Congress, House Committee on Appropriations, *Military Construction Appropriations for 1987, Part 2* (Washington, D.C.: U.S. Government Printing Office, 1986), p. 464.

93. Tom Bowman and Scott Shane, "Espionage from the Front Lines," *Baltimore Sun*, December 8, 1995, pp. 1A, 20A–21A.

94. Laurence Stern, "U.S. Tapped Top Russians' Car Phones," *Washington Post*, December 5, 1973, pp. A1, A16; Ernest Volkman, "U.S. Spies Lend an Ear to Soviets," *Newsday*, July 12, 1977, p. 7.

95. Stern, "U.S. Tapped Top Russians' Car Phones"; Volkman, "U.S. Spies Lend an Ear to Soviets"; Bill Gertz, "CIA Upset Because Perle Detailed Eavesdropping," *Washington Times*, April 15, 1987, p. 2A; Michael Frost and Michael Gratton, *Spyworld: Inside the Canadian and American Intelligence Establishments* (Toronto: Doubleday Canada, 1994), p. 60.

96. Jack Anderson, "CIA Eavesdrops on Kremlin Chiefs," *Washington Post*, September 16, 1971, p. F7.

97. Seymour Hersh, "The Wild East," *Atlantic Monthly*, June 1994, pp. 61–86. Possibly more on the operation is contained in the unredacted version of "'Night of the Living Coup': The 18/19 August 1991 Coup in Moscow," *Cryptologic Almanac* (50th Anniversary Series), November–December 2002, available at www.nsa.gov.

98. Howard Kurtz, "Pollard: Top Israelis Back Spy Ring," *Washington Post*, February 28, 1987, p. A8.

99. Arthur Gavshon and Desmond Rice, *The Sinking of the Belgrano* (London: Secker & Warburg, 1984), p. 205 n. 5; Bowman and Shane, "Espionage from the Front Lines." For more on the SCS, see Jeffrey T. Richelson, *The Wizards of Langley: Inside the CIA's Directorate of Science and Technology* (Boulder, Colo.: Westview, 2001), pp. 210–211, 257–260; and Aid, "All Glory Is Fleeting."

100. Julie Alger, National Security Agency, *A Review of the Technical Research Ship Program, 1961–1969*, 1970, available at www.cryptome.org; Mitchell B. Lerner, *The Pueblo Incident: A Spy Ship and the Failure of American Foreign Policy* (Lawrence, Ks.: University Press of Kansas, 2002); A. Jay Cristol, *The Liberty Incident: The 1967 Israeli Attack on the U.S. Navy Spy Ship* (Dulles, Va.: Brassey's, 2002); James Bamford, *The Puzzle Palace: A Report on NSA, America's Most Secret Agency* (Boston: Houghton-Mifflin, 1982), pp. 212–235.

101. Richard Halloran, "2 U.S. Ships Enter Soviet Waters Off Crimea to Gather Intelligence," *New York Times*, March 19, 1986, pp. A1, A11; George C. Wilson, "Soviet Ships Shadowed U.S. Vessels' Transit," *Washington Post*, March 20 1986, p. A33; Capt. Richard Sharpe, ed., *Jane's Fighting Ships, 1994–1995* (Surrey, U.K.: Jane's Information Group Limited, 1994), p. 792.

102. Halloran, "2 U.S. Ships Enter Soviet Waters off Crimea to Gather Intelligence"; Sharpe, *Jane's Fighting Ships, 1994–1995*, p. 768.

103. George C. Wilson, "U.S. Detects Slowdown in Shipments of Weapons to El Salvador," *Washington Post*, April 29, 1983, p. A13.

104. Richard Burt, "Technology Is Essential to Arms Verification," *New York Times*, August 14, 1979, pp. C1, C2; Murray Sayle, "KE 007: A Conspiracy of Circumstance," *New York Review of Books*, April 25, 1985, pp. 44–54.

105. Private information.

106. Robert Holzer and Neil Munro, "Navy Eyes Eavesdropping System," *Defense News*, November 25, 1991, p. 12.

107. Christopher Drew, Michael L. Millenson, and Robert Becker, "A Risky Game of Cloak-and-Dagger Under the Sea," *Chicago Tribune*, January 7, 1991, pp. 1, 8–9; Sherry Sontag and Christopher Drew, with Annette Lawrence Drew, *Blind Man's Bluff: The Untold Story of American Submarine Espionage* (New York: Public Affairs, 1998), p. 83.

108. Seymour Hersh, "Submarines of U.S. Stage Spy Missions Inside Soviet Waters," *New York Times*, May 25, 1975 pp. 1, 42.

109. Ibid.

110. Ibid.

111. Ibid.

112. *Jane's Fighting Ships, 1983–1984* (London: Jane's Publishing, 1983), p. 639.

113. Sharpe, *Jane's Fighting Ships, 1994–1995*, p. 774.

114. Private information.

115. "Pentagon Describes Damage to Sub After Arctic Collision," *New York Times*, February 28, 1992, p. A10; John H. Cushman, Jr., "Two Subs Collide off Russian Port," *New York Times*, February 19, 1992, p. A6; Bill Gertz, "Russian Sub's Sail Damaged in Collision,"

Washington Times, February 27, 1992, p. A4; John Lancaster, "U.S., Russian Subs Collide in Arctic," *Washington Post*, February 19, 1992, pp. A1, A24.

116. Bill Gertz, "Clinton Apologizes for Sub Collision," *Washington Times*, April 5, 1993, p. A7; Sharpe, *Jane's Fighting Ships, 1994–1995*, p. 773.

117. "Moscow Files Complaint with U.S. over Sub Incident," *Washington Post*, May 5, 1998, p. A16.

118. "Second U.S. Sub Monitors Iran's Fleet," *Washington Times*, February 12, 1993, p. A7; Sharpe, *Jane's Fighting Ships, 1994–1995*, p. 774; Richard J. Newman, "Breaking the Surface," *U.S. News & World Report*, April 6, 1998, pp. 28–42; William Arkin, "Sub Spying in Latin America: An Incredible Story," http://blogs.washingtonpost.com/earlywarning, January 31, 2006; "Attack Subs–SSN," www.navy.mil, accessed December 18, 2010.

119. Sontag and Drew, with Drew, *Blind Man's Bluff*, pp. 158–163; "Jimmy Carter: Super Spy?," www.defensetech.org/archives/001397.html, accessed February 27, 2011; Neil King Jr., "Spy Agency Taps into Undersea Cable," *Wall Street Journal Online*, May 22, 2001, www.zdnet.com; "Navy Commissions Super-Spy Submarine," *Washington Post*, February 20, 2005, p. A16.

9

MEASUREMENT AND SIGNATURE INTELLIGENCE

Imagery and signals intelligence can trace their identities as collection disciplines back to at least the early twentieth century. The use of the term "measurement and signature intelligence" (MASINT) as a category encompassing a number of distinct collection activities is much more recent. The U.S. Intelligence Community first classified MASINT as a formal intelligence discipline in 1986.[1]

Measurement and signature intelligence is defined in the most recent DOD Instruction on the subject as "Information produced by quantitative and qualitative analysis of physical attributes of targets and events to characterize, locate, and identify them." It also states that "MASINT exploits a variety of phenomenologies to support signature development and analysis, to perform technical analysis and to detect, characterize, locate, and identify targets and events." In addition, the instruction states that "MASINT is derived from specialized, technically-derived measurements of physical phenomena intrinsic to an object or event and it includes the use of quantitative signatures to interpret the data."[2]

Given the above definition, MASINT includes all technical collection other than SIGINT and traditional imagery intelligence (which include visible-light, radar, and infrared—but not multispectral, hyperspectral, or ultraspectral—imagery). MASINT's scope and diversity are indicated by the identification of its various components:

- radar (line of sight, bistatic, over-the-horizon)
- radio frequency (wideband electromagnetic pulse, unintentional radiation)
- geophysical data (acoustic, seismic, magnetic)
- nuclear radiation (X-ray, gamma ray, neutron)
- materials (effluents, particulates, debris)
- multispectral, hyperspectral, and ultraspectral imagery.[3]

It should not be surprising that, given the diversity of the phenomena being monitored and the means employed to monitor them, MASINT can be employed in pursuit of a large number of missions—both strategic and tactical. Thus, MASINT mission areas include support to military operations, defense acquisition and force modernization, arms control and treaty monitoring, proliferation, counterterrorism, environmental intelligence, and counternarcotics. A more detailed breakdown is given in Table 9.1.

Some MASINT missions are well-known, even if not thought of in terms of MASINT—for example, the detection of acoustic signals from submarines that allow their tracking and identification, the collection and analysis of seismic signals from nuclear detonations, and the use of radars to detect and monitor foreign missile tests.

Other missions, particularly tactical applications, may be less appreciated. Thus, the collection of electro-optical spectral signatures from an aircraft's exhaust, the measurement of an aircraft's radar cross section, and the gathering of its acoustic signatures can be used to determine range, speed, acceleration, climb rate, stability, turn radius, tactics, and proficiency, all of which are useful in combat. Such data can be loaded into an air defense system to aid in targeting such aircraft.[4]

It should be noted that MASINT's components lack the commonality of those of imagery and SIGINT. Visible-light, infrared, and radar imagery collection all produce an image from which intelligence is extracted. Similarly, SIGINT, in whatever form, involves the interception of a transmitted signal whose content is then mined for intelligence value. There is no similar commonality between multispectral imagery and acoustic intelligence, or between the employment of radar for monitoring foreign missiles and the detection of X-rays from nuclear detonations. In many ways, MASINT is more a description of the product, stemming from a particular type of analysis of the data produced by a variety of collection activities, than a coherent collection activity itself.

In addition, measurement of objects and the identification of signatures are a large portion of the work done by those interpreting and analyzing traditional imagery and signals intelligence data. Such observations, although important with respect to issues of the scope and organization of the MASINT effort, can, to a large extent, be put aside in surveying the collection systems that produce the data that are turned into measurement and signature intelligence.[5]

MASINT collection systems are operated in space, on aircraft, at ground stations, on surface ships, and below the oceans.

SPACE COLLECTION

The U.S. government operates at least five satellite systems that carry MASINT sensors. Those sensors fall into two categories—ones that produce non-imaging infrared data and ones that carry specialized nuclear detonation sensors.* As is the case

---

*Non-imaging infrared satellites have been described by the term Overhead Non-Imaging Infrared (ONIR) and, more recently, Overhead Persistent Infrared (OPIR). See Robert Clark, *The Technical Collection of Intelligence* (Washington, D.C.: CQ Press, 2010), pp. 78–80.

TABLE 9.1   MASINT Mission Areas

Support to Military Operations
Precision Guided Munitions Targeting
Intelligence Preparation of the Battlefield
Naval and Ground Combat
Space Control
Search and Rescue
Non-Cooperative Target Identification
Mission Planning
Indications and Warning
Tactical Warning/Attack Assessment
Theater Missile Defense
Scud Hunting
Air Defense
Strike Warfare
Peacekeeping

Defense Acquisition/Force Modernization
Signatures
Threat Definition
Countermeasures

Arms Control/Treaty Monitoring
Missile
Nuclear
Chemical and Biological

Proliferation
Missile
Nuclear
Chemical and Biological
Advanced Conventional Weapons

Environment
Natural Disasters
Pollution
Phenomena

Counterdrugs
Production
Transport
Storage

SOURCE: John L. Morris, *MASINT: Progress and Impact, Brief to NMIA*, November 1996 (Slide 6).

with many other MASINT sensors, some of the space MASINT sensors produce MASINT as a by-product of a more fundamental mission or are specialized MASINT sensors that are carried as secondary payload on satellites, often satellites not operated by the NRO or any other component of the Intelligence Community.

Satellite systems that carry non-imaging infrared sensors include the Defense Support Program (DSP) and highly-elliptically orbiting SIGINT satellites. The Space-Based Infrared System (SBIRS) program, DSP's planned successor, which already has some of its sensors carried on HEO SIGINT satellites, is projected to begin operations of dedicated geosynchronous satellites in 2011. In addition, several NRO satellites have carried experimental infrared sensors designated COBRA BRASS.

DSP satellites also are equipped with nuclear detonation (NUDET) detection sensors. In addition, the spacecraft of the Global Positioning System, the Defense Meteorological Satellite Program (DMSP), and the QUASAR (Satellite Data System) program carry NUDET sensors—although the sensors carried by different program spacecraft may target very different nuclear detonation signatures (e.g., X-rays, optical, gamma rays).

Furthermore, several commercial satellites, particularly those operated by Space Imaging and Digital Globe, provide multispectral and hyperspectral imagery.

The principal mission of the Defense Support Program satellites is to detect the launches of ICBMs and SLBMs, using an infrared sensor to monitor the missile's plume. In the 1970s, it was observed that DSP satellites could also detect the launches of intermediate-range ballistic missiles such as Scuds. Those missiles might be launched as part of a research and development program or military exercise, or during an actual military conflict. DSP data thus provide information on the level of such activities and, in the case of war, the specific targets. In addition, analysis of DSP infrared data allows determination of what type of fuel is being burned and identification of the spectral signatures associated with different missile systems.* DSP satellites have also provided intelligence on terrestrial events that generate sufficient infrared radiation, such as explosions resulting from missile and bomb attacks, accidental massive explosions of ammunition dumps, certain industrial processes, and aircraft explosions and crashes. Furthermore, DSP satellites have been used to monitor aircraft flying on afterburner, particularly Soviet naval Backfires during the Cold War—an effort designated SLOW WALKER.[6]

DSP satellites have also provided intelligence on foreign nuclear activity. The infrared sensor has detected the heat generated by surface nuclear tests. In addition, DSP satellites have carried several nuclear detonation sensors. The satellites' Advanced RADEC I sensor package consists of Bhangmeters, atmospheric fluorescence detectors, and an X-ray locator system. The Bhangmeters are optical sensors whose mission is to

---

*In 2007, for example, there were 120 foreign ballistic missile launches, according to the head of the Missile Defense Agency. See Peter Buxbaum, "Seeking More Help from Above," *Military Space & Missile Forum* 1, 2 (September 2008): 6–8.

detect the bright flash that would result from the fireball of a nuclear explosion. The air fluorescence sensor would record the bright pulse of visible (florescence) radiation resulting from the interaction of thermal X-rays from a high-altitude or exoatmospheric nuclear explosion with the low-density air in the upper portions of Earth's atmosphere. The X-ray locator employs several detectors to measure the direction and arrival time of X-rays from the near-Earth exoatmospheric nuclear detonations. The information provided by the most recent version of the locator (the Advanced Atmospheric Burst Locator, or AABL) allows estimates of yield, location, height of burst, frequency of detonations, and timing. The estimates have a smaller range of uncertainty than the estimates produced by previous sensors, and the improved sensors are able to detect events below the threshold reached by earlier versions.[7]

There have been several generations of DSP satellites since the initial launch in November 1970. The present version, designated DSP-1, is a 33-foot-long, 10-foot-diameter spacecraft weighing approximately 5,300 pounds. Detection is achieved by a 12-foot-long Schmidt telescope that is 39 inches in diameter. The telescope has a two-dimensional array of lead sulfide detectors at its focus to detect energy emitted by ballistic missile exhausts during the powered stages of their flights.[8]

DSP satellites have been placed in geosynchronous orbit from Cape Canaveral, Florida. The three-satellite constellation, with two spares, that became standard in the late 1970s and through the 1980s became a four-satellite operational constellation—with Atlantic, European, Indian Ocean, and Pacific slots. In addition, there were one or two retired satellites that could potentially be recalled to service if an operational satellite failed. The number of operational satellites at the moment is not clear, since the launch of DSP-23 (the last of the DSP spacecraft) failed and DSP-19 was retired in 2008.[9]

The ground segment included three dedicated ground stations, a main operating base for six Mobile Ground Terminals at Fort Greeley, Colorado, and a DSP multipurpose facility at Lowry Air Force Base, Colorado. The dedicated ground stations included the CONUS Ground Station at Buckley Air National Guard Base, Colorado; the Overseas Ground Station (also known as the Joint Defense Facility–Nurrungar) at Woomera Air Station, Australia; and the European Ground Station at Kapuan, Germany.[10]

The CONUS Ground Station at Buckley has been replaced by the SBIRS (see below) Mission Ground Station at Buckley and is operated by the 2nd Space Warning Squadron. It receives data from all the DSP satellites, either directly or via satellite and/or cable relay.

Buckley also hosts the Detachment 45 of the Air Force Technical Applications Center (AFTAC). AFTAC personnel stationed at Buckley are responsible for processing any nuclear detonation data provided by the nuclear detonation sensors aboard DSP spacecraft. In 1999, the manned sites at Nurrungar and Kapuan were closed and replaced by unmanned "bent pipes" at Pine Gap, Australia (Relay Ground Station–Pacific) and Menwith Hill, in the United Kingdom (Relay Ground Station–Europe), which simply receive the data from DSP satellites and relay them on to Buckley.[11]

In 1995, the Defense Department and Air Force, after a number of stops and starts, decided on a follow-on program to DSP—designated the Space-Based Infrared System (SBIRS). As with DSP, SBIRS would consist of four satellites in geosynchronous orbit, but they would have both scanning and staring sensors. In addition, as with DSP, highly-elliptically orbiting SIGINT satellites would carry infrared sensors—although as part of the SBIRS program—to permit coverage of northern polar regions that cannot be "seen" by geosynchronous SBIRS sensors. So far, two SBIRS sensors have been placed in HEO orbits, with the first launch of a dedicated SBIRS satellite into geosynchronous orbit scheduled for 2011.[12]

SBIRS satellites in geosynchronous orbits will have two sensors—a scanning sensor and a staring sensor. The scanning sensor will perform the strategic missile warning and technical intelligence missions, as well as the initial phase of the strategic missile defense mission. The staring sensor will perform the theater missile warning and defense missions and the battlespace awareness mission, and provide technical intelligence. The SBIRS payloads in highly elliptical orbit will carry a single infrared sensor. The SBIRS ground station will also be located at Buckley.[13]

The Nuclear Detonation (NUDET) Detection System (NDS) carried on board NAVSTAR Global Positioning System (GPS) satellites was developed to provide trans- and post-attack nuclear detonation monitoring. The primary function of the GPS satellites is to provide accurate location data for targeting and navigation purposes; the NDS is a major secondary function. At full strength, the GPS satellite constellation consists of twenty-one operational satellites plus three active spares in near-circular 11,000-mile orbits with an inclination of 55 degrees. The satellites are deployed in six planes of four satellites each. This arrangement guarantees that at least four to six satellites are in view at all times from any point on or near the earth.[14] Figure 9.1 shows the GPS constellation.

The NDS packages include X-ray and optical sensors, Bhangmeters, electromagnetic pulse (EMP) sensors, and a data-processing capability that can detect a nuclear weapons detonation "anywhere in the world at any time" and get its location down to less than 100 feet. The GPS Master Control Station is located at Schriever AFB, Colorado, with the Alternate Master Control Station at Vandenberg AFB, California. Schriever is also the home of AFTAC Detachment 46, which provides support for GPS NUDET operations. In addition, the ground segment consists of six dedicated monitor stations, ten NGA monitoring stations, and four ground antennas with uplink capabilities. NUDET data have been reported to be directly downlinked on a real-time basis to ground stations located at Diego Garcia Kwajalein Atoll; Ascension Island; and Kaena Point, Hawaii.[15]

The nuclear detonation detection equipment on GPS Block IIF satellites, the first of which was launched in May 2010 (with additional launches planned through 2014), includes the V-sensor—a broadband VHF receiver system operating in the low- to mid-VHF frequency range, designed to detect and geolocate electromagnetic pulses from nuclear detonations on a continuous worldwide basis. The V-sensor will be the size of a pack of cigarettes when stored but 6.5 feet long once it is deployed.

FIGURE 9.1   The NAVSTAR GPS Operational Constellation

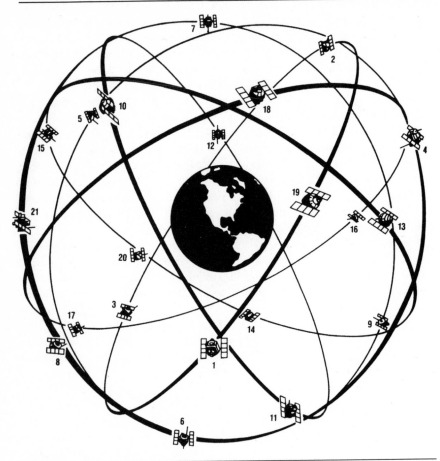

SOURCE: General Accounting Office, *Global Positioning System Acquisition Changes After Challenger's Accident* (Washington, D.C.: GAO, 1987), p. 12.

Data collection from a V-sensor will be triggered when the amplitude of a detected signal exceeds a preset amplitude in a predetermined number of sub-bands distributed within the receiver bandwidth. The triggering technique, along with an associated digital signal analysis algorithm, allows the instrument to (1) trigger on and detect weak signals of interest in the presence of strong interfering man-made carriers and (2) distinguish and discriminate between nuclear EMP and other man-made and naturally occurring events.[16]

DMSP satellites have hosted a variety of AFTAC sensors over the last several decades. These sensors have included the SSB Gamma Tracker (to track fallout and nuclear debris in the atmosphere), the SSB Gamma X-Ray Detector, and the SSB/A X-Ray Spectrometer (for the detection of X-Rays and gamma rays from bomb debris), as well as several that could monitor electromagnetic radiation. Usually, two DMSP satellites are in circular orbits of 450 nautical miles. DMSP ground stations are located at New Boston Air Force Station, New Hampshire; Thule Air Base, Greenland; Fairbanks, Alaska; and Kaena Point, Hawaii; and the stations transfer data to the Air Force Weather Agency at Offutt Air Force Base, Nebraska.[17]

Prior to the placement of SBIRS sensors on the highly-elliptically orbiting SIGINT satellites, such satellites, JUMPSEAT and TRUMPET, carried infrared sensors code-named HERITAGE. The sensors were designed to detect infrared emissions in a narrower time frame than those of DSP in order to permit detection of any short-burning anti-ballistic missiles that the Soviet Union/Russia might develop. Those sensors, some of which still may be in orbit, provided additional non-imaging infrared intelligence to the Intelligence Community. [18]

The U.S. decided in the mid-1970s to deploy MASINT sensors on a set of U.S. satellites in Molniya orbit. The Satellite Data System/QUASAR data relay satellites have carried nuclear detonation detection sensors, including, at least, Bhangmeters, since the third spacecraft in the program was launched in August 1978.[19]

In the late 1990s, and possibly beyond, various NRO satellites carried the COBRA BRASS sensor, which was intended to "demonstrate the utility of multispectral, fast-framing, staring sensor technology," particularly for the National Air and Space Intelligence Center. It was anticipated that the data might have some application for SBIRS missions of missile warning, missile defense, battlespace characterization, and technical intelligence. The COBRA BRASS Ground System is (or was) colocated with the ground station for the host satellite.[20]

Figure 9.2 shows a sample alert report for atmospheric tests detected by satellites.

Although there are no U.S. government satellites that produce multispectral imagery, there are several commercial satellites that do produce such imagery. Digital Globe's Quickbird satellite, which was launched in October 2001, operates in a sun-synchronous 280-mile orbit and produces multispectral images with 8-foot resolution. The company's Worldview-2 satellite, launched in October 2009, which operates in 477-mile orbit, also produces multispectral images, with a maximum resolution of 6-feet.[21]

GeoEye operates two satellites which produce multispectral imagery. Ikonos, launched in September 1999, orbits at 422 miles and returns multispectral images with 13-foot resolution. And GeoEye-1, launched in September 6, 2008, orbits at the same altitude as Ikonos and returns multispectral images with 5.4-foot resolution.[22]

AIRBORNE COLLECTION

Airborne MASINT systems are flown on Air Force and Navy aircraft that also serve as platforms for imagery and/or SIGINT sensors, including as platforms for imagery and/or SIGINT sensors; among these systems are the RC-135S COBRA BALL, the

FIGURE 9.2   Sample Alert Report Text: Atmospheric

30   CENR 55-5   Attachment 12   28 May 1992

    Figure A12-1.   (U) Sample Alert Report Text: Atmospheric
                         (This figure is classified SECRET)

SUBJECT: ALERT _____ (U)

1. (S) DATA RECORDED BY THE US ATOMIC ENERGY DETECTION SYSTEM (USAEDS) INDICATE AN ATMOSPHERIC NUCLEAR

EXPLOSION WITH A YIELD OF ABOUT _____ (_____) KT

OCCURRED AT _____ _____

(____) DEGREES _____ (_____) MINUTES NORTH,

_____ (_____) DEGREES

_____ (_____) MINUTES EAST, AT _____ COLON

_____ (_____) GMT ON _____ (_____) _____ 19 ____ .

2. (S) THE FOLLOWING SATELLITES/LOOK ANGLES (IN DEGREES) RECORDED THE EVENT:

_____ / _____

_____ / _____

_____ / _____

3. (S) THE LOCATION WAS OBTAINED FROM COMBINED INPUTS FROM ▮▮▮▮▮▮▮▮▮▮▮▮▮▮▮▮▮▮▮▮

.b.(1)

4. (S) SEISMIC DATA ARE/ARE NOT AVAILABLE FROM THIS EVENT.

5. (S) THE PRELIMINARY ESTIMATE OF YIELD OF ABOUT _____ (____) KT, WITH AN UNCERTAINTY RANGE ▮▮▮

OF _____ (____) TO _____ (____) KT, IS BASED ON ▮▮▮▮▮▮▮▮▮ A YIELD ESTIMATE OF

_____ (____) KT WAS OBTAINED FROM ▮▮▮▮▮▮▮▮▮▮

6. (S) THE PRELIMINARY ESTIMATE OF HEIGHT OF BURST IS _____ (_____) KILOMETERS.

7. (S) THE EARLIEST THAT ▮▮▮▮▮▮▮▮▮▮▮▮▮▮▮▮▮▮▮▮▮▮▮▮▮▮▮▮▮▮▮▮▮▮▮▮▮▮

_____ (_____) _____ 19 ___ . ▮▮▮▮▮▮▮▮▮▮

▮▮▮▮▮▮▮▮▮▮▮▮▮▮

8. (U) THE INFORMATION CONTAINED IN THIS DOCUMENT WILL BE SAFEGUARDED AS DIRECTED BY NATIONAL SECURITY DECISION

MEMORANDUM NO. 50.

DECL OADR.   OPR: AFTAC/DOB   INITIALS: _____   DATE: _____
==

SOURCE: AFTAC Regulation 55-5, "Alert Procedures," May 28, 1992.

P-3C ORION, and the P-3C IRON CLAD. In addition, a number of aircraft serve as platforms for sensors that can detect evidence of nuclear, chemical, or biological warfare activities.

In addition to the Advanced Telemetry System discussed in Chapter 8, COBRA BALL aircraft carry two Medium-Wave Infrared Arrays (MIRA); a Real-Time Optical System (ROTS), which records visible-light images using a combination of eight acquisition and five tracking sensors; and a Large Aperture Tracking System (LATS), which has a 12-inch-focal-length telescope with finer resolution for small targets picked up by the LATS. Each MIRA system is made up of six infrared cameras, and each camera's field of view marginally overlaps those on either side to produce a panoramic picture of slightly less than 180 degrees. The arrays have been modified to permit detection of cooler targets. A COBRA BALL can locate a missile launch within 100 yards, track missile flight at greater than 250 miles, and determine engine burnout and predict impact point within seconds.[23]

MASINT analysis of the data returned by COBRA BALL's infrared and optical sensors provides intelligence in a variety of areas. Analysis of the colors that appear around a reentry vehicle (RV) when heated by the friction of Earth's atmosphere can reveal the materials that the vehicle is composed of and whether it has a hardened titanium warhead for penetrating deep targets. In addition, plotting the warhead's flight path can indicate its speed and whether it can maneuver to avoid defensive missiles. Stability and accuracy of the RV can be estimated by calculating the speed-to-rotation ratio. Tracking the debris that surrounds a reentry vehicle allows analysts to extrapolate the quality of workmanship. Missiles manufactured during the Soviet era were "sloppy and dirty," and the warheads operated with "lots of debris."[24]

COBRA BALL's more recent missions have included monitoring Iran's ballistic missile tests. It has also been assigned missions outside the realm of foreign intelligence, including tracking the path of NASA's Compton Gamma Ray Observatory when it reentered the atmosphere in the spring of 2002.[25]

Prior to his extensive use for overland imagery purposes, the P-3C ORION, named after the Greek god of the hunt, was primarily an anti-submarine warfare aircraft. It is the third generation of the P-3 anti-submarine warfare aircraft that succeeded the Neptune P2V in the late 1950s. In its present configuration, the P-3C stands 33.7 feet high. It is 117 feet long and has a 99.7-foot wingspan. Its maximum speed is 473 miles per hour, and it has a service ceiling of 28,300 feet. Its endurance capability—sixteen hours—and maximum speed give it a range of 4,760 nautical miles. It can search up to 95,000 square nautical miles in an hour.[26]

The P-3C can carry up to eighty-four sonobuoys, expendable sonar systems that can be dropped into the water. Forty-eight of them are preset and loaded in external launch chutes prior to takeoff. The remaining thirty-six are carried internally, and their operating channels can be chosen during the mission. For many of the sonobuoys, it is possible to select the operating depth and length of transmission time. The acoustic operators on the P-3C can monitor up to sixteen sonobuoys simultaneously. A sonar-type recorder stores all acoustic data for reference so that the missions can be reconstructed in detail. [27]

In addition to sonobuoys, there are several nonacoustic detection systems on the P-3C. Its Magnetic Anomaly Detector (MAD) is used in concert with the Submarine Anomaly Detector to determine whether known submarine magnetic profiles are present. To get a good MAD reading, the plane must fly 200 to 300 feet above the water. An airborne search radar, designated AN/APS-115, is used to detect radar returns from ships or submarines on the surface and pick out periscopes at the waterline.[28]

Five P-3C aircraft were specially configured for the collection, analysis, and recording of high-quality acoustic data on Soviet submarines, sonars, and underwater communications equipment. These aircraft, known by the code name BEARTRAP, have a

4,000-nautical-mile range, an operational altitude of 200 to 10,000 feet, and an endurance capability of twelve hours. Enhancements of BEARTRAP antisubmarine warfare capabilities during fiscal year 1994 focused on the littoral water/regional conflict environment.[29]

Another version of the P-3C, which has been designated REEF POINT, STORM JIB, and more recently IRON CLAD, is a four-engine turboprop that can fly at 28,000 feet at 250 knots for up to twelve hours (but is not refuelable in flight). It has been described as being engaged in "all-weather, worldwide multisensor scientific and technical collection of naval and littoral targets," in support of joint task force, fleet, and maritime operations. In the past, the aircraft carried a wide variety of sensors. More recently, the planes' sensors have included the Directional Low-Frequency Analysis and Recording (DIFAR) system, which relies on signals from sonobuoys to locate targets to within 10–15 degrees of true target location, and the Tactical Optical Surveillance System (TOSS), an electro-optical surveillance system. The planes may also have been equipped, under the Adaptive Spectral Reconnaissance Program, with hyperspectral sensors.[30]

Four IRON CLAD aircraft are evenly split between Special Projects Patrol Squadron One (VPU-1), "Old Buzzards"—whose home port used to be Naval Air Station New Brunswick, Maine, but has relocated to Naval Air Station, Jacksonville—and Special Projects Patrol Squadron Two (VPU-2). VPU-2, the "Wizards," is headquartered at the Marine Corps Air Facility at Kaneohe Bay, Hawaii. VPU-1 focuses on the Atlantic and Mediterranean, and VPU-2, which has about 200 personnel assigned to it, operates extensively throughout the Pacific and Indian Ocean theaters.[31]

In Operation Desert Storm, IRON CLAD aircraft were used to photograph Iraqi fortifications, gather data on Iraq's electronic order of battle, and hunt for mobile Scuds. They have also been used to monitor developments in the Spratly Islands, whose ownership has been disputed by China and the Philippines.[32]

At one time, aerial sampling was extensively employed to detect the atomic particles that would be emitted by an atmospheric nuclear explosion or that might be "vented" by an underground test. Aircraft employed in aerial sampling operations included the U-2, the P-3, the WC-135, and the B-52. The WC-135s were equipped with the STARCAST camera system, designed to photograph high-speed objects in support of strategic research and development programs. Aerial sampling operations were conducted over the United States and the Southern Hemisphere. One version of the C-130, the HC-130, was outfitted with a seawater sampler for sorties flown against possible foreign underwater nuclear tests.[33]

Aircraft from the 55th Weather Reconnaissance Squadron (WRD) at McClellan Air Force Base, which operated six WC-135s, were used to monitor nuclear fallout from the 1986 Chernobyl accident, designated SPECIAL EVENT 86-05. The planes, which were deployed to RAF Mildenhall, flew missions over Germany, Switzerland, Italy, and the Mediterranean. A May 21, 1992, Chinese nuclear test at Lop Nor produced a large cloud of radioactive gas that, by early June, had passed over the Sea of Japan. A WC-135 flew into the cloud to collect nuclear particles. A

WC-135 was probably also used to monitor the effects of a plutonium leak from a nuclear plant in Siberia in July 1993.[34]

In subsequent years, the aerial sampling mission nearly faded into near oblivion. The C-130 sampling mission ended in 1990, and B-52 debris collection equipment was deactivated in 1993. Several WC-135s were transferred to Open Skies monitoring activities. In October 1993, the 55th WRS was deactivated. U-2 aircraft no longer carry aerial sampling equipment. All that remains are two WC-135Ws, designated CONSTANT PHOENIX and stationed at Offutt Air Force Base, Nebraska. The WC-135 is either a modified C-135B or a EC-135C. Crews are drawn from the 45th Reconnaissance Squadron at Offutt, while those operating the detection equipment are assigned to AFTAC Detachment 1 at Offutt.[35]

The WC-135 was deployed to Diego Garcia to conduct aerial sampling missions following the May 1998 Indian detonation of several nuclear devices. In the fall of 1998, the issue of whether that plane would remain operational was a subject of debate within the Clinton administration and was a topic of concern to several U.S. senators. Eventually, a decision was made to continue inclusion of the plane in the operational inventory. In October 2006, the WC-135 was ordered to fly from Kadena Air Base in Japan to gather air samples over the Sea of Japan, after North Korea's announcement that it had conducted a nuclear test. Missions in the European area are designated CREEK PHOENIX, whereas as those in the Pacific area are designated DISTANT PHOENIX.[36]

GROUND COLLECTION

MASINT collection systems operated from the ground involve a variety of different targets and employ assorted sensor systems. In addition, MASINT ground sensors include those employed for strategic purposes as well as for tactical purposes. Key MASINT ground systems include the radars operated by the Air Force Space Command for missile detection and tracking and the seismic stations operated by the Air Force Technical Applications Center to detect nuclear detonations. Whereas those systems produce strategic intelligence, the U.S. Army Intelligence and Security Command (INSCOM) has, for a number of years, operated a number of tactical MASINT collection systems.

The radars operated by the Air Force Space Command and the Air Force Intelligence, Surveillance, and Reconnaissance Agency include the COBRA DANE phased-array radar on Shemya, Alaska; the Norwegian-based CREEK CHART radar; and the COBRA SHOE radar* at a classified location.[37]

---

*For many years, at Pirinclik Air Base, Turkey, a satellite operation of Diyarbakir Air Station, the United States operated two radars—an AN/FPS-17 detection radar and an AN/FPS-79 tracking radar. In December 1995, the AN/FPS-17 was decommissioned, and in February 1997 the Department of Defense announced that U.S. operations at Pirinclik would cease and the facility would be turned over to Turkey. See Department of Defense, News Release No. 058–97, "Operations to End at Pirinclik Air Base Turkey," February 6,1997.}

The primary purpose of the COBRA DANE radar is to "acquire precise radar metric and signature data on developing [Russian] ballistic missile weapon systems for weapon system characteristics determination. The [Russian] developmental test to Kamchatka and the Pacific Ocean provide[s] the United States with the primary source for collection of these data early in the [Russian] developmental programs." Its corollary mission, missile warning, makes it part of the Integrated Tactical Warning and Attack Assessment (ITW/AA) network. COBRA DANE provides warning of all "Earth-impacting objects," including ballistic missiles targeted on the United States. Its secondary mission is space object tracking and identification.[38]

The COBRA DANE system consists of an AF/FPS-108 radar facility that measures 87 by 107 feet at its base; it rises approximately six stories, or 100 feet, in height and includes an attached one-story, 87-square-foot Precision Measurement Equipment Laboratory (PMEL). This facility overlooks the Bering Sea from a 230-foot-high bluff in the northwestern section of Shemya.[39]

The most important characteristic of COBRA DANE is that it is a phased-array radar. To observers relying only on their eyes or using binoculars, a phased-array radar is simply a dormant structure, sort of an electronic pyramid. This is in sharp contrast to the older, more traditional radar dish "sweeping its beam of microwave radiation along the horizon in search of distant objects." COBRA DANE consists of 15,360 radiating elements that occupy 95 feet in diameter on the radar's face. Each element emits a signal that travels in all directions. When the signals are emitted at the same time, only targets in the immediate vicinity of the array's perpendicular axis are detectable. By successively delaying the signals by a fraction of a wavelength, however, one can "steer" the beam to detect objects away from the perpendicular axis.[40]

COBRA DANE, which replaced the AN/FPS-17 and the AN/FPS-80 mechanical radar, achieved initial operating capability on July 13, 1977. It can detect (with a 99 percent probability) and track a basketball-sized object at a range of 2,000 miles with a 120-degree field of view, extending from the northern half of Sakhalin Island to just short of the easternmost tip of Russia near the Bering Strait. Its ability to provide information on the size and shape of the object, however, is available only over a 44-degree range center on the upper portion of Kamchatka, as indicated in Figure 9.3. COBRA DANE can simultaneously track up to 100 warheads when operating in an intelligence collection mode. It can also be employed for early warning and space surveillance; in those modes it can track up to 300 incoming warheads and up to 200 satellites, respectively. The final near-Earth trajectory of Russian reentry vehicles is not visible to COBRA DANE, however, owing to line-of-sight constraints imposed by the curvature of the earth.[41]

In September 2005, COBRA DANE was used for a new purpose. In a test for the Missile Defense Agency, the radar tracked a missile that was dropped by a U.S. Air Force C-17 cargo aircraft and then ignited. The radar's data was then fed into the missile defense fire control system.[42]

Far less is known about two other land-based radars—COBRA SHOE and CREEK CHART. COBRA SHOE, in operation since the late 1970s, may be an over-

FIGURE 9.3   Coverage of COBRA DANE Radar

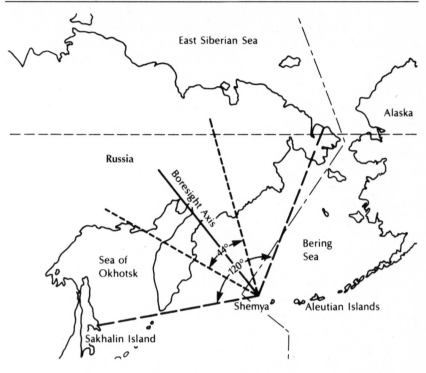

the-horizon (OTH) radar located at Ayios Nikolaos, Cyprus. CREEK CHART is a United States Air Forces Europe project of more recent origin, located in Norway and operated for the United States by the Norwegian Defense Intelligence Staff. CREEK CHART was scheduled to be replaced by the GLOBUS II radar (see Chapter 10).[43]

A second set of ground stations are those operated by the Air Force Technical Applications Center (AFTAC) for the purposes of monitoring compliance with test ban treaties and the collection of nuclear intelligence. The Limited Test Ban Treaty prohibits atmospheric testing; the Threshold Test Ban Treaty limits testing to underground tests of not more than 150 kilotons; and the Comprehensive Test Ban Treaty (CTBT) prohibits testing of any kind.* According to an official history of AFTAC,

---

*Although the CTBT has not been ratified by the U.S. Senate, the United States has not conducted any nuclear tests since signing the treaty in 1996. The other signators have also refrained from testing.

the "only technique of the USAEDS [that is] truly effective in the detection of underground nuclear detonations" is the seismic technique.[44]

Seismic detection relies on the fact that nuclear detonations, like earthquakes, generate waves that travel long distances either by passing deep through the earth (body waves) or by traveling along Earth's surface (surface waves). Teleseismic body and surface waves can be recorded by seismometers or seismic arrays at significant distances (over 1,240 miles) from the point of detonation. When the waves arrive at a seismic station, the resulting motion of the ground is recorded by seismometers and converted into a seismogram.[45]

Analysis of the data involves distinguishing between earthquakes (which originate from two bodies of rock slipping past each other) and detonations (a point source), filtering out background and instrument noise, and converting the seismic signal into an estimate of explosive yield, when appropriate. The conversion requires not only application of a mathematical formula but also data concerning the geology of test site, because a disturbance in a stable geological structure results in stronger body waves than a disturbance in a more molten geologic structure.[46]

At distances of less than 625 miles from an event, explosions of greater than a few kilotons can easily be distinguished from earthquakes. At greater distances, such distinctions become far more difficult to discern. Moreover, the actual recording of a seismic signal is disturbed by both instrumental and natural background noise, the latter setting a threshold of detectability. These limitations place a premium on situation monitoring stations or equipment in suitable locations and on development of techniques to enhance the signal-to-noise ratio obtained at any location. The simplest form of Earth-based monitoring equipment is a seismometer, which basically consists of a magnet fixed to the ground and a spring-suspended mass with an electric coil. According to the Stockholm International Peace Research Institute (SIPRI), "When seismic waves move the ground and the magnet attached to it, they leave the mass with the coil relatively unaffected. The relative motion of the magnet and coil generates a current in the coil which is proportional to their relative velocity." One method of enhancing the signal-to-noise ration is to place several seismometers in an array. An array allows the recording of seismic waves at a number of seismometers, which increases the data sets available for analysis.[47]

As a result of bilateral arrangements with the host governments, to which AFTAC has turned over previously U.S.-run seismic stations, and in accordance with the provisions of the CTBT, AFTAC will have access to data from an increased number of sites. The CTBT establishes an International Monitoring System (IMS), consisting of nationally run sites relying on seismic and other techniques. Data from those sites—such as ARCESS in Norway and KEV in Finland—as well as any additional data provided are transmitted to an International Data Center (IDC) in Vienna, Austria. Under the provisions of the treaty, each state party to the treaty will be able to receive all the data transmitted to the IDC.[48]

Even prior to the signing of the CTBT, AFTAC operations began to shift from a reliance on AFTAC-operated stations to a combination of AFTAC- and allied-government-operated stations. Most of the allied stations were either previously operated by AFTAC or established by AFTAC for the host government. The seismic arrays and seismometers operated by or for AFTAC are distributed throughout the world. Each detachment possesses broadband seismic detection capabilities and is responsible for detecting, recording, and analyzing all seismic activity that occurs in its area of responsibility, twenty-four hours a day.[49]

AFTAC seismic detection is carried out by the AFTAC Distributed Subsurface Network (ADSN), which consists of six subsystems and support networks. The collection element of the ADSN is the Seismic Field Subsystem (SFS), which consists of equipment at Cambridge Bay, Canada (Equipment Location [EL] 079); Flin Flon, Canada (EL 244); Chiang Mai, Thailand (Detachment 415); Alice Springs, Australia (Detachment 421); Wonju Air Station, Korea (Detachment 452); Eielson Air Force Base, Alaska (Detachment 460); and the Southern U.S. Stations in Lajitas, Shafter, and Marathon, Texas (ELs 190, 191, and 192, respectively).[50]

What used to be Detachment 313 at Sonesca, Spain, was turned over to the Spanish government in January 1996. Under the terms of a memorandum of understanding between AFTAC and the Spanish National Geographic Institute, AFTAC continues to receive data from the site, which includes two seismic arrays—a nineteen-instrument short-period array covering an area of about 125 square kilometers and a six-instrument long-period array covering an area of about 1,250 square kilometers. In addition, the Belbasi Seismic Research Station (Detachment 301) was turned over to the Turkish armed forces and the Kandili Seismic Center in 1999.[51]

Detachment 415 at Chiang Mai, Thailand, is actually operated by the Royal Thai Navy (RTN) Hydrographics Department, as a result of a memorandum of agreement between the U.S. Air Force and the RTN. The detachment has an eighteen-instrument short-period array for detecting vertical Earth motion. A five-instrument long-period array is used to detect vertical and horizontal Earth motion.[52]

Detachment 460 (Eielson Air Force Base) maintains forty-five seismic sites in seven arrays across Alaska, with the farthest site located 2,000 miles away from Eielson. The geological data collected by the detachment are the largest joint data feed to the U.S. Atomic Energy Detection System (USAEDS). Detachment 452 (Wonju Air Station) is located 50 miles south of the Demilitarized Zone and operates the second-largest seismic array. The arrays are laid out over a 600-square-mile area in north-central South Korea. A short-period array consisting of nineteen instruments detects vertical partial motion used for wave energy measurements. A long-period array consisting of six seismic instruments measures both vertical and horizontal Earth particle motions and provides data used for event discrimination and wave energy measurements. Both arrays contribute to the refinement of seismic magnitude calculations.[53]

The installation at Alice Springs, Australia, code-named OAK TREE, is operated by Detachment 421. The installation is officially known as the Joint Geological and

Geophysical Research Station, although there is no Australian participation. An underground seismic array located about 1.5 miles northeast of the detachment consists of twenty-two detectors arranged in a circular pattern over an area of 7 square miles. About thirteen of the seismometers are buried approximately 200 feet in the ground and are designed to pick up the long-period waves that pass through the surface layer of Earth. The remaining seismometers are buried 1.1 miles deep and are tuned to detect the short-period waves that pass through Earth's mantle and core. The seismometers are linked by cables to a central recording station where the signals are processed to provide an indication of the direction and speed at which they are traveling and the amplitude of the ground motion.[54]

AFTAC also obtains seismic data from stations it has set up in the Southern Hemisphere, but these are operated by foreign governments. This network—originally known as the Global Telemetered Seismic Network (GTSN), and subsequently as the Auxiliary Seismic Network (ASN)—is now known as the AFTAC Southern Network (ASN). The GTSN became operational in January 1995, and the ASN now consists of four stations in South America (Brazil, Paraguay, Argentina, Bolivia), four in Africa (South Africa, Botswana, Central African Republic, Ivory Coast), and one in Antarctica, and an experimental station at the Albuquerque Seismological Laboratory (ASL) for testing and debugging.[55] Figure 9.4 shows a sample alert report based on reporting from AFTAC seismic stations.

In addition to gathering seismic data, various AFTAC ground stations are part of a particulate sampling or Ground Filter Unit (GFU) network, established to back up and augment aerial sampling operations. The GFU is an electrically powered, ground-based, air-filtering unit. The unit draws free air into a transition cone, which flows through a filter paper and is then emitted back into the atmosphere. The filter paper containing airborne particles from the atmosphere is then removed and forwarded for analysis and classification.[56]

One AFTAC site that is part of the GFU network is Detachment 460 at Eielson Air Force Base. The detachment also operates the B/20–5, an automated cryogenic distillation device that employs very low temperatures to isolate rare elements (gases) contained in the atmosphere. The unit is designed to operate continuously over any preset sample run of twenty-four hours (or a multiple thereof) for periods of up to seven days. Samples are collected in 800-cc metal containers that are forwarded to the McClellan Central Laboratory for analysis.[57]

The prospect of the requirement to monitor CTBT compliance led to plans to deploy additional systems for NUDET detection monitoring. The IMS to be established in support of CTBT monitoring envisions eighty ground-based radionuclide collection sites around the world, with the United States responsible for eleven. The key equipment at the sites will be Radionuclide Aerosol Sampler/Analyzers (RASAs), which push large volumes of air through six rolls of filter paper strips that, after a decay period, are mechanically passed through a gamma-ray detector. The strips capture radioactive elements released into the atmosphere by a nuclear detonation, even days afterward.[58]

FIGURE 9.4   Sample Alert Report Text: CIS/PRC Underground Test Site Events

```
CENR 55-5      Attachment 12    28 May 1992                                    31

      Figure A12-2.  (U) Sample Alert Report Text:  CIS/PRC Underground Test Site Events
                     (This figure is classified SECRET)

SUBJECT:  ALERT ____ (U)

1. (S) DATA FROM ____ NORTH AMERICAN AND _____ OVERSEAS SEISMIC STATIONS OF THE US ATOMIC ENERGY DETECTION

SYSTEM (USAEDS) INDICATE AN UNDERGROUND EXPLOSION WITH A YIELD OF ABOUT _____ KT OCCURRED AT THE

_____  _____ TEST SITE, _____ DEGREES _____ MINUTES NORTH

_____DEGREES _____ MINUTES EAST, AT _____ GMT ON _____ 19___.  THE ERROR ELLIPSE

ASSOCIATED WITH THE ABOVE LOCATION HAS A ███████████████████████████████████████

████████████████████████████████████████████████

2. (S) DATA EVALUATED FROM ____ SATELLITES HAVING █████████████████████████████

████████████ITH THIS EVENT.

3. (S) THE PRELIMINARY ESTIMATE OF YIELD OF ABOUT _____ KT, WITH AN UNCERTAINTY RANGE ███████ OF _____

TO _____ KT, IS BASED ON A SEISMIC MAGNITUDE (Mb) OF ABOUT _____ AND AN ASSUMPTION THE DETONATION OCCURRED

AT THE _____ TEST SITE, THE MAGNITUDE-YIELD FORMULA _____ WAS USED IN

DETERMINING THE YIELD.

4. (S) SURFACE WAVE DATA _____

_____.

5. (S) THE EARLIEST THAT ████████████████████████████████████

19___.  AFTAC PLANS/DOES NOT PLAN TO CONDUCT ██████████████████████████

6. (U) THE INFORMATION CONTAINED IN THIS DOCUMENT WILL BE SAFEGUARDED AS DIRECTED BY NATIONAL SECURITY DECISION

MEMORANDUM NO. 50.



      _____


      _____


                  COORD: _____


                  DATE: _____



                  CLASSIFIED BY: AFTAC GSSCG 20 DEC 90
                  DECLASSIFY ON: OADR
===================================================================================
```

SOURCE: AFTAC Regulation 55-5, "Alert Procedures," May 28, 1992.

SEABORNE COLLECTION

A key seaborne collection element is the COBRA JUDY system on the USNS *Observation Island*, a missile range instrumentation ship. The collection program is managed by AFTAC, although the ship is operated by contractor personnel (with one Air Force officer on board). Emplaced on the 564-foot ship, which can travel at 20 knots, is a mechanically steered X-band parabolic dish antenna and an S-band phased-array radar. The S-band phased-array radar tracks missiles as they accelerate and tells the X-band radar where to look to focus on specific objects.[59]

The phased-array radar is essentially a 30-foot cube with one face tilted slightly inward. An antenna array 22.5 feet in diameter occupies an octagonal raised area on the cube's slanting face. In addition, on top of the superstructure there are two 32-foot-diameter geodesic radomes containing a complex of passive receiving antennas funded by the NSA.[60]

The deployment of COBRA JUDY was intended to permit the monitoring of the final near-Earth trajectories of Soviet (now Russian) reentry vehicles during the portion of their flight not "visible" to COBRA DANE because of Earth's line-of-sight constraints. In particular, the sensors provide information on the radar signatures of reentry vehicles and warheads. To enhance that capability, the X-band radar with dish antenna was added in 1985 to improve resolution and target separation, which may have resulted in the capability to distinguish between multiple warheads and penetration aides such as decoys and chaff.[61]

COBRA JUDY has also been used for missile warning. During Operation Iraqi Freedom in March 2003, the radar was used to detect launches of Iraqi Ababil-100 and Al Samoud missiles. It has also been used by the Missile Defense Agency during its anti-missile tests over the Pacific. COBRA JUDY is scheduled to be retired in 2012. The COBRA JUDY replacement program is scheduled to produce a replacement ship by that time. In June 2006, Raytheon, the prime contractor for the replacement ship, completed the final critical design review.[62]

Another radar that resides on a missile range instrumentation ship is GRAY STAR, which has also been known as COBRA GEMINI. Located on the USNS *Invincible*, GRAY STAR is a single-dish, dual-band X- and S-band radar system. Its principal mission is to support DIA MASINT requirements for ballistic missile data collection.[63]

A set of surface ships, operated by civilian contractors for the Military Sealift Command, with the common designation T-AGOS (Tactical Auxiliary Ocean Surveillance), and with numbers and names to distinguish one from another, deploys a Surveillance Toward-Array Sensor System (SURTASS) during missions to gather acoustic intelligence from great distances on foreign submarines. These includes the USNS *Victorious* (T-AGOS 19), USNS *Able* (T-AGOS-20), USNS *Effective* (T-AGOS 21), USNS *Loyal* (T-AGOS 22), and the USNS *Impeccable* (T-AGOS 23).[64]

The arrays gather Acoustic Intelligence (ACOUSTINT)—intelligence derived from the analysis of acoustic waves radiated either intentionally or unintentionally by a submarine into the surrounding ocean. This category of intelligence includes the underwater acoustic waves from submarines, which can be used to determine the "signature" of those vehicles in much the same manner as voice autographs of individuals can be developed.

SURTASS was developed with the Soviet submarine threat in mind, but since the end of the Cold War the focus has shifted "to include regional conflicts and the threat posed by diesel-electric submarines operating in littoral waters." Of particular interest are Chinese and North Korean submarines operating in Asian waters.[65]

UNDERSEA COLLECTION

As important as intelligence concerning the Soviet surface naval activities was during the Cold War, intelligence concerning underseas activities was even more important. Although the Soviet Union placed the preponderance of its strategic nuclear weapons capability on land, it also maintained sixty-two submarines armed with SLBMs. By the late 1980s, these submarines began to deploy the modern Typhoon SSBN armed with multiple warhead SS-N-20 missiles.

Additionally, Soviet attack submarines represented a threat to the U.S. SSBN fleet—the portion of the fleet equipped with long-range, nuclear-armed, ballistic missiles. In the midst of the transition from Poseidon to Trident submarines, the United States had only half the number of SSBNs possessed by the Soviet Union, although U.S. missiles were qualitatively superior to their Soviet counterparts. Since the submarines played a more significant role in U.S. nuclear strategy than Soviet SSBNs played in Soviet strategy, it was imperative to detect and track any possible threats to U.S. SSBNs.

Long before the mobile SURTASS sensors existed, the Navy had developed a fixed submarine detection and tracking system—a global network of large, fixed, sea-bottom hydrophones that passively listened for the sound generated by submarines. These arrays were collectively known as the Sound Surveillance System (SOSUS), although only about two-thirds of the arrays were part of the SOSUS network proper. The other third are or were part of allied systems. The SOSUS system was described by one U.S. admiral in 1979 as the "backbone of our ASW [Antisubmarine Warfare] detection capability." Along with SURTASS, SOSUS is part of the Integrated Undersea Surveillance System (IUSS). [66]

The SOSUS system was described by the Stockholm International Peace Research Institute (SIPRI) as follows:

Each SOSUS installation consists of an array of hundreds of hydrophones laid out on the sea floor, or moored at depths most conducive to propagation, and connected by submarine cables for transmission of telemetry. In such an array a sound wave arriving from a distant submarine will be successively detected by different hydrophones according to their geometric relationship to the direction from which the wave arrives. This direction can be determined by noting the order in which the wave is detected at the different hydrophones. In practice, the sensitivity of the array is enhanced many times by adding the signals from several individual hydrophones after introducing appropriate time delays between them. The result is a listening "beam" that can be "steered" in various sectors of the ocean by varying the pattern of time delays. The distance from the array to the sound source can be calculated by measuring the divergence of the sound rays within the array or by triangulating from adjacent arrays.[67]

Two phenomena have made it possible to productively deploy a system such as SOSUS. One is that the decline in signal intensity is much less during propagation through the ocean than through the earth, since the rate of absorption of sound energy in the ocean is very low. Second, the ocean has a layer of low-speed sound, called the Sound Fixing and Ranging (SOFAR) channel, that acts like a "waveguide." Sound energy moves horizontally in this channel, rather than downward to the sea floor, where interaction with the bottom can cause significant attenuation. In addition, the waveguide effect limits the "geometrical spreading" attenuation of the sound wave. As a result, the effect of spreading increases only linearly with distance from the source, rather than as the square of the distance from the source (as occurs with seismic body waves).[68]

Development work on SOSUS began in the early 1950s, at which time the first hydrophone arrays were given the unclassified designation CAESAR. By mid-1953 the Navy decided to install a SOSUS/CAESAR array on the continental shelf of the east coast of the United States. Within two years, the Navy decided to add arrays off the west coast as well and in Hawaii. The arrays have been progressively updated and the technology is now in its fifth or sixth generation of development.[69]

The CAESAR arrays proved extremely effective during the Cuban missile crisis of October 1962, when every Soviet submarine in the area was detected and closely trailed. As a result, the United States decided to expand and upgrade the network. An array was established to cover the Greenland–Iceland–United Kingdom (GIUK) Gap—the portion of the Atlantic through which Soviet submarines stationed at the Polyarnyy submarine base in the northwestern Soviet Union had to pass in order to head toward the United States. Even earlier warning was provided in this region by an array strung between Andoya, Norway, and Bear Island. [70]

Several arrays had been established in the Pacific by the late 1960s. An upgraded variation of CAESAR—designated COLOSSUS—was deployed on the west coast of the United States, extending from northern Alaska to the Baja Peninsula. COLOSSUS employed a more advanced form of sonar than CAESAR. Farther out in the Pacific, a 1,300-mile-long circular array, code-named SEA SPIDER, surrounds the Hawaiian Islands. Another Pacific array extended from Alaska and ran parallel to the Aleutian Islands. An array along the western side of the Kuril Islands allowed detection of Russian submarines exiting the naval base at Petropavlovsk or the Sea of Okhotsk.[71]

Construction began on an array known as the Azores Fixed Acoustic Range (AFAR) in September 1968 off the island of Santa Maria, the southernmost of the Azores group off the west coast of Africa. In May 1972, the system was commissioned by NATO with a dual mission—to track Soviet submarines approaching the Strait of Gibraltar and those passing around the Cape of Good Hope. An array in the Bosporus Strait between Yugoslavia and Turkey can detect submarines exiting the Black Sea port of Sevastopol. Yet another array was put in place along the coast of Taiwan and the Philippines, and there is an Indian Ocean array in vicinity of Diego Garcia. Other arrays were located off Turkey (in addition to the Bosporus array), Japan, Puerto Rico, Barbados, Canada (Argentia, Newfoundland), Italy, Denmark, Gibraltar, Galeta Island in Panama, and Guam.[72]

The hydrophones are sealed in tanks—approximately twenty-four to a tank—and cables transmit the data to facilities on shore. In earlier decades, the collected data were sent to one of a number of Naval Facilities (NAVFACs) and Naval Regional Processing Centers (NRPCs) positioned around the world. There has been a reported reduction in the number of NAVFACs over the years. Among the NAVFACs operating in 1993 were those at Adak, Alaska; Argentia, Newfoundland; Brawdy, Wales; Centreville Beach, California; Whidbey Island, Washington; and Keflavik, Iceland. However, all of the NAVFACs have since been closed. Data are now transmitted to two Naval Ocean Processing Facilities (NOPFs).[73]

The Whidbey Island NAVFAC has become an NOPF, with a staff of 273 U.S. and Canadian personnel (234 enlisted personnel, 25 officers, and 14 civilians). It receives remote data from unmanned relay centers at Coos Bay and Pacific Beach and elsewhere. The second NOPF is located at Dam Neck, Virginia, with 259 personnel (25 officers, 225 enlisted personnel, and 9 civilians). These two facilities are responsible for centralized reporting, correlation, localization, and tracking of submarine targets. They provide analysis and processing of underwater signals and transmit data to naval forces around the clock.[74]

The data collected about each submarine detected—its sonar echo and the noises made by the engine, its cooling system, and the movement of its propellers—can be translated into a recognition signal. A distinctive pattern can be determined that indicates not only a particular type of submarine—an Alfa-class attack submarine instead of a Typhoon-class ballistic-missile-carrying submarine, for example—but also the individual submarine. Thus the data, when analyzed, operate much like fingerprints or voiceprints do in identifying individuals.

Gradually, a fundamental change in Soviet submarine capabilities reduced the value of SOSUS. The first three generations of Soviet sea-based ballistic missile submarines—the SS-N-4 Snark, the SS-N-5 Serb, and the SS-N-6 Sawfly—had ranges of between 350 and 1,600 nautical miles. Beginning in 1973—with the operation of the SS-N-8, which had range of 4,200 nautical miles—Soviet subs did not have to exit Soviet home waters to hit targets in the United States. Soviet capability in this regard grew over the years, with the deployment of the SS-N-8 Mod 2, with its range of 4,900 nautical miles, and of the SS-N-18 and SS-N-20, with their ranges of 3,500 to 4,500 nautical miles. During the years preceding the Soviet collapse, Russians SSBNs conducted fewer operations off the Atlantic and Pacific coasts, reducing the value of the SOSUS arrays covering those areas. However, in the late 1990s, Russians subs were identified off each U.S. coast. And in August 2009 it was reported that a pair of nuclear-powered Russian attack submarines had been patrolling the eastern seaboard.[75]

As with DSP, SOSUS has been able to provide information about activities other than the primary strategic weapons systems it was created to monitor. One additional capability is the detection and tracking of surface ships. An even more surprising capability demonstrated by SOSUS is the tracking and identification of aircraft flying over the ocean. This capability was first discovered in 1965 and 1966, when the Norwegian SOSUS station detected Soviet Bear-D bombers flying over the Norwegian Sea.[76]

The same capabilities that made SOSUS such a valuable tool in monitoring Soviet submarine activity also make it able to detect nuclear and other detonations, whether conducted underwater or near the oceans. Thus, at one time AFTAC used nine hydroacoustic stations around the world to provide coverage of the North Pacific Ocean, the Atlantic Ocean, and the part of the Antarctic Ocean adjacent to the South Atlantic Ocean. Eight of the stations were collocated with SOSUS. AFTAC equipment was connected as near to the hydrophone cable shore terminal as possible, bypassing all host electronics to the maximum extent. Digital data were then encrypted and transmitted over dedicated circuits via satellite links to the main Hydroacoustics Operations Center at AFTAC headquarters. Operated twenty-four hours a day, the hydroacoustic data center is tasked with identifying the source of each recorded wave. In any given year, it receives data on more than 650,000 events from both natural and man-made sources.[77]

Thus, SOSUS arrays detected French nuclear tests in the Pacific in 1995 and what was probably the internal explosion that devastated the nuclear submarine *Kursk* before it sank in August 2000.[78]

While SOSUS, along with SURTASS, is part of the IUSS, SOSUS is also part of the Fixed Surveillance System (FSS). The FSS consists of SOSUS plus the Fixed Distributed System (FDS) and the FDS-Commercial (FDS-C). FDS "is a low frequency (LF) passive acoustic surveillance system employing fiber-optic technology" and "consists of long arrays and clusters of hydrophones distributed on the sea floor." FDS-C uses commercial off the shelf technology.[79]

Notes

1. U.S. Congress, House Permanent Select Committee on Intelligence, *IC 21: Intelligence Community in the 21st Century* (Washington, D.C.: U.S. Government Printing Office, 1996), p. 149.

2. Department of Defense Instruction Number 5105.28, "Measurement and Signature Intelligence (MASINT)," April 22, 2009, p. 13.

3. Department of Defense Instruction Number 5105. 28, "Management of Measurement and Signature Intelligence (MASINT)," February 9, 1993, p. 2; John L. Morris, *MASINT: Progress and Impact, Brief to NMIA*, November 19, 1996, Slide 1; Daniel B. Sibbet, "MASINT: Intelligence for the 1990s," *American Intelligence Journal* (Summer/Fall 1990): 23–26. Also see John Morris, "The Nature and Applications of Measurement and Signature Intelligence," *American Intelligence Journal* (Winter 1999–2000): 81–84; and John Macartney, "John, How Should We Explain MASINT?" *Intelligencer* (Summer 2001): 28–34.

4. Morris, *MASINT: Progress and Impact*, Slide 8; Capt. Chadwick T. Hawley, "MASINT: Supporting the Warfighter Today and Tomorrow!" *Communiqué*, May 1996, p. 14.

5. For a discussion of such issues, see U.S. Congress, House Permanent Select Committee on Intelligence, *IC-21: Intelligence Community in the 21st Century*, pp. 144–173; Office of the Inspector General, Department of Defense, PO 97–031 *Evaluation Report on Measurement and Signature*, June 30, 1997; and Jeffrey T. Richelson, "MASINT: The New Kid in Town," *International Journal of Intelligence and Counterintelligence* 14, 2 (Summer 2001): 149–192.

6. Jeffrey T. Richelson, *America's Space Sentinels: DSP Satellites and National Security* (Lawrence: University Press of Kansas, 1999); David A. Fulghum, "Offensive Gathers Speed," *Aviation Week & Space Technology*, March 24, 2003, pp. 22–23; "Ship Blast Spotted," *Aviation Week & Space Technology*, March 8,2004, p. 19.

7. U.S. Congress, Senate Committee on Armed Services, *Department of Defense Authorization for Appropriations for FY 1986, Part 6* (Washington, D.C.: U.S. Government Printing Office, 1980), p. 3449; Science Applications International Corporation, *Fifty Year Commemorative History of Long Range Detection: The Creation, Development, and Operation of the United States Atomic Energy Detection System* (Patrick AFB, Fla.: Air Force Technical Applications Center, 1997), pp. 124–126.

8. Richelson, *America's Space Sentinels*, pp. 125, 130.

9. Ibid., p. 162; Northrop Grumman, News Release, "Defense Support Program Satellite Decommissioned," July 31, 2008; Peter B. De Selding, "U.S. DSP-23 Satellite Drifts Near Vicinity of Other Craft," *Space News*, December 8, 2008, p. 4.

10. Richelson, *America's Space Sentinels*, p. 162.

11. Ibid., p. 224; Desmond Ball, *A Base for Debate: The U.S. Satellite Ground Station at Nurrungar* (Sydney: Allen & Unwin Australia, 1987), p. 50; "Space Group Activates, Serves as Space-Based Missile Warning Focal Point," *Guardian*, July 1996, p. 23; Michael M. Jacobs and Ronald R. Herm, "Missile Warning: A National Priority from Strategic to Tactical: Past, Present, and Future," *High Frontier* 2, 1, n.d., pp. 22–28; "Theater Ballistic Missile Warning," http://www.stratcom.mil/fact_sheets/fact_tbmw.html, accessed February 23, 2006.

12. Richelson, *America's Space Sentinels*, pp. 211–222; U.S. Air Force, Fact Sheet, "Space Based Infrared System," November 15, 2010, www.af.mil/information/factsheets.

13. U.S. Air Force, Fact Sheet, "Space Based Infrared System.

14. U.S. Congress, General Accounting Office, *Satellite Acquisition: Global Positioning Acquisition Changes After Challenger's Accident* (Washington, D.C.: GAO, 1987), pp. 8, 29; David A. Turner and Marcia S. Smith, *GPS: Satellite Navigation and Positioning and the DOD's Navstar Global Positioning System* (Washington, D.C.: Library of Congress, 1994), p. 5; Aerospace Corporation, *The Global Positioning System: A Record of Achievement*, n.d.; U.S. Air Force, Fact Sheet, "Global Positioning System," October 2006, http://www.afspc.af mil/library/factsheets.

15. U.S. Congress, House Committee on Appropriations, *Department of Defense Appropriations for 1983, Part 5* (Washington, D.C.: U.S. Government Printing Office, 1982), p. 16; U.S. Congress, House Committee on Appropriations, *Department of Defense Appropriations for 1984, Part 8* (Washington, D.C.: U.S. Government Printing Office, 1983), p. 337; U.S. Congress, House Committee on Armed Services, *Department of Energy National Security and Military Applications of Nuclear Energy Authorization Act of 1984* (Washington, D.C.: U.S. Government Printing Office, 1983), pp. 383–384; Paul Stares, *Space and National Security* (Washington, D.C.: Brookings Institution, 1987), p. 29; Charles A. Zraket, "Strategic Command, Control, Communications and Intelligence," *Science*, June 22, 1984, p. 1309; "Navstar Bloc 2 Satellites to Have Crosslinks, Radiation Hardening," *Defense Electronics*, July 1983,

p. 16; Department of the Air Force, *Supporting Data for Fiscal Year 1985* (Washington, D.C.: Department of the Air Force, 1984), pp. 394–395; AFSPACECOM Regulation 55–29, "Global Positioning System and Nuclear Detonation (NUDET) Detection System (GPS/NDS) Mission Requirements and Doctrine (MRD)," September 1, 1989, pp. 4, 6, 9; Turner and Smith, *GPS: Satellite Navigation and Positioning and the DOD's Navstar Global Positioning System*, p. 7; U.S. Air Force, Fact Sheet, "Global Positioning System," March 2007, wwwafmil/information/factsheets; Government Accountability Office, GAO-10–636, *Global Positioning System: Challenges in Sustaining and Upgrading Capabilities Persist*, September 2010, p. 6; Air Force Technical Applications Center, CENI 38–101, *Organization and Functions Chartbook*, June 2, 2003, p. 20.

16. D. M. Suszcynsky, A. Jacobsen, J. Fitzgerald, C. Rhodes, and E. Tech, Los Alamos National Laboratory, LA-UR-00–4956, *Satellite-Based Global Lightning and Severe Storm Monitoring Using VHF*, 2000, pp. 2–3; "Northrop Grumman Ships Nuclear Blast Sensors," *Space News* November 20, 2006, p. 9; U.S. Congress, House of Representatives, *Enactment of Provisions of H.R. 5408, The Floyd D. Spence National Defense Authorization Act for Fiscal Year 2001* (Washington, D.C.: U.S. Government Printing Office, 2000), p. 715; Amy Butler and Michael Mecham, "GPS IIF Fix Needed," *Aviation Week & Space Technology*, September 6, 2010, p. 35; Amy Butler, "Time for a Change," *Aviation Week & Space Technology*, April 12, 2010, pp. 44–47; National Nuclear Security Administration, "NNSA Launches New Detection Capability," May 28, 2010, http://nnsa.energy.gov.

17. Sylvia E. D. Ferry, *The Defense Meteorological Satellite System Sensors: An Historical Overview* (Los Angeles AFB, Calif.: DMSS Program Office, 1989), pp. 4–15; U.S. Air Force, Fact Sheet, "Defense Meteorological Satellite Program," accessed November 22, 2010.

18. Richelson, *America's Space Sentinels*, p. 74.

19. Jeffrey T. Richelson, *Spying on the Bomb: American Nuclear Intelligence from Nazi Germany to Iran and North Korea* (New York: W.W. Norton, 2006), p. 287.

20. "COBRA BRASS," www.wslfweb.org/docs/roadmap, accessed October 21, 2006.

21. "Quickbird," www.digitalglobe.com, accessed November 22, 2010; "Worldview-2," www.digitalglobe.com, accessed November 22, 2010.

22. "Imagery Sources," www.geoeye.com, accessed November 22, 2010.

23. David A. Fulghum, "Endurance Standoff Range Remain Crucial Attributes," *Aviation Week & Space Technology*, August 4, 1997, pp. 51–53.

24. David A. Fulghum, "Cobra Ball Revamped for Battlefield Missions," *Aviation Week & Space Technology*, August 4, 1997, pp. 48–50.

25. David A. Fulghum and John D. Morrocco, "First Arrow Battery Deployed Near Tel Aviv," *Aviation Week & Space Technology*, April 10, 2000, pp. 66–67; Robert Wall, "Compton Reentry Incident Free," *Aviation Week & Space Technology*, June 12, 2000, p. 34.

26. David Miller, *An Illustrated Guide to Modern Sub Hunters* (New York: Arco, 1984), p. 124; George A. Wilmoth, "Lockheed's Antisubmarine Warfare Aircraft: Watching the Threat," *Defense Systems Review* 3, 5 (1985): 18–25; U.S. Congress, Senate Committee on Armed Services, *Department of Defense Authorization for Appropriations for Fiscal Year 1986, Part 8* (Washington, D.C.: U.S. Government Printing Office, 1985), p. 4510; U.S. Navy Fact File, "P-3 Orion long range ASW aircraft," February 18, 2009, www.navy.mil/navydata.

27. Lori A. McClelland, "Versatile P-3C Orion Meeting Growing ASW Challenge," *Defense Electronics*, April 1985, pp. 132–141; Miller, *An Illustrated Guide to Sub Hunters*, p. 124; *P-3C Orion Update Weapon System* (Burbank, Calif.: Lockheed, n.d.), p. 17.

28. McClelland, "Versatile P-3C Orion Meeting Growing ASW Challenge"; *P-3C Orion Update Weapon System*, p. 18; Nicholas M. Horrock, "The Submarine Hunters," *Newsweek*, January 23, 1984, p. 38.

29. Private information; U.S. Congress, House Committee on Appropriations, *Department of Defense Appropriations for 1994, Part 1* (Washington, D.C.: U.S. Government Printing Office, 1993), p. 48.

30. Defense Airborne Reconnaissance Office, *Manned Airborne Reconnaissance Division*, 1995, p. 16; David A. Fulghum, "Navy Spying Masked by Patrol Aircraft," *Aviation Week & Space Technology*, March 8, 1999, pp. 32–33; "Lockheed Martin P-3B/C 'Iron Clad' Variants," *Jane's Aerospace*, April 2, 2001, www.janes.com.

31. Patrol Squadron Special Projects Unit Two, VPU-2 Inst. 5400.1H, "Squadron Organization and Regulations Manual (SORM)," February 7, 1995, p. 1-1; "Firms Specialize in Secret Aircraft," *Aviation Week & Space Technology*, August 4, 1997, p. 50; "Special Projects Patrol Squadron ONE [VPU-1] 'Old Buzzards,'" http://www.globalsecurity.org, accessed March 1, 2006; "Special Projects Patrol Squadron TWO [VPU-2] 'Wizards,'" http://www.globalsecurity.org, accessed June 2, 2006; Tom Kaminski, "United States Navy: Airpower Update 2006," *Combat Aircraft* 7, 9 (November 2006): 26–53; "VPU-1 History," wwwvpnavy.co/vpu1_historyhtml, accessed November 22, 2010. In late 1999, it was reported that the Navy was searching for funds to add a third IRON CLAD aircraft to each of the squadrons. See "Spooky," *Aviation Week & Space Technology*, November 22, 1999, p. 21.

32. Fulghum, "Navy Spying Masked by Patrol Aircraft."

33. Air Force Technical Applications Center, CENR 55–3, "Aerial Sampling Operations," October 22, 1982, pp. 2–7; Scott Weathers, Steve Greene, Greg Barge, Paul Schultz, and Chris Clements, *History of the 55th Weather Reconnaissance Squadron, July-December 1989* (McClellan AFB, Calif.: 55th WRS, December 31, 1989), p. 1.

34. Jerry King, Chris Lucey, Mike Lyons, Grant Phifer, and Leslie Yokoyama-Peralta, *History of the 55th Weather Reconnaissance Squadron, 1 Jan to 30 June 1986* (McClellan AFB, Calif.: 55th WRS, n.d.), p. 11; Bill Gertz, "Chinese Nuke Test Releases Gas Cloud," *Washington Times*, June 11, 1992, p. A5; James Rupert, "Plutonium Leak Reported at Russian Nuclear Plant," *Washington Post*, July 20, 1993, p. A14.

35. U.S. Air Force, Fact Sheet, "WC-135 CONSTANT PHOENIX," November 2009, www.af.mil/information/factsheets.

36. William B. Scott, "Sampling Missions Unveiled Nuclear Weapon Secrets," *Aviation Week & Space Technology*, November 3, 1997, pp. 54–57; Science Applications International Corporation, *Fifty Year Commemorative History of Long Range Detection*, pp. 66, 68; "USAF Aircraft Monitors Fallout of Nuclear Tests," *Jane's Defence Weekly*, May 20, 1998, p. 4; Bill Gertz, "Senators Back Keeping Atomic-Sniffing Jet," *Washington Times*, September 29, 1998, p. A6; Associated Press, "N. Korea Air Sample Has No Radioactivity," www.nytimes.com, October 13, 2006; Craig A. Kibbe, Dale W. McGavran, and Tracey M. Partelow, Air Combat Command, *History of the 55th Wing, 1 January 1997–30 June 1998, Volume 1*, p. 33.

37. Brigadier General Frank B. Campbell, Director of Forces, USAF, "Air Force TIARA Programs: Intelligence Support to the Warfighter," 1995, p. 3; "COBRA DANE," www.fas.org/spp/military/programs/track/cobra_dane.htm. Also see Melvin L. Stone and Gerald P. Banner, "Radars for the Detection and Tracking of Ballistic Missiles, Satellites, and Planets," *Lincoln Laboratory Journal* 12, 2 (200): 217–243.

38. Dr. Michael E. Papa, *Meeting the Challenge: ESD and the Cobra Dane Construction Effort on Shemya Island* (Bedford, Mass.: Electronic Systems Division, Air Force Systems Command, 1979), pp. 1–2; AFSPACECOM Regulation 55–123, "Cobra Dane Tactical Requirements and Doctrine," December 15, 1992, p. 4.

39. Del Papa, *Meeting the Challenge*, pp. 2–3.

40. Eli Brookner, "Phased-Array Radars," *Scientific American*, April 1985, pp. 94–102.

41. Philip J. Klass, "USAF Tracking Radar Details Disclosed," *Aviation Week & Space* Technology, October 25, 1976, pp. 41–46; del Papa, Meeting the Challenge, p. 38; Air Combat Command, *Searching the Skies: The Legacy of the United States Cold War Defense Radar* Program (Langley, Va.: ACC, 1997), p. 50.

42. "Cobra Dane Tracks Air-Launched Target," *Space News*, October 10, 2005, p. 16.

43. U.S Air Force, "Cobra Shoe Program Element Description," 1978; Lt. Gen. Nikolai Brunsitsin, *Openness and Espionage* (Moscow: 1990), p. 23; Campbell, Director of Forces, "Air Force TIARA Programs"; Chairman, JCS, Subject: OTH Radar in Turkey, April 21, 1967; J.W. Guest, Memorandum for Colonel McAuliffe, Subject: US Over-the-Horizon Radar Installations, April 21, 1967.

44. Science Applications International Corporation, *Fifty Year Commemorative History of Long Range Detection*, p. 71.

45. Ibid.

46. Ibid.

47. Henry R. Myers, "Extending the Nuclear Test Ban," *Scientific American*, January 1972, pp. 13–23; Lynn R. Sykes and Jack F. Evernden, "The Verification of a Comprehensive Nuclear Test Ban," *Scientific American*, October 1982, pp. 47–55; "The Comprehensive Test Ban," in *SIPRI Yearbook 1978: World Armaments and Disarmament* (New York: Crane, Russak, 1978), p. 317–359 at pp. 335 and 340.

48. Paul G. Richards and Won Young-kim, "Testing the Nuclear Test Ban Treaty," *Nature*, October 23, 1997, pp. 781–782.

49. 3400 Technical Training Wing, *Introduction to Detection Systems* (Lowry Air Force Base, Col.: 3400 TTW, October 18, 1984), p. 17.

50. Scientific Applications International Corporation, *Fifty Year Commemorative History of Long Range Detection*, pp. 77–78; Air Intelligence Agency, *Air Intelligence Agency Almanac*, August 1997, pp. 36, 41; Amy Webb, "Changing Technologies, Times and Politics . . . ," *Spokesman*, April 1996, pp. 20–21.

51. "Seismic Site Turned Over to Spanish Government," *Spokesman*, March 1996, p. 35; "Detachment 313–Sonseca, Spain," www.aftac.gov; "Turkey Assumes Former US Seismic Facility," *Jane's Defence Weekly*, December 1, 1999, p. 5.

52. Air Force Technical Applications Center, CENI 38–101, *Organization and Functions Chartbook*, p. 20.

53. Air Intelligence Agency, *Air Intelligence Agency Almanac*, pp. 37–38, 41; Air Force Technical Applications Center, CENI 38–101, *Organization and Functions Chartbook*, p. 20.

54. Desmond Ball, *A Suitable Piece of Real Estate: American Installations in Australia* (Sydney, Australia: Hale & Iremonger, 1980), pp. 84–85; Science Applications International Corporation, *Fifty Year Commemorative History of Long Range Detection*, p. 179; Air Force Technical Applications Center, CENI 38–101, *Organization and Functions Chartbook*, p. 20.

55. Science Applications International Corporation, *Fifty Year Commemorative History of Long-Range Detection*, pp. 79–80; Amy Webb, "National Data Center Will Support Comprehensive Test Ban Treaty," *Spokesman*, October 1995, pp. 26–27.

56. Science Applications International Corporation, *Fifty Years Commemorative History of Long Range Detection*, pp. 84–85; 3400 Technical Training Wing, *Introduction to Detection Systems*, p. 17.

57. Science Applications International Corporation, *Fifty Years Commemorative History of Long Range Detection*, pp. 107–108; 3400 Technical Training Wing, *Introduction to Detection Systems*, p. 17.

58. "Test Ban Checking," *Aviation Week & Space Technology*, May 4, 1998, p. 13; William B. Scott, "Debris Collection Reverts to Ground Sites," *Aviation Week & Space Technology*, November 3, 1997, pp. 57–59.

59. "USNS Observation Island (T-AGM 23)," www.msc.navy.mil, accessed April 10, 2010; Ben Iannotta, "Cobra Judy," *C4ISR Journal*, May 2007, pp. 32–33.

60. Kenneth J. Stein, "Cobra Judy Phased Array Radar Tested," *Aviation Week & Space Technology*, August 10, 1981, pp. 70–73; "X-Band Expands Cobra Judy's Repertoire," *Defense Electronics*, January 1985, pp. 43–44; *Science Applications International Corporation, Fifty Year Commemorative History of Long Range Detection*, p. 195.

61. Stein, "Cobra Judy Phased Array Radar Tested"; "X-Band Expands Cobra Judy's Repertoire."

62. U.S. Congress, Senate Select Committee on Intelligence, *Intelligence Authorization Act for Fiscal Year* 2007 (Washington, D.C.: U.S. Government Printing Office, 2006), p. 2; "Cobra Judy Replacement Moves Forward," *C4ISR Journal*, August 2006, p. 8; Coalition Media Center, Camp AS Sayliyah, Qatar, *Media Briefing Support Imagery: Attack on Ababil 100 Surface to Surface Missile*, March 28, 2003; Iannotta, "Cobra Judy."

63. "COBRA GEMINI," www.fas.org, accessed March 16, 2007; Air Force Technical Applications Center, CENI 38–101, *Organization and Functions Chartbook*, p. 8.

64. United States Navy, Fact File, "Ocean Surveillance Ships—T-AGOS," January 22, 2008, www.navymil/navydata; Military Sealift Command, "USNS Victorious (T-AGOS 19)"; Military Sealift Command, "USNS Able (T-AGOS 20)"; Military Sealift Command, "USNS Effective (T-AGOS 21)"; Military Sealift Command, "USNS Loyal (T-AGOS 22)"; "USNS Impeccable (T-AGOS 23)," all at www.msc.navy.mil/inventory, all accessed April 10, 2010.

65. Travis Graham, "SURTASS Ships Return from Deployment," www.northwestnavigatorcom, May 6, 2005; General Accounting Office, GAO-02-692, *Defense Acquisitions: Testing Need to* Prove SURTASS/LFA Effectiveness in Littoral Waters, June 2002, p. 1.

66. Testimony of Admiral Metzel in U.S. Congress, Senate Committee on Armed Services, *Department of Defense Authorization for Appropriations for Fiscal Year 1980, Part 6* (Washington, D.C.: U.S. Government Printing Office, 1979), p. 2925; Commander, Undersea Surveillance, "Commander Undersea Surveillance, IUSS Headquarters Staff," www.cus.navy.mil, accessed May 9, 2006.

67. Owen Wilkes, "Strategic Anti-Submarine Warfare and Its Implications for a Counterforce First Strike," in *World Armaments and Disarmament, SIPRI Yearbook 1979* (London: Taylor & Francis, 1979), p. 430.

68. Science Applications International Corporation, *Fifty Year Commemorative History of Long Range Detection*, p. 113.

69. U.S. Congress, House Committee on Appropriations, *Department of Defense Appropriations for Fiscal Year 1977, Part 5* (Washington, D.C.: U.S. Government Printing Office, 1976), p. 1255; Drew Middleton, "Expert Predicts a Big U.S. Gain in Sub Warfare," *New York Times*, July 18, 1979, p. A5; Chapman Pincher, "U.S. to Set Up Sub Spy Station," *Daily*

Express, January 6, 1973; Harvey B. Silverstein, "CAESAR, SOSUS and Submarines: Economic and Institutional Implications of ASW Technologies," *Ocean '78* (Proceedings of the Fourth Annual Combined Conference Sponsored by the Marine Technology Society and the Institute of Electrical and Electronics Engineers, Washington, D.C., September 6–8, 1978), p. 407; Commander, Undersea Surveillance, "Origins of the Sound Surveillance System (SOSUS)," www.cus.navy.mil/sosus.htm, accessed May 9, 2006; Edward C. Whitman, "SOSUS: The 'Secret Weapon' of Undersea Surveillance," *Undersea Warfare* 7, 2 (Winter 2005), wwwchinfonavy.mil; Gary E. Weir, National Geospatial Intelligence Agency, "The American Sound Surveillance System: Using the Ocean to Hunt Soviet Submarines, 1950–1961," 2007.

70. U.S. Congress, House Committee on Appropriations, *Department of Defense Appropriations for Fiscal Year 1977, Part 5*, p. 1255; Middleton, "Expert Predicts a Big U.S. Gain in Sub Warfare."

71. Defense Market Survey, "Sonar-Sub-Surface-Caesar," *DMS Market Intelligence Report* (Greenwich, Conn.: DMS, 1980), p. 1; Clyde Burleson, *The Jennifer Project* (Englewood Cliffs, N.J.: Prentice Hall, 1977), pp. 17–18, 24–25; Joel S. Wit, "Advances in Antisubmarine Warfare," *Scientific American*, February 1981, pp. 36 ff.; Silverstein, "CAESAR, SOSUS, and Submarines."

72. Howard B. Dratch, "High Stakes in the Azores," *The Nation*, November 8, 1975, pp. 455–456; "NATO Fixed Sonar Range Commissioned, *Armed Forces Journal International*, August 1972, p. 29; "Atlantic Islands: NATO Seeks Wider Facilities," *International Herald Tribune*, June 1981, p. 75; Richard Timsar, "Portugal Bargains for U.S. Military Aid with Strategic Mid-Atlantic Base," *Christian Science Monitor*, March 24, 1981, p. 9; Wit, "Advances in Antisubmarine Warfare."

73. William Arkin and Richard Fieldhouse, *Nuclear Battlefields: Global Links in the Arms Race* (Cambridge, Mass.: Ballinger, 1986), Appendix A; Ed Offley, "Turning the Tide: Soviets Score a Coup with Sub Progress," *Seattle Post-Intelligencer*, April 8, 1987, p. A5; USN-PLAD, p. 30, in United States Military Communications–Electronics Board, USMCEB Publication No. 6, Issue 25, *Message Address Directory* (Washington, D.C.: U.S. Government Printing Office, January 30, 1993); U.S. Congress, House Committee on Appropriations, *Department of Defense Appropriations for 1994, Part 1* (Washington, D.C.: U.S. Government Printing Office, 1993), p. 48; William J. Broad, "Scientists Oppose Navy Plan to Shut Undersea Monitor," *New York Times*, June 12, 1994, pp. 1, 18; Commander, Underseas Surveillance, "Past IUSS Sites—Decommissioned . . . But Never Forgotten," http://www.cus.navy.mil/pastussites.htm, accessed May 9, 2006.

74. William E. Burrows, *Deep Black: Space Espionage and National Security* (New York: Random House, 1986), p. 180 n.; "About NOPF Whidbey Island," www.naswi.navy.mil/nopf/ABOUT_NOPF.htm, accessed May 9, 2006; Commander, Undersea Surveillance, "Naval Ocean Processing Facility (NOPF) Whidbey Island, July 1987–Present," www.cus.navy.mil/nopfwi.htm, accessed April 10, 2010; Commander, Undersea Surveillance, "Naval Ocean Processing Facility (NOPF) Dam Neck, September 1979–Present," www.cus.navy.mil/nopfdn.htm, accessed April 10, 2010.

75. Robert P. Berman and John C. Baker, *Soviet Strategic Forces: Requirements and Responses* (Washington, D.C.: Brookings Institution, 1982), pp. 106–107; Bill Gertz, "Russian Sub Stalks Three U.S. Carriers," *Washington Times*, November 23, 1997, pp. A1, A5; Mark Mazzetti and Thom Shanker, "2 Russian Submarines Off East Coast of U.S. Evoke Echoes of Cold War," *New York Times*, August 5, 2009, p. A5.

76. Office of the Chief of Naval Operations, OPNAVINST C3501.204A, Subj: Projected Operational Environment (POE) and Required Operational Capabilities (ROC) Statements for the Integrated Underseas Surveillance Systems (IUSS), March 14, 1995; interview.

77. Science Applications International Corporation, *Fifty Year Commemorative History of Long Range Detection*, p. 114; 3400 Technical Training Wing, *Introduction to Detection Systems*, p. 18.

78. William J. Broad, "Anti-Sub Seabed Grid Thrown Open to Research Uses," *New York Times*, July 2, 1996, pp. C1, C7; Patrick E. Tyler and Steven Lee Myers, "Russian Admiral Acknowledges Explosion Inside Sub," *New York Times*, August 15, 2000, p. A6.

79. Department of Defense, *FY 2009 Budget, Congressional Justification Book—Military Intelligence Program, Volume I, Summary*, 2008, p. 53.

10

SPACE SURVEILLANCE

In addition to being concerned with events on land, sea, and in the air, the U.S. Intelligence Community is concerned with events in outer space—in "space situational awareness." An accurate understanding of the space activities of foreign nations is required for assessing foreign military space (including space intelligence) capabilities, selecting and implementing operations security measures, warning of actions (whether intended or not) that threaten U.S. space systems, warning of space systems or debris that could impact Earth or other space systems (including manned vehicles or the international space station), developing plans for the interception of satellite communications, preparing and implementing plans to neutralize foreign space systems, and monitoring compliance with several treaties (including the Outer Space Treaty, which prohibits the deployment of nuclear weapons in space).[1]

The foreign space activities that are monitored include launch preparations and launch, deployment into orbit, mission, orbital parameters, maneuvering, deployment of subsatellites, breakup of satellites, and reentry of satellites or debris into Earth's atmosphere. Space surveillance systems are also used to determine the size, shape, and other characteristics of space systems.[2]

During the Cold War, the driving force behind U.S. space surveillance activities was, of course, the Soviet Union. Of primary concern were the capabilities and employment of Soviet reconnaissance, navigation, communications, meteorological, and other military support satellites. The capabilities and orbits of Soviet reconnaissance satellites had to be factored into plans to provide operational security to U.S. military forces and research and development activities, including the plans of U.S. forces preparing for the April 1980 attempt to rescue U.S. hostages in Iran as well as the highly classified aeronautical activities at Area 51 in Nevada. In addition, Soviet anti-satellite testing was a significant concern of U.S. military officials. Even nonmilitary space activities, including space probes sent to Mars and Venus, were targets of the Intelligence Community.[3]

In response to the intelligence threat from Soviet imagery satellites, the United States initiated the Satellite Reconnaissance Advanced Notice (SATRAN) program, also known by the nickname STRAY CAT, in 1966. The SATRAN program became part of the Satellite Reconnaissance Operations Security Program.[4]

A complementary program has been the Navy's Fleet Support System/Satellite Vulnerability Program. By 1987, the Naval Space Surveillance System (NAVSPA-SUR) was providing satellite vulnerability information in four formats to Navy units:

- Large Area Vulnerability Reports (LAVR) provided satellite vulnerability information to units in established operating areas.
- Satellite Vulnerability Reports (SVR) provided tailored vulnerability information to units in a transit status or operating outside established operating areas.
- Safe Window Intelligence (SWINT) reports provided periods of time when the requesting units were not vulnerable to reconnaissance satellite coverage.
- One-line CHARLIE elements [which enable units to compute their own satellite vulnerability data] had been provided to units having the Reconnaissance Satellite Vulnerability Computer (RSVC) program, allowing the units to compute their own satellite vulnerability data.[5]

In 1988, the Naval Space Command (which was subsequently absorbed into the Naval Network Warfare Command) instituted the CHAMBERED ROUND program for support to deployed elements of the fleet and Fleet Marine Force. Under CHAMBERED ROUND, the Naval Space Command provided naval forces with tactical assessments of hostile space capabilities and specific reactions to their operations. The support was tailored to a unit's specific equipment, geographic area of interest, and intentions during their predeployment workups or while in transit to the theater of operations.[6]

Although the collapse of the Soviet Union resulted in a reduced Russian military space program, the remaining program is still of interest to the U.S. Intelligence Community. Operational security measures to prevent Russian imaging satellites from viewing particularly sensitive activities are still undertaken. Likewise, data concerning Russian communications satellites are required to support U.S. satellite communications intercept activities.[7]

Several other nations have used space systems for many years, particularly for communications. In January 1992, seventeen nations other than the United States and Russia, as well as five international organizations, owned and operated seventy-seven commercial or civilian communications satellites. The growing number of foreign military space programs led Congress, in the 1993 fiscal year, to require the Secretary of Defense to produce a report on the proliferation of military satellites.[8]

China orbited its first photographic reconnaissance satellite in 1975 and since then has orbited spacecraft with electronic intelligence, meteorological, and communications missions. Since 1995, there has been an explosion of foreign nations launching dedicated reconnaissance satellites—France, Israel, Japan, Germany, Italy,

India, and others—with more nations expected to follow. In addition, the numbers and capabilities of foreign commercial imagery satellites have grown significantly and can produce imagery with a resolution that can be readily exploited for intelligence purposes.[9]

Aside from imaging reconnaissance satellites, other nations operate a variety of military and civil satellites with other missions—including communications, navigation, meteorological, relay, and signals intelligence. In 2009, apart from the United States (which had 1,398 payloads in orbit), there were forty-nine nations with one or more spacecraft in orbit. The vast majority of satellites belonged to the United States and Russia, with Japan, China, and India also possessing a substantial space presence.[10]

Foreign space activities have on occasion threatened U.S. space assets. Prior to China's interference with the EP-3E SIGINT aircraft in 2001, Chinese statements implied that Beijing might seek to interfere with the operations of U.S. reconnaissance satellites. In 2006, China used a laser to illuminate a U.S. satellite. In the future, interference could be carried out by a Chinese anti-satellite system. On January 11, 2007, China successfully tested such a system, designated SC-19 by U.S. intelligence, after two failed attempts. The test involved firing a missile from the Xichang launch site in Szechuan province. The target, a Chinese weather satellite, FY-1C, had been launched in 1999 into a sun-synchronous 500-mile orbit. The satellite was destroyed when it was 715 miles from the launch site, resulting in two clusters of debris.[11]

Then in August 2010 a Chinese satellite, SJ-12, launched in June, undertook a series of orbital maneuvers to approach an older Chinese satellite, SJ-06F, at a very slow speed. The two satellites may have actually come into contact, as a result of a Chinese test of an orbital rendezvous capability. Developing a capability could be a prelude to construction of a space station, inspecting or servicing satellites, flying satellites in formation, or (if conducted at a higher speed) an anti-satellite capability.[12]

Unintended collisions are also of concern. In February 2009, a commercial Iridium communications satellite (which weighs almost 1,500 pounds when fully fueled) collided, at an altitude of 491 miles over northern Siberia, with Cosmos 2251, a defunct Russian military communications relay satellite that had been launched in 1993. Initial radar tracking detected about 600 pieces of debris from the collision.[13]

In response to concerns over threats to U.S. space systems, in August 2006 President George W. Bush signed a policy directive stating that the United States would "take those actions necessary to protect its space capabilities; respond to interference; and deny, if necessary, adversaries the use of space capabilities hostile to U.S. national interests." The succeeding directive, *National Space Policy of the United States of America*, signed by President Barack Obama in June 2010, similarly stated that "the United States will employ a variety of measures to help assure the use of space for all responsible parties, and consistent with the inherent right of self-defense, deter others from interference and attack, defend our space systems and contribute to the defense of allied space systems, and, if deterrence fails, defeat efforts to attack them."[14]

The 2010 space policy directive also stated that the United States would "develop, maintain, and use space situational awareness (SSA) information from commercial, civil, and national security sources to detect, identify, and attribute actions in space that are contrary to responsible use and the long-term sustainability of the space environment."[15]

Whereas the main means of observing activities on Earth are overhead systems, both spacecraft and aircraft, the vast majority of assets used for space situational awareness are located on the ground—although the current split between space and ground assets is not as one-sided as it has been in the past. The focal point of the U.S. space surveillance effort is the Strategic Command's Joint Space Operations Center (JSpOC) Space Situational Awareness Cell at Vandenberg AFB, California (formerly the Space Surveillance Center [SSC] at Cheyenne Mountain Air Force Base). The JSpOC, which maintains *The Space Catalogue*, a listing of orbiting objects, receives data from the three types of sensors—dedicated, collateral, and contributing—that make up the Space Surveillance Network (SSN). In 2010, JSpOC was tracking 1,300 satellites as well as calculating the trajectories of approximately 21,100 pieces of space debris. On any given day JSpOC tracks and monitors between forty and fifty possible collisions.[16] In addition to the SSN, the United States employs other systems for monitoring space activity.

DEDICATED SSN SENSORS

Dedicated SSN sensors are those that have a primary mission of space surveillance. They rely on a variety of techniques, including intermittent radar detection, optical collection, radio-frequency monitoring, and the establishment of an electronic radar fence. They are located at a number of sites in the United States, at sites in Norway, Diego Garcia, Spain, and in space.[17]

In April 1996, the Midcourse Space Experiment (MSX) spacecraft, designed by the Johns Hopkins University Applied Physics Laboratory, was placed into orbit, carrying three sensors. Its primary sensor, an infrared payload designated SPIRIT III, operated until late February 1997. Two others, ultraviolet and visible-light sensors, were employed until that time to identify ballistic missile signatures during the period between booster burnout and missile reentry. MSX's Space-Based Visible (SBV) telescope was employed to detect and track objects in space. In 1997, it became a contributing sensor in the Space Surveillance Network. In 1998, it was reported to have provided "more tracks of objects in the geosynchronous belt than any other Space Surveillance Network sensor." On October 1, 2000, it became a dedicated sensor in the SSN. In 2008, the Air Force shut down the satellite after the SBV sensor was determined to have degraded to the extent that it was no longer reliable.[18]

The termination of the MSX satellite meant an absence of any dedicated space-based SSN sensors—although as early as 1983 development of a space-based space surveillance system had been described by the Air Force Deputy Chief of Staff for

Research, Development, and Acquisition as the "primary thrust of the Space Surveillance Technology Program." The system was to provide full-Earth orbit coverage, reduce overseas basing of sensors, and provide near-real-time "operationally responsive coverage of objects and events in space." The Space-Based Surveillance System (SBSS) was to consist of four satellites in low-Earth orbit. The long-wave, infrared mosaic-staring sensor on each satellite was to view the volume of space from approximately 60 nautical miles to geosynchronous altitude. Subsequently, the program was absorbed into the Strategic Defense Initiative (SDI) and renamed the Space Surveillance and Tracking System (SSTS). It then became one of many SDI systems that eventually succumbed to budget restrictions.[19]

A new program with the same name as SBSS led to the September 25, 2010, launch from Vandenberg Air Force Base of the 2,275-pound Space-Based Space Surveillance Pathfinder Block 10 satellite into a 390-mile sun-synchronous orbit. The satellite, which has a seven-year design life, carries a 11.8-inch telescope and will be able to image satellites in geosynchronous orbit as well as ones at lower altitude. In mid-January 2011 it was reported that the satellite was progressing through its checkout phase and was expected to become operational in the spring.[20]

One improvement over the MSX satellite is that the SBSS telescope is gimballed rather than of fixed orientation. It can be operated twenty-four hours a day, seven days a week. In addition, it can reportedly detect objects that are half as dim as other systems and is expected to track ten times as many objects as the MSX satellite and deliver data to the ground twice as fast, with superior accuracy. It also is able to rapidly move from one target to another and to track a moving object—such as a satellite entering orbit.[21]

In spring 2010 the Air Force announced its intention to acquire a second SBSS satellite for launch in 2014, although in September it was announced that the final request for proposals for the new satellite would not take place any later than early 2011.[22]

Until the mid-1980s, the primary dedicated ground-based optical sensors consisted of a series of Baker-Nunn cameras that operated in twilight or darkness, when a satellite was illuminated by the sun but the earth's surface was in darkness. Measurement of the satellite's position against a known star field produced precise locational data. Over the course of the program, Baker-Nunn cameras were located at nearly a dozen sites, although they were not all operational at the same time. The last two sites to close were those at San Vito, Italy (1991), and St. Margarets, New Brunswick (1992). Baker-Nunn had also been located in Florida, California, Norway, Korea, and Chile.[23]

The role of the Baker-Nunn cameras in the U.S. space surveillance system has been assumed by the Ground-Based Electro-Optical Deep Space Surveillance (GEODSS) program, operated by three detachments of the 21st Operations Squadron, 21st Space Wing, Air Force Space Command, with the GEODSS Optical Command, Control, and Communications Facility (OC³F) center at Edwards Air Force Base. Detachment 1 is located at Socorro, New Mexico (specifically Stallion Station,

White Sands Missile Range); Detachment 2 at Diego Garcia, British Indian Ocean Territory; and Detachment 3 at Maui, Hawaii. The first three GEODSS sites began operations in 1983. (Previously, Detachment 2 was located at ChoeJong San, South Korea, and Diego Garcia was designated Detachment 4. The Korean site closed in 1993 as a result of poor tracking conditions.)[24]

The GEODSS sites each employ three one-meter telescopes equipped with "a highly sensitive digital camera technology" that is designated Deep STARE (STARE being an acronym for Surveillance Technology Advancement & Replacement for Ebsicons—the replacements being charge-coupled devices). The telescopes, which can be used either separately or in conjunction with one another, are capable of seeing objects 10,000 times dimmer than those detectable by the human eye. As with the Baker-Nunn system the sites operate only at night.[25]

According to an Air Force fact sheet,

> The Deep STARE system is able to track multiple satellites in the field of view. As the satellites cross the sky, the telescopes take rapid electronic snapshots, showing up on the operator's console as tiny streaks. Computers then measure these streaks and use the data to figure the current position of a satellite in orbit. Star images, which remain fixed, are used as reference or calibration points for each of the three telescopes.[26]

The system provides the capability to optically track objects higher than 3,000 nautical miles, out to geosynchronous orbit. More than 2,500 objects are in orbits more than 3,000 miles from Earth. The ability of GEODSS to reach geosynchronous altitude was demonstrated in 1985, when a GEODSS site photographed a Navy Fleet Satellite Communications (FLTSATCOM) satellite. At geosynchronous altitude, the GEODSS telescopes can detect a reflective object the size of a soccer ball. GEODSS is also able to search up to 17,400 square degrees per hour. Furthermore, some GEODSS installations are close enough together to provide overlapping coverage as a means of overcoming poor weather at an adjacent site.[27]

Like the Baker-Nunn system, GEODSS depends on the collection of light reflected by the objects under investigation and is operational only at night during clear weather. Additionally, sensitivity and resolution are downgraded by adverse atmospheric conditions. Unlike the earlier system, however, GEODSS is able to provide real-time data with a computer-managed instant video display of surveillance data. Furthermore, the computer automatically filters stars from the night-sky backdrop and then uses its memory of known space objects to determine the existence of new or unknown space objects, alerting the user when such objects are found.[28]

Prior to the closing of the Korea station, the stations' areas of coverage were 165W-050W for Stallion Station; 010W-140E for Maui, Hawaii; 010E-130E for Diego Garcia; and 070E-178E for ChoeJong San. GEODSS sensors were responsible for over 65 percent of all deep-space object tracking and identification and provide almost worldwide coverage of the equator.[29]

Operating in conjunction with the GEODSS is the Moron Optical Space Surveillance System (MOSS) at Moron, Spain, which was deployed in late 1997 and operated by Detachment 4, 21st Space Wing. It consists of a 22-inch telescope and the MOSS Space Operations Center (MOSC) van. MOSS fills GEODSS's gap in geosynchronous coverage.[30]

A second set of dedicated sensors, in operation since 1961, are those that are part of the Air Force Space Surveillance System (AFSSS), formerly the Naval Space Surveillance System (NAVSPASUR), which is operated by Detachment 1 of the 20th Space Control Squadron. The AFSSS consists of the Alternate Space Control Center at Dahlgren, Virginia, and the Air Force Space Fence—which detects and tracks satellites that pass through an electronic fence consisting of a fan-shaped radar beam with a 7,500-mile range, extending from San Diego, California, to Fort Stewart, Georgia. The beam cannot be steered; detection results when a satellite passes through the beam and deflects the beam's energy back to Earth, where it is detected by several arrays of dipole antennas—"a form of cheap, unsophisticated antenna not unlike a television receiving aerial."[31]

The central transmitter for the beam is located at Lake Kickapoo, Texas, and there are two smaller transmitting stations at Gila River, Arizona, and Jordan Lake, Alabama. The six receiver stations—at San Diego, California; Elephant Butte, New Mexico; Red River, Arkansas; Silver Lake, Mississippi; Hawkinsville, Georgia; and Tattnall, Georgia—are all located, as are the transmitting stations, across the southern part of the United States, along a great circle inclined about 33 degrees to the equator. All satellites with an inclination greater than 33 degrees (about 80 percent of the current population) pass through this circle twice each day. The data obtained are then transmitted in real time to Dahlgren. There are 57 personnel at Dahlgren (11 active-duty military, 41 DOD civilians, and 5 contractors), while the nine field sites are manned solely by 102 contractor personnel.[32]

Objects in low-inclination orbit (which includes geosynchronous satellites as well Israel's Offeq reconnaissance satellite) and very small objects are not routinely detectable with the fence. It does have a longitudinal width that goes from Africa (less than 15 degrees west longitude) to beyond Hawaii (greater than 165 degrees west longitude) and is capable of "seeing" out beyond 22,000 miles. On a typical day the system registers more than 160,000 observations, most generated by satellites in near-Earth orbit. There are more than 100 satellites that no sensor other than the fence routinely detects.[33]

For several years the Air Force has been planning to replace the current fence with a modernized Space Fence, which would have three stations, two outside of the United States, using an S-band radar to replace the VHF radar that is used by the current system. The expectation is that the new system would increase the number of space objects that could be tracked from 10,000 to 100,000. In 2007 it was hoped that the transition would be completed by 2013, but it now appears that initial deployment will not take place until 2014 or after. In 2009 the Air Force awarded contracts for first-phase work on the project, and in 2010 it issued requests for proposals to develop preliminary system designs, radar performance analysis, and prototypes. The whole project is expected to cost $3.5 billion.[34]

Also among SSN-dedicated sensors is the AN/FPS-85 phased-array radar operated by 20th Space Control Squadron (formerly the 20th Space Surveillance Squadron). The squadron headquarters are at Eglin Air Force Base, Florida—although the radar itself is located near the city of Freeport, about 25 miles east of the base. The radar, which was constructed in 1967 and became operational in December 1968, is 143 feet high and 318 feet long and has separate transmitter and receiver arrays. Its principal axis is aligned due south across the Gulf of Mexico, and it is capable of receiving and transmitting over an arc extending 60 degrees on either side. Most satellites pass through its beam, which has a range of 2,500 miles, twice a day. The radar provides tracking information on space objects in low-Earth orbit and has had a limited deep-space capability since 1988.[35]

The radar can track an object the size of a basketball at a distance of more than 22,000 miles. It can detect, track, and identify up to 200 satellites simultaneously. In a given year it collects more than 16 million observations of satellites, which make up 30 percent of the Space Surveillance Network total workload. It can also track space junk; in the early 1970s it located and tracked the glove lost by astronaut Ed White during a space walk.[36]

Another ground-based resource for space surveillance is a U.S. AN/FPS-129 radar, with an 89-foot mechanical dish, operated as a joint program by the Air Force Space Command and the Norwegian Military Intelligence Service. Designated HAVE STARE before being deployed to Vardo, Norway, forty miles from the Russian border, it is now known by its Norwegian project name—GLOBUS II. Its announced mission is to monitor space debris, and in 2001 it tracked approximately 100 deep-space objects each day. It can also be used as an imaging radar to produce high-resolution images or pictures of whatever it is pointed at, or it can be used for spectral data collection, such as reading exhaust fumes of a jet engine to determine aircraft type. The fact that the radar has the ability to obtain detailed radar imagery of Russian warheads and decoys, was originally developed for that purpose, and replaced another U.S. radar in Norway (CREEK CHART) that was used for that purpose raised suspicions and concerns in Norway and Russia that the real purpose was to provide data to a U.S. national missile defense system—a charge that was denied by both U.S. and Norwegian authorities.[37]

COLLATERAL SSN SENSORS

Collateral sensors are used for space surveillance, but they are designed primarily for other missions such as missile warning or intelligence collection. Collateral sensors include the three Ballistic Missile Early Warning System (BMEWS) sites; the two remaining PAVE PAWS sites;* and collection systems at Cavalier Air Station, North Dakota; Kaena Point, Hawaii; and the island of Ascension.[38]

The BMEWS is designed primarily to track missiles and to determine the number launched and their intended targets. The system is dispersed among three sites—Clear Air Force Station, Alaska; Thule Air Base, Greenland; and RAF Fylingdales, United Kingdom. The Air Force Space Command's 13th Space Warning Squadron at Clear, 85 miles southwest of Fairbanks, Alaska, operates an AN/FPS-123 phased-array radar, which had previously been employed as the PAVE PAWS radar in Texas. Its primary mission is to provide early warning of sea-launched and intercontinental ballistic missiles to the North American Aerospace Defense Command (NORAD). The radar system has a coverage arc of 240 degrees, extending from the Arctic Ocean to the Pacific Ocean and the west coast of the United States, and 3,000 nautical miles into space. An upgraded radar system for the site, the AN/FPS-132 is scheduled to be fielded and integrated into the Ballistic Missile Defense System (BMDS)in the 2013 fiscal year.[39]

The 12th Space Warning Squadron at Thule has operated an AN/FPS-120 phased-array-radar, also with the primary mission of warning of sea-launched and intercontinental ballistic missile attacks. Integration of its replacement radar, also an AN/FPS-132, into the BMDS is scheduled to be completed in fiscal year 2011. At the third BMEWS site, which shares the same primary mission as the other BMEWS sites, is at RAF Fylingdales, where the Air Force is represented by a liaison officer.** The AN/FPS-132, which has been integrated into the BMDS, tracks objects out to 3,000 nautical miles and by the end of a day tracks 55,000 objects (including many objects multiple times).[40]

Two of the original four PAVE PAWS sites, those at Eldorado Air Station in Texas and at Robins Air Force Base in Georgia, were placed in caretaker status, and the associated warning squadrons (the 8th and 9th Space Warning Squadrons) were deactivated. As noted above, the Eldorado radar was transferred to the Clear Air Force Station, where it replaced the mechanical radar previously operated by the Clear warning squadron. The remaining squadrons are located at Cape Cod Air Force Station (6th Warning Squadron–6th SWS) and Beale Air Force Base (7th Space Warning Squadron–7th SWS), with primary missions of detecting submarine-launched intercontinental ballistic missiles.[41]

---

*PAVE has been reported to be an acronym for Perimeter Acquisition Vehicle Entry, although a 2010 Air Force fact states that it is an Air Force program name. PAWS is an acronym for Phased Array Warning System. See U.S. Air Force, Fact Sheet, "PAVE PAWS Radar System," August 2010, www.asfspc.af.mil/library/factsheets.

**A third mission of the site is SWSUK—the Satellite Warning Service for the United Kingdom. The service "gives U.K. forces warning of surveillance by satellites of potentially hostile or other nations"—including both military and commercial intelligence gathering satellites. See U.S. Air Force, Fact Sheet, "RAF Fylingdales, U.K.," www.peterson.af.mil/library/factsheets, accessed March 9, 2010.

The Cape Cod warning squadron operates an AN/FPS-123, whose beams can sweep for 240 degrees and reach outward and upward for nearly 3,000 nautical miles. At its extreme range it can detect an object the size of a small car, while it can detect smaller objects at closer range. On a typical day, the 6th SWS performs approximately 2,600 satellite tracks and about 9,100 observations. The radar is scheduled to be upgraded in the 2012 fiscal year. The Beale squadron was upgraded in 2007 and operates an AN/FPS-132 radar, which has also been integrated into the Ballistic Missile Defense System.[42]

The Perimeter Acquisition Radar Characterization System (PARCS), run by the 10th Space Warning Squadron at Cavalier Air Station, North Dakota, is a vestige of the U.S. ABM system that was dismantled in 1975. With a 3,100 mile range, the PARCS, a single-faced phased-array radar, designated AN/FPQ-16, stands 121 feet high; its primary mission is to provide early warning of ICBM and SLBM attacks, but it "also provides surveillance, tracking, reporting, and space object identification (SOI) support for space surveillance and intelligence operations."[43]

The mission of the AN/FPQ-14 mechanical tracker at Kaena Point, Oahu, Hawaii, is to provide low-Earth satellite observation. The radar is tasked on a limited basis with supporting the space surveillance mission, primarily for high-priority objects requiring instantaneous observational data. The site is operated by civilians twenty-four hours a day, seven days a week. Kaena Point provides pointing data to the AMOS site (discussed below).[44]

On Ascension Island, located midway between the east coast of Brazil and the west coast of South Africa, are two radars. The primary radar is the AN/FPQ-15 tracker, which provides space and missile launch support to the Eastern Space and Missile Center (ESMC), near-Earth satellite observations to the Joint Space Operations Center Space Situational Awareness Operations Cell, and narrow-band space object identification data to Air Force Space Command intelligence components. The second radar is an AN/TPQ-18 tracker.[45]

CONTRIBUTING SSN SENSORS

Contributing sensors are those under contract or agreement to provide space surveillance data when requested by U.S. Air Force Space Command headquarters. Contributing sensors include a phased-array radar on Shemya Island, the Maui Space Surveillance System (MSSS), the Reagan Test Site on Kwajalein Atoll, and the Lincoln Space Surveillance Complex (LSSC).[46]

The phased array COBRA DANE (AN/FPS-108) and the mechanically steered AN/FPS-79 tracking radar, discussed in their MASINT role in Chapter 9, are and were, respectively, also contributing sensors. With its coverage extending northward over an arc from Kamchatka to the Bering Strait, COBRA DANE, which operates in the L-Band, can be used for tracking satellites in polar and near-polar orbits, out to 3,000 miles. By 2010 it had upgraded to allow it to perform a missile defense mission (the tracking of ballistic missiles with sufficient accuracy to allow the launch of interceptors) as well its traditional intelligence and space tracking missions.[47]

The two contributing sensors at Maui, Hawaii, form the Maui Space Surveillance System (MSSS). The Air Force Maui Optical System (AMOS) at Mt. Haleakala, Maui, is a photometric and laser facility assigned to the Air Force Materiel Command's Phillips Laboratory. Its basic mission is to conduct research and development of new and evolving electro-optical sensors as well as to provide support to the Air Force Space Command. It has also provided support to NASA and the Jet Propulsion Laboratory. AMOS experiments have included detection and tracking of orbital debris, observations of shuttle and satellite operations, and laser illumination of satellites.[48]

Mt. Haleakala's location, 10,000 feet above sea level, places AMOS's equipment above much of the atmosphere and the interference associated with it. The equipment includes a 5.2-foot Cassegrain telescope, a laser beam director, and an AMOS acquisition system. The space surveillance research and development work at AMOS includes metric, tracking, infrared space object identification, and compensated imaging.[49]

AMOS's laser was used to illuminate Soviet spacecraft at night for the purpose of telescope photography. It was also used to determine whether Soviet nuclear-powered radar ocean surveillance satellites were operating or properly shut down at the end of their missions. The visible-wavelength images of the satellites produced by AMOS were good enough to show a Soviet reactor glowing red-hot.[50]

AMOS's telescope has sufficiently high resolution to discern objects in a space shuttle's open payload bay. Such a capability could have been employed to obtain intelligence on Soviet shuttle missions, had the Soviet program reached operational status. Its telescope has allowed identification of objects as small as 3.1 inches in diameter in geosynchronous orbit. Another optical sensor, the AMOS Daylight Near-Infrared Imaging System (ADONIS), which underwent testing in 1993, extends AMOS capability to twenty-four hours a day.[51]

Collocated with the GEODSS and AMOS systems is the Maui Optical Tracking Identification Facility (MOTIF), code-named TEAL BLUE. MOTIF consists of two co-mounted, 48-inch Cassegrain telescopes capable of both near-Earth and deep-space satellite tracking and object identification using visual light and long-wave infrared imaging. One telescope is used primarily for infrared and light intensity measurements. The other is employed for low-light-level tracking and imagery. For satellites orbiting at 3,000 miles or less, MOTIF's sensors can measure reflectivity and heat emissions and provide images. MOTIF has identified objects as small as 8 centimeters in geosynchronous orbit.[52]

As of 1990, images could be taken for only a few hours after sunset or before dawn, when the telescopes were in darkness and the satellites were in the light. Planned improvements would allow one of the telescopes to operate for two hours before sunset or after sunrise by canceling out interference from the sun. As a result, the number of hours that MOTIF could be used daily would expand from six to ten.[53]

In 1997 the Air Force Materiel Command's Phillips Laboratory began testing another sensor at the Maui complex—the Advanced Electro-Optical System (AEOS), which is optimized for satellite tracking and space object identification. With a primary mirror 3.67 meters wide, it should permit detection and tracking of 4-inch pieces of debris in low-Earth orbit at a range of 186 miles. Today, it is jointly operated by the Air Force Office of Scientific Research and the National Science Foundation.[54]

Contributing sensors are also located at the Reagan Test Site on Roi-Namur Island and on the two largest islands of the hundred that make up the Kwajalein Atoll. The Advanced Research Projects Agency (ARPA) Lincoln C-Band Observable Radar (ALCOR), operated by the Army Space and Missile Defense Command, consists of a 40-foot antenna and provides wideband radar imaging data for space object identification on low-Earth orbit satellites. Support to the SSN is on a noninterference basis with the Kwajalein Missile Range support.[55]

ALCOR observed China's first satellite, launched in 1970. The images of the booster rocket-body revealed the dimensions of the object—information that was of great interest to the Defense Department because it provided insight into the size and payload capacity of Chinese ICBMs. In the following year, ALCOR imaged the Soviet Union's SALYUT-1 space station.[56]

A second radar located on Roi-Namur, the ARPA Long-Range Tracking and Instrumentation Radar (ALTAIR), is also operated by the Army Space and Strategic Defense Command. The ALTAIR is a 150-foot paraboloid antenna that provides metric data on spacecraft. The radar operates in a space surveillance mode for 128 hours per week. It has a capability against both near-Earth and deep-space objects and is capable of tracking one-third of the geosynchronous belt. Over 50 percent of the launches from Russia, China, and Japan pass through ALTAIR's coverage on their way to achieve orbit.[57]

Also located on Roi-Namur are the Target Resolution and Discrimination Experiment (TRADEX) and Millimeter Wave (MMW) radars. Like ALTAIR, TRADEX is a low-frequency dish radar that can pick up incoming objects as soon as they come over Kwajalein's horizon at a distance of approximately 2,400 miles. Like ALCOR, MMW operates at high frequencies, allowing it to image objects in space. MMW, the highest-resolution imaging radar in the space surveillance network, can detect details as small as 5 inches, which makes it of significant value to the Intelligence Community.[58]

The Millstone, Haystack, and Haystack Auxiliary (HAX) radars, located about half a mile apart at Westford, Massachusetts, are operated by the MIT's Lincoln Laboratory and form the Lincoln Space Surveillance Complex (LSSC). The Millstone Hill Radar is a deep-space, large-dish tracking radar capable of tracking 1-square-meter targets at geosynchronous altitude. It was the first radar to detect the radar signals reflected off Sputnik I in 1957. The Haystack Ultra-Wideband Satellite Imaging Radar (HUSIR) is a high-quality imaging radar that can resolve objects as small as 1 foot in diameter in low-Earth orbit. It has been described in congressional hearings as providing "images of orbiting satellites that we can get from no other location." It is a "long-range, high altitude capable radar which provides extremely good intelligence data and now has a real-time operational reporting capability." A planned upgrade will result in the radar being non-operational until August 2011. The Haystack Auxiliary Radar was deployed so that space surveillance efforts would not suffer when the Haystack was operating in a radio-astronomy mode. According to one account, it can produce "finer and sharper images of satellites than the Haystack [radar]."[59]

Figure 10. 1 shows the distribution of ground-based space surveillance sensors.

ADDITIONAL SPACE SURVEILLANCE CAPABILITIES

The Space Surveillance Network makes an average of 45,000 sightings of orbiting objects each day. Twenty percent of the objects and debris cannot be reliably tracked. More than 16,000 objects have been catalogued. A commander-in-chief of the (now disestablished) U.S. Space Command characterized the system as "predictive . . . rather than a constant surveillance system." Continuity on deep-space objects is sometimes difficult to maintain because the radars are part-time contributors, and the optical and electro-optical sensors are restricted to nighttime operation during clear weather.[60] The SSN does receive some additional help from other systems.

The United States has for many years made use of two space systems to provide intelligence on foreign space activities. The possibility of employing U.S. imagery satellites to photograph Soviet satellites was achieved no later than 1965, with the KH-4 satellite. Over a decade later, KH-11 satellites were used on occasion for "space-to-space" imagery operations.[61]

In addition, the Defense Support Program (DSP) satellites described in Chapter 9 have proven useful in monitoring foreign satellites. The employment of DSP sensors to detect space objects, including satellites and their debris, has been designated FAST WALKER. Most FAST WALKERs have been routine observations of foreign spacecraft. The infrared readings obtained by DSP sensors, resulting from the reflection of sunlight off the spacecraft, provided analysts at the CIA, DIA, and Air Force Foreign Technology Division (now the National Air and Space Intelligence Center) with data on spacecraft signatures and movements. Such data allowed analysts to estimate the path of the satellite and its mission.[62]

In addition, DSP sensors have provided data concerning the reentry of satellites and other man-made space platforms. In January 1978, DSP sensors detected the reentry of COSMOS 954, a Soviet ocean reconnaissance satellite with a nuclear reactor that the Soviets could not control. Unable to boost it into an orbit that would keep it in space, the Soviets could only watch as the satellite's orbit decayed to the point that reentry took place. At the Aerospace Corporation, the DSP track of the reentry was subjected to mathematical analysis and the impact point determined. A Nuclear Energy Search Team was dispatched to the approximate location in Canada where the analysts concluded the satellite would have crashed to Earth; the team

FIGURE 10.1 Location of Ground-Based Space Surveillance Sensors

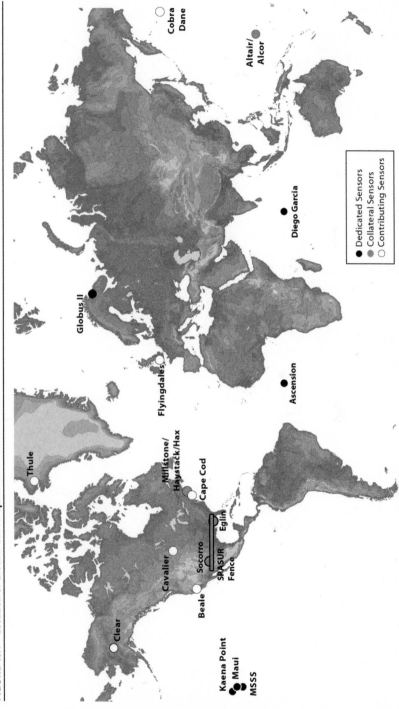

Source: Based on Air University, *Air University Space Primer*, 2009.

found a hunting party that had stumbled on the debris. In 1979, DSP sensors provided data on the reentry of Skylab, the 130,000-pound space station whose reentry threatened various populated areas.[63]

Among the satellite movements and debris that the DSP detected from the early 1970s to early 1980s were those associated with the Soviet anti-satellite (ASAT) program. From 1972 to 1982, the Soviets conducted sixteen anti-satellite tests. After an intercept satellite was placed in orbit by an SL-11 booster, ground controllers would maneuver the satellite so that after either one or two orbits, it passed sufficiently near the target satellite to permit its own guidance system to take over. When in range, an explosive charge aboard the intercept vehicle was detonated, sending a cloud of shrapnel at high speed to destroy the target. The DSP's monitoring of the launch, satellite movement, and aftermath contributed to U.S. intelligence analysis of the Soviet program. In 1996, a DSP satellite detected the descent of a malfunctioning Chinese FSW-1 reconnaissance satellite back to Earth and into the Atlantic Ocean. A DSP satellite also detected the launch of the kill vehicle used in China's January 11, 2007, anti-satellite test.[64]

In 2009, the Air Force launched two Space Tracking and Surveillance System (STSS) prototype satellites into a 840-mile circular orbit, with a 58-degree inclination, to test their capabilities with regard to missile detection and tracking. They may have the potential of contributing to the space surveillance mission as well.[65]

The ability to monitor foreign satellites is also available from the two 500-pound Micro-Satellite Technology Experiment (MiTEx) spacecraft launched from Cape Canaveral in June 2006 as part of a classified Defense Advanced Research Projects Agency technology development project. The satellites operate in geosynchronous orbit and have been employed to examine the DSP-23 satellite that failed shortly after launch.[66]

Notes

1. Gene H. McCall, Air Force Space Command, *Space Surveillance Requirements,* July 10, 1995, pp. 7–8; General Accounting Office, GAO/NSIAD 98–42, *Space Surveillance: DOD and NASA Need Consolidated Requirements and a Coordinated Plan,* GAO/NSIAD 98–42, December 1997, p. 12; U.S. Air Force, Fact Sheet, "Space Situational Awareness Integration Office," October 2006, www.afspc.mil/library/factsheets; Peter B. de Selding, "U.S.-France Agree on Space Surveillance as Top Priority," *Space News,* July 5, 2004, p. A4; Jeremy Singer, "Surveillance Remains Most Pressing Space Control Need," *Space News,* October 11, 2004, pp. A1–A2; Jeremy Singer, "Chilton Stresses Need for Space Situational Awareness," *Space News,* October 30, 2006, A2.

2. Air Force Space Command, *Space Surveillance Requirements,* pp. 12–13.

3. See Lt. Col. Michael R. Mantz, *The New Sword: A Theory of Space Combat Power* (Maxwell AFB, Ala.: Air University Press, 1995); Edna L. Jenkins and Dr. Paul W. Schumacher Jr., "Close Encounters: Parallel Processing Improves Space Debris Tracking," *Space Tracks,* Summer 1997, pp. 15–16; Dr. Paul W. Schumacher Jr., "Cataloging Space," *Space*

Tracks, Fall 1997, pp. 10–13; Nicholas L. Johnson, *Soviet Military Strategy in Space* (London: Jane's, 1987); and Nicholas L. Johnson and David M. Rodvold, *Europe and Asia in Space, 1993–1994* (Colorado Springs, Colo.: Kaman Sciences Corporation, n.d.).

4. Aerospace Defense Command, *ADCOM Command & Control*, November 30, 1980, pp. 8–12; USSPACECOM Regulation 200–1, "Satellite Reconnaissance Operations Security Support Program," August 18, 1989.

5. USSPACECOM Regulation 200–1, "Satellite Reconnaissance Operations Security Support Program"; Naval Education and Training Command, NAVEDTRA A 95–08–00–87, *Cryptologic* Technician Training Series, Module 8 Fleet Operations–Electronic Warfare, 1987.

6. Lt. Frank Murphy, "Chambered Round," *Space Tracks*, March–April 1991, pp. 8–9.

7. "News Breaks," *Aviation Week & Space Technology*, March 15, 1993, p. 23.

8. Johnson and Rodvold, *Europe and Asia in Space, 1993–1994*, passim.

9. Thomas G. Mahnken, "Why Third World Space Systems Matter," *Orbis*, Fall 1991, pp. 563–579; Theresa Hitchens, "European Eyes in the Sky," *Imaging Notes*, Fall 2006, pp. 20–24; Jeffrey T. Richelson, "The Whole World Is Watching," *Bulletin of the Atomic Scientists*, January–February 2006, pp. 26–35; Craig Covault, "India readies Israeli radar spysat to eye Pakistan," *Spaceflight Now* (www.spaceflightnow.com), April 18, 2009; "Delta 2 Lofts Italy's Final Cosmo-SkyMed Satellite," *Space News*, November 11, 2010, p. 8.

10. Rick W. Sturdevant, "Spacefarers and Satellite Operators: A Proliferation of Countries, Organizations, and Companies, 1957–2009," *High Frontier* 6, 2 (February 2010): 56–57.

11. Paul Mann, "Strategic Reconnaissance at Issue in Sino-U.S. Tiff," *Aviation Week & Space Technology*, April 9, 2001, pp. 32–33; Warren Ferster and Colin Clark, "NRO Confirms Chinese Laser Test Illuminated U.S. Spacecraft," *Space News*, October 2, 2006, p. 10; Vago Muradian, "Poke in the Eye," *C4ISR Journal*, November–December 2006, pp. 48–49; William J. Broad and David E. Sanger, "Flexing Muscle, China Destroys Satellite in Test," *New York Times,* January 19, 2007, pp. A1, A11; Colin Clark and Jeremy Singer, "China's ASAT Test Widely Criticized, U.S. Says No New Treaties Needed," *Space News*, January 22, 2007, pp. 1, 4; Craig Covault, "Space Control," *Aviation Week & Space Technology*, January 22, 2007, pp. 24–25; Joseph Kahn, "China Confirms Space Test; Denies Intent to Intimidate," *New York Times*, January 24, 2007, p. A8; Peter B. de Selding, "Debris from FY-1C Destruction Poses Long-Term Concern," *Space News*, January 29, 2007, p. 6; Michael R. Gordon and David S. Cloud, "U.S. Knew of China's Missile Test, but Kept Silent," *New York Times*, April 23, 2007, pp. A1, A9.

12. "Data Point to Chinese Orbital Rendezvous," *Space News*, August 30, 2010, p. 3; Stephen Clark, "China remains silent on satellite rendezvous," *Spaceflight Now* (www.spaceflightnow.com), September 8, 2010; Brian Weeden, "Dancing in the dark: The orbital rendezvous of SJ-12 and SJ-06F," *The Space Review* (www.thespacereview.com), August 30, 2010.

13. Andy Pasztor, "Satellite Destroyed in Orbital Collision," *Wall Street Journal*, February 12, 2009, pp. A1, A14; William Harwood, "Two satellites collide in orbit," *Spaceflight Now* (www.spaceflightnow.com), February 11, 2009.

14. George W. Bush, The White House, *U.S. National Space Policy*, August 31, 2006; Barack Obama, The White House, *National Space Policy of the United States of America*, June 28, 2010, p. 3.

15. Obama, *National Space Policy of the United States of America*, p. 7.

16. AFSPACECOM Regulation 55–10, "2nd Space Wing (SWG) Satellite Operations," October 13, 1989, p. 6; Jess Hall, "Command Activities 21st SPW at Peterson," *Space Trace*,

June 1992, p. 4; General Accounting Office, *Space Surveillance*, p. 10; "Media Advisory: Space Unit to Move from Cheyenne Mountain," September 15, 2006, www.afspc.af.mil/news; McCall, Air Force Space Command, *Space Surveillance*, p. 34; James Kitfield, "Crowded, Congested Space," *Air Force Magazine*, August 2010, pp. 24–29 at p. 27; Amy Butler, "Collision Avoidance," *Aviation Week & Space Technology*, July 6, 2009, pp. 18–19; U.S. Air Force, Fact Sheet, "Joint Space Operations Center," www.vandenberg.af.mil/library/factsheets, accessed December 1, 2010.

17. USSPACECOM Regulation 15–12, "Space Surveillance Network," June 1, 1992; Lt. Col. Glen Shepherd, Air Force Space Command, *Space Surveillance Network*, n.d., p. 4.

18. "MSX Satellite Passes Rocket Tracking Test," *Space News*, April 24–30, 1997, p. 10; "BMDO Needs More Money to Keep MSX Going," *Aerospace Daily*, April 1, 1997, pp. 1, 2; Kristi Marten, "MSX Turns Attention to Earth-Observing Objects," *APL News*, April 1998, p. 3; Shepherd, Air Force Space Command, Space Surveillance Network, n.d. (but 2005 or after); Jeremy Singer, "Air Force Plans SBSS Studies," *Space News*, February 27, 2006, p. 15; Jeremy Singer, "U.S. Air Force to Use MSX to Refine Satellite Design," *Space News*, November 13, 2000, p. 3; Grant H. Stokes, Curt von Braun, Ramaswamy Sridharan, David Harrison, and Jayant Sharma, "The Space-Based Visible Program," *Lincoln Laboratory Journal* 11, 2 (1998): 205–238; Jayant Sharma, Grant H. Stokes, Curt von Braun, George Zollinger, and Andrew J. Wiseman, "Toward Operational Space-Based Space Surveillance," *Lincoln Laboratory Journal* 13, 2 (2002): 309–333; Jeremy Singer, "Air Force Space Command Discontinues Use of MSX Satellite," *Space News*, June 16, 2008, p. 15; Amy Butler, "Space Gap," *Aviation Week & Space Technology*, June 16, 2008, pp. 29–30.

19. U.S. Congress, House Committee on Appropriations, *Department of Defense Appropriations for 1984, Part 8* (Washington, D.C.: U.S. Government Printing Office, 1983), pp. 506–508; Craig Covault, "SDI Delta Space Experiment to Aid Kill-Vehicle Design," *Aviation Week & Space Technology*, September 15, 1986, pp. 18–19.

20. Justin Ray, "Space surveillance project successfully blasts off," *Spaceflight Now* (www.spaceflightnow.com), September 26, 2010; Government Accountability Office, GAO-10–388SP, *Defense Acquisitions: Assessments of Selected Weapons Systems*, March 2000, pp. 125–126; Turner Brinton, "SBSS Satellite on Track to Enter Operations in Spring," *Space News*, January 17, 2011, p. 7.

21. Stephen Clark, "Space tracking satellite launch delayed indefinitely," *Spaceflight Now* (www.spaceflightnow.com), October 5, 2009; Government Accountability Office, GAO-09–326SP, *Defense Acquisitions: Assessments of Selected Weapon Programs*, March 2005, pp. 137–138; Jeremy Singer, "SBSS Facing Cost Growth, Launch Delay," *Space News*, June 11, 2007, p. 18; Amy Butler, "On Watch in Space," *Aviation Week & Space Technology*, April 14, 2008, pp. 32–33.

22. Stephen Clark, "Second SBSS Satellite scheduled for launch in 2014," *Spaceflight Now* (www.spacecflight.now), April 27, 2010; "Competition Delayed for SBSS Follow-On Satellite," *Space News*, September 20, 2010, p. 3.

23. USSPACECOM Regulation 55–6, "Space Surveillance Network Data User Support," April 15, 1991, p. 10; AFSPACECOM 002–88, "Statement of Operational Need (SON): Space Surveillance (S2)," August 7, 1989, p. A1-1; Curtis Peebles, *High Frontier: The U.S. Air Force and the Military Space Program* (Washington, D.C.: U.S. Government Printing Office, 1997), pp. 39–41.

24. U.S. Air Force, Fact Sheet, "Ground-Based Electro-Optical Deep Space Surveillance," November 2006 (accessed April 10, 2010 from www.af.mil/information/factsheets); AF-SPCMD 5–103, "Space Surveillance Squadrons (SPSS)," October 1, 1996; Peebles, *High Frontier*, pp. 39–40; Vincent Kiernan, "Portuguese Balk at U.S. Radar, Leaving Air Force with Blind Spot," *Space News*, October 9, 1989, p. 12; General Accounting Office, *Space Surveillance*, p. 12; www.af.mil/factsheets; Air University, *Air University Space Primer* (Maxwell AFB, Ala.: Air University, 2009), p. 251; McCall, Air Force Space Command, *Space Surveillance*, p. 10; Walter J. Facenda, Capt. David Ferris, C. Max Williams, and Dave Brisnehan, "Deep STARE Technical Advancements and Status" (2003), www.mitre.org.

25. U.S. Air Force, Fact Sheet, "Ground-Based Electro-Optical Deep Space Surveillance"; Facenda, Ferris, Williams, and Brisnehan, "Deep STARE Technical Advancements and Status."

26. U.S. Air Force, Fact Sheet, "Ground-Based Electro-Optical Deep Space Surveillance."

27. David M. Russell, "NORAD Adds Radar, Optics to Increase Space Defense," *Defense Electronics*, July 1982, pp. 82–86; Lt. Col. William C. Jeas and Robert Anctil, "The Ground-Based Electro-Optical Deep Space Surveillance (GEODSS) System," *Military Electronics/Countermeasures*, November 1981, pp. 47–51; "GEODSS Photographs Orbiting Satellite," *Aviation Week & Space Technology*, December 5, 1985, pp. 146–147; Office of Technology Assessment, *Anti-Satellite Weapons, Countermeasures and Arms Control* (Washington, D.C.: U.S. Government Printing Office, 1985), p. 55; USSPACECOM Regulation 55–12, "Space Surveillance Network (SSN)," p. 15; Dr. T. S. Kelso, "Space Surveillance," *Satellite Times*, September–October 1997, pp. 68–69.

28. "U.S. Upgrading Ground-Based Sensors," *Aviation Week & Space Technology*, June 16, 1980, pp. 239–242; Russell, "NORAD Adds Radar, Optics to Increase Space Defense."

29. Lt. Col. Michael Muolo, *Space Handbook: A War Fighter's Guide to Space, Volume 1* (Maxwell AFB, Ala.: Air University Press, 1993), pp. 98–99.

30. Air University, *Air University Space Primer*, p. 252; Peter B. de Selding, "U.S. Air Force to Widen Access to Detailed Space Surveillance Data," *Space News*, March 9, 2009, pp. 1,17; U.S. Air Force, Fact Sheet, "21st Space Wing," www.peterson.af.mil/library/factsheets, accessed March 9, 2010.

31. "Spacetrack," *Jane's Weapons Systems, 1982–1983* (London: Jane's Publishing, 1982), pp. 233–234; Russell, "NORAD Adds Radar, Optics to Increase Space Defense"; "The Arms Race in Space," *SIPRI Yearbook 1978: World Armaments and Disarmaments* (New York: Crane, Russak, 1978), pp. 104–130; Brendan Greeley Jr., "Navy Expanding Its Space Command to Bolster Readiness," *Aviation Week & Space Technology*, February 3, 1986, pp. 54–57; Office of the Chief of Naval Operations, OPNAV Instruction 5450.206, Subject: Naval Space Surveillance, Mission and Functions of, June 22, 1991; Schumacher, "Cataloging Space"; Gary R. Wagner, "High Desert Outpost," *Space Tracks*, Fall 1997, pp. 16–17; Roger Easton and Chester Kleczek, "Origins of Naval Space Surveillance," *Space Tracks*, May–June 1998, pp. 14–16; "Air Force Activates Space Surveillance Detachment at Dahlgren," *Domain*, Winter 2005, p. 22; "U.S. Air Force Takes Over Fence Space-Surveillance Network," *Space News*, October 18, 2004, p. 11; Gary R. Wagner, "Navy Passes Down the SPACE WATCH," *Domain*, Winter 2004, pp. 4–5; U.S. Air Force, Fact Sheet, "20th Space Control Squadron, Detachment 1," n.d., www.peterson.af.mil/library/factsheets, accessed December 3, 2010. On the history of NAVSPUR, see Gary R. Wagner, "The Longest Watch," *Space Tracks*, January

2001, pp. 12–14; Gary R. Wagner, "Pioneering Space Surveillance," *Space Tracks*, January 2001, p. 15; and "The Building of a National Treasure," *Domain*, Winter 2004, pp. 6–7.

32. "Spacetrack"; United States Space Command, "Space Surveillance Network (SSN)," p. 15; Schumacher, "Cataloging Space"; Kelso, "Space Surveillance"; U.S. Air Force, Fact Sheet, "20th Space Control Squadron, Detachment 1."

33. Schumacher, "Cataloging Space"; "A Constant Vigil," *Space Tracks*, March–April 1998, p. 5.

34. "T-Sat, Fence Schedules Move Right," *AeroSpace Briefing*, January 9, 2007, p. 1; Jeremy Singer, "U.S. Air Force T-Sat, Space Fence Could Be Facing Delays," *Space News*, January 15, 2007, p. 5; Jeremy Singer, "Air Force Seeks to Triple Funding for Space Surveillance," *Space News*, April 7, 2008, p. 5; "Space Fence Builders," *Aviation Week & Space Technology*, July 20,2009, p. 10; "U.S. Air Force Issues RFP for Space Fence Designs," *Space News*, November 1, 2010, p. 12.

35. U.S. Air Force Fact Sheet, "20th Space Control Squadron," www.peterson.af.mil/library/factsheets, accessed December 3, 2010; J. Mark Major, "Upgrading the Nation's Largest Space Surveillance Radar," *Technology Today*, September 1994; Peebles, *High Frontier*, p. 40; AFSPCMD 5–103, "Space Surveillance Squadrons (SPSS)"; "AN/FPS-85," *Jane's Weapons Systems, 1982–1983*, pp. 505–506; "The Arms Race in Space," pp. 114–124, at p. 116; John Hamre, *Strategic Command, Control, and Communications: Alternate Approaches for Modernization* (Washington, D.C.: Congressional Budget Office, 1981), p. 10; US-SPACECOM Regulation 55–12, "Space Surveillance Network (SSN)," p. 15; Science Applications International Corporation, *OUSD(A) Defense Space Systems Study, Final Report*, p. B-68; Air University, *Air University Space Primer*, pp. 252–253.

36. U.S. Air Force, Fact Sheet, "20th Space Control Squadron"; Major, "Upgrading the Nation's Largest Space Surveillance Radar."

37. Brian Orban, "Worldwide Support," *Guardian*, December 1995, pp. 3–6; Gordon Van Vleet, "'STAREway' into Space," *Guardian*, October 1995, pp. 14–15; "HAVE STARE," www.fas.org/spp/military/program/track/havestare.htm; Shepherd, Air Force Space Command, *Space Surveillance Network*, p. 4; Elizabeth Becker, "Russians Challenge U.S. over Radar in Norway," *New York Times*, February 22, 2000, p. A11; David Mulholland and Simon Saradzhyan, "Norwegian Radar Draws Russian Charge of Espionage," *Space News*, April 3, 2000, p. 8; Inge Sellevag, "Vardo Exposed," Bulletin of the Atomic Scientists, March–April 2000, pp. 26–29; Theodore A. Postol, "The Target Is Russia," *Bulletin of the Atomic Scientists*, March–April 2000, pp. 30–35; Gerard O'Dwyer, "Role of Arctic Radar Site Stirs Controversy in Norway," *Space News*, October 24, 2005, p. 12; McCall, Air Force Space Command, *Space Surveillance*, p. 12.

38. USPACECOM Regulation 55–12, "Space Surveillance Network"; Shepherd, Air Force Space Command, *Space Surveillance Network*, p. 6.

39. U.S. Air Force, Fact Sheet, "13th Space Warning Squadron," www.peterson.af.mil/library/factsheets,accessed March 9, 2010; Missile Defense Agency, Fact Sheet, "Upgraded Early Warning Radars (UEWR), AN/FPS-132," www.mda.mil, June 3, 2010.

40. U.S. Air Force, Fact Sheet, "12th Space Warning Squadron," www.peterson.af.mil/library/factsheets, accessed March 9, 2010; Missile Defense Agency, Fact Sheet, "Upgraded Early Warning Radars (UEWR), AN/FPS-132."

41. U.S. Air Force, Fact Sheet, "PAVE PAWS Radar System," August 2010, www.afspc.af.mil/library/factsheets.

42. U.S. Air Force, Fact Sheet, "6th Space Warning Squadron," www.peterson.af.mil/library/factsheets; U.S. Air Force, Fact Sheet, "PAVE PAWS Radar System"; U.S. Air Force, Fact Sheet, "7th Space Warning Squadron," www.peterson.af.mil/library/factsheets, accessed March 9, 2010; Missile Defense Agency, "Upgraded Early Warning Radars (UEWR), AN/FPS-132."

43. Air University, *Air University Space Primer*, p. 255; Stares, *Space and National Security*, p. 205; AFSPACOM Regulation 23–46, "10th Missile Warning Squadron (MWS)," June 12, 1987; U.S. Air Force, Fact Sheet, "10th Space Warning Squadron," www.peterson.af.mil/library/factsheets, accessed March 9, 2010.

44. Science Applications International Corporation, *OUSD(A) Defense Space Systems Study, Final Report*, pp. B-64, B-70.

45. USSPACECOM Regulation 55–12, "Space Surveillance Network (SSN)," p. 16; Science Applications International Corporation, *OUSD(A) Defense Space Systems Study, Final Report*, p. B-65; Air University, *Air University Space Primer*, pp. 255–256.

46. Shepherd, Air Force Space Command, *Space Surveillance Network*, p. 6; USSPACECOM Regulation 55–12, "Space Surveillance Network (SSN)," p. 17.

47. Stares, *Space and National Security*, p. 205; "The Arms Race in Space"; U.S. Air Force, "SAC Fact Sheet," August 1981; Missile Defense Agency, "COBRA DANE Upgrade," March 11, 2010.

48. Shepherd, Air Force Space Command, *Space Surveillance Network*, p. 6; Science Applications International Corporation, *OUSD(A) Defense Space Systems Study, Final Report*, p. B-64; Vincent Kiernan, "Air Force Begins Upgrades to Satellite Scanning Telescope," *Space News*, July 23–29, 1990, p. 8; "Air Force Maui Optical Station (AMOS)," http://www.fas.org/spp/military/program/track/amos.htm.

49. Science Applications International Corporation, *OUSD(A) Defense Space Systems Study, Final Report*, p. B-64; Kiernan, "Air Force Begins Upgrades to Satellite Scanning Telescope."

50. Craig Covault, "Maui Optical Station Photographs External Tank Reentry Breakup," *Aviation Week & Space Technology*, June 11, 1990, pp. 52–53.

51. Ibid.; Bruce D. Nordwall, "Air Force Uses Options to Track Space Objects," *Aviation Week & Space Technology*, August 16, 1993, pp. 66–68; Bruce D. Nordwall, "Optics/Laser Research Seeks to Improve Images," *Aviation Week & Space Technology*, August 16, 1993, p. 69.

52. Stares, *Space and National Security*, p. 204; John L. Piotrowski, "C³I for Space Control," *Signal*, June 1987, pp. 23–33; Science Applications International Corporation, *OUSD (A) Defense Space Systems Study, Final Report*, p. B-72; Kiernan, "Air Force Begins Upgrades to Satellite Scanning Telescope," p. 8; Air University, *Air University Space Primer*, p. 253.

53. Kiernan, "Air Force Begins Upgrades to Satellite Scanning Telescope."

54. William B. Scott, "Satellite-Tracking Telescope Readied for USAF Service," *Aviation Week & Space Technology*, July 21, 1997, p. 57; "Telescope That Tracks Satellites Is Unveiled," *Space News*, July 14–20, 1997, p. 22; Air Force Research Laboratory, "AFOSR and NSF Joint Initiatives for U.S. Civilian Research at the 3.67m Advanced Electro-Optical System (AEOS) Telescope at the Air Force Maui Optical Station (AMOS) on Hawaii," September 15, 2006, www.afosr.af.mil.

55. Science Applications International Corporation, *OUSD(A) Defense Space Systems Study, Final Report*, p. B-62; USSPACECOM Regulation 55–12, "Space Surveillance Network (SSN)," p. 17; Stephen M. Hunt, "Space Surveillance Always Tracking at the U.S. Army Kwajalein Atoll's Reagan Test Site," *Army*, December 2003, accessed through www.findarticles.com.

56. William W. Camp, Joseph T. Mayhan, and Robert O'Donnell, "Wideband Radar for Ballistic Missile Defense and Range-Doppler Imaging of Satellites," *Lincoln Laboratory Journal* 12, 2 (2000): 267–280.

57. Science Applications International Corporation, *OUSD (A) Defense Space Systems Study, Final Report*, p. B-63; USSPACECOM Regulation 55–12, "Space Surveillance Network (SSN)," p. 17; Air University, *Air University Space Primer*, p. 256; Hunt, "Space Surveillance Always Tracking at the U.S. Army's Kwajalein Atoll's Reagan Test Site."

58. Tony Reichhardt, "Catch a Falling Missile," *Air & Space*, December 1997–January 1998, pp. 26–37; Camp, Mayhan, and O'Donnell, "Wideband Radar for Ballistic Missile Defense and Range-Doppler Imaging of Satellites"; McCall, *Space Surveillance*, p. 24.

59. U.S. Air Force, "SAC Fact Sheet"; Defense Marketing Service, *Codename Handbook 1981* (Greenwich, Conn.: DMS, 1981), p. 168; Stares, *Space and National Security*, p. 205; U.S. Congress, House Committee on Appropriations, *Department of Defense Appropriations for 1981, Part 8* (Washington, D.C.: U.S. Government Printing Office, 1980), p. 241; Science Applications International Corporation, *OUSD(A) Defense Space Systems Study, Final Report*, p. B-71; USSPACECOM Regulation 55–12, "Space Surveillance Network (SSN)," p. 17; Air University, *Air University Space Primer*, p. 256; Melvin L. Stone and Gerald P. Banner, "Radars for the Detection and Tracking of Ballistic Missile, Satellites, and Planets," *Lincoln Laboratory Journal* 12, 2 (2000): 217–243; Camp, Mayhan, and O'Donnell, "Wideband Radar for Ballistic Missile Defense and Range-Doppler Imaging of Satellites"; William P. Delaney and William W. Ward, "Radar Development at Lincoln Laboratory: An Overview of the First Fifty Years," *Lincoln Laboratory Journal* 12, 2 (2000): 147–166; Richard F. Colarco, "Space Surveillance Network Sensor Development, Modification, and Sustainment Programs," www.amostech.com/TechnicalPapers/2010.cfm.

60. AFSPACECOM 002–08, "Statement of Operational Need (SON): Space Surveillance (S2)," p. 3; William J. Broad, "New Space Challenge: Monitoring Weapons," *New York Times*, December 8, 1987, pp. C1, C6.

61. [Deleted] Chief, Systems Analysis Staff, Memorandum for: Mr. William A. Tidwell, Subject: Use of KH-4 to Photograph Orbiting Satellites, October 1, 1965; private information.

62. AFSPACECOM Regulation 55–55, "Space Based Sensor (SBS) Large Processing Station (LPS) and European Ground Station (EGS) Tactical Requirements Doctrine (TRD)," September 30, 1992, p. 38; interview. One exceptional sighting occurred on May 5, 1984, which some in the UFO community have suggested was a detection of a UFO. A detection did take place, but the object detected was of terrestrial origin. See Jeffrey T. Richelson, *America's Space Sentinels: DPS Satellites and National Security* (Lawrence: University Press of Kansas, 1999), pp. 106–107.

63. Gus W. Weiss, "The Life and Death of Cosmos 954," *Studies in Intelligence*, Spring 1978; Jack Manno, *Arming the Heavens: The Hidden Military Agenda for Space, 1945–1995* (New York: Dodd, Mead, 1984), p. 148; private information.

64. Stares, *Space and National Security*, pp. 85–87; interviews; Craig Covault, "Chinese Military Satellite Poses Falling-Debris Risk," *Aviation Week & Space Technology*, November 27, 1995, p. 56; "FSW-1 Sinks into Atlantic," *Aviation Week & Space Technology*, March 18, 1996, p. 62; Covault, "Space Control."

65. Government Accountability Office, *Defense Acquisitions*, pp. 143–144; Justin Ray, "Delta 2 rocket launches missile defense satellites," *Spaceflight Now* (wwwspaceflightnow.com),

September 25, 2009; "STSS Eyed for Possible Space Surveillance Role," *Space News*, March 26, 2007, p. 3; John Watson and Keith P. Zondervan, "The Missile Defense Agency's Space Tracking and Surveillance System," *Crosslink*, Spring 2008, pp. 15–19.

66. Craig Covault, "Secret inspection satellite boost space intelligence ops," www.spaceflight.now, January 14, 2009; 45th Space Wing Public Affairs, "Cape launches Delta II, MiTEx satellite, *Air Force Print News Today* (www.afspc.af.mil/news), June 23, 2006.

11

HUMAN INTELLIGENCE

During the Cold War, the increasing ability to collect information through technical means reduced the need to rely on human sources for many types of intelligence—such as the coordinates of missile silos, the location of bomber bases, or the technical characteristics of missile systems.* However, human sources were not inconsequential then and are even more important today. Those sources include intelligence offices and their agents, attachés, diplomats, defectors and émigrés, detainees, and travelers.

Much valuable information, particularly that contained in documents, is accessible only through human sources. Such sources can be used to fill gaps—in some cases important gaps—left by technical collection systems. Sometimes intelligence gaps are the result of the inherent limitations of technical collection systems; with proper security, discussions are often immune to interception or eavesdropping. Also, technical systems cannot photograph policy documents or weapons systems manuals locked in vaults. Nor can they acquire weapons systems or systems components.

Thus, one objective of human intelligence (HUMINT) activities is the acquisition of planning documents, technical manuals, contingency plans, and weapons systems blueprints. As Amrom Katz observed, "The analysts . . . want the designer's plan, notebooks, tests on components, test of materials, conversations between designer and customer."[1] In most cases, the analysts must settle for images and electronic data concerning test activities.

Obtaining a comprehensive overview of a particular program, whether it be a nuclear, missile, or biological weapons program, can be difficult to achieve when relying solely on technical sources of information. It has been reported that in the experience of intelligence officials, a "program's workings become clear only when described by the participants."[2]

---

*The United States did, in 1962, wonder about how well the Soviets might do in using human sources to locate the precise location of U.S. missile silos and conducted an experiment to try to determine the likelihood of Soviet success. See Walter W. Romig, "Spy Mission to Montana," *Studies in Intelligence* 13, 1 (Winter 1969): 77–84.

Certain stages of military R&D are simply not available for technical monitoring. Once plans have reached the testing stage, a variety of U.S. technical collection systems can be employed. But when the weapon is being designed and its characteristics debated, technical collection can be of very limited utility, particularly if information security is stringent. It is desirable to know about the characteristics of weapons systems when they have reached the testing stage, but it is also important to collect information about any activity in design organizations. Even nations that purchase weapons abroad may develop their own modified versions. For example, Iraq developed modified versions of the Scud missiles that it purchased from the Soviet Union, and Pakistan's Prithvi missiles were developed from weapons that originated in North Korea.

U.S. intelligence objectives go beyond the deployment and technical characteristics of foreign government weapons systems, however. The Intelligence Community wants to know the intentions and plans of foreign governments—both hostile and friendly—with respect to foreign, defense, and economic policy. An understanding of both the processes and the people can lead to more accurate estimates of future actions. Some data on such matters may be obtained through open sources or by technical means (particularly communications intelligence), but there may be gaps that can be addressed only by human intelligence.

Human intelligence plays a critical role in monitoring terrorist groups and their facilities. Although training facilities may be monitored by overhead imagery, the most essential data are the location of leaders and other key personnel and the discernment of their intentions and plans. Human intelligence, along with COMINT and intelligence from liaison arrangements, offers the best chance of gathering such data. In addition, when engaged in combat with a terrorist group—such as al-Qaeda in Afghanistan—human collectors in the vicinity can provide critically important intelligence when technical collection systems are not overhead or are unable to provide real-time data.

HUMINT is generally classified into two basic categories: clandestine HUMINT and overt HUMINT. Clandestine HUMINT involves a secret relationship with a foreign source to provide classified data, or the direct and secret collection of intelligence by a U.S. intelligence officer. Overt HUMINT involves open activities conducted by Defense attachés and State Department personnel, as well as the debriefing of defectors, émigrés, and travelers. The use of harsh interrogation methods to extract intelligence from detainees raises the question of whether a third category of HUMINT should be added—possibly designated "coerced HUMINT."

Statistics derived from twelve 1994 intelligence reviews provide some measure, although not necessarily a perfect one, of the value of HUMINT at that time. Of the 376 specific intelligence issues, HUMINT was judged as making a "critical contribution" in 205 of those issues. In regard to terrorism, HUMINT items represented 75 percent of the critical items. The figures for some other key issues were over 50 percent for narcotics, over 40 percent for nonproliferation, and over 33 percent for economics.[3]

During the 1991 Persian Gulf War, overt HUMINT was employed, in real time, "to nominate, target, and destroy key Iraqi command, control, communications, and other military targets." HUMINT was used, in conjunction with imagery, not only to aid in the destruction of military facilities but to identify mosques and hospitals and to permit U.S. war planners to avoid targeting civilian facilities. One source provided information that, according to an Army intelligence history, "significantly contributed to the impact of the air campaign, which undoubtedly saved many American and coalition lives."[4]

OFFICERS AND DIPLOMATS

The core of U.S. human intelligence operations is composed of the intelligence officers of the CIA's National Clandestine Service. These officers are U.S. citizens who generally operate under the cover of U.S. embassies and consulates—an approach that provides them with secure communications (within the embassy and to other locations), protected files, and diplomatic immunity.

Others operate under "non-official cover" (NOC). Such NOCs may operate as businessmen, sometimes under the cover of working at the overseas office of a U.S. firm. In 1995 it was reported that 110 CIA officers were serving as NOCs, and that RJR Nabisco, General Electric, IBM, Bank of America, Pan Am, Rockwell International, and other major corporations had allowed CIA officers to pose as overseas employees. In other cases, the CIA officer might work for a front company established by the CIA. Thus, for example, Valerie Plame, an officer with the Counterproliferation Division, operated overseas while ostensibly being employed by the CIA-created Brewster Jennings & Associates.[5]

However, in 2008 it was reported that the CIA had shut down all but two of as many as twelve front companies set up in Europe and elsewhere in the aftermath of the September 11 attacks and that the Bush administration had planned to expand overseas operations by 50 percent. The companies were to have had six to nine case officers plus support staff. The agency apparently concluded that the companies were "ill-conceived and poorly positioned" for collecting intelligence on terrorist groups and networks dealing in the proliferation of unconventional weapons.[6]

CIA officers generally seek to recruit foreign nationals as agents as well as to cultivate knowledgeable foreigners who may provide information, either as "unwitting" sources or outside of a formal officer-agent relationship. CIA stations in foreign countries are headed by the Chief of Station(COS) and vary substantially in size, from just a few officers to more than 150, as was the case in the Philippines in the late 1980s. The COS and his or her officers operate under a variety of cover positions that vary from embassy to embassy, including political counselor, second secretary, and economic attaché.[7]

DIA human intelligence officers, including attachés who operate as part of the Defense Attaché System, constitute a second group of intelligence officers. The functions of the Defense attachés include

- identifying and gaining cooperation of human sources believed to possess the ability to furnish intelligence information;
- identifying and capturing collection opportunities presented by trade fairs, military demonstrations, parades, symposia, convocations, conferences, meetings, and the like;
- traveling to identified geographic target areas to observe, photograph, and report information specifically needed by consumers/users;
- identifying, establishing contact with, and maintaining liaison with foreign military officers, who by virtue of rank, position, or assignment can furnish potential intelligence information or are considered to be future leaders;
- gaining and maintaining area reality to observe and report political, sociological, psychological, and economic developments of potential value in gauging military plans, capabilities, and intentions of foreign governments and their military forces and their stability;
- identifying and gaining access to assist in the acquisition and exploitation of foreign military equipment and materiel.[8]

In addition to cultivating sources and collecting open source material, Defense attachés may engage in direct collection activities, which may constitute more than open observation, at least in the view of foreign security services. That was the belief of the Russian Federal Security Service (FSB) in 1999 when assistant Army attaché Lt. Col. Pete Hoffman hired a local taxi to drive to the training facility of the 242nd Airborne Training Center at the village of Posyotok Svetlyl. In 2008, Russia expelled two military attachés who had made an uninvited visit that March to the Novosibirsk Aviation Production Association in Siberia, a factory that manufactures Sukhoi-34 fighter bombers.[9]

Over two decades earlier, in May 1986, the Nicaraguan government charged that two military officers, including the U.S. embassy's military attaché, were discovered traveling without permits in a restricted war zone and suggested that they were involved in espionage activity. The two were found traveling near the town of Siuna, a remote area in north-central Nicaragua that had been a focus of combat between the Sandinista Army and guerrilla forces.[10]

In early 1987, Col. Marc B. Powe, the attaché at the U.S. embassy in Baghdad, was given two weeks to leave Iraq after he was accused of spying on and photographing truckloads of tanks and other military equipment in Kuwait in early December. Powe, who also served as attaché to Kuwait, had discovered a convoy of Soviet military equipment in Kuwait en route to Baghdad, and Kuwaiti authorities spotted him photographing the convoy and taking notes.[11]

In early 1989, two U.S. attachés, Col. Clifford Robert Ward and Maj. Robert Siegel, were apprehended on the perimeter of a Palestinian commando base, twenty-five miles from Damascus. Taken into custody by armed guerillas of the Popular Front for the Liberation of Palestine–General Command (PFLP-GC), Ward and Siegel were reported to have been carrying cameras, maps, binoculars, and telephoto lenses.[12]

At the beginning of August 1995, two U.S. Air Force officers, Col. Joseph Wei Chan and Capt. Dwayne Howard Florenzie, were expelled from China after being apprehended on July 28 and accused of spying on restricted military zones along the southeastern coast of China. The two attachés, assigned to the U.S. Consulate General's office in Hong Kong, were charged with sneaking into restricted areas and "illegally acquiring military intelligence by photographing and videotaping" the areas before being detained "on the spot" by Chinese soldiers.[13]

The attachés had entered China on July 23 on visas issued for the purpose of consulting with officials at the U.S. embassy in Beijing and the Consulate General in Guangzhou. But their actual objective was reported to be the monitoring of ongoing Chinese military exercises north of Taiwan. The officers were said to be looking for Chinese Su-27 warplanes that had been moved to an airfield up the coast from Canton and close to Taiwan.[14]

The American officers were riding bicycles and wearing civilian clothes, had photographic equipment stored away in their backpacks, and were "observing" and "carrying along with the normal business" of military attachés when they were picked up by the Chinese, according to a Defense Department spokesman.[15]

Five months later, in early January 1996, a similar incident took place near a military base in Siaxi, in Guangdong province in southern China. The Chinese detained Air Force Col. Bradley Gerdes, the assistant military attaché, whose spying, Beijing said, "had seriously encroached upon China's sovereignty and compromised the national security of China."[16]

On January 8, Gerdes and a Japanese military attaché were stopped near a military area on Hainan Island, off the southern tip of China, after allegedly sneaking into a military airport near the city of Zhanjiang, the headquarters of the South China Fleet. Chinese authorities confiscated film and videotapes, according to a Foreign Ministry spokesman. The attachés may have been checking unconfirmed rumors of a temporary deployment of Su-27 fighter-bombers around Hainan Island, which China first used in an exercise off Taiwan in November 1995.[17]

In July 1998, Maj. Thomas Gillen, the deputy U.S. Army attaché in Mexico, and his assistant conducted an information-gathering mission in Mexico's explosive Chiapas region. The trip resulted in their being detained for four and a half hours by suspicious residents of the remote village of Los Platanos, which had been the scene of fighting in June between local pro-government forces and the leftist Zapatista National Liberation Army.[18]

The U.S. Special Operations Command's Intelligence Support Activity (ISA) also provides human intelligence through both recruiting of sources as well as direct collection by its members. Subsequent to Iraq's invasion of Kuwait in August 1990, ISA managed to infiltrate several of its personnel into Kuwait, posing as expatriate oil workers. It also sent in a number of specially trained Kuwaitis to gather intelligence on what was happening inside the occupied territory.[19]

A fourth source of HUMINT reporting comes from Foreign Service officers stationed in U.S. embassies and consulates. These officers include those with political, economic, or cultural assignments. According to the 1995 congressional testimony of Under Secretary of State Peter Tarnoff, "The Foreign Service is a primary collector and producer of diplomatic and overseas reporting." That reporting, according to Tarnoff, accounts for a significant contribution, particularly in the political and economic areas, of the data that go into national intelligence production.[20]

In certain situations, such individuals can provide valuable additional on-the-ground reporting. A case in point occurred during late May and June 1989, when U.S. diplomats stationed in Beijing reported on the critical events unfolding in China. On June 3, 1989, the day preceding the now-infamous events in Tiananmen Square, a cable from the U.S. embassy in Beijing to the State Department reported that "ten to fifteen thousand helmeted, armed troops moved into Beijing during the late afternoon/early evening hours of June 3," provided information on the location of troop trucks and troops' weapons, and confirmed that elite airborne troops were moving from the south. The cable also noted that the embassy had received reports of trucks being surrounded and stopped by city residents and that Defense Attaché Office personnel were checking the western suburbs.[21]

Drug Enforcement Administration investigations officers (or their sources) may also provide human intelligence—the vast majority of which, as expected, is related to narcotics trafficking. Such intelligence is transmitted not only to DEA but also to the CIA's Crime and Narcotics Center. In addition, some may be related to terrorism. In a 2008 audit the Department of Justice's inspector general found that, among eighty-one cables sampled, three concerned terrorism. One was related to Stinger missiles and other heavy arms for sale via a terrorist group seeking to attack coalition forces in Afghanistan. The other two concerned Taliban drug trafficking to finance terrorist activities and the identification of a significant terrorist cell training and operations activity in a specific district of Afghanistan.[22]

AGENTS AND ASSETS

Agents are foreign nationals recruited by U.S. intelligence officers to collect information in their home country or in a third nation, or individuals who volunteer their services. Obviously, the identities of present U.S. agents are not known publicly. However, revelations of recent years indicate the types of assets, some of whom were operating until quite recently, and the types of information acquired.

During the Cold War, the primary target was, of course, the Soviet Union. Despite the closed nature of Soviet society and the size and intensity of the KGB's counterintelligence operation, the CIA had a number of notable successes. The most significant was Col. Oleg Penkovsky, a Soviet military intelligence (GRU) officer with significant connections. In 1961 and 1962, Penkovsky passed great quantities of material to the CIA and British Secret Intelligence Service, including information on Soviet strategic capabilities and nuclear targeting policy.* Additionally, he provided a copy of the official Soviet MRBM (Medium-Range Ballistic Missile) manual, which was of crucial importance at the time of the Cuban Missile Crisis.[23]

In subsequent years the CIA was able to penetrate the Soviet Foreign Ministry, Defense Ministry and General Staff, GRU, KGB, at least one military research facility, and probably several other Soviet organizations. Individuals providing data to the CIA included some stationed in the Soviet consulates and embassies and some assigned to the United Nations or other international organizations. One unfortunate measure of success in terms of recruiting Soviet citizens was the number of Russian nationals whom Aldrich Ames was able to betray in his first years as an asset of the KGB.[24]

Included in the group was one agent who had already been compromised by former CIA officer Edward Lee Howard—Adolf G. Tolkachev, an electronics expert at the Moscow Aviation Institute. Tolkachev was, according to a U.S. official, "one of our most lucrative agents" who "saved us billions of dollars in development costs" by telling the United States about the nature of Soviet military aviation efforts. Over the years, Tolkachev passed on information concerning Soviet research efforts in electronic guidance and countermeasures, advanced radar, and stealth technologies. As a result of that intelligence, the Air Force "completely reversed its direction on a multi-million dollar electronics package for one of its latest fighter aircraft." Tolkachev was arrested in 1985 and subsequently executed.[25]

Such operations did not cease with the end of the Cold War and the collapse of the Soviet Union. In September 1995, a worker at a Defense Ministry research institute in St. Petersburg was arrested on suspicion of having provided the United States with secret information on Russia's new attack submarine. In 1997, a former Russian diplomat was convicted of having spied since his recruitment in 1976.[26]

U.S. operations continued in Europe, Africa, the Middle East, Southwest Asia, and Latin America over the past several decades. In early 1997, the German government ordered a CIA officer expelled. According to one account, the officer had been accused of trying to recruit senior German officials to provide information on high-technology projects. According to another account, the officer was gathering information about a third country, probably Iran, and was ordered to leave because the operation had not been cleared with the German government.[27]

In 1993, the CIA targeted Henri Plagnol, an advisor to Premier Edouard Balladur of France, although how successful they were has been a matter of dispute. At approximately the same time, the agency also approached Thierry Miléo, who handled cable and satellite issues for Minister of Communications Alain Carignon, and

---

*As was the case with other penetrations of the Soviet national security establishment, Penkovsky sought out the CIA rather than being recruited by the agency. Similarly, post–World War II penetrations of the U.S. national security apparatus by Soviet intelligence resulted from insiders approaching the Soviet representatives rather than being identified and recruited.

offered him cash in exchange for information on the French negotiating strategy on telecommunications. In another instance, an employee of French Telecom, the national telephone company, was asked to "sell documents and information on France international structure and networks," according to the report of the French security service, the Directorate for Territorial Surveillance (DST). Both targets reported the overtures to the DST, which encouraged them to continue contacts with the CIA officers. Among those involved in the operation was one NOC, who represented herself as an employee of a Texas foundation interested in world economics.[28]

HUMINT operations in the Middle East have targeted Israel, Egypt, the Palestine Liberation Organization, Iraq, and Iran. An Israeli army officer, Maj. Yosef Amit, apparently began providing the CIA with information in 1982. In 1987, he was secretly sentenced to twelve years' imprisonment for espionage. The Egyptian government has apparently been extensively penetrated by the CIA. The agency has also had a variety of sources in the Palestine Liberation Organization.[29]

In the aftermath of the U.S. invasion of Iraq in 2003, it was revealed that Naji Sabri, Saddam Hussein's last foreign minister, had been a CIA asset. Sabri first began spying for France's Directorate General of External Security (DGSE), which subsequently turned him over to the CIA more than six months before the war to provide intelligence on Iraqi nuclear, biological, and chemical weapons programs. Reportedly, Sabri told the CIA that while Hussein had ambitions to reestablish a nuclear weapons program it was not active, and that no biological weapons were being produced or stockpiled, although research was taking place. With respect to chemical weapons, he is alleged to have stated that some existed but not under military control.[30]

Not long before the invasion, the CIA's Iraq Operations Group recruited a network of more than eighty agents, designated DB/ROCKSTARS—DB being the CIA digraph for Iraq. Each was equipped with a satellite telephone to send the intelligence to a communications station atop a mountain in northern Iraq. After one of the agents was captured and shown on Iraqi television along with his Thurya telephone, thirty of the eighty-seven ROCKSTARS halted communications with the CIA.[31]

ROCKSTARS assets included agents in the Republican Guard, regular army, and security services. Intelligence obtained included the location of surface-to-surface missiles and anti-aircraft positions, which would then be confirmed by satellite imagery. A ROCKSTARS asset headed the security unit in the Iraqi port of Umm Qasr and provided information on the location of mines and security forces—information that would make it easy for U.S. Marines to seize the port.[32]

Two days before the invasion was scheduled to begin, one of the agents reported that there was a heightened level of activity at the Dora Farms compound, outside Baghdad, which was used by Saddam Hussein's wife and which Saddam had also used. The heightened activity included the stocking of food and supplies and the arrival of a significant security presence (follow-up satellite imagery would show thirty-six vehicles). One of the agents reported that he had seen Saddam, who had left for a meeting but was to return to sleep. The information led President Bush to authorize an attack on the compound, employing cruise missiles and F-117 aircraft, in an effort to kill Saddam. Saddam survived, apparently because he was not at the facility when it was attacked.[33]

In April 1989, a number of Iranian military officers were arrested and charged with spying for the United States. Before the detection of the network, which was coordinated from Frankfurt, it apparently produced valuable military intelligence about Iranian operations in the Persian Gulf at a time when U.S. naval forces were confronting Iranian forces.[34]

In mid-2004, the CIA acquired, through an Iranian source, a laptop computer that contained studies for essential features of a nuclear warhead, including a sphere of detonators to trigger a nuclear explosion. The documents also examined the question of how to position a heavy ball—presumably consisting of fissile material—inside the warhead so as to guarantee stability and accuracy as it descended toward its target. In addition, they specified an explosion about 2,000 feet above the target—the preferred altitude for a nuclear detonation.[35]

The documents on the pilfered computer also included sophisticated drawings of a 130-foot-deep underground shaft, with remote-controlled sensors to measure pressure and heat—the type of shaft used for an underground nuclear test. A test control team was to be located six miles away. There were also designs, with the most recent ones dated February 2003, for a small-scale facility to produced UF4, uranium tetraflouride, or "green salt," an intermediate product in the transformation of uranium into gaseous form. Absent from the documents was evidence—in the form of construction orders or payment invoices—that the projects had gotten beyond the drawing-board stage.[36]

In April 2010, it was reported that turmoil in Iran had "prompted a growing number of the country's officials to defect or leak information to the West, creating a new flow of intelligence about [Iran's] secretive nuclear programs." Several months later, in October, Iranian officials stated that some personnel at the nation's nuclear facilities had passed secret information to the West in exchange for money.[37]

CIA targets in Southwest Asia have included India, Afghanistan, and al-Qaeda. In India, in 1977, six individuals were arrested and charged with spying for the United States. The six had access to secret reports of the external affairs, chemical, and petroleum ministries as well as information about India's main aircraft design and production center, plus drawings of Soviet-made guns, missiles, and radar. And, according to a former senior Indian government, in the early 1990s a top Indian civil servant was providing information about India's nuclear program to the CIA. A former member of the nation's Research and Analysis Wing (RAW) stated: "We know the Americans had somebody inside. They knew about plans to test nuclear weapons and stopped us in the early 1990s." In 2006, a former Indian intelligence official who worked for Microsoft was arrested, followed by the departure of a senior U.S. embassy official.[38]

For several years prior to the terrorist attacks of September 11, 2001, the CIA paid a team of about fifteen Afghans to regularly track Osama bin Laden in Afghanistan—

an effort that had mixed results. About once a month, the team pinpointed bin Laden's presence in a specific facility—intelligence that was confirmed by satellite imagery or communications intelligence. After 9/11, Afghan recruits used satellite telephones to provide the U.S. government with exact locations of several buildings housing Taliban fighters and weapons on the west end of Kandahar—intelligence that led to a bombing attack on October 5, 2001.[39]

In addition, a few days after the 9/11 attacks, a CIA-led team code-named JAW-BREAKER was dispatched to Afghanistan to work with the Northern Alliance and provide intelligence, in anticipation of the arrival of U.S. combat troops. Information sources for the team included Taliban soldiers co-opted by the North Alliance (NA) as well as civilians residing within NA territory who had friends or relatives on the Taliban side and were willing to risk passing through enemy lines to collect intelligence. From September 27 to October 26, 2001, the collection effort resulted in over 400 intelligence reports, which allowed U.S. aircraft to attack Taliban and al-Qaeda positions "with great accuracy and a minimum of collateral damage."[40]

In 2008 it was reported that al-Qaeda had remained impervious to penetration, but eighteen months later U.S. and international officials were touting improved recruitment of spies within the terrorist organization. One former CIA official referred to "our penetration of al-Qaeda." Dennis Blair, the Director of National Intelligence at the time, told reporters that the primary means of determining which terrorist organizations pose a direct threat is "to penetrate them and learn whether they're talking about making attacks against the United States."[41]

In Asia, China has been the most important HUMINT target. At least one penetration of the Chinese establishment has involved someone with access to information on Chinese nuclear relations with a variety of foreign nations. That source was able to gain intelligence on a number of sensitive issues in the 1980s:

- China's nuclear exports to Argentina and South Africa
- Chinese technicians assisting at a suspected Pakistani bomb developments site
- Chinese scientific delegations who were spending a substantial amount of time at a centrifuge plant in Kahuta where Pakistani scientists were attempting to produce enriched uranium
- Pakistani scientists from a secret facility at Wah showing a nuclear weapon design to some Chinese physicists in late 1982 or early 1983, seeking Chinese evaluation of whether the design would yield a nuclear blast
- the triggering mechanism for the Pakistani bomb, which appeared to be very similar to one used by China in its fourth nuclear test.[42]

In 1995, the United States received documents delivered by a walk-in to the Taiwanese security services, who claimed to be a missile expert. Among the documents he delivered were a twenty-page memo from 1988 prepared for China's First Ministry of Machine Building, which employed missile designers and builders, and a five-year strategic plan for China's future missile forces describing the characteristics of both Chinese and American weapons. Taiwan passed the information and walk-in to the CIA station in Taiwan.[43]

The walk-in made frequent trips back to China and returned with more documents—over seven hundred, totaling 13,000 pages. A CIA translation team was flown to Taiwan to begin working on them, while a CIA polygrapher tested the walk-in and found his answer to the question of whether he was working on behalf of a foreign intelligence agency to be deceptive. He was then flown back to the United States so that the CIA and FBI could try to determine whether the entire operation had been managed by China's intelligence services. Ultimately, it was concluded that he was likely to be a double agent.[44]

Information about the Taiwanese nuclear program was provided by a long-time agent, Col. Chang Hsien-Yi, the Deputy Director of the Institute for Nuclear Energy Research. Chang had been recruited by the CIA when he was a military cadet and defected in 1987. The information he provided indicated that the Taiwanese were in the process of building a secret installation that could be used to produce plutonium. Construction of the installation would have violated Taiwanese commitments to the United States not to undertake nuclear weapons research. U.S. pressure forced the Taiwanese to stop work on the secret installation and to shut down its largest civilian reactor, which the United States felt had military potential.[45]

HUMINT operations in Latin America have targeted Cuba, El Salvador, Nicaragua, Colombia, and Argentina. The operations in Cuba highlighted the potential dangers of HUMINT operations. During 1987, Cuban television showed films of apparent CIA officers operating in Cuba picking up and leaving material at dead drops. The program claimed that from September 1977 thirty-eight of the sixty-nine diplomats permanently accredited to the U.S. diplomatic mission in Havana had been CIA officers. Apparently, a significant number of Cubans had been operating as double agents, feeding information to the CIA under the supervision of Cuban security officials. The Cubans apparently decided to reveal the operations after the defection of a senior intelligence officer.[46]

In Central America, the head of El Salvador's Treasury Police, Nicolas Carranza, was an informant of the CIA in the late 1970s. In Nicaragua, Gen. Reynaldo Perez Vega, the second-ranking officer in the National Guard under Anastasio Somoza, was a CIA asset. In March 1986, with the Sandinista regime in power, three Nicaraguans were accused of attempting to infiltrate the Interior Ministry. One, a sublieutenant in the ministry, was allegedly recruited by the CIA in 1983 and tasked to provide information on connections between the Sandinistas and leftist guerrillas in Colombia and El Salvador.[47]

Given the concern with transnational targets—including terrorist groups, drug and criminal cartels, and proliferation networks—the United States also seeks to recruit assets in such organizations. One such asset was Urs Tinner, whose father owned or was associated with a number of Swiss precision engineering firms—and who had supplied A. Q. Khan starting in the mid-1970s. In 2000, Tinner was recruited by the CIA, possibly after he found himself in trouble with French authorities and a French security official tipped off the CIA. Subsequently, Tinner persuaded his father and brother to join him in working for the CIA. They were able, for payments that may have totaled as much $10 million, to provide the CIA with secret information concerning both the Iranian and Libyan nuclear programs.[48]

In 2002, Urs Tinner went to work for Scomi Precision Engineering (SCOPE), a Malaysian-based company established by associates of Pakistan's A. Q. Khan, ostensibly to produce high-tech components for use in the oil industry. Tinner actually supervised production of centrifuge components, which were loaded on a ship, the *BBC China*, headed for Libya—information that he apparently gave to the CIA. The ship was intercepted by agents of the United States and other countries. The interception led, in part, to Libya ending its nuclear program and providing the United States with intelligence about its nuclear suppliers.[49]

Overt and controlled (i.e., clandestine) sources for military intelligence organizations have also provided a variety of information. During the 1993 fiscal year, Army intelligence sources reported on mass murders and other atrocities committed by Bosnian Serbs against Bosnian Muslims, the rise in membership of neo-Nazi organizations in Germany, the activities of the Algerian Front Islamique de Salvation (FIS), a planned campaign of violence against U.S. interests and personnel by a member of the Panama National Police, Russian-directed energy programs, the status of Cuba's biological warfare program, the purchase of advanced tunnel-boring equipment by North Korea, and a planned coup d'état in Afghanistan supported by Russia.[50]

DEFECTORS AND ÉMIGRÉS

Defectors and émigrés also sometimes serve as valuable intelligence sources. Thus, during the Cold War, the United States established a coordinated Defector Program managed by the CIA-led Interagency Defector Committee (IDC).[51]

A defector may be able to resolve uncertainties concerning data acquired through technical collection systems. For example, one defector was asked to

> look at an elaborate analysis of something U.S. cameras had detected by chance when there was an opening in the clouds that normally shrouded a particular region. Learned men had spent a good deal of time trying to figure out what it was and concluded that it was something quite sinister, an Air Force officer said. "Viktor took one look at it and convincingly explained why what we thought was so ominous was in fact comically innocuous."[52]

During the 1980s, CIA sources included defectors from Cuba and Nicaragua, such as Rafeael del Pino Diaz and Roger Miranda Bengoechea. Diaz apparently held important aviation posts in the 1960s, including head of Cuban Airlines and the

Cuban Aviation Agency. He also claimed to be the Cuban Air Force's Deputy Chief of Staff, although the Cuban government asserted that he had been relegated to organizing a museum about the history of the Cuban Air Force.[53]

Roger Miranda Bengoechea, a senior military officer, was chief contact for all military advisors in Nicaragua, which probably gave him knowledge concerning the Cuban presence in that country. He had toured all Sandinista military bases the week prior to his defection. Miranda, who made frequent trips to Mexico for medical reasons, may have been passing information to the CIA before his defection. According to the Nicaraguan Defense Minister, Miranda had made copies of Air Force plans as well as documents concerning artillery brigades and other Managua installations.[54]

Iraqi defectors provided U.S. intelligence agencies with information on Iraqi weapons of mass destruction programs in the years between the 1991 Gulf War and the 2003 invasion of Iraq, although much of the information was fabricated. A senior Iraqi scientist, Khidhir Abdul Abas Hamza, who fled his country in 1994, provided the CIA with important details concerning the Iraqi nuclear program. Hamza, the highest-ranking scientist ever to defect from Baghdad, was able to provide information on the origins of the nuclear program, the role of foreign suppliers, the treatment of nuclear scientists in Iraq, and Iraqi success in perfecting methods of uranium enrichment.[55]

In October 1994, the Iraqi National Congress "provided a steady stream of low-ranking walk-ins from various Iraqi army and Republican Guard units who generally had interesting information," according to a Senate report. Then, in the summer of 1995, two of Saddam Hussein's sons-in-law defected to Jordan, where they were interrogated by U.S. officials. One defector was Lt. Gen. Hussein Kamel Hassan, who headed the industry ministry and military industrialization program, which included the nuclear weapons and biological weapons program. The other, Lt. Col. Saddam Kamel Hassan, headed the presidential security detail. (Not surprisingly, after they decided to return to Iraq, they were killed.)[56]

Among the best known of the Iraqi defectors is the one given the code name CURVEBALL, who resided in Germany under the care of that nation's Federal Intelligence Service (BND). CURVEBALL claimed to be a chemical engineer who had worked in a laboratory built on a trailer bed, which produced biological weapons. The CIA did not have direct access to CURVEBALL and did not even know his name, Ahmed Hassan Mohammed, until after the war. The BND claimed, falsely as it would turn out, that CURVEBALL did not speak English and hated Americans. His assertions were accepted by WINPAC analysts who believed his information was too detailed to be a fabrication.[57]

Although it was eventually accepted after the war that CURVEBALL was not who he had claimed to be and that his information was fabricated, another Iraqi defector had been judged as early as 2002 to be a fabricator. A former major in the Iraqi intelligence service, he was debriefed twice by DIA and claimed that Iraq had built mobile research labs to test biological agents. By May 2002 DIA had posted a "fabrication notice" on the major on a classified computer network.[58]

At least three Iraqi defectors were introduced to the U.S. Intelligence Community through Ahmad Chalabi's Iraqi National Congress. One, who claimed to be a physicist who worked on isotope separation, was rejected outright after the initial contact. Another, Adnan Ihsan Saeed al-Haideri, met U.S. intelligence officers in Turkey, while a third, Mohammed Harith, met with U.S. intelligence officers in Amman. Harith claimed to have worked on the development of mobile biological weapons vans.[59]

Another "defector" from a Middle East nation who proved to be less than reliable was "Ahmad Behbahani," who appeared on *60 Minutes* in 2000, claiming that the bombing of Pan Am 103 over Lockerbie, Scotland, in December 1988 was the result of a joint Iranian-Libyan operation. But the CIA and FBI concluded that the "defector" was not Ahmad Behbahani and that he had not directed foreign assassination and terrorism operations for Iraq.[60]

Today, the most desirable defectors come from China, North Korea, and Iran. In December 2000, Xu Junping, the director of the American and Oceanic Office of the Foreign Affairs Bureau of the Ministry of National Defense and a student at Harvard in 1999, defected during a visit to the United States, where, according to one report, he had a mistress. According to a China expert at the RAND Corporation, "Someone at his level, especially operating in a political hothouse like Beijing, would have access to a wide range of formal and informal information, ranging from high-level gossip about the military and civilian leadership to the basic stuff of daily life in the PLA." He also added, "All of his information, high and low, would be extremely valuable to his current custodians . . . since our collective knowledge about even the most mundane aspects of PLA life are so limited."[61]

In 1997, two high-level North Korean officials defected. One was the country's chief ideologist, Hwang Jan Yop, who defected to South Korea. He reportedly told his South Korean, and then U.S., interrogators about North Korea's strategy for nuclear war, their nuclear and chemical weapons programs, and the identities of North Korean agents in South Korea. However, one Clinton administration official remarked that Hwang didn't have "as much knowledge as we hoped" and had "no direct knowledge of military matters." Some of his information was characterized as "old, dated, not true."[62]

A more useful defector was Chang Sung Kil, the North Korean ambassador to Egypt prior to his defection to the United States in 1997. It was believed that Chang could provide the CIA with a "wealth of information about his country's sensitive dealings with Middle East nations." Of particular interest were North Korean sales of Scud-B missiles to Egypt and sales of other arms to Iran and Syria. Some of that information may have been provided prior to his defection; it was reported that Chang had been recruited by the CIA well before his defection.[63]

Other North Korean defectors include Ju-Hwal Choi, a former official of the Ministry of the People's Army, and Young-Hwan Ko, a former Ministry of Foreign

Affairs official. They were able to tell a Senate committee (and presumably the CIA) about the production and employment of rockets by the 4th General Bureau, the production of chemical weapons by the 5th General Bureau, and North Korean missile exports.[64]

In 2004 it was reported that a stream of information concerning the Iranian nuclear program had come from defecting nuclear scientists (and possibly from some who remained behind). The defections, at least from 2004, were the objective of a CIA program designated BRAIN DRAIN and designed to lure scientists away from the Iranian nuclear program.[65]

In 2009, one scientist who had apparently been providing information to the CIA while in Iran, defected while on a pilgrimage to Saudi Arabia. Shahram Amiri, a thirty-two-year-old radiation detection specialist, worked at Malek Ashtar University, an institution linked to the Revolutionary Guards and involved in nuclear weapons research. Amiri also worked at a number of Iranian nuclear facilities, possibly including the Lavizan facility in Tehran—which was razed in 2003 and 2004 after questions had been raised by atomic inspectors about its possession of highly enriched uranium. According to one report, he was also able to provide information on the Iranian projects to develop nuclear warheads that could fit on missiles.[66]

In 2010, Amiri released a video claiming, implausibly, that he had been kidnapped and drugged by the CIA, possibly due to some combination of homesickness and Iranian government threats to harm the family he left behind if he didn't return home. Not long afterward, he returned home to Tehran, and the Iranian government subsequently claimed that he had served as an Iranian double agent. However, U.S. officials asserted that Amiri provided "significant, original information that's checked out."[67]

Other Iranian officials have also defected. One, Ali Reza Asgari, a former deputy defense minister who once commanded the Revolutionary Guards, disappeared in Turkey in February 2007, and the information he provided was "fully available" to U.S. intelligence, according to newspaper reports. According to one Iranian dissident, Asgari "had very precious intelligence about the Iranian nuclear program." In March 2007, it was reported that Iran had lost contact with Col. Amir Muhammad Shirazi, an officer in the Quds unit of the Revolutionary Guards who was stationed in Iraq.[68]

In recent years, the United States has sought intelligence from both Iraqi and Iranian émigrés. In October 2002, the Defense Intelligence Agency assumed responsibility for a program previously administered by the State Department—the Intelligence Collection Program (ICP). The ICP placed primary emphasis upon "debriefing Iraqi citizens worldwide who can establish and maintain a continuous flow of tactical and strategic information regarding Iraq, in general, and the Saddam Hussein regime, in particular."[69]

Those Iraqi citizens were provided by the Iraqi National Congress (INC), which had an interest in providing intelligence that would help justify a U.S. invasion of

Iraq. The approximately twenty sources that DIA debriefed included fabricators, at least some of whose fabrications were known to the INC, as well as individuals who provided useful information. After the invasion, the DIA reported that the intelligence provided by these sources "covered a myriad of information and was not uniform in quality, accuracy, and utility. In some cases, [the ICP] provided solid intelligence leads, corroborated other information, and contributed to our knowledge base. In other cases, the information was of low or no value."[70]

Specifically, the INC sources provided intelligence "that identified sensitive site locations used by CENTCOM for coalition strikes," as well as information on forged travel documents of known terrorists and on violations of UN sanctions. In addition, an INC-provided source identified a senior member of al-Qaeda previously unknown to the U.S. Intelligence Community and provided a photograph to assist in his capture. Information obtained through the ICP also led to the arrest of two of the fifty-five Iraqi high-value targets sought after the defeat of Saddam's regime.[71]

The Iranian émigré community in Los Angeles has long been the target of the CIA's station in Los Angeles in its efforts to glean intelligence about Iran. For several years, the station has cultivated contacts with members of the community, seeking information from Iranians who have traveled to Iran or communicated with relatives in their native country.[72]

DETAINEES AND POWS

In past wars, prisoners of war (POWs) were a potential source of intelligence about an adversary's plans and capabilities. However, the Geneva Convention provides extensive protections to such prisoners. A POW is required to provide only a very limited amount of information (name, rank, serial number), and signatories to the convention have clear obligations and limits concerning treatment of POWs.

However, those captured and detained as a result of the U.S. war on terror that followed the attacks of September 11 have been considered by the Bush and Obama administrations to be not prisoners of war but unlawful enemy combatants. The legal rationale for this determination is founded on the fact that members of al-Qaeda (or its offshoots) target civilians, do not wear uniforms, and do not belong to a conventional army. Taliban fighters were also judged not to be POWs because they did not serve under a legitimate government. Because al-Qaeda fighters do not legally qualify as lawful enemy combatants, the United States determined that it may not only ask those captured and detained for more information than a POW is obligated to provide but also subject those fighters to harsher interrogation methods to extract desired information.[73]

Those detained were held in a variety of installations around the world, operated by different agencies. At U.S. bases at Kandahar and Bagram in Afghanistan, the latter of which is still in operation, Army interrogators questioned detainees. At one time, Kandahar had a detainee population of over 500. Best known is the facility at

Guantanamo Bay, Cuba—first known as Camp X-Ray and then Camp Delta. The newest detention facility there has been designated Camp 6. As of June 2005, there were more than 500 detainees at Guantanamo. Currently, there are about 170.[74]

Other detainees have been reported to have been interrogated at the joint British-American base on Diego Garcia and at U.S. military bases in the northeastern United States. Still others were held at sites operated by the CIA. In addition, the CIA operated a number of "black sites" until September 2006, when the fourteen prisoners from those sites were transferred from Guantanamo Bay. A year earlier, it had been reported that thirty-six detainees were being held at those facilities.* Among the nations mentioned as hosts to possible CIA detention facilities were Afghanistan, Thailand, Romania (Mihail Kogalniceanu airfield), Lithuania, and Poland (the Kejkuty intelligence facility).[75]

Detainees were apprehended in a variety of ways. Some were swept up in conventional military operations. Others were captured in raids conducted by special forces personnel, such as those conducted by Task Force Hatchet—a group of Rangers and special operations forces that conducted raids across Afghanistan in search of al-Qaeda and Taliban leadership figures. Still others were acquired by CIA operations, such as the joint CIA-Thai operation that resulted in the August 2003 capture of the operations chief of Indonesia's al-Qaeda affiliate, Jemaah Islamiyah, or operations conducted by the CIA and Pakistani intelligence units. In addition, some suspects were arrested by foreign nations and turned over to the United States.[76]

The individuals detained and interrogated varied greatly in terms of the threat they represented and their potential intelligence value. According to one former Army interrogator, al-Qaeda trained tens of thousands of fighters at its camps in Afghanistan: "There are hundreds of lower-level Al Qaeda alumni who were all but anonymous. Some may be harmless, others not." Some were detained because of information, not always accurate, that indicated their involvement in terrorist operations—such as Mohamed Mansur Jabarah, a Canadian citizen, arrested for being part of an al-Qaeda cell that intended to blow up the U.S., Israeli, British, and Australian embassies in Singapore. Others held at Guantanamo included a businessman who had lived in the United States between 1971 and 1987, who was charged with aiding an al-Qaeda operative planning to bomb American targets, and a man captured in Afghanistan who is believed to be the twentieth hijacker.[77]

That presumed twentieth hijacker, Mohamed al-Kahtani, according to a Defense Department press release, clarified the relationship of Jose Padilla and shoe-bomber Richard Reid with al-Qaeda, provided information on infiltration routes and methods used by al-Qaeda to slip past unprotected borders, explained how

---

*In April 2007, the CIA transferred another al-Qaeda leader to the Pentagon, who they had held since the previous fall. See Mark Mazzetti and David S. Cloud, "CIA Held Qaeda Leader in Secret Prison for Months," *New York Times*, April 2, 2007, p. A7.

bin Laden evaded capture and provided information on his health, and provided detailed information on about thirty of bin Laden's bodyguards, who are held at Guantanamo.[78]

The detainees held at the CIA's black sites were those considered "high-value targets"—a term reflecting the fact that it was not only senior al-Qaeda leaders who could provide potentially valuable intelligence. Such intelligence might come from those involved in transferring funds to finance the group's operations, or those responsible for logistics, or those involved in training fighters. In fact, the fourteen high-value targets who were transferred to Guantanamo Bay in September 2006 included several key operatives, according to a DNI summary: 'Ali 'Abd al-'Aziz 'Ali (a "Pakistani-based al-Qaeda operative"), Ahmed Khalfan Ghailani (an al-Qaeda forger and travel facilitator),* Hambali (operations chief for the Indonesian Jemaah Islamiya), Mustafa Ahmad al-Hawsawi (a financial facilitator), Mohammed Nazir Bin Lep (one of Hambali's key lieutenants), Majid Khan (who had been tasked by Khalid Sheikh Mohammed to conduct research on poisoning U.S. water reservoirs, among other projects), Abdal-Rahim Hussein Muhammed Abdu (al-Qaeda's operations chief in the Arabian Peninsula until his capture in 2002), Abu Faraj al-Libi (a communications conduit to bin Laden), Abu Zubaydah (a senior al-Qaeda operations official), Ramzi Bin al-Shibh ("a key facilitator" of the September 11 attacks), Zubair (a JI operational planner under Hambali), Walid Bin 'Attash (an operational planner), Khalid Sheikh Mohammed, and Gouled Hassan Dourad ("head of a Mogadishu-based facilitation network of al-Ittihad al-Islami").[79]

Interrogators were allowed to use more than the standard array of psychological ploys in trying to extract intelligence from the detainees. The army interrogation training manual in force until fall 2006 focused on sixteen basic alternatives, but it prohibited torture. However, the manual did not provide guidance to those

---

*Ghailani was the first to be tried in a U.S. civilian court, where he faced charges of murder and conspiracy to use weapons of mass destruction, stemming from his role in the 1998 attacks on U.S. embassies in Tanzania and Kenya. Abu Zubaydah and Ramzi Bin al-Shibh were two of four residents of the black sites who had been transported to Guantanamo in 2003 and then back to a black site for fear that the Supreme Court might rule that they must have access to legal counsel. Ultimately, Ghailani, whose statements were withheld from the jury, was acquitted of all but one count, which was sufficient to result in a life sentence. See Tina Susman, "Trial Begins for Embassy Blast Suspect," *Los Angeles Times*, October 13, 2010, p. A8; Adam Goldman and Matt Apuzzo, "Guantanamo prisoners moved earlier than disclosed," www.washingtonpost.com, August 7, 2010; Benjamin Weiser, "Defendant's Statements Were Kept from Jury," *New York Times*, November 18, 2010, p. A26; and Benjamin Weiser, "U.S. Jury Acquits Former Detainee of Most Charges," *New York Times*, November 18, 2010, pp. A1, A26; Benjamin Weiser, "Ex-Detainee Gets Life Sentence in Embassy Blasts," January 25, 2011, www.nytimes.com.

working at CIA facilities, nor was the manual explicit as to what acts constituted torture. Authorized CIA techniques* included water-boarding and water-dousing (both of which were meant to make prisoners feel like they were drowning), hard slapping, isolation, sleep deprivation, liquid diets, stress positions, and withholding of pain medication.[80] Additional details are provided in Figure 11.1.

One detainee, held at the Kandahar facility, provided, according to one of the interrogators, "critical intelligence about the Hamburg al-Qaeda cell, betray[ed] many other enemy fighters, and expose[d] a never-before-understood connection between al-Qaeda and Islamic groups across North Africa." Another prisoner told of assignments involving a planned poison attack on the U.S. embassy in Rome, which was followed by the arrest of eight Moroccans (who were eventually acquitted) and the discovery of 8.8 pounds of a cyanide-based compound, a tourist map with the U.S. embassy circled, and maps showing the location of underground utility lines near the embassy. Still another provided details about al-Qaeda's European recruitment and procurement activities, as well as information on bin Laden's security detachment and movements.[81]

Abu Zubaydah provided information, some of which proved to "be quite valuable," according to an American official. His disclosures led to the arrest of Jose Padilla in 2002, first charged with planning a dirty-bomb attack on an American city. He also confirmed Khalid Sheikh Mohammed's role as the mastermind of the September 11 attacks and provided information that led to the capture of 9/11 plotter Ramzi bin al-Shibh. JI operations chief Hambali told CIA interrogators about al-Qaeda plans to attack two American-managed hotels in Bangkok as well as airlines using the international airport—information that led airlines using the airport to alter their schedules.[82]

According to a CIA assessment, Khalid Sheikh Mohammed, one of three individuals to be water-boarded, "shed light on the plots, capabilities, the identity and location of [al-Qaeda] operations, and affiliated terrorist organizations and networks." He also provided considerable detail on the "traits and profiles" that al-Qaeda sought

---

*Under direction from President Obama, the only techniques permitted, irrespective of the agency handling the interrogation, are those specified in the relevant Army Field Manual. In addition, he established a High-Value Detainee Interrogation Group (HIG) to conduct HVD interrogations. The group consists of three to five mobile interrogation teams (MIT), drawn primarily from the FBI, with some CIA and DOD participation. The charter for the group, "Charter for Operations of Interagency High-Value Detainee Interrogation Group," was issued by the National Security Council on April 19, 2010. See Barack Obama, "Ensuring Lawful Interrogations," January 22, 2009, www.whitehouse.gov; Adam Entous, "Obama starts deploying interrogation teams," www.reuters.com, May 18, 2010; Anne E. Kornblut, "New Unit to Question Key Terror Suspects," www.washingtonpost.com, August 24, 2009; Evan Perez and Siobhan Gorman, "Interrogation Team Is Still Months Away," *Wall Street Journal*, January 22, 2010, p. A5; and DOD Directive 3115.13, "DoD Support to High-Value Detainee Interrogation Group," December 9, 2010, p. 3.

FIGURE 11.1   Enhanced Interrogation Techniques

Enhanced Interrogation Techniques

◆ The attention grasp consists of grasping the detainee with both hands, with one hand on each side of the collar opening, in a controlled and quick motion. In the same motion as the grasp, the detainee is drawn toward the interrogator.

◆ During the walling technique, the detainee is pulled forward and then quickly and firmly pushed into a flexible false wall so that his shoulder blades hit the wall. His head and neck are supported with a rolled towel to prevent whiplash.

◆ The facial hold is used to hold the detainee's head immobile. The interrogator places an open palm on either side of the detainee's face and the interrogator's fingertips are kept well away from the detainee's eyes.

◆ With the facial or insult slap, the fingers are slightly spread apart. The interrogator's hand makes contact with the area between the tip of the detainee's chin and the bottom of the corresponding earlobe.

◆ In cramped confinement, the detainee is placed in a confined space, typically a small or large box, which is usually dark. Confinement in the smaller space lasts no more than two hours and in the larger space it can last up to 18 hours.

◆ Insects placed in a confinement box involve placing a harmless insect in the box with the detainee.

◆ During wall standing, the detainee may stand about 4 to 5 feet from a wall with his feet spread approximately to his shoulder width. His arms are stretched out in front of him and his fingers rest on the wall to support all of his body weight. The detainee is not allowed to reposition his hands or feet.

◆ The application of stress positions may include having the detainee sit on the floor with his legs extended straight out in front of him with his arms raised above his head or kneeling on the floor while leaning back at a 45 degree angle.

◆ Sleep deprivation will not exceed 11 days at a time.

◆ The application of the waterboard technique involves binding the detainee to a bench with his feet elevated above his head. The detainee's head is immobilized and an interrogator places a cloth over the detainee's mouth and nose while pouring water onto the cloth in a controlled manner. Airflow is restricted for 20 to 40 seconds and the technique produces the sensation of drowning and suffocation.

SOURCE: Inspector General, Central Intelligence Agency, Special Review, 20073-7123-IG, *Counterterrorism Detention and Interrogation Activities (September 2001-October 2003)*, May 7, 2004, p. 15.

in Western recruits after 9/11 and, according to the agency, provided insight into how al-Qaeda might conduct surveillance of potential targets in the United States. In addition, he provided information on his use of the JI network for Western operations, "setting off a chain of detentions and reporting that ultimately led to the capture not only of Hambali, but of his brother and a cell of JI operatives." He and other detainees also provided leads to an "elusive operative" who, prior to 9/11, had been tasked to case financial buildings in major East Coast cities. In 2003, information from detainees led to the disruption of a plot to attack London's Heathrow Airport using hijacked commercial airlines.[83]

Information from either a defector or detainee contributed to the U.S. ability to kill Abu Musab al-Zarqawi, the leader of al-Qaeda in Iraq. That individual revealed that Zarqawi often met with a religious advisor—Sheik Abdel Rashid Rahman. As a result, Rahman's movements were monitored by human, electronic, and overhead surveillance—the first two probably by members of the Intelligence Support Activity operating as part of a special forces task force. Eventually, U.S. special forces located Zarqawi in an isolated house near the village of Habib, eight miles west of Baghdad. Zarqawi was killed when U.S. forces dropped a 500-pound bomb on the house.[84]

In May 2010, Mullah Abdul Ghani Baradar, the highest-ranking Taliban leader in custody, was being detained in Pakistan, having been apprehended in January by Pakistani forces. He was providing CIA personnel with information on Mullah Omar's strategy with respect to negotiations and explaining a new Taliban code of conduct intended to avoid civilian casualties.[85]

TRAVELERS

Travelers who are not intelligence officers may often be able to provide useful intelligence information. At one time, before the United States developed satellites to penetrate the Soviet interior and other denied areas, travelers played a more significant role in intelligence activities than they do today.[86]

During at least the mid-1980s the United States Air Forces Europe (USAFE) conducted a traveler collection program designated CREEK GRAB. The USAFE regulation on CREEK GRAB—Regulation 200–6—stated,

> During peacetime, USAF military and DAF [Department of the Air Force] civilian personnel, other US employees, and contractors may occasionally have opportunities to acquire information of intelligence value either while performing their normal duties or by pure chance. . . . USAFE personnel must be able to respond effectively to unexpected opportunities for foreign intelligence collection in peacetime as well as wartime.[87]

Among those considered potential intelligence contributors are not just travelers but also amateur radio operators, persons in contact with foreign friends and relatives, and persons living adjacent to sites where foreign military aircraft have landed or crashed. Regulation 200-6 also outlined procedures for photographing aircraft, specifying that photographs of the following items could be particularly useful:

- cockpit interior
- weapons systems controls, panel instruments
- seat (s)
- weaponry
- electronic gear (avionics, radar, black boxes, etc.)
- propulsion system (air intake, variable geometry, fuel parts, and fuel tankages)
- documents, maintenance records.[88]

CIA-trained military travelers have been used in Africa to provide political intelligence as well as information relevant in ensuring the security of U.S. forces employed in humanitarian and peacekeeping operations. Specific information provided by the travelers has included threats to U.S. military personnel, the general security threat, as well as the status of airfields and ports. During political upheaval in one country, "the collectors provided extensive data on five neighboring countries, two of which were either considered or used as forward staging areas for US troops. The US military regularly relied on their detailed reporting on airports and air fields."[89]

The CIA's National Resources Division seeks to interview businesspeople, tourists, and professionals, either because of specific contacts they may have had during their foreign travels or because of the sites of their travel—for example, Iran or China. The information sought may include the health and attitudes of a national leader, the military activities in a particular region, or the developments in foreign and science technology.[90]

The CIA has also received intelligence from Americans who were invited to visit China, meet with Chinese nuclear scientists, and visit Chinese nuclear facilities. Those Americans included George Keyworth, shortly before becoming President Ronald Reagan's scientific advisor in 1981, former Los Alamos chief Harold Agnew in 1989, and, from 1990 to 1999, Danny Stillman—first in his capacity as chief of Los Alamos laboratory's intelligence division and then as a private citizen.[91]

Stillman's nine visits included tours of Chinese nuclear facilities, equipped with video recorders and camera. Stops included the Southwest Institute of the Chinese Academy of Physics, from which he and his deputy brought back a brochure of pictures of the facility, which was often blanketed by cloud cover. Other facilities he visited were Fudan University and the Shanghai Institute of Nuclear Research, where scientists worked on neutron initiators and sources. He also toured the headquarters of the Chinese Academy of Engineering Physics, China's equivalent to the Los Alamos, Livermore, and Sandia labs. In addition, there were visits to the Northwest Institute of Nuclear Technology, which designed and produced diagnostic equipment to monitor nuclear tests, and the Lop Nor nuclear test site. Reports on what he saw on those visits and material he brought back were provided to the CIA, along with the names of more than 2,000 Chinese scientists working at the nuclear weapons facilities.[92]

In 2001 and 2002, the CIA recruited about thirty Iraqis who were living in the United States and had relatives in Iraq; these individuals agreed to travel to their homeland in search of information about Iraqi WMD programs. One of those recruited was Dr. Sawsan Alhaddad, of the Cleveland Clinic. In May 2002, she was asked to travel to Iraq to speak with her brother, Saad Tawfiq, an electrical engineer living in Baghdad, whom the CIA had identified as a key figure in the Iraqi nuclear weapons program. She was given a set of questions to ask and was trained in the art of secret writing. Dr. Alhaddad's brother told her that although Saddam was certain to resume the nuclear weapons program if sanctions were lifted, there was no ongoing program at the time.[93]

Notes

1. Amrom Katz, "Technical Collection Requirements for the 1980s," in *Intelligence Requirements for the 1980s: Clandestine Collection*, ed. Roy Godson (New Brunswick, N.J.: Transaction 1982), pp. 101–117 at pp. 106–107.

2. Judith Miller, "Baghdad Arrests a Germ Specialist," *New York Times*, March 24, 1998, pp. A1, A11.

3. John I. Millis, "Our Spying Success Is No Secret," *Wall Street Journal*, October 12, 1994, p. A15.

4. U.S. Army, Office of the Deputy Chief of Staff for Intelligence, *Annual Historical Review, 1 October 1990 to 30 September 1991*, 1993, pp. 4–10 to 4–12.

5. Robert Dreyfuss, "The CIA Crosses Over," *Mother Jones*, January–February 1995, pp. 40ff; Greg Miller, "CIA spy plan for post-9/11 era crumbles," *Los Angeles Times*, February 17, 2008, pp. A1, A27. The utility of NOCs is discussed in Walter Pincus, "Agencies Debate Value of Being Out in the Cold," *Washington Post*, January 12, 1996, p. A18.

6. Miller, "CIA spy plan for post-9/11 era crumbles."

7. Philip Agee and Louis Wolf, eds., *Dirty Work: The CIA in Western Europe* (Secaucus, N.J.: Lyle Stuart, 1978), pp. 131–132.

8. Defense Intelligence Agency, *Capabilities Handbook, Annex A, to the Department of Defense Plan for Intelligence Support to Operational Commanders*, 1983, p. 352. Also see Robert Baldi, "Jack-of-All Trades," *INSCOM Journal* (April–June 1999): 34–38.

9. Bill Gertz and Rowan Scarborough, "Inside the Ring," *Washington Times*, August 13, 1999, p. A8; C. J. Chivers, "Factory Visit Tied to Ouster Of Attachés From Russia," *New York Times*, May 14, 2008, p. A6.

10. Nancy Nusser, "U.S. Officials Cited as Spies by Managua," *Washington Post*, May 10, 1986, p. A14.

11. Richard Mackenzie, "A Gulf War Intrigue: The Tale of the Colonel's Camera," *Washington Times*, April 20, 1987, p. 9A.

12. Nora Boustany and Patrick E. Tyler, "Syria Suspects U.S. Attachés Meant to Aid Israel," *Washington Post*, March 13, 1989, p. A28.

13. Steven Mufson, "China Expels Two U.S. Attachés Accused of Spying," *Washington Post*, August 3, 1995, pp. A1, A27.

14. Martin Sieff, "Two American Officers Ordered Out of China," *Washington Times*, August 4, 1995, p. A15.

15. Linda Chong, "Expelled Americans Arrive in Hong Kong," *Washington Times*, August 5, 1995, p. A15.

16. Tim Weiner, "China Detains U.S. Attaché and Seeks Recall," *New York Times*, January 17, 1996, p. A26; Steven Mufson, "U.S. and Japanese Attachés Detained Twice, China Says," *Washington Post*, January 18, 1996, p. A19.

17. Mufson, "U.S. and Japanese Attachés Detained Twice, China Says"; Martin Sieff, "Detained U.S. Military Aide to Be Sent Home from China," *Washington Times*, January 18, 1996, p. A13.

18. Molly Moore, "U.S. Attaché, Aide Strayed into Chiapas Face-Off," *Washington Post*, July 29, 1998, p. A17.

19. Michael Smith, *The Killer Elite: The Inside Story of America's Most Secret Special Operations Team* (London: Weidenfeld and Nicolson, 2006), p. 172.

20. Peter Tarnoff, "Intelligence Support of Foreign and National Security Policy in a Post–Cold War World," presentation to the U.S. Congress, Senate Select Committee on Intelligence, September 20, 1995.

21. Amembassy Beijing to Sec State Wash DC, Subject: SITREP No. 28: Ten to Fifteen Thousand Armed Troops Stopped at City Perimeter by Human and Bus Barricades, June 3, 1989.

22. U.S. Department of Justice, Audit Report 08–23, *The Drug Enforcement's Administration's Use of Intelligence Analysts*, May 2008, p. xvi.

23. See Jerrold L. Schecter and Peter S. Deriabin, *The Spy Who Saved the World: How a Soviet Colonel Changed the Course of the Cold War* (New York: Scribner's, 1992).

24. John Barron, *The KGB Today: The Hidden Hand* (New York: Reader's Digest Press, 1983), p. 428; Ernest Volkman, *Warriors of the Night: Spies, Soldiers and American Intelligence* (New York: Morrow, 1985), p. 224; David Martin, "A CIA Spy in the Kremlin," *Newsweek*, July 21, 1980, pp. 69–70; Ronald Kessler, "Moscow's Mole in the CIA," *Washington Post*, April 17, 1988, pp. C1, C4; Peter Samuel, "1977 Spy Data on SS-20's Cast Shadow over INF Talks," *New York City Tribune*, November 17, 1987 p. 1; Walter Pincus, "U.S. May Have Discounted Some Soviet Missiles," *Washington Post*, April 17, 1988, p. A6; Peter Earley, *Confessions of a Spy: The Real Story of Aldrich Ames* (New York: Putnam, 1997), pp. 143–144; David Wise, *Nightmover: How Aldrich Ames Sold the CIA to the KGB for $4.6 Million* (New York: HarperCollins, 1995).

25. William Kucewicz, "KGB Defector Confirms Intelligence Fiasco," *Wall Street Journal*, October 17, 1985, p. 28; Barry G. Royden, "Tolkachev, a Worthy Successor to Penkovsky," *Studies in Intelligence* 47, 3 (Fall 2003): 5–33; Joseph W. Wippl, "The CIA and Tolkachev vs. the KGB/SVR and Ames: A Comparison," *International Journal of Intelligence* 23, 4 (Winter 2010): 636–646.

26. "Russian Arrested as U.S. Spy," *Washington Post*, September 26, 1996, p. A22; "Russians Assail U.S. Spy 'Trick,'" *Washington Post*, November 5, 1996, p. A15; Gareth Jones, "Russian Sentenced in Spying," *Washington Times*, July 4, 1997, p. A9.

27. William Drozdiak, "Bonn Expels U.S. Officials for Spying," *Washington Post*, March 9, 1997, pp. A1, A25; Walter Pincus, "Expelled CIA Agent Was Not Gathering Data on Germany, Sources Say," *Washington Post*, March 11, 1997, p. A11.

28. William Drozdiak, "France Accuses Americans of Spying, Seeks Recall," *Washington Post*, February 23, 1995, pp. A1, A20; Craig R. Whitney, "France Accuses 5 Americans of Spying: Asks They Leave," *New York Times*, February 23, 1995, pp. A1, A12; Walter Pincus, "Agencies Debate Value of Being Out in the Cold," *Washington Post*, January 12, 1996, p. A18; Kim Willsher, "French Official Was CIA Contact," *Washington Times*, September 9, 2003, p. A15.

29. Wolf Blitzer, "U.S. Changed Rules of the Spy Game," *Jerusalem Post International Edition*, March 28, 1987, pp. 1, 2; Bob Woodward, *Veil: The Secret Wars of the CIA, 1981–1987* (New York: Simon & Schuster, 1987), pp. 87, 161; David Hoffman, "Israel Army Major Was a Spy," *Washington Post*, June 3, 1993, p. A18.

30. Walter Pincus, "Ex-Iraqi Official Unveiled as Spy," www.washingtonpost.com, March 23, 2006.

31. Bob Woodward, *Plan of Attack* (New York: Simon & Schuster, 2004), pp. 144, 335–337; James Risen, *State of War: The Secret History of the CIA and the Bush Administration* (New York: Free Press, 2006), pp. 130–131.

32. Woodward, *Plan of Attack*, p. 352.

33. Ibid., pp. 144, 374, 380–399; Risen, *State of War*, pp. 130–131.

34. Youssef M. Ibrahim, "Teheran Is Said to Arrest Officers on Charges of Spying for U.S.," *New York Times*, April 22, 1989, p. 5; Stephen Engelberg and Bernard E. Trainor, "Iran Broke C.I.A. Spy Ring, U.S. Says," *New York Times*, August 8, 1989, p. A6.

35. William J. Broad and David E. Sanger, "Relying on Computer, U.S. Seeks to Prove Iran's Nuclear Aims," *New York Times*, November 13, 2005, pp. 1, 2.

36. Ibid.

37. Joby Warrick and Greg Miller, "Iranian technocrats, disillusioned with government, offer wealth of intelligence to U.S.," www.washingtonpost.com, April 25, 2010; Ali Akbar Dareimi, Associated Press, "Iran acknowledges espionage at nuclear facilities," October 9, 2010, www.rr.com.

38. Sanjoy Hazarika, "In Secret Trial, India Sentences 6 for Spying for U.S.," *New York Times*, October 30, 1986, p. A5; Randeep Ramesh, "Top Indian Civil Servant 'Was CIA Spy,'" www.guardian.co.uk, July 28, 2006.

39. Bob Woodward, "CIA Paid Afghans to Track Bin Laden," *Washington Post*, December 23, 2001, pp. A1, A12; Eric Slater, "These Spies Called the Shots in Strikes Against Taliban," www.latimes.com, February 14, 2002.

40. Gary C. Shroen, *First In: An Insider's Account of How the CIA Spearheaded the War on Terror in Afghanistan* (New York: Ballantine Books, 2005), pp. 111–112.

41. Craig Whitlock, "After a Decade at War with West, Al-Qaeda Still Impervious to Spies," www.washingtonpost.com, March 20, 2008; Karen DeYoung and Walter Pincus, "Success Against Al-Qaeda Cited," www.washingtonpost.com, September 30, 2009.

42. Jack Anderson and Dale Van Atta, "Nuclear Exports to China?" *Washington Post*, November 3, 1985, p. C7; Patrick E. Tyler and Joanne Omang, "China-Iran Nuclear Link Is Reported," *Washington Post*, October 23, 1985, pp. A1, A19; Joanne Omang, "Nuclear Pact with China Wins Senate Approval," *Washington Post*, November 22, 1985, p. A3; Patrick E. Tyler, "A Few Spoken Words Sealed China Atom Pact," *Washington Post*, January 15, 1986, pp. A1, A20–A21.

43. Jeffrey T. Richelson, *Spying on the Bomb: American Nuclear Intelligence from Nazi Germany to North Korea and Iran* (New York: W.W. Norton, 2006), p. 417.

44. Ibid.; Walter Pincus and Vernon Loeb, "China Spy Probe Shifts to Missiles," *Washington Post*, October 19, 2000, pp. A1, A18-A19.

45. Stephen Engelberg and Michael R. Gordon, "Taipei Halts Works on Secret Plant to Make Nuclear Bomb Ingredient," *New York Times*, March 23, 1988, pp. A1, A15; Tim Weiner, "How a Spy Left Taiwan in the Cold," *New York Times*, December 28, 1997, p. A7.

46. "Cuban TV Purports to Show U.S. Spies," *Washington Times*, July 8, 1987, p. A8; Lewis H. Duiguid, "Spy Charges Strain U.S.-Cuban Ties," *Washington Post*, July 25, 1987, p. A17; Michael Wines and Ronald J. Ostrow, "U.S. Duped by Cuban Agents, Defector Says," *Los Angeles Times*, August 12, 1987, pp. 1,14.

47. Philip Taubman, "Top Salvador Police Official Said to Be CIA Informant," *New York Times*, March 22, 1984, pp. A1, A4; Stephen Kinzer, "Sandinistas Tap Heroine as Envoy, But Some in U.S. Oppose Her," *New York Times*, March 22, 1984, pp. A1, A4; Stephen Kinzer, "Nicaragua Says It Has Cracked CIA Spy Ring," *New York Times*, March 15, 1986, p. 3.

48. Mark Hosenball and Christopher Dickey, "A Shadowy Nuclear Saga," *Newsweek*, October 30, 2006, p. 48; William J. Broad and David E. Sanger, "In Nuclear Net's Undoing, A Web of Shadowy Deals," *New York Times*, August 25, 2008, pp. A1, A8; Gordon Corera, *Shopping for Bombs: Nuclear Proliferation, Global Insecurity, and the Rise and Fall of the A.Q. Khan Network* (New York: Oxford, 2006), p. 114; David Albright, *Peddling Peril: How the Secret Nuclear Trade Arms America's Enemies* (New York: Free Press, 2010), pp. 208–212, 222–226.

49. Hosenball and Dickey, "A Shadowy Nuclear Saga."

50. Department of the Army, Office of the Deputy Chief of Staff for Intelligence, *Annual Historical Review, 1 October 1992 to 30 September 1993*, n.d., pp. 4–32 to 4–42.

51. E. Howard Hunt, *Undercover: Memoirs of an American Secret Agent* (New York: Berkeley, 1974), p. 80.

52. John Barron, *MiG Pilot* (New York: Avon, 1981), p. 186.

53. John M. Goshko and Julia Preston, "Defector Arrives for Debriefing: Cuba Plays Down Military Role," *Washington Post*, November 4, 1987, p. A10.

54. Glenn Garvin and John McCaslin, "Key Nicaraguan Aide Dubs Military Defector U.S. Spy," *Washington Times*, November 4, 1987, p. A10.

55. Judith Miller and James Risen, "Defector Describes Iraq's Atom Bomb Push," *New York Times*, August 15, 1998, pp. A1, A4; Judith Miller and James Risen, "C.I.A. Almost Bungles Intelligence Coup with Iraqi Refugee," *New York Times*, August 15, 1998, p. A4.

56. U.S. Congress, Senate Select Committee, *Report of the Select Committee on Intelligence on the Use by the Intelligence Community of Information Provided by the Iraqi National Congress Together with Additional Views*, September 8, 2006, p. 8; Daniel Williams, "U.S. Questions Top-Level Iraqis," *Washington Post*, August 12, 1995, p. A15; "Saddam's Sons-in-Law Talk to U.S. After Pair's Defection," *Washington Times*, August 12, 1995, p. A6; Kevin Fedavko, "Dead on Arrival," *Time*, March 4, 1996, p. 44; William J. Broad and Judith Miller, "Iraq's Deadliest Arms: Puzzles Breed Fears," *New York Times*, February 26, 1998, pp. A1, A10–A11.

57. Bob Drogin and Greg Miller, "Iraqi Defector's Tales Bolstered U.S. Case for War," www.latimes.com, March 28, 2004; Bob Drogin and John Goetz, "How U.S. Fell Under Spell of 'Curveball,'" www.latimes.com, November 20, 2005; Joby Warrick, "Warnings on WMD 'Fabricator' Were Ignored, Ex-CIA Aide Says," www.washigtonpost.com, June 25, 2006; Tyler Drumheller, *On the Brink: An Insider's Account of How the White House Compromised American Intelligence* (New York: Carroll & Graf, 2006). The primary work on the CURVEBALL saga is Bob Drogin, *CURVEBALL: Spies, Lies, and the Con Man Who Caused a*

War (New York: Random House, 2007). Also see John Goetz and Bob Drogin, "'Curveball' lies low and denies it all," *Los Angeles Times*, June 18, 2008, pp. A1, A4.

58. Drogin and Miller, "Iraqi Defector's Tales Bolstered U.S. Case for War."

59. Bill Gertz, "Iraqi Groups Aided CIA Intelligence," *Washington Times*, June 12, 2003, p. A22.

60. "Defector Blames Iran for Pan Am Bombing," *Washington Post*, June 4, 2000, p. A10; John Lancaster, "Defector Ties Iran to Bombings," *Washington Post*, June 6, 2000, p. A2; Vernon Loeb, "Iranian Defector Claiming Terrorist Links Is Called an Impostor," *Washington Post*, June 11, 2000, p. A25; Bill Carter, "'60 Minutes' Faces Doubts on Reported Terrorist 'Czar,'" *New York Times,* June 16, 2000, p. A18.

61. James Risen, "Defection of Senior Chinese Officer Is Confirmed," *New York Times*, March 24, 2001, p. A6; John Pomfret, "Senior Chinese Military Officer Defects to U.S.," *Washington Post*, March 13, 2001, p. A18; John Pomfret, "Defector Described as 'Walk-In,'" *Washington Post*, March 31, 2001, p. A14.

62. Kevin Sullivan, "Key Defector Warns Again of North Korean War Plans," *Washington Post*, July 10, 1997, p. A23; Nicholas D. Kristof, "North Korean Defector's 'Spy List' Proves a Hot Topic in Seoul," *New York Times*, September 5, 1997, p. A9; Kevin Sullivan, "N. Korea Defector Takes Questions, Raises Them," *Washington Post*, July 11, 1997, p. A27; Bill Gertz, "Hwang Says N. Korea Has Atomic Weapons," *Washington Times*, June 5, 1997, p. A12.

63. R. Jeffrey Smith, "North Korean May Bring Arms Data," *Washington Post*, August 27, 1997, pp. A1, A24; Stephen Lee Myers, "Defecting Envoy from North Korea to Get U.S. Asylum," *New York Times*, August 21, 1997, pp. A1, A9; Bill Gertz, "CIA Seeks Missile Data from Defector," *Washington Times*, August 27, 1997, pp. A1, A10; "North Korean Defector Reportedly a CIA Agent," *Washington Times*, August 31, 1997, p. A2; Tony Emerson, "The CIA Lands a Big Fish," *Newsweek*, September 8, 1997, p. 54.

64. U.S. Congress, Senate Committee on Governmental Affairs, Report 105–50, *Compilation of Hearings on National Security Issues* (Washington, D.C.: U.S. Government Printing Office, 1998), pp. 467–495.

65. Louis Charbonneau, "Iran Keeps Tabs on Nuclear Officials," *Washington Times*, April 29, 2004, p. A17; Siobhan Gorman and Farnaz Fassihi, "In Iran, a Defector Disappears Again," *Wall Street Journal*, July 16, 2010, p. A11.

66. Nazila Fathi, "Videos Deepen Mystery of Iranian Scientist," *New York Times*, June 9, 2010, p. A4; David E. Sanger, "Iranian's Saga Takes a U-Turn Toward Bizarre," *New York Times*, July14, 2010, pp. A1, A10; David E. Sanger, "Going Home, But to What End?," *New York Times*, July 18, 2010, Section 4, p. 3.

67. Fathi, "Video Deepens Mystery of Iranian Scientist"; Siobhan Gorman, Farnaz Fassihi, and Jay Solomon, "As Iranian Scientist Surfaces, Intrigue Builds," *Wall Street Journal*, July 14, 2010, p. A9; Gorman and Fassihi, "In Iran, a Defector Disappears Again," p. A11; William Yong and Robert F. Worth, "Iran Now Says Nuclear Scientist Was Operating as Double Agent," *New York Times*, July 22, 2010, p. A4.

68. Dafna Linzer, "Former Iranian Defense Official Talks to Western Intelligence," www.washingtonpost.com, March 8, 2007; Sebnem Arsu, "German Official Adds to Mystery of Iranian Missing in Turkey," *New York Times*, Marcy 14, 2007, p. A11; Michael Young, "By Way of Defection," www.reason.com, March 15, 2007; Borzou Daragahi, "Iranian dissident's case throws light on a key defection," *Los Angeles Times*, March 29, 2008, p. A8.

69. U.S. Congress, Senate Select Committee on Intelligence, *Report of the Select Committee on Intelligence on the Use by the Intelligence Community of Information Provided by the Iraqi National Congress Together with Additional Views*, pp. 30–31.

70. Ibid., p. 93.

71. Ibid., pp. 142–143.

72. Greg Miller, "U.S. Lacks Reliable Data on Iran Arms," www.latimes.com, November 27, 2004.

73. Daniel Eisenberg and Timothy J. Burger, "What's Going On at Gitmo," *Time*, June 2, 2005, pp. 30–31.

74. John Mintz, "Al Qaeda Interrogations Fall Short of the Mark," *Washington Post*, April 21,2002, pp. A1, A20; Chris Mackey and Greg Miller, *The Interrogators: Task Force 500 and America's Secret War Against Al Qaeda* (Boston: Back Bay Books, 2005), pp. 149, 217; Eisenberg and Burger, "What's Going On at Gitmo?"; Andrew C. McCarthy, "Gitmo Follies," www.nationalreview.com, December 11, 2010.

75. Simon Elegant, "The Terrorist Talks," *Time*, October 13, 2003, pp. 46–47; William K. Rashbaum, "Captured Qaeda Member Gives Details on Group's Operations," *New York Times*, July 27, 2002, p. A8; Mackey and Miller, *The Interrogators*, p. 149; Glenn Kessler, "Rice to Go on Offense over Secret Prisons," www.washingtonpost.com, December 3, 2005; "Poland Suppresses CIA Prisons Report," www.abc.net.au, December 24, 2005; Craig Whitlock, "European Probe Finds Signs of CIA-Run Secret Prisons," www.washingtonpost.com, June 8, 2006: "U.S. Use of Romanian Base Is Described," *Los Angeles Times*, November 22, 2005, p. A12; Douglas Jehl, "Report Warned on C.I.A.'s Tactics in Interrogation," *New York Times*, November 9, 2005, pp. A1, A16; Ryan Lucas, Associated Press, "Polish Intelligence Base Focus of Probe," December 17, 2005, www.comcastnet; "Allegations of secret CIA prison," *Los Angeles Times*, November 6, 2009, p. A27.

76. Mackey and Miller, *The Interrogators*, pp. 151, 254; Deb Reichmann, Associated Press, "Bush Says Cooperation Thwarted 2002 Attack," February 9, 2006, www.comcast.net; Raymond Bonner, "Qaeda Operative Said to Give C.I.A. Inside Information," *New York Times*, September 20, 2003, p. A3; William K. Rashbaum, "Captured Qaeda Member Gives Details on Group's Operations," *New York Times*, July 27, 2002, p. A8.

77. Mackey and Miller, *The Interrogators*, p. xxvii; Rashbaum, "Captured Qaeda Member Gives Details on Group's Operations"; Carol J. Williams, "Detainee Refuses Surgery," *Los Angeles Times*, November 23, 2006; Adam Zagorin and Michael Duffy, "Inside the Interrogation of Detainee 063," *Time*, June 20, 2005, pp. 26–33.

78. Office of the Assistant Secretary of Defense (Public Affairs), No. 592–05, "Guantanamo Provides Valuable Intelligence Information," June 12, 2005, www.defenselink.mil.

79. Director of National Intelligence, "Biographies of High Value Detainees Transferred to the US Naval Base at Guantanamo Bay," September 6, 2006, www.dni.gov. Also on Abu Zubaydah, see Central Intelligence Agency, "Psychological Assessment of Zain al-'Abedin al-Abideen Muhammad Hassan, a.k.a. Abu Zubaydah," January 31, 2003. For decidedly different assessments of Zubaydah, see George J. Tenet with Bill Harlow, *At the Center of the Storm: My Years at the CIA* (New York: HarperCollins, 2007), pp. 240–243; and Ron Suskind, *The One Percent Doctrine: Deep Inside America's Pursuit of Its Enemies Since 9/11* (New York: Simon & Schuster, 2006), p. 95.

80. Mackey and Miller, *The Interrogators*, pp. xxviii, 95, 285; Dana Priest, "Covert CIA Program Withstands New Furor," www.washingtonpost.com, December 30, 2005.

81. Mackey and Miller, *The Interrogators*, pp. 13, 173, 253.

82. Curt Anderson, Associated Press, "Prosecutors Identify Al Qaeda Informant in Padilla Case," www.boston.com, November 18, 2006; Philip Shenon, "Officials Says Qaeda Suspect Has Given Useful Information," *New York Times*, April 26, 2002, p. A12; Bonner, "Qaeda Operative Said to Give C.I.A. Inside Information"; James Risen, "Traces of Terror: The Intelligence Reports; September 11 Suspect May Be Relative of '93 Plot Leader," www.nytimes.com, June 5, 2002; Office of the Director of National Intelligence, "Summary of the High Value Terrorist Detainee Program," September 6, 2006, www.dni.gov.

83. Central Intelligence Agency, *Khalid Shayk Muhammad: Preeminent Source on Al-Qa'ida*, July 13, 2004, p. 1; Office of the Director of National Intelligence, "Summary of the High Value Terrorist Detainee Program," p. 3.

84. Office of the Director of National Intelligence, "Summary of the High Value Terrorist Detainee Program," p. 4; Solomon Moore and Gregory Miller, "U.S. Tracks Aide to Zarqawi's Door; Bush Says War Is Far from Over," *Los Angeles Times*, June 9, 2006, pp. A1, A24; Dexter Filkins, Mark Mazetti, and Richard A. Oppel, "How Surveillance and Betrayal Led to Hunt's End," *New York Times*, June 9, 2006, pp. A1, A11; Ellen Knickmeyer, "Zarqawi's Hideout Was Secret Till Last Minute," www.washingtonpost.com, June 11, 2006; Mark Bowden, "The Ploy," *The Atlantic*, May 2007, pp. 54–68.

85. Eric Schmitt, "Questioning of Captured Taliban Leader Offers Insight into How the Group Works," *New York Times*, May 6, 2010, p. A13.

86. See Jeffrey T. Richelson, *American Espionage and the Soviet Target* (New York: Morrow, 1987), pp. 52–55.

87. United States Air Force Europe, USAFE Regulation 200–6, "CREEK GRAB," May 31, 1986, p. 2.

88. Ibid., p. 15.

89. The Central Intelligence Agency Lieutenant General Vernon A. Walters Award presented to The Operational Architect for a New Collection Capability, NMIA XXIV Anniversary and Awards Banquet, June 5, 1998, www.nmia.org/1998Awards/CIAAward98.htm.

90. Victor Marchetti and John Marks, *The CIA and Cult of Intelligence* (New York: Dell, 1980), pp. 236–237.

91. Richelson, *Spying on the Bomb*, pp. 408–409.

92. Ibid., p. 409.

93. Risen, *State of War*, pp. 85–108.

12

OPEN SOURCES, TECHNICAL SURVEILLANCE AND EMPLACED SENSORS, AND DOCUMENT AND MATERIEL EXPLOITATION

Significant intelligence concerning other nations and foreign organizations can be obtained through means other than remote technical or clandestine human source collection. Included in this category are open sources, technical surveillance and emplaced sensors, document or video exploitation, and materiel exploitation. These techniques can reveal information about personalities, plans, as well as capabilities.

Open source acquisition involves the acquisition of any verbal, written, or electronically transmitted material that can be legally obtained. Electronic surveillance and emplaced sensors also contribute to the intelligence gathered by the CIA and other intelligence organizations. The electronic surveillance usually takes the form of bugging or phone tapping. Although technical in nature, it is not a remote-sensing activity, and installation of the surveillance devices requires trained personnel. Emplaced sensors are installed at fixed locations in the target's territory to continuously monitor communications or other signals, in contrast to intermittent reconnaissance from overhead platforms.

Other significant aspects of intelligence collection are document/video and materiel exploitation. The acquisition and analysis of key foreign documents or videos and the acquisition of foreign weapons and communications systems yield information that often cannot be acquired through overhead collection. For example, detailed information on the technological capability of tanks (or other weapons systems) can be used to design countermeasures. Although the weapons designed for the armed forces of the Soviet Union are now less threatening in the hands of the Russian armed forces, the Soviet (and Russian) export of weapons systems and technology to North Korea, Syria, Iran, and other nations of concern makes intelligence on these weapons systems—and on any modifications— extremely valuable.

OPEN SOURCES

Open sources can be divided into six categories:

- Media: newspapers, magazines, radio, television.
- Internet-specific: blogs, discussion forums.
- Public data: government reports, budgets, hearings, telephone directories, press conferences, speeches.
- Professional and academic: journals, conferences, symposia, academic papers, dissertations, theses.
- Commercial data: commercial imagery, financial and industrial assessments.
- Gray literature: defined in 1995 by the U.S. Interagency Gray Literature Working Group as "foreign or domestic open source material that is usually available through specialized channels and may not enter normal channels or systems of publication, distribution, bibliographic control, or acquisition by booksellers or subscription agents." Gray literature includes, but is not limited to, technical reports, preprints, patents, working papers, business documents, unpublished works, dissertations, and newsletters.[1]

Open sources, according to one account, can provide (1) early information on emerging crises and regional instability; (2) biographic details on key leaders, dissidents, and opposition leaders as well as terrorists and criminals; (3) information on the security implications of geography, demographics, and national infrastructure; (4) indications of domestic and foreign policy changes; (5) information on the organization, equipment, and deployment of military forces; (6) insights into the security implications of nationality, ethnicity, and religion; (7) strategies underlying information-warfare approaches; and (8) insights about criminal organizations.[2]

In 1948, Director of Central Intelligence Roscoe Hillenkoeter wrote that "80 percent of intelligence is derived from such prosaic sources as foreign books, magazines and radio broadcasts, and general information from people with a knowledge of affairs abroad." Far more recently, the former head of the CIA's bin Laden unit commented that "open source information contains 90% of what you need to know," the same figure given by a deputy director of national intelligence, while a former senior DNI staffer put the figure at 95%.[3]

In open societies, a variety of data concerning political, military, and economic affairs is available through print and online versions of newspapers, magazines, trade journals, academic journals, and government publications. These published sources may yield intelligence concerning the internal disputes plaguing a European political party, French or Russian arms developments, Japanese defense and trade policy, or advances in computer or laser technologies.

Of course, in closed societies much less information is available; direct reporting on these societies' internal regimes and military affairs in particular is largely absent. Furthermore, all reporting is conducted under the eye of government censors. Even in a closed society, however, there is a significant amount of intelligence that can be gleaned from legally obtainable documents, including newspapers, magazines, collected speeches, academic journals, and even official documents on military affairs.

Intelligence on terrorist groups can also be obtained from open sources. Although these organizations strive to maintain secrecy about their operations and location, they make public threats against those whose actions they seek to alter, and they actively recruit followers and attempt to energize those who already subscribe to their doctrines. Such groups now employ the Internet extensively to accomplish these objectives.

In addition, data on a plethora of non-governmental organizations (NGOs)—from political organizations to human rights and environmental groups—whose activities may be of interest or concern to national security officials are available from the public information generated by those groups as well as from reporting by media sources and academic studies.

After World War II and during the Cold War, the prime focus of U.S. open source collection was the Soviet Union. From August 1947 through April 1951, all articles in Soviet scientific and technical journals were abstracted, and some were translated in full. In 1952, 87 Soviet journals were available for review; by 1954, that number had nearly doubled to 165 and by April 1956 it had virtually doubled again—to 328. The journals contained information on Soviet research and development in, or related to, atomic energy, missiles, electronics, and atomic, biological, and chemical warfare. In addition, there were about 3,000 books and monographs per year that were surveyed for scientific and technical intelligence.[4]

The U.S. Intelligence Community examined other components of Soviet open source literature for information of political and military intelligence value. In addition to general circulation organs such as *Pravda* and *Izvestia*, the CIA and other agencies examined the 11 major Soviet military journals and approximately 500 books on military affairs published in the Soviet Union each year.[5]

Among the translations of Soviet reports, the one that had the most impact on U.S. research and development capabilities occurred in 1971, when the Foreign Technology Division produced a translation of a paper by Pytor Ufimtsev of the Moscow Institute of Radio Engineering, titled "The Method of Edge Waves in the Physical Theory of Diffraction." The paper became, according to Ben Rich, former head of the Lockheed Skunk Works, "the Rosetta Stone breakthrough for stealth technology."[6]

The introduction of *glasnost* in the Soviet Union in 1985, and the union's subsequent dissolution in 1991 into the Russian Federation and other independent political entities, dramatically increased the availability of open source intelligence concerning that area of the world. The type of military intelligence that could be obtained from Russian open sources was qualitatively different from that acquired under the Soviet regime—both because of greater press freedom and because of the Russian desire to sell weaponry to remedy the nation's dire economic situation. Thus, for example, an August 1993 broadcast from Moscow reported on how a lack of funding threatened the MiG-29M program. That same month, *Rossiyskaya*

Gazeta reported on an air defense missile demonstration at Kapustin Yar. In December 1993, in an unprecedented public announcement, the government of Russia revealed that the first unit of its fourth-generation attack submarine, to be named the *Severodvinsk*, was laid down. The November 4, 1994, issue of *Nezavisimaya Gazeta* included an interview concerning the future of the Russian strategic forces with a scientist employed by the Defense Ministry. In early 1995, *Izvestia* contained "an unusually detailed description" of the silo-based Topol-M ICBM, including information on its accuracy as well as the time between launch command and the missile leaving its silo.[7]

In early 1997, a retired Russian colonel, in an article in the mass-circulation newspaper *Komsomolskaya Pravda*, wrote about the deterioration of the Russian command-and-control system. His article echoed the comments that Defense Minister Igor Rodionov made in a letter to President Yeltsin. The article was subsequently discussed in a CIA report outlining Rodionov's concerns about command and control.[8]

Russian open source material is also considered valuable with respect to understanding Russian organized crime. In 1997, the Foreign Broadcast Information Service Gray Literature Coordinator outlined the strategic value of this type of intelligence:

> The combination of Russian culture and Soviet past makes open source material particularly valuable for studying Russian organized crime. . . . First, during the emergence of a relatively free press following the years of constricting CPSU control, the exposé became a popular style of reporting. Criminal groups are regularly portrayed and detailed by daring crime reporters, some of whom have paid with their lives. Second, because of the nexus of Russian crime, politics, and the media, Russian criminal leaders appear to be image conscious and often use the press to defend themselves as honest businessmen. At the same time, however, they rarely miss an opportunity to attack their opponents—viciously exposing other groups for their criminal ties and activity. Third, Russian criminals have in the past been motivated to attract Western business partners or allies. For this reason, they provide business data to various research firms that are publicly available—allowing interested parties to understand their business methods, sophistication, and business sense.[9]

Even the insignia patches associated with special Russian military units can yield information of value to U.S. intelligence analysts. In November 2006, the DNI Open Source Center produced a report entitled "Russia: Insignia Collectors Websites Identify Special Leadership Facilities Unit," which noted that the patches shown on the website identified components of the Special Facilities Service, which was responsible for the construction of leadership bunkers.[10]

Chinese open sources can also be exploited to produce intelligence. In a mid-1980s assessment, the journal *Knowledge of Ships* was judged to generally provide low-quality and unreliable naval information but on one occasion to contain useful data. One article, "The Role of the Guided Missile Speedboat in Engagement," stated that the "planners" were considering assigning an anti-aircraft mission to one or two of the six boats in a typical OSA or KOMAR squadron.[11]

Another Chinese journal, *Journal of Shipbuilding*, focused on research topics in marine engineering in considerable detail and demonstrated that the Chinese were actively exploiting U.S., British, Soviet, Japanese, and German work in the field. Examination of the journal also revealed that the instruments being employed by China for test purposes were of German, Japanese, and Chinese manufacture and that the Chinese experiments generally picked up where the exploited source stopped—either advancing the testing process a step further or seeking empirical verification of a theory propounded by the source.[12]

According to one analyst, "From the technical intelligence perspective the publication can be valuable in providing new information about marine engineering topics of interest in China, an appreciation of the foreign sources being exploited by the Chinese, and the results of their experiments in the field." This information, when combined with other intelligence, "offers a reasonably accurate assessment of where China stands in this area of technology." Also of interest to intelligence analysts is *Contemporary Military Affairs*, in which the Pacific and Indian Ocean theaters of operation receive good coverage.[13]

Press reports also provide useful information to those tracking the organization and operations of the People's Liberation Army. For example, a February 4, 1987, report in the Xinhua press disclosed the existence of a training center for reserve paratroop personnel, apparently the first such center in China. The article stated that the center included a small airport, parachute training and drop zones, an area to stage tactical exercises, and lecture rooms.[14]

Chinese views on information warfare, the new military revolution, Taiwan, the future security environment, and high-technology warfare can also be judged, at least in part, through a review of a variety of published sources. Those sources have included *On Meeting the Challenge of the New Military Revolution* (by Lt. Gen. Huai Guomo), *Latest Trends in China's Military Revolution, Logical Concept of Information Warfare, Information Warfare and Training of Skilled Commanders*, and *Exploring Ways to Defeat the Enemy Through Information*. In 2010, it was reported that U.S. intelligence agencies had obtained a copy of a 2007 book—*Information Warfare Theory*, written by the president of the PLA Information Engineering University—that promised to "provide new insights into the Chinese military's information-warfare plans."[15]

A 2003 assessment of the utility of Chinese open sources in studying the PLA examined research directories, encyclopedias and dictionaries, monographs and books, magazines and journals, and electronic databases. The author concluded that "open source materials have proven useful in shedding light on the traditionally opaque issue of Chinese strategic doctrine" and that "Chinese sources can provide broad insights into force planning debates and discussion within the PLA."[16]

Even the controlled Iranian press may yield useful information on Iran's nuclear decisionmaking and nuclear strategy. For example, a speech by Hasan Rohani, Iran's chief nuclear negotiator from October 2003 to August 2005, to the Supreme Cultural Revolution Council—"Beyond the Challenges Facing Iran and the IAEA Concerning the Nuclear Dossier"—was published in the Iranian press in late September 2005. According to a non-governmental evaluation of the speech, it provided "an interesting analysis of Iran's domestic scene and of the decisionmaking process" and reinforced the "cynical view that Iran's main objective in negotiating is to gain time," as Rohani told the council that during negotiations with the EU-3, Iran agreed to suspend activities only in the areas where it was not experiencing technical problems and that Iran completed the Isfahan Uranium Conversion Facility in the midst of the negotiations.[17]

The volume of open source material around the world dwarfs what was available a few decades ago, in part due to the explosion in printed matter. The number of periodicals worldwide grew from 70,000 in 1972 to 116,000 in 1991. A 1997 study on the Chinese media reported that there were more than 2,200 newspapers, in contrast to 42—almost all party papers, limited to propaganda and officials speeches—thirty years earlier. The same study estimated that 7,000 magazines and journals were being published in the PRC. In December 1992, there were 1,700 newspapers that did not exist in 1989 in Russia and the other former Soviet states. At that time, the CIA's Foreign Broadcast Information Service (FBIS) monitored more than 3,500 publications in fifty-five foreign languages.[18]

The DIA and military service intelligence organizations acquire foreign S&T (science and technology) publications and materials, publications concerning foreign weapons systems, training and doctrine manuals, military organization and planning documents, and map and town plans. In 1992, a database of foreign scientific and technical information references and abstracts contained about 10 million records, of which approximately 6 million were unclassified. And as of late 1992, the CIA had identified 8,000 commercial databases worldwide.[19]

In addition to accessing databases both within and outside the Internet, an analyst can access a variety of material—written and video—through the Internet. A report by an analyst with the Office of the Assistant Secretary of Defense for Special Operations and Low-Intensity Conflict concluded that the Internet could provide useful intelligence information by providing reports on current events, "analytical assessments by politically astute observers on or near the scene of those events, many of whom offer unique insights," and information about the plans and operations of politically active groups.[20]

The report also noted that "a great deal of message traffic on the Internet is idle chit-chat with no intelligence value" and that the accuracy of much of the information on the Internet is suspect, requiring validation. As a result, an alternative use of the Internet is to "cue higher confidence means of U.S. intelligence collection, by alerting us to potentially important factors and allowing us to orient and focus our collection more precisely."[21]

For the Asian Studies Detachment (ASD) of INSCOM's 501st Military Intelligence Brigade, the Internet does provide a substantial amount of data. In late 2005 it was reported that approximately half of the ASD's cited sources consisted of Internet-derived information and that this percentage was growing.[22]

In 2000, monitoring of online publications in Taiwan provided warning that the first group from a total of forty Su-30 MKK ground attack aircraft took off from Russia on their way to China. As part of the Intelligence Community's effort to track the activities of terrorist groups, the DNI Open Source Center, as of 2005, closely monitored 150 to 300 jihadist websites. In 2010 the website of al-Qaeda in the Arabian Peninsula began to publish the magazine *Inspire*, containing articles on encryption, "Mujahedeen 101," and how to build a bomb in the kitchen. Its second issue, which ran to seventy-four pages, encouraged jihadists to engage in "lone-wolf" attacks with firearms, such as a shooting rampage at a restaurant.[23]

The DNI Open Source Center also monitors blogs. In 2006, the center director commented that "a lot of blogs now have become very big on the Internet, and we're getting a lot of rich information on blogs that are telling us a lot about social perspectives and everything from what the general feeling is to . . . people putting information on there that doesn't exist anywhere else." Chinese bloggers have become an important source of information on China's military buildup. Meanwhile, Farsi is among the top five languages employed by bloggers, and snapshots posted on Iranian blogs have shown how young women were following or defying the mullah's edicts on head coverings and skirt lengths—one indicator of the public's mood.[24] Subsequently, the protests and Green Revolution that began with the disputed presidential election of 2009 generated written and video blogs that Iranian analysts at CIA, INR, and elsewhere undoubtedly scrutinized.

Monitoring of the numerous jihadist websites provides information on the messages being conveyed to those who access them, as well as declarations from prominent terrorists. As of 2006, there were over 4,000 pro-al-Qaeda sites, chat rooms, and message boards, which recruit members, spread propaganda, and broadcast news. The online publication *Sada-al-Jihad* (Echo of Jihad) translated and posted a speech by Abu Musab al-Zarqawi and posted video messages and images of violence. An hour-long video, posted in 2004, "The Winds of Victory," included pictures of suicide bombings and other attacks. And in early October 2010, jihadist websites carried two audio recordings by bin Laden—containing a wide range of comments on current events.[25]

The Internet provided information of relevance to U.S. military interrogators at Kandahar, Afghanistan, during the U.S. operations against the Taliban and al-Qaeda—including data on some London mosques and their fundamentalist imams. The Intelligence Community has also gleaned online information about some other rather obscure groups. For example, although there was no information available from classified U.S. computer networks on China's Uighurs, who had been agitating for an independent Muslim state, data were accessed from the Internet.[26]

The monitoring of radio and television broadcasts can also be valuable. In 1988, the Air Force Intelligence Service observed: "Broadcasts can provide information on development of new weapons systems, deployment and modifications of existing systems, military operations, and daily life in the armed forces of foreign countries. High-level personalities can be identified—the West can better understand a country's foreign and internal policies by viewing the broadcasts and analyzing statements by leadership."[27]

Through the FBIS and its partner, the BBC Monitoring Service, the United States obtained a vast amount of information concerning political, military, and economic events throughout the world. In a 1992 speech, then Deputy DCI Admiral William O. Studeman described the value of foreign broadcasts: "Each week FBIS monitors 790 hours of television from over 50 countries in 29 languages. Foreign TV programs, such as news programs and documentaries, give analysts a multidimensional feel for a country that other open source media cannot provide. TV allows us to broaden our knowledge of more restrictive societies."[28]

Just as the number of publications in China has increased dramatically, so has the number of radio and television outlets. In late 1997, it was estimated that there were 700 broadcast TV stations, 3,000 cable stations, and 1,000 radio stations. During May 1989, U.S. monitoring of Chinese radio broadcasts provided important information on the support for the student protesters in Beijing. The reports indicated that 40,000 students, teachers, and writers in Chengdu marched in support of democracy in mid-May. Guangdong provincial radio reported a march of 30,000 students. Altogether, radio reports indicated that there had been demonstrations of more than 10,000 people in at least nine other provinces.[29]

During Operation Desert Shield, the CIA and other intelligence agencies found that the television appearances of Saddam Hussein and other Iraqi officials provided useful information. CIA doctors and psychologists examined interviews with Iraqi leaders to look for signs of stress and worry. DIA analysts studied TV reports, particularly those from Baghdad, that might show scenes of military vehicles in the background. They would freeze the frames and try to compare a vehicle's unit designation with the lists of Iraqi equipment in DIA computers in order to determine whether anything new had been added to the force.[30]

U.S. intelligence analysts also studied transcripts of radio broadcasts "by both sides [in the Yugoslav crisis] to gain insights into the intensity of the conflict." At the theater/tactical level, in support of U.S. forces in the region, the intelligence component of the Army's 1st Infantry Division, headquartered in Tuzla, monitored Serbian, Bosnian, and Croatian media. It produced the daily *Tuzla Night Owl*, whose approximately ten pages contained excerpts of media reports on political, economic, and military developments in the region, such as "Investigation of Black Marketing Denied," "Bosnians Have Chemical Weapons?," and "Milosevic Pressures RS Socialist Party."[31]

Monitoring of Arab television stations became a higher priority in the post–Cold War era. One station, Al-Manar, according to a DNI Open Source Center analysis, "uses its newscasts, talk shows on political, social, and cultural issues, and education and religious programming to push Hizaballah's pro-Palestinian agenda and to educate its viewers in line with its Shiite principles." It also notes that "Al-Manar continues its negative treatment of the United States but has dropped the more incendiary anti-U.S. material seen in the past."[32]

The U.S. Central Command and other agencies have fielded a computer system that monitors newscasts of Al-Jazeera and other Arabic television stations and translates them in real time. In addition, the system flags passages and excerpts that might be of interest to intelligence analysts.[33]

Of even greater interest than such stations are some of the videotapes that these stations, particularly Al-Jazeera, play—videotapes containing messages from Osama bin Laden, his deputy Ayman al-Zawahiri, and, until his death in June 2006, Abu Musab al-Zarqawi, the leader of al-Qaeda in Iraq. Among the data they seek to extract are the time and place the tapes were made, the health of the speaker, and indications of upcoming attacks, which might be suggested by code words, images, or particular phrases. In May 2006, it was reported that analyses of the tapes produced by the three al-Qaeda leaders indicated "differing motives and political interests of al-Qaeda's leadership—including the possible emergence of a rivalry between bin Laden and Zarqawi.[34]

Video of Fidel Castro has also been of interest to U.S. leaders and medical intelligence analysts since Castro's health began to deteriorate in late 2006. Photos and video released by the Cuban government, in the face of reports of Castro's then temporarily relinquishing power for medical reasons, showed a bandage covering his neck and a bulge under his running suit. The former was believed to hide the location where he was receiving dialysis, while the latter was believed to conceal a colostomy bag.[35]

The appearances of Kim Jong-Il—and what those appearances reveal about his health—have also been of concern to the U.S. Intelligence Community. Thus, analysts were undoubtedly interested in North Korean television's showing of still pictures of Kim chatting with soldiers and watching a military training exercise—a month after his absence from an important anniversary had inspired rumors of his having suffered a stroke.[36]

Analysis of an Iranian video revealed that Iran's claims that it had successfully fired a submarine-launched missile might have been false and that the video purporting to show that launch was an attempted act of deception. U.S. intelligence analysts discovered that the plume of smoke from the missile shown in the video was an exact match to a video of an earlier Chinese test. "It's an identical launch," according to a Pentagon official. "The plume, everything is the same."[37]

Video footage taken at the Dingxin missile test center and Yangliang flight test center, components of China's Flight Test Establishment, and posted on the Internet provided insight into the Chinese air force's air-to-air and air-to-surface missile programs. Imagery, which undoubtedly has been studied by analysts with the National Air and Space Intelligence Center, has included firings of China's PL-12 radar guided air-to-air missile as well as variants of the KD-88 air-to-surface missile.[38]

Videos of interest may also appear on sites such as YouTube. The site has been used extensively by American-born but Yemen-based cleric Anwar Awlaki, whom U.S. officials have designated as a "global terrorist." Awlaki has appeared on over 700 videos with 3.5 million page views on the site. Quite likely, the CIA has a copy of each of his appearances and examines them in an effort to determine both his exact location and any shifts in his message.[39]

To facilitate the collection and availability of open source information the Intelligence Community has established the Open Source Information System (OSIS)/Intelink-U database. Information available in that database includes *Armies of the World*, the CIA's *World Factbook*, *Patterns of Global Terrorism*, country handbooks, OSC reports, and trade show imagery and brochures, as well as data on foreign medical capabilities, worldwide health issues, land mines and de-mining, infectious diseases, and a number of other topics.[40]

The assorted varieties of open source data have allowed open source units in the Intelligence Community to produce reports on a wide range of topics. Reports from the Asian Studies Detachment have examined North Korean underground facilities as well as PLA air force and space science and technology developments. During the Russian-Georgian conflict and the upheaval in Pakistan, finished intelligence delivered to policymakers "routinely integrated open sources and analyses based on open sources, including mainstream media, video, and blogs."[41]

Unclassified publications of the Open Source Center in 2009 and 2010 included

- *Brazil—Survey of Nuclear Agencies, Facilities* (February 9, 2009)
- *Afghanistan—Geospatial Analysis Reveals Patterns in Terrorist Incidents* (April 20, 2009)
- *North Korean Media Campaign Suggests Long-Term Planning for Hereditary Successor* (May 6, 2009)
- *Venezuela—Chavez Moves to Silence Opposition Media* (August 3, 2009)
- *Japanese Media Expresses Confidence in Japan's Future Role in Space Development* (September 30, 2009)
- *Structure of Iran's State-Run TV IRIB* (December 16, 2009)
- *Taiwan: Unofficial Military Websites* (January 12, 2010)
- *Cuba—Military's Profile in State Media Limited, Positive* (February 26, 2010)
- *Kremlin Allies Expanding Control of Runet Provokes Only Limited Opposition* (February 28, 2010)
- *South Africa's Nuclear Nonproliferation Posture Remains Consistent* (April 9, 2010)
- *German Left-Wing Crime Increase Adds to Public Security Concerns* (April 27, 2010)[42]

TECHNICAL SURVEILLANCE AND EMPLACED SENSORS

The technical surveillance and emplaced sensor operations conducted by the CIA and other intelligence units constitute another important aspect of intelligence gathering. These methods supplement human intelligence activities and can provide detailed information not available by other means. Technical penetration of a residence offers twenty-four-hour coverage and captures the exact conversations that occur. Such operations in foreign embassies can provide information on the plan, policies, and activities of diplomats and intelligence agents.

Two prominent forms of technical surveillance are "bugs" and telephone taps. A bug, or audio device, that will transmit all conversations in a room to a monitoring site is planted by experts from the Office of Technical Service of the National Clandestine Service. Planting such a device is a complex operation. According to an article in the CIA's *Studies in Intelligence,*

> the setting up of an audio installation must be the execution of a "perfect crime." It must be perfect not only in that you don't get caught, but also in that you give no inkling, from the inception of an operation until its termination sometimes five years later, that such an operation was even contemplated; any show of interest in your target would alert the opposition to lay on countermeasures.[43]

The operation involves surveillance of the site, acquisition of building and floor plans, and determination of the color of the interior furnishings and the color texture of the walls. Activity in the room, as well as the movements of security patrols, is noted. When the information is acquired and processed, it is employed to determine the time of surreptitious entry and the materials needed to install the device in such a way as to minimize the probability of discovery.[44]

During the early 1970s, one target of CIA audio devices was Nguyen Van Thieu, the President of South Vietnam. Presents given to Thieu by the CIA—television sets and furniture—came equipped with audio devices, allowing the agency to monitor his personal conversations. The CIA also attempted to install devices in the office and living quarters of the South Vietnamese observer to the Paris Peace Talks.[45]

Another Asian ally that been subject to CIA and NSA technical penetration is South Korea. A substantial part of the evidence against Tongsun Park concerning his alleged attempts to bribe U.S. congressmen came from tape recordings of incriminating conversations inside the South Korean presidential mansion.[46]

Audio devices and telephone taps have, at least in the past, produced much of the CIA's intelligence on Latin America. A report on clandestine collection activities in Latin America during the 1960s revealed that the CIA had managed to place audio devices in the homes of many key personnel, including cabinet ministers.[47]

During E. Howard Hunt's tenure in Mexico City, the CIA bugged or tapped several Iron Curtain embassies. During his tenure in Uruguay, the CIA station conducted technical penetrations of embassies and the living quarters of key personnel. During Philip Agee's time in Uruguay, seven telephone lines were being monitored. Included were phones of the Soviet and Cuban embassies, consulates, and commercial offices.[48]

More recently, the CIA may have bugged the rooms of Iraqi and Iranian delegates to a November 1996 OPEC meeting in Vienna. Decorators found bugging devices in the walls at the hotel during a subsequent renovation. It was reported that the German Federal Intelligence Service (Bundesnachrichtendienst—BND) told its Austrian counterpart that the CIA eavesdropped on the delegates. In 1997, a member of the U.S. embassy in Austria, presumably a CIA officer, left Austria after being arrested for wiretapping the phone of a North Korean diplomat in Vienna.[49]

In 1982 or 1983, a unit of INSCOM—then known as the Quick Reaction Team (QRT), subsequently as the Technical Analysis Unit—placed an electronic listening device in a Panamanian apartment belonging to Gen. Manuel Antonio Noriega. Paying bribes to the maids who cleaned the apartment and to the guards who protected it, a QRT member was able to place a listening device in Noriega's conference room. The six 90-minute tapes that resulted did not produce any substantial intelligence information.[50]

QRT members also bugged the apartment of a Cuban diplomat in Panama. When the diplomat was away, agents slipped into his apartment and wired it with microtransmitters; again the take was of little value.[51]

In 1983, the QRT targeted Soviet representatives on several occasions during their visit to the United States. Soviet officials who traveled to Livermore, California, home of the Lawrence Livermore National Laboratory, had their rooms bugged by QRT agents. The bugging was repeated when the Soviets moved on to Denver. This time the results were more useful; sensitive discussions were recorded and leads obtained on possible Soviet agents in the United States.[52]

In early 2002, it was revealed that a joint FBI-NSA operation had attempted to place listening devices aboard Boeing 767 300 ER aircraft that had been purchased for China's president and refitted at San Antonio International Airport. However, in October 2001, shortly before its initial voyage, Chinese military communication experts discovered at least twenty-seven listening devices aboard the plane.[53]

An even more daring operation, conducted by the CIA, was designated CK/TAW and involved the taping of underground communications lines that linked the Krasnaya Pakhra Nuclear Weapons Research Institute in Troitsk to the Soviet Ministry of Defense headquarters in Moscow—a tap that produced intelligence on Soviet particle beam and laser weapons research. TAW ceased working around 1985 and may have been betrayed by Edward Lee Howard, Aldrich Ames, or both. Another technical surveillance operation that was betrayed to the Soviets around 1985 was designated ABSORB. The operation involved secretly placing radiation detection devices with cargoes traveling on the Trans-Siberian railroad in order to pick up the radiation emitted from missiles in the vicinity of the train tracks, radiation that could be used to determine the number of warheads on each missile.[54]

Technical surveillance operations may also employ lasers. A laser beam can be directed at a closed window from outside and used to detect the vibrations of the sound waves resulting from a conversation inside the room. The vibrations can be transformed back into the words that were spoken. Such a device was successfully tested in West Africa in the 1960s, but at the time did not seem to function properly anywhere else than in the United States.[55] Subsequent advances made it a viable intelligence collection technique.

Another class of technical surveillance systems are emplaced sensors, which can be employed to monitor communications signals or other emissions. Emplaced sensors may have the same purpose as sensors placed on spacecraft, aircraft, ships, or other mobile platforms. However, placing them covertly in a single location rather than on a mobile platform offers two advantages. In many cases, no mobile platform operating from a distance could produce the necessary intelligence—because it could not pick up the signals emitted from the target. Second, an emplaced sensor can monitor a facility or activity continuously.

Such operations are as sensitive as certain HUMINT operations; if the target is aware of the operation, it can be easily neutralized. There are also significant risks for those involved in installing the sensors. Former DCI Stansfield Turner recalled the "very risky planting of a sensing device to monitor a secret activity in a hostile country. The case officer had to do the placement himself, escaping surveillance and proceeding undetected to a location so unusual that had he been found he would have undoubtedly paid with his life."[56]

In 1965, the CIA planted a nuclear-powered device on the summit of Nanda Devi in Garhwal, India. The device was intended to monitor Chinese missile tests from the Shuangchengzi test center in north-central China. After it was swept away in an avalanche, a second device was placed, in 1967, on the summit of the neighboring 22,400-foot Nanda Kot. The device remained in place for a year before being removed.[57]

In 1974 and 1975, and possibly subsequently, the U.S. Navy and Israel Defense Forces conducted a joint operation designated CLUSTER LOBSTER. The operation involved planting an acoustic and magnetic sensor/recorder package in the Strait of Gubal. The tapes yielded valuable information on Soviet mine-sweeping operations.[58]

East Germany was also the target of emplaced sensor operations. In one operation, nuclear detection equipment was installed in a series of road posts on an East German road. The equipment transmitted its data back to an antenna on a pile of rubble in West Berlin. In another instance, seismic monitoring devices were placed underground near a road. The data they transmitted (to a satellite) allowed intelligence analysts to differentiate among seven different weight classes (e.g., jeep, passenger car, truck, tank).[59]

Some of the most exotic emplaced sensors were those used in an attempt to monitor various Soviet weapons programs. One was a round device camouflaged as a tree stump and discovered near a military facility that could transmit the data collected to a satellite. Another looked like a tree branch and was discovered in the late 1980s near a military airfield. According to a 1990 Soviet publication, it was an "automatic device for gathering intelligence on the parameters of the optronic control systems and laser sights used in the Air Force." The publication went on to state that the "optronic sensor enables it to receive scattered radiation from laser sights or missile control systems. The received laser beams are transformed into a numerical code and recorded by the electronic memory." The data could then be transmitted to a satellite.[60]

In 1994, it was reported that the Defense Intelligence Agency was developing Unattended Ground Sensors (UGS) and Unattended MASINT Sensors (UMS) (the latter code-named STEEL RATTLER), employing imagery and acoustic sensors to covertly monitor activity around critical targets such as North Korean nuclear facilities. UGS/UMS may be used to monitor nuclear power plants, deeply buried bunkers, mobile missile launch sites, and weapons-manufacturing facilities. A high-speed digital signal processor board inside the UGS would handle both the processing for the acoustic sensor and the image compression for the imager.[61]

Another risky operation occurred in 1999, when a team of CIA officers from the joint CIA-NSA Special Collection Service covertly entered southeastern Afghanistan to install a remote-controlled SIGINT collection system near a collection of al-Qaeda camps near the town of Khost.[62]

Emplaced sensors may also be used to provide warning of approaching enemy troops. In 2005, it was reported that "the U.S. military is developing miniature electronic sensors disguised as rocks that can be dropped from aircraft and used to help detect the sound of approaching enemy combatants." It was expected that the devices, no larger than golf balls and employing tiny silicon chips and radio-frequency identification technology, would be able to detect the sound of a human footfall at 20 to 30 feet. The devices were expected to be ready for use by early 2007.[63]

DOCUMENT EXPLOITATION

Important intelligence can also be obtained from the exploitation of documents as well as videotapes and audiotapes (not intended for public release) seized during military operations, such as those obtained in Grenada, Afghanistan, and Iraq. On October 25, 1983, U.S. forces, including special forces, invaded the island of Grenada in response to the overthrow of the Marxist government of Maurice Bishop by a hard-line faction that executed Bishop. The perceived importance of the documents seized resulted in President Ronald Reagan's signing of National Security Decision Directive 112, "Processing and Disposition of Documents Acquired by U.S. Forces in Grenada," of November 15, 1983. The directive stated that "the documents acquired by U.S. Forces in Grenada represent a unique resource, which is of significant potential value to U.S. national security interests. It is vital that this resource be protected and carefully utilized to obtain maximum benefit." [64]

The directive went on to specify subjects that it was hoped the documents could shed additional light on, many of which involved Cuban activities. A few months after the directive was issued, a secret memorandum noted that DIA had received about 4,800 documents and that at least 3,000 additional documents were en route to DIA for processing. In addition, the memo noted that "hundreds—if not thousands—more documents may still be identified for exploitation."[65]

Among the results of the exploitation process were a December 19, 1983, Interagency Intelligence Assessment—*Grenada: A First Look at Mechanism of Control and Foreign Involvement*—and an August 20, 1984, follow-up memorandum to holders of the interagency assessment. The August 1984 study notes that the December 1983 assessment was based on 3,500 documents that had been processed at the time, while the new study relied on an additional 8,000 documents.[66]

The August 1984 assessment covered the New Jewel movement—specifically, the coup that overthrew Bishop, interworkings with the People's Revolutionary Government, political indoctrination, and relations with the Catholic Church. It also examined the Grenadian Revolutionary Armed Forces—its organization, armed strength, weapons—as well as the Ministry of Interior. Significant attention was also devoted to Cuba's influence in Grenada—Cuban military advisors and Cuba's use of Grenada and the Port Salines Airport. "Growing Soviet Influence," was the title of another section, while yet another dealt with Soviet-Cuban cooperation. In a final section titled "Dealing with Other Nations," the assessment focused on Vietnam and narcotics.[67]

Among the documents recovered by the CIA and U.S. military forces in Afghanistan after the beginning of U.S. military operations in 2001 were manuals written in Arabic that outlined the step-by-step construction of booby traps and improvised explosive devices. In another instance, they were able to acquire a notebook with cell-phone and fax numbers for Mullah Omar, Osama bin Laden, and senior al-Qaeda commanders. Also discovered, in December 2001, was a set of documents describing attempts by a Pakistani scientist to obtain anthrax spores and equipment needed to convert them into biological weapons.[68]

In addition, a reporter who inadvertently bought a computer that had been used by the number-two and number-three al-Qaeda officials—Ayman al-Zawahiri and Mohammed Atef—turned it over to the CIA. Among the items discovered on the hard drive were statements describing the pursuit of biological weapons: "A germ attack is often detected days after it occurs, which raises the number of victims. . . . Defense against such weapons is very difficult. . . . I would like to emphasize what we previously discussed: that looking for a specialist is the fastest, safest, and cheapest way." Other correspondence on the computer revealed that al-Qaeda had hired an expert who built a rudimentary laboratory and had established a charitable foundation as a front for the group's chemical weapons program.[69]

In addition to correspondence, the documents of the hard drive included "budgets, training manuals for recruits, and scouting reports for international attacks"; they "shed light on everything from personnel matters and petty bureaucratic sniping to theological discussions and debates about the merits of suicide operations." The computer also contained "video files, photographs, scanned documents, and Web pages" that constituted the organization's Internet-based publicity and recruitment effort. Hundreds of pages of additional documents found in a house in Kabul, reportedly used by al-Qaeda, indicated that the group was interested in developing a nuclear weapon. Among those items was a twenty-five-page document containing information about nuclear weapons, including a design for the device.[70]

In January 2007, U.S. forces conducted two raids on Iranian targets in Iraq—the Iranian Liaison Office in Ibril and the Ibril airport—in response to Iranian arming, funding, and training of Iraqi militant groups. In addition to detaining five Iranians, the forces confiscated "vast amounts of documents and computer data," which undoubtedly were scrutinized by analysts at CENTCOM and in Washington.[71]

In early 2008, "American investigative teams" were in Bogota, Colombia, and Washington, D.C., examining documents pulled from laptops and hard drives belonging to the Marxist Revolutionary Armed Forces of Colombia (FARC), which had been seized by the Colombian military. The documents apparently showed that the Venezuelan government had provided about $300 million to the FARC and offered to provide rockets to the rebels.[72]

MATERIEL EXPLOITATION

Particularly valuable intelligence also comes from the acquisition of new or used foreign weapons systems, communication equipment, and other devices of military significance. In many cases, information on small systems cannot be obtained by overhead reconnaissance or signals intelligence. In any case, possession of the actual system adds significant new information to whatever is already known. The acquisition and analysis—materiel exploitation—of such systems, a function of all military scientific and technical intelligence units, allow scientists to determine not only the capabilities of the system but how such capabilities are achieved. Such knowledge can then be exploited to improve U.S. systems and to develop countermeasures.

According to Army Regulation 381–26, materiel exploitation enables

- the production of scientific and technical intelligence in support of force, combat, and materiel development;
- the assessment of foreign technology, design features, and scientific developments for infusion into U.S. developmental efforts;
- the support of U.S. systems and developmental testing/operational testing by providing adversary systems for use in evaluating U.S. systems capabilities;
- the development of systems in support of simulations of foreign systems.[73]

During the course of the Cold War, U.S. materiel acquisition activities focused primarily on Soviet and Chinese systems. In Indonesia, in the 1960s, the CIA conducted an operation designated HA/BRINK. In one phase of the operation, CIA operatives entered a warehouse holding SAM-2 missiles, removed the guidance system from one of them, and took it with them. The acquisition allowed U.S. Air Force scientists to equip B-52s with appropriate countermeasures. HA/BRINK also obtained the designs and workings of numerous Soviet weapons—the surface-to-surface Styx naval missile, the W-class submarine, the KOMAR guided-missile patrol boat, a RIGA-class destroyer, a SVERDLOV cruiser, a TU-16 BADGER bomber, and a KENNEL air-to-surface missile.[74]

In 1979, the CIA and DIA planned Operation GRAY PAN, which involved the theft of a Soviet-made anti-aircraft gun and armored personnel carrier that the Soviets had sold to the Iranian Army.[75]

In a more recent version of HA/BRINK, the CIA purchased, from retired officers of the Indian Army and Air Force, details on weapons furnished to India by the Soviet Union. The Indian officers involved included a major general and a lieutenant colonel in the Indian Army, and a vice-marshal of the Indian Air Force.[76]

The most significant ground forces equipment the CIA obtained during the Cold War was the T-72 tank; only the T-80 is newer. In 1981, the Army Intelligence Support Activity, in an operation code-named GRAND FALCON, attempted to obtain a T-72 and other equipment (including a MiG-25) from Iraq in exchange for U.S. 175-mm cannons. Ultimately, Iraqi officials vetoed the deal. A CIA attempt to acquire at T-72 from Romania also failed in 1981. Another unsuccessful ISA attempt to acquire a T-72, at the urging of Lt. Col. Oliver North, involved the attempted delivery of U.S.-made machine guns to Iran in October 1986 in exchange for a T-72 captured from Iraq. By March 1987, the CIA had acquired several T-72s.[77]

The United States acquired advanced Soviet aircraft from pilots who defected, or purchased the aircraft from third parties. Once obtained, the planes were examined thoroughly by Foreign Technology Division (FTD) offices and scientists. Thus, when a MiG-25 pilot defected from the Soviet Union with his plane, landing in Japan, examination of the airplane was a high priority. Before being returned to the Soviet Union, the entire MiG-25 was disassembled at Hyakuri Air Base in Japan. The engines, radar, computer, electronic countermeasures, automatic pilot, and communications equipment were placed on blocks and stands for mechanical, metallurgical, and photographic analysis.[78]

This examination, as well as the pilot's debriefing, sharply altered Western understanding of the plane and its missions. Among the discoveries was a radar more powerful than that installed in any other interceptor and fighter. In addition, the Soviet designers had used vacuum tubes rather than transistors.[79] (Although vacuum tubes represent a more primitive technology than transistors, they are resistant to the electromagnetic pulse [EMP] created by nuclear detonations.)

The MiG-25 was far from the first MiG obtained for purposes of exploitation. In early 1951, the Allied Air Force Commander in Korea was asked to make every effort to obtain a complete MiG-15 for analysis. As a result, a MiG that was shot down off Korea was retrieved within a short time. Portions of another MiG were recovered by helicopter. Air Technical Intelligence Center personnel landed, ran up to the crashed plane, threw grenades into it to separate assemblies small enough to carry, and left under hostile fire. In 1953, a defecting North Korean pilot flew an intact MiG-15 to South Korea. Several years later, Israel supplied the U.S. with a MiG-21.[80]

From 1977 through 1988, at Tonopah Test Range in Nevada, Air Force, Navy, and Marine pilots flew against a variety of MiGs (including the MiG-17,-21,-23, and possibly the-25 and-27) and possibly the Su-27, in a program designated CONSTANT PEG—the objective being to give the pilots an advantage should they ever meet such aircraft in combat. The Soviet aircraft eventually received new designations, so the MiG-23 became the YF-113G.[81]

In some instances, Soviet equipment was sold to the United States by nominal Soviet allies—particularly Romania. During the final ten years of the Ceauşescu regime, the CIA was able to buy advanced Soviet military technology through Ceauşescu's two brothers, one of whom was the deputy defense minister. The equipment from Romania included:

- the latest version of the Shilka, one of the more effective Soviet antiaircraft systems;
- mobile rocket launchers that had been modified and improved by the Romanian military;
- radar systems used in identifying targets and directing the firing of various Soviet AA weapons.[82]

In other cases, materiel exploitation follows from the completion of a recovery operation in which parts of a satellite that have returned to Earth, or a crashed airplane, or a sunken ship are retrieved. During the 1960s, Project MOON DUST focused on the "national-level coordination of information concerning the decay and deorbit of space debris [including rocket boosters], regardless of country of origin." When sightings and/or recovery were considered possible, attachés were notified to maintain watch and consider action for recovery.[83]

In 1970, the United States recovered a nuclear weapon from a Soviet aircraft that had crashed into the Sea of Japan; in 1971, the Navy recovered electronic eavesdropping equipment from a sunken trawler; and in 1972, a joint U.S.-British operation recovered electronic gear from a Soviet plane that had crashed earlier that year into the North Sea. In 1975, in Project AZORIAN, the CIA recovered part of a Golf-II submarine that had sunk northwest of Hawaii.[84]

The repeated recovery of Soviet test warheads that landed in ocean waters was known as Operation SAND DOLLAR. By international agreement, the Soviet Union was required to specify the impact areas for such tests. U.S. radars tracked the warheads to determine the precise points of impact. What appeared to be civilian drilling ships were sent to the Pacific test range after the tests had been completed to recover nose cones that had not self-destructed. Ships were guided to the proper locations by computers coordinated with U.S. satellites, and the objects were located by sonar and magnetometer devices. Scientists at FTD then analyzed the design and construction of captured nose cones.[85]

In the aftermath of the 1973 Yom Kippur War, the United States received from Israel a variety of Soviet materiel. In addition to a Soviet AMD-500 mine, the Israelis provided SA-2, SA-3, SA-6, and SA-7 missiles.[86]

In 1983, during Operation BRIGHT STAR, personnel from INSCOM's 513th Military Intelligence Group were able to examine and evaluate Soviet and other foreign communications equipment that had been left behind in Somalia. The

INSCOM personnel examined and repaired eighty-one pieces of Soviet and other foreign communications equipment.[87]

In the 1980s, the CIA acquired several advanced Soviet military helicopter gunships, specifically the Mi-24 HINDs, from both Pakistan and Chad. The helicopters were obtained by Pakistan and Chad as a result of the defection of a Soviet pilot from Afghanistan and Chad's victory over Libya in their border war. It has been reported that as a result of acquiring the helicopters, the United States discovered how to penetrate the Mi-24s defense systems with Stinger surface-to-air missiles. In 1983, the Deputy Under Secretary of Defense had refused to sanction an operation to acquire a Mi-24 from Iraq in exchange for permission for Iraq to buy up to 100 Hughes helicopters because he believed that the background of the Iraqi intermediary meant that "the potential for causing embarrassment to the U.S. Government is too great."[88]

The end of the Cold War and the collapse of the Soviet Union did not decrease the emphasis on acquiring Soviet-and Russian-produced weapons systems. In addition to providing intelligence about innovative aspects of current Russian weapons systems, acquisition operations provide a hedge against any future conflict. But of much greater importance is the extent to which Soviet weapons systems are the foundations for other nations' military arsenals, and Russia continues to sell advanced weaponry. For example, in 1990, the Soviet Union exported a variety of high-tech aircraft—the Su-7, Su-24, MiG-21, MiG-23, MiG-29, Mi-17, and Mi-24. In 1998, significant portions of the Iraqi, Libyan, North Korean, and Syrian air forces were made up by Soviet aircraft.[89]

In March 1991, the United States recovered the nose section of a MiG-29 FULCRUM A from Jalibah Air Base in Iraq. It provided analysts at the National Air and Space Intelligence Center (NASIC) with a SLOTBACK I radar and with the FULCRUM's infrared search-and-track system, a heat-seeking targeting device—both of which were subject to "much study." In 1992, NASIC acquired an MiG-23 FLOGGER after it had been bought by a U.S. citizen from the Finnish company that Russia had sold it to, only to have it seized by the Bureau of Alcohol, Tobacco, and Firearms because the buyer brought the plane's 23-mm cannon into the country illegally. For over five years, it was housed at the center's Foreign Materiel Exploitation Facility.[90]

In October 1997, the United States signed an agreement with the Republic of Moldava to purchase twenty-one MiG-29 nuclear-capable fighters—one FULCRUM B trainer, six FULCRUM A, and fourteen advanced FULCRUM C. Allegedly, the primary goal was to prevent their being sold to Iran, but acquisition also "represented something of an intelligence coup," since the planes were the first MiG-29s to be acquired by the United States. The aircraft were characterized by NASIC as "one of the leading threat aircraft in the world today." They were disassembled and flown to NASIC headquarters at Wright-Patterson Air Force Base, after which the center's materiel exploitation experts "began the highly complex task of studying the aircraft's capabilities and limitations." It was suggested that the nuclear wiring system and nuclear safeguards on the aircraft would be of particular interest to analysts at NASIC, since other versions obtained by the United States were not set up for the delivery of nuclear weapons.[91]

In 1999, under a program designated Project BAIL, the Defense Department purchased several Su-27 jet engines for testing and intelligence purposes. At that time, China was flying hundreds of Su-27 sorties over the Taiwan Straits.[92]

In addition to aircraft, a large number of Third World nations possess Soviet-made tanks and surface-to-air missiles. In particular, Soviet-produced SAMs form a significant part of the Syrian, Libyan, Iranian, Cuban, and North Korean arsenals.[93]

The vast analyses of Soviet weapons conducted by Army, Navy, and Air Force scientific and technical intelligence organizations during the Cold War served as the basis for understanding Iraqi capabilities during Operations Desert Shield and Desert Storm. In April 1991, the Army received, from Germany, T-55 and T-72 tanks, assorted signals and communications equipment, and small battlefield weapons, automatic rifles, and mortars. The equipment had been inherited from the East German Army. Furthermore, in late 1992, the CIA was reported to be involved in a program of buying high-technology from former Soviet republics.[94]

Russia has also sought to export its most modern surface-to-air missile systems, the S-300 PMU (designated the S-10 GRUMBLE by the United States) and S-300V (SA-12A/B GLADIATOR/GIANT). Not surprisingly, the United States acquired both systems. It also acquired, from Eastern European governments, thirty-one Scud-B missiles and four MAZ 543 transporter-erector-launchers, in a program designated WILLOW SAND. The missiles have been employed both in theater missile defense exercises and as subjects of intelligence exploitation by the DIA's Missile and Space Intelligence Center.[95]

Notes

1. Richard A. Best Jr. and Alfred Cumming, Congressional Research Service, *Open Source Intelligence (OSINT): Issues for Congress*, December 5, 2007, p. 6; "We've Launched," http://graylit.osti.gov/whatsnew.html, August 2000; "Gray Literature," www.csulb.edu/library/subj/gray_literature.

2. Graham H. Turbiville Jr., Lt. Col. Karl E. Prinslow, and Lt. Col. Robert E. Waller, "Assessing Emerging Threat Through Open Sources," *Military Review*, September–October 1999.

3. Roscoe H. Hillenkoeter, "Using the World's Information Sources," *Army Information Digest*, November 1948, pp. 3–6; Hamilton Bean, "The DNI's Open Sources Center: An Organizational Communication Perspective," *International Journal of Intelligence and Counterintelligence* 20, 2 (Summer 2007): 240–257. It should be noted that not only will the percentage of information that can be obtained from open sources vary from issue to issue but the intelligence available only from clandestine sources may be the most important in many cases. Thus, for example, one may do extensive reporting on al-Qaeda based on open sources and yet find that those sources are not likely to yield information on the next planned attack. For some of the debate on the value of open sources, see Arthur J. Hulnick, "The Downside of Open Source Intelligence," *International Journal of Intelligence and Counterintelligence* 15, 4 (Fall, 2002): 565–579; Stephen C. Mercado, "Sailing the Sea of OSINT in the Information

Age," *Studies in Intelligence* 48, 3 (2004): 45–55; Stephen C. Mercado, "Reexamining the Distinction Between Open Information and Secrets," *Studies in Intelligence* 49, 2 (2005), www.cia.gov; Robert W. Pringle, "The Limits of OSINT: Diagnosing the Soviet Media, 1985–1989," *International Journal of Intelligence and Counterintelligence* 16, 4 (Summer 2002): 280–289; and Amy Sands, "Integrating Open Sources into Transnational Threat Assessments," in Jennifer E. Sims and Burton Gerber, eds., *Transforming U.S. Intelligence* (Washington, D.C.: Georgetown University Press, 2005), pp. 63–78.

4. J. J. Bagnall, "The Exploitation of Russian Scientific Literature for Intelligence Purposes," *Studies in Intelligence* 2, 3 (Summer 1958): 45–49. Also see Joseph Becker, "Comparative Survey of Soviet and U.S. Access to Published Information," *Studies in Intelligence* 1, 4 (Fall 1957): 35–46.

5. Andrew Cockburn, *The Threat: Inside the Soviet Military Machine* (New York: Random House, 1983), p. 22; Jonathan Samuel Lockwood, *The Soviet View of U.S. Strategic Doctrine* (New Brunswick, N.J.: Transaction, 1983), p. 5.

6. Bruce Ashcroft, "Air Force Materiel Exploitation," *American Intelligence Journal* (Autumn–Winter 1994): 79–82; Ben Rich with Leo Janos, *Skunk Works* (Boston: Little, Brown, 1994), p. 19.

7. "Lack of Funding Threatens 'MiG-29M,'" FBIS-SOV–93–164, August 26, 1993, pp. 32–33; "Air Missile Defense Demonstration Observed," FBIS-SOV–93–164, August 26, 1993, pp. 33–34; Office of Naval Intelligence, *Office of Naval Intelligence Command History 1994*, 1995, p. 55; "Top-Secret Scientist on Future of Strategic Rocket Forces," FBIS-SOV–94–215, November 7, 1994, pp. 34–35; "Topol-M Silo-Based SS-25 Upgrade Said More Accurate Than MX," *Aerospace Daily*, January 24, 1995, p. 113.

8. David Hoffman, "Cold-War Doctrines Refuse to Die," *Washington Post*, March 15, 1998, pp. A1, A24–A25; Bill Gertz, *Betrayal: How the Clinton Administration Undermined American Security* (Washington, D.C.: Regnery, 1999), pp. 229–230.

9. Michael S. Moore, "Use of Open Source Material for Studying Russian Organized Crime," in *1997 Open Source Conference for the Intelligence and Law Enforcement Communities*, September 16–18, 1997, McLean, Virginia.

10. Alan Thomson, *A Sourcebook on the Russian Federation Main Directorate of Special Programs (GUSP) and the Special Installations Service (SSO)*, November 14, 2006, p. 1.

11. Carl B. Crawley, "On the Exploitation of Open Source Chinese Documents," *Naval Intelligence Quarterly* 2, 4 (1981): 7–9.

12. Ibid.

13. Ibid.

14. Intelligence Center, Pacific, *IPAC Daily Intelligence Summary* 24–87, February 6, 1987, p. 2.

15. M. Ehsan Ahrari, "Chinese Prove to Be Attentive Students of Information Warfare," *Jane's Intelligence Review*, October 1997, pp. 469–473; Michael Pillsbury, *China Debates the Future Security Environment* (Washington, D.C.: NDU Press, 2000), particularly pp. 325–354; Bill Gertz, "Inside the Ring," www.washingtontimes.com, June 2, 2010.

16. Evan S. Medeiros, "Undressing the Dragon: Researching the PLA Through Open Source Exploitation," in *A Poverty of Riches: New Challenges and Opportunities in PLA Research*, ed. James C. Mulvenon and Andrew N.D. Yang (Santa Monica, Calif.: RAND, 2003), pp. vi,133, 137.

17. Chen Kane, "Nuclear Decision Making in Iran: A Rare Glimpse," *Middle East Brief* 5 (May 2006), especially pp. 2–5.

18. "Remarks by Admiral William O. Studeman, Deputy Director of Central Intelligence," to the First International Symposium on National Security and National Competitiveness: Open Source Solutions, December 1, 1992, Mc Lean, Virginia, pp. 12, 20; Todd Hazelbarth, *The Chinese Media: More Autonomous and Diverse—Within Limits* (Washington, D.C.: CIA Center for the Study of Intelligence, September 1997), p. 1.

19. "Remarks by A. Denis Clift, Chief of Staff, Chief of Staff, Defense Intelligence Agency," to the First International Symposium on National Security and National Competitiveness: Open Source Solutions; "Remarks by William O. Studeman," p. 12.

20. Charles Swett, Office of the Assistant Secretary of Defense for Special Operations and Low Intensity Conflict, *Strategic Assessment: The Internet*, July 17, 1995, p. 25.

21. Ibid., p. 26.

22. David A. Reese, "50 Years of Excellence: ASD Forges Ahead as the Army's Premier OSINT Unit in the Pacific," *Military Intelligence Professionals Bulletin*, October–December 2005, pp. 27–29.

23. Susan B. Glasser, "Probing Galaxies of Data for Nuggets," www.washingtonpost.com, November 25, 2005; Jeremy W. Peters, "Terrorists' Magazine, Now in English," *New York Times*, July 2, 2010, p. A8; Shaun Waterman, "In online journal, al Qaeda pushes 'lone-wolf' attacks," www.washingtontimes.com, October 13, 2010. The first issue of *Inspire* was supposed to run sixty-four pages, but only three pages were initially available due to a computer bug, which was possibly the result of hackers.

24. Bill Gertz, "CIA Mines 'Rich' Content from Blogs," www.washingtontimescom, April 19, 2006; Scott Shane, "A T-Shirt-and-Dagger Operation," *New York Times*, November 13, 2005, Section 4, p. 5.

25. Scott Shane, "The Struggle for Iraq: The Internet; The Grisly Jihadist Network That He Inspired Is Busy Promoting Zarqawi's Militant Views," www.nytimes.com, June 9, 2006; Arnaud de Borchgrave, Thomas Sanderson, and John MacGaffin, *Open Source Information: The Missing Dimension of Intelligence* (Washington, D.C.: Center for Strategic and International Studies, 2006), p. 3; Scott Shane, "Bin Laden, Resurfacing in Audio Recordings, Urges Aid for Pakistan Flood Victims," *New York Times*, October 3, 2010, p. 5.

26. Chris Mackey and Greg Miller, *The Interrogators: Task Force 500 and America's Secret War Against Al-Qaeda* (Boston: Back Bay Books, 2005), pp. 86, 161.

27. Air Force Intelligence Service, "Video Intelligence (VIDINT)," 1988.

28. Kalev Leetaru, "The Scope of FBI and BBC Open Source Media Coverage, 1979–2008," *Studies in Intelligence* 54, 1 (March 2010): 17–37; "Remarks by William O. Studeman," p. 15.

29. Hazelbarth, *The Chinese Media*, p. 1; Robert Pear, "Radio Broadcasts Report Protests Erupting All Over China," *New York Times*, May 23, 1989, p. A14.

30. "Live, from Baghdad," *Newsweek*, September 24, 1990, p. 4.

31. "Remarks by William O. Studeman," p. 5; 1st Infantry Division, *Tuzla Night Owl*, November 30, 1997, p. 1.

32. DNI Open Source Center, "Al-Manar Promotes 'Resistance,' Tones Down Anti-U.S. Material," December 8, 2005, available at www.fas.org.

33. "Attitude Check," *C4ISR*, November–December 2006, p. 50.

34. David Johnson and Mark Mazzetti, "Some See Hints of Disharmony in Qaeda Tapes," *New York Times*, May 1, 2006, pp. A1, A11.

35. Katherine Shrader, Associated Press, "U.S: Castro's Health Is Deteriorating," November 12, 2006, www.comcast.net; Carmine Gentile, "Suspicions Growing That Castro Is Terminally Ill," www.washingtontimes.com, November 23, 2006; private information.

36. Choe Sang-Hun, "North Korean TV Shows Photos of Elusive Leader," *New York Times*, October 12, 2008, p. 8.

37. Julian E. Barnes, "Video of Iranian Missile Test Is Fake, Pentagon Says," *Los Angeles Times*, September 10, 2006, p. A12.

38. Douglas Barrie, "Chinese Rockets," *Aviation Week & Space Technology*, May 7, 2007, pp. 40–41.

39. Brian Bennett, "Terror Watch on YouTube," *Los Angeles Times*, December 13, 2010, pp. A1, A7.

40. Office of the Director, COSPO, *OSIS/Intelink-U Brochure*, n.d.

41. Reese, "50 Years of Excellence"; Michael Hayden, "Director's Remarks at the DNI Open Source Conference 2008," September 12, 2008, www.cia.gov.

42. Available on the website of the Federation of American Scientists.

43. Alfred Hubest, "Audiosurveillance," *Studies in Intelligence* 4, 3 (Summer 1960): 39–46.

44. Victor Marchetti and John Marks, *The CIA and the Cult of Intelligence* (New York: Knopf, 1974), p. 189.

45. John Stockwell, *In Search of Enemies: A CIA Story* (New York: W. W. Norton, 1978), p. 107; Thomas Powers, *The Man Who Kept the Secrets: Richard Helms and the CIA* (New York: Knopf, 1974), p. 189.

46. Steven Weissman and Herbert Krosney, *The Islamic Bomb* (New York: Times Books, 1981), p. 151.

47. Marchetti and Marks, *The CIA and the Cult of Intelligence*, p. 189.

48. E. Howard Hunt, *Undercover: Memoirs of an American Secret Agent* (New York: Berkley, 1974), pp. 80, 126; Philip Agee, *Inside the Company: A CIA Diary* (New York: Stonehill, 1975), pp. 346–347.

49. "Weekly Notes," *Washington Times*, April 16, 1997, p. A10; "Intelligence Monitor," *Jane's Intelligence Review*, July 1997, p. 336; Tim Weiner, "U.S. Diplomat Leaves Austria After Being Caught Wiretapping," *New York Times*, November 6, 1997, p. A10.

50. Steve Emerson, *Secret Warriors: Inside the Covert Military Operations of the Reagan Era* (New York: Putnam, 1988), p. 111.

51. Ibid., p. 112.

52. Ibid., p. 116.

53. John Pomfret, "China Finds Bugs on Jet Equipped in U.S.," *Washington Post*, January 19, 2002, pp. A1, A21; James Risen and Erich Lichtblau, "Spy Suspect May Have Told Chinese of Bugs, U.S. Says," *New York Times*, April 15, 2002, p. A12.

54. Robert Wallace and H. Keith Mellon, *Spycraft: The Secret History of the CIA's Spytechs from Communism to Al-Qaeda* (New York: Dutton, 2008), p. 138; Pete Earley, *Confessions of a Spy: The Real Story of Aldrich Ames* (New York: Putnam, 1997), pp. 19, 117, 197.

55. Marchetti and Marks, *The CIA and the Cult of Intelligence*, pp. 190–191.

56. Stansfield Turner, *Secrecy and Democracy: The CIA in Transition* (Boston: Houghton Mifflin, 1985), pp. 59–60.

57. Jeffrey T. Richelson, *The Wizards of Langley: Inside the CIA's Directorate of Science and Technology* (Boulder, Colo.: Westview, 2001), p. 93.

58. Naval Intelligence Command, *Naval Intelligence Command (NAVTINTCOM) History for CY-1975, Basic Narrative*, 1976, p. 18.

59. Interview; "Seismic Sensors," *Intelligence Newsletter*, January 17, 1990, p. 2.

60. Lt. Gen. Nikolai Brusnitsin, Openness and Espionage (Moscow, 1990), p. 15; NBC, *Inside the KGB: Narration and Shooting Script*, May 1993, p. 39.

61. Barbara Starr, "Super Sensors Will Eye the New Proliferation Frontier," *Jane's Defence Weekly*, June 4, 1994, p. 19.

62. Matthew M. Aid, "All Glory Is Fleeting: Sigint and the Fight Against International Terrorism," *Intelligence and National Security* 18, 4 (Winter 2003): 72–120; Barton Gellman, "Broad Effort Launched After '98 Attacks," *Washington Post*, December 19, 2001, pp. A1, A26.

63. Jeremy Grant, "U.S. Military 'Rocks' Spy World," www.FT.com, May 26, 2005.

64. Ronald Reagan, National Security Decision Directive 112, "Processing and Disposition of Documents Acquired by U.S. Forces in Grenada," November 15, 1983.

65. John Horton, National Intelligence Officer for Latin America, Memorandum for: Director of Central Intelligence, Subject: Grenada: Exploitation Status Report, January 10, 1984.

66. Interagency Intelligence Assessment, *Grenada: A First Look at Mechanisms of Control and Foreign Involvement*, December 19, 1983; Director of Central Intelligence, *Grenada: A First Look at Mechanisms of Control and Foreign Involvement*, Interagency Intelligence Assessment Memorandum to Holders of NIC M 83–10021, August 20, 1984, p. 1.

67. Director of Central Intelligence, *Grenada: A First Look at Mechanisms of Control and Foreign Involvement*, Interagency Intelligence Assessment Memorandum to Holders of NIC M 83–10021, pp. 3–14.

68. Gary Bernsten and Ralph Pezzullo, *JAWBREAKER—The Attack on Bin Laden and Al-Qaeda: A Personal Account by the CIA's Key Commander* (New York: Crown, 2005), pp. 206, 294, 303–304; Joby Warrick, "Suspect and a Setback in Al-Qaeda Anthrax Case," www.washingtonpost.com, October 11, 2006.

69. Alan Cullison, "Inside Al-Qaeda's Hard Drive," *Atlantic Monthly*, September 2004, www.theatlantic.com.

70. Ibid.; Mike Boettcher and Ingrid Arnesen, "Al Qaeda Documents Outline Serious Weapons," www.CNN.com, January 25, 2002.

71. Robin Wright and Nancy Trejos, "U.S. Troops Raid 2 Iranian Targets in Iraq, Detain 5 People," www.washingtonpost.com, January 12, 2007.

72. Alexei Barrioneuvo, "U.S. Studies Rebels' Data for Chavez Link," *New York Times*, March 14, 2008, p. A8; José de Cordoba and Jay Solomon, "Chavez Aided Colombia Rebels, Captured Computer Files Show," *Wall Street Journal*, May 9, 2008, pp. A1, A13; José de Cordoba and David Gauthier-Villars, "Interpol Says Colombia Didn't Alter Seized Files," *Wall Street Journal*, May 16, 2008, p. A5.

73. AR 381–26, *Army Foreign Materiel Exploitation Program*, March 6, 1987, p. 3.

74. John Barron, *The KGB Today: The Hidden Hand* (New York: Reader's Digest, 1983), pp. 233–234; *Statement of Facts, United States of America v. David Henry Barnett, K 80–0390*, United States District Court, Maryland, 1980.

75. "What the U.S. Lost in Iran," *Newsweek*, December 28, 1981, pp. 33–34.

76. William J. Eaton, "CIA Reportedly Caught Buying Indian Military Secrets," *Los Angeles Times*, December 15, 1983, p. 4.

77. Emerson, *Secret Warriors*, p. 185; Michael Wines and Richard E. Meyer, "North Apparently Tried a Swap for Soviet Tank," *Washington Post*, January 22, 1987, p. A37; Richard Halloran, "U.S. Has Acquired a T-72 Tank," *New York Times*, March 13, 1987, p. A12; Benjamin Weiser, "One That Got Away: Romanians Were Ready to Sell Soviet Tank," *Washington Post*, May 6, 1990, p. A30.

78. John Barron, *MiG Pilot* (New York: Avon, 1981), pp. 172–173.

79. Ibid.

80. Foreign Technology Division, *FTD 1917–1967* (Dayton, Ohio: FTD, 1967), p. 24; Steve Davies, *Red Eagles: America's Secret MiGs* (New York: Osprey, 2008), p. 18.

81. David Fulghum, "MiGs in Nevada," *Aviation Week & Space Technology*, November 27, 2006, p. 69; Peter Grier, "Constant Peg," *Air Force Magazine*, April 2007, pp. 86–89; Davies, *Red Eagles: America's Secret MiGs.*

82. Benjamin Weiser, "Ceauşescu Family Sold Military Secrets to U.S.," *Washington Post*, May 6, 1990, pp. A1, A30.

83. Air Force Office of the Assistant Chief of Staff, Intelligence, *History, Directorate of Collection, AFNIC, 1 July–31 December 1968*, pp. 250–251. Also see James David, "Was It Really 'Space Junk'? U.S. Intelligence Interest in Space Debris That Returned to Earth," *Astropolitics* 3, 1 (Spring 2005): 43–65.

84. [Deleted], "Project AZORIAN: The Story of the Hughes Glomar Explorer," *Studies in Intelligence* 29, 3 (Fall 1985); Norman Polmar and Michael White, *Project AZORIAN: The CIA and the Raising of the K-129* (Annapolis, Md.: Naval Institute Press, 2010); "The Great Submarine Snatch," *Time*, March 31, 1975, pp. 20–27; William J. Broad, "Russia Says U.S. Got Sub's Atom Arms," *New York Times*, June 30, 1993, p. 4; "CIA Raising USSR Sub Raises Questions," *FBIS-SOV-92-145*, July 28, 1992, pp. 15–16.

85. Roy Varner and Wayne Collier, *A Matter of Risk* (New York: Random House, 1977), p. 26; Willard Bascom, *The Crest of the Wave: Adventures in Oceanography* (New York: Harper & Row, 1988), pp. 241–242; William J. Broad, *The Universe Below: Discovering the Secrets of the Deep Sea* (New York: Simon & Schuster, 1996), pp. 69–70.

86. Naval Intelligence Command, *Naval Intelligence Command History for CY-1973*, April 29, 1974, p. 20.

87. U.S. Army Intelligence and Security Command, *Annual Historical Review, FY 1983*, September 1984, p. 72.

88. James Bruce, "CIA Acquires Soviet MI-24 and T-72," *Jane's Defence Weekly*, March 28, 1987, p. 535; James Brooke, "Chad Reaps a Windfall in War Booty," *New York Times*, August 17, 1987, p. A4; Brig. Gen. Harry E. Soyster, Acting ACS for Intelligence, Memorandum Thru Director, Defense Intelligence Agency, for Deputy Under Secretary of Defense (Policy), Subject: Possible Acquisition Opportunity (U)—Action Memorandum, April 11, 1983; Gen. Richard O. Stilwell (Ret.), Deputy Undersecretary of Defense (Policy), Memorandum for the Assistant Chief of Staff for Intelligence, Department of the Army, [day and month illegible], 1983.

89. *Statement of Rear Admiral Thomas A. Brooks, USN, Director of Naval Intelligence*, Before the Seapower, Strategic, and Critical Materials Subcommittee of the House Armed Services Committee on Intelligence Issues, March 7, 1991, p. 36; Paul Quinn-Judge, "CIA Buys Ex-Soviet Arms, US Aide Says," *Boston Globe*, November 15, 1992, pp. 1, 14; Bill Gertz, "Soviets Flee with Secrets," *Washington Times*, January 1, 1991, pp. A1, A6; "World Military Aircraft Inventory," *Aviation Week & Space Technology*, January 12, 1998, pp. 222–238.

90. National Air and Space Intelligence Center, "Have Nose," www.wpafb.af.mil/naic/havenose.html, accessed February 12, 2006; Rob Young, "NAIC Donates MiG-23 to AF Museum," Spokesman, September 1999, p. 4.

91. National Air and Space Intelligence Center, "MiG-29 Purchase," www.wpafb.af.mil/naic/mig29s.html, accessed February 12, 2006; National Air and Space Intelligence Center, "Blue 62," www.wpafb.af.mil/naic/blue62.html, accessed February 12, 2006; Steven Lee Myers, "U.S. Is Buying MiG's So Rogue Nations Will Not Get Them," *New York Times*,

November 5, 1997, pp. A1, A6; David A. Fulghum, "Moldovan MiG-29s to Fly for USAF," *Aviation Week & Space Technology*, November 10, 1997, pp. 37–38; Brian Barr and Rob Young, "Russian Aircraft Cross Borders: Moldovan MiGs Call NAIC Home," *Spokesman*, January 1998, pp. 4–5.

92. Bill Gertz and Rowan Scarborough, "Inside the Ring," *Washington Times*, September 3, 1999, p. A6.

93. Quinn-Judge, "CIA Buys Ex-Soviet Arms, US Aide Says."

94. Richard H.P. Sia, "U.S. Army Gets Soviet Weapons from Germany," *Philadelphia Inquirer*, May 5, 1991, p. 14-E.

95. Nikolay Novichkov and Michael A. Dornheim, "Russian SA-12, SA-10 on World ATBM Market," *Aviation Week & Space Technology*, March 3, 1997, p. 59; David Hughes, "U.S. Army to Assess Russian SA-10 SAM System," *Aviation Week & Space Technology*, January 2, 1995, p. 60; Jeff Gerth, "In a Furtive, Frantic Market, America Buys Russian Arms," *New York Times*, December 24, 1994, pp. 1, 7; Barbara Starr, "USA Fields 'Scuds' to Test Theatre Missile Defense," *Jane's Defence Weekly*, May 7, 1997, p. 3.

13

COOPERATION WITH FOREIGN SERVICES

Despite its huge investments in technical and human intelligence, the United States relies on liaison arrangements and cooperative agreements with foreign intelligence and security services for a significant portion of its intelligence. As then Defense Secretary Caspar Weinberger explained in 1985: "The United States has neither the opportunity nor the resources to unilaterally collect all the intelligence information we require. We compensate with a variety of intelligence sharing arrangements with other nations in the world."[1]

The United States can benefit in several ways with respect to such arrangements and liaison relationships. The ability to monitor events in a foreign country can be enhanced because an ally is particularly well situated to conduct a variety of technical collection operations against the target. The United States has often helped establish collection sites, in exchange for access to the information collected. In the case of nations where the United States has no diplomatic representation, allied intelligence services can run agents on behalf of the United States. Allies can also provide additional manpower to collect or process intelligence, particularly the vast quantities of intelligence produced by technical collection systems. In addition, the commentary and analysis presented by allied analysts can improve understanding of foreign developments.[2]

At the same time, there are several risks involved in such arrangements. The cooperating service may be penetrated by an adversary, and the information provided by the United States might wind up in an adversary's hands. For example, in the 1970s the product of the U.S. CANYON COMINT satellite was provided to the U.K., which in turn provided translators to process the vast quantity of intercept material. One of those involved in the translation effort was also reporting to Soviet military intelligence. Reliance on a liaison relationship may also allow the partner insights into the collection techniques employed against it—as when one article in an NSA journal referred to Third Parties (to the UKUSA Agreement) as "allies and targets." Alternatively, the partner may provide a skewed view of reality to the United States in an attempt to influence decisions in accord with its preferences. In addition, the presence of U.S. collection facilities in a country may tempt that nation to use those facilities as a means of blackmail or retaliation—as when Turkey shut down U.S. missile monitoring facilities in the mid-1970s in a dispute with the United States over arms sales. Finally, the cooperating nation may be both cooperating to some extent but also providing data on U.S. operations to American targets—as the Pakistani Inter-Services Intelligence has been accused of doing.[3]

Some arrangements are long-standing and highly formalized and involve the most sensitive forms of intelligence collection. Others are less wide-ranging and reflect limited common interests between the United States and particular nations. In addition, exchange arrangements may involve different components of the intelligence communities in the United States and other nations. Whereas some arrangements may involve links between the CIA and a nation's counterpart agency, others may involve cooperation between the NSA, DIA, or ONI and their foreign counterparts.

The most important arrangements are the multilateral and bilateral arrangements between the United States and the United Kingdom, Australia, Canada, and New Zealand concerning the collection and distribution of signals intelligence and ocean surveillance data. In addition, the creation and growth of geospatial intelligence organizations in United Kingdom, Australia, and Canada has created an expanded pool of imagery interpreters available to exploit the imagery produced by U.S. electro-optical and radar imagery satellites. This extensive five-nation relationship has resulted, in recent years, in the creation of the dissemination category "FIVE EYES"—as in "REL TO FVEY (RELEASE TO FIVE EYES)."

The United States is also involved in intelligence sharing and cooperation, to varying degrees, with Germany, Israel, Japan, Jordan, Mexico, Peru, and Pakistan. In addition, the United States provides intelligence support to the United Nations and the International Atomic Energy Agency.

FIVE EYES

The U.S.-British military alliance in World War II necessitated a high degree of cooperation with respect to intelligence activities. It was imperative that the United States and Britain, as the main allied combatants in the European and Pacific theaters, establish a coordinated effort in the acquisition of worldwide intelligence and its evaluation and distribution.

The most important aspect of that cooperation was in the area of signals intelligence. An apparently limited agreement on SIGINT cooperation was reached in December 1940. That was followed by the visit of four U.S. officers, including two members of the Army Signal Intelligence Service, to the British Government Code and Cipher School in January 1941. In June of that year the United States and Britain agreed to exchange signals intelligence concerning Japan. But it was not until October 2, 1942, that the United States and Britain signed an agreement for extensive cooperation in the area of naval SIGINT. That was followed by a May 17, 1943, agreement generally known as the British-U.S. Communications Intelligence Agreement (BRUSA), which provided for extensive cooperation between the U.S. Army's

SIGINT agency and the British Code and Cypher School. SIGINT cooperation also included Canada, Australia, and New Zealand.[4]

The intelligence relationships among Australia, Britain, Canada, New Zealand, and the United States that were forged during World War II did not end with the war. Rather, they became formalized and grew stronger. At about the time World War II ended, the already ongoing cooperation between the United States and the United Kingdom to target and exploit Soviet communications was assigned the code name BOURBON. On March 5, 1946, the United States and Britain signed the British-U.S. Communications Intelligence Agreement, which absorbed the BOURBON effort. Both countries agreed to exchange the products of the operations relating to the collection of foreign communications traffic, the acquisition of communications documents and equipment, traffic analysis, cryptanalysis, and acquisition of information regarding communications organizations—their practices, procedures, and equipment. The agreement stipulated that the exchange would be unrestricted except for specific exclusions at the request of either party.[5]

The agreement also specified the terms of any interaction with Third Parties, defined as all individuals or authorities other than those of the United States, the British Empire, and the British Dominions. Specifically, it was agreed that "each party will seek the agreement of the other to any action with third parties, and will take no such action until its advisability is agreed upon" and that "each party will ensure that the results of any such action are made available to the other."[6]

In 1954, at the behest of the British, U.S. bilateral SIGINT relationships with Britain and Canada developed into the UKUSA Agreement, also known as the UKUSA Security Agreement or "Secret Treaty." The primary emphasis of the agreement was to provide a division of SIGINT collection responsibilities between the First Party (the United States) and the Second Parties (Australia, Britain, Canada, and New Zealand).* The specific agencies now involved are the National Security Agency, the Australian Defence Signals Directorate (DSD), the British Government Communications Headquarters (GCHQ), the Canadian Communications Security Establishment (CSE), and the New Zealand Government Communications Security Bureau (GCSB).[7]

Under the present division of responsibilities, the United States is responsible for SIGINT in Latin America, most of Asia, Russia, and northern China. Australia's area of responsibility includes its neighbors (such as Indonesia), southern China, and the nations of Indochina. Britain is responsible for Africa and the former Soviet Union west of the Urals. The polar regions of Russia are the responsibility of Canada, and New Zealand's area of responsibility is the Western Pacific. Specific tasking assignments are specified in the SIGINT Combined Operating List.[8]

Britain's geographical position gives it a significant capability for long-range SIGINT collection against certain targets in Russia and former Soviet states such as

---

*Third Parties to the treaty have included Austria, Thailand, Japan, South Korea, Norway, Denmark, Germany, Italy, Greece, and Turkey.

the Ukraine. Britain's historical role in Africa led to its assumption of SIGINT responsibility for that area. Canada's responsibility for northern Russia stems from its geographical location, which gives it "unique access to communications in . . . northern [Russia]." The areas of responsibility for Australia and New Zealand clearly result from their geographical location.[9]

The UKUSA component of the FIVE EYES relationship is more than an agreement to coordinate separately conducted intelligence activities and share the intelligence collected. Rather, it is cemented by the presence of U.S. facilities on British, Canadian, and Australian territory; by joint operations (U.S.-U.K., Australian-U.S., and U.K.-Australian) within and outside UKUSA territory; and, in the case of Australia, by the presence of U.K. and U.S. staff at DSD facilities.[10]

In addition to specifying SIGINT collection responsibilities, the agreement addresses access to the collected intelligence and security arrangements for the handling of data. Standardized code words (e.g., in the past, UMBRA for the highest-level signals intelligence), security agreements that all employees of the respective SIGINT agencies must sign, and procedures for storing and disseminating code-word material are all implemented under terms of the agreement.[11]

Thus, in 1967, the "COMINT Indoctrination" declaration, which all British-cleared personnel had to sign, included in the first paragraph the statement "I declare that I fully understand the information relating to the manner and extent of the interception of communications of foreign powers by H. M. Government and *other cooperating Governments*, and intelligence produced by such interception known as Communications Intelligence (COMINT) is information covered by Section 2 of the Official Secrets Act 1911 (as amended)" (emphasis added). The requirements for standardized code words (see Chapter 19), security arrangements, and procedures for the handling and dissemination of SIGINT material are detailed in a series of International Regulations on SIGINT (IRSIG) that was in its third edition as of 1967.[12]

In one case, U.S.-Canadian-British cooperation in the SIGINT area was the result of a U.S. inability to process the data produced by a U.S. COMINT satellite program. The CANYON program commenced operations with a launch in April 1968 and was followed by five additional successful launches through 1977. The satellites produced such a heavy volume of intercepted communications that the United States recruited the British and Canadian SIGINT agencies to help in the processing, thus granting those two nations access to the intercepted communications. However, one of the individuals assigned by the British to work on the processing of the intercepts was Geoffrey Prime, who also reported to Soviet intelligence.[13]

One of the best examples of UKUSA cooperation is the ECHELON program. As noted in Chapter 8, despite press reports to the contrary, ECHELON is not the overall UKUSA collection program but one limited to the interception of the traffic through selected civilian communication satellites, particularly the INTELSAT spacecraft in geosynchronous orbit. The computer dictionaries at each site search intercepted material for key words submitted by analysts from each of the UKUSA partners, and intercepts that contain those key words are automatically forwarded to those analysts. In addition to the U.S. intercept facilities that are part of the ECHE-LON network, there are ECHELON stations operated by the DSD (at Geraldton, Australia, which targets communications concerning the North Korean military, Pakistani nuclear weapons technology, and Japanese trade ministry plans), the CSE (at Leitrim, which apparently targets Latin American communications), the GCHQ (at Morwenstow, near Bude, Cornwall), and the GCSB (at Waihopai).[14]

As of yet, there is no similar agreement with regard to space SIGINT, as the United States is still the only UKUSA nation with a space SIGINT capability. In the case of Britain, the decision to cancel an indigenous SIGINT satellite program, code-named ZIRCON, was followed by a February 1987 decision to purchase a share in the ORION system at the cost of $750 million. ZIRCON had originally been conceived by GCHQ director Brian Tovey "to keep the special relationship sweet and to take his organization into space."[15]

With regard to ocean surveillance, cooperation exists on a level similar to that in the SIGINT area, with British and Australian stations feeding into the U.S. Ocean Surveillance Information System (OSIS). Several Australian stations contribute significantly to OSIS. Those stations are located at Pearce, Western Australia; Cabarlah, Queensland; and Shoal Bay, New Territories. The Cabarlah station on the east coast of Australia is operated by the DSD, and its main function is monitoring transmissions through the Southwest Pacific. The Pearce station has as its primary purpose the monitoring of naval and air traffic over the Indian Ocean. In the early 1980s, a Pusher antenna was installed for the purpose of intercepting, monitoring, direction finding, and analyzing radio signals in a portion of the HF band.[16]

The most important station for monitoring the Southeast Asian area is the DSD station at Darwin (Shoal Bay), which originally had a very limited direction-finding capability. However, contracts signed in 1981 provided for the procurement of modern DF equipment to enable the station to "participate fully in the OSIS." Canadian stations at Halifax and a joint U.S.-British station on Ascension Island (which monitors naval traffic in the South Atlantic) contribute to the monitoring of naval movements in the Atlantic Ocean.[17]

Overhead maritime surveillance is the subject of the 1977 agreement among Australia, New Zealand, and the United States, the Agreement for the Coordination of Maritime Surveillance and Reconnaissance, in the South-Southwest Pacific and Eastern Indian Oceans.[18]

In addition to cooperating on collection activities, the UKUSA nations are involved in cooperative arrangements concerning defense intelligence analysis, holding periodic conferences dealing with a wide range of scientific and defense intelligence matters. Thus, U.S. analysts have participated in the Annual Land Warfare Technical Intelligence Conference, the International Scientific Intelligence Exchange, the Quadripartite Intelligence Working Party on Chinese Guided Missiles, and the Tripartite Defense Intelligence Estimates Conference.[19]

U.S., Canadian, and U.K. representatives regularly attend the Annual CANUKUS Maritime Intelligence Conference. Air Force intelligence representatives from each nation have also met to examine topics such as Soviet surface-to-air missiles. In addition, U.S. and U.K. military intelligence representatives have participated in the U.S./U.K. Chemical Warfare Intelligence Conference and the U.S./U.K. Armor Conference (held at the CIA).[20]

The National Center for Medical Intelligence Center (formerly the Armed Forces Medical Intelligence Center) is involved in medical intelligence exchanges with Australia, Canada, and the United Kingdom through the Quadripartite Medical Intelligence Exchange (QMIX), which maintains its own website. NCMI is a member of the Quadripartite Medical Intelligence Committee. Other members include the Canadian and U.S. medical liaison officers and the Australian scientific attaché.[21]

In 1974, a senior U.S. intelligence official wrote, with respect to U.S. participation in the Quadripartite Medical Intelligence Exchange: "I believe that an objective study would show that the U.S. is ahead of the game, keeping [deleted] analysts informed of activities here allows them to channel their work into more productive areas. And, in spite of the small size of the [deleted] intelligence groups, they keep coming up with nuggets in the form of unique analysis which have been very helpful to us."[22]

The UKUSA nations also cooperate in matters of counterintelligence and counterterrorism. Beginning in the 1950s, representatives of the United States, Canada, Australia, New Zealand, and the United States met every eighteen months for a week-long conference on counterintelligence matters of common interest. Subjects have included joint operations, research of old cases, investigation of penetrations, assessment of defectors, and technical and communications advances.[23]

Another example of cooperation among four of the five UKUSA nations is STONE GHOST—a "database comprised of worldwide intelligence products, applications, databases and services." STONE GHOST's infrastructure comprises more than thirty-eight U.S. Intelligence Community servers and sites (including ones operated by the CIA, the Department of Homeland Security, and the combatant commands), as well as sites operated by the participating nations' military intelligence organizations. This database operates at the Top Secret/Special Intelligence level and is accessible to cleared individuals in the United States, Australia, Canada, and the United Kingdom.[24]

AUSTRALIA

In addition to their participation in UKUSA activities, each of the member nations has bilateral exchange programs with the United States. One consequence of Australian participation in Operation Iraqi Freedom and its aftermath was an increased sharing of intelligence. In late August 2005, the Australian Minister of Defence stated, "In recent years, we have obtained unprecedented access to U.S. intelligence and tactical planning."[25]

For a number of years, Australia has had access to U.S. satellite imagery, which could be exploited by imagery interpreters employed by the Defence Intelligence

Organization (DIO). The risks of sharing such information were illustrated in May 1999, when a former employee of the DIO, Jean-Philippe Wispelaere, was arrested after he disembarked from his flight from London to Washington. He was charged with trying to sell a variety of documents to an unspecified foreign government, through its embassy in Bangkok—claiming to be an employee of the National Imagery and Mapping Agency, presumably to both hide his identity and explain how he was in possession of the overhead imagery.[26]

Despite that incident, it is likely that U.S. provision of imagery has increased in subsequent years—in part because of an even greater general sharing of intelligence but also due to Australia's creation of a new agency along the lines of NGA. In 1998, the imagery intelligence function was separated from the DIO and placed in the newly established Australian Imagery Organization (AIO). AIO developed the ability to exploit digital imagery—of the sort returned by U.S. electro-optical imagery satellites. In November 2000, after the completion of an Australian government study, AIO was merged with other military units to form the Defense Imagery and Geospatial Organisation (DIGO).[27]

Given the growing expertise in geospatial intelligence, the creation of a counterpart organization in NIMA/NGA, the Australian involvement in Iraq and Afghanistan, and the increasing number of images produced by NRO satellites, it is highly likely that the United States has provided an increasing number of images to Australia—to analyze for its own intelligence purposes as well as for those of the U.S. Intelligence Community.

U.S.-Australian intelligence cooperation also extends to the sharing of space surveillance data. On November 8, 2010, Secretary of Defense Robert Gates and Minister for Defence Stephen Smith signed the "Australian–United States Space Situational Awareness Partnership Statement of Principles." The statement called for the two nations to "investigate the potential for jointly establishing and operating space situational awareness facilities in Australia to support the United States space surveillance network and to support the development of Australia's space situational awareness." It also calls for both nations to share space situational awareness information and technical data.* Talks were scheduled to begin in January 2011 about placement of U.S. Space Fence sites in Australia.[28]

CANADA

Canada and the United States have signed a variety of bilateral intelligence arrangements and have worked together on a number of projects. U.S.-Canadian joint estimates produced in the late 1950s focused on Soviet capabilities and likely actions in the event of a major Soviet attack on North America. Those documents considered

---

*In February 2011 the United States also assigned a preliminary agreement with France on cooperation in space situational awareness. See Peter B. de Selding, "France, U.S. Sign Agreement for Space Surveillance Cooperation," *Space News*, February 14, 2011, p. A2.

factors such as Communist bloc political stability and economic support; the internal threat to North America; Soviet weapons of mass destruction; aircraft, including bombers, transport aircraft, and tanker aircraft; guided missiles; naval weapons; electronics; ground, naval, and surface strength and combat effectiveness; Soviet worldwide strategy; and Soviet capabilities to conduct air and airborne missile, naval amphibious, and internal operations against North America. Preparation of such estimates continued on a yearly basis, at least into the 1980s, under the title *Canadian–United States Intelligence Estimate of the Military Threat to North America.*[29]

In March 1966, the United States and Canada signed the *Canadian–United States Communications Instructions for Reporting Vital Intelligence Sightings* (CIRVIS/MERINT). That agreement specified the type of information to be reported by airborne or land-borne observers, which included the following:

- hostile or unidentified single aircraft or formations of aircraft that appear to be directed against the United States or Canada or their forces
- missiles
- unidentified flying objects
- hostile or unidentified submarines
- hostile or unidentified groups of military vessels
- individual surface vessels, submarines, or aircraft of unconventional design, or engaged in suspicious activity, or observed in a location or on a course that may be interpreted as constituting a threat to the United States, Canada, or their forces
- any unexplained or unusual activity that may indicate a possible attack against or through Canada or the United States, including the presence of any unidentified or other suspicious ground parties in the Polar Region or other remote or sparsely populated areas.[30]

The agreement also specified eleven types of information that should be provided in any MERINT report, including a description of the object sighted (covering each of nine different aspects of the object), a description of the course of the object and the manner of observation, and information on weather and wind conditions.[31]

Furthermore, the agreement specified that seaborne vessels submit MERINT reports concerning such topics as

- the movement of unidentified aircraft (single or in formation)
- missile firings
- the movement of . . . unidentified submarines
- the movement of . . . unidentified groups of surface combatants
- any airborne, seaborne, ballistic, or orbiting objects that the observers feels may constitute a military threat against the United States or Canada or may be of interest to military and civilian government officials

- individual surface ships, submarines, or aircraft of unconventional design or engaged in suspicious activities or observed in unusual locations
- any unexplained or unusual activity that may indicate a possible attack against or through the United States or Canada, including the presence of any unidentified or suspicious ground parties in the Polar Region or other remote or sparsely populated areas.[32]

Canada's SIGINT relationship with the United States is defined by the CANUS Agreement (as well as the UKUSA Agreement), which was initially drafted more than six decades ago. On September 15, 1950, Canada and the United States exchanged letters giving formal recognition to the *Security Agreement Between Canada and the United States of America* (which was followed exactly two months later by the *Arrangement for the Exchange of Information Between the U.S., U.K., and Canada*).[33]

Negotiations for the CANUS Agreement had been taking place since at least 1948. There was some concern on the part of U.S. intelligence officials that original drafts of the agreement provided for too much exchange. Thus, a 1948 memorandum by the Air Force's Acting Director of Intelligence noted that one paragraph of the proposed agreement "was not sufficiently restrictive. In effect, it provides for complete exchange of information. Not only is it considered that the Canadians will reap all the benefits of complete exchange but wider dissemination of the information. It is believed that the exchange should be related to mutually agreed COMINT activities on a 'need to know' basis."[34]

In the 1970s, U.S.-Canadian SIGINT cooperation led the Canadian SIGINT organization to conduct a feasibility study of embassy-based eavesdropping operations. The overall program, code-named PILGRIM, involved eavesdropping operations in India, China, Venezuela, Mexico, the Soviet Union, Romania, Morocco, Jamaica, and the Ivory Coast. More recently, Canada provided the United States with an intelligence assessment based on communications intelligence concerning Afghanistan: "Afghanistan: Taliban Challenges, Regional Concerns," dated October 17, 1996.[35]

Officers from the Canadian Security Intelligence Service (CSIS) have also gathered intelligence on the ground in Afghanistan—playing "a crucial and long-standing role as interrogators of a vast swath of captured Taliban fighters," according to a Canadian press account. While the primary focus of the interrogations would be on threats to Canadian troops in Afghanistan, such information would also be of interest to the CIA and other U.S. intelligence organizations. The Canadian Minister of Defence acknowledged that both Afghan officials and NATO were kept informed.[36]

Canada has also been a partner in the Sound Surveillance System (SOSUS), first becoming involved when one of its first naval facilities, in Shelburne, Nova Scotia, opened. In 1972, Canada expanded its role in SOSUS and sent a small detachment to work with U.S. personnel at the U.S. Naval Facility at Argentia, Newfoundland. By the early 1980s, it had expanded its capabilities and Canadian participation had grown, with additional Canadian Forces personnel being assigned to the Naval

Ocean Processing Facility at Dam Neck, Virginia, the Naval Facility at Bermuda, and at Headquarters, Commander, Underseas Surveillance Pacific, Ford Island, Hawaii. A Canadian detachment was also formed at the Whidbey Island Naval Facility. In 1994, the Canadian Offshore Surveillance Center at Halifax, Nova Scotia, opened to process all acoustic information gathered in Argentia.[37]

Along with Australia, the U.K., and Germany, Canada has established an agency for imagery interpretation—the Canadian Forces Joint Imagery Centre (CFJIC). On June 21, 2001, CFJIC was formed from the merger of the Canadian Forces Photographic Unit and the imagery intelligence component of the then Director General of Intelligence. CFJIC apparently provided assistance to NGA with respect to imagery interpretation related to Hurricane Katrina disaster relief. Two CFJIC Liaison Officers were stationed at NGA headquarters by 2006.[38]

The CFJIC was brought together with the Canadian Mapping and Charting Establishment and other organizations into the Directorate of Geospatial Intelligence, which provided assistance to NGA in its response to the 2010 earthquake in Haiti.[39]

Canada is also planning to provide the United States with space surveillance data. Launch of a satellite, designated Sapphire, is scheduled for July 2011. The satellite's ground element, the Satellite Sensor Systems Operations Centre, "will function as the interface between the Sapphire system and the U.S. Joint Space Operations Center."[40]

GERMANY

Germany's foreign intelligence service, the BND or Bundesnachrichtendienst (Federal Intelligence Service), began life in the aftermath of World War II as the Gehlen Organization—run by Reinhard Gehlen, the former head of Hitler's Foreign Armies East, who reported to the CIA. With West Germany's transition from an occupied country to an independent state, the Gehlen Organization became the BND.[41]

In 2003, despite Germany's opposition to the U.S. invasion of Iraq, the BND provided intelligence to the United States in support of the military effort—although exactly how much has been a matter of dispute. According to one account, on April 7, 2003, German military intelligence operatives who had been dispatched to Baghdad before the war drove by a chicken restaurant in the city's well-to-do Mansour district and noticed a convoy of armored vehicles similar to those used by Saddam Hussein. The information was passed from the BND to the Defense Intelligence Agency and served as the catalyst for a B-1 strike on the site, which occurred less than forty-five minutes later.* While the strike killed at least a dozen people, none of them were Saddam Hussein or his two sons as had been hoped.[42]

German intelligence assistance, through its intelligence officers in Baghdad, also involved the provision of coordinates of civilian sites, including hospitals, foreign

---

*This is one of the allegations denied by German officials—in this case, the foreign minister. See Jeffrey Fleishman, "Official Denies Germany Aided U.S. in Iraq War," *Los Angeles Times*, January 21, 2006, p. A7.

embassies, and places of worship, so that they would not be hit in U.S. air attacks. They also provided information on the possible location of a missing U.S. pilot. [43]

Furthermore, according to an account in the *New York Times*, German intelligence personnel in Baghdad provided a copy of Saddam Hussein's plan for the defense of Baghdad, which gave the United States "an extraordinary window into Iraq's top-level deliberations, including where and how Mr. Hussein planned to deploy his most loyal troops."* The plan had been unveiled at a December 18, 2002, strategy session that included Hussein and his commanders. In February 2003, a German intelligence officer serving as a representative to the Central Command in Qatar provided the plan to a DIA official who worked at the command. [44]

That liaison officer provided twenty-five reports to the United States, which answered eighteen of thirty-three specific requests for information made during the first few months of the Iraq war in what was "a systematic exchange" between U.S. intelligence officials and the Germans. Eight of the reports concerned the mood and provisioning of the residents of Baghdad, while another eight focused on the nature of the military and police presence in the city. Two reports provided coordinates of military forces. [45]

A less controversial aspect of U.S.-German intelligence cooperation concerns geospatial intelligence—specifically, the cooperation between NGA and the Bundeswehr Geoinformation Office (BGIO). In 1994, the BGIO began exchanging topographic products with the Defense Mapping Agency—two years before DMA was absorbed by the National Imagery and Mapping Agency. [46]

In 2000, the director of the BGIO decided that Germany should expand its role as a provider of international geopspatial data, which required the office to build a new production facility in Euskirchen, Germany. With support from NIMA, BGIO established a test bed to develop and test digital production processes. In February 2001, NIMA and BGIO expanded their geospatial coproduction relationship. On September 15, 2004, NGA and BGIO signed an agreement to promote greater exchange, and as a result, BGIO sent digital data to NGA for inclusion in the agency's Geospatial Intelligence Feature Database (GIFD). In the spring of 2008, a BGIO liaison officer position was established at NGA's facility in Reston, Virginia. In April 2009, NGA officials met with BND officials to discuss Germany's plans for expansion of its satellite reconnaissance effort. [47]

ISRAEL

One of the strongest Western intelligence links is that between the United States and Israel. These arrangements involve the Mossad (the Central Institute for Intelligence and Special Tasks), AMAN (the Israeli Defense Forces Intelligence Branch) and its

---

*Germany also denied this assertion, which is based on a classified report by the Joint Forces Command. See Richard Bernstein and Judy Dempsey, "Germany Denies Giving U.S. Iraq's Plan to Defend Baghdad," *New York Times*, February 28, 2006, p. A9.

Unit 8200 (responsible for SIGINT), and a variety of U.S. intelligence agencies—the CIA, the FBI, the DIA, the NSA, the National Air and Space Intelligence Center, and the National Ground Intelligence Center.

The intelligence liaison between the United States and Israel dates back to 1951, when Prime Minister David Ben-Gurion arrived in the United States for a fund-raising drive. Ben-Gurion also paid an unpublicized visit to DCI Walter Bedell Smith and his deputy, Allen Dulles. At that meeting, Ben-Gurion offered, and the CIA accepted, the concept of a liaison relationship between the U.S. and Israeli intelligence communities. In October 1951, James Jesus Angleton, then Director of the CIA's Staff A (Foreign Intelligence), arrived in Israel to establish a cooperative arrangement. Angleton continued to direct the liaison relationship with Israel until his forced retirement in 1975.[48]

Angleton had developed extensive contacts with future Israeli intelligence officials during his World War II activities in Europe with the Office of Strategic Services. In 1957, he set up a liaison unit to deal with the Mossad. This unit was responsible for producing Middle East intelligence for both services. In addition, the CIA received intelligence from Mossad networks in the Soviet Union.[49]

By the early 1970s, the United States and Israel had established a joint debriefing operation to interview émigrés from the Soviet Union. The joint operation was located in Tel Aviv under Mossad auspices, with CIA officers participating. After Angleton's dismissal as counterintelligence chief in 1975, the liaison unit was abolished, and the Israeli account was moved to the appropriate Directorate of Operations regional division of the CIA. The CIA also began to operate more independently of the Mossad and by the late 1970s was operating on the West Bank.[50]

Through this relationship with the Israeli services, the U.S. Intelligence Community gained access to Soviet weapons systems and data on their wartime performance. Such exchanges took place after the 1967 and 1973 Arab-Israeli wars. Israel furnished the United States with captured Soviet air-to-ground and ground-to-air missiles and anti-tank weapons. Also furnished were Soviet 122 and 130 mm artillery pieces, along with ammunition for evaluation and testing. Additionally, extensive joint analyses conducted after the 1973 war produced eight 200- and 300-page volumes of intelligence. These analyses influenced subsequent developments in U.S. weapons tactics and military budgets.[51]

In early 1983, the Israeli government offered to share military intelligence gained during the war in Lebanon. The offer included details of an "Israeli invention" that was alleged by Prime Minister Menachem Begin to be the key to Israel's ability to destroy Syria's Soviet-made surface-to-air missiles during the war. However, Secretary of Defense Caspar Weinberger rejected a proposed agreement for sharing that information, feeling that it would have trapped the United States into undesirable long-range commitments to Israel. Administration officials argued that the information had already been learned through normal military contacts.[52]

As a condition for sharing the information, Israel insisted on sending Israeli experts to the United States with captured weapons for U.S. analysis, stipulating that the United States share the results of the analysis. Israel also insisted on the right to veto the transfer of information and analysis to third-party countries, including members of NATO, and on measures to ensure that the data remained secret. According to diplomats, the Israelis expressed fears that Soviet intelligence agents who had penetrated Western governments would find out what Israel had learned and would then pass that information along to the Soviet Union's Arab allies. Subsequently, an agreement was reached that continued the flow of information.[53]

The CIA also obtained infantry weapons that Israel captured from the PLO, an effort designated Operation Tipped Kettle. In late 1982, DCI William Casey requested Department of Defense assistance in obtaining those weapons that Israel had captured during the Lebanon war. As a result, in May 1983, three hundred tons of weapons were provided by Israel to DOD without charge. The weapons were moved by the U.S. Navy from Israel to the United States and turned over to the CIA at dockside.[54]

In late 1983, as the situation in Lebanon deteriorated and Syrian intransigence continued, the United States conducted a reassessment of U.S. policy in the Middle East. The effort resulted in the top-secret National Security Decision Directive 111, "Next Steps Toward Progress in Lebanon and the Middle East." The directive reportedly specified a "tilt" toward Israel and expanded U.S.-Israeli strategic cooperation.[55]

The expanded cooperation reportedly involved greater sharing of satellite reconnaissance data, including data on Saudi Arabia and Jordon. William J. Casey, during his first three years as Director of Central Intelligence, provided the Israelis with access to satellite imagery and other reconnaissance data that they had been denied under the Carter administration. The head of AMAN from 1979 to 1983, Maj. Gen. Yehoshua Saguy, said in early 1984 that the CIA was providing Israel with access to data from reconnaissance satellites, and "not only the information but the photos themselves." Under the Carter administration, DCI Stansfield Turner had refused to provide the satellite imagery that had been shared during George Bush's tenure as DCI in 1976–1977.[56]

After 1981, the satellite photos were often referred to as "Casey's gifts" inside the Israeli intelligence community, and they were considered invaluable. After Israel used some of the photos to aid in targeting Iraq's Osirak reactor, and a review determined that Israel had received imagery of targets in Libya, Pakistan, and other nations a considerable distance from Israel, Deputy DCI Bobby Ray Inman restricted Israeli access to photographs of targets within 250 miles of the Israeli border.[57]

Another aspect of the expanded cooperation was reported to be greater Israeli access to the "take" of Cyprus-based SR-71 flights. The United States had been sharing such data with Israel, Egypt, and Syria on a "highly-selective basis" as a result of an agreement signed in 1974 after the October War of 1973. The information previously transmitted to Israel primarily concerned Egyptian or Syrian military developments but was not expanded to cover a "broader range." Israel did not, however, receive everything it wanted. In December 1975, Israel requested a dedicated satellite and a system of ground stations that would "directly access" the KH-11 as it passed over the Middle East.[58]

In return for intelligence from the United States, Israel supplied the United States with intelligence on the Middle East, including both reports from agents and finished intelligence analyses. Some U.S. officials were not impressed by the political intelligence, however. One CIA official said that he was "appalled at the lack of quality of the political intelligence on the Arab world. . . . Their tactical military intelligence was first rate. But they didn't know their enemy. I saw this political intelligence and it was lousy, laughably bad. . . . It was gossip stuff mostly."[59]

The United States and Israel have also exchanged intelligence during crisis situations. During the 1973 war, Israel received data obtained by the RHYOLITE satellite. In 1976, the United States supplied Israel with both aerial and satellite reconnaissance imagery of Entebbe airport to supplement the information obtained by Israeli agents in preparation for the Israeli hostage rescue mission. During the 1985 hijacking of the *Achille Lauro*, Israel provided the United States with the location of the ship on several occasions, the location of the ship's hijackers when they were in Egypt, and the identification number and call sign of the plane carrying the hijackers seconds after it took off from Egypt.[60]

The United States and Israel also exchanged intelligence during Operation Desert Shield and Operation Desert Storm. Israel provided the United States with data on Iraqi air defenses, and the United States granted Israel increased access to U.S. satellite imagery. Once again, Israel pressed for establishment of a receiving station to allow real-time access.[61]

In October 1997, it was reported that the AMAN had provided the CIA and the DIA with information about a transfer of sensitive technology from China to Iran. The Israeli report stated that China's Great Wall Industries was providing Iran with "telemetry infrastructure" to support a program to develop two medium-range ballistic missiles.[62]

Israel also assisted the United States in its efforts to discover further details of Iraqi nuclear, chemical, and biological warfare activities. Israeli imagery interpreters analyzed overhead photography obtained by U.S. U-2 aircraft operating in support of the UN Special Commission (UNSCOM) in light of data contained in Israeli databases about the targets. Israeli intelligence personnel also processed other forms of data obtained by UNSCOM and provided the commission with raw reports from defectors and other human sources. In September 1994, Israel provided UNSCOM with details concerning the deception and concealment activities of the Special Security Organization, headed by Saddam's son Qusay.[63]

A key part of the relationship between the CIA and Mossad was the personal element, according to Efraim Halevy, the chief of the Mossad from 1998 to 2002. In his memoirs, Halevy wrote:

> I often recall, with a whiff of nostalgia, the one-on-one meetings that I had with George Tenet, the director of the CIA, throughout my four-and-a-half-year tenure as head of the Mossad. We always had these meetings just before or immediately

after the full sessions with our respective staffs, and we felt free to discuss anything and everything that was on our minds. . . . We could talk intimately on the situations in the countries neighboring Israel and assess what might happen based on our personal knowledge of the principal players and their strengths, aims, and weaknesses.[64]

JOINT TERRORISM INTELLIGENCE CENTERS

In the aftermath of 9/11, the CIA established joint counterterrorism intelligence centers (CTICs) in about two dozen countries, adding to the two that had been created in the 1990s to monitor and apprehend Islamic militants traveling from Saudi Arabia, Yemen, Egypt, and Chechnya to participate in the conflict in Bosnia and in other parts of the former Yugoslavia. At the centers currently operating, U.S. and foreign intelligence officers work together to track and capture suspected terrorists and to destroy or penetrate their networks. The centers make decisions on a daily basis "on when and how to apprehend suspects, whether to whisk them off to other countries for interrogation and detention, and how to disrupt al-Qaeda's logistical and financial support."[65]

CTICs were established in Europe, the Middle East, and Asia. "CTICs were a step forward in codifying, organizing liaison relationships that elsewhere would be more ad hoc," according to a former counterterrorism official."[66]

One of the CITCs, known as Alliance Base, is located in Paris, with the French foreign intelligence service, the General Directorate of External Security (DGSE), in the lead. The CIA is a key participant, and the center also has case officers from Canada, Australia, and Germany. The Paris center selects a case, chooses a lead country for an operation, and that country's service directs the operation.[67]

It has been reported that in the aftermath of the terrorist attacks of September 11, 2001, President Jacques Chirac ordered the French intelligence services to place no limits on the information concerning terrorism that it would share with U.S. intelligence services. The French also detained about sixty suspects between the end of 2001 and mid-2005. In addition, France permitted the United States to fly armed Predator drones from the French airbase in Djibouti. In return, France was given access to detainees held at Guantanamo Bay, and French interrogators traveled there to gather evidence for use in French courts.[68]

JORDAN

According to one report, "Jordan's General Intelligence Directorate, or GID, has surpassed Israel's Mossad as America's most effective counterterrorism agency in the Middle East." A former CIA operations officer explained, "They're going to get more information [from a terrorism suspect] because they're going to know his language, his culture, his associates—and more about the network he belongs to."

According to the same officer, Jordanians were particularly valued for their skill in interrogating captives and recruiting assets, due to their "expertise with radicalized militant groups and Shia/Sunni culture."[69]

CIA-GID cooperation has, reportedly, helped disrupt several terrorist plots, including the 2000 "millennium" plan to attack tourists at hotels and other sites.[70]

Cooperation began several decades ago. In the 1980s, the two services conducted a joint campaign to subvert and cripple the Abu Nidal's organization—at the time, one of the world's most dangerous terrorist groups. The project involved creation of bogus foreign bank accounts that falsely showed Nidal's aides receiving mysterious payments from overseas sources. As a result, Nidal had many of them executed. In 1995, Jordan turned over to the CIA several dozen Russian gyroscopes and accelerometers intended for Iraq that they had seized. In the summer of 2001, the Jordanians provided the United States with communications intercepts indicating an upcoming terrorist attack on the United States.[71]

The GID has also cooperated with the United States by serving as a rendition partner, interrogating a number of individuals detained or apprehended by the CIA after they have been delivered to the GID. One example is Jamal Mari, a Yemeni citizen who was seized in Karachi by Pakistani security forces. After being held in a secret prison for several weeks, he was turned over to American intelligence officials, who believed that he was working for a charity group in Pakistan with ties to al-Qaeda. U.S. officials then transported him to Jordan where he spent four months before being returned to U.S. custody, presumably after a number of interrogations.[72]

Also long-standing is U.S. financial support for the GID. According to one former U.S. intelligence official, "It is not a huge sum of money to us, but it's a significant amount of money for [the GID] and allows them to buy a lot of equipment, mostly technical stuff that they otherwise could not afford." That financial support probably extends to paying, at least in part, for the CIA-GID bilateral operations center established after the 9/11 attacks.[73]

According to a 2010 account, the relationship has progressed to the point that "the CIA liaison in Amman enjoys full, unescorted access to the GID's fortress-like headquarters.[74]

MEXICO

According to a 2004 report on Mexican intelligence, the nation's Center for Intelligence and National Security (CISEN—Centro de Inteligencia y Seguridad Nacioal) has liaison relationships with over forty foreign intelligence services from twenty-eight nations. Of those, the CIA is the "foremost strategic partner" and, along with other U.S. intelligence organizations, provides "valuable information on drug cartels," which includes satellite intelligence related to drug production within Mexico.[75]

According to a 2010 fact sheet, the Office of the DNI "surged intelligence support to Mexico to help combat drug cartels and their impact on Mexican governance and U.S. border security."[76]

PAKISTAN

In 2009, the United States began providing Pakistan with data collected by Predator and Reaper drones flying along the border of Pakistan and Afghanistan, although, as reported at the time, it was not clear whether the cooperation would continue. The United States also offered to provide Pakistan with a large volume of imagery, including real-time video feeds and communications intercepts—in an attempt to placate Pakistani concerns about the way the drones were employed. The United States, however, did not provide data on the drone's technical operations.[77]

In addition to providing imagery the United States has, since 9/11, "funneled hundreds of millions of dollars" to the Directorate of Inter-Services Intelligence, paying for as much as a third of the organization's budget. The directorate also received payments for the capture or killing of militants, as part of a CIA clandestine reward. It received $10 million for its role in the capture of Abu Zubaydah and $25 million for the capture of Khalid Sheikh Mohammed. In addition, ISI officers have been brought to the CIA training facility in North Carolina.[78]

In early 2010, it was reported that the United States would provide Pakistan with a dozen unarmed Shadow surveillance drones, which are smaller than the Predator. Later that year, the CIA sent additional intelligence collection and technical personnel to Pakistan, with plans to establish a joint military intelligence processing center. The center was probably among the subjects discussed between the chief of ISI and CIA director Leon Panetta during the latter's September visit to Pakistan.[79]

But by early 2011, it was being reported that CIA-ISI "deteriorated sharply in recent months" and that the ISI was, generally, no longer providing the CIA with targeting information for drone strikes. The deterioration was attributed to Pakistani anger over U.S. comments questioning Pakistan's commitment to combating militants and Pakistan's concern that the CIA was establishing its own network to avoid reliance on the ISI—as well as over the U.S. belief that ISI leaked the name of the agency's station chief, leading to his recall. The arrest of a CIA contractor for killing the individuals who apparently attempted to rob him further exacerbated tensions.[80]

UNITED KINGDOM

Bilateral intelligence relations between the United States and the United Kingdom include human intelligence, signals intelligence, and radio and television broadcast monitoring. The British–United States Communications Intelligence Agreement (BRUSA) is still in force and regulates the bilateral part of the British-U.S. SIGINT relationship.

A second set of agreements known as the Burns-Templer agreements were struck between 1948 and 1950, named for the chief negotiators—U.S. Assistant Secretary of Defense James Burns and vice chief of the imperial staff, Gerald Templer. The most significant agreement, concluded in 1950, "allowed the two intelligence communities to pool their resources in 'a full and frank exchange to greatest practicable degree of all classified military information and intelligence." The 1950 agreement, which remains in force, led to sharing of information on Soviet guided missile technology as well as on the sales of arms to Eastern Bloc nations.[81]

Another highly formalized arrangement consists of the agreement to divide up, on a geographic basis, the responsibility for monitoring public radio and television broadcasts—mainly news and public affairs broadcasts. The specific organizations involved are the British Broadcasting Corporation (BBC) Monitoring Service and the DNI's Open Source Center (OSC) (formerly the Foreign Broadcast Information Service). Together, these two organizations monitor most of the world's significant news reports and other broadcasts. Both the BBC Monitoring Service and the OSC have a network of overseas stations that operate with varying degrees of secrecy to gather raw material.[82]

Post–World War II cooperation between the BBC Monitoring Service and the United States was formalized in 1947, as the result of an exchange of letters between the head of the Foreign Broadcast Information Branch of the CIA's Office of Operations and the head of the Monitoring Service. The basic provisions were noted in a 1950 document, the two-page "FBIS-BBC Reciprocal Agreement, Basic Provisions." The agreement divided the monitoring tasks among the small number of stations then operating, provided for FBIS personnel to be stationed at BBC headquarters to select material, and required FBIS to provide material to satisfy BBC requirements. It also provided for a joint planning FBIS-BBC Monitoring Service Coordination Committee.[83]

The 1950 document also noted that "the organization of mutually complementary operations requires continuous consultation and cooperation between the Services in respect to the location of monitoring stations, the allocation of monitoring coverage, the standardization of operational principles and procedures, their communications networks, and all other matters of mutual concern."[84]

The cooperation began as an openly acknowledged arrangement, which is clearly stated in the BBC Annual Report for 1948–1949: "There [is] close cooperation between the BBC's Monitoring Service and its American counterpart, the Foreign Broadcast Information Branch of the United States Central Intelligence Agency, and each of the two services maintained liaison units at each other's stations for the purpose of a full exchange of information."[85]

The area of responsibility for the Monitoring Service is roughly equivalent to the GCHQ's area of responsibility for SIGINT collection—Europe, Africa, and western Russia. Thus, the Monitoring Service maintained a remotely controlled listening post on top of the British embassy in Vienna to monitor VHF radio and television broadcasts originating in Hungary and Czechoslovakia. It also maintained listening posts in Accra, Ghana, and Abidjan, Ivory Coast. In 1976–1977, the Monitoring Service turned over responsibility for monitoring Far East broadcasts to the FBIS. To compensate, it stepped up its reporting of events in Portugal and Spain to meet CIA requirements.[86]

From 1979 to 2009, according to the BBC's Summary of World Broadcasts (SWB), relatively large increases occurred in coverage of Iran and Pakistan while there was little change in coverage of other Middle East nations. Meanwhile, coverage of Russia and China declined, with the decline in China coverage substantial.[87]

The United Kingdom has also had significant access to U.S. satellite imagery, beginning with the CORONA program. In 1996, it was reported that Britain was going to provide part of the funding for a new generation of U.S. imagery satellites, which would allow it greater access to the imagery produced by the system.[88]

In late January 2000, a massive computer failure at NSA prevented the agency, for three days, from processing intelligence gathered by its myriad collection systems. During that time, GCHQ worked to fill the gap—providing information in support of military operations and intelligence on ongoing world events and crises.[89]

THE UNITED NATIONS AND INTERNATIONAL ATOMIC ENERGY AGENCY

The United States has shown satellite imagery and provided other intelligence to the United Nations and some of its agencies, including the International Atomic Energy Agency (IAEA).

U.S. satellite imagery was provided to the board of the IAEA to convince the members that North Korea was violating its commitments under the Nuclear Nonproliferation Treaty by seeking to secretly store nuclear waste from its Yongbyon reactor—waste that would be reprocessed to extract plutonium for nuclear weapons. On February 22, 1993, the representatives from thirty-five member states of the IAEA Board of Governors met in Vienna, in closed session. They examined a series of black-and-white images that showed a storage facility under construction as well as what appeared to be an older facility at Yongbyon being covered with dirt and later planted with trees and shrubs. The images were intended to provide convincing proof that North Korea had buried nuclear waste under a camouflaged mound and constructed a new facility to serve as a decoy. The board approved a resolution demanding that North Korea permit inspections, "without delay," of waste storage sites.[90]

In November 1993, a team of inspectors from IAEA conducted an examination of previously unchecked buildings at Iranian nuclear sites, looking for evidence of a clandestine nuclear weapons program. The targets of the unannounced inspection included sites that the U.S. Intelligence Community suspected might be involved in nuclear-related work—isolated and camouflaged buildings, surrounded by tall wire fencing and tight security.[91]

In July 2005, senior U.S. intelligence officials briefed the top echelon of the IAEA in Vienna on the contents of a laptop computer provided by an Iranian source (discussed in Chapter 11). At the same time, the United States hoped to benefit from the IAEA's inspections in Iran throughout 2005 and 2006. In late 2005, Iran was not as forthcoming as the IAEA (and the U.S. government) had hoped it would be in responding to the agency's requests for information. However, the agency was provided access, during visits in October and November, to buildings of interest at Parchin, where environmental samples were taken, and inspectors reported that they "did not observe any unusual activities in the buildings visited." They also reported that the UF6 (uranium hexafluoride) being produced at the uranium conversion facility at Esfahan "has remained under Agency containment and surveillance measures." In contrast to those items of information, another that the IAEA reported—that civil engineering and construction of the reactor at Arak was continuing—came directly from intelligence derived from U.S. satellite reconnaissance activities.[92]

At the end of January 2006, the IAEA had more to contribute, providing data that U.S. intelligence officials would have been more than a little pleased to have acquired through a spy or communications intercept. Iran showed the international agency more than sixty documents concerning uranium metal. Included was a fifteen-page document describing the procedures for the reduction of UF6 to metal in small quantities and the casting of enriched and depleted uranium metal into hemispheres, both of which relate to the production of nuclear weapon components. Iranian officials claimed that the document, along with other material, had been provided by A. Q. Khan's network, at the network's own initiative. However, Iran did not permit the agency to make a copy. Iran also provided some documentation on some of its efforts to acquire dual-use technology, including laser equipment and electric-drive equipment.[93]

Notes

1. Declaration of the Secretary of Defense, *United States of America v. Jonathan Jay Pollard, Defendant*, United States District Court for the District of Columbia, Criminal No. 86–02070 (AER), p. 22.

2. See Jeffrey T. Richelson, "The Calculus of Intelligence Cooperation," *International Journal of Intelligence and Counterintelligence* 4, 3 (Fall 1990): 307–324; H. Bradford Westerfield, "America and the World of Intelligence Liaison," *Intelligence and National Security* 11, 3 (July 1996): 523–560; Commission on the Roles and Capabilities of the United States Intelligence Community, *Preparing for the 21st Century: An Appraisal of U.S. Intelligence* (Washington, D.C.: U.S. Government Printing Office, 1996), p. 128; Stéphen Lefebvre, "The Difficulties and Dilemmas of International Intelligence Cooperation," *International Journal of Intelligence and Counterintelligence* 16, 4 (Winter 2003–2004): 527–542; and Jennifer Sims, "Foreign Intelligence Liaison: Devils, Deals, and Details," *International Journal of Intelligence and Counterintelligence* 19, 2 (Summer 2006): 195–217.

3. Richard J. Aldrich, *GCHQ: The Uncensored Story of Britain's Most Secret Intelligence Agency* (London: Harper Press, 2010), p. 376; [deleted], "Third Party Nations: Partners and Targets," *Cryptologic Quarterly* 7, 4 (Winter 1989): 15–22; Richelson, "The Calculus of Intel-

ligence Cooperation"; Sims, "Foreign Intelligence Liaison"; Mark Mazzetti, "When Spies Don't Play Well with Their Allies," *New York Times*, January 20, 2008, Section 4, pp. 1, 6.

4. On the British-U.S. World War II SIGINT alliance, see Bradley F. Smith, *The Ultra-Magic Deals* (Novato, Calif.: Presidio, 1993). On Canadian participation, see John Bryden, *Best Kept Secret: Canadian Secret Intelligence in the Second World War* (Toronto: Lester, 1993). On Australian–New Zealand involvement, see Jeffrey T. Richelson and Desmond Ball, *The Ties That Bind: Intelligence Cooperation Among the UKUSA Countries* (Boston: Allen & Unwin, 1985), pp. 3–4; and Desmond Ball, "Allied Intelligence Cooperation Involving Australia During World War II," *Australian Outlook* 32, 4 (1978): 299–309.

5. State-Army-Navy Communication Intelligence Board and London Signal Intelligence Board (Signators), "British–U.S. Communication Intelligence Agreement," March 5, 1946, pp. 3–4; "The Days of BOURBON," *Cryptologic Almanac 50th Anniversary Series*, January–February 2002.

6. State-Army-Navy Communication Intelligence Board and London Signal Intelligence Board (Signators), "British–U.S. Communication Intelligence Agreement," pp. 4–5.

7. Ball, "Allied Intelligence Cooperation Involving Australia During World War II"; Duncan Campbell, "Threat of the Electronic Spies," *New Statesman*, February 2, 1979, pp. 140–144; John Sawatsky, *Men in the Shadows: The RCMP Security Service* (New York: Doubleday, 1980), p. 9 n.; Transcript of "The Fifth Estate—The Espionage Establishment," broadcast by the Canadian Broadcasting Company, 1974; Matthew Aid, *The Secret Sentry: The Untold History of the National Security Agency* (New York: Bloomsbury, 2009), pp. 12–13; [deleted], "Six Decades of Second Party Relations," *Cryptologic Almanac (50th Anniversary Series)*, January–February 2002.

8. Private information; Seymour Hersh, *"The Target Is Destroyed": What Really Happened to Flight 007 and What America Knew About It* (New York: Random House, 1986), pp. 48 n.

9. Chapman Pincher, *Inside Story: A Documentary of the Pursuit of Power* (New York: Stein & Day, 1979), p. 157; Sawatsky, *Men in the Shadows*, p. 9 n.

10. Desmond Ball, *A Suitable Piece of Real Estate: American Installations in Australia* (Sydney: Hale & Iremonger, 1980), p. 40.

11. Campbell, "The Threat of the Electronic Spies."

12. See Richelson and Ball, *The Ties That Bind*, pp. 148–149.

13. Christopher Anson Pike, "CANYON, RHYOLITE and AQUACADE: US Signals Intelligence Satellites in the 1970s," *Spaceflight* 37, 11 (November 1995): 381–383; Mark Urban, *UK Eyes Alpha: The Inside Story of British Intelligence* (London: Faber and Faber, 1996), p. 58; private information.

14. Nicky Hager, *Secret Power: New Zealand's Role in the International Spy Network* (Nelson, N.Z.: Craig Potter, 1986), pp. 42–56; Jeffrey Richelson, "Desperately Seeking Signals," *Bulletin of the Atomic Scientists* 56, 2 (March–April 2000): 47–51.

15. Urban, *UK Eyes Alpha*, pp. 60–63; Duncan Campbell, "The Parliamentary Bypass Operation," *New Statesman*, January 23, 1987, pp. 8–12; James Bamford, *Body of Secrets: Anatomy of the Ultra-Secret National Security Agency, from the Cold War to the Dawn of a New Century* (New York: Doubleday, 2001), pp. 400–401.

16. Desmond Ball, "The U.S. Naval Ocean Surveillance Information System (NOSIS)–Australia's Role," *Pacific Defence Reporter*, June 1982, pp. 40–49.

17. "Britannia Scorns to Yield," *Newsweek*, April 19, 1982, pp. 41–46.

18. Centre for Peace Studies, The University of Auckland, "New Zealand International Military Connections; Agreements and Arrangements," 1986.

19. Joint Intelligence Organization, *Fourth Annual Report, 1974* (Canberra: JIO, 1974), pp. F1–F2; Department of the Army, Office of the Deputy Chief of Staff for Intelligence, *Annual Historical Review, 1 October 1993 to 30 September 1994*, n.d., pp. 6–11.

20. Navy Field Operational Office, *Command History for CY 1981*, April 15, 1982, p. 5; Assistant Chief of Staff for Intelligence, Air Force, *History of the Assistant Chief of Staff, Intelligence Hq., United States Air Force, 1 July 1974–31 December 1974*, n.d., p. 9; Department of the Army, Office of the Assistant Chief of Staff, Intelligence, *Annual Historical Review, 1 October 1985–30 September 1986*, n.d., pp. 4–5.

21. Armed Forces Medical Intelligence Center, *Organization and Functions of the Armed Forces Medical Intelligence Center*, April 1986, p. vii; Lynn A. McNamara, "AFMIC Responds to Tsunami Disaster," *Communiqué* 17, 1 (January 2005): 10–11.

22. David S. Brandwein, "Confessions of a Former USIB Committee Chairman," *Studies in Intelligence* 18, 2 (Summer 1974): 43–50.

23. Tom Mangold, *Cold Warrior, James Jesus Angleton: The CIA's Master Spy Hunter* (New York: Simon & Schuster, 1991), p. 292.

24. Elizabeth K. Krug, "Analysts and Collectors: TAKE NOTE!," *Communiqué*, March–April 2006, pp. 30–31.

25. Rod McGuirk, "Report: U.S., Australia Share Spy Secrets," www.newsday.com, September 1, 2005.

26. Robert Suro, "Australian Arrested on Spy Charge," *Washington Post*, May 18, 1999, p. A9; Jerry Sepper, "Court Jails Australian in a Sale of U.S. Secrets," *Washington Times*, May 18, 1999, pp. A1, A11; David Johnston, "U.S. Arrests an Australian in Spying Case," *New York Times*, May 18, 1999, p. A3.

27. Philip Flood, *Report into the Inquiry into Australian Intelligence Agencies* (Canberra, 2004), pp. 139–146.

28. Stephen Smith and Robert M. Gates (Signators), "Australian–United States Space Situational Awareness Partnership: Statement of Principles," November 8, 2010; Turner Brinton, "U.S., Australia Sign Agreement on Space Situational Awareness," *Space News*, November 15, 2010, p. 4. On the history of space surveillance in Australia, see G.W. Newsam, "Surveillance of Space in Australia," 2008, available at www.amostech.com.

29. Canadian-U.S. Joint Intelligence Committee, *Soviet Capabilities and Probable Course of Action Against North America in a Major War Commencing During the Period 1 January 1958 to 31 December 1958* (Washington, D.C.: CIA, March 1, 1957), Declassified Documents Reference System (DDRS) 1981–169A; U.S. Congress, Senate Committee on Armed Services, *Department of Defense Authorization for Appropriations for Fiscal Year 1984, Part 5* (Washington, D.C.: U.S. Government Printing Office, 1983), p. 2708.

30. Joint Chiefs of Staff, *Canadian–United States Communications Instructions for Reporting Vital Intelligence Sightings* (CIRVIS/MERINT), March 1966, p. 2-1.

31. Ibid., pp. 2–4 to 2–6.

32. Ibid., p. 3-1.

33. *Canada-U.S. Arrangements in Regard to Defence, Defence Production, Defence Sharing* (Washington, D.C.: Institute for Policy Studies, 1985), p. 31.

34. Walter Agee, Deputy Director of Intelligence, "Memorandum for the Coordination of Joint Operations: Proposed U.S.–Canadian Agreement," RG 341, Entry 214, File Nos. 2–1900 through 2–1999, Military Reference Branch, National Archives.

35. Mike Frost as told to Michel Gratton, *Spyworld: Inside the Canadian and American Intelligence Establishments* (Toronto: Doubleday Canada, 1994), p. 15, 274–275; Intelligence

Advisory Committee, "Afghanistan: Taliban Challenges, Regional Concerns," October 17, 1996.

36. The Canadian Press, "CSIS played critical role in Afghan prisoner interrogations: documents, sources," www.metronews.ca, March 8, 2010.

37. . Lt. Rodney R. Bickford, "Canadian Undersea Surveillance," *Proceedings*, March 1995, pp. 70–71.

38. Lt. Col. R. S. Williams, "Your Canadian Partner," *Pathfinder* 4, 1 (January–February 2006): 9; Ed Batchelor, "Canada Responds to Haiti Earthquake," *Pathfinder* 8, 6 (November–December, 2010): 16.

39. "Operational interaction with Canada valued," www.forces.gc.ca, January 21, 2008; Ed Batchelor, "Canada Responds to Haiti Earthquake," *Pathfinder* 8, 6 (November–December 2010): 16; Col. D.H.N. Thompson, "Meet Canada's Directorate of Geospatial Intelligence," *Pathfinder* 7, 2 (March/April 2009): 3–4.

40. Paul Maskell and Lorne Oram, "Sapphire: Canada's Answer to Space-Based Surveillance of Orbital Objects," 2008, available at www.amostech.com.

41. See Jeffrey T. Richelson, *A Century of Spies: Intelligence in the Twentieth Century* (New York: Oxford University Press, 1995), pp. 232–236; James H. Critchfield, *Partners at the Creation: The Men Behind Postwar Germany's Defense and Intelligence Establishments* (Annapolis, Md.: Naval Institute Press, 2003); and Mary Ellen Reese, *General Reinhard Gehlen: The CIA Connection* (Fairfax, Va.: George Mason University Press, 1990).

42. Bob Drogin, "German Spies Aided in U.S. Attempt to Kill Hussein in Aerial Attack," *Los Angeles Times*, January 12, 2006, p. A3.

43. Richard Bernstein, "Germans Ask How Agents Helped U.S.," *New York Times*, January 21, 2006, p. A6; Michael R. Gordon, "German Intelligence Gave U.S. Iraqi Defense Plan, Report Says," *New York Times*, February 27, 2006, pp. A1, A9.

44. Gordon, "German Intelligence Gave U.S. Iraqi Defense Plan, Report Says."

45. Richard Bernstein and Michael R. Gordon, "Berlin File Says Germany's Spies Aided U.S. in Iraq," *New York Times*, March 2, 2006, pp. A1, A12.

46. David Fontenot and Kevin Firmin, "Germany Expands Co-Production Capabilities," *Pathfinder* 4, 1 (January–February 2006): 30–31.

47. Ibid.; Heidi Whitesell, "NGA Welcomes New German Geospatial Liaison," August 4, 2008, www.nga.mil; Joshua Keating, "Germany planning secret satellite recon?," January 3, 2011, http://wikileaks.foreignpolicy.com.

48. Andrew Cockburn and Leslie Cockburn, *Dangerous Liaisons: The Inside Story of the U.S.-Israeli Covert Relationship* (New York: HarperCollins, 1991), p. 41; also see Ephraim Kahana, "Mossad–CIA Cooperation," *International Journal of Intelligence and Counterintelligence* 14, 3 (Fall 2001): 409–420.

49. Judith Perera, "Cracks in the Special Relationship," *The Middle East*, March 1983, pp. 12–18.

50. Cockburn and Cockburn, *Dangerous Liaisons*, p. 187.

51. Richard Halloran, "U.S. Offers Israel Plan on War Data," *New York Times*, March 13, 1983, pp. 1, 13.

52. Edmund Walsh, "Begin Offers to Give War Intelligence to U.S.," *Washington Post*, October 15, 1982, p. A18; Richard Hallorn, "U.S. Said to Bar Deal with Israel," *New York Times*, February 10, 1983, pp. A1, A7.

53. Halloran, "U.S. Said to Bar Deal with Israel"; Bernard Gwertzman, "Israelis to Share Lessons of War with Pentagon," *New York Times*, March 22, 1983, pp. 1, 12.

54. Richard Armitage, Assistant Secretary of Defense/International Security Affairs, Memorandum for the Secretary of Defense, Subject: Obtaining PLO Weapons from Israel—INFORMATION MEMORANDUM, n.d.; Lincoln P. Bloomfield, Jr., Special Assistant to the ASD/ISA, Memorandum for the Assistant General Counsel (Legal Counsel), Subject: Request for Documents on "Tipped Kettle," April 17, 1987, available at www.dod.mil/pubs/foi.

55. Ronald Reagan, National Security Decision Directive 111, "Next Steps Toward Progress in Lebanon and the Middle East," October 28, 1983. The directive has been released in heavily sanitized form. The tilt toward Israel is reported in Bernard Gwertzman, "Reagan Turns to Israel," *New York Times Magazine*, November 27, 1983, pp. 62ff.

56. Bob Woodward, "CIA Sought 3rd Country Contra Aid," *Washington Post*, May 19, 1984, pp. A1, A13.

57. "Statement of Bobby Ray Inman on Withdrawing His Nomination," *New York Times*, January 19, 1994, p. A14; E. L. Zorn, "Israel's Quest for Satellite Intelligence," *Studies in Intelligence*, Winter–Spring 2001, pp. 33–38.

58. "U.S. to Share More Recon Data, Tighten Air Links with Israel," *Aerospace Daily*, December 8, 1983, pp. 193–194; Zorn, "Israel's Quest for Satellite Intelligence."

59. Charles Babcock, "Israel Uses Special Relationship to Get Secrets," *Washington Post*, June 15, 1986, p. A1.

60. "How the Israelis Pulled It Off," *Newsweek*, July 19, 1976, pp. 42–47; David Halevy and Neil C. Livingstone, "The Ollie We Knew," *Washingtonian*, July 1987, pp. 77 ff.

61. Theodore Sanger, "The Israelis: A Not Very Hidden Agenda," *Newsweek*, September 10, 1990, p. 20; Gerald F. Sieb and Bob Davis, "Fighting Flares Again at Saudi Town; Allied Planes Attack Big Iraqi Column," *Wall Street Journal*, February 1, 1991, p. A12; Martin Sieff, "Israelis Press U.S. for Direct Access to Intelligence Data," *Washington Times*, November 28, 1992, p. A7.

62. Bill Gertz, "U.S. Offers Deal to Stop China's Nuke Sales," *Washington Times*, October 14, 1997, pp. A1, A11.

63. Barton Gellman, "Israel Gave Key Help to U.N. Team in Iraq," *Washington Post*, September 29, 1998, pp. A1, A12.

64. Efraim Halevy, *Man in the Shadows: Inside the Middle East with a Man Who Led the Mossad* (New York: St. Martin's Press, 2006), pp. 215–216.

65. Dana Priest, "Foreign Network at Front of CIA's Terror Fight," *Washington Post*, November 18, 2005, pp. A1, A12.

66. Ibid.

67. Dana Priest, "Help from France Key in Covert Operations," *Washington Post*, July 3, 2005, pp. A1, A16.

68. Ibid.

69. Ken Silverstein, "U.S., Jordan Forge Closer Ties in Covert War on Terrorism," *Los Angeles Times*, November 11, 2005, pp. A1, A10–A11; Joby Warrick, "Jordan emerges as key CIA counterterrorism ally," www.washingtonpost.com, January 4, 2010.

70. Warrick, "Jordan emerges as key CIA counterterrorism ally."

71. Silverstein, "U.S., Jordan Forge Closer Ties in Covert War on Terrorism"; Warrick, "Jordan emerges as key CIA counterterrorism ally"; R. Jeffrey Smith, "U.N. Inspectors or Spies? Iraq Data Can Take Many Paths," *Washington Post*, February 16, 1998, pp. A1, A20.

72. Silverstein, U.S., Jordan Forge Closer Ties in Covert War on Terrorism."

73. Ibid.; Warrick, "Jordan emerges as key CIA counterterrorism ally."

74. Warrick, "Jordan emerges as key CIA counterterrorism ally."

75. Christophe Leroy, "Mexican Intelligence at a Crossroads," *SAIS Review* 14, 1 (Winter-Spring 2004): 107–129; American Embassy, Mexico to State Department, Subject: Weekly Narcotics Roundup: August 13–17, August 22, 1990, p. 1.

76. Office of the Director of National Intelligence, "ODNI Fact Sheet," October 2010, www.dni.gov.

77. Eric Schmitt and Mark Mazzetti, "In a First, U.S. Provides Pakistan with Drone Data," *New York Times*, May 14, 2009, p. A12.

78. Greg Miller, "CIA pays for support in Pakistan," *Los Angeles Times*, November 15, 2009, pp. A1, A28.

79. Karen DeYoung, "U.S., Pakistan bolster joint efforts, treading delicately," www .washingtonpost.com, April 29, 2010; Karin Brulliard and Karen DeYoung, "U.S., Pakistan chiefs of intelligence meet," www.washingtonpost.com, September 30, 2010.

80. Adam Entous, Julian E. Barnes, and Tom Wright, "Spy Feud Hampers Antiterror Efforts," *Wall Street Journal*," February 18, 2011, pp. A1, A8; Alex Rodriguez and Ken Dilanian, "CIA's Ties to Pakistan Are Fraying," *Los Angeles Times*, February 26, 2011, p. A3; June Perlez, "Pakistani Spy Agency Demands That C.I.A. Account for Contractors," *New York Times*, February 26, 2011, p. A4.

81. Michael B. Petersen, "60 Years of a 'SPECIAL RELATIONSHIP,'" *Communiqué*, January–February 2010, pp. 15–16.

82. Duncan Campbell and Clive Thomas, "BBC's Trade Secrets," *New Statesman*, July 4, 1980, pp. 13–14. For a history of the early years of FBIS, see Joseph E. Roop, *Foreign Broadcast Information Service, History–Part I: 1941–1947* (Washington, D.C.: Central Intelligence Agency, April 1969), available at www.foia.cia.gov.

83. Louise D. Davison, "Historical Note on the 'Agreement' Between the Foreign Broadcast Information Service (CIG/CIA) and the British Broadcasting Corporation Monitoring Service, 1947," August 23, 1971; "FBIS-BBC Reciprocal Arrangement, Basic Provisions," 1950.

84. "FBIS–BBC Reciprocal Arrangement, Basic Provisions."

85. Campbell and Thomas, "BBC's Trade Secrets."

86. Ibid.

87. Kalev Leetaru, "The Scope of FBIS and BBC Open Source Media Coverage, 1979–2008," *Studies in Intelligence* 54, 1 (Extracts March 2010): 17–37 at 33.

88. Acting Assistant Director, Special Activities, DR/CIA, Memorandum for: Special Requirements Staff, DD/R, Subject: Accessibility of LANYARD Take to the British, January 31, 1963; James Adams, "Britain in Spy Satellite Talks," *Sunday Times*, January 14, 1996.

89. Ben MacIntryre, "UK Spied for US as Computer Bug Hit," www.londontimes.com, April 27, 2000.

90. Joel S. Wit, Daniel B. Poneman, and Robert L. Gallucci, *Going Critical: The First North Korean Nuclear Crisis* (Washington, D.C.: Brookings Institution, 2004), p. 20; R. Jeffrey Smith, "North Korea and the Bomb: High Tech Hide-and-Seek," *Washington Post*, April 27, 1993, pp. A1, A11.

91. Steve Coll, "Nuclear Inspectors Check Sites in Iran," *Washington Post*, November 20, 1993, pp. A13, A16.

92. Mohamed El Baradei, Director General, International Atomic Energy Agency, "Implementation of the NPT Safeguards Agreement in the Islamic Republic of Iran," November 18, 2005, pp. 4–5; Alissa J. Rubin, "Iran Still Not Opening Up to the IAEA," *Los Angeles Times*,

November 19, 2005, p. A3; Nazila Fathi, "Iran Parliament Votes to Close Atomic Sites to U.N. Monitors," *New York Times*, November 21, 2005, p. A10.

93. Deputy Director General for Safeguards, IAEA, "Developments in the Implementation of the NPT Safeguards Agreement in the Islamic Republic of Iran and Agency Verification of Iran's Suspension of Enrichment-Related and Reprocessing Activities," January 31, 2006, pp. 2–3.

14

ANALYSIS

Just as the U.S. intelligence collection effort is vast and distributed across a number of different organizations, the effort to produce finished intelligence is extensive and involves a variety of organizations, analytical techniques, and products.

ANALYSTS

The CIA distinguishes several different types of foreign intelligence analysts, most tied to specific subject matter—political, leadership, economic, military, weapons systems, foreign media, terrorism, and foreign intelligence activities. Political analysts evaluate "the goals and motivations of foreign government and entities" and examine "their culture, values, society and ideologies; their resources and capabilities; their political and decision making processes; the strengths and weaknesses of their strategies for achieving their goal; and the implications of all of the above for US interests."[1]

Leadership analysts "produce assessments of foreign leaders and other key decisionmakers in the political, economic, military, science and technology, social and cultural fields." Also contributing to such analyses are psychological/psychiatric analysts, "who research, analyze, and write assessments of foreign leaders, societal impacts of disease and disaster, and decision making groups." Economic analysts "assess foreign economic policies and foreign financial issues—licit as well as illicit that affect US security interests." The illicit financial activities and networks they examine include those of terrorist and criminal organizations, those involved in weapons proliferation, money launderers, and corrupt governments and companies.[2]

Military analysts evaluate weapons systems, military resources, and the intentions and war-fighting capabilities of foreign governments as well as of terrorist and insurgent groups. They also examine peacekeeping activities, civil-military relations, denial and deception, regional security arrangements, arms control, and nonproliferation regimes. Science, technology, and weapons analysts, with backgrounds in science and engineering, examine foreign weapons development, proliferation, information warfare, and emerging technologies.[3]

Foreign media analysts "review and assess foreign open media sources, including Internet sites, newspapers, press agencies, television, radio and specialized publications," which allows them to "identify trends and patterns." Counterterrorism analysts "monitor and assess the leadership, motivations, plans and intentions of foreign terrorist groups and their state and non-state sponsors." Counterintelligence threat analysts "identify, monitor and analyze the efforts of foreign intelligence entities against US persons, activities and interests, including the threats posed by emerging technologies to US operations and interests."[4]

Organizations solely devoted to foreign intelligence analysis, or with substantial analytical components, include the National Intelligence Council, the National Counterterrorism Center, the National Nonproliferation Center, several Intelligence Community committees (including the Joint Atomic Energy Intelligence Committee and the Weapons and Space Systems Intelligence Committee), the Central Intelligence Agency, the Defense Intelligence Agency, the Bureau of Intelligence and Research, the National Geospatial Intelligence Agency, the National Ground Intelligence Center, the National Air and Space Intelligence Center, and the Office of Naval Intelligence, as well as the Energy Department's Office of Intelligence and Counterintelligence, the intelligence units of the national laboratories, and the unified command joint intelligence centers. Domestic intelligence analysis is largely the province of the Department of Homeland Security and the FBI.

ANALYTICAL TECHNIQUES

In the past, finished intelligence reports were largely, although not exclusively, based on the judgments reached by analysts after reviewing the data—whether technical data about an ICBM or comments by foreign political figures. Other studies might have examined data through the use of basic statistical analysis, such as the number and severity of terrorist incidents, or, less frequently, through the use of Bayesian analysis (in which new evidence or observations are used to revise an estimate that a hypothesis is true).

Today's analytical products reflect the increasing use of a number of new analytical techniques, particularly with respect to the structure and activities of terrorist groups. These techniques include clustering (which allows analysts to exploit the most useful data sets first), link analysis (which helps establish relationships between a known problem and unknown actors), time series analysis (to identify time trends), visualization (which permits analysts to see complex data in new forms), and automated database population (which eliminates the need for maintaining databases). Thus, among the classes of analysts identified by the CIA is the "targeting analyst," who uses "network analysis techniques and specialized tools to identify and detail key threats to the US."[5]

Among the best-known of the new techniques are data mining and social network analysis. Data mining involves the use of algorithms to discover previously undetected but valid patterns and relationships in large data sets. One of the best-known data mining efforts was ABLE DANGER, initiated in late 1999 by the U.S. Special Operations Command to uncover terrorists and their activities. In addition, after 9/11 the National Security Agency initiated new data mining projects. Social network analysis, also used in support of counterterrorism, employs mathematics, anthropology, psychology, and sociology to uncover social networks—sets of actors and the relation or relations that define them.[6]

Social network analysis was used to aid in the December 2003 capture of Saddam Hussein, according to a U.S. Army field manual. New items of information "led to coalition forces identifying and locating more of the key players in the insurgent network," including not only highly visible ones but also "lesser ones who sustained and supported the insurgency." The result was the production of detailed diagrams showing the structure of the former Iraqi dictator's personal security apparatus and the relationships among the individuals identified.[7]

During the summer of 2003, intelligence analysts from the 4th Infantry Division constructed link diagrams "showing everyone related to Hussein by blood or tribe." The diagrams "led counterinsurgents to the lower-level, but nonetheless highly trusted, relatives and clan members harboring Hussein and helping him move around the countryside." Later in the year, operations produced new intelligence about Hussein's whereabouts, which led commanders to design a series of raids to capture key individuals and leaders of the former regime who could lead counterinsurgents to him."[8]

Among the most recent innovations in analysis is the establishment of collaborative analysis. The first of these efforts, Intellipedia, has been an attempt to create an Intelligence Community version of Wikipedia, with three levels of classification—Top Secret/SI/TK/Noforn, Secret/Noforn, and Controlled Unclassified. Its genesis was a 2004 paper by a CIA employee titled "The Wiki and the Blog: Toward an Adaptive Intelligence Community." Policymakers can participate. By September 2008, Intellipedia had more than 40,000 registered users and 349,000 active pages.[9]

A more restrictive work space, in that it is for analysts only, is A-Space. The goal is "to create a common collaborative workspace where IC analysts in diverse locations can work together, in a new simultaneous fashion, on common projects. It allows posting of "emerging insights" during the course of their research—so that other analysts can see and comment on the work in progress. As of September 2008, A-Space was open to 9,000 analysts.[10]

CATEGORIES OF INTELLIGENCE PRODUCTS

The analytical products produced by U.S. intelligence organizations can be characterized in a number of ways. One way is by reference to the designated consumers. Specifically, there are national products (for the President and National Security Council), departmental products (for the Departments of State, Defense, and Treasury), and military service/military command products (for the Army or the European Command).

An alternative approach is to distinguish the outputs by the nature of the product: current intelligence, warning intelligence, estimates, reports and studies, periodicals, databases, and maps. The second approach is more reflective of the fact that consumers of intelligence products may receive many different types of products originating in several areas of the Intelligence Community. For example, Anthony Lake, President Clinton's first national security advisor, read not only the *President's Daily Brief* each morning but also the *Secretary's Morning Summary*. Likewise, an analyst who is responsible for producing finished intelligence on nuclear proliferation or a policymaker who helps formulate decisions in the area may receive reports from the National Intelligence Council, the Joint Atomic Energy Intelligence Committee, the CIA, the DIA, and the Department of Energy, in addition to reports from other organizations. In turn, the report of the analyst, wherever he or she is located, may find its way not only to readers in a particular department but also to those in other departments, and even to those at the national level.*

CURRENT INTELLIGENCE

Current intelligence is intelligence pertinent to a topic of immediate interest, such as military movements in Beijing during early June 1989, terrorist attacks in Israel, London, or Madrid, or the activities of al-Qaeda or the Taliban in Pakistan or Afghanistan. Such intelligence is generally transmitted without the opportunity for extensive evaluation that is possible in other types of reports; it is also more likely to be a product based on one or two sources than an all-source product.

A variety of products, whose sensitivity and consumers vary, fall into the current intelligence category. The most restricted and sensitive current intelligence is the *President's Daily Brief*—"a compilation of current intelligence items of high significance to national policy concerns prepared six days a week." The PDB, which began as the *President's Intelligence Checklist* during the administration of John F. Kennedy and took its present name in December 1964, is tailored to meet the daily intelligence requirements as defined by the President. Because it contains information from the most sensitive U.S. sources, it has been the most restricted of current intelligence products—at times being distributed only to the President, Vice President, the Secretaries of State and Defense, the National Security Advisor, the Chairman of the Joint Chiefs of Staff, and possibly a few other key officials.[11]

According to Cord Meyer, a former CIA official, the PDB "is a powerful tool for focusing the attention of the President on potential crisis areas and for alerting him to situations that may require rapid policy adjustment." It has also been described as being "designed to give policy officials an understanding about what happened in

---

*The final section of this chapter focuses on domestic intelligence analysis, irrespective of whether the product is current intelligence, estimative intelligence, or some other variety of intelligence.

the world during the past 24 hours, and what is likely to happen during the next 24 hours."[12]

The size and organization of the PDB may change from president to president. Under Gerald Ford, the brief was rather lengthy, but it was reduced to a maximum of about fifteen pages under Jimmy Carter, although DCI Stansfield Turner occasionally appended longer "trend pieces" at the end. Carter would often write in the margins of the PDB to request more information. During the Clinton administration it was nine to twelve pages long and printed in four-color graphics, and during the Bush administration it apparently consisted of six to eight relatively short (one- to two-page) articles or briefs covering a wide variety of topics. Appended to the PDB is the *National Terrorism Brief* (NTB), prepared by the National Counterterrorism Center.[13]

An article in the December 4, 1998, issue was titled "Bin Ladin Preparing to Hijack US Aircraft and Other Attacks." According to the item, motivation for the hijacking plans was "to obtain the release of Shayk 'Umar 'Abd al-Rahman, Ramzi Yousef, and Muhammad Sadiq 'Awada." The August 6, 2001, PDB carried an article titled "Bin Ladin Determined to Strike in US." It began by noting that "clandestine, foreign government, and media reports indicate Bin Ladin since 1997 has wanted to conduct terrorist attacks in the U.S." It also stated that "Al-Qa'ida members— including some who are US citizens—have resided in or traveled to the US for years, and the group apparently maintains a support structure that could aid attacks."[14] Figure 14.1 shows the entire August 6, 2001, President's Daily Brief.

A key subject in the PDB of September 21, 2001, concerned the question of whether there was an Iraqi connection with the terrorist attacks of ten days earlier. The May 26, 2009, issue of the PDB contained an article titled "North American al Qaeda trainees may influence targets and tactics in the United States and Canada."[15]

During the Bush administration, the CIA noted that "it has become common for the President and his senior advisors who also receive PDB materials to ask follow-up questions." Members of the analytic briefing team return after the briefings and task Intelligence Community personnel to provide answers to the questions that have been raised. The answers were contained in the *Presidential Daily Brief Memoranda*.[16]

During the Bush administration there were several additional changes associated with the PDB. According to one study, after 9/11 the PDB was "elevated . . . to unprecedented levels of importance," with Bush spending as much as an hour on the PDB briefing.* Initially the responsibility of the Director of Central Intelligence, the briefing became the responsibility of the DNI after that position was established. In

---

*The study also concluded that there was an overemphasis on the PDB, which had a variety negative effects on overall analytic effort—including skewing incentives with respect to topic selection, use of hyperbolic language, an excessive attachment to classified sources, and catering of subject matter to presidential policy preferences. See Kenneth Lieberthal, *The U.S. Intelligence Community and Foreign Policy: Getting Analysis Right* (Washington, D.C.: Brookings Institution, 2009), pp. 11–12.

FIGURE 14.1 Excerpt from *President's Daily Brief,* August 6, 2001

Bin Ladin Determined To Strike in US

Clandestine, foreign government, and media reports indicate Bin Ladin since 1997 has wanted to conduct terrorist attacks in the US. Bin Ladin implied in US television interviews in 1997 and 1998 that his followers would follow the example of World Trade Center bomber Ramzi Yousef and "bring the fighting to America."

After US missile strikes on his base in Afghanistan in 1998, Bin Ladin told followers he wanted to retaliate in Washington, according to a ███████████ service.

An Egyptian Islamic Jihad (EIJ) operative told an ███████ service at the same time that Bin Ladin was planning to exploit the operative's access to the US to mount a terrorist strike.

The millennium plotting in Canada in 1999 may have been part of Bin Ladin's first serious attempt to implement a terrorist strike in the US. Convicted plotter Ahmed Ressam has told the FBI that he conceived the idea to attack Los Angeles International Airport himself, but that Bin Ladin lieutenant Abu Zubaydah encouraged him and helped facilitate the operation. Ressam also said that in 1998 Abu Zubaydah was planning his own US attack.

Ressam says Bin Ladin was aware of the Los Angeles operation.

Although Bin Ladin has not succeeded, his attacks against the US Embassies in Kenya and Tanzania in 1998 demonstrate that he prepares operations years in advance and is not deterred by setbacks. Bin Ladin associates surveilled our Embassies in Nairobi and Dar es Salaam as early as 1993, and some members of the Nairobi cell planning the bombings were arrested and deported in 1997.

Al-Qa'ida members—including some who are US citizens—have resided in or traveled to the US for years, and the group apparently maintains a support structure that could aid attacks. Two al-Qa'ida members found guilty in the conspiracy to bomb our Embassies in East Africa were US citizens, and a senior EIJ member lived in California in the mid-1990s.

A clandestine source said in 1998 that a Bin Ladin cell in New York was recruiting Muslim-American youth for attacks.

We have not been able to corroborate some of the more sensational threat reporting, such as that from a ███████████ *service in 1998 saying that Bin Ladin wanted to hijack a US aircraft to gain the release of "Blind Shaykh" 'Umar 'Abd al-Rahman and other US-held extremists.*

(continues)

— Nevertheless, FBI information since that time indicates patterns of suspicious activity in this country consistent with preparations for hijackings or other types of attacks, including recent surveillance of federal buildings in New York.

The FBI is conducting approximately 70 full field investigations throughout the US that it considers Bin Ladin-related. CIA and the FBI are investigating a call to our Embassy in the UAE in May saying that a group of Bin Ladin supporters was in the US planning attacks with explosives.

addition, analysts began presenting verbal "deep dives" into an issue of particular concern to the President. The former deputy director for analysis estimated that almost 100 deep dives, involving over 200 analysts, were given to President Bush by September 2008.[17]

The second regular current intelligence publication, prepared by the CIA in consultation with the Defense Intelligence Agency (DIA), the State Department's Bureau of Intelligence and Research (INR), and the National Security Agency (NSA), is the *Worldwide Intelligence Review* (WIRe), previously known as the *Senior Executive Intelligence Brief* (SEIB) and, for decades before that, as the *National Intelligence Daily* (NID). The NID was the idea of former DCI William Colby, who had repeatedly recommended during the mid-1960s that the CIA's daily intelligence report, then known as the *National Intelligence Digest*, be issued in newspaper format to emphasize the more important items and to offer its readers a choice between a headline summary and in-depth reports. Subsequently, the newspaper format was judged to be too inflexible, and the publication reverted to magazine format.[18]

The SEIB was a daily publication that contained six to eight relatively short articles or briefs on a variety of subjects, similar to the PDB. It was prepared by the CIA but was coordinated with other Intelligence Community production organizations. Although the brief had no classification limits, it excluded some of the more sensitive information contained in the PDB, since it could be distributed to several hundred senior policymakers in the executive branch. Dissenting views were noted either in the text of the article or in a separate paragraph.[19]

SEIBs have included articles such as "Sudan: Regime Exploits US Attack" (September 4, 1998), "Indonesia: Militia Terrorism Intensifying in East Timor" (May 22, 1999), "Russia: Ambitious Nuclear Test Program This Year" (June 4, 1999), "Nepal: New King May Try to Expand Monarchy's Power" (June 4, 2001), "Iraq: Nuclear-Related Procurement Efforts (October 18, 2001), "Lebanon: Many Suspects in Assassination" (January 26, 2002), "FARC-AUC Conflict Intensifying" (May 8, 2002), "Iraq: Terrorists Are Threat to US Forces at War's Outset" (March 21, 2003), and "Iraq: Russian, French Oil Companies Want Post-War Role" (March 21, 2003).[20]

The State Department's INR produces the *Secretary's Morning Summary* seven days a week. It includes approximately a dozen brief reports with comment and three or four longer articles—all related to policy issues. A supplementary Weekend Edition covers selected issues in detail. Topics of the Weekend Edition have included "China's Forecast: Cloudy with Summer Storm Possible" (February 9–10, 1991) and "China's Defense Conversion: Lessons for the USSR?" (June 29–30, 1991). In addition to limited dissemination within the State Department, the *Morning Summary* is provided to the White House, National Security Council, and key ambassadors.[21]

The Defense Department's premier current intelligence product is the *Defense Intelligence Digest* (DID), formerly the *Military Intelligence Digest* (MID), which began publication in 1993. It is produced in a magazine format and published Monday through Friday and focuses on the events of the past day or two, or on issues expected to arise over the following few days. The MID is a joint publication by the DIA, the military service intelligence organizations, and the unified commands that contains items likely to be of interest to national-level policymakers on military or military-related topics. General areas covered include regional security, nuclear security and proliferation, and strategy and resources. On March 14, 1994, the *Digest's* articles included "Iraq: Ecological Warfare." The January 24, 1997, issue carried a report on a Russian program code-named FOLIANT, which concerned the production of a highly lethal nerve gas agent, A-232. The February 2, 1998, issue carried a report on Iraqi concealment of Scud missiles, while a February 2000 issue carried an article titled "Iraq: Unmanned Aerial Vehicle Program." An April 7, 2009, issue of the DID listed new unsubstantiated reports of former Guantanamo Bay detainees allegedly involved in terrorism.[22]

Two additional Defense Department current intelligence products are the *NMJIC Executive Highlights* (EH) and the *Defense Intelligence Terrorism Summary* (DITSUM). The EH is published Monday through Friday based on data from the DIA and the NSA and contains articles on crisis or near-crisis situations. The September 7, 2000, issue of *Executive Highlights* carried an article on Russian testing activities at Novaya Zemlya, while the February 12, 2002, edition included an article titled "Niamey signed an agreement to sell 500 tons of uranium a year to Baghdad." It is intended to keep the Secretary of Defense, the Chairman of the Joint Chiefs of Staff, and other key decisionmakers informed of developments that might require immediate action by the United States.[23]

The DITSUM is a compilation of information and analysis concerning terrorism threats and developments that could affect DOD personnel, facilities, and interests. DITSUM articles include brief notes on terrorism, regional terrorism developments, and in-depth special analyses. It also contains a monthly terrorism review by combatant commands. A 2002 issue contained a discussion of chemical and biological weapons training in Iraq. The DITSUM is distributed Monday through Friday in the Washington area in hard-copy form and in an electronic message version to military commands outside the area.[24]

Two specialist current intelligence products are the *National SIGINT File* (which replaced the *SIGINT Digest* in October 1997) and the *World Imagery Report*. The former is distributed in hard-copy form on weekdays in the Washington area and electronically to customers in the field and contains the most significant daily intelligence derived from SIGINT. The *World Imagery Report* is a video-format compilation of current intelligence items derived from imagery collection.[25]

Other current intelligence may also be conveyed by video rather than paper or electronic formats. By the early 1990s the DIA was distributing finished intelligence via television through the Defense Intelligence Network (DIN), formally known as the Joint Worldwide Intelligence Communications System. For approximately twelve hours a day, five days a week, the DIN broadcast Top Secret reports to defense intelligence and operations officers at the Pentagon and nineteen other military commands in the United States.[26]

In addition to having anchors who reported finished intelligence, the DIN showed satellite reconnaissance photos, reported communication intercepts, and carried reports from defense attachés overseas. Reporting began at 6:15 A.M., with a 30-minute "Global Update." At 6:45 the head of the DIA J-2 conducted a 45-minute interview show featuring visiting briefers who gave classified reports on developing events. "Global Update" resumed at 8:00 A.M. and continued at the top of each hour, updated as required and interspersed with special features. In addition, there were regular features, such as "Regional Intelligence Review" and "Military Trends and Capabilities."[27]

WARNING INTELLIGENCE

Warning intelligence products "identify and focus on developments that could have sudden and deleterious effects on U.S. security or policy." Among the national-level products that are dedicated specifically to warning is the *Strategic Warning Committee's Watchlist*, a weekly report that tracks and assigns probabilities to potential threats to U.S. security or policy interests within the following six months. The September 15, 2000, issue contained an item on Colombia, which discussed the threat from "rising insurgent violence and a weak economy." The *Watchlist* is produced by the interagency Strategic Warning Committee, which also produces the *Strategic Warning Committee's Atrocities Watchlist*.[28]

A product that can be initiated by the National Intelligence Officer for Warning or, through that office, by an element of the Intelligence Community is the *Warning Memorandum*. The memorandum is a special warning notice that focuses on "a potential development of particularly high significance to U.S. interests."[29]

The Defense Intelligence Agency also issues a number of regular and special warning reports designed to guide U.S. commands around the world. *The Weekly Intelligence Forecast* and *The Weekly Warning Report* include assessments from the various commands. In addition, *The Quarterly Warning Forecast* reviews a wide range of potential events that could affect U.S. security interests. The DIA and the commands also publish two ad hoc products as issues arise: the *Warning Report*, an assessment of a specific warning issue that is considered to require the immediate, specific attention of senior U.S. officials within the Washington area; and the *Watch Condition Change*, a notification of a change in the threat level presented by a specific warning problem.[30]

Defense warning system forecasts are a set of DIA periodicals that "provide evaluation of critical threat issues that could reach crisis proportions in the period covered." The *Weekly Warning Forecast* covers the following two-week period, whereas the *Quarterly Warning Forecast* focuses on the two- to six-month period. The *Annual Warning Forecast* focuses on the coming year. The forecasts are distributed in hard copy to members of the Defense Warning System and other decisionmakers in the Washington area and in message form to other recipients.[31]

ESTIMATES

The best-known estimative intelligence products are the National Intelligence Estimates (NIEs), which attempt to project existing military, political, and economic trends into the future and to estimate for policymakers the likely implications of these trends.

In 1980, the House Committee on Foreign Affairs described an NIE as "a thorough assessment of a situation in the foreign environment which is relevant to the formulation of foreign, economic, and national security policy, and which projects probable future courses of action and developments." A Congressional Research Service (CRS) report explained that NIEs "represent the highest and most formal level of strategic analysis by the U.S. Intelligence Community." They are not predictions of the future, however, but judgments as to the likely course of events.[32]

Another CRS memorandum explained that NIEs "represent the coordinated judgments of the Intelligence Community, and thus represent the most authoritative assessment of the [Director of National Intelligence] with respect to a particular national security issue." In addition, the author noted that "coordination of NIEs involves not only trying to resolve any interagency differences but also assigning confidence levels to the key judgments and rigorously evaluating the sources for them."[33]

Based on inputs from the Intelligence Community, the NIEs are produced by the National Intelligence Council. NIEs are intended for a variety of customers, from the President and National Security Council to other senior policymakers to analysts.[34]

NIEs produced in the last years of Soviet rule include *Soviet Forces and Capabilities for Strategic Nuclear Conflict Through the 1990s*, *Soviet Aerodynamic Counterstealth and Stealth Capabilities*, *The Soviet System in Crisis: Prospects for the Next Two Years*, and *Trends and Developments in Warsaw Pact Theater Forces and Doctrine Through the 1990s*. In late December 1991, in the aftermath of the failed coup and imminent dissolution of the Soviet state, the Intelligence Community was commissioned to produce at least ten new NIEs concerning subjects such as food, fuel, the consumer distribution system, economic stagnation, and the potential for civil disorder, ethnic strife, military conditions, control over nuclear weapons and technology, and nuclear forces.[35]

NIEs focusing on other subjects and areas of the world that were produced in the 1980s included *Nicaragua: Prospects for Sandinista Consolidation* (February 1985); *Nicaragua: Prospects of Insurgency* (March 1986); and *State-Sponsored Terrorism, Terrorist Use of Chemical and Biological Warfare*, and *The International Narcotics Trade: Implications for U.S. Security* (November 1985).[36]

NIEs produced during the first half of the 1990s included *The Global Energy Environment into the Next Century* (1990), *Saddam Husayn: Likely to Hang On* (1992), *North Korea: Outlook for War and Warning* (1993), *Emerging Missile Threats to North America During the Next Fifteen Years* (1995), *The Foreign Terrorist Threat in the United*

States (1995), and *Monitoring the Comprehensive Test Ban Treaty over the Next Ten Years* (1997), as well as 1993 NIEs on the North Korean nuclear weapons program and the Intelligence Community's ability to monitor the Chemical Weapons Convention. During the 1994 fiscal year, NIEs were completed or started on South Africa, Zaire, Iraq, sub-Saharan Africa, European peacekeeping trends, Russia and former Soviet states, France, the former Yugoslavia, and Greece-Turkey. The Intelligence Community also produces an annual NIE on global humanitarian emergencies.[37]

NIEs produced since 1998 concerning Iraq, weapons of mass destruction, or terrorism include *Iraqi Military Capabilities Through 2003* (April 1999), *Worldwide Biological Warfare Programs: Trends and Prospects Update* (December 2000), *Iraq's Continuing Programs for Weapons of Mass Destruction* (October 2002), *Nontraditional Threats to the U.S. Homeland Through 2007* (November 2002), *Foreign Missile Developments and Ballistic Missile Threat Through 2003* (February 2003), and *Trends in Global Terrorism: Implications for the United States* (April 2006).[38]

Among the NIEs published in 2007 were *Implications of the NIE "The Terrorism Threat to the US Homeland"* and what proved to be the controversial *Iran: Nuclear Intentions and Capabilities.* In addition to its substance, the estimate contained an explanation of estimative language and the relationship of the terms used (from *remote* to *almost certainly*). That estimate contained the judgment (with high confidence) that in the fall of 2003, Iran halted its nuclear weapons program—wherein the term *nuclear weapons program* was defined to mean nuclear weapon design and weaponization work and covert uranium conversion- and enrichment-related work.[39]

In late 2010 NIEs were completed on the situations in Afghanistan and Pakistan. The essence of the estimates, which were disputed by some military officers, asserted, according to media reports, that Pakistan's government was unwilling to halt its covert support for members of the Afghan Taliban who were attacking U.S. troops and that such support would make it difficult for American strategy in Afghanistan to succeed. An updated NIE on the Iranian nuclear program was prepared in early 2011, which reportedly concluded that there was a split among Iran's rulers over whether to continue the pursuit of nuclear weapons.[40]

NIEs are distilled into a separate *President's Summary*, which is distributed to the highest levels of the foreign policymaking community. Other national estimative products include *Special Estimates* (formerly Special National Intelligence Estimates), "short, tightly focused papers . . . designed to provide consumers with policy-relevant analysis needed under a short deadline," and *Update Memorandums*, which update a previous NIE "when new evidence, analysis, or perspective is available." In addition, *NIC Memorandums* (NICMs) are mini-NIEs, longer than *Special Estimates* but shorter than NIEs. A 1994 *Special Estimate* focused on Russian government failures to halt the spread of Russian arms and weapons technology.[41]

A shorter estimative product is the *Intelligence Community Brief,* which is a quickly prepared six-page paper focusing on a particular issue. It is produced under the auspices of a National Intelligence Officer, who is expected to either resolve any disagreements or note ones that have not been resolved. Briefs have included *The BW Threat to the Global and US Agricultural Sectors* (March 2001) and *Smallpox: How Extensive a Threat?* (December 2001).[42]

For many years, the DIA produced a DOD version of the NIEs and SNIEs—the *Defense Intelligence Estimates* (DIEs) and *Special Defense Intelligence Estimates* (SDIEs). Those estimates originated in late 1969 or early 1970 as a means of expressing independent DIA judgments on estimative issues prior to U.S. Intelligence Board meetings. The estimates often covered topics similar to those covered by NIEs and SNIEs; however, they also tended to deal in depth with military issues that were treated only briefly in NIEs and SNIEs. Being departmental estimates, they were produced without interdepartmental coordination.[43]

The DIEs and SDIEs were replaced by *Defense Intelligence Assessments* in the late 1980s. The assessments are intended to respond to "broad consumer interest by presenting comprehensive analysis on a policy-relevant event, situation, issue, or development in 5 to 25 pages." The assessments are targeted at planning and policy staff at various levels.[44]

Assessments have included *USSR: Advanced Conventional Munitions on the Future Battlefield* (1990); *Implications of Directed Energy Weapons in a Ground Combat Environment over the Next Twenty Years* (1990); *South Africa: Defense Forces Transition to Majority Rule* (1991); *East Africa in the 1990s: The Evolving Challenge to United States Security* (1990); and *Balkan Instability—Europe's Vulnerable Underbelly* (1991).[45]

Defense Intelligence Assessments concerning Iraq or al-Qaeda include *Usama Bin Laden/Al-Qaida Information Operations* (September 1999); *Iraq's Nuclear, Biological, and Chemical Weapons and Missile Programs: Progress, Prospects, and Political Vulnerabilities* (May 2000); *Iraq's Weapons of Mass Destruction and Theater Ballistic Missile Programs: Post 11 September* (January 2002); and *Iraq's Reemerging Nuclear Program* (September 22, 2002).[46]

Another DIA estimative product is the *Defense Intelligence Report*, "a concise report that addresses a topic of interest to senior policy makers and commanders." A January 2010 report, prepared by the agency's National Center for Medical Intelligence, was titled *Haiti: Health Risks and Health System Impacts Associated with Large-Scale Earthquake.*[47]

Estimative intelligence produced by the State Department's Bureau of Intelligence and Research is sometimes contained in the Bureau's Intelligence Research Report series but is mainly found in memorandums circulated within the department. The Drug Enforcement Administration also produces an estimative product—the annual *Narcotics Intelligence Estimate*—and a compendium of worldwide production, smuggling, and trafficking trends and projections.[48]

In January 2008, the U.S. Coast Guard's Intelligence Coordination Center produced a 63-page estimate, *National Maritime Threat Assessment*. It contains sections on alternative analysis, analytic assumptions, four types of threats (international terrorists, domestic extremists, lone offenders, and insider saboteurs), and the outlook for the future.[49]

REPORTS AND STUDIES

The Intelligence Community (through the National Intelligence Council [NIC], the CIA's Directorate of Intelligence, the DIA, the INR, and other agencies) also produces a variety of reports and studies whose main focus is the analysis of political, economic, military, or social matters. Intelligence Community analytical products include *Intelligence Community Assessments* (ICAs), which are research papers of twenty to thirty pages that provide a "detailed logic trail on key national security issues," and *Sense of the Community Memos* (SOCM), which are one-page memos that evaluate current or day-to-day events.[50]

Intelligence Community Assessments that have been published since 1998 include *The Foreign Biological and Chemical Weapons Threat to the United States* (July 1998); *Iraq: Steadily Pursuing WMD Capabilities* (December 2000); *Regional Consequences of Regime Change in Iraq* (January 2003); and *Principal Challenges in Post Saddam Iraq* (January 2003). *Sense of Community Memos* included *Iraq: Saddam's Next Moves* (March 4, 1999) and *Niger: No Recent Uranium Sales to Iraq* (April 5, 2003).[51]

Among the interagency products that have been produced since 1995 are the CIA-DIA Joint Intelligence Memorandum, *Chinese Nuclear Testing: Racing Against a Comprehensive Test Ban* (October 5, 1994); the October 19, 1995, report by the DCI Interagency Balkan Task Force, *Croatia: Tomislav Mercep's Role in Atrocities*, prepared by analysts from CIA, DIA, and NSA; and a February 1999 study, *Iraq: WMD and Delivery Capabilities After Operation Desert Fox*, produced by CIA, NIMA, DIA, and CENTCOM analysts. A joint CIA-FBI product is *Al-Qa'ida Remains Intent on Defeating US Immigration Inspections*.[52]

The Joint Atomic Energy Intelligence Committee produced *Iran's Nuclear Program: Building a Weapons Capability* (February 1993); *Iraq's Nuclear Weapons Program: Elements of Reconstitution* (September 1994); *Reconstitution of Iraq's Nuclear Weapons Program: An Update* (October 1997); and *Reconstitution of Iraq's Nuclear Weapons Program: Post Desert Fox* (June 1999).[53]

A 2005 examination of Intelligence Community analytical products identified four types of analytical products. Those products include the 25-page Intelligence Assessments (IA),which are the primary form of in-depth research and can focus on larger analytic questions or include great detail on a more narrow, complex issue. In addition, there is the Strategic Perspective Series (SPS), which focuses on a key strategic issue and often cuts across analytic disciplines or regions, such as Muslims in the European Union or China's global strategic ambitions. Serial Fliers (SFs) are short, concise memorandum-style products, generally a few pages in length, on a single topic of current relevance. There are also Research Projects/Papers, which are the primary means employed to explore new analytic research areas—and may culminate in an IA, SPS, or SF.[54]

CIA analytical products have included *Political Instability: The Narcotics Connection* (March 1987); *South Africa: The Dynamics of Black Politics* (March 1987); *The Abu Nidal Terror Network: Organization, State Sponsors, and Commercial Enterprises* (July 1987); *Chemical and Biological Weapons: The Poor Man's Atomic Bomb* (December 1988); *Rising Political Instability Under Gorbachev: Understanding the Problem and Prospects for Resolution* (April 1989); and *Gorbachev's Future* (May 23, 1991).[55]

More recent CIA reports include *Rodionov's Concerns About Nuclear Command and Control, Prospects for Unsanctioned Use of Russian Nuclear Weapons*, a report on the links between the Russian Mafia and the banking industry, and a report on the Russian biological warfare program. Reports concerning Latin America have included *Colombia-Venezuela: Continuing Friction Along the Border* (October 1, 1997); *Peru: President Manipulating Judiciary* (May 20, 1998); and *Colombia: Burgeoning Coca Industry in Norte de Santander* (August 17, 2000). The prospects of the Indian government were the subject of *India: Problems and Prospects for the BJP Government* (April 13, 1998). A July 2, 1999, report was entitled *Russia: Developing Nuclear Warheads at Novaya Zemlya?* while an August 2002 report was titled *Terrorists: Recruiting and Operating Behind Bars.*[56]

Reports concerning Iraq include *Iraq's Remaining WMD Capabilities* (August 1996); *Iraq and al-Qaida: Interpreting a Murky Relationship* (June 21, 2002); *Iraq: Expanding WMD Capabilities Pose Growing Threat* (August 1, 2002); *Iraq's Hunt for Aluminum Tubes: Evidence of a Renewed Uranium Enrichment Program* (September 2002); and *Saddam's Timeline for Using WMD* (October 2002).[57]

A more recently established type of CIA report is that produced by the CIA's Red Cell, which is responsible for taking an "out-of-the-box" approach to provoke thought and offer alternative viewpoints. A February 5, 2010, Secret report bore the title "What If Foreigners See the United States as an 'Exporter of Terrorism'?," which focused on the implications of U.S.-born individuals who engage in terrorism against non-U.S. targets. A month later, in March 2010, another Red Cell Special Memorandum was titled "Afghanistan: Sustaining West European Support for the NATO-led Mission—Why Counting on Apathy Might Not be Enough."[58]

DIA produces a series of reports under the title *Defense Analysis Report—Terrorism*, which include updates on the participation of former detainees at Guantanamo Bay in terrorist activities subsequent to their release. A January 2009 report noted that of "the 531 Guantanamo Bay (GTMO) detainees transferred from Department of Defense custody, 18 are confirmed and 43 are suspected to be subsequently reengaging in terrorist activities."[59]

Analytical studies by the State Department's INR were, for many years, published under three titles: Current Analyses, Assessments and Research, and Policy Assessments. Those studies analyzed recent or ongoing events, assessed prospects and implications for the following six months, assessed past trends or projected events beyond six months, or analyzed the context or results of past policies or assessed policy options. The distinct series were subsequently merged into a single Intelligence

Research Report series, although INR has since produced products labeled as "Assessments" and "Briefs."[60]

INR products over the past two decades have included *China: Looking In and Looking Out* (July 25, 1990); *DPRK: Grappling with Food Shortage* (April 4, 1996); *China/North Korea: Food Aid?* (March 16, 1996); and *Niger Sale of Uranium to Iraq Is Unlikely* (March 1, 2002).[61]

Department of Energy intelligence products include the department's Technical Intelligence Notes, such as *Iraq: High Strength Aluminum Tube Procurement* (April 11, 2001); *Iraq's Gas Centrifuge Program: Is Reconstitution Underway?* (August 17, 2001); *Iraq: Seeking Additional Aluminum Tubes* (December 2001); *Iraq: Nuclear Reconstitution Efforts Underway?* (July 22, 2002); and *Iraq: Gas Centrifuge Program Recounted* (November 8, 2002).[62]

The military service intelligence organizations also produce their own analytical reports, sometimes as designated (by the DIA) producers within the Defense Intelligence Production Program. NGIC products concerning Iraq have included *Iraq: Specialty Aluminum Tubes Are an Exercise in Deception* (November 25, 2002), *Iraq: Current Chemical Warfare Capabilities* (October 23, 2001), *Iraq's UAV CW Delivery Capabilities—An Unlikely Threat* (March 25, 2003), and *Complex Environments: Battle of Fallujah I, April 2004* (n.d.). Other products, *NGIC Assessments*, have included *China: Joint Venture with Royal Dutch/Shell Group to Exploit Oil-Shale Reserves in Northeastern China* (March 18, 2005); *Foreign Ground Forces Exercise and Training Assessment (EXTRA): China (Guangzhou Military Region)—January 2003 to December 2004* (September 12, 2005); *China: Constructing the World's First Large Direct-Coal-Liquefaction Plant* (February 2, 2007); and *China: Z-10 Attack Helicopter Program—2007 Update* (May 21, 2008).[63]

The Office of Naval Intelligence (ONI) has produced *Chinese Space-Based Remote Sensing Programs and Ground-Processing Capabilities* (September 1994); *Worldwide Threat to U.S. Navy and Marine Forces [deleted] Volume II: Country Study—China* (December 1993); and *Chinese Exercise Strait 961: 8–25 March 1996* (May 1996). In 1995, it produced Special Intelligence Studies on *Algeria: Air Defenses*; *Iraqi Threat to Naval Forces—95*; *Cuban Helicopter Operations, Training, and Tactics*; and *Maritime Surveillance Capabilities—Iran.*[64]

In the last several years, ONI has also produced a number of large unclassified studies, including *China's Navy 2007*; *The People's Liberation Army Navy: A Modern Navy with Chinese Characteristics* (August 2009); and *Iran's Naval Forces: From Guerilla Warfare to a Modern Naval Strategy* (Fall 2009).

The National Air and Space Intelligence Center periodically produces the unclassifed *Ballistic and Cruise Missile Threat*. Among its 2009 and 2010 products are the open source studies *Chinese Air Research Association* (June 2, 2009) and *Current and Potential Applications of Chinese Aerostats (Airships)* (March 23, 2010).[65]

Unclassified DEA intelligence reports have included *China: Country Brief* (February 2004); *Heroin Signature Program 2002* (March 2004); *Heroin Trafficking in Russia's Troubled East* (October 2003); *The Drug Trade in the Caribbean: A Threat*

Assessment (September 2003); *Changing Dynamics of Cocaine Production in the Andean Region* (June 2002); and *Russian Organized Crime Groups* (January 2002).[66]

PERIODICALS

A substantial part of the outcome of the intelligence analysis effort is conveyed in a variety of weekly or monthly publications. The CIA publishes the *Economic Intelligence Weekly* (EIW), which analyzes major foreign economic developments and trends and is distributed to top- and mid-level policymakers. The offices within the CIA's Directorate of Intelligence also publish periodic collections of articles, ranging from weekly to monthly, which may have either a regional or topical focus, depending on the publishing office. Included among those publications are the *Eurasian Intelligence Weekly*, the *European Monthly Review*, the bimonthly *Arms Trade Report*, and the *International Energy Statistical Quarterly.*[67]

The *Economic Intelligence Weekly* carried an article on May 25, 1995, titled "Japan Threatens to Reduce Grant Aid to China," and subsequent articles titled "Azerbaijan's Energy Strategy Threatens Caspian Export Projects" (July 17, 1999) and "Caspian Gas: Turkey Shifting Focus to Azerbaijan as Supplier" (August 5, 2000). The *Eurasian Intelligence Weekly* has carried articles on Russian nuclear activities, including "Ministries at Odds over US Nuclear Testing Initiative" (August 18, 1995) and "Russians Deny Nuclear Test Took Place" (March 1996).[68]

Three additional periodicals are published by what were known as DCI centers. The *Terrorism Review* is a monthly publication of the CIA's Counterterrorist Center that addresses current trends in international terrorism activity and methods. It also tracks international terrorist incidents. Articles that appeared in the *Terrorism Review* when it was published on a weekly basis included "The Shia Urged Toward Martyrdom" (January 24, 1985); "Iran: Spreading Islam and Terrorism" (March 1, 1984); "Islamic Jihad: Increasing Threat to U.S. Interests in Western Europe" (February 2, 1984); and "The Surprising Absence of the Red Brigades" (March 25, 1985). More recent articles include "Libya Maintains Ties to International Terrorist Activity" (January 1999), and "Prointegrationists Pose Threat to Foreign Interests in East Timor" (September 1999).[69]

The *International Narcotics Review* is published monthly by the CIA's Crime and Narcotics Center and evaluates worldwide deployments related to narcotics. In addition, the *Proliferation Digest* is published monthly by the Directorate of Intelligence, with contributions from all offices in the directorate. It has contained articles such as "China's Nuclear Test Program Faces Delays" (October 30, 1994), "Russian Nuclear Device in Kazakhstan" (June 30, 1995), "Libya: Pursuing WMD and Missile Programs in Search of Power and Prestige" (March 1999), and "Proliferation Will Worsen in Next Decade" (March 2000).[70]

A number of other periodicals are also produced by the State Department's Bureau of Intelligence and Research. Among the most recently established is *Peacekeeping Perspectives*, a biweekly journal on multilateral conflict management and humanitarian operations. It provides the government's only comprehensive review of current or projected peacekeeping operations and humanitarian issues.[71]

In the early 1990s, INR journals included *African Trends*, *East-Asia Pacific Dynamics*, *Economic Commentary*, *Inter-American Highlights*, *Strategic Forces Analysis Biweekly*, *War Watch Weekly*, and *Western Europe and Canada Issues and Trends*. Each journal consisted of short essays, brief analyses of intelligence reporting, and selected chronologies.[72]

The National Air and Space Intelligence Center produces the *Foreign Missile Update* "to provide a timely update of activities and developments of foreign countries in the area of ballistic missiles." In November 1996, the update carried a report titled "Chinese ICBM Capability Steadily Increasing."[73]

Regular DEA intelligence publications include the *Monthly Digest of Drug Intelligence* and *Quarterly Intelligence Trends*. Among the articles that have appeared in the *Quarterly* is "The Southeast Asian Banking System" (Winter 1994).[74]

LEADERSHIP PROFILES

Both the CIA and DIA devote extensive effort to preparing biographical sketches of key civilian and military officials, respectively. The sketches serve as both reference and analytical documents, providing basic information on the individual, as well as exploring his or her motivations and attempting to provide explanations for past and likely future actions. CIA leadership profiles are often prepared for a particular meeting or event.[75]

Before the demise of the Soviet Union, the CIA produced Biographic Handbooks that provided biographies of key Soviet officials who made and implemented policy, as well as biographies of many lesser individuals. Thus, for example, the April 1977 *Biographic Handbook, USSR Supplement IV*, included profiles on twenty-one officials, including the chief editor of *Pravda*, the chairman of the State Committee for Prices, the Minister of Construction, and the chairman of the board for the State Bank.[76] The biography of Eduard Shevardnadze, then a Georgian party official and later foreign minister, is shown as Figure 14.2.

A few years earlier, in 1974, the CIA prepared a nine-page Biographic Report on Yitzhak Rabin, who served as Israeli prime minister on a number of occasions, including in the 1990s. The report contained seven subheadings: "Prime Minister," "The Sons of the Founding Generation," "Military Hawk/Political Dove," "The General as Ambassador," "Exodus Hero," "Strong Belief and Extreme Caution," and "A Fighting Family."[77]

In January 1991, the CIA produced the *Political and Personality Handbook of Iraq*, which examined Saddam's Iraq (specifically the structure of the government, the Ba'ath Party, and the security services), Saddam's inner circle, Saddam's outer circle, and key military commanders. Twelve years later, DIA prepared *Iraqi Key Regime Personalities*, containing brief biographies of the high-value targets that the U.S.

FIGURE 14.2   Biography of Eduard Shevardnadze

USSR   **Eduard Amvrosiyevich SHEVARDNADZE**
First Secretary, Central Committee, Communist Party of Georgia

One of the youngest regional Party leaders in the Soviet Union, Eduard Shevardnadze (pronounced shevardNAHDzeh) became first secretary of the Georgian Communist Party in
September 1972, at the age of 43. He was a newcomer to the Georgian Party hierarchy,
having served in the government for the previous 7 years as republic minister of internal
affairs, charged with the preservation of law and order. The chief factor in Shevardnadze's
promotion was his experience as a police administrator.

In the Soviet Union, Georgia has long been known as an enclave of high living and
fast runners. Its most important economic activity, wine production, is one of the oldest
and the best loved branches of Georgian agriculture. Georgians are freedom loving and
individualistic; they have always lived by looser rules than other Soviet nationalities, first
because former Premier Josif Stalin (himself a Georgian by birth) indulged them, and later,
apparently, because the pattern had been established.

Disciplinarian in a Loose Republic

Former police official Shevardnadze, who has nurtured an image as a firm, austere discipli-
narian (the Georgians refer to him as the "boss"), has tried since 1972 to overturn the habits
of generations regarding easy virtue, political corruption, underground capitalism and heavy
drinking. The Georgians are not giving in easily. Shevardnadze's cleanup campaign met
with early and continued foot dragging, and during his first years as Georgian Party leader
he encountered considerable bureaucratic opposition. Speakers at an August 1973 Party
Plenum hinted at disorders among the public at large, and rumors of anonymous threats
against Shevardnadze and his family were prevalent throughout 1973.

Several recent developments indicate that Shevardnadze's cleanup campaign in Georgia
has been intense, broad and continuous. An underground Soviet publication that appeared
in 1975 claimed that nearly 25,000 persons had been arrested in Georgia in the past 2 years.
(A Soviet who visited Georgia in late 1974 reported that 13,000 Party and Komsomol members
had been arrested.) In addition, the republic's second secretary, Al'bert Churkin, was dis-
missed in April 1975 for gross errors and shortcomings.

During 1976 there was a series of bomb and arson attacks in the republic as Shevardnadze
continued his all-out campaign against corruption, nationalism and ideological deviation
in Georgia. The attacks may have been intended to blacken Shevardnadze's reputation by
showing his inability to control the Georgian situation; there were rumors that the first
secretary was on the way out because of the disorders. A long hard-hitting report delivered
by Shevardnadze in July 1976 seemed to indicate that despite the disturbances he was still
in control. His repeated allusions to approval of his campaign by the central authorities
in Moscow, however, betrayed a certain unease about his authority in the republic.

Views on Agriculture

In 1975, when Georgia was suffering from the Soviet Union's general harvest failure,
Shevardnadze set forth several new ideas on agriculture. In a report delivered to a local
Party meeting, he attacked the existing program for construction of large mechanized livestock
facilities—a pet project of top Soviet agricultural officials—and proposed instead to divert
a part of the material and money to help expand the feed base. Shevardnadze also made
several proposals designed to strengthen the position of individual farmers. For example,

(continues)

he asked that the feed allotment be ensured for livestock owned by individuals; that unwanted land (swamp lands or rocky areas) be turned over to the population, with technical assistance and fertilizer provided by the state; and that individual farmers form cooperative associations. Little has been heard of these proposals since 1975, but they are indicative of Shevardnadze's surprisingly pragmatic leadership style, which may serve him well in the face of continuing political problems in his republic.

Early Life and Career

A native Georgian, Eduard Amvrosiyevich Shevardnadze was born on 25 January 1928. He was the son of a teacher and was educated as a historian at a pedagogical intitute, but he began his career as a Komsomol functionary in 1946. He rose through the ranks to become first secretary of the Georgian Komsomol Central Committee in December 1957. Shevard- nadze was elected a nonvoting member of the Bureau of the Georgian Party Central Com- mittee, his first Party post, in 1958; and 3 years later he advanced from nonvoting to voting membership on the Bureau of the All-Union Komsomol Central Committee.

Political Eclipse and Recovery

In 1961 Shevardnadze was released without explanation as Komsomol chief and removed from his position on the Party Bureau. His career in eclipse, he served for 3 years in minor Party posts in Tbilisi, the Georgian capital. He began his political comeback in 1965, when he was appointed Georgian minister for the protection of public order, a title later changed to minister of internal affairs. His career may have benefited at this stage from an associa- tion with Aleksandr Shelepin, at that time a member of the Communist Party of the Soviet Union (CPSU) Politburo: When Shevardnadze became Georgian Komsomol chief, Shelepin was first secretary of the All-Union Komsomol, and when he was named minister, Shelepin's influence in Moscow was at its peak.

In July 1972 Shevardnadze was elected a voting member of the republic's Party Bureau and first secretary of the Tbilisi City Party Committee. Shevardnadze did not serve as first secretary for long—2 months later he became Georgian Party chief. He has been a Deputy to the USSR Supreme Soviet since 1974.

Travel

While he was Komsomol first secretary, Shevardnadze made several trips abroad to attend youth conferences, visiting Belgium, Tunisia and France. Since becoming republic first secretary, he has increased his contacts with foreign officials through travel and attendance at official functions. During 1974 he headed a CPSU delegation to the Austrian Communist Party Congress, attended a dinner in Moscow given by CPSU General Secretary Leonid Brezhnev for the President of France, met with Senator Edward Kennedy in Georgia, and traveled with Politburo member Nikolay Podgorny to Sofia. He accompanied Brezhnev to the Hungarian Party Congress in March 1975.

Shevardnadze has a brother, Ippokrat, who has been active in the Georgian Party appa- ratus. No further personal information on Shevardnadze is currently available.

CIA/DDI/OCR
JZebatto   1 April 1977

SOURCE: Central Intelligence Agency, *Biographic Handbook USSR,* Supplement 4 (Washington, D.C.: CIA, April 1977).

wanted to capture. The entry for Amir Hamudi Hasan al-Sadi, Saddam's science advisor, stated: "has knowledge of Iraq's WMD programs and personnel . . . [ellipsis in original]oversaw interaction of the National Monitoring Directorate (NMD) with UN inspections . . . holds a doctorate from University of London in chemical engineering."[78]

In 1996, the CIA prepared a profile, a little over two pages long, titled *Usama Bin Ladin: Islamic Extremist Financier*, that examined his background, his actions in response to the Soviet invasion of Afghanistan, his stay in Sudan, and his support of Islamic jihadist training and operations.[79]

The DIA prepares military leadership profiles (formerly known as biographic sketches) of foreign military officers, even junior officers. The agency prepared its first sketch of Andres Rodriguez no later than April 1966, at which time he was commander of the 1st Cavalry Division of the Paraguayan Army. In February 1989, he led the coup that deposed Paraguay's longtime dictator, Alfredo Stroessner.[80]

Each sketch usually runs several single-spaced pages and provides information on the subject's position, significance, politics, personality, personal life, and professional career. An October 2003 military leadership profile of General Cao Gangchuan notes his positions, including Minister of National Defense and Vice Chairman of the Central Military Commission.

It notes that "Cao is primarily concerned with military, not political, matters and likely will adhere to the party line on a range of issues." It also states that "Cao emphasizes applying Jiang Zemin's 'three represents' by highlighting science and technology to 'realize new development of weaponry.'" The sketch is reproduced as Figure 14.3.

Sketches of Iraqi military officials completed prior to the Persian Gulf War include those for Lt. Gen. Husayn Rahsid Mohammad Hasan (December 18, 1990), chief of the General Staff at the time; and Lt. Gen. Ayyad Futayih Khalifa Al Rawi (October 18, 1990), commander of the Iraqi Republican Guard forces.[81]

REFERENCE DOCUMENTS AND DATABASES

The DIA also produces or delegates production of the Defense Intelligence Reference Document (DIRD) series. A DIRD can be a onetime or recurring (often encyclopedic) study on military forces and force capabilities, infrastructure, facilities, systems and equipment, or associated topics for military planning and operations. A DIRD may consist of fold-out wall charts intended as reference aids or may be a more typical book-length publication.[82]

A May 1995 DIRD, prepared by the National Ground Intelligence Center, concerned *Nonlethal Technologies—Worldwide*. The 81-page document covered a variety of nonlethal effectors—chemical, biotechnical, acoustic, electromagnetic, kinetic, and information. The section on electromagnetic efforts examined laser weapons in the United Kingdom, France, China, Israel, and several other countries.[83]

394

FIGURE 14.3 Military Leadership Profile of Lieutenant General Cao Gangchuan

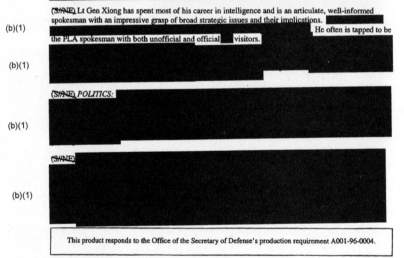

CHINA
Lieutenant General *XIONG* Guangkai
January 2000

Military
Leadership
Profile

UNCLASSIFIED

(U) *NAME*: Lieutenant General *Xiong* Guangkai (pronounced shee-yong) (STC 3574/0342/2818), People's Liberation Army (PLA).

(U) *POSITION*: Deputy Chief of the General Staff (DCOGS) since January 1996; President, Chinese Institute for International and Strategic Studies (CIISS) since December 1996; and Alternate Member, Central Committee (CC), Communist Party of China (CPC) Congress, since October 1992.

(C) *SIGNIFICANCE*: Lt Gen Xiong is responsible for managing the PLA General Staff's foreign affairs and intelligence apparatus.

(U) Photo date: 1998

(U) COPYRIGHT WARNING: Further dissemination of the photograph in this publication is not authorized.

(b)(1)

(S//NF) Lt Gen Xiong has spent most of his career in intelligence and is an articulate, well-informed spokesman with an impressive grasp of broad strategic issues and their implications. He often is tapped to be the PLA spokesman with both unofficial and official visitors.

(b)(1)

(b)(1)

(S//NF) *POLITICS*:

(b)(1)

(S//NF)

(b)(1)

This product responds to the Office of the Secretary of Defense's production requirement A001-96-0004.

Derived from: Multiple Sources
Declassify on: Source marked "OADR"
Date of Source: January 2000

SECRET//NOFORN//MR

Lieutenant General *XIONG* Guangkai

(b)(1)

(S//NF)

(b)(1)

(C//NF) *PERSONAL DATA:* Xiong Guangkai was born 15 March 1939 in Nanchang, Jiangxi Province. He speaks excellent German, English, Japanese, and some French.

(b)(1)

(S//NF)

(b)(1)
A capable and talented officer, he has moved up in the military hierarchy because of hard work and merit more than political influence.

(b)(1)

(C//NF)

(b)(1)

(S//NF) *CAREER:* Lt Gen Xiong began his military career in 1956, following graduation from the Beijing Foreign Language University. From 1958 to 1960 he studied Russian and English at the Beijing Foreign Language Institute.

(b)(1)

(S//NF) From 1981 to 1982, Lt Gen Xiong attended the PLA Military Academy.

(b)(1)
In early 1986, he visited the United States as a member of a CIISS delegation to Washington, DC. In May that year, he returned to the United States as

SECRET//NOFORN//MR

(*Continues*)

FIGURE 14.3 (continued)

Lieutenant General *XIONG* Guangkai

(b)(1) part of a delegation led by then-COGS Gen Yang Dezhi. ████████████ Lt Gen Xiong visited the United States again in May 1987 as part of then-CMC Vice Chairman Yang Shangkun's delegation. ████

(b)(1)

(S//NF) In 1988, Lt Gen Xiong was named Director of the MID and, when the PLA rank system was restored — also in 1988 — was awarded the rank of major general.

(b)(1)

(b)(1) (S//NF) From October 1992 until January 1996, Lt Gen Xiong was assigned as an Assistant COGS ████ In March 1995, he visited the United States and met with Secretary ████ In January 1996, Lt Gen Xiong was selected as a DCOGS████ In December 1996, he accompanied CMC Vice Chairman Gen Chi Haotian on a visit to the United States. In November and December 1997, he visited France, Russia, and Japan and attended the first regular session of the Sino-US Defense Consultative Talks in Washington. Also in December, he was named President of CIISS.

(b)(1) (S//NF) ████ In August 1998, he led a delegation on a visit to North Korea, South Korea, Vietnam, and Australia. In September 1998, he visited the United States as part of a delegation led by CMC Vice Chairman Gen Zhang Wannian. In February 1999, he accompanied Gen Chi Haotian on a trip to Pakistan, Cuba, and Mexico. In June 1999, he accompanied Gen Zhang Wannian on a trip to Russia. In August 1999, he visited North Korea. In November 1999, he led a delegation to France and Russia.

(b)(3)

(Reverse Blank)

More recent NGIC-produced DIRDs include *Assessment of Chinese Radiofrequency Weapon Capabilities* (April 2001) and *Chinese Ground Propulsion Technology* (July 2002).

The former DIRD includes sections on research on high-power radiofrequency generation and high-power radiofrequency susceptibility and propagation. It also contains sections on evidence for radiofrequency weapon development programs and postulated Chinese RF weapons. The later DIRD contains an overview of Chinese engines as well as sections on military ground propulsion, engine subsystems, and engine specifications and parameters.[84]

A 1996 DIRD, prepared by the Office of Naval Intelligence, is *Foreign Oceanographic Research and Development with Naval Implications—China*. DIRDs prepared by the National Air and Space Intelligence Center include *Iraq L-29 UAV Conversion* (December 30, 1999) and *Foreign Weaponized Unmanned Aerial Vehicles* (December 2001). The latter contains sections on electronic warfare systems, unmanned attack drone systems, unmanned combat aerial vehicles, and advanced concepts.[85]

One database is the Terrorist Identities Datamart Environment (TIDE), a collection of data about individuals that the Intelligence Community believes might be threats to the United States. It serves as a database from which watch lists distributed to airlines, law enforcement, border posts, and U.S. consulates are generated. At its inception in 2003 there were fewer than 100,000; it grew to about 435,000 by 2007.[86]

A DNI-sponsored project is the Library of National Intelligence (LNI), whose goal is to "create an authoritative repository for all disseminated intelligence products"—thus making it a database of intelligence reports. As of September 2008, there were 750,000 products in the LNI, with 20,000 being added each week.[87]

Databases also include signature libraries or manuals. Among the material compromised by Jonathan Jay Pollard was the RAISIN manual, which "lists the physical parameters of every known signal . . . and links all the known communications links then used by the Soviet Union." Other libraries contain chemical signatures, which would allow an analyst to identify the laboratory or plant that produces a specific chemical, as well as the signatures of nuclear material and the signals of foreign instrumentation.[88]

DOMESTIC INTELLIGENCE ANALYSIS

With respect to domestic intelligence, the FBI and Department of Homeland Security are the two major producers. Among the FBI's products is the 2004 SECRET/NOFORN assessment, *The Terrorist Threat to the US Homeland: An FBI Assessment*. The key issue examined in the estimate was the risk of another attack on the United States by foreign or domestic terrorists. Among the specific topics examined were the threats posed by al-Qaeda and other Sunni extremists, the threats posed by other Islamic extremists groups, domestic terrorism, and Islamic extremist terrorism trends.[89]

Other FBI intelligence assessments include *Tactics Used by Eco-Terrorists to Detect and Thwart Law Enforcement Operations* (April 15, 2004). The bureau's *White Supremacist Recruitment of Military Personnel Since 9/11* (July 7, 2008) noted that "military experience is found throughout the white supremacist extremist movement as the result of recruitment campaigns by extremist groups and self-recruitment by veterans sympathetic to white supremacist causes." Its October 2006 assessment, *White Supremacist Infiltration of Law Enforcement*, concluded that "the primary threat from infiltration or recruitment arises from the areas of intelligence collection and exploitation, which can lead to investigative breaches and can jeopardize the safety of law enforcement sources and personnel."[90]

As of early 2010, there were at least seven different types of products produced by the DHS Office of Intelligence & Analysis. The *Homeland Security Threat Assessment* is an annual threat assessment that "represents the analytical judgements of DHS and assesses the major threats to the homeland for which the nation must prepare and respond." It is produced in classified and unclassified versions.[91]

The 2008 report, *Homeland Security Threat Assessment: Evaluating Threats 2008–2013*, examined six different kinds of enduring threats: demographics and travel security; border security; chemical, biological, radiological, and nuclear security; health security; critical infrastructure; and homegrown extremism and radicalization. It also examined six "high consequence threats of uncertain probability"—subdivided into the same six categories.[92]

Two additional products are the *Intelligence Warning*, which contains urgent intelligence, and the *Intelligence Note*, which "contains timely information or analysis on a current topic." The *Homeland Security Assessment* consists of an in-depth analysis on a single topic. The office also produces *Homeland Security Monitors* on a monthly basis in collaboration with other DHS components. The monitors include the Border Security Monitor, the Cyber-Security Monitor, and the Cuba-Gram. Other products include *Reference Aids*, which might describe the appearance of an anthrax lab or the most recent information on improvised explosive devices. Issues of *Perspective* are longer-term analytical pieces.[93]

Homeland Security intelligence assessments include "Online Extremist Propagandists Target U.S. Muslims" (November 5, 2007); "The Domestic Terrorism Threat: Lone Wolves, Small Cells, and Leaderless Resistance" (July 5, 2005); "Racist Skinheads: A Potential Terrorist Threat" (November 3, 2006); and "Recent Al-Qa'ida Propaganda May Resonate with Minorities" (August 21, 2007).[94]

Further Homeland Security intelligence products include the June 30, 2009, note titled "2009 Fourth of July Security Awareness" as well as the 2007 Homeland Security Assessment, "Potential Terrorist Threat to the U.S. Information Infrastructure," which reported that "Islamic terrorist groups . . . have a growing appreciation of information technology to support their operations, and could parlay their cyber knowledge into attacks on homeland information infrastructure." Among the products produced in 2006 and 2007 by the Homeland Infrastructure

Threat and Risk Analysis Center (HITRAC)—then a part of the Homeland Security intelligence office—were *Strategic Sector Assessment: Government Facilities Sector* and *Strategic Sector Assessment: Commercial Facilities Sector.* The intelligence and analysis office also publishes the *Domestic Extremist Digest,* which has carried articles such as "Explosive Device Left at Texas Abortion Clinic" and "Alleged Earth Liberation Front Claim at Arson."[95]

A January 2009 assessment focused on the expectation that left-wing extremists were likely to increase their use of cyber attacks over the next decade. The seven-page study examined the appeal of cyber attacks, why they are expected to become an attractive future strategy, potential targets, and potential indicators.[96]

Some DHS assessments have proved controversial. An October 2007 intelligence note titled *Nation of Islam: Uncertain Leadership Succession Poses Risk* produced concern from the general counsel and intelligence oversight officer for the intelligence and analysis office. As a result the note was recalled a few hours after distribution. The oversight officer subsequently determined that the intelligence and analysis office had violated internal guidelines by collecting and retaining information on the Nation of Islam and other U.S. persons named in the intelligence note for more than 180 days without having determined whether the group or its members constituted a terrorist threat.[97]

Another product that produced significant controversy was the 2009 study, *Rightwing Extremism: Current Economic and Political Climate Fueling Resurgence in Radicalization and Recruitment.* One paragraph among the study's key findings that led to protest was the statement that "the possible passage of new restrictions on firearms and the return of military veterans facing significant challenges reintegrating into their communities could lead to the potential emergence of terrorist groups or lone wolf extremists capable of carrying out violent attacks."[98]

In addition to their departmental products, the DHS and FBI produce joint assessments. A March 12, 2007, Joint Homeland Security Assessment was titled *Fraudulent Intention: Terrorist and Criminal Intent* while a July 2, 2007, joint assessment bore the title *Glasgow Airport Illustrates Varied Terrorist Tactics to Attack Transportation Infrastructure.* The latter assessment noted the June 30, 2007, crash of an SUV loaded with compressed air cylinders into the doors of the Glasgow International Airport. In late November 2008, after the attacks in Mumbai, India, the FBI and the DHS intelligence and analysis office released a situational awareness update titled *Islamic Militant Group Attacks Multiple Locations in Mumbai, India.*[99]

Other joint products in which the DHS intelligence and analysis office and the FBI have produced in cooperation with additional agencies include the joint threat assessments for the inauguration of Barack Obama and the 2009 Super Bowl. The inaugural assessment, prepared in concert with the National Counterterrorism Center, the National Geospatial-Intelligence Agency, Northern Command, and several regional fusion centers as well as the Capitol Police, examined international and domestic terrorism threats, the criminal threat environment, the foreign intelligence and cyber threat environments, the weapons of mass destruction threat environment, threats to facilities, the transportation threat environment, and other scenarios of concern.[100]

The Super Bowl assessment, prepared by the same national entities along with the Florida Fusion Center, considered some of the same sources of threats. Among the scenarios of concern examined were those involving improvised explosive devices, suicide bombers, security breaches and inside threats, and noted intelligence gaps.[101]

Notes

1. "Political Analyst," www.cia.gov/careers, accessed October 19, 2010.

2. "Leadership Analyst," "Psychological/Psychiatric Analyst," and "Economic Analyst," all at www.cia.gov/careers, accessed October 19, 2010.

3. "Military Analyst" and "Science, Technology, and Weapons Analyst," both at www.cia.gov/careers, accessed October 19, 2010.

4. "Open Source Officer (Foreign Media Analyst)," "Counterterrorism Analyst," and "Counterintelligence Threat Analyst," all at www.cia.gov/careers, accessed October 19, 2010.

5. John Gannon, address to Washington College of Law at American University, Washington, D.C., October 6, 2000, www.cia.gov; "Targeting Analyst," www.cia.gov/careers, accessed October 19, 2010.

6. See Jeffrey W. Seifert, Congressional Research Service, *Data Mining: An Overview*, December 16, 2004; Mary DeRosa, *Data Mining and Data Analysis for Counterterrorism* (Washington, D.C.: Center for Strategic and International Studies, 2004); Office of the Director of National Intelligence, *2009 Data Mining Report for the Period of February 1, 2009 Through December 31, 2009*, n.d.; Inspector General, Department of Defense, *Alleged Misconduct by Senior DOD Officials Concerning the ABLE DANGER Program and Lieutenant Colonel Anthony A. Shaffer, U.S. Army Reserve*, September 18, 2006; Anthony A. Shaffer, *Operation Dark Heart: Spycraft and Special Ops on the Frontlines of Afghanistan—And the Path to Victory* (New York: St. Martin's, 2010), passim; Stuart Koschade, "A Social Network Analysis of Jemaah Islamiyah: The Applications to Counterterrorism and Intelligence," *Studies in Conflict & Terrorism* 29 (2006): 559–575; and Patrick Radden Keefe, "Can Network Theory Thwart Terrorists?" *New York Times Magazine*, March 12, 2006, pp. 16, 18.

7. Department of the Army, FM 3–24, *Counterinsurgency*, December 2006, p. B-14.

8. Ibid.

9. Kenneth Lieberthal, *The U.S. Intelligence Community and Foreign Policy: Getting Analysis Right* (Washington, D.C.: The Brookings Institution, 2009), p. 4; Steve Vogel, "For Intelligence Officers, a Wiki Way to Connect the Dots," www.washingtonpost.com, August 27, 2009.

10. Lieberthal, *The U.S. Intelligence Community and Foreign Policy*, p. 4.

11. Central Intelligence Agency, *A Consumer's Guide to Intelligence* (Washington, D.C.: CIA, July 1995), p. 30; Walter Pincus, "PDB, the Only News Not Fit for Anyone Else to Read," *Washington Post*, August 27, 1994, p. A7; Cord Meyer, *Facing Reality: From World Federalism to the CIA* (New York: Harper & Row, 1980), p. 352; Zbigniew Brzezinski, *Power and Principle: Memoirs of the National Security Adviser, 1977–1981* (New York: Farrar, Straus &

Giroux, 1983), p. 224; Alfred Cumming, Congressional Research Service, Memorandum to: Sen. Dianne Feinstein, Subject: Congress as a Consumer of Intelligence Information, December 14, 2005, p. 5; Russell Jack Smith, *The Unknown CIA: My Three Decades with the Agency* (New York: Berkley, 1992), pp. 173–174; William Newton, "The President's Daily Brief," *Studies in Intelligence* 26, 4 (Winter 1982): 57–66; Lieberthal, *The U.S. Intelligence Community and Foreign Policy*, p. 9.

12. Meyer, *Facing Reality*, p. 352; Loch K. Johnson, "Glimpses into the Gems of American Intelligence: *The President's Daily Brief* and the National Intelligence Estimate," *Intelligence and National Security* 23, 3 (June 2008): 333–370 at 333.

13. Loch K. Johnson, "Making the Intelligence 'Cycle' Work," *International Journal of Intelligence and Counterintelligence* 1, 4 (Winter 1986–1987): 1–23; Pincus, "PDB, the Only News Not Fit for Anyone Else to Read"; Cumming, Congressional Research Service, Memorandum to: Sen. Dianne Feinstein, Subject: Congress as a Consumer of Intelligence Information, pp. 5, 12; Richard J. Kerr and Peter Dixon Davis, "Ronald Reagan and the President's Daily Brief," *Studies in Intelligence*, Winter 1998–1999, pp. 51–56; Johnson, "Glimpses into the Gems of American Intelligence, p. 337; George Tenet with Bill Harlow, *At the Center of the Storm: My Years at the CIA* (New York: HarperCollins, 2007), p. 31.

14. Central Intelligence Agency, "Bin Ladin Preparing to Hijack US Aircraft and Other Attacks," December 4, 1998 (declassified July 12, 2004); Central Intelligence Agency, "Bin Ladin Determined to Strike in US," *President's Daily Brief*, August 6, 2001, in Thomas S. Blanton, ed., National Security Archive Electronic Briefing Book No. 116, *The President's Daily Brief*, April 12, 2004, Section I, www.nsarchive.org.

15. Murray Waas, "Key Bush Intelligence Briefing Kept from Panel," www.nationaljournal.com, November 22, 2005; Bob Woodward, *Obama's Wars* (New York: Simon & Schuster, 2010), pp. 120–121.

16. Cumming, Congressional Research Service, Memorandum to: Sen. Dianne Feinstein, Subject: Congress as a Consumer of Intelligence Information, p. 12; United States District Court for the District Columbia, *United States of America v. I. Lewis Libby*, March 3, 2006, *Government's Response to Court Orders of February 23 and February 27, 2006*, p. 6.

17. Lieberthal, *The U.S. Intelligence Community and Foreign Policy*, pp. 10–11.

18. Ibid. p. 39; William Colby with Peter Forbath, *Honorable Men: My Life in the CIA* (New York: Simon & Schuster, 1978), p. 354; letter, Arthur S. Hulnick, CIA Office of Public Affairs, to author, April 7, 1988; Nathan Nielsen, "The National Intelligence Daily," *Studies in Intelligence* 20, 1 (Spring 1976): 39–51; Cumming, Congressional Research Service, Memorandum to: Sen. Dianne Feinstein, Subject: Congress as a Consumer of Intelligence Information, p. 10.

19. Central Intelligence Agency, *A Consumer's Guide to Intelligence*, 1995, p. 30; Meyer, *Facing Reality*, pp. 353–354; Cumming, Congressional Research Service, Memorandum to: Sen. Dianne Feinstein, Subject: Congress as a Consumer of Intelligence Information, p. 11; private information.

20. U.S. Congress, Senate Select Committee on Intelligence, *Report on the U.S. Intelligence Community's Prewar Intelligence Assessments on Iraq*, July 7, 2004, p. 36; "Russia: Ambitious Nuclear Test Program This Year," *Senior Executive Intelligence Brief*, June 4, 1999, p. 8. Others are available at the CIA's Electronic Reading Room, www.foia.cia.gov.

21. Central Intelligence Agency, *A Consumer's Guide to Intelligence*, 1995, p. 30.

22. Susan McFarland and Mike Zwicke, "MID: Providing Insights for Policymakers and Warfighters," *Communiqué*, September 1996, pp. 12–13; Bill Gertz, "Russia Dodges Chemical Arms Ban," *Washington Times*, February 4, 1997, pp. A1, A20; Bill Gertz, "Hidden Iraqi Scuds Threaten Israel, Gulf Countries," *Washington Times*, February 11, 1998, pp. A1, A12; Cumming, Congressional Research Service, Memorandum to: Sen. Dianne Feinstein, Subject: Congress as a Consumer of Intelligence Information, p. 11; U.S. Congress, Senate Select Committee on Intelligence, *Report on the U.S. Intelligence Community's Prewar Intelligence Assessments on Iraq*, pp. 233, 396; Defense Intelligence Agency, "Unsubstantiated Cases," *Defense Intelligence Digest*, April 7, 2009, available at www.dia.mil/public_affairs/foia.

23. Central Intelligence Agency, *A Consumer's Guide to Intelligence*, 1995, p. 31; *NMJIC Executive Highlights* No. 170–00, September 7, 2000; Senate Select Committee on Intelligence, *Report on the U.S. Intelligence Community's Prewar Intelligence Assessments on Iraq*, p. 38.

24. Central Intelligence Agency, *A Consumer's Guide to Intelligence*, 1995, p. 31; letter from Kathleen P. Turner, Defense Intelligence Agency, to Hon. John D. Rockefeller IV, October 26, 2005.

25. Central Intelligence Agency, *A Consumer's Guide to Intelligence*, 1995, p. 31; James Bamford, *Body of Secrets: Anatomy of the Ultra-Secret National Security Agency, from the Cold War Through the Dawn of a New Century* (New York: Doubleday, 2001), p. 515.

26. George Lardner Jr. and Walter Pincus, "On This Network, All the News Is Top Secret," *Washington Post*, March 3, 1992, pp. A1, A9.

27. Ibid.

28. Central Intelligence Agency, *A Consumer's Guide to Intelligence*, 1995, p. 36; U.S. Congress, Senate Select Committee on Intelligence, *Report on the U.S. Intelligence Community's Prewar Intelligence Assessments on Iraq*, p. 397; DCI Strategic Warning Committee, *The DCI Strategic Warning Committee's Watchlist*, September 15, 2000, p. 10.

29. Central Intelligence Agency, *A Consumer's Guide to Intelligence*, 1995, p. 36.

30. Ibid., pp. 36–37.

31. Ibid., p. 37.

32. U.S. Congress, House Committee on Foreign Affairs, *The Role of Intelligence in the Foreign Policy Process* (Washington, D.C.: U.S. Government Printing Office, 1980), p. 235; Richard A. Best Jr., Congressional Research Service, *Intelligence Estimates: How Useful to Congress?*, November 21, 2006, p. 1.

33. Cumming, Congressional Research Service, Memorandum to: Sen. Dianne Feinstein, Subject: Congress as Consumer of Intelligence Information, p. 10. For more on NIEs (past and present), see Johnson, "Glimpses into the Gems of American Intelligence," and Lieberthal, *The U.S. Intelligence Community and Foreign Policy*, pp. 12–15.

34. Central Intelligence Agency, *A Consumer's Guide to Intelligence*, 1995, p. 35.

35. Office of Naval Intelligence, *Office of Naval Intelligence 1989 Command History*, n.d., Intelligence Division section, pp. 1–2; U.S. Congress, Senate Select Committee on Intelligence, *Nomination of Robert M. Gates to Be Director of Central Intelligence* (Washington, D.C.: U.S. Government Printing Office, 1991), p. 131; John M. Broder, "CIA Scrambles to Evaluate Breakaway Soviet Republics," *Los Angeles Times*, December 12, 1991, p. A14; Sam Vincent Meddis, "Soviet Disunion Keeps U.S. Spymasters Busy," *USA Today*, December 11, 1991, p. 6A.

36. U.S. Congress, Senate Select Committee on Intelligence, *Nomination of Robert M. Gates to Be Director of Central Intelligence*, pp. 121, 123; private information; Peter Kornbluh,

Nicaragua: The Price of Intervention (Washington, D.C.: Institute for Policy Studies, 1987), p. 243 n. 22; Bob Woodward, *Veil: The Secret Wars of the CIA, 1981–1987* (New York: Simon & Schuster, 1987), p. 400; Brian Barger and Robert Parry, "Nicaraguan Rebels Linked to Drug Trafficking," *Washington Post*, December 27, 1985, p. A22; Office of Naval Intelligence, *Office of Naval Intelligence (ONI) Annual History 1985, Annex C*, September 1986, p. 4; U.S. Congress, *Department of Energy and Water Development Appropriations for 1992, Part 6* (Washington, D.C.: U.S. Government Printing Office, 1991), p. 828.

37. Department of the Army, *Office of the Deputy Chief of Staff for Intelligence Historical Review, 1 October 1992 to 30 September 1993*, n.d., p. 6–4; Department of the Army, *Office of the Deputy Chief of Staff for Intelligence Historical Review, 1 October 1994 to 30 September 1995*, n.d., p. 3–23; Department of the Army, *Office of the Deputy Chief of Staff for Intelligence Historical Review, 1 October 1993 to 30 September 1994*, n.d., pp. 6–6, 6–8; U.S. Congress, Senate Select Committee on Intelligence, *Intelligence Analysis of the Long-Range Missile Threat to the United States* (Washington, D.C.: U.S. Government Printing Office, 1997), p. 14; Martin Sieff, "N. Korea Has Nuke or Is Close to It, CIA Believes," *Washington Times*, December 22, 1993, p. 12; Stephen Engelberg with Michael R. Gordon, "Intelligence Study Says North Korea Has Nuclear Bomb," *New York Times*, December 26, 1993, pp. 1, 8; U.S. Congress, Senate Select Committee on Intelligence, *Current and Projected National Security Threats to the United States* (Washington, D.C.: U.S. Government Printing Office, 1997), pp. 38, 87–88; Jeffrey Richelson, ed., National Security Archive Electronic Briefing Book 167, *Saddam's Iron Grip: Intelligence Reports on Saddam Hussein's Regime*, October 18, 2005, Document 10.

38. U.S. Congress, Senate Select Committee on Intelligence, *Report on the U.S. Intelligence Community's Prewar Intelligence Assessments on Iraq*, p. 227; The Commission on the Intelligence Capabilities of the United States Regarding Weapons of Mass Destruction, *Report to the President of the United States* (Washington, D.C.: U.S. Government Printing Office, 2005), pp. 197 n. 3, 215 n. 239, 238 n. 631; *Declassified Key Judgments of the National Intelligence Estimate "Trends in Global Terrorism: Implications for the United States,"* April 2006, www.dni.gov.

39. Edward Gistaro and Michael Leiter, "Implications of the NIE *The Terrorism Threat to the US Homeland*," Statement for the Record, House Permanent Select Committee on Intelligence and House Armed Services Committee, July 25, 2007; National Intelligence Council, *Iran: Nuclear Intentions and Capabilities*, November 2007, Key Judgments, www.dni.gov. For more on the Iran NIE, see David Sanger, *The Inheritance: The World Obama Confronts and the Challenges to American Power* (New York: Harmony Books, 2009), pp. 3–13, 17–20; and Richard A. Best Jr., Congressional Research Service, *Intelligence Estimates: How Useful to Congress?*, November 24, 2010, pp. 10–12.

40. Elisabeth Bumiller, "U.S. Intelligence Offers Dim View of Afghan War," *New York Times*, December 15, 2010, pp. A1, A12; Ken Dilanian and David S. Cloud, "Grim reports cast doubt on war progress," *Los Angeles Times*, December 15, 2010, pp. A1, A8; Adam Entous, "U.S. Spies: Iran Split on Nuclear Program," *Wall Street Journal*, February 17, 2011, pp. A1, A14; Greg Miller and Joby Warrick, "U.S. report finds debate in Iran on building nuclear bomb," www.washingtonpost.com, February 19, 2011.

41. Central Intelligence Agency, *A Consumer's Guide to Intelligence*, 1995, p. 35; Bill Gertz, "Yeltsin Can't Curtail Arms Spread," *Washington Times*, September 27, 1994, p. A3.

42. Cumming, Congressional Research Service, Memorandum to: Sen. Dianne Feinstein, Subject: Congress as a Consumer of Intelligence Information, p. 10; U.S. Congress, Senate Select Committee on Intelligence, *Report of the U.S. Intelligence Community's Prewar Intelligence Assessments on Iraq*, p. 145.

43. Harold P. Ford, *Estimative Intelligence: The Purposes and Problems of National Intelligence Estimating* (Washington, D.C.: Defense Intelligence College, 1989), p. 136.

44. Central Intelligence Agency, *A Consumer's Guide to Intelligence*, 1995, p. 31.

45. Titles obtained under the Freedom of Information Act.

46. Defense Intelligence Agency, *Usama Bin Ladin/Al-Qaida Information Operations*, September 1999; U.S. Congress, Senate Select Committee on Intelligence, *Report on the U.S. Intelligence Community's Prewar Intelligence Assessments on Iraq*, pp. 185, 232; The Commission on the Intelligence Capabilities of the United States Regarding Weapons of Mass Destruction, *Report to the President of the United States*, p. 200 n. 41.

47. Central Intelligence Agency, *A Consumer's Guide to Intelligence*, 1995, p. 35; Defense Intelligence Agency, *Haiti: Health Risks and Health System Impacts Associated with Large-Scale Earthquake*, January 14, 2010.

48. Central Intelligence Agency, *A Consumer's Guide to Intelligence*, 1995, p. 35; U.S. Congress, House Committee on Appropriations, *Department of Commerce, Justice and State, the Judiciary and Related Agencies Appropriations for FY 1986, Part 7* (Washington, D.C.: U.S. Government Printing Office, 1985), p. 492.

49. U.S. Coast Guard Intelligence Coordination Center, *National Maritime Terrorism Threat Assessment*, January 7, 2008, p. 7.

50. Cumming, Congressional Research Service, Memorandum to: Sen. Dianne Feinstein, Subject: Congress as a Consumer of Intelligence Information, p. 10.

51. U.S. Congress, Senate Select Committee on Intelligence, *Report on the U.S. Intelligence Community's Prewar Intelligence Assessments on Iraq*, pp. 71, 215, 386, 390; The Commission on the Intelligence Capabilities of the United States Regarding Weapons of Mass Destruction, *Report to the President of the United States*, pp. 198 n. 23, 200 n. 41, 247 n. 834.

52. Central Intelligence Agency and Defense Intelligence Agency, *Chinese Nuclear Testing: Racing Against a Comprehensive Test Ban*, October 5, 1994; DCI Interagency Balkan Task Force, *Croatia: Tomislav Mercep's Role in Atrocities*, October 19, 1995, www.foia.cia.gov; Central Intelligence Agency and Federal Bureau of Investigation, *Al-Qa'ida Remains Intent on Defeating US Immigration Inspections*, May 30, 2003.

53. Joint Atomic Energy Intelligence Committee, *Iran's Nuclear Program: Building a Weapons Capability*, February 1993; The Commission on the Intelligence Capabilities of the United States Regarding Weapons of Mass Destruction, *Report to the President of the United States*, p. 198 n. 14, n. 18, n. 22.

54. Cumming, Congressional Research Service, Memorandum to: Sen. Dianne Feinstein, Subject: Congress as a Consumer of Intelligence Information, p. 11.

55. Bill Gertz, "NATO Candidates Armed Rogue States," *Washington Times*, February 19, 1997, pp. A1, A16. Other titles are obtained from documents released by the CIA.

56. Bill Gertz, "Mishaps Put Russian Missiles in 'Combat' Mode," *New York Times*, May 12, 1997, pp. A1, A10; Bill Gertz, "Most of Russia's Biggest Banks Linked to Mob, CIA Says," *Washington Times*, December 5, 1994, pp. A1, A12; Bill Gertz, "16 Biological Weapons Sites Identified in Ex-Soviet Union," *Washington Times*, March 3, 1992, p. A3; Bill Gertz, "Renegades Pose Nuke Danger," *Washington Times*, October 22, 1996, pp. A1, A18; Central

Intelligence Agency, "Terrorists: Recruiting and Operating Behind Bars," August 20, 2002, available at www.fas.org; Central Intelligence Agency, *Colombia-Venezuela: Continuing Friction Along the Border*, October 1, 1977, www.foia.cia.gov; Central Intelligence Agency, *Peru: President Manipulating Judiciary*, May 20, 1998, www.foia.cia.gov; Central Intelligence Agency, *Colombia: Burgeoning Coca Industry in Norte de Santander*, August 17, 2000, www.foia.cia.gov; Central Intelligence Agency, *Russia: Developing New Nuclear Warheads at Novaya Zemlya?* July 2, 1999; Central Intelligence Agency, *India: Problems and Prospects for the BJP Government*, April 13, 1998.

57. U.S. Congress, Senate Select Committee on Intelligence, *Report on the U.S. Intelligence Community's Prewar Intelligence Assessments on Iraq*, p. 186; The Commission on the Intelligence Capabilities of the United States Regarding Weapons of Mass Destruction, *Report to the President of the United States*, pp. 198 n. 23; 200 n. 41, 247 n. 834.

58. CIA Red Cell, "What If Foreigners See the United States as an 'Exporter of Terrorism'?," February 5, 2010; CIA Red Cell, "Afghanistan: Sustaining West European Support for the NATO-Led Mission—Why Counting on Apathy Might Not Be Enough," March 11, 2010.

59. Defense Intelligence Agency, *Defense Analysis Report—Terrorism: Former Guantanamo Bay Detainee Terrorism Trends*, January 7, 2009, available at www.dia.mil/public_affairs/foia.

60. Central Intelligence Agency, *A Consumer's Guide to Intelligence*, 1995, p. v.

61. Robert A. Wampler, ed., National Security Archive Electronic Briefing Book 205, *North Korea's Collapse? The End is Near—Maybe*, October 26, 2006, Document 4; INR, *China: Looking In and Looking Out*, July 25, 1990.

62. U.S. Congress, Senate Select Committee on Intelligence, *Report on the U.S. Intelligence Community's Prewar Intelligence Assessments on Iraq*, p. 48; The Commission on the Intelligence Capabilities of the United States Regarding Weapons of Mass Destruction, *Report to the President of the United States*, pp. 199 n. 32, n. 35, 209 n. 160.

63. The Commission on the Intelligence Capabilities of the United States Regarding Weapons of Mass Destruction, *Report to the President of the United States*, p. 210 n. 111, p. 245 n. 82; National Ground Intelligence Center, *Complex Environments: Battle of Fallujah I, April 2004* (n.d.), available at www.wikileaks.org; *NGIC Assessments* obtained by the National Security Archive under the Freedom of Information Act.

64. Documents obtained under the Freedom of Information Act; Office of Naval Intelligence, *Office of Naval Intelligence Command History 1995*, 1996, pp. 54–55.

65. National Air and Space Intelligence Center, NASCI-OS-0037–2010, *Current and Potential Applications of Chinese Aerostats (Airships)*, March 23, 2010.

66. Drug Enforcement Administration, "Intelligence Reports," www.justice.gov/dea/pubs/intel.htm, accessed October 27, 2010.

67. Central Intelligence Agency, *A Consumer's Guide to Intelligence*, 1995, pp. 32–33.

68. "Japan Threatens to Reduce Grant Aid to China," *Economic Intelligence Weekly*, May 25, 1995, pp. 17–18; "Azerbaijan's Energy Strategy Threatens Caspian Export Projects," *Economic Intelligence Weekly*, July 17, 1999, www.foiaciagov; "Caspian Gas: Turkey Shifting Focus to Azerbaijan as Supplier," *Economic Intelligence Weekly*, August 5, 2000, www.foia.cia.gov; "Ministries at Odds over US Nuclear Testing Initiative," *Eurasian Intelligence Weekly*, August 18, 1995; "Russians Deny Nuclear Test Took Place," *Eurasian Intelligence Weekly*, March 15, 1996.

69. Central Intelligence Agency, *A Consumer's Guide to Intelligence*, 1995, p. 33; issues of *Terrorism Review* partially released under the Freedom of Information Act; Vernon Loeb, "Where the CIA Wages Its New War," *Washington Post*, September 9, 1998, p. A17; "Prointegrationists Pose Threat to Foreign Interests in East Timor," *Terrorism Review*, September 1999, pp. 1–4, www.foia.cia.gov.

70. Central Intelligence Agency, *A Consumer's Guide to Intelligence*, 1995, p. 33; "China's Nuclear Test Program Faces Delays," *Proliferation Digest*, October 30, 1994, p. 10; "Russian Nuclear Device in Kazakhstan," *Proliferation Digest*, June 30, 1995, pp. 11–12; "Libya: Pursuing WMD and Missile Programs in Search of Power and Prestige," *Proliferation Digest*, March 1999, p. 37, www.foia.cia.gov; "Proliferation Will Worsen in Next Decade," *Proliferation Digest*, March 2000, p. 1, www.foia.cia.gov.

71. Central Intelligence Agency, *A Consumer's Guide to Intelligence*, 1995, p. 34.

72. Central Intelligence Agency, *A Consumer's Guide to Intelligence*, 1993, p. 22.

73. Bill Gertz, *Betrayal: How the Clinton Administration Undermined American Security* (Washington, D.C.: Regnery, 1999), p. 253.

74. "The Homepage of Richard Mangan," www.fau.edu/dcj/faculty/rmangan.html, accessed October 28, 2010.

75. Cumming, Congressional Research Service, Memorandum to: Sen. Diane Feinstein, Subject: Congress as a Consumer of Intelligence Information, p. 11.

76. Central Intelligence Agency, *Biographic Handbook USSR, Supplement IV*, April 1977.

77. Central Intelligence Agency, *Biographic Report: Yitzhak RABIN, Prime Minister of Israel*, June 1974.

78. Richelson, ed., National Security Archive Briefing Book 167, *Saddam's Iron Grip*, Document 6; Defense Intelligence Agency, *Iraqi Key Regime Personalities*, 2003, p. 63.

79. Central Intelligence Agency, *Usama Bin Ladin: Islamic Extremist Financier*, 1996.

80. Defense Intelligence Agency, "Biographic Sketch: Andres Rodriguez," April 1966.

81. Sketches and profiles released under the Freedom of Information Act.

82. Central Intelligence Agency, *A Consumer's Guide to Intelligence*, 1995, p. 32.

83. National Ground Intelligence Center, NGIC-1147–101–95, *Nonlethal Technologies—Worldwide (U)*, May 1995, pp. vii–ix.

84. National Ground Intelligence Center, NGIC-1867–0285–01, *Assessment of Chinese Radio Frequency Weapon Capabilities*, April 2001, p. v; National Ground Intelligence Center, NGIC-1841–0178–02, *Chinese Ground Propulsion Technology*, July 2002, p. v.

85. Office of Naval Intelligence, *Foreign Oceanographic Research and Development with Naval Implications*, 1996; National Air Intelligence Center, NAIC-1361–2253–00, *Iraq L-29 UAV Conversion*, December 30, 1999; National Air Intelligence Center, *Foreign Weaponized Unmanned Aerial Vehicles*, December 2001, pp. v–vii.

86. Karen DeYoung, "Terror Database Has Quadrupled in Four Years," www.washington post.com, March 25, 2007.

87. Lieberthal, *The U.S. Intelligence Community and Foreign Policy*, p. 4.

88. M. E. "Spike" Bowman, "The Drumbeats for Clemency for Jonathan Jay Pollard Reverberate Again," *The Intelligencer*, Winter/Spring 2011, pp. 31–34; Robert Clark, *The Technical Collection of Intelligence* (Washington, D.C.: CQ Press, 2010), pp. 242, 244, 276.

89. Federal Bureau of Investigation, *The Terrorist Threat to the US Homeland: An FBI Assessment*, April 15, 2004, passim.

90. Federal Bureau of Investigation, *Tactics Used by Eco-Terrorists to Detect and Thwart Law Enforcement Operations*, April 15, 2004; Federal Bureau of Investigation, *White Supremacist Recruitment of Military Personnel Since 9/11*, July 7, 2008, p. 3; Federal Bureau of Investigation, *White Supremacist Infiltration of Law Enforcement*, October 17, 2006, p. 3.

91. Mark A. Randol, Congressional Research Service, *The Department of Homeland Security Intelligence Enterprise: Operational Overview and Oversight Challenges for Congress*, March 19, 2010, p. 9.

92. Office of Intelligence and Analysis, Department of Homeland Security, *Homeland Security Threat Assessment: Evaluating Threats 2008–2013*, 2008, p. 3; "Border Internet Cited in U.S. Terror Threat," *Los Angeles Times*, December 26, 2008, p. A22.

93. Randol, Congressional Research Service, *The Department of Homeland Security Intelligence Enterprise*, pp. 9–10.

94. Office of Intelligence and Analysis, Department of Homeland Security, *Homeland Security Threat Assessment*, p. 37.

95. Office of Intelligence and Analysis, Department of Homeland Security, "2009 Fourth of July Security Awareness," June 30, 2009; Office of Intelligence and Analysis, Department of Homeland Security, *Potential Terrorist Threat to the U.S. Information Infrastructure*, June 5, 2007; Homeland Infrastructure Threat and Risk Analysis Center, Department of Homeland Security, *Strategic Sector Assessment: Commercial Facilities Sector*, January 23, 2007; Homeland Infrastructure Threat and Risk Analysis Center, Department of Homeland Security, *Strategic Sector Assessment: Government Facilities Sector*, December 8, 2006; Office of Intelligence and Analysis, Department of Homeland Security, *Domestic Extremist Digest* 2, 2 (2007).

96. Office of Intelligence and Analysis, Department of Homeland Security, *Leftwing Extremists Likely to Increase Use of Cyber Attacks over the Coming Decade*, January 26, 2009.

97. Charles E. Allen, Memorandum for: Gus Coidebella, Acting General Counsel, and Richard Skinner, Inspector General, Department of Homeland Security, Subject: Intelligence Oversight Inquiry into the Production and Dissemination of Office of Intelligence and Analysis Intelligence Note, March 28, 2008, www.eff.org; Spencer S. Hsu and Carrie Johnson, "Documents show DHS improperly spied on Nation of Islam in 2007," www.washington post.com, December 17, 2009.

98. Office of Intelligence and Analysis, Department of Homeland Security, *Rightwing Extremism: Current Economic and Political Climate Fueling Resurgence in Radicalization and Recruitment*, April 7, 2009, p. 2; Eli Lake, "Federal agency warns of radicals on right," www.washingtontimes.com, April 14, 2009.

99. Office of Intelligence and Analysis, Department of Homeland Security, and Federal Bureau of Investigation, Joint Homeland Security Assessment, *Fraudulent Identification: Terrorist and Criminal Intent*, March 12, 2007; Office of Intelligence and Analysis, Department of Homeland Security, *Glasgow Airport Illustrates Varied Terrorist Tactics to Attack Transportation Infrastructure*, July 2, 2007; "Statement for the Record of Charles E. Allen," in U.S. Congress, Senate Committee on Homeland Security and Governmental Affairs, *Lessons from the Mumbai Terrorist Attacks—Parts I and II* (Washington, D.C.: U.S. Government Printing Office, 2010), p. 65.

100. Department of Homeland Security, Washington Regional Threat and Analysis Center, United States Capitol Police, Maryland Coordination and Analysis Center, Federal Bureau of Investigation, National Counterterrorism Center, Virginia Fusion Center, National

Geospatial Intelligence Agency and United States Northern Command, *56th Presidential Inauguration: Joint Threat Assessment*, January 7, 2009, pp. 2–7.

101. Department of Homeland Security, National Counterterrorism Center, National Geospatial-Intelligence Agency, Federal Bureau of Investigation, United States Northern Command, and Florida Fusion Center, *Super Bowl XLIII: Joint Special Event Threat Assessment*, January 16, 2009, pp. 2–7.

15

COUNTERINTELLIGENCE

Counterintelligence is often associated with the catching of spies. However, it is necessary to distinguish between counterintelligence and counterespionage. Counterespionage is a narrower activity than counterintelligence and is concerned with simply preventing the illicit acquisition of secrets by a foreign government or other foreign organization. Counterintelligence is concerned with understanding, and possibly neutralizing, all aspects of the intelligence operations (both human and technical, including both traditional technical collection activities and cyber activities aimed at the acquisition of stored data) of foreign nations and groups.

Foreign intelligence operations may be intended to acquire U.S. national security secrets; manipulate and distort the facts and reality presented to United States policymakers by manipulating the intelligence collected or through covert influence operations; detect, disrupt, and counter U.S. national security operations, including clandestine collection and special operations; and acquire critical technologies and other information to enhance their military capabilities or for economic gain.[1]

Counterintelligence was defined by President Ronald Reagan's Executive Order 12333, which is still partially in force, as both "information gathered" and "activities conducted" in order "to protect against espionage, other intelligence activities, sabotage or assassination conducted on behalf of foreign powers, organizations or persons, or international terrorist activities but not including personnel, physical documents or communications security."[2]

Thus, as defined in Executive Order 12333, counterintelligence incorporates a wide range of activities, some of which were not traditionally considered to be within the realm of counterintelligence. The definition stresses the *counter* aspect and lets the term *intelligence* represent activities below the conventional military level, including terrorist attacks and sabotage, irrespective of whether they are performed by an intelligence organization. Some would also consider counterdeception and counter–illicit technology transfer to be part of the list of counterintelligence subcategories.[3] Such a view essentially combines traditional counterintelligence, positive intelligence designed to counter any form of hostile activity, and a framework (counterdeception) for the analysis of positive intelligence.

The traditional notion of counterintelligence, the one that is employed here, focuses on information gathered and activities conducted with the purpose of understanding and possibly neutralizing the activities of foreign intelligence services. In this view there are four basic functions of counterintelligence activity:

- collection of information on foreign (including terrorist) intelligence and security services and their activities, employing open and clandestine sources;
- evaluation of defectors;
- research and analysis concerning the structure, personnel, and operations of foreign intelligence and security services;
- operations for the purpose of disrupting and neutralizing intelligence and security services engaging in activities hostile to the United States.

These activities serve to fulfill the objectives stated in *The National Counterintelligence Strategy of the United States of America*, issued in 2009:

- Secure the nation against foreign espionage and electronic penetration.
- Protect the integrity of the U.S. Intelligence System.
- Support national policy and decisions.
- Protect U.S. economic advantage, trade secrets and know-how.
- Support U.S. Armed Forces.[4]

TARGETS

Foreign intelligence and security service communities that are targets of U.S. intelligence collection and analysis by a variety of U.S. agencies—including, but not limited to, the CIA, the NSA, the FBI, the DIA, the Army Counterintelligence Center (ACIC), the Air Force Office of Special Investigations (AFOSI), and the Naval Criminal Investigative Service (NCIS)—include those belonging to friendly as well as hostile governments.

Some nations that are allies of the United States employ their intelligence services to engage in activities—such as industrial espionage—inimical to U.S. economic interests. Most prominently, the French Directorate General of External Security (DGSE) has penetrated several U.S. companies, including IBM, Texas Instruments, and Bell Textron. A French government document, apparently obtained by the CIA, indicated a broad effort to obtain information about the work of U.S. aerospace companies. Other allies, including Germany, Israel, Japan, and South Korea, have also been involved in economic espionage.[5]

Of course, the intelligence communities of several nations have also been involved in operations inimical to U.S. national security. The Russian, Israeli, South Korean, Cuban, and Chinese intelligence services have penetrated the CIA, FBI, Office of Naval Intelligence, and other national security institutions—as indicated by the cases of Aldrich Ames (CIA), Harold Nicholson (CIA), Larry Wu-Tai Chin

(CIA), Ana Bellen Montes (DIA), Walter Kendall Myers (INR), Edwin Pitts (FBI), Robert Hanssen (FBI), Robert S. Kim (ONI), Jonathan Pollard (Naval Investigative Service), John Walker (Navy), James Wilbur Fondren Jr. (Pacific Command), and Peter Lee (Los Alamos National Laboratory).[6]

An attempted Chinese penetration of the CIA may have taken place in 2010. Glenn Duffie Shriver was indicted in the Eastern District of Virginia and charged with making false statements to the CIA in a 2007 employment application and 2010 interview—specifically, that he had not had any contact with or received money from any foreign government or intelligence service. The indictment charged that he had met with PRC intelligence officers on several occasions and received $70,000 from them.[7]

Collectively, Ames, Nicholson, Pitts, and Hanssen were able to provide information about the identities of Soviets/Russians providing intelligence to the CIA, about technical surveillance operations (ABSORB and TAW, discussed in Chapter 12), and about the identities of CIA personnel. Pollard provided an enormous number of documents, including more than 800 Top Secret documents, to Israel's Scientific Liaison Bureau (LAKAM). Montes provided information on highly sensitive U.S. intelligence operations directed against Cuba. Among his duties, Chin, who worked for the CIA's Foreign Broadcast Information Service (FBIS), "reviewed, translated and analyzed classified documents from covert and overt human and technical collection sources," and Peter Lee examined the feasibility of detecting submerged submarines via radar imagery. Both provided intelligence on their activities to Chinese intelligence.[8]

A 1999 report by the CIA's Counterintelligence Center stated that Russian intelligence was sabotaging international peacekeeping operations in the Balkans. In addition, it was reported that the Russian Foreign Intelligence Service (SVR) had spied on personnel of the UN Special Commission responsible for investigating Iraq's compliance with its pledge to eliminate its capacity for producing weapons of mass destruction and that the SVR may have passed some of the information collected to Iraq. Subsequent to the March 2003 invasion of Iraq, a Joint Forces Command study stated that the SVR had passed information, sometimes inaccurate information, about U.S. war plans and troop movements. In addition, the Russian Federal Security Service (FSB) has recruited Russian scientists from technological institutes and weapons factories to train Iranian scientists in missile development.[9]

For years, the Soviet Union, and later Russia, maintained a communications intelligence facility at Lourdes, Cuba, which was a significant target for U.S. counterintelligence. The facility, whether or not it provided Moscow with advance knowledge of U.S. war plans during Operation Desert Storm, was one of the world's largest intercept facilities, and it was capable of intercepting a wide range of communications within the United States and between the United States and Europe.[10]

Today, there is a Chinese SIGINT facility in Cuba, which undoubtedly targets some of the same communications links that the Lourdes facility intercepted. These SIGINT facilities, and the activities of a number of other, sometimes allied, countries are targets for U.S. counterintelligence collection, including those used for economic and industrial espionage. For example, France has systematically monitored the telephone conversations and cable traffic of many businesses based in the United States. Other nations in pursuit of economic, business, and industrial intelligence also operate signals intelligence ground stations that intercept U.S. government and commercial communications.[11]

In recent years, the intelligence services of nations such as Iran, Iraq, Pakistan, Syria, and North Korea have been of even greater concern than in the past—including their operations in the United States. For example, Iraqi intelligence officers successfully spied on UN weapons inspectors in 1996 and 1997 and, after learning of the inspectors' targets, moved quickly to hide suspected weapons caches. Iraqi intelligence also recruited a member of the German Foreign Ministry to provide data during the Gulf War, including Western assessments of Iraqi missile capabilities.[12]

According to testimony by then DCI John Deutch, Iranian agents contacted officials at nuclear facilities in Kazakhstan on several occasions, attempting to acquire nuclear-related materials. In 1992, Iran unsuccessfully approached the Ulba Metallurgical Plant to obtain enriched uranium. The following year, three Iranians believed to have connections to Iran's intelligence service were arrested in Turkey while seeking to acquire nuclear material from smugglers from the former Soviet Union.[13]

In 1996, the CIA reported that, in 1995, there had been "several instances of suspected Iranian surveillance of US persons and facilities abroad." The report went on to state, "These incidents involved brazen techniques, especially the frequent use of easily traced diplomatic vehicles. The surveillance probably was a matter of intimidation rather than planning for terrorist attacks, but the information collected could facilitate future planning for terrorist operations."[14]

The following year it was reported that Iranian agents in Bosnia were engaged in extensive operations and had infiltrated the U.S. program to train the Bosnian army. In addition, for several years the VAVAK component of the Ministry of Intelligence and Security left a trail of dead bodies across Europe and the Middle East—the result of a campaign to assassinate Iranian dissidents. The campaign was orchestrated by a Committee for Special Operations, which included the country's spiritual leader, president, foreign minister, and high security officials.[15]

Pakistan's Inter-Services Intelligence Directorate (ISI) is another foreign intelligence service of concern to the United States. Even when it was thought that the higher-levels of the ISI might be committed to operations against the Taliban, there was still concern about the loyalties of those at lower levels. More recently, it was reported that the organization's "S Wing," responsible for operations against India and Afghanistan operates with a certain degree of autonomy. And leaked documents suggested that Pakistan was permitting ISI representatives "to meet directly with the Taliban in secret strategy sessions to organize networks of militant groups that fight against American soldiers in Afghanistan, and even hatch plots to assassinate Afghan leaders."[16]

The intelligence organizations of terrorist/insurgent organizations—particularly al-Qaeda, the Taliban, and Hezbollah—are also of concern to U.S. counterintelligence organizations. In 2007, a CIA officer pleaded guilty to charges of illegally seeking to extract from government computers classified information on Hezbollah (although she was not charged with passing the information to Hezbollah or any other terrorist group). More dramatically, and tragically, an apparently valuable source in al-Qaeda blew himself up, also killing four CIA officers, three agency contractors, and a Jordanian intelligence officer, at the CIA's base in Khost Province—in an operation apparently orchestrated by al-Qaeda.[17]

COLLECTION

Information desired about foreign intelligence and security services, which may ultimately be used to neutralize any hostile activities directed against the United States, includes data on their facilities, leadership, personnel at headquarters and in the field, means of communication, methods of operation, and areas of interest, and may come from a variety of sources.[18]

Open sources concerning friendly and hostile services may include official government documents (e.g., telephone directories, brochures, yearly reports, parliamentary hearings, and reports of commissions of inquiry), books and articles (including those written by former officers of a service of interest), and newspapers. Examples of such sources include Russian newspaper articles on that nation's reconnaissance satellites, a book written by a former member of Israel's Mossad, investigative books on the German Federal Intelligence Service (BND) or the Russian Federal Security Service (FSB), and official publications such as the Canadian Security Intelligence Review Committee's annual report on the Canadian Security Intelligence Service.[19]

In the case of closed societies, open source material is limited; nevertheless, even in these countries analysts may get some useful insights into high-ranking personnel or some aspects of internal operations from occasional government-approved accounts of intelligence and security service actions.

Information about friendly services may also come from liaison and training arrangements. For example, Dominic Perrone of the U.S. Military Liaison Office at the U.S. Embassy in Rome, was able, in 1978, to gather inside information on the effectiveness, or lack thereof, of the newly established Italian intelligence and security services (the SISMI, or Military Security and Information Service, and the SISDE, or Democratic Security and Information Service) from several sources inside the Italian government. As a result, Perrone was able to prepare a 4,000 word report for the DIA that indicated that the resources devoted to SISDE's antiterrorist activities were making effective counterespionage impossible, that the commander of SISDE was not qualified for his job, and that both SISDE and SISMI were performing poorly.[20]

Liaison with allied services also provides information about the activities of hostile services, such as when the French Directorate for Territorial Surveillance (DST) provided the CIA with information from its agent—Vladimir Vetrov, code-named FAREWELL—in Directorate T of the KGB. Beginning in 1981, FAREWELL provided the DST with more than 4,000 documents on Soviet scientific and technical espionage, including information on the Soviet Union's plans to steal Western technological secrets and on internal assessments of its covert technology acquisition activities. Specifically, FAREWELL provided (1) a complete, detailed list of all Soviet organizations involved in scientific and technical intelligence; (2) reports on Soviet plans, accomplishments, and annual savings in all branches of the military industry due to illegal acquisition of foreign technology; (3) a list of all KGB officers throughout the world involved in scientific and technical espionage; and (4) the identities of the principal agents recruited by the officers of "Line X" in ten Western nations, including the United States, West Germany, and France. French President François Mitterrand informed President Reagan about FAREWELL in 1981 and gave him a sample of the intelligence material the agent had transmitted. Several weeks later, the head of the DST, Marcel Chalet, visited Vice President Bush in Washington to discuss FAREWELL.[21]

Several types of human sources may provide useful information. The first is the agent who holds an official position within a hostile service. This type is either a mole (someone recruited prior to their entry into the service, such as Kim Philby) or a "defector-in-place" (someone who agrees to provide information after having attained an intelligence or security position, such as FAREWELL). An individual may agree to provide information for ideological or financial reasons or as the result of coercion or blackmail, which might be based on evidence of sexual or financial misbehavior.

The United States had some significant successes during the Cold War in penetrating the Soviet military intelligence service, the Chief Intelligence Directorate (GRU) of the Soviet General Staff. In the late 1950s and early 1960s, Peter Popov and Oleg Penkovsky, both colonels in the GRU, volunteered their services to the CIA. In addition to providing detailed information on the physical layout of the GRU headquarters, they identified GRU agents and described their personalities. The CIA also began receiving information in the early 1960s from GRU officer Dmitri Polyakov, who reached the rank of major general, was eventually betrayed by Aldrich Ames and executed in 1988. Polyakov was only one of a number of CIA sources, recruited in the 1970s and early 1980s, in the Soviet intelligence apparatus (primarily the KGB) who was betrayed by Ames. More recently, in November 2002, a Russian military court convicted Col. Alexander Sypachev, identified as a Russian intelligence agent, of espionage. He had been accused of preparing a two-page report about Russian intelligence personnel for U.S. contacts.[22]

The CIA also apparently penetrated the Indian Research and Analysis Wing (RAW), India's principal foreign intelligence agency. In 1987 a senior RAW official,

K.V. Unnikrishnan, was reported to have been stationed in Madras, where he was responsible for coordinating Tamil insurgency activities. Unnikrishnan was reportedly blackmailed with compromising photographs of himself and a "stewardess."[23]

The second type of human source is the defector. Defectors provide information concerning various aspects of an intelligence or security service's structure, operations, and leadership. The CIA certainly reaped an intelligence bonanza when Maj. Hunter Bolanos of the Nicaraguan Directorate General of State Security (Direccion General de Seguridad del Estado, DGSE) defected in 1983. For almost the entire period from January 1980 to May 7, 1983, Bolanos had special responsibility for surveillance of the U.S. embassy and CIA activities in Nicaragua. He provided information on the structure of the DGSE, the number of Nicaraguans in the DGSE (2,800–3,000), the presence of foreign advisors to the DGSE (70 Soviets, 400 Cubans, 40–50 East Germans, 20–25 Bulgarians), and the Soviet provision of sophisticated eavesdropping devices.[24]

Similarly, senior intelligence officers who have defected from Cuba and China have provided the United States with new information on intelligence and counterintelligence operations in those nations. In June 1987, Maj. Florentino Apillaga Lombard defected to the United States from the Cuban DGI (General Directorate of Intelligence) and proceeded to inform CIA officials that the great majority of CIA "assets" in Cuba were actually double agents working for the Cuban government. In 1986, Yu Zhensan, the former head of the Foreign Affairs Bureau of the PRC's Ministry of State Security, defected and provided the United States with extensive information about Chinese intelligence operations abroad, including the names of Chinese agents, as well as the names of suspected agents from other nations operating in China. Before defecting, he apparently provided the United States with information leading to the arrest of FBIS employee and long-term Chinese mole Larry Wu-Tai Chin.[25]

During the Cold War, the United States benefitted from information provided by a substantial number of KGB and GRU defectors. As a result, the CIA was able to develop a detailed, albeit not complete, picture of the structures and activities of those organizations.

Before his redefection, KGB official Vitaly Yurchenko provided the CIA with information concerning several Soviet penetrations of the U.S. Intelligence Community— information that led to the discovery that former CIA officer Edward Lee Howard and former NSA employee Ronald Pelton had been providing information to the Soviet Union. He also stated that Pelton and naval spy John Walker were the KGB's most prized assets in the United States.[26]

In June 1986, it was reported that the head of KGB operations in North Africa and liaison to the Palestine Liberation Organization, Oleg Agranians, had defected to the United States. Agranians, who may have been working for the CIA for the three years prior to his defection, apparently supplied the names of KGB agents in Tunisia, Algeria, Morocco, and Libya.[27]

The changing domestic situation in the Soviet Union during the Gorbachev era and the subsequent collapse of the Soviet Union led to the defection of numerous KGB officers. In 1990, Igor Cherpinski, reportedly the KGB's station chief in Belgium, defected. In 1991, Sergi Illarionov, a KGB colonel based in Genoa, defected and helped Western security services identify the KGB's European networks. Aldrich Ames relationship with the KGB was apparently revealed by a defecting SVR officer, code-named AVENGER, who also led them to another Soviet intelligence officer who provided information on Robert Hanssen. In 2000 or early 2001, Sergei Tretykov, a senior aide to the Russian ambassador, and an SVR officer, defected.[28]

And it was apparently the defection, in June 2010, of the SVR officer, identified only as Col. Shcherbakov, who was responsible for supervising illegals operating in the United States, that helped the U.S. break up a network of ten Russian agents. The agents were arrested and traded for prisoners being held in Russia.[29]

A third type of human source on foreign counterintelligence services and activities is surveillance by CIA and other U.S. intelligence personnel. In 1999, it was reported that a major CIA operation in Germany involved monitoring of Iranian intelligence personnel in Frankfurt, which was believed to serve as their base of operations in Europe.[30]

Documents from the intelligence services of a collapsed or deposed regime may provide valuable information about the regime's intelligence operations and covert procurement activities—or similar operations and activities of the regime's allies. For example, the CIA apparently acquired the archives of the East German Ministry of State Security (MfS), better known as the STASI, from a Russian source for between $1 million and $1.5 million, which allowed the agency to identify thousands of East German agents around the world, agents who might have transitioned from East German spies to spies for another hostile government.[31]

In the wake of the fall of Saddam Hussein's government, the CIA seized a large set of files from the newly defunct Iraqi Intelligence Service. That seizure, according to a report in late 2003, "is spurring U.S. investigators of weapons procurement network and agents of influence who took money from the government of Saddam Hussein." The records, which would stretch ninety-four miles if laid out from end to end, contained the names of virtually every Iraqi intelligence officer, as well as the names of their agents. The CIA, was also, in 2003, busy examining files of the Special Security Organization.[32]

Beyond human sources and documents, technical collection also provides data of value for counterintelligence. Intercepted communications from within a country or to embassies overseas can reveal either the activities of the internal security or foreign intelligence service. For example, the United States interception and decoding of Soviet communications traffic in the 1940s paid off significantly in the late 1940s, 1950s, and beyond when the traffic was partially decrypted under the VENONA program. From the 1960s until the collapse of the East German regime, the targets of the U.S. Army's Field Station Berlin included the communications of the MfS. In addition, intercepts of signals from foreign reconnaissance satellites can provide information on what targets are being imaged by those satellites.[33]

Satellite imagery is decidedly less useful than human sources, open sources, or COMINT in providing information about most activities of foreign intelligence services. It can, however, provide information on the precise location and layout of intelligence and security service complexes—information that may prove particularly useful if a direct attack on such facilities is authorized. For example, reconnaissance flights in support of UN inspectors provided information on the regional centers of the Iraqi Special Security Organization. And in periods before and after the March 2003 U.S. invasion of Iraq, U.S. reconnaissance satellites photographed the headquarters of the Special Security Organization as well as the Iraqi Intelligence Service, producing pre- and post-strike imagery. In addition, satellite imagery can provide information on the presence and capabilities of SIGINT facilities and ground stations, whether Chinese facilities in the 1960s or the more recent Soviet/Russian GRU LOW EAR intercept dishes.[34]

EVALUATION OF DEFECTORS

The evaluation and debriefing of defectors are additional responsibilities of a counterintelligence organization. The United States has provided political asylum to officials from the Soviet Union and Russia, China, Nicaragua, Cuba, and a number of Eastern European nations. Since 2005 it appears that a number of Iranian officials have defected and have been willing to provide information to Western intelligence agencies. One, Ali Reza Asgari, a former deputy defense minister who once commanded the Revolutionary Guards, disappeared in Turkey in February 2007, and the information he provided was "fully available" to U.S. intelligence, according to newspaper reports. In March 2007, it was reported that Iran had lost contact with Col. Amir Muhammad Shirazi, an officer in the Quds unit of the Revolutionary Guards, who was stationed in Iraq.[35]

Debriefers seek information on the personnel, policies, structure, capabilities, and activities of whatever government component, especially a hostile intelligence service, employed the defector—as well as information about activities outside his component. In addition to eliciting information, debriefers seek to determine the reliability of the information offered.

When dealing with defectors, debriefers must determine where the defectors' knowledge begins and ends. Exaggeration or fabrication in the face of depleted information is one possibility. Complicating the debriefers' task is the fact that many defectors hold back valid information as insurance for continued protection.[36]

The inability to determine conclusively the bona fides of defectors can lead to paralysis of intelligence collection operations in one or more nations, creation of unwarranted suspicions about and damage to the careers of valuable intelligence officers, failure to fully exploit valuable information, or reliance on false information in making policy or conducting military operations.

Thus, for example, the 1962 defection of KGB officer Anatoli Golitsin to the CIA in Helsinki, Finland, combined with the suspicions of CIA Counterintelligence Chief James Angleton, produced a mole hunt that ruined the careers of several CIA officers, led other KGB defectors to be treated with unjustified suspicion, and helped immobilize CIA clandestine collection operations in the Soviet Union throughout much of the 1960s.[37]

In the case of Vitaly Yurchenko, the CIA's counterintelligence officials and analysts were faced with the task of assessing whether he was a legitimate defector who subsequently changed his mind or a plant who intended to redefect from the very beginning. Yurchenko, a KGB staff officer with twenty-five years of service, requested political asylum in the United States at the U.S. embassy in Rome on August 1, 1985.[38]

From August 1975 until August 1980, Yurchenko was the security officer at the Soviet embassy in Washington, where he was responsible for the security of Soviet facilities and citizens in Washington, for protecting classified information, and for handling foreign visitors. In September 1980, he became chief of Department K of the First Chief Directorate—a position he retained until March 1985. His responsibilities included, but were not limited to, investigating suspected incidents of espionage involving KGB personnel and information leaks concerning the directorate. From April to July 1985, he was deputy chief of the First Department, which carried out operations against the United States and Canada.[39]

Three months after his defection Yurchenko appeared at a press conference at the Soviet embassy in Washington, claiming to have been kidnapped, drugged, and kept in isolation at a CIA safehouse in Fredericksburg, Virginia. His "escape" was due, according to Yurchenko, to a "momentary lapse" by his captors. (In fact, he walked out of a Georgetown restaurant without opposition from his CIA escort.) Two days later, after a visit from U.S. officials to determine whether he was acting of his own free will, Yurchenko flew back to Moscow, where he held a two-hour press conference at which he and other Soviet officials accused the United States of "state terrorism." Subsequent reports that he had been executed were proved incorrect when he was spotted walking on a Moscow street.[40]

Following Yurchenko's defection, U.S. officials speculated on the reasons for his actions. If Yurchenko was a plant who had planned to redefect from the beginning, KGB motives could have been to gather information on CIA treatment and debriefing of defectors, or to embarrass the CIA and discourage the agency from accepting defectors. Among those suggesting that Yurchenko was a plant were President Reagan, Senator Patrick Leahy (then vice chairman of the Senate Select Committee on Intelligence), and other officials who considered Yurchenko's information to be largely "historical."[41]

Others suggested that Yurchenko had been a legitimate defector who had changed his mind. Reasons given for an actual change included his rejection by the wife of a Soviet official stationed in Canada (and whom he visited almost immediately after his arrival in the United States); the great publicity generated by his defection; a general homesickness for "Mother Russia" often experienced by Soviet defectors; and a specific longing to be reunited with his family—especially his sixteen-year-old son. Among those doubting a staged defection was then FBI chief William H. Webster, who said that Yurchenko had provided the United States with valuable information on the roles of Edward Lee Howard and Ronald Pelton.[42]

In early 1993, DCI Robert Gates stated that the CIA had concluded that Yurchenko was a bona fide defector. According to Gates: "My view, and I think the view of virtually everybody in this building, is that Yurchenko was genuine. He provided too much specific information, including in the counterintelligence arena, that has been useful, for him, in my judgment to have been a plant."[43]

In more recent years, cases from Iraq and Iran have provided examples of the requirement to properly assess defectors and their claims—as to both the validity of their information and their stability.

In 2001 the DIA debriefed a number of defectors who claimed to have information about Saddam Hussein's weapons of mass destruction (WMD) efforts. One told his debriefers about an alleged "Substitute Sites" program, which involved the use of government company buildings, private villas, and underground wells to conceal storage and production facilities. Another defector, introduced to Western intelligence by the Iraqi National Congress (INC), reported on what he claimed were Iraq's WMD efforts as well as on its support of foreign terrorist groups. The CIA would determine that he had embellished and exaggerated his access.[44]

In the period leading up to the U.S. invasion of Iraq in 2003, INC introduced additional defectors to U.S. intelligence representatives. In one of its reports on U.S. intelligence and the war, the Senate Select Committee on Intelligence noted that the INC-provided individuals who were debriefed by DIA included both fabricators as well as individuals who provided useful information. The report also stated that after the invasion DIA reported that intelligence provided by the INC sources "covered a myriad of information and was not uniform in quality, accuracy, and utility. In some cases, [the Intelligence Collection Program—INC] provided solid intelligence leads, corroborated other information, and contributed to our knowledge base. In other cases the information was of little or no value."[45]

Among the most prominent defectors associated with the 2003 war as well as with U.S. claims concerning Iraqi WMD activities was known by the code name CURVEBALL. CURVEBALL, who had defected to the Germans and was in custody of the BND, claimed that Iraq was operating mobile biological weapons laboratories. That appeared to confirm other information, and the claim became a key element in Colin Powell's February 5, 2003, presentation to the United Nations. Assessment of CURVEBALL was hindered, rather dramatically, by the BND's refusal to grant the CIA access to him—claiming, falsely (as would later be discovered) that CURVEBALL did not speak English and did not like Americans.[46]

Reminiscent of the Yurchenko case, Iranian nuclear scientist Shahram Amiri (discussed in greater detail in Chapter 11), apparently defected in 2009 and redefected in 2010, but not until providing the CIA with information on Iranian nuclear activities. As with Yurchenko, Amiri claimed mistreatment and coercion by the CIA, leaving the agency to assess the original intent of his defection and the reliability of the information provided.[47]

RESEARCH AND ANALYSIS

It is fundamental to both intelligence and counterintelligence missions that there exist individuals with the ability to decipher, understand, and report on the personalities, structure, facilities, tradecraft, and past and current operations of other nations' intelligence and security services. Only with such knowledge can positive intelligence collection operations be planned and conducted effectively. Likewise, only with such knowledge can effective penetration, disruption, and neutralization activities be carried out.

One significant output of research on foreign intelligence services conducted within the U.S. Intelligence Community is contained in reports prepared by the CIA's Counterintelligence Center (CIC), which is the successor to the agency's Counterintelligence Staff.

The CIC prepares reports on all intelligence communities of interest, both hostile and friendly. Some of the reports detail the origins of the intelligence services, their structure, function, mode of operation, and the arrangements for control by a higher authority. Thus, for example, the 47-page study *Israel: Foreign Intelligence and Security Services*, published in March 1977, focused in its first section on the background and development of the Israeli services, objectives, and structure; the relationship between the government and the services; and professional standards. The second, third, and fourth sections focused on the other three major Israeli intelligence and security units—the Mossad, the Shin Bet, and AMAN, respectively.* In each case, the report examined the service's function, organization, administrative practice (including training), and methods of operation. Additionally, liaison with other Israeli and foreign services was considered. The three penultimate sections examined the Foreign Ministry's Research and Political Planning Center, the National Police, and key officials, while the final section commented on principal sources.[48]

In 1985, the CIA's Counterintelligence Staff produced the 24-page *Iraq: Foreign Intelligence and Security Services*. The study examined the background and development of the services in general and included a section on key personalities as well as individual chapters on the Iraqi Intelligence Service, the Directorate of Military Intelligence, the Directorate General of Security. (The functions, organizations, and administrative practices of each service are explored in these chapters.)[49] The study's table of contents is shown in Figure 15.1.

---

*A more recent, more limited, and perhaps more immediately useful type of product concerning Israel is the CIA's July 25, 2006, report, *Assessment of the Counterintelligence Environment in Israel*, cited in Army Counterintelligence Center, *Wikileaks.org—An Online Reference to Foreign Intelligence Services, Insurgents, or Terrorist Groups?*, March 18, 2008, p. 27.

FIGURE 15.1 Table of Contents: Iraq: Foreign Intelligence and Security Services

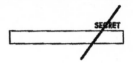

TABLE OF CONTENTS

FIGURES

SECRET

(REVERSE BLANK)   iii

A 1984 study titled *Soviet Intelligence: KGB and GRU* discussed the background and development of the Soviet services, national intelligence objectives and structure, the relationship between the Communist Party/government and the services, the internal security and counterintelligence operations of the KGB, and the foreign operations of the KGB and GRU.[50]

The intelligence structure of Russia is significantly different from that of the Soviet Union. Today there are three key services: the Foreign Intelligence Service (SVR), the Federal Security Service (FSB), and the Chief Intelligence Directorate (GRU) of the General Staff.[51] Any present studies of the Russian services probably examine their Soviet heritage, the transition from the Soviet structure to the early post-Soviet structure and, then, to today's structure (a transition that involved the creation, abolition, merging, and renaming of key institutions), and their present organization, size, targets, and key personalities.

Such studies are likely to be far more detailed examinations of the questions that appeared in the unclassified September 1992 CIA study, *The Russian Security Services: Sorting Out the Pieces*. This seven-page study contains a diagram of the evolution of the Russian services (except the GRU) between August 1991 and September 1992, a brief description of the organizations at the time of publication, and short biographies of service heads.[52]

Counterintelligence studies are also prepared by the Defense Intelligence Agency and military service intelligence and security components. The DIA prepared a November 15, 1978, Intelligence Appraisal titled *Italy: Reorganization of the Intelligence and Security Services*, which discussed the background and structure of Italy's services, key personalities, intelligence reforms, and outlook for the future. Studies prepared by the Army Intelligence and Threat Analysis Center, absorbed into the National Ground Intelligence Center in 1995, included *Italy: A Counterintelligence Assessment* (April 1984), which reviewed the country's security and intelligence organizations as well as various threats—including terrorism, wartime sabotage, and espionage; *The DST: An Organization in Flux* (September 1986); *France: A Counterintelligence Assessment* (June 1981); *GRU Activity in the Washington, D.C. Area* (April 1983); and *The Cuban Intelligence Threat in Panama* (May 1978).[53]

Among the products of the Army Counterintelligence Center are its 2006 study, *Iraqi Insurgent and Militia Group Intelligence Capabilities to Counter US Counter-Improvised Explosive Device Systems* and its 2007 product, *Multidiscipline Counterintelligence Threat Assessment for the Counter Radio Control Improvised Explosive Device Electronic Warfare (CREW-2) Program*. But perhaps its best-known product, given the unwanted publicity it received, is its 2008 report, *Wikileaks.org—An Online Reference to Foreign Intelligence Services, Insurgents, or Terrorist Groups?*[54]

The report's key judgments included the observation that Wikileaks represented "a potential force protection, counterintelligence, [operations security, and information security] threat to the Army" and that the "recent unauthorized release" of classified Defense Department information provided foreign intelligence services, foreign terrorist groups, insurgents, and other foreign adversaries with "potentially actionable information for targeting US forces." The report also suggested that "the identification, exposure, termination of employment of or legal actions against current or former insiders, leakers, or whistleblowers could damage or destroy this center of gravity and deter others from using Wikileaks.org to make such information public."[55]

DISRUPTION AND NEUTRALIZATION

The neutralization of the activities of foreign intelligence services can be accomplished by various means. Penetration of a hostile service can be used not only to gather information but to damage the service's operations. In 1980, the Polish civilian intelligence and security service, the SB, began receiving classified information from James D. Harper, a Silicon Valley engineer. Harper, through his wife, who worked for a southern California defense contractor, obtained copies of well over 100 pounds of classified reports, which he sold to the SB for more than $250,000. Most were Confidential or Secret documents pertaining to the U.S. Minuteman missile and ballistic missile defense programs, including the 1978 *Minuteman Defense Study (Final Report)*, the 1981 *Report on the Task Force on U.S. Ballistic Missile Defense*, and a 1978 Martin-Marietta Corporation study titled *Endoatmospheric Nonnuclear Kill Technology Requirements and Definition Study*. The CIA discovered Harper's activities via its penetration of the SB. When arrested, Harper was preparing to deliver an additional 150 to 200 pounds of documents.[56]

A second means of neutralizing a hostile intelligence service is by passing information to a third country that will lead that country to take action against the officers and agents of the hostile service. In many cases, the CIA passes such information on as a natural result of its liaison with a friendly security service, such as when it provided the British Security Service with information on East German intelligence operations in the United Kingdom. At the time of the defection of GRU officer Sergei Bokhane (code-named GT/BLIZZARD), who had been stationed in Greece, he provided information on at least three Greeks involved in spying for the Soviet Union. Included was Michael Megalokonomos, who, when apprehended, was in possession of a code book, a microfilm reading device, a radio capable of picking up special frequencies, and instructions on how to work a radio transmitter. Also named by Bokhane was Nikos Pipitsoulis, who sold an electrical device to Soviet officials for $43,000. In addition, a lieutenant commander working in the data processing unit at Greek defense headquarters was involved in passing information on to the Soviet Union. The information provided to the CIA by Bokhane was passed on to Greek security authorities, leading to the arrest of the three agents.[57]

On other occasions the recipient of the information may be a hostile nation. In the spring of 1983, when the Iranian Communist (Tudeh) Party had been closed down, the CIA provided a list of Soviet agents and collaborators operating in Iran to the Khomeini regime and its security service (SAVAMA). As a result, 18 Soviet diplomats were expelled, 200 suspects were executed, and Tudeh Party leaders were imprisoned.[58]

Another method of neutralization entails running double agents. One CIA double agent operation that came to light is one that backfired. In 1959, Captain Nikolai Federovich Artamanov, the youngest commanding officer of a destroyer in Soviet naval history, defected to Sweden. Information about Artamanov was transferred to the United States by the CIA station chief in Sweden.[59]

Artamanov was subsequently recruited by the Office of Naval Intelligence (ONI) to come to the United States. In his debriefing, he provided the ONI with information on the Soviet use of trawlers for intelligence collection, Soviet nuclear strategy, and Soviet destroyer tactics against submarines. Subsequently, he was given a new name, Nicholas Shadrin, and a position as a translator in the Naval Science and Technical Intelligence Center. In 1966, Shadrin went to work for the Defense Intelligence Agency and was also approached by a Soviet intelligence officer who tried to recruit him. Shadrin reported the offer to the FBI, which persuaded Shadrin, despite his initial reluctance, to become a double agent, to "accept" the Soviet offer, and to feed the KGB CIA-doctored information.[60]

After several years of pretending to work for the KGB, Shadrin began to make trips abroad to meet his controller. He never returned from a December 20, 1975, meeting in Vienna. According to temporary defector Vitaly Yurchenko, Shadrin was, by accident, fatally chloroformed while struggling in the backseat of a sedan with Soviet agents trying to spirit him out of Vienna.[61]

During George Tenet's tenure at the CIA, the agency conducted a disruption campaign against Iran's Ministry of Intelligence and Security (MOIS). Agency officers approached ministry officers—on the streets or wherever they had the opportunity—and asked if they would be willing to work for the CIA or sell information. Those approaches "undoubtedly ruined some careers," according to Tenet, as well as occasionally producing actual intelligence dividends.[62]

The military, particularly the Army, also runs double agent operations. According to the 1982 version of U.S. Army Regulation 381–47, offensive counterintelligence operations, such as double agent operations, "may require engagement in unorthodox operations and activities. These unorthodox activities may be at variance with recognized standards or methods normally associated with the military service. They will be undertaken only when authorized by the commander of a counterintelligence unit or higher authority."[63]

Double agent operations often are initiated after a member of the U.S. armed forces reports an approach made by a foreign intelligence officer. In 1984, there were 481 incidents of soldiers being approached by people suspected of being Soviet bloc intelligence officers or sympathizers.[64]

Under the direction of counterintelligence authorities, the service personnel maintain contact with the foreign intelligence officers, providing a combination of low-grade factual and false, but apparently valuable, information supplied by the military services. Such operations yield information on the intelligence targets of hostile services, allow identification of the intelligence officers and agents of hostile services, tie up hostile service resources, and permit the transmission of disinformation concerning the plans and capabilities of U.S. military forces.[65]

One operation involved Chief Warrant Officer Janos Szmolka, who had left Hungary to become a U.S. citizen and eventually joined the U.S. Army. Stationed in West Germany, he went on authorized leaves to Budapest to visit his mother in 1978 and 1979. On his third trip he was approached by a man described as a Hungarian intelligence officer, who offered to ensure better living conditions for Szmolka's family in exchange for information.[66]

Szmolka returned to West Germany and reported the offer to his superiors. For the next four years, under the direction of Army counterintelligence officers, he was in contact with Hungarian agents in Europe and the United States. In 1980, under normal rotation procedures, he was transferred to the States; and in 1982, when the Army desired to uncover the Hungarian intelligence network in the United States, Szmolka was instructed to inform the Hungarians, through coded letters, that he had valuable information to turn over. On April 17, 1982, he went to the Confederate monument in Augusta, Georgia, near his post at Fort Gordon, to meet a Hungarian agent. Federal agents arrested Otto A. Gilbert, an expatriate Hungarian and naturalized U.S. citizen, and charged him with espionage. Gilbert received a reduced sentence in exchange for information about Hungarian intelligence.[67]

Disruption and neutralization may be targeted not only on foreign intelligence collection operations but also on foreign service acquisition technology operations—which, in turn, may be conducted on behalf of either the civilian or military sector. The information provided by FAREWELL allowed the CIA to devise an operation that led the KGB's "Line X" to acquire altered, defective products—including contrived computer chips and flawed turbines—as well as misinformation about stealth aircraft and space defense.[68]

Notes

1. Office of the National Counterintelligence Executive, *The National Counterintelligence Strategy of the United States*, March 2005, p. 1.

2. Ronald Reagan, "Executive Order 12333: United States Intelligence Activities," December 4, 1981, in *Federal Register* 46, no. 235 (December 8, 1981): 59941–59955 at 59943.

3. See, for example, William Harris, "Counterintelligence Jurisdiction and the Double Cross System by National Technical Means," in *Intelligence Requirements for the 1980s: Counterintelligence*, ed. Roy Godson (New Brunswick, N.J.: Transaction, 1980), pp. 53–82.

4. Office of the National Counterintelligence Executive, *The National Counterintelligence Strategy of the United States of America*, 2009, pp. 1–5.

5. Jay Peterzell, "When 'Friends' Become Moles," *Time*, May 28, 1990, p. 50; "Parlez-Vous Espionage?," *Newsweek*, September 23, 1991, p. 40; Douglas Jehl, "U.S. Expanding Its Effort to Halt Spying by Allies," *New York Times*, April 30, 1993, pp. A1, A10; R. Jeffrey Smith, "U.S. to Protest Industrial Spying by Allies," *Washington Post*, April 30, 1993, p. A39; John J. Fialka, *War by Other Means: Economic Espionage in America* (New York: W.W. Norton, 1997); Peter Schweitzer, *Friendly Spies: How America's Allies Are Using Economic Espionage to Steal Our Secrets* (New York: Atlantic Monthly Press, 1993); General Accounting Office, GAO/NSIAD-96–64, *Weaknesses in U.S. Security Arrangements with Foreign-Owned Defense Contractors*, 1996, pp. 22–26.

6. On the Myers and Fondren cases, see Evan Perez, "Spy for Cuba, Unrepentant, Gets Life," *Wall Street Journal*, July 17–18, 2010, p. A3; and Department of Justice, "Recent Espionage-Related Prosecutions Involving China," n.d., p. 1.

7. Department of Justice, "Recent Espionage-Related Prosecutions Involving China," p.1.

8. David Wise, *Nightmover: How Aldrich Ames Sold the CIA to the KGB for $4.6 Million* (New York: HarperCollins, 1995); David Wise, *Spy: The Inside Story of How the FBI's Robert Hanssen Betrayed America* (New York: Random House, 2002); Nicholas Eftimiades, *Chinese Intelligence Operations* (Annapolis, Md.: Naval Institute Press, 1994), pp. 21–37; "Physicist Admits to Spying for China," *Washington Times*, December 10, 1997, p. A9; *United States of America v. Larry Wu-Tai Chin aka Chin Wu-Tai in the United States District Court for the Eastern District of Virginia, Alexandria Division*, Criminal No. 85–00263-A, January 2, 1986, pp. 2–3; National Counterintelligence Executive, *American Revolution into the New Millennium: A Counterintelligence Reader*, Volume 4, n.d., pp. 434–439, www.ncix.gov/history; Director of Central Intelligence, *The Jonathan Jay Pollard Espionage Case: A Damage Assessment*, October 30, 1987; Bill Gertz, "China's Spies 'Very Aggressive' Threat to U.S.," www.washington times.com, March 6, 2007.

9. R. Jeffrey Smith, "Did Russia Sell Iraq Germ Warfare Equipment?" *Washington Post*, February 12, 1998, pp. A1, A35; Peter Spiegel and Greg Miller, "Russians Told Iraqi Regime of U.S. Troop Movements," *Los Angeles Times*, March 25, 2006, pp. A1, A7; Thom Shanker, "U.S. Inquiry Finds Russians Passed Spy Data to Iraq in '03," *New York Times*, March 25, 2006, p. A7; Mark Kramer, "Did Russia Help Saddam During the War?," http://www.wash ingtonpost.com, April 2, 2006; Kim Murphy, "Russia Denies Slipping U.S. War Plans to Iraq," *Los Angeles Times*, March 26, 2006, p. A32; Daniel Williams, "Russian Spy Agency Linked to Iran," *Washington Post*, March 23, 1998, p. A14; Bill Gertz, "U.S. Official Claims Russia Cutting Aid to Iran on Missiles," *Washington Times*, March 11, 1998, p. A5; Bill Gertz, "Russian Spies Active in Balkans, CIA Says," *Washington Times*, March 23, 1999, p. A14; Kevin M. Woods with Michael R. Pease, Mark E. Stout, Williamson Murray, and James G. Lacey, Joint Forces Command, *Iraqi Perspectives Project: A View of Operation Iraqi Freedom from Saddam's Senior Leadership*, 2006, pp. 138–139, 144–145.

10. Juan O. Tamayo, "Soviets Spied on Gulf War Plans from Cuba, Defector Says," *Miami Herald*, April 3, 1998, p. 21A; William Rosenau, "A Deafening Silence: US Government Policy and the Sigint Facility at Lourdes," *Intelligence and National Security* 9, 4 (October 1994): 723–734.

11. National Counterintelligence Executive, *American Revolution into the New Millennium: A Counterintelligence Reader*, Volume 4, pp. 202–203; Interagency OPSEC Support Staff, *Intelligence Threat Handbook*, n.d., pp. 18–50.

12. Tim Weiner, "U.S. Says Iraq Spied on Inspectors to Know When to Hide Weapons," *New York Times*, November 25, 1997, pp. A1, A6; Alan Cowell, "German Military Official Spied for Iraq in Gulf War," *New York Times*, November 18, 1997, p. A14.

13. John Deutch, "The Threat of Nuclear Diversion," Statement for the Record to the Permanent Subcommittee on Investigations of the Senate Committee on Governmental Affairs, March 20, 1996, p. 4.

14. Central Intelligence Agency, "Iranian Surveillance of US Persons and Facilities in 1995," January 1996, www.foia.cia.gov.

15. Mike O'Connor, "Spies for Iranians Are Said to Gain a Hold in Bosnia," *New York Times*, November 28, 1997, pp. A1, A8; Alan Cowell, "Berlin Court Says Top Iran Leaders Ordered Killings," *New York Times*, April 11, 1997, pp. A1, A10; Carl Anthony Wege, "Ira-

nian Intelligence Organizations," *International Journal of Intelligence and Counterintelligence* 10, 3 (Fall 1997): 287–298; U.S. Department of State, *Patterns of Global Terrorism, 1997,* 1998, p. 31.

16. Mark Mazzetti, Jane Perlez, Eric Schmitt, and Andrew W. Lehren, "Pakistan Spy Unit Aiding Insurgents, Reports Suggest," *New York Times,* July 26, 2010, pp. A1, A12; Julian E. Barnes, Matthew Rosenberg, and Habib Khan Totakhill, "Pakistan Urges on Taliban," *Wall Street Journal,* October 7, 2010, pp. A1, A14.

17. Philip Shenon, "C.I.A. Officer Admit Guilt in Seeking Hezbollah Files," *New York Times,* November 14, 2007, p. A17; Department of Justice, "Former Employee of CIA and FBI Pleads Guilty to Conspiracy, Unauthorized Computer Access and Naturalization Fraud," November 13, 2007; Sheryl Gay Stolberg and Mark Mazzetti, "Suicide Bombing Puts a Rare Face on C.I.A.'s Work," *New York Times,* January 7, 2010, pp. A1, A18; Robert Baer, "A Dagger to the CIA," www.gq.com, April 2010; Stephen Farrell, "Video Bolsters Pakistani Link to C.I.A. Deaths," *New York Times,* January 10, 2010, pp.1, 10; "CIA Blast Blamed on Double Agent," *Wall Street Journal,* January 5, 2010, pp. A1, A10; Mark Magnier, "CIA spy said he gave secrets to militants," *Los Angeles Times,* January 10, 2010, p. A24; Joby Warrick, "In new video, CIA bomber says he lured targets with doctored intelligence," www.washingtonpost.com, March 1, 2008.

18. Department of the Army, AR 381–47, *U.S. Army Counterintelligence Operations,* June 15, 1982, p. 2.

19. "Russian Newspaper Says Spy Satellite Was Expensive Test Dummy," *Aerospace Daily,* June 11, 1997, p. 399; Erich Schmidt-Eenboom, *Schnuffer ohne Nase: Der BND–Die Un-heimliche Macht im Staate* (Dusseldorf: ECON Verlag, 1993); Andrei Soldatov and Irina Borogan, *The New Nobility: The Restoration of Russia's Security State and the Enduring Legacy of the KGB* (New York: Public Affairs, 2010); Victor Ostrovsky and Claire Hoy, *By Way of Deception: The Making and Unmaking of a Mossad Officer* (New York: St. Martin's Press, 1990); Security Intelligence Review Committee, *Annual Report 1995–1996* (Ottawa: SIRC, 1996).

20. Dominic Perrone, "I&SS, Status of SISDE/SISMI Anti-Terrorist Orientation," *Covert Action Information Bulletin* (April–May 1979): 6–9.

21. Thierry Wolton, *Le KGB en France* (Paris: Bernard Grasser, 1986), pp. 248–249.

22. Tom Mangold, *Cold Warrior, James Jesus Angleton: The CIA's Master Spy Hunter* (New York: Simon & Schuster, 1991), pp. 227–236; David Wise, *Molehunt: The Secret Search for Traitors That Shattered the CIA* (New York: Random House, 1991), pp. 153–154; David Wise, *Nightmover,* p. 105, passim; "Russian Convicted of Spying," *Washington Post,* November 12, 2002, p. A21.

23. Iderjit Badhwar, "Spy-Catching," *India Today,* September 20, 1987, p. 33.

24. Don Oberdorfer and Joanne Omang, "Nicaraguan Bares Plan to Discredit Foes," *Washington Post,* June 19, 1983, pp. 1, 4.

25. Jack Anderson and Dale Van Atta, "Cuban Defector Impeaches CIA Spies," *Washington Post,* March 21, 1988, p. B15; Jack Anderson and Dale Van Atta, "CIA Recruits Were Castro's Agents," *Washington Post,* March 23, 1988, p. D11; Jack Anderson and Dale Van Atta, "CIA, Cubans in Looking-Glass War," *Washington Post,* March 25, 1988, p. E5; "Chinese Official Said Exposer of CIA Turncoat," *Washington Post,* September 5, 1986, p. A18; Michael Wines, "Spy Reportedly Unmasked by China Defector," *Los Angeles Times,* September 5, 1986, pp. 1, 12; Daniel Southerland, "China Silent on Reported Defection of Intelligence Official," *Washington Post,* September 4, 1986, p. A30.

26. "Did Yurchenko Fool the CIA?," *Newsweek,* November 18, 1985, pp. 34–39.

27. "High-Ranking KGB Agent Defects," *Washington Post*, June 20, 1986, p. A5.

28. "Defection of KGB Agent Causes Stir," *Washington Times*, June 6, 1990, p. A11; Bill Gertz, "CIA Learning from KGB Defector," *Washington Times*, March 5, 1992, p. A3; Mike Mattson, "A Counterintelligence Cold Case File: The Fourth Mole," *The Intelligencer* (Winter/Spring 2009): 39–50 at 43; James Risen, "Defection of Senior Chinese Officer Is Confirmed," *New York Times*, March 24, 2001, p. A6.

29. Clifford J. Levy, "Defector Aided in Thwarting Russian Spies, Article Says," *New York Times*, November 12, 2010, p. A6; Sergei L. Loiko, "Russian spy saga has new twist: An alleged defector," *Los Angeles Times*, November 12, 2010, p. A3.

30. William Drozdiak, "Germans Force U.S. to Recall 3 CIA Agents in Spy Case," *Washington Post*, September 30, 1999, pp. A17, A20.

31. William Drozdiak, "The Cold War in Cold Storage," *Washington Post*, March 8, 1999, p. A17.

32. Steve Coll, "Seized Intelligence Files Spur U.S. Investigations," *Washington Post*, November 3, 2003, p. A15.

33. Robert Louis Benson and Michael Warner, eds., *VENONA: Soviet Espionage and the American Response, 1939–1957* (Washington, D.C.: National Security Agency/Central Intelligence Agency, 1996); Markus Wolf with Ann McElvoy, *Man Without a Face: The Autobiography of Communism's Greatest Spymaster* (New York: Times Books, 1997), p. 294; private information.

34. Barton Gellman, "Raids May Strike at Power Structure," *Washington Post*, February 17, 1998, pp. A1, A9; Jeffrey T. Richelson, ed., National Security Archive Electronic Briefing Book No. 88, *Eyes on Saddam*, April 30, 2003, www.nsarchive.org; Central Intelligence Agency, CIA/PIR-1017/65, *Tung-Ching-Shan Electronic Intercept Site*, China, June 1965; Jeffrey T. Richelson, *America's Secret Eyes in Space: The US KEYHOLE Spy Satellite Program* (New York: Harper & Row, 1990), p. 245.

35. Dafna Linzer, "Former Iranian Defense Official Talks to Western Intelligence," www.washingtonpost.com, March 8, 2007; Sebnem Arsu, "German Official Adds to Mystery of Iranian Missing in Turkey," *New York Times*, Marcy 14, 2007, p. A11; Michael Young, "By Way of Defection," www.reason.com, March 15, 2007.

36. Ralph Blumenthal, "Moscow Moves Rapidly in Defections to the U.S.," *New York Times*, November 7, 1985, p. A12.

37. See Wise, *Molehunt*; Mangold, *Cold Warrior*.

38. Central Intelligence Agency, "Vitaly Sergeyevich Yurchenko," November 8, 1985, p. 1.

39. Ibid., pp. 2–3.

40. "Did Yurchenko Fool the CIA?"; Celestine Bohlen, "Yurchenko Regales Moscow Audience," *Washington Post*, November 15, 1985, p. A33; "How Yurchenko Bade C.I.A. Adieu," *New York Times*, November 7, 1985, p. A12; Stephen Engelberg, "U.S. Is Convinced That K.G.B. Agent Wants to Go Home," *New York Times*, November 6, 1985, pp. A1, A12.

41. "Did Yurchenko Fool the CIA?"; Stephen Engelberg, "President Sees a Soviet 'Ploy' in 3 Defections," *New York Times*, November 7, 1985, pp. A1, A12; Stephen Engelberg, "Washington Ponders Yurchenko: A Troubled Spy or Actor?" *New York Times*, November 10, 1985, p. 20; Bob Woodward, "CIA Takes Serious Look at Theory That Yurchenko Was Double Agent," *Washington Post*, November 20, 1985, p. A35; Stephen Engelberg, "U.S. Aides Split on Yurchenko's Authenticity," *New York Times*, November 8, 1985, p. A10.

42. John Mintz, "FBI Chief Doubts Defection of Yurchenko Was Staged," *Washington Post*, December 2, 1985, pp. A1, A14; Joel Brinkley, "Publicity Said to Have Upset Defector," *New*

York Times, November 14, 1985, p. A12; Christopher Wren, "K.G.B. Man Reportedly Met with Envoy's Wife," *New York Times*, November 9, 1985, p. 4; Arkady N. Shevchenko, "A Lesson of the Yurchenko Affair," *New York Times*, November 12, 1985, p. 35; Dale Russakof, "In Yurchenko Case, Truth Remains a Covert Factor," *Washington Post*, November 10, 1985, pp. A1, A40–A41.

43. "Gates Calls '85 Defector Bona Fide," *Washington Post*, January 16, 1993, p. A7.

44. Jeffrey T. Richelson, *Spying on the Bomb: American Nuclear Intelligence from Nazi Germany to Iran and North Korea* (New York: W. W. Norton, 2006), pp. 470–471.

45. U.S. Congress, Senate Select Committee on Intelligence, *Report of the Select Committee on Intelligence on the Use by the Intelligence Community of Information Provided by the Iraqi National Congress Together with Additional Views*, September 8, 2006, pp. 30–31, 93.

46. Bob Drogin, *CURVEBALL: Spies, Lies, and the Con Man Who Caused a War* (New York: Random House, 2007), pp. 112–114.

47. Siobhan Gorman, Farnaz Fassihi, and Jay Solomon, "As Iranian Surfaces, Intrigue Builds," *Wall Street Journal*, July 14, 2010, p. A9.

48. Central Intelligence Agency, *Israel: Foreign Intelligence and Security Services*, March 1977.

49. Central Intelligence Agency, *Iraq: Foreign Intelligence and Security Services*, August 1985, p. iii in Jeffrey T. Richelson, ed., National Security Archive Electronic Briefing Book No.167, *Saddam's Iron Grip: Intelligence Reports on Saddam Hussein's Reign*, October 18, 2005, Document 5, www.nsarchive.org.

50. Central Intelligence Agency, *Soviet Intelligence: KGB and GRU*, 1984.

51. See Amy Knight, *Spies Without Cloaks: The KGB's Successors* (Princeton, N.J.: Princeton University Press, 1996); J. Michael Waller, *Secret Empire: The KGB in Russia Today* (Boulder, Colo.: Westview Press, 1994); and Soldatov and Borogan, *The New Nobility*.

52. Central Intelligence Agency, *The Russian Security Services: Sorting Out the Pieces*, September 1992.

53. Documents obtained under the Freedom of Information Act.

54. Army Counterintelligence Center, *Wikileaks.org—An Online Reference to Foreign Intelligence Services, Insurgents, or Terrorist Groups?*, March 18, 2008. References to the first two reports mentioned are on p. 28.

55. Ibid., p. 3.

56. "Partners in Espionage," Security Awareness Bulletin, August 1984, pp. 1–8; Linda Melvern, David Hebditch, and Nick Anning, *Techno-Bandits: How the Soviets Are Stealing America's High-Tech Future* (Boston: Houghton Mifflin, 1984), p. 242; *Affidavit of Allen M. Power, Federal Bureau of Investigation, Submitted to State and Northern District of California, City and County of San Francisco*, October 16, 1983, pp. 1–2; "For Love of Money and Adventure," *Time*, October 31, 1983, pp. 39–40; Howard Kurtz, "California Man Charged with Spying," *Washington Post*, October 18, 1983, pp. A1, A4; David Wise, "How Our Spy Spied Their Spy," *Los Angeles Times*, October 23, 1983, pp. 1, 6.

57. "Greece Charges Three as Spies After U.S. Tip," *Washington Post*, September 17, 1985, p. A29; Mattson, "A Counterintelligence Cold Case File," p. 45.

58. Bob Woodward and Dan Morgan, "Soviet Threat Toward Iran Overstated, Casey Concluded," *Washington Post*, January 13, 1987, pp. A1, A8.

59. Henry Hurt, *Shadrin: The Spy Who Never Came Back* (New York: McGraw-Hill, 1981), p. 52.

60. Ibid., pp. 52–82; 140–151.

61. Ibid., p. 206; Patrick E. Tyler, "Missing U.S. Agent Dead," *Washington Post*, October 30, 1985, p. A9.

62. George Tenet with Bill Harlow, *At the Center of the Storm: My Years at the CIA* (New York: HarperCollins, 2007), p. 124.

63. Department of the Army, AR 381–47, *U.S. Army Offensive Counterintelligence Operations*, p. 7.

64. Richard Halloran, "Overtures to Soldiers to Spy for Soviet Bloc Said to Rise," *New York Times*, June 29, 1985, pp. A1, B5.

65. "Former Counterspy for Army Is Indicted on Subversion Charges," *New York Times*, April 10, 1984, p. A20.

66. Ibid.

67. Ibid.

68. Gus Weiss, "The Farewell Dossier," *Studies in Intelligence* 39, 5 (1996): 121–126.

16

COVERT ACTION

Traditionally, covert action involved activities designed to influence foreign governments, events, organizations, or persons in support of U.S. foreign policy in such a way that the involvement of the U.S. government was not apparent. During the Reagan and George H.W. Bush administrations, the practice of the "overt-covert operation" emerged—the clearest examples being the attempt to overthrow the Sandinista government and the support provided to the Afghan resistance. In the George W. Bush and Barack Obama administrations, targeted killings fell into the category of an activity that traditionally would be considered a covert action activity but was conducted openly.

During the Cold War, U.S. covert operations included (1) political advice and counsel; (2) subsidies to individuals; (3) financial support and technical assistance to political parties or groups; (4) support to private organizations, including labor unions and business firms; (5) covert propaganda; (6) training of individuals; (7) economic operations; (8) paramilitary or political action operations designed to overthrow or support a regime; and, up until the mid-1960s, (9) attempted assassination.[1]

Many of those activities, such as paramilitary or political action operations, were highly visible and designed to achieve a specific objective—the overthrow of a regime or the defeat of an insurgent force. Many behind-the-scenes political and propaganda activities have also been designed to achieve a specific objective, such as the electoral defeat of a political candidate or party.

Other low-visibility operations involving propaganda or aid to individuals or organizations were more focused on the enhancement of long-term U.S. objectives and the countering of similar Soviet activities rather than the achievement of a specific objective in the near term. Furthermore, a high-visibility operation might be conducted without expectation of "success." When the United States began aiding the Afghan rebels, after the 1979 Soviet invasion, there was no expectation of actually inducing Soviet withdrawal but simply one of draining Soviet resources and keeping international attention on the Soviet role in Afghanistan.

Thus, beginning in 1946, and extending for various periods of time, the United States, principally through the Central Intelligence Agency, engaged in a wide variety of covert action operations. These included support to political parties and labor unions in France and Italy; support to resistance groups in the Soviet Union; masterminding the overthrow of the Guatemalan and Italian governments; a full-scale covert action campaign (including attempted assassination) directed against the Cuban regime of Fidel Castro; political action in an attempt to prevent Salvador Allende from becoming president of Chile and then to remove him once he attained that position; propaganda operations directed against the Soviet SS-20 deployment in Europe and against the Sandinista regime in Nicaragua; paramilitary operations in Afghanistan and Nicaragua; and political support operations in El Salvador and Panama.[2]

The years between the end of the Cold War and the terrorist attacks of September 11, 2001, represent the first era of post–Cold War covert action. The Soviet collapse meant the end of that worldwide ideological conflict—a conflict that led to covert support of publications in Western Europe and elsewhere that advanced Western democratic values and sought to undermine the propaganda of the Soviet Union and other Marxist entities. In contrast, no similar worldwide ideological conflict was being waged between the United States and its allies on one side and Iraq, North Korea, and Libya on the other.

In addition, activities such as the support of political parties or broadcasting that would have been conducted as covert operations are now often done overtly. Thus, for example, the National Endowment for Democracy (NED) provided support to the Nicaraguan political parties who ran against the Sandinistas in the 1990 election. A September 22, 1989, National Security Directive declared that "the Department of State shall undertake a vigorous *overt* program to support a free and fair election process. Every effort will be made, consistent with U.S. law, to assist the democratic opposition to compete effectively with the Sandinista regime." Furthermore, the directive specified that "there shall be *no covert* assistance to political or other groups in Nicaragua in the upcoming election campaign."[3]

In 1995, the Agency for International Development (AID) began providing funds, which totaled $26 million by May 1998, to Indonesian human rights and free speech groups, including the Indonesian Legal Aid Society, headed by a leading figure in the Indonesian democracy movement. Altogether, AID provided funds to thirty non-governmental organizations in Indonesia. Prior to the 2000 Serbian election, AID and the NED provided support to student groups, labor unions, independent media outlets, and Serbian heavy-metal bands that participated in street concerts as part of a voter registration drive. Likewise, some of the broadcast operations, such as Radio Free Asia and Radio Free Iran (approved by Congress 1997), are openly acknowledged and funded rather than being conducted as covert operations.[4]

The emergence of a number of rogue states that previously might have been restrained by the Soviet Union also had an impact on U.S. policy. Although undermining these states politically was one objective of U.S. covert action policy, an equally or more critical concern was impeding the acquisition of technologies that would facilitate the production of weapons of mass destruction (WMD) and potentially destroying facilities used to produce such weapons.

During this period, there were three major transnational targets: proliferation of weapons of mass destruction, terrorism, and international narcotics trafficking. Proliferation could involve the acquisition of technologies and information from Europe, their transportation (by physical or electronic means) to the acquiring nation, and, finally, the exploitation of the technologies to produce weapons of mass destruction. Likewise, terrorism could be planned in Lebanon or Afghanistan, funded through Switzerland, and carried out in London, Paris, New York, or Africa. Ultimately, narcotics trafficking involved leadership, production facilities, transportation, transit points, and delivery to a variety of nations. In each case, operations could be directed toward a number of points, and a number of techniques could be employed, in an attempt to disrupt or neutralize such activities.

There were other important aspects to the first era of post–Cold War covert action. The greater prevalence of underground targets—designed to avoid overhead surveillance and to protect the facility from attack—added a new dimension to any paramilitary operation that sought to destroy such targets. In addition, new means became available for covert operators to employ. Among the most important of the new techniques was cyber warfare, which can be employed to deprive hostile parties of the financial resources needed to perform terrorist acts or acquire WMD technologies.[5]

The changes in both targets and techniques employed meant that covert action operations were now planned and carried out by not only the CIA but also other organizations. Cyberwar operations were assumed by the NSA and by the three military SIGINT organizations. In addition, the United States Special Operations Command and its subsidiary organizations (discussed in Chapter 5) now played a significant role in the operations designed to neutralize WMD or narcotics production facilities.

After the 1998 attacks on U.S. embassies in Africa, the CIA was authorized to use covert means to disrupt and preempt terrorist operations planned abroad by al-Qaeda. President Clinton signed three Memoranda of Notification, which first authorized the killing of bin Laden, then expanded the authorization to several senior al-Qaeda officials, and, last, authorized the shooting down of private civilian aircraft on which they flew.[6]

The 9/11 attacks ushered in a new era of covert action. Almost all of the aspects of the first post–Cold War era of covert action mentioned above still pertain. But the United States has now found itself facing a new worldwide ideological conflict—this time, with militant Islam (also referred to as Islamic totalitarianism or Islamofascism). If that was not apparent immediately after the September 11 attacks, it has become so in subsequent years.*

---

*As numerous analyses have noted, militant Islam is not a centrally directed movement, and it has become even less so since the onset of U.S. military actions against the Taliban and al-Qaeda. Militant Islam includes al-Qaeda-affiliated and al-Qaeda-inspired organizations. Nevertheless, it adheres to a common ideology and seeks, through terrorism and intimidation, to force significant changes in Western behavior (including those of cartoonists) and policies (domestic and foreign) with the long-term aspiration, if not plan, of establishing an Islamic world. It also makes leaders of the post-Stalin Soviet Union seem like libertarians by comparison.

The attacks also led to far more widespread use of prisoner renditions and an unapologetic willingness to engage in targeted killings of Taliban and al-Qaeda leaders. President Bush signed a Presidential Finding calling for the destruction of bin Laden and his organization, and for doing "whatever necessary" to achieve that result. Al-Qaeda's communications, security apparatus, and infrastructure were among the specific elements to be destroyed. Furthermore, the Bush administration concluded, based on two classified memoranda (one written in 1998 and one after the 9/11 attacks), that executive orders banning assassination did not prevent singling out individuals to be killed if those individuals were engaged in an ongoing terrorist war against the United States.[7]

In December 2009, the Director of the CIA presented President-elect Obama with a list of fourteen covert action operations in progress. The covert actions included those that were authorized to

- conduct secret, lethal counterterrorism operations in more than sixty nations;
- stop or delay Iran's development of nuclear weapons;
- deter North Korea from adding to its nuclear weapons arsenal;
- engage in counterproliferation operations to prevent select nations from developing weapons of mass destruction;
- conduct lethal and other operations in support of the U.S. forces in Afghanistan or independently;
- run a variety of lethal operations in Iraq;
- aid secret efforts to halt genocide in the Darfur region of Sudan;
- provide Turkey with intelligence and other support to prevent the Kurdish Workers' Party (PKK) in northern Iraq from establishing a separatist enclave within Turkey;
- counter narcotics production and trafficking;
- perform propaganda operations; and
- conduct rendition, detention, and interrogation operations.[8]

In addition to such operations conducted by the CIA, a set of operations was ordered on September 30, 2010, when the then commander of the Central Command, Gen. David H. Petraeus, signed the Joint Unconventional Warfare Execute Order. Reportedly, the order's goals are to create networks that could "penetrate, disrupt, defeat or destroy" al-Qaeda and other militant groups as well as "prepare the environment" for future attacks by U.S. or local military forces.[9]

AFGHANISTAN

In 1998, the CIA began sending teams of officers into northern Afghanistan in an attempt to convince the leader of the Northern Alliance (NA), Ahmed Shah Massoud, to marshal his forces to capture and possibly kill Osama bin Laden. Massoud was offered large amounts of money if he and his opposition forces could apprehend or kill the al-Qaeda leader. The effort to recruit Massoud in this effort followed the failed attempt to kill bin Laden with a cruise missile attack on a site where bin Laden was scheduled to meet with 200 to 300 members of al-Qaeda. In 1999, members of the Special Activities Division (SA) secretly entered Afghanistan, at least once, to prepare a desert airstrip to extract bin Laden, should he be captured, or to evacuate U.S. tribal allies should they be cornered.[10]

In the aftermath of 9/11, President Bush decided to seek to destroy not only al-Qaeda but the Taliban regime that had given bin Laden and his organization a home, after their expulsion from the Sudan. The CIA's Counterterrorism Center (CTC) conceived a plan that involved sending in teams of CTC, Special Activities Division, and Special Forces personnel to various parts of Afghanistan to work with the Northern Alliance and other Afghan opposition groups. The teams were to be headed by a Farsi- or Dari-speaking officer, with a deputy from the SA.[11]

By the evening of September 26, the first JAWBREAKER team, also designated the Northern Alliance Liaison Team (NALT), had arrived in the Panjshir Valley in northeastern Afghanistan. Part of the team's mission was to provide intelligence to U.S. forces, as well as to assist the Northern Alliance collection, including COMINT collection, efforts. But it also had a covert action mission: to convince the Northern Alliance to accept U.S. military forces into the area and to provide the Alliance with financial support.[12]

Thus, the first JAWBREAKER team provided Gen. Mohammad Fahim Khan, the overall leader of the Northern Alliance, with $1 million to assist him in preparing his forces for upcoming battles. The team also gave $500,000 to the head of the NA intelligence organization. In mid-October, the team provided an additional $1.7 million to General Fahim and Dr. Abdullah Abdullah, the Alliance's foreign minister. Of that sum, $750,000 was to help General Fahim bring his forces to full combat-readiness, while another $250,000 was to be used to purchase humanitarian supplies for the civilian populations living near the battlefields. A further $250,000 was intended for Gen. Ostad Atta, a senior Northern Alliance commander. The remaining $450,000 was for the daily operation of the NA's intelligence organization and for possible bribes to persuade Taliban commanders to defect to the Northern Alliance.[13]

In early October 2001, a CIA-led team in southern Afghanistan, the ECHO Team, met with Hamid Karzai, then a popular tribal leader who had been forced out of Afghanistan and was organizing resistance to the Taliban from Pakistan. Karzai had been the first Pashtun leader to offer to cooperate with the United States in establishing a military resistance in the southern part of the country. In their discussions, the ECHO Team and Karzai prepared the foundation of support for his return and arranged airdrops of weapons and ammunition for his supporters.[14]

The CIA would supply the Taliban's opposition in the south—including Karzai's forces and those led by the former governor of Kandahar—with AK-47 assault rifles, from agency holdings, and with other light weaponry. In addition, it provided uniforms and food. The CIA also made contacts with other tribal leaders, offering weapons, money, and other benefits to induce them to join the opposition to the Taliban. CIA representatives also used money and threats in an effort to get dissident Taliban commanders to switch sides.[15]

Afghanistan has also been the site of both failed and successful attempts at targeted killing. In May 2002, former Afghan prime minister Gulbuddin Hekmaytar, the leader of a hard-line Islamic group, was the target of, or one of a group that was the target of, a Hellfire missile fired from a Predator. Hekmaytar had been planning to attack Karzai's government and possibly Karzai himself. The missile missed Hekmaytar but killed some of his followers. An administration official stated that the missile was trying to hit a group of people from his organization, not solely Hekmaytar, who "sadly" survived.[16]

In addition to current Predator strikes on targets in Afghanistan, U.S. and Afghani forces continue to pursue and kill Taliban insurgents on the ground. In early 2010, it was reported that "small teams of Army commandos, Navy Seals and Central Intelligence Agency operatives have intensified the pace of what the military often calls 'kill-capture missions'—hunting down just one or two insurgents at a time. . . ."[17]

In addition, the CIA trained and deployed, in response to authorization from President George W. Bush, a 3,000-member paramilitary force, consisting mostly of Afghans and known as Counterterrorism Pursuit Teams (CTPT). One of those is apparently the Paktita Defense Force, described as "one of six C.I.A.-trained Afghan militias that serve as a special operations force against insurgents throughout Afghanistan." The teams' primary function is to kill or capture Taliban insurgents, although they also have conducted pacification operations as well as cross-border operations into Pakistan.[18]

GST

On September 17, 2001, President Bush authorized a global counterterrorist effort, which consisted of dozens of component programs. This program, known within the CIA as GST (an abbreviation for the actual codeword), included efforts to capture suspected al-Qaeda officials with the assistance of foreign intelligence services, the maintenance of secret prisons ("black sites"), and the use of enhanced interrogation techniques. Other GST components involved the improvement of the CIA's ability to sort through international financial data and to monitor the communications of suspects around the world. The authorization also created paramilitary units to hunt and kill designated targets anywhere in the world.[19]

The acquisition of suspected al-Qaeda personnel has been accomplished through a variety of means: abductions by CIA officers, arrests by foreign governments and transfer to U.S. custody, and raids—sometimes conducted in concert with or by foreign intelligence services or special forces—in Pakistan, Afghanistan, and other nations. For example, in March 2002, Pakistani special forces took al-Qaeda official Abu Zubaydah into custody and turned him over to the United States, and a joint U.S.-Pakistani operation resulted in the arrest of chief 9/11 planner Khalid Sheikh Mohammed.[20]

In November 2001, Muhammad Saad Aqbal Madni was arrested by Indonesia's State Intelligence Agency (BAKIN) after being informed by the CIA that he was an al-Qaeda operative who had worked with shoe-bomber Richard Reid. Madni was then sent to Egypt for interrogation. In 2002, in a case of mistaken identity, the CIA arranged for Khalid el-Masri, a German citizen of Lebanese parents, to be detained during a visit to Macedonia and sent to Afghanistan for interrogation. In February 2003, the CIA apparently snatched a radical Muslim cleric, Hassan Mustafa Osama Nasr, also known as Abu Omar, off the street in Milan, Italy.[21]

In October 2001, Jamil Qasim Saeed Mohammed, a Yemeni student of microbiology wanted in connection with the attack on the USS *Cole*, was transported from Pakistan to Jordan on a U.S.-registered Gulfstream jet. The rendition followed his being surrendered to U.S. authorities in Karachi by Pakistan's Inter-Services Intelligence Directorate (ISI). The Gulfstream was one of twenty-six planes owned by the CIA, ten of which had been acquired after 2001. The planes are owned by shell companies with no employees and operated by actual companies controlled by or tied to the CIA. In addition to two different types of Gulf Stream jets (Gulfstream III and Gulfstream V), the fleet included a Boeing Business Jet, a DC-3, a Hercules transport, a DeHavilland Twin Otter, a Learjet 35, and a Beech Super King 200. A report to the European Parliament in spring 2006 estimated that this CIA fleet had made 1,000 flights.[22]

The "black sites" maintained under the program included, at various times, facilities in eight countries, including Thailand (where Abu Zubaydah was held), Afghanistan (code-named SALT PIT), Guantanamo Bay in Cuba, and apparently Romania, Poland, and Djibouti. These facilities held between thirty and forty al-Qaeda members. In September 2006, President Bush transferred the remaining fourteen al-Qaeda "high-value targets" from the secret prisons to Guantanamo Bay, due to their declining value as intelligence sources and the controversy in Europe that resulted from their disclosure, as a prelude to their trials.[23]

About seventy others arrested or captured under the GST program were transferred to the custody of foreign governments—a practice known as rendition.* The governments—or, more precisely, the internal security services—of Afghanistan, Algeria, Pakistan, Uzbekistan, Morocco, Egypt, and Jordan are among those that have received individuals who have been rendered by the United States for interrogation.[24]

---

*At least one terrorism-rendition had taken place prior to the 9/11 attacks. CIA officers worked with the Albanian security service to seize five Egyptian members of Islamic Jihad who were suspected of planning to bomb the U.S. embassy in Albania's capital, Tirana. The five were soon flown to Egypt, where two were executed. See Andrew Higgins and Christopher Cooper, "A CIA-Backed Team Used Brutal Means to Crack Terror Cell, *Wall Street Journal*, November 20, 2001, pp. A1, A10. On earlier renditions to the United States, see Daniel Benjamin and Steven Simon, *The Age of Sacred Terror* (New York: Random House, 2002), pp. 251–252. According to those authors a rendition qualifies as an 'extraordinary rendition' only if an individual is removed from the country without the approval of the host government. See Daniel Benjamin and Steven Simon, *The Next Attack: The Failure of the War on Terror and a Strategy for Getting it Right* (New York: Owl, 2006), p. 256.

IRAN

The covert operation directed by President Reagan's National Security Council that ended in the Iran-Contra affair was highly publicized, but other covert operations—directed by the CIA—were not. CIA operations during the Reagan and Bush years were designed to aid Iranian paramilitary and political exile groups, counter Soviet influence in Iran, and give the United States a role of its own in the event that the Khomeini regime collapsed. The initial goal was to knit together a coalition of exile groups and their supporters still in Iran so that if the opportunity arose they could be a significant factor in shaping the future of Iran.[25]

The covert action included providing several million dollars to units composed largely of Iranian exiles in eastern Turkey. The larger of the paramilitary groups had 6,000 to 8,000 men under the command of former Rear Admiral Ahmad Madani, the commander of the Iranian navy under the Shah, who was court-martialed for "being against the government" and became the first defense minister in the Khomeini regime. The second unit, which consisted of fewer than 2,000 men, was commanded by Gen. Bahram Aryana, chief of staff of the Iranian army under the Shah. The paramilitary groups were intended to perform two functions: In the event of a Soviet invasion of Iran, they could harass the flanks of the Soviet armed forces, and in the event of a civil war or domestic upheaval, they would be able to enter Iran to protect and bolster any centrist forces.[26]

The CIA was also reported to be financing Iranian exile groups said to be situated principally in France and Egypt. Support was made available to groups both on the Left (up to but not including Bani-Sadr) and the Right (up to but not including the monarchist factions).[27]

The CIA established and financed a radio station in Egypt to broadcast anti-Khomeini information. In 1987, regular features included reports on long food lines, pockets of opposition and small uprisings against the clergy and revolutionary guards, torture and killings by the government, and gains made by Iranian Communists and agents of the Soviet Union. In September 1986, the CIA provided a miniaturized suitcase television transmitter for a clandestine broadcast to Iran by the Shah's son. The broadcast disrupted two channels of Iranian television for 11 minutes at 9 P.M. on September 5.[28]

In addition, the CIA supplied information to Iraq to aid the country in its war with Iran. The agency secretly provided Iraq with detailed intelligence to assist with Iraqi bombing raids on Iran's oil terminals and power plants. In 1984, when some feared that Iran might overrun Iraq, the United States began supplying Iraq with intelligence that reportedly enabled Iraq to calibrate mustard gas attacks on Iranian ground troops.[29]

In early 1985, Iraq began receiving regular satellite information from Washington, particularly after Iraqi bombing raids. It is not clear whether the Iraqis were receiving actual photos or information derived from the photos at that point. In any case, in August 1986, the CIA established a direct, Top Secret, Washington-Baghdad link to provide the Iraqis with better and more timely satellite intelligence. The Iraqis would thus receive information from satellite images "several hours" after a bombing raid in order to assess damage and plan the next attack. By December 1986, the Iraqis were receiving selected portions of the actual photos taken by KH-11 and SR-71 overhead platforms. According to one account, some of the information or images provided were incomplete or doctored—with the size of Soviet troop strength on the Iranian border being inflated—in order to advance the administration's goals.[30]

A more recent objective of U.S. covert action programs with respect to Iran has been to retard Iran's progress toward development of nuclear weapons. One operation revolved around the Tinners' (see Chapter 11) sale of allegedly high-quality vacuum pumps to Iran—pumps needed so that the centrifuges employed for uranium enrichment can operate inside a vacuum seal. The pumps, though produced in Germany, were first purchased by the Oak Ridge and Los Alamos laboratories and altered so that they would break down under operational conditions. In 2010, a study estimated that Iranian centrifuges were operating at only 20 percent efficiency. An International Atomic Energy Agency report indicated that there were 3,936 uranium enrichment centrifuges operating at the Natanz site while 4,592 were not operating. Also a victim of sabotage was a power supply purchased from Turkey. But in 2006, after the Iranians installed the power supply at their Natanz uranium enrichment facility, it failed, causing 50 centrifuges to explode.[31]

CIA responsibility is plausible, although not certain, with respect to the faulty power supply—given President Bush's authorization, in 2009, to undermine electrical systems, computer systems, and other networks associated with Iran's nuclear program. The same can be said about the "Stuxnet" computer worm that experts concluded may have been developed with the specific objective of changing the rotor speed of Iranian centrifuges, first increasing their speed and then lowering it, with the apparent intention of causing extensive vibrations or distortions that would destroy the centrifuges. The worm, which targeted Siemens software systems and took over industrial control systems, also has affected facilities in India, Indonesia, and the United States, although 60 percent of the computers infected were in Iran.[32]

PAKISTAN

In 1999, the CIA trained and equipped approximately sixty special forces personnel from Pakistan's Inter-Services Intelligence Directorate (ISI), whose mission was to apprehend or kill Osama bin Laden. The operation was arranged by Pakistani Prime Minister Nawaz Sharif and his intelligence chief with the Clinton administration, in exchange for economic benefits. The plan was canceled later that year when Sharif was overthrown by a military coup, and his successor, Gen. Pervez Musharraf, refused to continue the operation. NSA intercepts also indicate that the training effort had been compromised.[33]

More recent covert actions in Pakistan have involved targeted killings of al-Qaeda leadership employing Hellfire-armed Predator unmanned aerial vehicles. An apparent

Predator attack killed a former Taliban commander, Nek Mohammed, in South Waziristan in June 2004, along with five others. On May 10, 2005, Haithem al Yemeni, a potential successor to Abu Faraj al Libi, who had been captured a week earlier, was killed in Pakistan by a Hellfire missile. In December 2005, a Hellfire was used to kill Hamza Rabia, identified by American officials as al-Qaeda's chief of international operations, at a safe house located in Asorai, in western Pakistan.[34]

In January 2006, based on intelligence suggesting that Ayman al-Zawahiri, Osama bin Laden's deputy, was visiting a home in a village in the northwestern region of Pakistan, the CIA attempted to kill Zawahiri with a Hellfire missile. The attack on the target within the village of Damadola occurred at 12:30 A.M. on January 13. However, Zawahiri had left the village two hours earlier.[35]

Local officials claimed that eighteen civilians had been killed in the attack, as well as at least eleven militants, including seven Arab fighters and four Pakistani militants from Punjab province. In addition, according to Pakistani officials, although Zawahiri was not among the dead, two and possibly three senior members of al-Qaeda and Zawahiri's son-in-law appeared to be among those killed. One of those (Midhat Mursi al-Sayid Umar, also known as Abu Khabab al-Masri) was an expert on explosives and poisons and was on the United States' "most wanted" list. He had operated an al-Qaeda camp in eastern Afghanistan and had prepared a training manual with recipes for crude chemical and biological weapons. Another of the believed dead, Abu Ubayda al-Misri, was chief of insurgency operations in the southern Afghanistan province of Kunar. Zawahiri's son-in-law was in charge of al-Qaeda propaganda in the region.[36]

Starting in August 2008, drone strikes against al-Qaeda and Taliban officials and training facilities in Pakistan were stepped up and have become a common occurrence. From 2004 to 2007 there were 4 strikes. Then in 2008 there were 34. By the end of 2009 there had been 99 strikes inside Pakistan—employing both Predator and Reaper drones. In 2010, there had been 74 additional strikes by the end of September. In mid-December 2010, it was reported that there had been over 100 Predator strikes in that year. The expansion in the number of strikes followed a 2008 policy change in which individuals could be targeted not only as a result of having been identified as approved targets but also as the result of a "pattern of life analysis." In early 2010 it was reported that the size of the Reaper fleet was expected to more than double—from 6 to 14—by 2011.[37]

The attacks have killed a number of senior al-Qaeda and Taliban officials. In early 2009 it was reported that the attacks had killed 9 of al-Qaeda's 20 leaders. The strikes have continued a particularly successful campaign to kill or capture a succession of al-Qaeda operations chiefs (other than the ones who were captured). The latest victim, in May 2010, was Sheikh Sa'id al-Masri, who was believed to have been a key al-Qaeda official behind the attempt of Najibullah Zazi to blow up the New York subway as well as having provided funds to three of the September 11 hijackers.[38]

One official that the strikes missed, or at least didn't kill outright, was Baitullah Mehsud, the leader of the Pakistani Taliban, who was believed to be responsible for the assassination of former prime minister Benazir Bhutto and for scores of suicide bombings. He was first reported killed in a January attack, then reported to have been badly wounded and to have died from his injuries. Then, in March 2010, it was reported that he was still alive but sidelined as result of his injuries.[39]

The strikes have forced the al-Qaeda and Taliban officials to forego use of their satellite phones and to avoid large gatherings, resorting instead to communication by courier and to stealthy movements in small groups. In addition, outside fighters have resorted to hideouts in tunnels dug into the mountainside in the Datta Khel area.[40]

Intelligence concerning a terrorist plot aimed at Europe led the United States to further increase the pace of drone strikes in Pakistan's tribal regions in October 2010. The strikes succeeded in killing several terrorists with German citizenship. Of particular interest with respect to the European plot were three German brothers, one of whom, Imram al Amani, was killed in an early October attack.[41] Notable deaths due to the drone campaign are summarized in Table 16.1.

SERBIA

In the early 1990s, CIA officers in the Balkans brought the lead conspirator in a plot to unseat Serbian strongman Slobodan Milosevic to CIA headquarters to speak with senior officials of the agency's Central European Division. He and a few other Serbian government insiders were ready to overthrow Milosevic and had the backing of key generals from the Yugoslav army and air force.[42]

The motivation for the coup plotters apparently included their perception of Milosevic as unpredictable and possibly unstable, and the fear that his long-term designs on Kosovo and Montenegro would result in a conflict with the West. They wanted financial support for the coup and Washington's promise to lift economic sanctions, as well as a pledge to fast-track loans from the International Monetary Fund and World Bank if the plot succeeded. The CIA turned down the deal.[43]

In May 1999, President Clinton did approve a different action aimed at Milosevic, when he signed a Presidential Finding authorizing CIA training of Kosovar rebels in sabotage—possibly including severing telephone lines, fouling gasoline reserves, and blowing up buildings—as a way to undermine public support for the regime. In addition, the CIA, presumably using National Security Agency hackers, was ordered to tap into Milosevic's foreign bank accounts and, according to one U.S. official, to "diddle with Milosevic's bank accounts."[44]

SOMALIA

CIA covert action in Somalia in 2005 and the first part of 2006 had several aims, including neutralizing a small number of al-Qaeda members believed to be hiding in the country. The CIA operation, run from the agency's station in Nairobi, Kenya, involved channeling hundreds of thousands of dollars to secular warlords within

TABLE 16.1 Notable Deaths in Pakistan Due to Drone Campaign

Name	*Position*
Saad bin Laden	Son of Usama bin Laden
Khalid Habib	Deputy to Sheikh Sa'id al-Masri, al Qaeda's No. 3
Rashid Rauf	Mastermind of the 2006 trans-Atlantic airliner plot
Abu Khabab al-Masri	Led al-Qaeda's chemical and biological weapons effort
Abu al-Hassan al-Rimi	Led al-Qaeda's operations against forces in Afghanistan
Usama al-Kini	Planned September 2008 attack on Marriott in Islamabad
Sheikh Ahmed Salim Swedan	Usama al-Kini's lieutenant; on FBI's terrorist most wanted list
Abu Sulaiman al-Jaziri	Senior external operations planner and facilitator for al Qaeda
Abu Jihad al-Masri	Senior operational planner and propagandist for al Qaeda
Abdullah Azzam	Senior aide to Sheikh Sa'id al-Masri
Najmiddin Kamolitdinovich Jalolov	Leader of the Islamic Jihad Union
Saleh al-Somali	Member of al-Qaeda's inner circle
Mohammed Haqqani	Brother of Sirajuddin Haqqani, Taliban-al-Qaeda leader
Hussein Yemeni	al-Qaeda bomb expert
Mohammed Qari Zafar	Taliban commander
Sheikh Mansoor	Egyptian Canadian al-Qaeda leader
Mahmud Mahdi Zeidan	Jordanian Taliban commander
Sheikh Sa'id al-Masri	Al-Qaeda operations chief (2007–2010)

SOURCES: Jay Solomon, Siobhan Gorman, and Matthew Rosenberg, "U.S. Plans New Drone Attacks in Pakistan," *Wall Street Journal*, March 26, 2009, pp. A1, A18; Jonathan Karl and Matthew Cole, "CIA Kept bin Laden Son's Death Secret for Months," http://abcnews.go.com, July 23, 2009; Siobhan Gorman and Peter Spiegel, "Drone Attacks Target Pakistan Militants," *Wall Street Journal*, September 17, 2009, p. A8; Mark Mazzetti and Souad Mekhennet, "Qaeda Planner In Pakistan Killed by Drone," *New York Times*, December 12, 2009, p. A8; Zahid Hussain, "Another Militant Is Killed by Drone," *Wall Street Journal*, February 20–21, 2010, p.A6; David S. Cloud, "Suspect in CIA Attack Slain," *Los Angeles Times*, March 18, 2010, pp. AA1, AA6; David S. Cloud, "CIA Drones Have Broader List of Targets," *Los Angeles Times*, May 6, 2010, pp. A1, A6; Siobhan Gorman, "Al Qaeda Is Again Forced to Fill Risky No. 3 Post," *Wall Street Journal*, June 2, 2010, p. A12.

Somalia, with the objective of killing or capturing the suspected al-Qaeda members. The operation occasionally involved Nairobi-based CIA officers arriving at warlord-controlled airstrips in Mogadishu, carrying large amounts of money to be dispersed to the Somali warlords.[45]

The plan to enlist the warlords in this effort was largely due to apprehension about deploying large numbers of American personnel in Somalia; the 1994 attempt to capture warlord Mohammed Farah Aidid had resulted in the deaths of eighteen American Special Forces personnel and the withdrawal of U.S. personnel from the country. Since November 2002, however, U.S. representatives had had success in their contacts with Somali clansmen, who provided intelligence about suspected al-Qaeda members in Somalia. As a result, Suleiman Abdalla Salim Hemed, a suspected al-Qaeda operative, was turned over to U.S. officials in April 2003. However, the plan failed to achieve further results, and Islamic militias took control of the country in early June 2006. That control was short-lived, being terminated by invading Ethiopian troops, covertly supported by the U.S. military, that December.[46]

In early January 2007, an AC-130 gunship was used to launch an attack on al-Qaeda members in southern Somalia. Among the targets of the attack was Abu Talha al-Sudani, who had been described as an explosives expert with a close relationship with bin Laden and, more recently, as a close associate of Gouled Hassan Dourad, head of a Mogadishu-based network that supported al-Qaeda. Sudani had also been named by some as the financier for the individuals believed responsible for the 1998 bombings of the U.S. embassies in Kenya and Tanzania.[47]

YEMEN

On November 2, 2002, a Hellfire missile launched from a Predator struck a car carrying six men as it was traveling through the desert, one hundred miles east of Sanaa, the capital of Yemen. The Predator detected the vehicle as it moved along a highway toward the city of Marib. All six men were killed, including the target of the attack—Qaed Salim Sinan al-Harethi. Harethi was believed to be one of the leaders of al-Qaeda in Yemen and was suspected of involvement in the bombing of the Navy destroyer USS *Cole* in October 2000. All six men, including one who was a U.S. citizen, were al-Qaeda operatives, according to the United States. According to another account, four were members of the Aden-Ayban Islamic Army, a terrorist sect with ties to al-Qaeda. The U.S. citizen had recruited Muslims to attend al-Qaeda training camps, according to the FBI.[48]

In late 2009 and the first half of 2010 the U.S. military, with CIA drones being tied up in attacks on Pakistani targets, conducted a number of strikes designed to eliminate members of al-Qaeda of the Arabian Peninsula (AQAP)—which was responsible for the failed bombing of a U.S.-bound aircraft on Christmas Day, 2009.

A December 17, 2009, cruise missile attack was believed to have hit an al-Qaeda training facility in Abyan Province. A week later, on December 24, a cruise missile attack killed five al-Qaeda members, although it missed the primary targets—the

AQAP leader and deputy chief. A March attack killed Jamil al-Anbari, an al-Qaeda operative, in Mudiyah, while a May 25 attack in Marib Province, which was targeted on what was believed to be a group of al-Qaeda members, killed the province's deputy governor. In the midst of the December 2009 and spring 2010 attacks, the Yemeni government—possibly with intelligence and other assistance from the United States—conducted an airstrike that killed at least five senior AQAP members, including the group's military commander.[49]

In August 2010, it was reported that the CIA and U.S. special operations forces had positioned drones and surveillance equipment in Yemen and other nations with the intention of stepping up operations against AQAP. In November of the same year, it was reported that "U.S. officials said . . . Predators have been patrolling the skies over Yemen for several months in search of leaders and operatives of . . . AQAP" but as a result of the cruise missile strikes earlier in the year the AQAP leaders "went to ground."[50]

Notes

1. "The Bissell Philosophy," appendix to Victor Marchetti and John Marks, *The CIA and the Cult of Intelligence* (New York: Knopf, 1974), p. 387; U.S. Congress, Senate Select Committee to Study Governmental Operations with Respect to Intelligence Activities, *Alleged Assassination Plots Involving Foreign Leaders* (Washington, D.C.: U.S. Government Printing Office, 1976).

2. For histories of U.S. covert action, see William J. Daugherty, *Executive Secrets: Covert Action and the Presidency* (Lexington: University Press of Kentucky, 2004); John Prados, *Safe for Democracy: The Secret Wars of the CIA* (Chicago: Ivan R. Dee, 2006); and Gregory F. Treverton, *Covert Action: The Limits of Intervention in the Postwar World* (New York: Basic Books, 1987).

3. George Bush, National Security Directive 25, "U.S. Policy Toward the February 1990 Nicaraguan Election," September 22, 1989. It should be noted that a Secret Annex to NSD-25, "[Deleted] NSD-25 on U.S. Policy Towards the February 1990 Nicaraguan," was issued on the same day as NSD-25.

4. Tim Weiner, "U.S. Has Spent $26 Million Since '95 on Suharto Opponents," *New York Times,* May 20, 1998, p. A11; John Lancaster, "U.S. Funds Help Milosevic's Foes in Election Fight," *Washington Post,* September 19, 2000, pp. A1, A8; U.S. Congress, Senate Committee on Foreign Relations, *Broadcasting to China: Applying the Lessons from European Freedom Radios* (Washington, D.C.: U.S. Government Printing Office, 1992); U.S. Congress, Senate Committee on Foreign Relations, *The Radio Free China Act S. 2985* (Washington, D.C.: U.S. Government Printing Office, 1992); Kennon H. Nakamura and Susan B. Epstein, Congressional Research Service, *Radio Free Asia,* June 3, 1994; Elaine Sciolino, "Pleased Yet Wary, U.S. Offers Gestures of Support for Iran," *New York Times;* March 26, 1998, pp. A1, A10; Elaine Sciolino, "White House Agrees to Radio Broadcasts to Iran," *New York Times,* April 15, 1998, p. A3.

5. Walter Pincus, "CIA Turns to Boutique Operations, Covert Action Against Terrorism, Drugs, Arms," *Washington Post,* September 14, 1997, p. A6; Craig Covault, "Cyber Threat Challenges Intelligence Capability," *Aviation Week & Space Technology,* February 10, 1997, pp. 20–21.

6. Bob Woodward and Vernon Loeb, "CIA's Covert War on Bin Laden," *Washington Post*, September 14, 2001, pp. A1, A14; Barton Gellman, "Broad Effort Launched After '98 Attacks," *Washington Post*, December 19, 2001, pp. A1, A26.

7. Bob Woodward, "CIA Told to Do 'Whatever Necessary' to Kill Bin Laden," *Washington Post*, October 21, 2001, pp. A1, A22; Barton Gellman, "CIA Weighs 'Targeted Killing' Missions," *Washington Post*, October 28, 2001, pp. A1, A19.

8. Bob Woodward, *Obama's Wars* (New York: Simon & Schuster, 2010), pp. 52–53.

9. Mark Mazzetti, "U.S. Said to Order an Expanded Use of Secret Action," *New York Times*, May 25, 2010, p. A1, A12.

10. James Risen, "U.S. Pursued Secret Efforts to Catch or Kill bin Laden," *New York Times*, September 30, 2001, pp. A1, B3; Gellman, "Broad Effort Launched After '98 Attacks."

11. Gary Bernsten and Ralph Pezzullo, *Jawbreaker: The Attack on bin Laden and Al-Qaeda: A Personal Account by the CIA's Key Field Commander* (New York: Crown, 2005), p. 74.

12. Gary C. Schroen, *First In: An Insider's Account of How the CIA Spearheaded the War on Terror in Afghanistan* (New York: Ballantine, 2005), pp. 22, 38, 75, 78.

13. Ibid., pp. 96, 101, 195.

14. Ibid., p. 274.

15. David S. Cloud, "CIA Supplies Anti-Taliban Forces in South," *Wall Street Journal*, December 7, 2001, p. A4; Alan Sipress and Walter Pincus, "U.S. Making Covert Drive for Fashtun Support," *Washington Post*, November 4, 2001, p. A18; Alan Sipress and Vernon Loeb, "CIA's Stealth War Centers on Eroding Taliban Loyalty and Aiding Opposition," *Washington Post*, October 10, 2001, pp. A1, A16.

16. "CIA Effort to Kill Ex-Warlord Fails," *Washington Times*, May 10, 2002, p. A8; Walter Pincus and Thomas E. Ricks, "CIA Fails in Bid to Kill Afghan Rebel with a Missile," *Washington Post*, May 10, 2002, pp. A24–A25. Also see Alex S. Wilner, "Targeted Killings in Afghanistan: Measuring Coercion and Deterrence in Counterterrorism and Counterinsurgency," *Studies in Conflict & Terrorism* 33, 4 (April 2010): 307–329.

17. Michael M. Phillips, "U.S. Steps Up Missions Targeting Taliban Leaders," *Wall Street Journal*, February 2, 2010, pp. A1, A10.

18. Woodward, *Obama's Wars*, pp. 8, 367; Mark Mazzetti and Dexter Filkins, "U.S. Commanders Push to Expand Raids in Pakistan," *New York Times*, December 21, 2010, pp. A1, A12.

19. Dana Priest, "Covert CIA Program Withstands New Furor," www.washingtonpost.com, December 30, 2005.

20. Dana Priest, "CIA Holds Terror Suspects in Secret Prisons," www.washingtonpost.com, November 2, 2005.

21. Rajiv Chandrasekaran and Peter Finn, "U.S. Behind Secret Transfer of Terror Suspects," *Washington Post*, March 11, 2002, pp. A1, A15; Don Van Natta Jr., "Germans Looking into Complicity in Seizure by U.S.," *New York Times*, February 21, 2006, pp. A1, A8; Dana Priest, "Italy Knew About Plan to Grab Suspect," *Washington Post*, June 30, 2004, pp. A1, A18; Steve Henricks, *A Kidnapping in Milan: The CIA on Trial* (New York: W. W. Norton, 2010).

22. Chandrasekaran and Finn, "U.S. Behind Secret Transfer of Terror Suspects"; Scott Shane, "C.I.A. Expanding Terror Battle Under Guise of Charter Flights," *New York Times*, May 31, 2005, pp. A1, A10; Dan Bilefsky, "European Inquiry Flew 1,000 Flights in Secret," *New York Times*, April 27, 2006, p. A12; Stephen Gray, *Ghost Plane: The True Story of the CIA Torture Program* (New York: St. Martin's Press, 2006), pp. 45, 62, 79, 105, 190, 248.

23. Priest, "CIA Holds Terror Suspects in Secret Prisons"; Jennifer K. Elsea and Julie Kim, Congressional Research Service, *Undisclosed U.S. Detention Sites Overseas: Background and Legal Issues*, September 12, 2006, p. 3; Sheryl Gay Stolberg, "President Moves 14 Held in Secret to Guantanamo; Seeks Tribunals," *New York Times*, September 7, 2006, pp. A1, A20.

24. Priest, "CIA Holds Terror Suspects in Secret Prisons"; Craig Whitlock, "European Probe Finds Signs of CIA-Run Secret Prisons," www.washingtonpost.com, June 8, 2006.

25. Leslie H. Gelb, "U.S. Said to Aid Iranian Exiles in Combat and Political Units," *New York Times*, March 7, 1982, pp. 1, 12.

26. Ibid.

27. Ibid.

28. Ibid.; Bob Woodward, "CIA Curried Favor with Khomeini Exiles," *Washington Post*, November 19, 1986, pp. A1, A28.

29. Bob Woodward, "CIA Aiding Iraq in Gulf War," *Washington Post*, December 15, 1986, pp. A1, A18–A19.

30. Ibid.; Stephen Engelberg, "Iran and Iraq Got 'Doctored' Data, U.S. Officials Say," *New York Times*, January 12, 1987, pp. A1, A16.

31. Eli Lake, "Operation Sabotage," *The New Republic*, July 22, 2010, pp. 16–17; William J. Broad and David E. Sanger, "In Nuclear Net's Undoing, a Web of Shadowy Deals," *New York Times*, August 25, 2008, pp. A1, A8; "Covert Action Suspected in Iranian Nuclear Troubles," *Global Security Newswire*, http://gsn.nti.org, July 23, 2010.

32. David E. Sanger, "Iran Fights Malware Attacking Computers," *New York Times*, September 26, 2010, pp. 4, 9; Robert McMillan, "Was Stuxnet Built to Attack Iran's Nuclear Program?," www.pcworld.com, accessed September 21, 2010; "Iran nuclear agency is working to defeat a computer worm," *Los Angeles Times*, September 26, 2010, p. A4; Siobhan Gorman, "Computer Worm Hits Plant in Iran," *Wall Street Journal*, September 27, 2010, p. A12; Paul A. Kerr, John Rollins, and Catherine A. Theohary, Congressional Research Service, *The Stuxnet Computer Worm: Harbinger of an Emerging Warfare Capability*, December 9, 2010; David A. Albright, Paul Brannan, and Christina Walrond, Institute for Science and International Security, *Skynet Malware and Natanz: Update of ISIS December 22, 2010 Report*, February 15, 2010; William J. Broad, "Worm in Iran Was Perfect for Sabotaging Nuclear Centrifuges," *New York Times*, November 19, 2010, pp. A1, A4; Joby Warrick, "Iran's Natanz nuclear facility recovered quickly from Stuxnet cyberattack," www.washingtonpost.com, February 16, 2011.

33. Bob Woodward and Thomas E. Ricks, "CIA Trained Pakistanis to Nab Terrorist But Military Coup Put an End to 1999 Plot," *Washington Post*, October 3, 2001, pp. A1, A18; Gelman, "Broad Effort Launched After '98 Attacks."

34. "Airstrike by U.S. Draws Protests from Pakistanis," *New York Times*, January 15, 2006, pp. 1, 4; Josh Meyer, "CIA Expands Use of Drones in Terror War," *Los Angeles Times*, January 29, 2006, pp. A1, A28–A29.

35. "Airstrike by U.S. Draws Protests from Pakistanis"; Carlotta Gail and Ismail Khan, "American Strike in January Missed by Al Qaeda's No. 2 by a Few Hours," *New York Times*, November 10, 2006, p. A10.

36. "Airstrike by U.S. Draws Protests from Pakistanis"; Carlotta Gall and Douglas Jehl, "Strike Aimed at Qaeda Figure Stirs More Pakistan Protests," *New York Times*, January 16, 2005, p. A3; Carla Gall and Douglas Jehl, "U.S. Raid Killed Qaeda Leaders, Pakistanis Say," *New York Times*, January 19, 2006, pp. A1, A8.

37. Peter Bergen and Katherine Tiedeman, New American Foundation, "Revenge of the Drones, Appendix 1," October 19, 2009, p. 1; Greg Miller and Julian E. Barnes, "Drone plan

opens new front," *Los Angeles Times*, December 14, 2009, pp. A1, A24; Bill Roggio and Alexander Mayer, "Analysis: US air campaign in Pakistan heats up," www.longwarjournal.org, January 5, 2010; Scott Shane and Eric Schmitt, "C.I.A. Deaths Prompt Surge in Drone War," *New York Times*, January 23, 2010, pp. A1, A3; David S. Cloud, "CIA drones have broader list of targets," *Los Angeles Times*, May 6, 2010, pp. A1, A6; Mark Mazzetti, "C.I.A. Intensifies Drone Campaign," *New York Times*, September 28, 2010, pp. A1, A12; Helene Cooper and David E. Sanger, "U.S. Will Widen War on Militants Inside Pakistan," *New York Times*, December 17, 2010, pp. A1, A14.

38. Mark Mazzetti and David E. Sanger, "Obama Expands Missile Strikes Inside Pakistan," *New York Times*, February 21, 2009, pp. A1, A6; David E. Sanger and Eric Schmitt, "U.S. Weighs Taliban Strike in Pakistan," *New York Times*, March 18, 2009, pp. A1, A8; Siobhan Gorman, "Qaeda Aide Believed Dead," *Wall Street Journal*, June 1, 2010, p. A11; David S. Cloud, "Al Qaeda's No. 3 man likely dead," *Los Angeles Times*, June 1, 2010, pp. AA1, AA6; Siobhan Gorman, "Al Qaeda Is Again Forced to Fill Risky No. 3 Post," *Wall Street Journal*, June 2, 2010, p. A12. For a skeptical account of the effectiveness of drone strikes, see Greg Miller, "Increased U.S. drone strikes in Pakistan killing a few high-value militants," www.washingtonpost.com, February 20, 2011. It has also been reported that the CIA may be decreasing the number of drone strikes to reduce civilian casualties. See Ken Dilanian, "CIA may be tempering its drone use," *Los Angeles Times*, February 22, 2011, p. A9.

39. Pir Zubair Shah, Sabrina Tavernise, and Mark Mazzetti, "U.S. and Pakistan Say Taliban 'Chief' Is Believed Dead," *New York Times*, August 8, 2009, pp. A1, A6; Jane Perlez and Pir Zubair Shah, "Pakistani Taliban Leader Is Believed to Have Been Killed in January Attack," *New York Times*, February 1, 2010, p. A4; Tom Wright and Zahid Hussain, "Pakistan Revives Initial Account of Mehsud's Death," *Wall Street Journal*, April 30, 2010, p. A12.

40. Jane Perlez and Pir Zubair Shah, "Drones Batter Qaeda and Allies Within Pakistan," *New York Times*, April 5, 2010, pp. A1, A6.

41. Tom Wright and David Crawford, "Drone Strike Killed European Plotters," *Wall Street Journal*, October 9–10, 2010, p. A10; Mark Mazzetti and Souad Mekhennet, "Drones Kill Militants from West in Pakistan," *New York Times*, October 5, 2010, p. A6. For an assessment of the drone war in Pakistan, see Brian Glyn Williams, "The CIA's Covert Predator Drone War in Pakistan, 2004–2010: The History of an Assassination Campaign," *Studies in Conflict & Terrorism* 33, 10 (October 2010): 871–792.

42. Gregory L. Vistica, "The Plot to Get Slobo," *Newsweek*, April 12, 1999, p. 36.

43. Ibid.

44. Gregory L. Vistica, "Cyberwar and Sabotage," *Newsweek*, May 31, 1999, p. 38.

45. Mark Mazzetti, "Efforts by C.I.A. Fail in Somalia, Officials Charge," *New York Times*, June 8, 2006, pp. A1, A10.

46. Ibid.; Karen DeYoung, "U.S. Sees Growing Threats in Somalia," www.washingtonpost.com, December 18, 2006; Stephanie McCrummen, "In Somalia, Confusion Remains in Command," www.washingtonpost.com, January 6, 2007; Jeffrey Gettleman, "U.S. Aiding Somalia in Its Plan to Retake Its Capital," www.nytimes.com, March 5, 2010.

47. Karen DeYoung, "U.S. Strike in Somalia Targets Al-Qaeda Figure," www.washingtonpost.com, January 9, 2007.

48. Walter Pincus, "U.S. Strikes Kills Six in Al Qaeda," *Washington Post*, November 5, 2002, pp. A1, A22; David Johnston and David E. Sanger, "Fatal Strike in Yemen Was Based on Rules Set Out by Bush," *New York Times*, November 6, 2002, p. A14; Dana Priest, "CIA Killed U.S. Citizen in Yemen Missile Strike," *Washington Post*, November 8, 2002, pp. A1,

A22; "They Didn't Know What Hit Them," *Time*, November 18, 2002, pp. 58–59; Seymour M. Hersh, "Manhunt," *New Yorker*, December 23 and 30, 2002, pp. 66–74.

49. Scott Shane, Mark Mazzetti, and Robert F. Worth, "A Secret Assault on Terror Widens on Two Continents," *New York Times*, August 15, 2010, pp. 1, 10–11; Robert F. Worth, "Senior Members of Al Qaeda in Yemen Killed in Strike, Officials Say," *New York Times*, January 16, 2010, p. A4; Adam Entous and Siobhan Gorman, "U.S. Eyes Expanded Strikes in Yemen," *Wall Street Journal*, August 25, 2010, pp. A1, A9.

50. Entous and Gorman, "U.S. Eyes Expanded Strikes in Yemen"; Greg Miller, Greg Jaffe, and Karen DeYoung, "U.S. drones on hunt in Yemen," www.washingtonpost.com, November 7, 2010.

U.S. satellite photograph of Shifa Pharmaceutical Plant, Sudan. This degraded photo was released after the U.S. attack in August 1998 on the plant in retaliation for attacks on two U.S. embassies in Africa. Photo credit: U.S. Department of Defense.

Defense Communications Electronics Evaluation and Testing Activity at Fort Belvoir, Virginia, the U.S. receiving station for KH-11 and advanced KH-11 imagery. Photo credit: Robert Windrem.

The U-2 reconnaissance aircraft. U-2s first began operating in 1956 and are still in service, performing both imagery and SIGINT missions. Photo credit: Lockheed.

The Global Hawk UAV is capable of operating up to 3,000 nautical miles from its launch point and staying on station for twenty-four hours. It can carry electro-optical, infrared, and synthetic aperture sensors. Photo credit: Teledyne Ryan Aeronautical.

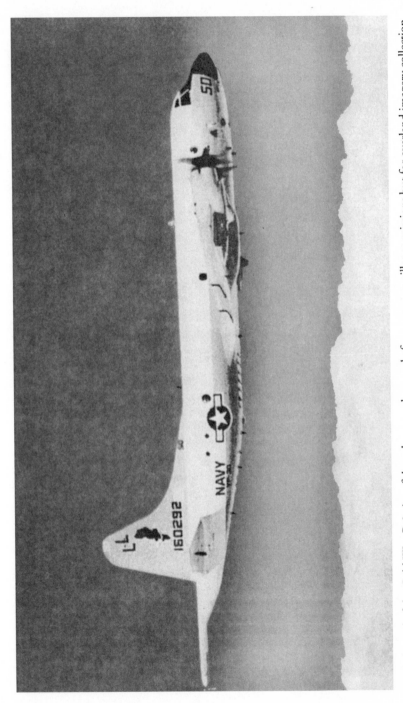

With the end of the Cold War, P-3 aircraft have been used not only for ocean surveillance missions but for overland imagery collection. Photo credit: Lockheed.

454

LACROSSE/ONYX radar imagery satellite under construction. Photo credit: National Reconnaissance Office.

Menwith Hill has served as the ground station for the VORTEX SIGINT satellite and is now the ground station for a new SIGINT satellite program. Photo credit: Duncan Campbell.

Joint Defense Space Research Facility at Alice Springs, Australia (Pine Gap), the ground control station for RHYOLITE, ORION, and advanced ORION satellites. Photo credit: Desmond Ball.

An artist's drawing of the Defense Support Program satellite. Although the primary function of DSP satellites is the detection of foreign missile launches, they also provide data used in the production of measurement and signature intelligence (MASINT). Photo credit: U.S. Air Force.

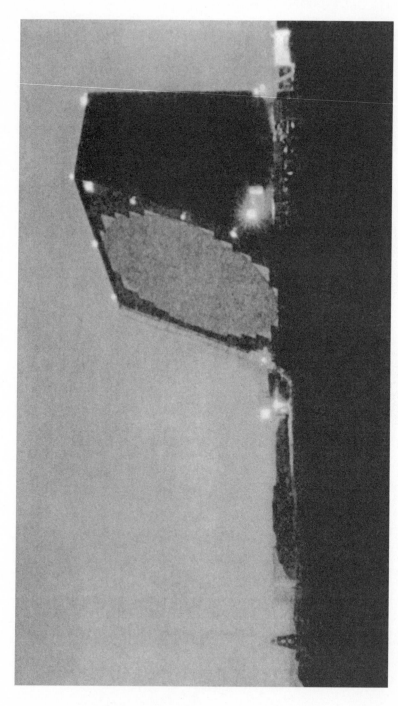

COBRA DANE phased-array radar, Shemya Island. COBRA DANE is used to track Russian missile warheads as they descend to Earth during tests. Photo credit: Raytheon.

The TEAL BLUE space surveillance site in Hawaii. Photo credit: Bob Windrem.

The COBRA JUDY phased-array radar on the USNS *Observation Island* has been used to monitor the end phase of Soviet and Russian ballistic missile tests. Photo credit: Raytheon.

The COMBAT SENT version of the RC-135 collects the emanations of foreign radars.
Credit: U.S. Air Force

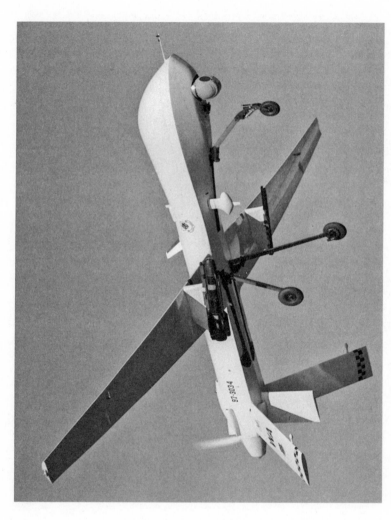

The MQ-1B version of the Predator can carry both imagery sensors for intelligence and target location, as well as two Hellfire missiles. Credit: U.S. Air Force.

17

MANAGING NATIONAL INTELLIGENCE

Prior to World War II, although the intelligence activities of the War and Navy departments certainly had national implications, those activities were managed on a departmental basis. The War Department's G-2 and the Navy's Office of Naval Intelligence had been established to fulfill departmental requirements, and their activities were guided by those requirements.

World War II was the first time the United States operated a national intelligence agency—the Office of Strategic Services. With the postwar creation of the position of Director of Central Intelligence, as well as the establishment of the National Security Council and Central Intelligence Agency, intelligence was considered to be a national as well as a departmental activity. The President was engaged in issuing executive orders to guide intelligence activities as well as approving sensitive collection and covert action operations—sometimes during meetings of the National Security Council (NSC) or its subgroups. The NSC issued its own directives to guide intelligence activities. The Director of Central Intelligence was given the charter of leading, if not commanding, the Intelligence Community on behalf of the President and the nation.

In performing that job, the Director of Central Intelligence (DCI) built up an apparatus—consisting of staffs, councils, and committees—and was empowered to issue directives covering the full range of intelligence activities that applied not only to the CIA but other members of the Intelligence Community. He also had organizations with national missions placed directly under him—such as the National Intelligence Council and, more recently, the Terrorist Threat Integration Center (and its successor, the National Counterterrorist Center)—while he had a considerable say in, but not direct control over, the activities of other organizations, such as the National Reconnaissance Office and National Security Agency.

Then, as a result of the 9/11 attacks and the report of the commission appointed to investigate those attacks, the position of DCI was abolished. The new Director of National Intelligence (DNI) has greater powers than the DCI had and is not tied to the job of managing the CIA. Some of the DCI's apparatus was transferred to the nation's new intelligence director, while other parts of that apparatus were eliminated.

What did not change was the continued involvement of the President and National Security Council in directing national intelligence activities.

THE PRESIDENT AND THE NATIONAL SECURITY COUNCIL

Direction of the national intelligence effort begins with the actions of the President and National Security Council—as manifested by the issuing of orders and directives and by the decisions of NSC groups that review intelligence activities.

The most visible documents issued by the President concerning intelligence activities are unclassified executive orders. Executive orders governing intelligence were issued in the Ford, Carter, Reagan, and George W. Bush administrations. The Bush order is an extensive amendment to Reagan's Executive Order 12333, "United States Intelligence Activities," of December 4, 1981. The amendments consume eighteen single-spaced pages in the Federal Register.[1]

The Bush order deletes the entire first part of Reagan's order and substitutes new text. Part 1 designates the Director of National Intelligence as the head of the Intelligence Community and principal intelligence advisor to the President and NSC. It also establishes the obligations and responsibilities of the DNI, including establishing objectives and priorities for the Intelligence Community, formulating policies with respect to intelligence and counterintelligence arrangements with foreign governments, and ensuring the development of programs to protect intelligence sources and methods from unauthorized disclosures. In addition, it permits the DNI to establish Functional and Mission Managers and designates the directors of the National Security Agency, Central Intelligence Agency, and National Geospatial-Intelligence Agency as the functional managers for their respective disciplines.[2]

The order specifies that the DNI "shall oversee and direct the implementation of the National Intelligence Program budget," while heads of Intelligence Community elements are directed to "provide all programmatic and budgetary information necessary to support the Director in developing the National Intelligence Program."[3]

The revised first part also specifies Intelligence Community elements and the responsibilities of the element directors as well as of those executive branch departments that contain intelligence elements. The CIA is directed, under the guidance of the DNI, to "coordinate the implementation of intelligence and counterintelligence relationships between elements of the Intelligence Community and the intelligence or security services of foreign governments or international organizations. The order further specifies that the Department of State shall "collect (overtly or through publicly available sources) information relevant to the United States' foreign policy and national security concerns," while the Department of Energy shall "provide expert scientific, technical, analytic, and research capabilities to other agencies within the Intelligence Community."[4]

Presidents also issue presidential decision and study directives, usually classified, with the titles of those directives changing with each administration. Presidential Directives (PDs) and Presidential Review Memoranda (PRM) in the Carter administration became National Security Decision Directives (NSDDs) and National Security Study Directives (NSSDs) in the Reagan administration, which became National Security Directives (NSDs) and National Security Reviews (NSRs) in the administration of George H. W. Bush. In the Clinton administration there were Presidential Decision Directives (PDDs) and Presidential Review Directives (PRDs). When George W. Bush assumed the presidency, he replaced the PDDs and PRDs with a single series—the National Security Presidential Directives (NSPDs).[5]

Although the titles of the directives change from administration to administration, they generally remain in force until explicitly canceled or replaced by a successor administration. At least seven Reagan NSDDs concerned intelligence matters. NSDD-17 of January 4, 1982, "National Security Directive on Cuba and Central America," dealt with covert operations in that region. NSDD-19 of January 12, 1982, is titled "Protection of Classified National Security Council and Intelligence Information," and NSDD-22 of January 29, 1982, concerned the "Designation of Intelligence Officials Authorized to Request FBI Collection of Foreign Intelligence." NSDD-42 of July 4, 1982, "National Space Policy," dealt, in part, with space reconnaissance. NSDD-84 of March 11, 1983, "Safeguarding National Security Information," specified new security review requirements for individuals permitted access to code word information. NSDD-159 of January 18, 1985, specified "Covert Action Policy Approval and Coordination Procedures"; NSDD-196 of November 1, 1985, concerned the "Counterintelligence/Countermeasure Implementation Task Force"; NSDD-202, "Soviet Noncompliance with Arms Control Agreements," of December 20, 1985, dealt, in part, with the impact of a new methodology for assessing the yield of Soviet nuclear weapons tests; NSDD-204 of December 24, 1985, concerned "Transfer of National Intelligence Collection Tasking Authority"; and NSDD-286 dealt with covert action procedures.[6]

Bush administration National Security Directives concerning intelligence matters included a February 1989 NSD on support to the Afghan resistance; NSD-30 of November 2, 1989, on "National Space Policy"; an August 1990 NSD on covert action directed against Iraq; the October 5, 1990, NSD-47 on "Counterintelligence and Security Countermeasures"; NSD-63 of October 21, 1991, on "Single Scope Background Investigations"; and NSD-67 of March 30, 1992, on "Intelligence Capabilities, 1992–2005."[7]

The only two known Clinton Presidential Decision Directives to deal directly with intelligence matters are PDD-24 on "U.S. Counterintelligence Effectiveness," which was the product of an interagency review mandate by Presidential Review Directive-44, and PDD-35 on intelligence priorities. Similarly, there are only two known NSPDs from the Bush administration concerning intelligence: NSPD 5 (May 9, 2001), which directed a review of U.S. intelligence, and NSPD 26 (February 2003), which focused on intelligence priorities.[8] None of the Obama administration's Presidential Policy or Study Directives concerning intelligence have become known publicly.

More detailed guidance across much of the spectrum of intelligence activities was provided from the beginning of the post–World War II era in the form of National

Security Council Intelligence Directives (NSCIDs), which were revised periodically up to February 17, 1972, when updated versions of all eight current NSCIDs were reissued.

A project to produce an omnibus NSCID in the 1970s was never completed. Consideration was given in the 1980s to further updating the directives, but it was decided to issue new guidance through the Director of Central Intelligence Directives that were derived from the NSCIDs, which have never been rescinded.[9] The numbers and names of the NSCIDs are listed in Table 17.1.

NSCID No. 1, "Basic Duties and Responsibilities," was first issued in 1947 and subsequently updated in 1952, 1958, 1961, 1964, and 1972. The NSCID No. 1 of February 17, 1972, assigned four major responsibilities to the DCI:

1. planning, reviewing, and evaluating all intelligence activities and the allocation of all intelligence resources
2. producing national intelligence required by the President and national consumers
3. chairing and staffing all intelligence advisory boards
4. establishing and reconciling intelligence requirements and priorities with budgetary constraints.[10]

NSCID No. 1 also (1) instructs the DCI to prepare and submit to the Office of Management and Budget (OMB) a consolidated budget, (2) authorizes the issuance of Director of Central Intelligence Directives as a means of implementing the NSCIDs, and (3) instructs the DCI to protect sources and methods.[11]

NSCID No. 2 of February 1972 makes the DCI responsible for planning how the overt collection and reporting capabilities of the various government departments will be utilized and makes the CIA responsible for conducting, as a service of common concern, radio broadcast monitoring. The Department of State is charged with overt collection of political, sociological, economic, scientific, and technical information; military-pertinent scientific and technical intelligence; and economic intelligence.[12]

The 1972 version of NSCID No. 3 makes the Department of State responsible for the production of political and sociological intelligence on all countries and economic intelligence on the countries of the "Free World." It makes the Department of Defense (DOD) responsible for the production of military intelligence and scientific and technical intelligence pertinent to the missions of DOD components. The CIA is assigned responsibility for economic and scientific and technical intelligence plus "any other intelligence required by the CIA." In practice, this clause has meant that the CIA is heavily involved in the production of political and military intelligence, especially strategic intelligence. In addition, atomic energy intelligence is decreed, by NSCID No. 3, to be the responsibility of all National Foreign Intelligence Board (NFIB) agencies.[13]

TABLE 17.1   NSCIDs Issued on February 17, 1972

Number	Title
1	Basic Duties and Responsibilities
2	Coordination of Overt Activities
3	Coordination of Intelligence Production
4	The Defector Program
5	U.S. Espionage and Counterintelligence Activities Abroad
6	Signals Intelligence
7	Critical Intelligence Communications
8	Photographic Interpretation

Originally, NSCID No. 4 concerned Priority National Intelligence Objectives (PNIOs)—a system for prioritizing collection efforts. The PNIO system has been eliminated; hence, NSCID No. 4 now bears the title "The Defector Program" and presumably concerns the inducement of defections and the responsibilities of the CIA and other agencies in the program.[14]

NSCID No. 5, "U.S. Espionage and Counterintelligence Activities Abroad," is the successor to versions issued in 1947, 1951, 1958, and 1961. The directive authorizes the DCI to "establish the procedures necessary to achieve such direction and coordination, including the assessment of risk incident upon such operations as compared to the value of the activity, and to ensure that sensitive operations are reviewed pursuant to applicable direction."[15]

NSCID No. 6, "Signals Intelligence," serves as the charter for the NSA. The February 1972 version defines the nature of SIGINT activities and directs the Director of NSA (DIRNSA) to produce intelligence "in accordance with objectives, requirements and priorities established by the Director of Central Intelligence and the United States Intelligence Board." It further authorizes the DIRNSA "to issue direct to any operating elements engaged in SIGINT operations such instructions and assignments as are required. All instructions issued by the Director under the authority provided in this paragraph shall be mandatory, subject only to appeal to the Secretary of Defense."[16]

NSCID No. 7 establishes the Critical Intelligence Communications (CRITIC) system. This system governs procedures and criteria for the transmission of particularly important intelligence to top officials, including the President, within the shortest possible period of time. The information may concern an imminent coup, the assassination of a world leader, or, as in September 1983, the shooting down of a civilian airliner. The information acquired may be via HUMINT, SIGINT, or IMINT. It has been NSA's goal to have a CRITIC message on the President's desk within 10 minutes of the event.[17]

The original NSCID No. 8 was issued on May 25, 1948, and was titled "Biographic Data on Foreign Scientific and Technological Personalities." Before the end of 1961, the NSCID dealt, instead, with "Photographic Interpretation." NSCID No. 8 of February 1972 continued the National Photographic Interpretation Center (NPIC) as a service of common concern to be provided by the DCI. Additionally, it specified that the Director of the NPIC was to be selected by the DCI with the concurrence of the Secretary of Defense.[18]

THE DIRECTOR OF NATIONAL INTELLIGENCE

Ever since the Central Intelligence Agency was established in July 1947, there have been controversy and conflict over the role of the DCI in managing agencies other than the CIA—both because existing agencies and their departments sought to protect their bureaucratic turf and because it was feared that increased authority for the DCI could result in a reduction in the responsiveness of military organizations to the requirements of the military.

Notable milestones over the years have included DCI Walter Bedell Smith's successful fight to establish that the Intelligence Advisory Committee, consisting of the chiefs of the nation's intelligence agencies, existed to provide him with advice rather than to serve as a board of directors. Allen Dulles (1953–1961) fought and won a number of battles to prevent the Defense Department from gaining control of key institutions and programs for the collection and analysis of intelligence. His successor, John McCone, became embroiled in bitter battles between the CIA's Directorate of Science and Technology and the leadership of the National Reconnaissance Office over control of satellite programs—at one point drafting a memorandum that would have abolished the NRO. During his tenure as DCI, Richard Helms (1966–1973) complained that while he was ostensibly responsible for the activities of the entire Intelligence Community, he controlled only 15 percent of its resources, with almost all of the remaining 85 percent in the hands of the Secretary of Defense.

Over the years, presidents took a number of actions to enhance the authority of the DCI, some of which followed one or more of the multitude of studies undertaken to examine the workings of the Intelligence Community. Investigations into Intelligence Community performance have been conducted since at least 1949—by private citizens or government officials appointed by the DCI, by interagency groups, by the Office of Management and Budget, by internal CIA panels, and by congressional committees and other entities. Often the options considered have included ones far more radical than the administration has been willing to adopt. Among the more radical proposals had been the creation of an intelligence czar—a Director of National Intelligence who would replace the DCI as the President's primary intelligence advisor and who would be responsible for the entire Intelligence Community's activities.

As a result of the events of September 11, 2001, the Congressional Joint Inquiry and the National Commission on Terrorist Attacks Upon the United States examined the issue of intelligence organization and recommended the creation of a Director of National Intelligence, with two main areas of responsibility: (1) overseeing national intelligence centers on specific subjects of interest across the U.S. government, and (2) managing the National Intelligence Program and overseeing the agencies that contribute to it.[19]

Indeed, creation of a DNI was one of the committee's principal recommendations. The proposal was eventually supported by the Bush administration, but opposition from the Pentagon and then the chairman of the House Armed Services Committee blocked passage of legislation creating a DNI. With a compromise reached on December 6, 2004, the road was finally cleared to establish a Director of National Intelligence.

The *Intelligence Reform and Terrorism Prevention Act of 2004* (IRTPA) did not give the DNI complete power over the NRO, NSA, or NGA, which remained located within the Department of Defense, although it confirmed the increased authority that President Bush gave the DCI in August 2004 and further increased his authority with regard to those and other organizations in several areas. Under the act, the Director of Management and Budget, under the exclusive direction of the DNI, is to apportion—or direct how congressionally appropriated funds are to flow from the Treasury Department—to each of the Cabinet-level agencies containing Intelligence Community elements. Thus, the DNI is in a better position to control the pace of spending and can withhold funds until recipients comply with DNI spending priorities. The DNI also has the authority to allot appropriations directly at the sub-Cabinet agency and department level, giving him or her an additional opportunity to control spending. The IRTPA also requires the DNI to inform Congress if a departmental comptroller refuses to act in accordance with a DNI spending directive. The DCI had neither authority.[20]

The DNI is also charged with the responsibility to "develop and determine" the National Intelligence Program budget and ensure the effective execution of the budget and monitor its implementation. In addition, the DNI is permitted, with OMB approval, to unilaterally transfer funds up to $150 million, provided that the sum is less than 5 percent of the affected agency's or department's budget. DCIs could effect such a transfer only with the concurrence of the agency or department head, which could take several months to negotiate.[21]

The DNI is also able to transfer Intelligence Community personnel for up to two years, without the concurrence of the agency or department head—a concurrence that DCIs were required to obtain. If the DNI establishes any new national intelligence centers in addition to the two that already exist (he has the authority to create another four), the director has the authority to transfer up to 100 personnel to staff the new center.[22]

With regard to appointments, agency or department heads having jurisdiction over the appointment must seek the concurrence of the DNI. Without the DNI's concurrence the position cannot be filled. The DNI also has approval authority over major acquisitions. Although the DCI had significant impact on a number of acquisition decisions in the past—primarily concerning satellite reconnaissance systems—he had no statutory authority. The DNI, as a result of the legislation, serves as the executive milestone decision authority on major acquisitions. His power is limited to the extent that acquisitions concern Defense Department programs. In that case, he shares power with the Secretary of Defense. If they cannot reach agreement, it is up to the President to resolve the dispute.[23]

The IRTPA enhanced the DNI's tasking authority over that possessed by the DCIs by stating that the DNI shall "manage and direct the tasking of, collection, analysis, production, and dissemination of national intelligence . . . by approving requirements and resolving conflicts." In 2010, the DNI reached agreement with the Secretary of Defense such that the entire National Intelligence Program budget would be under the purview of the DNI by 2013.[24]

Subordinate to the DNI are approximately 1,500 individuals—deputy directors, assistant deputy directors, mission managers and their staffs, a counterintelligence organization, and the two national centers created by the IRTPA.[25]

At this time, the structure of the DNI's office is being reorganized. The current chart for the DNI's office is shown as Figure 17.1.

NATIONAL INTELLIGENCE BOARD

The National Intelligence Board is the successor to the National Foreign Intelligence Board and United States Intelligence Board. Its functions include advising the DNI on production, review, and coordination of national intelligence; on interagency exchanges of national intelligence data; on sharing of Intelligence Community products with foreign governments; on protection of intelligence sources and methods; and on activities of common concern and other matters that may be referred to it by the DNI. Its membership includes the DNI as chairman; the Principal Deputy DNI; the chairman of the National Intelligence Council; the Deputy DNI for Collection; the directors of CIA, DIA, NGA, NSA, INR, the National Counterintelligence Executive, and the FBI National Security Branch; the assistant secretaries for intelligence analysis of the Treasury and Homeland Security Departments; the director of the Energy Department Office of Intelligence and Counterintelligence; and the Under Secretary of Defense for Intelligence.[26]

JOINT INTELLIGENCE COMMUNITY COUNCIL

The Joint Intelligence Community Council (JICC) includes the DNI, as chair, the Secretary of State, the Secretary of the Treasury, the Secretary of Defense, the Attorney General, the Secretary of Energy, the Secretary of Homeland Security, and others that the President may designate. It assists the DNI in developing and implementing a joint unified national intelligence effort by advising the DNI on requirements, developing budgets, managing finances, monitoring and evaluating the performance of the Intelligence Community, and ensuring timely execution of DNI programs, policies, and directives.[27]

FIGURE 17.1   Organization of the Office of the Director of National Intelligence

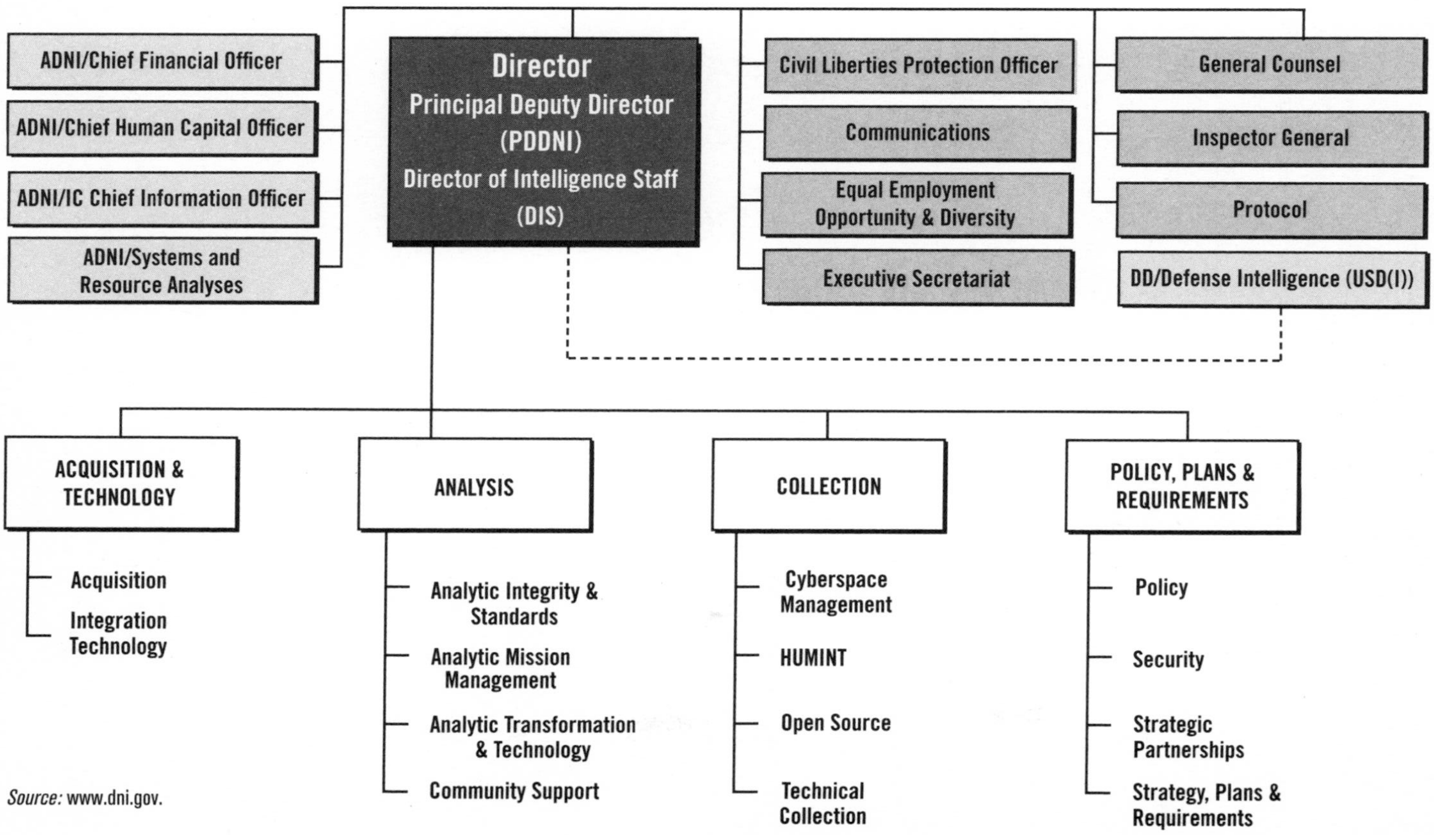

- Director
  Principal Deputy Director (PDDNI)
  Director of Intelligence Staff (DIS)

- General Counsel
- Inspector General
- Protocol
- DD/Defense Intelligence (USD(I))

- Civil Liberties Protection Officer
- Communications
- Equal Employment Opportunity & Diversity
- Executive Secretariat

- ADNI/Chief Financial Officer
- ADNI/Chief Human Capital Officer
- ADNI/IC Chief Information Officer
- ADNI/Systems and Resource Analyses

ACQUISITION & TECHNOLOGY
- Acquisition
- Integration
- Technology

ANALYSIS
- Analytic Integrity & Standards
- Analytic Mission Management
- Analytic Transformation & Technology
- Community Support

COLLECTION
- Cyberspace Management
- HUMINT
- Open Source
- Technical Collection

POLICY, PLANS & REQUIREMENTS
- Policy
- Security
- Strategic Partnerships
- Strategy, Plans & Requirements

Source: www.dni.gov.

INTELLIGENCE COMMUNITY EXECUTIVE COMMITTEE

The Executive Committee (EXCOM) is a senior advisory group, consisting of "the DNI and Directors of the 16 IC elements," that "advises and supports the DNI, conducts in-depth discussions on critical issues such as intelligence support to Afghanistan and Pakistan and terrorist finance, and enables proper resource allocation," according to a DNI fact sheet.[28]

PROGRAM MANAGER GROUP

The Program Manager Group, chaired by the Principal DDNI, advises and assists the DNI in identifying requirements, developing budgets, managing finance, and monitoring and evaluating the performance of the Intelligence Community. The group consists of the heads of the CIA, the DIA, the NGA, the NRO, the FBI National Security Branch, the DDNIs, the ADNI/CoS, and others as directed by the Principal DNI.[29]

NATIONAL INTELLIGENCE PROGRAM

Until 2005, the allocation of resources for national intelligence activities was governed by the National Foreign Intelligence Program. The nonmilitary components of the NFIP were the Central Intelligence Agency Program, the State Department Intelligence Program, the Community Management Staff, and the intelligence elements of the FBI, the Department of Energy, and the Department of the Treasury. There were five DOD components: the Consolidated Cryptologic Program (CCP), the General Defense Intelligence Program (GDIP), the Navy Special Reconnaissance Activities, the National Reconnaissance Program (NRP), and the Defense Foreign Counterintelligence Program.[30]

The CCP, managed by NSA, included all SIGINT resources in the NFIP. The GDIP included all non-SIGINT, non-reconnaissance programs. Specifically, the GDIP included eight activities: general military intelligence production, imagery collection and processing, HUMINT, nuclear monitoring, R&D procurement, field support, general support, and scientific and technical intelligence production. The CCP and GDIP, when combined, formed the Consolidated Defense Intelligence Program.

The Naval Special Reconnaissance Activities program allocates attack submarines (SSNs) and other craft for sensitive reconnaissance missions. The NRP specifies the spending, procurement, and operational activities of the NRO.[31]

One component of the Intelligence Reform and Terrorism Prevention Act of 2004 was the redesignation of the NFIP as the National Intelligence Program—a change that highlighted the Director of National Intelligence's role in domestic intelligence.[32]

NATIONAL INTELLIGENCE COUNCIL

The National Intelligence Council (NIC) was the DCI's principal vehicle for producing National Intelligence Estimates, Special Estimates, and Interagency Intelligence Memoranda, and now performs its mission on behalf of the DNI. Its origins go back to 1950, when an Office of National Estimates (ONE) was established within the CIA. This office, tasked with drafting national estimates, consisted of the Board of National Estimates and its staff. The board consisted of seven to twelve senior officials with expertise in particular areas who were initially drawn from academia and subsequently from the CIA.[33]

The ONE suffered a decline in prestige and influence during the Nixon administration for a variety of reasons, including Henry Kissinger's unhappiness with its product. In June 1973, the BNE chairman was forced to retire. DCI William Colby decided not to replace him and abolished the ONE.[34]

Colby gave two reasons for his decision:

One, I had some concern with the tendency to compromise differences and put out a document which was less sharp than perhaps was needed in certain situations. Second, I believed that I needed the advantage of some individuals who could specialize in some of the major problems not just as estimative problems but as broad intelligence problems. They could sit in my chair, so to speak, and look at the full range of an intelligence problem: Are we collecting enough? Are we processing the raw data properly? Are we spending too much money on it? Are we organized right to do the job?[35]

Colby created the National Intelligence Officer (NIO) system, whereby specific individuals were held solely responsible for producing a particular estimate. In a 1987 memo on "The Integrity and Objectivity of National Foreign Estimates," the then Deputy Director for Intelligence, Richard J. Kerr, observed,

The role of the National Intelligence Officer, in our judgment, is critical. An impartial estimative process requires the full expression of views by participating agencies and the clear identification for our consumers of areas of agreement and, often most importantly, disagreement. In order to fight what is often an unhealthy desire to reach consensus, the NIO must, above all, see himself as a manager of the process, the one who ensures that the tough questions are addressed, that consensus views represent real agreement, and not papered-over differences, and that minority views are fully expressed. It has been our experience that when the NIO subordinates this responsibility to the advocacy of a particular analytic line that the integrity of the estimative process suffers.[36]

Initially, NIOs were purposely not given a staff but were expected to draw on the resources of the CIA, DIA, INR, and other analytical units to produce the required estimates. On January 1, 1980, with the establishment of the National Intelligence Council, the NIOs were given not only a collective identity but also an Analytic Staff.[37]

When BNE/ONE was established it was part of the CIA. Under DCI John Mc-Cone, the BNE was attached to the DCI's office and made responsible to him alone. During the Carter administration, the NIOs became part of the National Foreign Assessment Center (NFAC) and thus reported to the CIA's Deputy Director for National Foreign Assessment.[38]

One of the Reagan administration's first actions concerning intelligence was converting the NFAC back to the Directorate of Intelligence. With that change, the NIOs were once again placed under the control of the DCI. Subsequently, the NIC was moved back within the Directorate of Intelligence. In 1992, however, DCI Robert Gates announced plans to move the NIC out of the CIA and into an independent facility.[39]

The NIOs primary functions are to

- advise the DNI;
- interact regularly with senior intelligence consumers and support their current and longer-term needs;
- produce estimative intelligence;
- interact with outside experts for their knowledge and insights;
- help assess the capabilities and needs of Intelligence Community analytic producers;
- promote collaboration among Intelligence Community analytic producers on strategic warning, advanced analytical tools, and methodologies;
- articulate substantive priorities to guide intelligence collection, evaluation, and procurement.[40]

The three top officials of the NIC are the Chairman, Vice Chairman, and Director of Analysis and Production Staff. As of late 2010, there were thirteen NIOs. Seven had regional responsibilities: Africa, East Asia, Europe, Near East, Russia and Eurasia, South Asia, and the Western Hemisphere. The remaining six NIOs are responsible for Economics Issues, Military Issues, Science and Technology, Transnational Threats, Warning, and Weapons of Mass Destruction and Proliferation.[41]

As of December 2010, five of the NIOs had come from the CIA, while another two came from other intelligence organizations (Z Division and DIA). The others came from the Institute of Peace, the Council on Foreign Relations, the Army, the DOD, and the National Defense University. One position was vacant.[42]

When Robert Gates transferred the NIC out of the CIA's Directorate of Intelligence, he also transferred three DCI interagency intelligence production committees to the NIC—the Joint Atomic Energy Intelligence Committee (JAEIC), the

Weapons and Space Systems Intelligence Committee (WSSIC), and the Scientific and Technical Intelligence Committee.[43]

The JAEIC was created "to foster, develop and maintain a coordinated community approach to the problems in the field of atomic energy intelligence, to promote interagency liaison, and to give added impetus and community support to the efforts of individual agencies."[44]

In 1965, DCID 3/3, "Production of Atomic Energy Intelligence," noted that atomic energy intelligence was the responsibility of all NFIB committees and further declared that "the mission of the Joint Atomic Energy Intelligence Committee (JAEIC) shall be to foster, develop and maintain a coordinated community approach to the problems in the field of atomic energy intelligence, to promote interagency liaison and to give impetus and community support to the efforts of individual agencies."[45]

The JAEIC discusses items related to nuclear intelligence. Its specific responsibilities include assessing the adequacy of the U.S. nuclear intelligence program and its ability to effectively monitor compliance with various nuclear testing treaties; evaluating the methodology used in estimating the yield of foreign nuclear detonations; assessing major developments in foreign nuclear weapons powers; considering the possible impact of nuclear energy programs on proliferation in nations not yet possessing nuclear weapons; providing national decisionmakers with advice on the possible authorization of U.S. foreign sales in the nuclear energy area; and providing warning of a country "going nuclear."[46]

Its products have included a 1976 assessment of "The Soviet Atomic Energy Program," a 1989 assessment of Iraq's ability to build an atomic weapon, and the 1992 study on the "Geology of the Qinggir Underground Nuclear Test Site." It may also commission work, such as the tasking of a national laboratory intelligence unit to produce a study on the state of nuclear materials security in Russia. JAEIC components have included a Nuclear Test Intelligence Subcommittee and a Nuclear Weapons Logistics Working Group.[47]

The failure to convene a second meeting of the JAEIC in 2002 to examine the varied views in the Intelligence Community about the implications of Iraq's purchase of aluminum tubes became a subject of controversy. An August 2002 meeting was to be followed by a meeting later in the month, but this was cancelled, as was a scheduled September meeting.[48]

The Weapons and Space Systems Intelligence Committee (WSSIC) was created in 1956 as the Guided Missile Intelligence Committee and subsequently became the Guided Missile and Astronautics Intelligence Committee (GMAIC). In addition to coordinating the guided missile and astronautics intelligence activities of the Intelligence Community during the Cold War, the WSSIC performed technical studies on Soviet missiles as inputs to the NIEs. These papers were coordinated in the same manner as NIEs but were directed at informing the Intelligence Community. The WSSIC also assigned designators and code names for such systems.[49]

The WSSIC's Biological and Chemical Warfare Working Group reviewed all available intelligence concerning the suspected biological warfare incident at Sverdlovsk in 1979. It concluded that there was a high probability that the Soviets maintained an active biological warfare program. Earlier committee products concerned Soviet tank developments, the air defense capabilities of Soviet nuclear-equipped surface-to-air missiles, and estimates of Soviet ICBM silo hardness. More recently, the committee produced a report concluding that Chinese-supplied M-11s in Pakistan should be considered operational.[50]

The Scientific and Technical Intelligence Committee (STIC) is responsible for "advising and assisting the [DNI] with respect to the production, coordination, and evaluation of intelligence on foreign scientific and technical developments that could affect U.S. national security."[51]

STIC products have included "Soviet R&D Related to Particle Beam Weapons" (October 1976), "Collection Guide: Chinese Students and Visitors from Important Institutes Seeking Critical Technologies" (1986), and "A Preliminary Assessment of Soviet Kinetic Energy Weapons Technology" (1986). In the 1991 fiscal year, its Collection Subcommittee examined "existing and planned approaches to S&T intelligence collection identified gaps, and provided a forum for discussion of S&T collection issues."[52]

The National Intelligence Production Board (NIPB), formerly known as the Intelligence Producers Council (IPC), operates under the NIC, is chaired by the chairman of the NIC, and is composed of senior Intelligence Community production managers, including the chairmen of the DNI production committees. In addition to advising the DNI on production matters, it "oversees several Community programs that focus on minimizing unnecessary duplication of effort and maximizing efforts to meet consumer needs."[53]

NATIONAL COUNTERTERRORISM CENTER

In his January 2003 State of the Union address, President Bush announced plans to establish a Terrorist Threat Integration Center (TTIC), outside of the CIA organizational structure, but reporting to the Director of Central Intelligence. A Director of Central Intelligence Directive, DCID 2/4, followed, formally establishing the center and specifying its missions. On May 1, 2003, the center opened with fifty officers from the Departments of State, Defense, Justice, and Homeland Security and from the Intelligence Community. It was expected to have several hundred officers by the time it moved into a new facility in May 2004, with the FBI Counterterrorism Division and CIA Counterterrorist Center relocating to that facility at the same time.[54]

The center was assigned four key missions. It was responsible for providing terrorist threat assessments to U.S. national leaders, ensuring information sharing across agency lines, integrating domestic and foreign intelligence related to terrorist threats, and optimizing the use of terrorist threat–related information, expertise, and capabilities to conduct threat analysis and guide collection strategies. By December 2003, the TTIC was producing a daily terrorist threat matrix, a daily terrorist threat report for the Executive Branch, a daily terrorist situation report, spot commentaries, threat warnings, Intelligence Community assessments, and special analysis reports.[55]

A major recommendation of the National Commission on Terrorist Attacks Upon the United States in its July 2004 report was the creation of a National Counterterrorism Center (NCTC), to be built on the foundation of the TTIC. The center, as envisioned by the commission, would be a center for not only joint intelligence but also joint operational planning and would be staffed by personnel from the CIA, FBI, and other agencies.[56]

With respect to intelligence, the NCTC "should lead strategic analysis, pooling all-source intelligence, foreign and domestic, about transnational terrorist organizations with global reach," the Commission wrote. The center, the Commission believed, should develop net assessments, comparing terrorist capabilities with U.S. defenses and countermeasures, and provide warning and task collection assets both within and outside the United States.[57]

The Commission recommended that the NCTC's operational planning functions should include assigning operational responsibilities to agencies such as the State Department, the CIA, the FBI, the Defense Department and the combatant commands, and the Department of Homeland Security. While the NCTC would not direct the actual execution of operations, it would track their implementation by the operational agencies. It would also "look across the foreign-domestic divide and across agency boundaries, updating plans to follow through on cases."[58]

In response to the Commission's recommendation, President Bush issued an executive order in late August 2004 establishing a National Counterterrorism Center, under the supervision of the Director of Central Intelligence. Consistent with the Commission's recommendations, the order assigned the NCTC the responsibility for being the U.S. government's primary organization for analyzing and integrating all intelligence possessed by the government pertaining to terrorism and counterterrorism, with the exception of "purely domestic counterterrorism information." And, as the Commission recommended, the NCTC was assigned the mission of strategic operational planning for counterterrorism activities. It was also assigned the recommended missions of information sharing and serving as a central bank of knowledge.[59]

Two months later, Congress passed the Intelligence Reform and Terrorism Prevention Act, which, in effect, transferred the NCTC from the former office of the Director of Central Intelligence to the office of the Director of National Intelligence. The primary NCTC missions in the legislation were essentially identical to those outlined in the executive order. However, with respect to the planning of counterterrorist operations, the NCTC reports to the President, whereas it reports to the DNI with respect to budget and programs of the NCTC and the activities of the NCTC's Directorate of Intelligence.[60]

Since it was formally launched in December 2004, the NCTC has established a database, the Terrorist Identities Datamart Environment (TIDE), based on all-source information from the Intelligence Community, which has more than 450,000 entries and 200,000 unique terrorist identities. A "very, very small fraction" of that number includes U.S. citizens, with the "vast majority" being "non-U.S. persons" who do not live in the United States. A key provider of names is the National Security Agency. To facilitate information sharing, the NCTC manages a classified counterterrorism website, NCTC OnLine (NOL), which has 5,000 cleared customers. NOL contains approximately 5 million different intelligence products and reports.[61]

It also produces continually updated reports called Threat Threads, with as many as twelve Threads being produced simultaneously. It has also produced the National Action Plan to Combat Foreign Fighters in Iraq, completed in June 2006, and the 200-page National Implementation Plan, the overall plan to guide counterterrorist activities.[62]

The Center carries out its responsibilities through its two directorates—the Directorate of Intelligence and the Directorate of Strategic Operational Planning. It also maintains a 24-hour operations center, which can display an Arab satellite news channel, a radar map over New York City, or the feed from a Predator drone over Afghanistan. An NCTC watch team of at least a dozen people is on duty around the clock, while the CIA and FBI also maintain their own watch centers in the same space.[63]

As shown in Figure 17.2, the NCTC is composed of five directorates. The Directorate of Intelligence "leads the production and integration of counterterrorism analysis for the U.S. Government." The Directorate of Strategic Operational Planning "directs the U.S. Government's planning efforts to focus all elements of national power against the terrorist threat." The Directorate of Mission Management provides "strategic management" of all national intelligence related to the Intelligence Community's counterterrorism mission. It sets analytic and collection priorities and leads strategic planning, evaluation, and budgeting activities. The Directorate of Information Sharing and Knowledge Development "ensures Federal Government agencies can access the information they need through systems such as NCTC Online (NOL) and the Terrorist Identities Datamart Environment." Finally, the Directorate of Operations Support "provides the common intelligence picture for the counterterrorism community with 24 hours a day/7 days a week situational awareness."[64]

NATIONAL COUNTERPROLIFERATION CENTER

The National Commission on Terrorist Attacks Upon the United States suggested the possibility of establishing a center focusing on proliferation of weapons of mass destruction under a Director of National Intelligence. In its March 2005 report, the Commission on the Intelligence Capabilities of the United States Regarding Weapons of Mass Destruction explicitly recommended that the President "establish a National Counter Proliferation Center (NCPC) that is relatively small (i.e., fewer than 100 people) and that manages and coordinates analysis and collection on nuclear, biological, and chemical weapons across the Intelligence Community."[65]

FIGURE 17.2   Organization of the National Counterterrorism Center

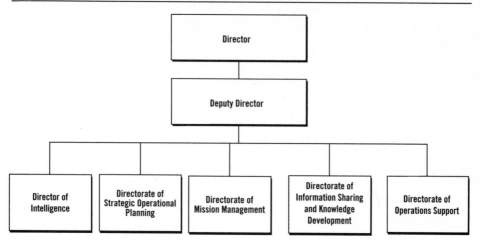

Even before that report was issued, a provision of the Intelligence Reform and Terrorism Prevention Act of 2004 specified that no later than eighteen months after the enactment of the legislation, the President was required to establish a National Counterproliferation Center. Its responsibilities would include serving as the primary organization for analyzing and integrating all intelligence possessed or acquired by the United States pertaining to proliferation, ensuring that agencies had full access to all-source intelligence needed to support their counterproliferation activities, coordinating the counterproliferation plans and activities of various departments and agencies, and conducting strategic operational counterproliferation planning for U.S. government agencies. The legislation did provide a provision that the President could waive any of the requirements of the section if the President determined that the provisions would not materially improve U.S. counterproliferation capabilities.[66]

On August 8, 2005, in compliance with the IRTPA, DNI John Negroponte appointed Kenneth C. Brill to be the Counterproliferation Mission Manager as well as the Director of the future National Counterproliferation Center—making him the principal advisor to the DNI on issues and matters related to the proliferation of weapons of mass destruction.[67]

Because President Bush waived some of the new requirements, the new center was not the precise counterpart to the NCTC that the intelligence reform act envisioned. Thus, it did not replace the CIA's Weapons Intelligence, Nonproliferation, and Arms Control Center (WINPAC). Rather, the new center is responsible for coordinating strategic planning within the Intelligence Community to enhance intelligence support to the United States' efforts to halt the proliferation of weapons of mass destruction and related delivery systems. It is chartered to "work with the Intelligence

Community to identify critical intelligence gaps or shortfalls in collection, analysis or exploitation, and develop solutions to ameliorate or close [such] gaps." It is also responsible for working with the Intelligence Community to identify long-term proliferation threats and requirements and to develop strategies "to ensure the IC is positioned to address these threats and issues."[68]

It is also responsible for maintaining contact with organizations within and outside the Intelligence Community that might help identify new methods or technologies that can improve the community's capabilities to detect and prevent future proliferation threats.[69] This presumably includes contacts with the CIA, NSA, NRO, the national laboratories, and private firms, among others.

The organization chart of the NCPC is shown as Figure 17.3.

NATIONAL COUNTERINTELLIGENCE POLICY BOARD

The National Counterintelligence Policy Board was established in May 1994 by PDD-24 and consists of senior executive representatives from the DNI, the CIA, the Defense Department, the State Department, and the Justice Department (including the FBI), the Department of Homeland Security, and the Department of the Energy. The board considers, develops, and recommends counterintelligence policy and planning directives to the President's national security advisor.

Subordinate to the policy board is the National Counterintelligence Operations Board.[70]

NATIONAL COUNTERINTELLIGENCE EXECUTIVE

The office of the National Counterintelligence Executive (NCIX), established in 1995, has six functions: (1) producing annual foreign intelligence threat assessments and other analytic counterintelligence products, (2) producing an annual national counterintelligence strategy for the U.S. government, (3) establishing priorities for counterintelligence collection, investigation, and operations, (4) producing counterintelligence program budgets and evaluations reflecting strategic priorities, (5) producing in-depth espionage damage assessments, and (6) providing for counterintelligence awareness and outreach. The NCIX also chairs the National Counterintelligence Policy Board.[71]

NATIONAL INTELLIGENCE COORDINATION–CENTER

The National Intelligence Coordination–Center (NIC-C) was established on October 1, 2007, with the objective of improving strategic management of national collection activities. In addition to the Center's director, there are two deputy directors—Domestic and Defense.[72]

There are four aspects to the NIC-C effort. One is Collection Mission Management, which seeks to "determine what needs to be done." Personnel seek to "ingest"

FIGURE 17.3   Organization of the National Counterproliferation Center

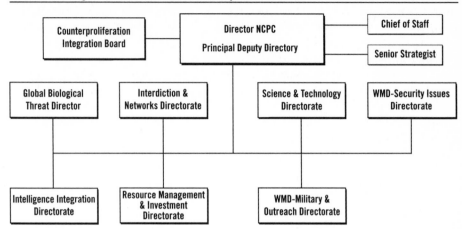

strategic requirements and reconcile and align them with the National Intelligence Priorities Framework and the requirements of the combatant commands. A second aspect is Collection Situational Awareness, "understand[ing] what is happening." Specifically, that element is responsible for creating a mechanism to "inform, integrate, and initiate collection activities across the Intelligence Community (IC), Defense and Homeland collection enterprise as well as informing collection activities of the priorities of the DNI and other senior decision makers."[73]

A third aspect is Collection Assessment—"understand[ing] the value of the effort." This component of the NIC-C effort assesses collection programs or targets via cost/benefit/risk analysis and makes recommendations to improve the value and efficiency of the collection effort. The final aspect is Global Maritime and Air Intelligence integration, whose primary objective is to "provide integrated mission management to ensure unity of effort" across the IC and other agencies.[74]

INTELLIGENCE COMMUNITY DIRECTIVES

While National Security Council Intelligence Directives, first issued in 1947, were intended to provide broad policy guidance to the Intelligence Community, there was a need for more detailed guidance on the multiple issues associated with each NSCID. The main mechanism for providing that more detailed guidance was the Director of Central Intelligence Directive (DCID)—with each DCID being of the form "DCID x/y," where x represented the NSCID that the DCID pertained to and y represented the number in that particular series of DCIDs.

When Jimmy Carter's executive order on intelligence activities covered issues not addressed in the NSCIDs, there was internal discussion of the need to revise them. A similar discussion followed Ronald Reagan's Executive Order 12333. Instead, the decision was made to issue DCIDs regardless of any non-matching aspects of the NSCIDs and the executive order. In effect, the DCIDs were decoupled from the NSCIDs that had originally served as the basis for their promulgation.[75]

Following the creation of the office of the Director of National Intelligence, the DNI created three new series of documents: Intelligence Community Policy Memorandums (ICPMs), Intelligence Community Policy Guidance (ICPG), and Intelligence Community Directives (ICDs). The ICPMs are issued to provide policy direction to the Intelligence Community prior to the issuance of an ICD on that same subject. ICPMs that were issued in the early years of the DNI's office have naturally been replaced by ICDs over time. An ICPG is subsidiary to an ICD and provides more detailed implementation information. The ICPMs and ICDs, with the exception of some early ICDs, are divided into nine series covering the following topics:

- 100: Enterprise Management
- 200: Intelligence Analysis
- 300: Intelligence Collection
- 400: Customer Outcomes
- 500: Information Management
- 600: Human Capital
- 700: Security and Counterintelligence
- 800: Science and Technology
- 900: Mission Management

ICD 204, issued in September 2007, rescinded DCID 2/3 and established roles and responsibilities for the National Intelligence Priorities Framework (NIPF). It declares the NIPF to be "the DNI's sole mechanism for establishing national intelligence priorities." It also defines the NIPF as consisting of intelligence topics approved by the President, a process for assigning priorities to countries and nonstate actors relevant to the approved intelligence topics, and a matrix showing those priorities.[76]

ICD 902, "Global Maritime and Air Intelligence Integration," was issued in January 2009 to "provide policy and direction to the Intelligence Community (IC) elements for integrating activities and information sharing to improve, develop, and enhance maritime and air domain intelligence to effectively identify and respond to national security threats." It specifies that "a national intelligence center for the integration of strategic maritime information will be established at the National Maritime Intelligence Center."[77] A number of additional ICDs are discussed in Chapter 19.

Table 17.2 lists the set of directives that had been released.

DNI COMMITTEES

In 1976, in the interval between the abolition of the United States Intelligence Board (USIB) and the creation of the NFIB, the USIB committees were redesignated as

TABLE 17.2   Intelligence Community Directives

ICD Number	Title	Date
101	Intelligence Community Policy System	January 16, 2009
102	Process for Developing Interpretive Principles and Proposing Amendments to Attorney General Guidelines for the Collection, Retention, and Dissemination of Information Regarding U.S. Persons	November 17, 2009
103	Intelligence Enterprise Exercise Program	July 14, 2008
104	Budgeting for Intelligence Programs	May 17, 2006
106	Intelligence Community Strategic Enterprise Management	November 20, 2008
108	Intelligence Community History Programs	August 27, 2007
109	Independent Cost Estimates	April 26, 2010
110	Intelligence Community Equal Opportunity and Diversity	July 1, 2009
113	Functional Managers	May 19, 2009
200	Management, Integration, and Oversight of Intelligence Analysis	January 8, 2007
202	National Intelligence Board	July 16, 2007
203	Analytic Standards	June 21, 2007
204	Roles and Responsibilities for the National Intelligence Priorities Framework	September 13, 2007
205	Analytic Outreach	July 16, 2008
206	Sourcing Requirements for Disseminated Analytic Products	October 17, 2007
207	National Intelligence Council	June 9, 2008
208	Write for Maximum Utility	December 17, 2008
300	Management, Integration, and Oversight of Intelligence Collection and Covert Action	October 3, 2006
301	National Open Source Enterprise	July 11, 2006
302	Document and Media Exploitation	July 16, 2007
304	Human Intelligence	March 6, 2008
500	DNI Chief Information Officer	August 7, 2008
501	Discovery and Dissemination or Retrieval of Information Within the Intelligence Community	January 21, 2009

(continues)

TABLE 17.2   Intelligence Community Directives *(continued)*

ICD Number	Title	Date
503	Intelligence Community Information Technology Systems	September 15, 2008
601	Human Capital—Joint Intelligence Community Duty Assignments	September 4, 2009
602	Human Capital - Intelligence Community Critical Pay	August 16, 2006
610	Competency Directories for the Intelligence Community Workforce	September 1, 2008
612	Intelligence Community Core Contract Personnel	October 30, 2009
623	Appointment of Highly Qualified Experts	October 16, 2008
650	National Intelligence Civilian Compensation Program: Guiding Principles and Framework	April 28, 2008
651	Performance Management System Requirements for the Intelligence Community Civilian Workforce	November 21, 2008
652	Occupational Structure for the Intelligence Community Civilian Workforce	May 14, 2008
653	Pay-Setting and Administration Policies for the Intelligence Community Civilian Workforce	May 14, 2008
654	Performance-Based Pay for the Intelligence Community Civilian Workforce	April 28, 2008
655	National Intelligence Awards Program	May 23, 2007
656	Performance Management System Requirements for Intelligence Community Senior Civilian Officers	April 28, 2008
700	Protection of National Intelligence	September 21, 2007
701	Security Policy Directive for Unauthorized Disclosures of Classified Information	March 14, 2007
702	Technical Surveillance Countermeasures	February 18, 2008
703	Protection of SCI and Sources & Methods	date not available
704	Personnel Security Standards and Procedures Governing Eligibility for Access to Sensitive Compartmented Information and Other Controlled Access Program Information	October 1, 2008
705	Sensitive Compartmented Information Facilities	May 26, 2010

ICD Number	Title	Date
706	Controlled Access Program Oversight Committee (CAPOC)	date not available
707	Center for Security Evaluation	October 17, 2008
710	Classification and Control Markings System	September 11, 2009
801	Acquisition	August 15, 2006
900	Mission Management	December 21, 2006
901	Program Management Posture Adjustment Notification	June 23, 2008
902	Global Maritime and Air Intelligence Integration	January 14, 2009

SOURCES: "Director of National Intelligence Community Directives," www.fas.org/irp/dni/icd, accessed December 23, 2010; Office of the Director of National Intelligence, "Policy Documents," www.dni.gov/electronic_reading_room.htm, accessed March 19, 2010.

DCI committees. DCI committees that have been retained subsequent to the implementation of the Intelligence Reform and Terrorism Prevention Act of 2004 now report to the DNI.

DNI committees, in addition to the collection and analysis committees discussed with respect to the NIC and in Chapter 19, may include the Technology Transfer Intelligence Committee (TTIC), the Foreign Denial and Deception Committee, the Economic Intelligence Committee (EIC), the Foreign Intelligence Priorities Committee (FIPC), the Critical Intelligence Problems Committee (CIPC), the Information Handling Committee (IHC), the Foreign Language Committee, the Narcotics Intelligence Issues Committee (NIIC), the Interagency Intelligence Committee on Terrorism (IICT), the Interagency Defector Committee (IDC), the Strategic Warning Committee, the Community Nonproliferation Committee (CNC), the Open Source Committee (OSC), the Community Counterintelligence and Security Countermeasures Committee (CCSCC), and the Advanced Research and Development Program Committee.[78]

The Technology Transfer Intelligence Committee was formed in 1981 to deal with what was perceived to be a growing hemorrhage of critical technology to the Soviet Union. The TTIC draws on scientific and technical analysis through the military intelligence services and elsewhere in the Intelligence Community. The TTIC's functions would include, but not be limited to, advising the DNI on the effectiveness of the Intelligence Community's role in support of U.S. government policy on technology transfer issues, preparing—when requested—interagency intelligence assessments on the significance of technology transfer, and providing guidance to collection activities on technology transfer issues.[79]

The TTIC's products have included "Soviet Requirements for Western Technology: A Forecasting Methodology" (May 1987), "National Security and Export Controls: A Decision Aid" (September 1988), and "Israel: Marketing U.S. Strategic Technology" (September 1990).[80]

The Economic Intelligence Committee would be responsible for assisting the DNI in the production of foreign economic intelligence and provides support to agencies charged with formulating U.S. international economic policy. A subcommittee produces the Economic Alert List (EAL), which highlights the current economic information needs of all agencies participating in the Combined Economic Reporting Program (CERP).[81]

The Critical Intelligence Problems Committee was created in 1958—as the Critical Collection Problems Committee (CCPC)—to examine particularly difficult collection problems regardless of the technique involved and to suggest ways to improve the collection, processing, and production efforts against the problem targets. In 1971, one subject considered by the CCPC was narcotics intelligence, and it has had a Narcotics Working Group. In 1975, the CIPC prepared the "Study on Intelligence Activities Against International Terrorism." In 1985, it sponsored a conference on combat intelligence analysis and produced at least three studies—on combat intelligence analysis, cruise missile collection, and Strategic Defense Initiative intelligence. Two years later, it produced the study "Soviet Enigma Satellites."[82]

The Foreign Intelligence Priorities Committee (now probably the National Intelligence Priorities Committee) was the executive agent for managing the DCI's "Foreign Intelligence Requirements Categories and Priorities" in DCID 1/2. An October 20, 1986, order of the FIPC raised the collection of intelligence related to American MIAs to "Priority One," although that priority level was formally reserved for information considered "vital to U.S. survival."[83]

The Foreign Language Committee is responsible for evaluating the effectiveness of programs to recruit, train, and retain personnel with adequate foreign language competence for elements of the Intelligence Community, as well as for recommending new initiatives to ensure the availability of the required foreign language competence.[84]

The Strategic Warning Committee is chaired by the National Intelligence Officer for Warning. Its members include the Directors of DIA and NSA, the CIA's Director of Intelligence, and the Assistant Secretary of State for Intelligence and Research. The committee meets weekly to discuss a variety of warning issues and to coordinate warning products. It has produced, among other products, a Watchlist, which includes Special Warning Notices, and Watch Notes.[85]

The Advanced Research and Development Committee has worked with research and development authorities in the imagery, energy, and defense sectors to produce a Critical Technologies List that would guide investment decisions in key areas such as sensors, communications, data storage and management, advanced processing, and enabling technology.[86]

The Information Handling Committee has been responsible for all aspects of information handling—supervising research and development of information handling systems, developing rules and procedures for the exchange of information between agencies, and establishing education of training programs in information science.[87]

The Interagency Intelligence Committee on Terrorism advised and assisted the DCI in "coordinating national intelligence on terrorism issues and [promoting] effective use of intelligence resources for [counterterrorism]." The committee has representatives from agencies across the intelligence, law enforcement, military, and regulatory communities. In May 1996, the committee published a report titled "Aum Shinrikyo: Insights into the Chemical and Biological Terrorist Threat."[88]

Notes

1. George W. Bush, Executive Order 13470, "Further Amendments to Executive Order 12333, United States Intelligence Activities," July 30, 2008, *Federal Register*, August 4, 2008, pp. 45325–45342.

2. Ibid., pp. 45325–45328.

3. Ibid., pp. 45326, 45331.

4. Ibid., pp. 45333–45337.

5. Two compilations of declassified National Security directives on microfiche are National Security Archive, *Presidential Directives on National Security from Truman to Clinton* (Alexandria, Va.: Chadwyck-Healey, 1994), and National Security Archive, *Presidential Directives on National Security from Truman to Bush* (Alexandria, Va.: Chadwyck-Healey, 2002).

6. On NSDD-17, see Raymond Bonner, "President Approved Policy of Preventing 'Cuba Model' States," *New York Times*, April 7, 1983, pp. 1, 16. On NSDD-42, see U.S. Congress, House Committee on Science and Technology, *National Space Policy* (Washington, D.C.: U.S. Government Printing Office, 1982), p. 13. NSDDs 17, 19, 22, 42, 84, 196, 202, and 204 were obtained in whole, or in part, under the Freedom of Information Act by the National Security Archive. NSDD-159 was released during the Iran-Contra hearings.

7. Elaine Sciolino, "Pakistan Keeping Afghan Aid Role," *New York Times*, February 26, 1989, p. 15; "Saudi Help for the CIA," *Newsweek*, September 10, 1990, p. 6; Bill Gertz, "Despite Thaw in Cold War, Bush Heats Up Counterspy Operations," *Washington Times*, October 24, 1990, pp. A1, A6; Edward D. Shaefer Jr., *Strategic Planning for the Office of Naval Intelligence: Vision and Direction for the Future* (Washington, D.C.: Office of Naval Intelligence, 1992), p. 10; NSD-67, "Intelligence Capabilities, 1992–2005," March 30, 1992.

8. National Security Council, Fact Sheet, "U.S. Counterintelligence Effectiveness," May 1994; William J. Clinton, "Remarks at the Central Intelligence Agency in Langley, Virginia, July 14, 1995," White House, July 14, 1995. PDD-35 established six priority ranks as tiers: Tier 0, crisis coverage; Tier 1, countries that are enemies/potential enemies; Tier 1A, topics of highest priority; Tier 2, other countries of high priority; Tier 3, low-priority countries (some coverage); and Tier 4, low-priority countries (not covered). See Defense Science Board, *Defense Mapping for Future Operations* (Washington, D.C.: Office of the Under Secretary of Defense for Acquisition and Technology, 1995), p. E-9; and Federation of American Scientists, "National Security Presidential Directives [NSPD] George W. Bush Administration," www.fas.org, accessed October 8, 2006.

9. Douglas F. Garthoff, *Directors of Central Intelligence as Leaders of the U.S. Intelligence Community, 1946–2005* (Washington, D.C.: Center for the Study of Intelligence, 2005), p. 158 n.

10. NSCID No.1, "Basic Duties and Responsibilities," February 17, 1972, *Declassified Documents Reference Service* (DDRS), 1976–167G.

11. Ibid.

12. NSCID No. 2, "Coordination of Overt Collection Activities," February 17, 1972, *DDRS* 1976–253D.

13. NSCID No. 3, "Coordination of Intelligence Production," February 17, 1972, *DDRS* 1976–253E.

14. U.S. Congress, House Permanent Select Committee on Intelligence, *Annual Report* (Washington, D.C.: U.S. Government Printing Office, 1978), p. 70.

15. NSCID No. 5, "U.S. Espionage and Counterintelligence Activities Abroad," February 17, 1972, *DDRS* 1976–253F.

16. Department of Justice, *Report on Inquiry into CIA-Related Electronic Surveillance Activities* (Washington, D.C.: Department of Justice, 1976), pp. 77–78.

17. National Security Agency/Central Security Service, *NSA/CSS Manual 22–1* (Fort George G. Meade, NSA, 1986), p. 1; Department of Defense Directive S-5100.9, "Implementation of National Security Council Directive No. 7," March 19, 1960; James Bamford, *The Puzzle Palace: A Report on NSA, America's Most Secret Agency* (Boston: Houghton Mifflin, 1982), p. 104; Seymour M. Hersh, *"The Target Is Destroyed": What Really Happened to Flight 007 and What America Really Knew About It* (New York: Random House, 1986), p. 53.

18. NSCID No. 8, "Photographic Interpretation," February 17, 1972, *DDRS* 1976–253G.

19. National Commission on Terrorist Attacks Upon the United States, *The 9/11 Commission Report: Final Report of the National Commission on Terrorist Attacks Upon the United States* (New York: W.W. Norton, 2004), p. 411 (hereafter cited as *The 9/11 Commission Report*).

20. Richard A. Best Jr., Alfred Cumming, and Todd Masse, Congressional Research Service, *Director of National Intelligence: Statutory Authorities*, April 11, 2005, p. 3.

21. Ibid., p. 4.

22. Ibid.

23. Ibid., pp. 4–5.

24. Ibid., p. 5; Ellen Nakashima, "Control of intelligence budget will shift," www.washingtonpost.com, November 3, 2010.

25. . David E. Kaplan and Kevin Whitelaw, "Playing Defense," *U.S. News & World Report*, November 13, 2006, pp. 43–53; "Getting Smarter About Intelligence," *C4ISR Journal*, March 2007, pp. 45–46.

26. Intelligence Community Directive 202, "National Intelligence Board," July 16, 2007.

27. Office of the Director of National Intelligence, ICD-1, "Policy Directive for Community Leadership," May 1, 2006, p. 16.

28. Office of the Director of National Intelligence, "ODNI Fact Sheet," October 2010, p. 5.

29. Office of the Director of National Intelligence, ODNI News Release No. 09–07, "Director McConnell Announces Organizational Changes at ODNI," March 23, 2007.

30. Caspar Weinberger, *FY 1983 Report of the Secretary of Defense Caspar Weinberger*, p. III-88; Department of Defense Inspector General, *Defense Intelligence Agency Inspection Report 91-INS-06*, 1991, p. 14.

31. Department of Defense, Memorandum for Correspondents No. 264-M, September 18, 1992.

32. U.S. Congress, Senate Committee on Governmental Affairs, *Summary of Intelligence Reform and Terrorism Prevention Act of 2004*, December 6, 2004, p. 1.

33. Lawrence Freedman, *U.S. Intelligence and the Soviet Strategic Threat* (Princeton, N.J.: Princeton University Press, 1986), p. 31; Richard A. Best, *The National Intelligence Council: Issues and Options for Congress*, January 10, 2011, pp. 3–4.

34. Freedman, *U.S. Intelligence and the Soviet Strategic Threat*, p. 54.

35. Ibid.

36. Richard J. Kerr, Deputy Director for Intelligence, Memorandum for Chairman, National Intelligence Council, Subject: The Integrity and Objectivity of National Foreign Intelligence Estimates, May 12, 1987, p. 1. The memo is reprinted in U.S. Congress, Senate Select Committee on Intelligence, *Nomination of Robert M. Gates*, Volume 2 (Washington, D.C.: U.S. Government Printing Office, 1992), pp. 106–108.

37. U.S. Congress, House Select Committee on Intelligence, *U.S. Intelligence Agencies and Activities: Fiscal Costs and Procedures, Part I* (Washington, D.C.: U.S. Government Printing Office, 1975), p. 389; U.S. Congress, House Committee on Foreign Affairs, *The Role of Intelligence in the Foreign Policy Process* (Washington, D.C.: U.S. Government Printing Office, 1980), p. 135.

38. Freedman, *U.S. Intelligence and the Soviet Strategic Threat*, p. 31.

39. U.S. Congress, Senate Select Committee on Intelligence, *Nomination of John N. McMahon* (Washington, D.C.: U.S. Government Printing Office, 1982), pp. 48–49; Robert M. Gates, Director of Central Intelligence, "Statement of Change in CIA and Intelligence Community," April 1, 1992, pp. 21, 22.

40. National Intelligence Council, "NIC Mission," www.dni.gov/nic, accessed December 25, 2010.

41. National Intelligence Council, "NIC Organization," www.dni.gov/nic, accessed December 25, 2010.

42. Ibid.

43. U.S. Congress, Senate Select Committee on Intelligence and House Permanent Select Committee on Intelligence, *S. 2198 and S. 421 to Reorganize the United States Intelligence Community* (Washington, D.C.: U.S. Government Printing Office, 1993), p. 15.

44. DCID 3/3, "Production of Atomic Energy Intelligence," April 23, 1965, *DDRS 1980–131G*.

45. Ibid.

46. The JAEIC's role in evaluating the U.S. capability to monitor compliance with the Threshold Test Ban Treaty is mentioned in Attachment to Memorandum, Holsey G. Handyside, Deputy Assistant Secretary, International Nuclear and Technical Programs, Department of Energy for Leslie H. Brown, Senior Deputy Assistant Secretary for Oceans and International, Environmental and Scientific Affairs, Department of State, "Response to Congressional Questions on Nuclear Explosives," March 7, 1980.

47. U.S. Congress, House Committee on Energy and Commerce, *Nuclear Nonproliferation: Failed Efforts to Curtail Iraq's Nuclear Weapons Program* (Washington, D.C.: U.S. Government Printing Office, 1992), p. 20; William J. Broad, "Warning on Iraq and Bomb Bid Silenced in '89," *New York Times*, April 20, 1992, pp. A1, A5; NIE 11–3/8–76, *Soviet Forces for International Conflict Through the Mid-1980s, Volume 1, Key Judgements and Summary*, 1976, p. iii; Air Force Intelligence Agency, *History of the Air Force Intelligence Agency, 18 April 1987–31 December 1989, Volume 1, Narrative and Appendices*, 1990; Air University, Special Bibliography Series, Special Bibliography No. 207, Supplement No. 5, *China: Military Capabilities* (Maxwell AFB, Ala.: Air University, February 1993), p. 14; Andrew and Leslie Cockburn, *One Point Safe* (New York: Anchor Books, 1997), p. 188; R. Jeffrey Smith, "U.S.

Officials Acted Hastily in Nuclear Test Accusation," *Washington Post*, October 20, 1997, pp. A1, A6–A7.

48. Jeffrey T. Richelson, *Spying on the Bomb: American Nuclear Intelligence from Nazi Germany to Iran and North Korea* (New York: W. W. Norton, 2006), p. 480.

49. DCID 3/4, "Production of Guided Missile and Astronautics Intelligence," April 23, 1965, *DDRS* 1980–132A; John Prados, *The Soviet Estimate: U.S. Intelligence Analysis and Russian Military Strength* (New York: Dial, 1982), pp. 59–61, 202; U.S. Congress, House Committee on Appropriations, *Department of Defense Appropriations for 1978, Part I* (Washington, D.C.: U.S. Government Printing Office, 1977), p. 224.

50. Department of the Army, *Office of the Assistant Chief of Staff for Intelligence, Annual Historical Review, 1 July 1975–30 September 1976*, n.d., pp. 39–40, NIE 11–3/8–76, *Soviet Strategic Forces for International Conflict Through the Mid-1980s, Volume 1: Key Judgments and Summary*, p. iii; Andrew Koch, "Pakistan Persists with Nuclear Procurement," *Jane's Intelligence Review*, March 1997, pp. 131–133.

51. Central Intelligence Agency, *A Consumer's Guide to Intelligence*, p. 57.

52. Department of the Army, Office of the Deputy Chief of Staff for Intelligence, *Annual Historical Review, 1 October 1990 to 30 September 1991*, n.d., p. 4–30.

53. Central Intelligence Agency, *A Consumer's Guide to Intelligence*, p. 43; National Intelligence Council, *A Guide to the National Intelligence Council*, p. 41.

54. Director of Central Intelligence, "Terrorist Threat Integration Center Begins Operations," May 1, 2003, www.cia.gov; John O. Brennan, "Responses from John O. Brennan to Post-Hearing Questions," December 4, 2003, p. 8.

55. White House, Fact Sheet, "Strengthening Intelligence to Better Protect America," January 28, 2003, www.whitehouse.gov; John O. Brennan, "Responses from John O. Brennan to Post-Hearing Questions."

56. *The 9/11 Commission Report*, p. 403.

57. Ibid., p. 404.

58. Ibid.

59. George W. Bush, "Executive Order: National Counterterrorism Center," August 27, 2004, www.whitehouse.gov.

60. Todd M. Masse, Congressional Research Service, *The National Counterterrorism Center: Implementation Challenges and Issues for Congress*, March 24, 2005, Summary and p. 6.

61. John Scott Reid, "Statement for the Record: Senate Foreign Relations Committee," June 13, 2006, p. 5; National Counterterrorism Center, *Managing Information in the Age of Information Sharing: A Case Study*, April 20, 2005, p. 9; Walter Pincus and Dan Eggen, "325,000 Names on Terrorism List," www.washingtonpost.com, February 15, 2006; Karen DeYoung, "Terror Database Has Quadrupled in Four Years," www.washingtonpost.com, March 25, 2007; Russell Travers, Statement for the Record to House Committee on the Judiciary, "Sharing and Analyzing Information to Prevent Terrorism," March 24, 2010.

62. Kevin Whitelaw, "The Eye of the Storm," www.usnews.com, October 29, 2006.

63. Ibid. For a recent discussion of the NCTC, see Richard A. Best, Jr., Congressional Research Service, *The National Counterterrorism Center (NCTC)—Responsibilities and Potential Concerns*, January 15, 2010.

64. Director of National Intelligence, *National Intelligence: A Consumer's Guide*, 2009, p. 24.

65. *The 9/11 Commission Report*, p. 413; Commission on the Intelligence Capabilities of the United States Regarding Weapons of Mass Destruction, *Report to the President of the United States* (Washington, D.C.: U.S. Government Printing Office, 2005), p. 567.

66. United States Congress, House of Representatives, *Intelligence Reform and Terrorism Prevention Act of 2004 Conference Report*, December 7, 2004, pp. 40–41.

67. "National Counterterrorism Center—Ambassador Kenneth Brill," www.dni.gov, accessed December 30, 2006.

68. Office of the Director of National Intelligence, News Release No. 9–05, "ODNI Announces Establishment of National Counterproliferation Center (NCPC)," December 21, 2005, www.dni.gov.

69. Ibid.

70. "National Counterintelligence Policy Board," www.dni.gov/ncix, accessed January 2, 2007; Office of the National Counterintelligence Executive, *The National Counterintelligence Strategy of the United States*, 2009, p. ii.

71. "NCIX: National Counterintelligence Executive," www.dni.gov/ncix, accessed January 2, 2007.

72. Office of the Director of National Intelligence, "National Intelligence Coordination Center," n.d., www.dni.gov/nicc.htm, accessed December 25, 2010.

73. Ibid.

74. Ibid.

75. "Old" DCID categories were Production of Sources and Methods (Category 1), Selected Services Common Concern (2), DCI Advisory Bodies (3), Espionage, Counterintelligence, and Foreign Liaison Activities (5), Warning, Critical Communications, and Emergency Planning (6), and Other DCI Policies and Procedures (7). The newer categories were Management (1), Analysis and Production (2), Collection (3), Program and Budget (4), Relationships (5), Security (6), and Other (7). See Director of Central Intelligence, "Index of Director of Central Intelligence Directives," n.d.

76. Intelligence Community Directive 204, "Roles and Responsibilities for the National Intelligence Priorities Framework," September 13, 2007.

77. Intelligence Community Directive 902, "Global Maritime and Air Intelligence Integration," January 14, 2009.

78. Letter, Lee S. Strickland, CIA Information and Privacy Coordinator, to the author, June 5, 1987; Naval Intelligence Command, *Naval Intelligence Command Historical Review, 1976*, 1977, p. 3; Office of Naval Intelligence, *Office of Naval Intelligence (OP-92) Command History 1990*, n.d., Assistant for Counternarcotics Section, p. 2; Department of the Army, Office of the Deputy Chief of Staff for Intelligence, *Annual Historical Review, 1 October 1987–30 September 1988*, n.d., p. 2–37; Eagle Research Group, *ERG Support to OTA* (Arlington, Va.: ERG, December 14, 1990), p. 11; Central Intelligence Agency, *A Consumer's Guide to Intelligence*, pp. 53–57; Hayden B. Peake, "The Intelligence Officer's Bookshelf," *Studies in Intelligence* 50, 4 (2006): 59–78.

79. National Academy of Sciences, *Scientific Communication and National Security* (Washington, D.C.: National Academy Press, 1983), pp. 72, 141–142; DCID 3/13, "Technology Transfer Intelligence Community," December 3, 1981.

80. Edward T. Pound, "U.S. Sees New Signs Israel Resells Its Arms to China, South Africa," *Wall Street Journal*, March 13, 1992, pp. A1, A6.

81. Central Intelligence Agency, *A Consumer's Guide to Intelligence*, p. 53; Konrad Ege, "CIA Targets African Economies," *Counter Spy*, July–August 1982, pp. 30–38.

82. Department of Justice, *Report on Inquiry into CIA-Related Economic Surveillance Activities*, pp. 72–73; Office of Naval Intelligence, *Office of Naval Intelligence (ONI) Annual History 1985*, pp. 5, 9; DCID 3/8, "Critical Intelligence Problems Committee," April 6, 1983; Edward C. Mishler, *History of the Air Force Office of Special Investigations, 1 July 1975–31 December 1976, Volume I, Narrative* (Washington, D.C.: AFOSI, 1978), p. 23.

83. Central Intelligence Agency, *A Consumer's Guide to Intelligence*, p. 54; Bob Woodward and John Mintz, "Despite Vast U.S. Hunt, Perot Says POWs Held," *Washington Post*, June 21, 1992, p. A18.

84. DCID 3/15, "Foreign Language Committee," March 5, 1982.

85. Central Intelligence Agency, *A Consumer's Guide to Intelligence*, p. 36; DCI Strategic Warning Committee, "The DCI Strategic Warning Committee's Watchlist," September 15, 2000, www.foia.cia.gov.

86. Director of Central Intelligence, *Annual Report FY 1994, Director of Central Intelligence*, September 1995, p. 7.

87. DCID 3/4, "Information Handling Committee," May 4, 1982; Naval Intelligence Activity, *Calendar Year 1991 History, Naval Intelligence Activity (NIA), 1 January–30 September 1991*, 1992, p. 6; Putney, *History of the Air Force Intelligence Service, 1 January–31 December 1983, Volume 1, Narrative and Appendices*, p. 95.

88. General Accounting Office, GAO/NSIAD-97–254, *Combating Terrorism: Federal Agencies' Efforts to Implement National Policy and Strategy*, September 1997, pp. 22–23, 32; U.S. Congress, Senate Select Committee on Intelligence, *Current and Projected National Security Threats to the United States* (Washington, D.C.: U.S. Government Printing Office, 1997), p. 51.

18

MANAGING DEFENSE INTELLIGENCE

During the years that the Director of Central Intelligence served as the President's chief intelligence advisor and head of the Intelligence Community, that community included national agencies located within the Defense Department—the National Security Agency, the National Reconnaissance Office, and since 1996, the National Geospatial-Intelligence Agency. Although after 1977 the DCI had authority to approve their budgets, day-to-day management was the responsibility of the Secretary of Defense and those officials he designated to handle intelligence matters.

Over the years, management of the national intelligence agencies within the Defense Department and other defense intelligence agencies—particularly the Defense Intelligence Agency—was handled by the Secretary and key aides. During the 1970s, there was an Assistant Secretary of Defense (Intelligence), while more recently an under secretary was responsible for intelligence along with command, control, communications, and computers. In 2001, Secretary of Defense Donald H. Rumsfeld proposed the creation of an Under Secretary of Defense for Intelligence, USD (I), which was established by Congress.[1]

Other mechanisms for managing defense intelligence, most of which predate the creation of the USD (I) position, include the Military Intelligence Board, chaired by the director of DIA and including military service intelligence chiefs; and Department of Defense Directives, which specify the functions of different agencies, or policies for the conduct of intelligence activities—from the collection of signals intelligence to the interrogation of detainees.

THE USD (I)

Within a very short time of assuming the position of Secretary of Defense, Donald Rumsfeld concluded that he needed an official directly below him in the chain of command whose sole responsibility would be managing the department's intelligence activities. One catalyst for Rumsfeld's conclusion was a meeting in April 2001 to discuss the intelligence lost after the crash landing of an EP-3 in China, which was attended by officials from eleven different military intelligence units. Another catalyst was the long-standing reluctance of the DCI to deal with lower-level subordinates of the Defense Secretary in settling budget issues.[2]

In August 2002, Rumsfeld stated that he wanted a single "more senior person overseeing those aspects of intelligence that are in the Department of Defense." A former senior Pentagon official in the Clinton administration said at the time that "it would be a step forward" if a new under secretary "serves as an action officer for the department's intelligence budget," since trying to work out different budget issues took "a huge piece of the secretary's time."[3]

During his tenure as Director of Central Intelligence (1961–1965), John McCone believed that he could better carry out his responsibilities if there was a single Defense Department official responsible for supervising the Department's intelligence operations. And in the spring of 2002, Rumsfeld was able to persuade DCI George Tenet of the desirability of an arrangement whereby he and other senior CIA officials would have a single point of contact on intelligence policy and resources matters. However, Rumsfeld's proposal was greeted with some concern by those who feared that such an official, with his sole focus on intelligence and his day-to-day authority over the national intelligence agencies, would become a serious competitor to the Director of Central Intelligence.[4]

Despite such concerns, Congress quickly approved the creation of the position within the National Defense Authorization Act of 2002, and in March 2003 Rumsfeld's nominee, Stephen Cambone, was confirmed by the Senate. The office's responsibilities were first outlined in a memo, "Implementation Guidance on Restructuring Defense Intelligence—and Related Matters," which also specified an initial personnel strength of 114 employees. That memo was superseded on November 23, 2005, by Department of Defense Directive 5143.01, "Under Secretary of Defense for Intelligence (USD [I])," signed by Rumsfeld—but coordinated with the Director of National Intelligence. (In May 2007, the Secretary of Defense and the DNI agreed that the USD [I] should also be designated as Director of Defense Intelligence within the DNI's office.)[5]

The directive specified that the under secretary would serve as senior Defense Department intelligence, counterintelligence, and security official below the Secretary and Deputy Secretary as well as the primary representative of the Secretary to the office of the Director of National Intelligence and other Intelligence Community members. It also specified the under secretary's responsibilities with respect to human capital; planning, programming, budgeting, and execution; acquisition; defense intelligence; counterintelligence; security policy; information operations; and other areas—including coordination with the Under Secretary for Defense Policy on intelligence matters related to counterterrorism.[6]

Thus the under secretary is responsible for

- identifying candidates to serve as directors of the NRO, NSA, NGA, and DIA;
- proposing DOD resource programs, formulating budget estimates, recommending resource allocations and priorities, and monitoring the implementation of approved policy and planning guidance;

- overseeing all Defense intelligence budgetary matters to ensure compliance with the budget policies issued by the DNI for the NIP;
- exercising acquisition authority delegated by the DNI;
- overseeing all DOD intelligence policies and activities, including Sensitive Reconnaissance Operations (SRO) Program policy;
- overseeing DOD HUMINT and related activities;
- developing, coordinating, and overseeing the implementation of Defense Department policy, programs, and guidance for DOD counterintelligence;
- overseeing the implementation of policy regarding the protection of Sensitive Compartmented Information;
- coordinating, overseeing, and assessing the efforts of DOD components to plan, program, and develop capabilities in support of Information Operations requirements.[7]

The office originally consisted, in addition to the under secretary and principal deputy under secretary, of four deputy under secretaries—for intelligence and warfighting support; preparation and warning; counterintelligence and security; and policy, resources, and requirements. In June 2008 the office was restructured based on four core functions (joint force operations, technical intelligence, programs and resources, and HUMINT/CI and security), a restructuring dictated by a memo by then USD (I) James Clapper.[8] That structure, shown in Figure 18.1, remained as of spring 2010.

DEFENSE INTELLIGENCE EXECUTIVE BOARD (DIEB)

The Defense Intelligence Executive Board was established in 1994 "as the senior corporate advisory body to the Secretary of Defense for review and oversight of Defense intelligence programs and activities." In addition, it was established to serve as "the senior management body providing planning, programming, and budget oversight of the Joint Military Intelligence Program (JMIP)."[9]

The DIEB charter specified that the board would meet at least twice a year and focus on requirements and capabilities, policy, interoperability, resources, priorities and goals, and resolution of issues.[10]

MILITARY INTELLIGENCE PROGRAM

The Joint Military Intelligence Program (JMIP) was established in 1995 to "improve the effectiveness of DOD intelligence activities when those activities involve resources from more than one DOD Component; when users of the intelligence data are from more than one DOD Component; and/or when centralized planning, management, coordination, or oversight will contribute to the effectiveness of the effort."[11]

There were three major program aggregations within the JMIP: the Defense Cryptologic Program (DCP), the Defense Imagery and Mapping Program

FIGURE 18.1 Organization of the Office of the Under Secretary of Defense (Intelligence)

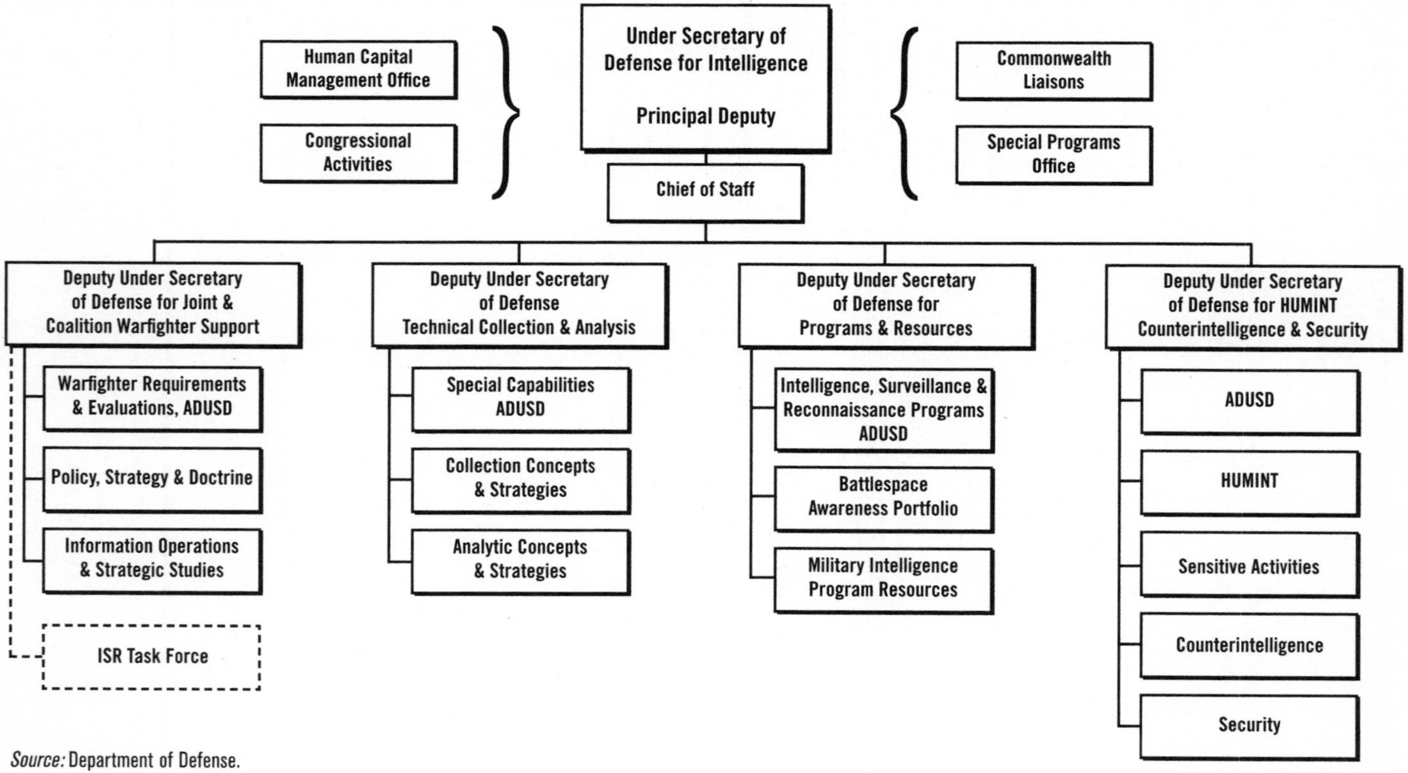

Source: Department of Defense.

(DIMAP), and the Defense General Intelligence and Applications Program (DGIAP). Each program was made up of resources that had previously been funded within the Tactical Intelligence and Related Activities (TIARA) program. The DGIAP consisted of five subordinate programs: the Defense Airborne Reconnaissance Program (DARP), the Defense Intelligence Counterdrug Program (DICP), the Defense Intelligence Agency's Tactical Program (DIATP), the Defense Space Reconnaissance Program (DSRP), and the Defense Intelligence Special Technologies Program (DISTP).[12]

Creation of the JMIP stripped the TIARA program of two of its three elements—the Defense Space Reconnaissance Program (formerly the Defense Reconnaissance Support Program) and the Tactical Cryptologic Program—leaving the Reconnaissance, Surveillance, and Target Acquisition component.

In 1995, the Air Force TIARA program was divided into six components: Battle Management (JOINT STARS); Processing and Dissemination (including CONSTANT SOURCE, the Combat Air Intelligence System, and the Combat Intelligence System); Surveillance and Reconnaissance (including SPACETRACK, PACER COIN, and SENIOR SCOUT); Tactical Warning/Attack Assessment (including the Missile Early Warning System); Manpower and Training (including the U.S. Space Command's Space Warfare Center); and Scientific and Technical Collection (the COBRA JUDY sea-based phased-array radar).[13]

On September 1, 2005, the Department of Defense, through a memorandum signed by the Acting Secretary of Defense, "Establishment of the Military Intelligence Program," combined the JMIP and TIARA programs to form the Military Intelligence Program (MIP).[14]

The contents of the MIP for the 2009 fiscal year are listed in the table of contents of the FY 2009 Congressional Budget Justification Book.[15] Those pages are shown as Figure 18.2.

MILITARY INTELLIGENCE BOARD

Another mechanism for the coordination of military intelligence is the Military Intelligence Board (MIB), chaired by the Director of the DIA. The board was established on August 15, 1961, to assist in the development of the DIA activation plan and in the selection of personnel. However, it has remained in existence as a mechanism for coordinating Defense positions on DOD intelligence issues among the Director of the DIA, the Joint Staff J2, and the service intelligence chiefs.[16]

The MIB met on an irregular basis during the first thirty years of its existence. During operations DESERT SHIELD and DESERT STORM, the director of the DIA restructured the board as an advisory and decisionmaking body chaired by the director of DIA with significant new members, including the director of the NSA.[17]

The MIB is convened by the Director of the DIA. It has no executive authority. Its recommendations and the actions of its chairman are not permitted to alter the missions, responsibilities, functions, authorities, and resources assigned to any Defense

FIGURE 18.2 Military Intelligence Program Elements

UNCLASSIFIED
Project Highlights Table of Contents

ARMY

- Aerial Common Sensor
- Airborne Reconnaissance - Low
- All Source Analysis System
- Army Foreign Language Program
- Army Tactical Unmanned Aircraft System
- Biometrics for Intelligence
- Counterintelligence Support to Combatant Commands and Defense Agencies
- Counterintelligence/HUMINT Information Management System
- Critical Information Infrastructure Protection
- Cryptologic/SIGINT Related Skill Training
- Distributed Common Ground/Surface Systems
- Future Combat Systems
- General Intelligence Skill Training
- HUMINT Training JCOE
- Intelligence Force Structure
- Intelligence Staff Support
- Intelligence Support to Detainee Operations
- Intelligence Support to the Common Operational Picture
- Joint Tactical Ground Station
- Mapping and Geodesy
- National Guard Intelligence
- Operational Human Intelligence (HUMINT)
- Project Foundry
- Prophet
- Research and Critical Technology Protection
- Reserve Intelligence
- Tactical Exploitation of National Capabilities and Program Support
- TROJAN

NAVY

- Advanced Technology and Sensors
- Aerial Common Sensor
- Broad Area Maritime Surveillance
- COBRA JUDY Replacement
- Counterintelligence Support to Force Protection
- Cryptologic Direct Support
- Distributed Common Ground/Surface Systems
- EP-3E/ARIES II
- Fixed Surveillance System
- GLOBAL HAWK High Altitude Endurance Unmanned Aircraft System
- Information Warfare (IW)-Exploit
- Intelligence Support to the Common Operational Picture
- Marine Corps Tactical Unmanned Aircraft System
- Maritime Intelligence Support
- PIONEER Unmanned Aircraft System
- Research and Critical Technology Protection

- Small Tactical Unmanned Aircraft System/Tier II UAS
- Special Project Aircraft
- Submarine Support Equipment Program
- Surveillance Towed Array Sensor System
- Tactical Control System
- Tactical Exploitation of National Capabilities

USAF

- Advanced Technology and Sensors
- Airborne SIGINT Enterprise
- GLOBAL HAWK High Altitude Endurance Unmanned Aircraft System
- Intelligence Continuity and Enablers
- Intelligence Equipment
- Network Centric Collaborative Targeting
- Nuclear Detonation Detection System
- Podded Reconnaissance
- PREDATOR Medium Altitude Endurance Unmanned Aircraft System
- Space Based Infrared System High
- Tactical Cryptologic Program, Reserve and Guard Units
- Tactical Information Program
- U-2

USMC

- Angel Fire
- Communication Emitter Sensing and Attacking System
- Counterintelligence/HUMINT Equipment Program
- Intelligence Analysis System Modification Kit
- Intelligence Broadcast Receiver
- Intelligence Equipment Readiness
- Joint STARS Connectivity
- Marine Corps Operational Intelligence Support
- Radio Reconnaissance Equipment Program
- Tactical Exploitation Group
- Technical Control and Analysis Center
- Topographical Production Capability
- USMC Unmanned Aircraft System Family of Systems

CIFA

- Counterintelligence Education, Training, and Development
- Counterintelligence Mission Support
- Counterintelligence Support to Combatant Commands and Defense Agencies

DIA

- Analysis Enabling
- Distributed Common Ground/Surface Systems
- Enterprise Management Operations & Support
- HUMINT Enabling

UNCLASSIFIED
Project Highlights Table of Contents

DIA *(continued)*

Intelligence Support to Information Operations
Intelligence Support to the COCOMs
MASINT Enabling
MASINT Operations
Transnational Analysis

NGA

Advanced Airborne TPED
GeoScout Block II
Personnel Support Project
Purchases (Commercial Remote Sensing)

NSA

Advanced Technology and Sensors
Aerial Common Sensor
Airborne Cryptologic Capabilities
Distributed Common Ground/Surface Systems
Electronic Intelligence Programs
Intelligence Support to Information Operations
Maritime Cryptologic Capabilities
Rapid Technology Insertion
RC-135
Real-Time Architecture Development
Technical Response to Cryptologic Operations
U-2

OSD

Foreign Materiel Acquisition and Exploitation
Intelligence Management (OSD)
Intelligence Support to Information Operations

SOCOM

Distributed Common Ground/Surface Systems
Hostile Forces Tagging, Tracking and Locating
Intelligence Staff Support
Joint Threat Warning System
Optimal Placement of Unattended Sensors
Special Operations Command Research, Analysis, and
    Threat Evaluation System
Special Operations Forces Organic Intelligence, Surveillance,
    and Reconnaissance
Special Operations Tactical Video System

Source: Department of Defense, *FY 2009 Budget, Congressional Justification Book, Military Intelligence Program,* Vol. 1, "Summary," March 4, 2008.

Department component by the Secretary or Deputy Secretary of Defense. The Deputy Secretary of Defense, the Chairman of the Joint Chiefs of Staff, and the Under Secretary of Defense for Intelligence may convene and preside over special meetings of the MIB.[18]

MIB members, in addition to the Director of the DIA, include the Deputy Director of the DIA, the Directors of NSA and NGA, and the service intelligence chiefs. In addition, there are three groups associated with the MIB, although they are not subordinate to it: the Council of Defense Intelligence Producers, the Military Target Intelligence Committee, and the Council on Functional Management.[19]

The MIB coordinates intelligence support to military operations and provides a forum for discussion and development of a coordinated military intelligence position on issues going before the NIB. It also provides oversight and direction to the defense intelligence functional managers for collection, production, and infrastructure.[20]

The MIB meets approximately once a week and has considered topics such as Iraq, Korea, intelligence support to Operation Desert Storm, intelligence support to the European Command, Operation Joint Endeavor, the NIMA Implementation Plan, the Quadrennial Defense Review, and National Intelligence Estimates. The DIA convened the board in preparation for Operation ENDURING FREEDOM.[21]

In 1994, former DIA Director James B. Clapper Jr. described the role played by the Military Intelligence Board: "MIB proved its worth during the Gulf War when it played a critical role in fostering greater cooperation within the military intelligence community. Since that time MIB has met virtually every week and provided a forum for senior community leaders to oversee program development, review integrated programs and budgets, resolve programmatic issues of mutual concern, and deal with substantive intelligence matters.[22]

DEFENSE COUNTERINTELLIGENCE BOARD

The Defense Counterintelligence Board (DCIB) was established by a 1983 directive on Defense Department counterintelligence. The Board is responsible for advising and assisting the Deputy Under Secretary of Defense for Intelligence (Counterintelligence and Security) on counterintelligence matters under the purview of the executive order on intelligence activities, overseeing the implementation of counterintelligence policy, advising on the need for and allocation of counterintelligence resources, and reviewing and evaluating reforms of counterintelligence organizations.[23]

The Board is convened and chaired by the Director of Counterintelligence in the office of the Deputy Under Secretary of Defense for Intelligence (HUMINT, Counterintelligence and Security). Full members include representatives from the Office of the Secretary of Defense, each of the military service counterintelligence organizations, the Defense Security Service, the Defense Threat Reduction Agency, and the Defense Intelligence Agency. Associate members include, but are not limited to, representatives from the NRO, the NSA, and the Marine Corps Counterintelligence/HUMINT Branch.[24]

DIRECTIVES, INSTRUCTIONS, AND DTMs

The most important departmental regulations on intelligence matters are the DOD Directives, Instructions, and Directive-Type Memoranda (DTM), which concern both intelligence policies and the operations of specific organizations. DOD Directive C-5230.23 of November 18, 1983, on "Intelligence Disclosure Policy," specifies the functions of various DOD officials in the disclosure process. Thus, the Director of DIA is to "coordinate within and for the Department of Defense, proposed disclosures of classified U.S. intelligence to senior foreign officials," and the Deputy Under Secretary of Policy is to "resolve conflicts among DOD components relating to disclosure of classified U.S. intelligence to senior foreign officials."[25]

Other DOD directives, instructions, and DTMs concerning foreign intelligence policy and activities include "DOD Intelligence Interrogations, Detainee Debriefings, and Tactical Questioning" (3115.09 and DTM 09–031, October 9, 2008), "Signals Intelligence" (Directive O-3115.07, September 15, 2008), "Foreign Materiel Program (FMP)" (C-3325.01E, October 10, 2006); "Management and Execution of Defense Human Intelligence (HUMINT)" (S-5200.37, February 9, 2009), "Transfer of National Intelligence Collection Authority" (S-3325.02, March 16, 2009), "DoD Cover and Support Activities" (S-5105.61 and DTM-08–050, May 6, 2010), and "Videotaping or Otherwise Electronically Recording Strategic Intelligence Interrogations of Persons in the Custody of the Department of Defense" (DTM 09–031, May 10, 2010).[26]

Other directives or instructions concern counterintelligence activities. These include "Counterintelligence" (Directive O-5240.02), "DOD Counterintelligence Functional Services" (Instruction 5240.16, May 21, 2005), "Counterintelligence Collection" (Instruction S-5240.17, January 12, 2009), "Counterintelligence (CI) Analysis and Production (Instruction 5240.18, November 17, 2009), "Counterintelligence Support to the Defense Critical Infrastructure Program (Instruction 5240.19, August 27, 2007), "Counterintelligence (CI) Inquiries" (O-5240.21, May 14, 2009), "Counterintelligence Support to Force Protection" (Instruction 5240.22, September 24, 2009), and "Counterintelligence (CI) Activities in Cyberspace" (Instruction S-5240.23, December 13, 2010).[27]

Still other DOD directives or instructions specify the missions and functions of the Principal Deputy Under Secretary of Defense for Intelligence (PDUSD [I]) (Directive 5143.02, August 18, 2010), the National Reconnaissance Office (Directive 5105.23, March 27, 1964), the National Security Agency (Directive 5100.20, January 26, 2010), the Defense Intelligence Agency (Directive 5105.21, March 18, 2008), the National Geospatial-Intelligence Agency (Directive 5105.60, July 29, 2009), the Defense Counterintelligence (CI) and Human Intelligence Center (DCHC) (Instruction O-5100.93, August 13, 2010), the National Center for Medical Intelligence (Instruction 6420.1, March 20, 2009), and the Defense Special Missile and Aerospace Center (Instruction 5100.43, September 24, 2008).[28]

Notes

1. Initially, Rumsfeld envisioned the Pentagon's intelligence chief being an assistant secretary but then concluded that an under secretary would be more effective. See Bradley Graham, *By His Own Rules: The Ambitions, Successes, and Ultimate Failures of Donald Rumsfeld* (New York: Public Affairs, 2009), p. 367.

2. James Risen and Thom Shanker, "Rumsfeld Moves to Strengthen His Grip on Military Intelligence," *New York Times*, August 3, 2002, pp. A1, A8; Walter Pincus, "Pentagon May Get New Intelligence Chief," *Washington Post*, August 19, 2002, p. A11.

3. Pincus, "Pentagon May Get New Intelligence Chief."

4. Douglas F. Garthoff, *Directors of Central Intelligence as Leaders of the U.S. Intelligence Community, 1946–2005* (Washington, D.C.: CIA, 2005), p. 48; Graham, *By His Own Rules*,

pp. 366–367; Risen and Shanker, "Rumsfeld Moves to Strengthen His Grip on Military Intelligence."

5. Margan A. Carlstrom, "OUSD (I) Charts Its Course," *Communiqué*, May–June 2006, pp. 12–14; Paul Wolfowitz, Memorandum, Subject: Implementation Guidance on Restructuring Defense Intelligence—and Related Matters," May 8, 2003; Donald H. Rumsfeld, Department of Defense Directive 5143.01, "Under Secretary of Defense for Intelligence (USD [I])," November 23, 2005; Office of the Director of National Intelligence, ODNI News Release No. 16–07, "Under Secretary of Defense for Intelligence to Be Dual-Hatted as Director of Defense Intelligence," May 24, 2007.

6. Rumsfeld, Department of Defense Directive 5143.01, "Under Secretary of Defense for Intelligence (USD [I])," pp. 2–6.

7. Ibid., pp. 2–6; Stephen Cambone, Memorandum, Subject: Guidance for the Conduct and Oversight of Defense Human Intelligence (HUMINT), December 14, 2004.

8. James R. Clapper, Jr., Memorandum, Subject: Reorganization of the Office of the Under Secretary of Defense for Intelligence, June 18, 2008.

9. "Defense Intelligence Executive Board Charter," attachment to: John Deutch, Memorandum, Subject: Defense Intelligence Executive Board (DIEB), May 14, 1994.

10. Ibid.

11. DOD Directive 5205.9, "Joint Military Intelligence Program," April 7, 1995.

12. Ibid.; U.S. Congress, House of Representatives, Report 105–508, *Intelligence Authorization Act for Fiscal Year 1999* (Washington, D.C.: U.S. Government Printing Office, 1998), p. 7.

13. Brig. Gen. Frank B. Campbell, Director of Forces, USAF, "Air Force TIARA Programs: Intelligence Support to the Warfighter," 1995.

14. Rumsfeld, Department of Defense Directive 5143.01, "Under Secretary of Defense for Intelligence (USD [I])"; Office of the Director of National Intelligence, *Report on the Progress of Director of National Intelligence in Implementing the "Intelligence Reform and Terrorism Prevention Act of 2004*," May 2006, p. 6; U.S. Congress, House of Representatives, Report 109–411, *Intelligence Authorization Act for Fiscal Year 2007* (Washington, D.C.: U.S. Government Printing Office, 2006), p. 15.

15. Department of Defense, *FY 2009 Budget Congressional Justification Book: Military Intelligence Program, Volume I, Summary*, 2008, pp. 17–19.

16. Lt. Col. Steve Palm, "DOD's Military Intelligence Board," *Communiqué*, April–May 1997, p. 13.

17. "Military Intelligence Board," www.dia.mil/history, accessed September 10, 2010.

18. Department of Defense Directive 5105.21, "Defense Intelligence Agency (DIA)," February 18, 1997, pp. 2–3.

19. Palm, "DOD's Military Intelligence Board."

20. Ibid.

21. Ibid.; Director of Central Intelligence, *The 2001 Annual Report of the United States Intelligence Community*, February 2002, Support to Military Operations.

22. James B. Clapper, Jr., "Challenging Joint Military Intelligence," *Joint Forces Quarterly*, Spring 1994, pp. 92–99.

23. Department of Defense Directive 5240.2, "DOD Counterintelligence," June 6, 1983; Department of Defense Directive 5240.2, "DOD Counterintelligence," May 22, 1997, p. 15.

24. Department of Defense Directive 5240.2, "DOD Counterintelligence," May 22, 1997, p. 15.

25. Department of Defense Directive C-5230.23, "Intelligence Disclosure Policy," November 18, 1983.

26. Available at www.dtic.mil/whs/directives and www.dtic.mil/whs/instructions, both accessed November 7, 2010.

27. Ibid.

28. Ibid.

19

MANAGING INTELLIGENCE COLLECTION, COVERT ACTION, AND INFORMATION ACCESS

Management of four different types of collection—imagery, SIGINT, MASINT, and HUMINT—reflects both the commonality and diversity of the operations and collection systems employed by the Intelligence Community. Imagery is collected largely by satellites and aircraft, while SIGINT and MASINT are also collected by significant numbers of ground- and sea-based and undersea platforms. And, of course, human collection is a quite different method of collection.

Managing covert action is yet another aspect of the management task. Inadequate management can result not only in an inefficient use of resources but in serious international political consequences—as President John F. Kennedy discovered after the failure of the April 1961 Bay of Pigs operation. A further management task is the control over access to information about intelligence collection activities and covert action operations.

MANAGING SATELLITE IMAGING

For many years, the job of translating general imagery collection priorities into the targeting of systems against installations or activities was the responsibility of the Committee on Imagery Requirements and Exploitation (COMIREX). COMIREX was established on July 1, 1967, by Director of Central Intelligence Directive 1/13, as the successor to the Committee on Overhead Reconnaissance (COMOR). COMOR's responsibilities included coordination of collection requirements for the development and operation of all imaging satellites. As these programs grew, the number of photographs increased substantially, resulting in serious duplication of imagery exploitation activities. One solution to this problem involved replacing COMOR with COMIREX. COMIREX's membership consisted of representatives from all United States Intelligence Board/National Foreign Intelligence Board agencies, plus the intelligence chiefs of the Army, Navy, and Air Force. The committee was staffed by personnel from the CIA and the DIA.[1]

The functions of COMIREX were summarized by former COMIREX chairman Roland S. Inlow:

> COMIREX performs the interagency coordination and management functions needed to direct photographic satellite reconnaissance, including the process of deciding what targets should be photographed and what agencies should get which photos to analyze. It also evaluates the needs for, and the results from, photographic reconnaissance, and oversees security controls that are designed to protect photography and information derived from photography from unauthorized disclosure.[2]

COMIREX dealt with three basic questions with regard to the establishment of targets and priorities:

1. What installations/areas were to be imaged?
2. What systems were to be targeted on specific installations/areas?
3. What was to be the frequency of coverage?

When the United States operated a single type of imaging satellite system (the KH-11), COMIREX's decision problem with regard to the second question was simple, but as different versions of the KH-11 satellites, the LACROSSE/ONYX, and MISTY satellites joined the constellation, the decision became more complicated. In any case, there are always significant areas of contention among consumers over priorities and targeting. In addition, there are a multitude of technical questions with regard to the imagery of targets that must be factored into decisions concerning items 1 and 2, including the angle and altitude at which the image is to be obtained.

Conflicts over satellite imagery targeting priorities occur for a variety of reasons. Current intelligence requirements may conflict with long-term requirements—as when coverage of the Iran-Iraq battlefield meant bypassing some opportunities for monitoring the Iraqi nuclear program. Strategic and tactical intelligence requirements may also conflict. Day-to-day coverage, revealing movements of troops or weapons and small changes in capabilities, may be of interest to military commanders; at the national level, in the absence of a crisis, such information is of little interest. COMIREX served to prioritize the claims of the CIA, the DIA, the military services, and other consumers with the objective of distributing a strictly limited resource in such a way as to at least minimally satisfy the legitimate requests of several competitive bureaucracies.

In the area of imagery exploitation, COMIREX allocated interpretation tasks among the National Photographic Interpretation Center, the CIA's Office of Imagery Analysis, the imagery exploitation components of the DIA, and the military service intelligence organizations. The basic division of labor was spelled out in COMIREX's National Tasking Plan for Imagery Processing and Exploitation.[3] With NGA's absorption (when it was NIMA) of NPIC, the CIA's Office of Imagery

Analysis, and the DIA's imagery exploitation component, NGA now must decide which interpretation tasks it will perform itself, and which it will assign to military service intelligence organizations.

Following its creation after the 1991 Gulf War, the Central Imagery Office assumed responsibility for tasking satellites and exploitation components. According to DCID 2/9 of June 1, 1992, "Management of National Imagery Intelligence," the CIO was to "perform those Intelligence Community responsibilities previously vested in COMIREX." Tasking was to be done by a central imagery tasking authority "in accordance with intelligence requirements established by the DCI in peacetime and the Secretary of Defense in wartime." The CIO was also to produce the National Tasking Policy for Imagery Exploitation to allocate interpretation tasks among the different agencies.[4]

NIMA's Central Imagery Tasking Office was the successor to the CIO tasking function. Today, it is NGA's Source Operations and Management Directorate—specifically its Source Operations Group—that is responsible for receiving requests for satellite imagery coverage from the organizations requiring such cover—both within and outside the Intelligence Community. The directorate then produces the tasking for the NRO's imagery satellites.[5]

Among the innovations in imagery tasking that took place during the 1970s was COMIREX's establishment of the COMIREX Automated Management System (CAMS). CAMS used operations research procedures to take the requirements from different customers and create a tasking plan to optimize satellite operations in pursuit of those requirements and established priorities. In 1996, NIMA established the Requirements Management System to supersede CAMS. As of 1998, the system could be accessed from over eighty locations throughout the world.[6]

MANAGING SIGINT

Management of the United States Unified Cryptologic System (UCS) is vested in the Director of the NSA by National Security Council Directive No. 6. The most recently available version of that directive, the version of February 17, 1972, is still "operative."[7] In addition to defining the components of SIGINT (COMINT and ELINT), the directive states,

> The Secretary of Defense is designated as Executive Agent of the Government for the conduct of SIGINT activities in accordance with the provisions of this directive and for the direction, supervision, funding, maintenance and operation of the National Security Agency. The Director of the National Security Agency shall report to the Secretary of Defense, the Director of Central Intelligence, and the Joint Chiefs of Staff. The Secretary of Defense may delegate, in whole or part, authority over the Director of the National Security Agency within the Office of the Secretary of Defense.

It shall be the duty of the Director of the National Security Agency to provide for the SIGINT mission of the United States, to establish an effective unified organization and control of all SIGINT collection and processing activities of the United States, and to produce SIGINT in accordance with the objectives, requirements and priorities established by the Director of Central Intelligence Board. No other organization shall engage in SIGINT activities except as provided for in this directive.

Except as provided in paragraphs 5 and 6 of this directive (re unique responsibilities of CIA and FBI) the Director of the National Security Agency shall exercise full control over all SIGINT collection and processing activities. . . . The Director of the National Security Agency is authorized to issue direct to any operating elements engaged in SIGINT operations such instructions and assignments as are required. All instructions issued by the Director under the authority provided in this paragraph shall be mandatory, subject only to appeal to the Secretary of Defense. . . .

The Armed Forces and other departments and agencies often require timely and effective SIGINT. The Director of the National Security Agency shall provide such SIGINT . . .

The intelligence components of the individual departments and agencies may continue to conduct direct liaison with the National Security Agency in the interpretation and amplification of the requirements and priorities established by the Director of Central Intelligence (emphasis in original).[8]

One means of managing the SIGINT system is through the U.S. Signals Intelligence Directives (USSIDs) issued by the Director of the NSA. The numbering scheme for the directives is keyed to the different types of subject matter covered by the directives. Thus, the USSID numbering system can be described as follows:

USSID	1–99	Policy
USSID	100–199	Collection
USSID	200–299	Processing
USSID	300–399	Analysis and Reporting
USSID	400–499	Standards
USSID	500–599	Administration
USSID	600–699	Training
USSID	700–799	ADP
USSID	1000–	Tasking[9]

A listing of known USSIDs is given in Table 19.1.

As indicated in the extract from NSCID No. 6 above, although the Secretary of Defense is the executive agent, and the Director of NSA is the program manager of the UCS, requirements and priorities are to be established by the National Intelligence Board and the National SIGINT Committee. The committee is the successor

TABLE 19.1   U.S. Signals Intelligence Directives

Number	Title/Subject	Date
3	SIGINT Security	August 1972
4	SIGINT Support to Military Commanders	July 1, 1974
18	Legal Compliance and Minimization Procedures	July 27, 1993
40	ELINT Operating Policy	October 1970
52	SIGINT Support to Electronic Warfare Operations	n.a.
56	Exercise SIGINT	n.a.
58	SIGINT Support to MIJI	n.a.
101	COMINT Collection Instructions	Dec. 1, 1989
110	Collection Management Procedures	Dec. 18, 1987
150	SIGINT Numerical Tasking Register	Feb. 1, 1985
240	ELINT Processing, Analysis, and Reporting	n.a.
300	SIGINT Reporting	n.a.
301	Handling of Critical (CRITIC) Information	Nov. 25, 1987
302	SIGINT Alert Systems	n.a.
316	Non-Codeword Reporting System	June 19, 1987
319	Tactical Reporting	n.a.
325	AIRBOAT Procedures	n.a.
326	Electronic Warfare Mutual Support Procedures	n.a.
341	Technical ELINT Product Reporting	n.a.
369	Time-Sensitive SIGINT Reporting	n.a.
402	Equipment and Manning Standards for SIGINT Positions	Sept. 8, 1986
404TM	Technical Extracts from Traffic Analysis (TEXTA)	Dec. 14, 1988
505	Directory of SIGINT Organizations	n.a.
550	Technical SIGINT Support Policies, Procedures, and Responsibilities	n.a.
601	Technical Support for Cryptologic Training	n.a.
602	Specialized Operational Training	n.a.
701	Sanitizing and Declassifying ADP Storage Devices	Sept. 30, 1976
702	Automatic Data Processing Systems Security	Sept. 1980
1045	SIGINT Tasking for USM-45, Misawa	Jan. 16, 1980
1600	SIGINT Tasking for US Army Tactical SIGINT Units	June 7, 1989

SOURCES: U.S. Congress, House Permanent Select Committee on Intelligence, *Annual Report* (Washington, D.C.: U.S. Government Printing Office, 1978), pp. 70, 72; Working Group on Computer Security, *Computer and Telecommunications Security* (Washington, D.C.: National Communications Security Committee, July 1981), pp. 110, 157; Defense Intelligence College, *Instructional Management Plan: Advanced Methods of Intelligence Collection,* March 1984; Department of the Army AR 350-3, "Tactical Intelligence Readiness Training (REDTRAIN)," November 20, 1984, p. 7; Department of the Army, *FM 34-1, Intelligence and Electronic Warfare Operations,* July 1987, Ref. 2; Department of the Army, *FM 34-40-12, Morse Code Intercept Operations (U),* August 26, 1991, Ref. 3; U.S. European Command, ED 40-6, Operations and Administration of JIC, April 25, 1989; Private information.

to a series of predecessors. As of 1950, prior to the creation of the NSA, the work was divided between the Armed Forces Security Agency Council's Intelligence Requirements Committee (AFSAC/IRC) and the U.S. Communications Intelligence Board's Intelligence Committee (USIB/IC). The AFSAC/IRC was primarily responsible for targeting and setting priorities for intercepts of military traffic. The USIB/IC was primarily concerned with nonmilitary traffic.[10]

Following the creation of the NSA, NSCID No. 9 of December 9, 1952, reconstituted the USCIB to operate under the Special Committee of the NSC for COMINT, which consisted of the Secretary of State, the Secretary of Defense, and the Attorney General and was assisted by the DCI. In 1958, when the USCIB and the Intelligence Advisory Committee were merged into the USIB, two committees were created: the COMINT Committee and the ELINT Committee (by means of DCID 6/1 and DCID 6/2, respectively, both issued on October 21, 1958). The ELINT and COMINT committees were merged to form the SIGINT Committee by DCID 6/1 of May 31, 1962.[11]

The responsibilities of the National SIGINT Committee (as it is now known) are extensive, as indicated by DCID 6/1 of May 12, 1982, reprinted in Figure 19.1. They include developing specifications for SIGINT collection requirements, monitoring the responsiveness of U.S. and cooperating foreign SIGINT agencies, and developing policies for the conduct of SIGINT liaison and the security of SIGINT-obtained information. In the 1993 fiscal year, the key SIGINT Committee activities included the development of a new architecture for SIGINT satellites, the review and approval of selected allied relationships, the review of foreign military sales requests, and several special evaluations.[12]

Prior to the Middle East war in 1973, the USIB SIGINT Committee recommended that the Middle East be a priority target for intelligence collection if hostilities erupted. The NSA was asked to evaluate the intelligence collected and to determine appropriate targets. Upon the outbreak of war, the NSA implemented these policies under the SIGINT Committee's guidance. The committee discussed and approved the DIA's recommendation to change the primary target of one collector.[13]

In addition to validating requirements and tasking collection assets, the SIGINT Committee examines the relationships between U.S. SIGINT agencies and foreign agencies. Thus, in 1972 the committee developed a new set of objectives regarding SIGINT relations with Japan.[14]

The SIGINT Committee operated for many years with two permanent subcommittees—the SIGINT Requirements Validation and Evaluation Subcommittee (SIRVES) and the SIGINT Overhead Reconnaissance Subcommittee (SORS). SIRVES was established in the 1970s, as a successor to the Evaluation Subcommittee, to, among other things, oversee the National SIGINT Requirements System (which is discussed in more detail below). SIRVES restructured the key SIGINT requirements covering the former USSR and Eastern Europe. SORS was established in the 1960s, with the arrival of satellite SIGINT collection. It was "responsible for receipt, approval, and subsequent generation of intelligence guidance in response to tasks to

FIGURE 19.1   DCID 6/1, The SIGINT Committee

SECRET
NOFORN

DIRECTOR OF CENTRAL INTELLIGENCE DIRECTIVE[1]
SIGINT Committee
(Effective 12 May 1982)

Pursuant to the provisions of Section 102, the National Security Act of 1947, and Executive Order 12333, there is established a Signals Intelligence (SIGINT) Committee.

1. Mission

The mission of the SIGINT Committee is to advise and assist the Director of Central Intelligence (DCI) and the Director, National Security Agency (DIRNSA) in the discharge of their duties and responsibilities with respect to Signals Intelligence as specified in Executive Order 12333, to monitor and assist in coordinating within the Intelligence Community the accomplishment of objectives established by the DCI, and to promote the effective use of Intelligence Community SIGINT resources.

2. Functions:

Under the general guidance of the Deputy Director of Central Intelligence, the SIGINT Committee shall:

a. advise the DCI on the establishment of SIGINT requirements, priorities, and objectives;

b. develop statements, based on the DCI's objectives and priorities, of collection and exploitation requirements for COMINT, ELINT, foreign instrumentation signals, nonimagery infrared, coherent light, and nonnuclear electromagnetic pulse (EMP) sources. (These statements will provide guidance for resource programming, mission planning, and reporting. Each statement should take into account practical limitations, costs, and risk factors.)

c. monitor and evaluate the responsiveness of present and programmed United States and cooperating foreign SIGINT resources to United States needs for intelligence information;

d. monitor the impact on SIGINT programs of information needs levied by intelligence comsumers;

e. advise and make recommendations on the dissemination and sanitization of SIGINT or information derived therefrom and the release of disclosure of SIGINT or derived information to foreign governments or international organizations in which the United States Government participates;

f. develop and recommend to the DCI policies, directives, and guidance for the conduct of SIGINT arrangements with foreign governments;

g. assess and report to the DCI on the potential impact on current and future United States SIGINT capabilities of providing cryptographic assistance to foreign governments; and

---

[1]This directive supersedes DCID No. 6/1, 18 May 1976.

SECRET

Classified by: DCI
Declassify on: OADR

(continues)

SECRET
NOFORN

h. review, develop, and recommend to the DCI policies for the protection, through classification and compartmentation, of COMINT, ELINT, and other SIGINT or of information about them or derived from them and procedures enabling United States Government entities outside of the Intelligence Community to receive and use SIGINT.

3. Intelligence Community Responsibilities

Upon request of the Committee Chairman, Intelligence Community elements shall provide information pertinent to the Committee's mission and functions within DCI-approved security safeguards.

4. Composition and Organization

The Committee Chairman will be appointed by the Director of Central Intelligence.

The members of the committee will be representatives designated by Intelligence Community principals.

The Chairman will establish subcommittees or task forces as required.

With the approval of the DCI, the Committee Chairman may invite representatives of relevant United States Government entities to participate as appropriate.

The Committee will be supported by an Executive Secretariat.

William J. Casey
Director of Central Intelligence

SECRET

be levied on national resources" and "continually monitors requirements and provides collection and processing guidance for both long- and short-term needs."[15]

In the mid-1990s two new groups were established—the Weapons and Space Systems Advisory Group (WSSAG) and the National Emitter Intelligence Subcommittee (NEIS). The WSSAG was created to "coordinate SIGINT on foreign weapons and space systems," whereas the NEIS is concerned with SIGINT production on foreign radars and other noncommunications signals. The committee may also employ working groups and task forces on a short-term basis—such as the Third Party Ad Hoc Working Group of 1972.[16]

In March 2004, the DCI signed a new charter for the National SIGINT Committee. As a result, SIRVES became the National SIGINT Analysis and Production Subcommittee while SORS became the National SIGINT Collection Subcommittee, which is responsible for providing a perspective on the relative merit of SIGINT collection assets. In addition, two groups established in the 1990s have been merged into the National Emitter, Weapons, and Space Subcommittee (NEWSS).[17]

A second DNI committee that might on occasion have input on the subject of SIGINT requirements is the Critical Intelligence Problems Committee (CIPC). On January 31, 1972, the DCI requested the Critical Collection Problems Committee (CCPC), as the CIPC was then known, to conduct a review of intelligence efforts against narcotics. In a section titled "SIGINT Information on Narcotics and Dangerous Drugs," the CCPC report of October 1972 noted in part

1. No SIGINT resources are dedicated solely to the intercept of narcotics information. The SIGINT which is now being produced on the international narcotics problem is a by-product of SIGINT reporting on other national requirements. . . .
5. The effective use of SIGINT information in support of ongoing operations while at the same time protecting the source has been a problem.
6. Successful usage of the SIGINT product is largely contingent upon close collaboration between the SIGINT producers and the appropriate customer agencies.[18]

The CCPC therefore recommended that the "NSA, in conjunction with the interested customers, particularly BNDD and Customs, make appropriate determination of what COMINT support is required on the narcotics problem and that the requisite priorities be established through the SIGINT Committee."[19]

As noted above, under congressional pressure a National SIGINT Requirements System was established in 1975, after USIB approval. Under this system, a formal community review and approval procedure must be conducted for each requirement before it can be validated and placed on the National SIGINT Requirements List (NSRL). Today, the NSRL is the basic guidance document for the NSA and specifies SIGINT targets according to well-defined priorities, including cross-references to DNI and other national requirements documents. The system does not, however, prevent the Director of the NSA from determining which specific signals to intercept in fulfillment of requirements. Nor does it prevent the Secretaries of State and Defense or military commanders from directly tasking NSA in a crisis and then informing the DNI and SIGINT Committee afterward.[20]

The yearly statement of objectives, requirements, and priorities is given in the yearly Consolidated Cryptologic Program (CCP) and Defense Cryptologic Program (DCP), formerly the Tactical Cryptologic Program (TCP). The TCP "was established in 1979 to correct the problem of disparate requirements competing for limited available funding within the NFIP which resulted in inadequate treatment of Service tactical support needs."[21]

MANAGING SENSITIVE RECONNAISSANCE MISSIONS

Reconnaissance conducted by satellite is relatively nonintrusive because it does not require actual violation of a target nation's airspace. Further, with the exception of Russia and China, no nation possesses the means to destroy U.S. satellites. And even during the Cold War, the likely costs to the Soviet Union of interfering in an obvious way with such satellites were likely to be far greater than the potential benefits.

When airborne overflights or air, sea, or submarine missions close to a nation's borders are involved, the potential for an international incident is much greater. Early Cold War aircraft reconnaissance missions directed at the Soviet Union involved this risk because they approached or penetrated the margins of Soviet and East European territory to collect several varieties of intelligence, including the signatures and operating frequencies of air defense systems.[22]

Over the years, incidents occurred involving air and sea missions. In 1962, during the Cuban missile crisis, one U-2 strayed into Soviet territory and another was shot down during a flight over Cuba. In 1967, the Israeli Air Force bombed the USS *Liberty* while it was collecting signals intelligence in the midst of the Six Day War. In 1968, the USS *Pueblo* was seized by North Korea during a SIGINT mission off the North Korean coast, and in 1969, an EC-121 SIGINT aircraft was shot down by North Korean forces while it patrolled off the same coast.

The North Koreans also made hundreds of attempts to shoot down overflying SR-71s and, as noted previously, in 2003 attempted to force a RC-135 to land in North Korea. Also noted in Chapter 8 was the collision between an EP-3 and Chinese fighter that forced the U.S. plane to make an emergency landing on Hainan Island. In addition, there have been several incidents involving U.S. submarines conducting HOLYSTONE-type missions, including collisions with Soviet submarines.[23]

The U.S. system for the management of these missions reflects many considerations. Many of the missions are proposed by and conducted in support of the unified military commands. Others are clearly designed to provide national intelligence. In either case, such missions could cause an international incident, and thus they require national-level approval and close monitoring.

Special Navy reconnaissance programs are the initial responsibility of the "National Underwater Reconnaissance Program Executive Committee" and are managed by the National Underwater Reconnaissance Office.[24]

Missions originating from the unified commands go through a chain of supervisory offices and divisions, beginning with the command's joint reconnaissance center.

Until the mid-1990s, a national Joint Reconnaissance Center (JRC) operated as part of the J-3 (Operations) Directorate of the Joint Chiefs of Staff and colocated with the National Joint Military Center. The JRC was established on October 24, 1960, as the result of the loss of an RB-47 over the Barents Sea and President Eisenhower's desire to avoid a repetition.[25]

The JRC acted as an initial approval authority for reconnaissance plans developed by unified and component commands. It also developed a Joint Reconnaissance Schedule (JRS)—"several inches thick and filled with hundreds of pages of highly technical data and maps"—that monitored the progress of the missions and provided the National Military Command Center with real-time information regarding the status and disposition of forces, mission activity, and other reconnaissance-related information. Figure 19.2 shows a 1980 request related to planning for a possible second mission to rescue U.S. hostages in Iran.

The JRC, operating through three branches, performed several functions:

- receiving, reviewing, evaluating, and submitting for approval to the JCS the reconnaissance plans, programs, and schedules originated by the commanders of the unified commands, the military services, and other governmental agencies;
- preparing the planning guidance for the execution of reconnaissance operations of special significance or sensitivity;
- reviewing intelligence support plans, and preparing policy guidance, planning, analysis, and review of reconnaissance-related activities that support trans- and post-nuclear attack operations;
- monitoring the missions approved by the JRC and ensuring that all incidents were brought to the attention of appropriate authorities;
- displaying on a current basis all peacetime military reconnaissance and some other sensitive operations.[26]

Those functions are now performed by the Reconnaissance Operations Division (ROD) of the J-3 Directorate, as the JRC has been retitled.[27] As indicated in Figure 19.3, the ROD consists of Airborne and Maritime branches, with sections for different platforms and components for Administration/Security and Liaison/Support.

MANAGING MASINT

As discussed in Chapter 9, measurement and signature intelligence consists of a number of collection activities that lack the common features of imagery and SIGINT activities. The decision to treat these activities as components of a single disci-

FIGURE 19.2 SR-71 Mission Request

THE JOINT CHIEFS OF STAFF
WASHINGTON, D.C. 20301

3 November 1980

THE JOINT STAFF

MEMORANDUM FOR DIRECTOR, JOINT RECONNAISSANCE CENTER

Subject: SR 71 Mission Request

1. (U)(TS) Request consideration be given to conducting several SR 71 surveillance missions of the Persian Gulf during the next 3-6 weeks.

2. (U)(TS) Purpose of mission is to determine locations of major oil rig concentrations and typical flow pattern of Gulf shipping to assist in selection of low level air penetration routes.

3. (U)(TS) Recognize that missions could raise Soviet/Iran/ME speculation; however, given irregular scheduling, direct association with any US military planning will probably be low. On the other hand, periodic SR 71 missions would provide "reason" for increased tanker support in the area prior to the execution of any US military contingency action.

JAMES B. VAUGHT
Major General, USA

CLASSIFIED BY JCS, J-3,
DECLASSIFY ON 3 NOV 2000

---

pline has led to the creation of organizations to manage MASINT across the Intelligence Community.

The senior official for MASINT management is the Measurement and Signature Intelligence Community Executive (MCE), who reports to the DDNI for Collection and "works to resolve MASINT issues in concert with the relevant IC members." The senior body for MASINT management, established in 1986, is the MASINT Committee. The committee is responsible for providing advice to Defense Department and Intelligence Community leaders, fostering technology and information exchange, supporting community coordination, developing policy and guidance for future programs, validating and prioritizing requirements, and monitoring and evaluating the fulfillment of requirements.[28]

FIGURE 19.3   Reorganization of the JCS Reconnaissance Operations Division

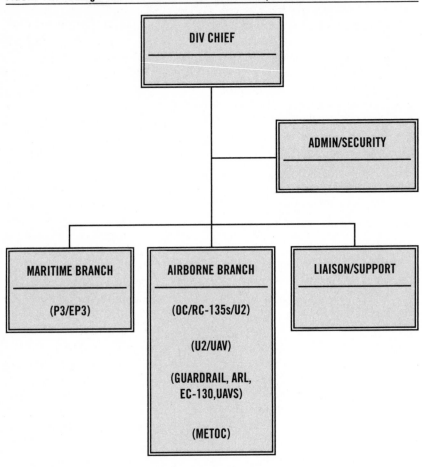

The structure of the committee, circa 2001, is shown in Figure 19.4. As the chart indicates, the committee contained seven working groups related to collection disciplines. What the committee lacks is tasking authority equivalent to that of the NGA Source Operations and Management Directorate or the National SIGINT Committee.

MANAGING HUMINT

Throughout the Cold War and beyond, the fundamental guidance for U.S human intelligence activities—clandestine as well as overt—was contained in National Security Council Intelligence Directive No. 5, whose most recent and still current version is "U.S. Espionage and Counterintelligence Abroad," of February 17, 1972, and the Director of Central Intelligence Directives derived from NSCID No. 5.*

The DCID's governing aspects of the HUMINT effort—including DCID 5/1, "Espionage and Counterintelligence Activities Abroad" (December 19, 1984) and DCID 3/2, "Coordination of Overt Collection Abroad" (November 26, 2001)—were rescinded in part and in whole respectively by ICD 304, originally issued in March 2008, and amended in July 2009.[29]

The current version of ICD 304 "delineates the roles and responsibilities of the DNI, the National HUMINT Manager (NHM), and those principal agencies or departments that conduct HUMINT activities [including counterintelligence activities using human sources]"—specifically, the Central Intelligence Agency, the Federal Bureau of Investigation, and the Department of Defense.[30]

The directive delegates to the Deputy Director of National Intelligence for Collection (DDNI/C) the DNI's authorities and responsibilities with regard to establishing objectives, priorities, and guidance for national HUMINT activities; resolving conflicts in collection requirements; and evaluating the effectiveness of national HUMINT activities. In addition, the directive assigns the DDNI/C responsibility, in conjunction with other officials, for advising the DNI on HUMINT resource allocations in the National Intelligence Program and Military Intelligence Program.[31]

The directive also designates the Director of the Central Intelligence Agency as National HUMINT Manager (NHM)—a position that the director has delegated to the Director of the National Clandestine Service. The NHM's responsibilities include production of an integrated national HUMINT plan containing goals and performance objectives, integrating national HUMINT collection capabilities into the National Intelligence Coordination Center, and creating and implementing command standards for HUMINT activities—including source validation, training, collection requirements, evaluation, reporting, and cover support.[32]

Additional NHM responsibilities include developing and implementing procedures to de-conflict HUMINT operations and activities conducted by Intelligence Community organizations or funded by the National Intelligence Program, as well as negotiating written agreements with other U.S. Government "entities engaged in collection activities involving clandestine methods, or that collect intelligence through HUMINT or counterintelligence activities"—such as the June 2005 "Memorandum of Understanding Concerning Overseas and Domestic Activities of the Central Intelligence Agency and Federal Bureau of Investigation."

---

*Another aspect of human intelligence—defectors—was the subject of NSCID No. 4, "The Defector Program," February 17, 1972. Among the DCIDs issued under its authority were DCID 4/1, "The Interagency Defector Committee," and DCID 4/2, "The Defector Program Abroad." See DCID 4/2, "The Defector Program Abroad," June 26, 1959, in *Documents from the Espionage Den (53): U.S.S.R., the Aggressive East*, section 4 ("Tehran: Muslim Students Following the Line of the Imam," n.d.), pp. 4–11; U.S. Congress, House Permanent Select Committee on Intelligence, *Annual Report*, p. 70.

FIGURE 19.4 Organization of the MASINT Committee

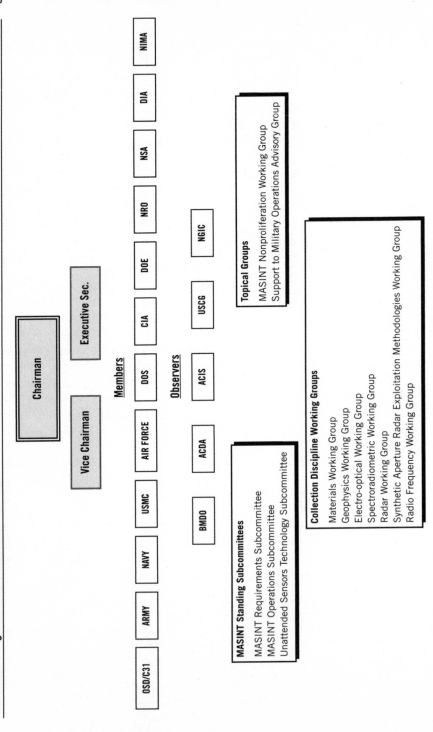

In addition, the NHM is authorized to establish committees, boards, or other means of facilitating HUMINT collaboration and integration. Among the committees and boards that exist are the National HUMINT Board of Governors (which has also been known as the HUMINT Enterprise National Board of Governors) and the National HUMINT Committee. The board of governors was established by early 2007 to "oversee efforts to more fully integrate . . . national human intelligence resources." Its membership includes agencies that "use clandestine methods or tradecraft to pursue law enforcement, counterintelligence, drug enforcement or military missions, plus organizations that enable HUMINT operations," according to a 2007 statement from the CIA's director. The director also reported that leaders of twenty-one agencies, bureaus, and departments attended the board's first meeting.[33]

Among those attending were leaders of the National Clandestine Service, the DIA, the FBI, the Special Operations Command, the Department of Energy and Homeland Security, the National Security Agency, and the National Reconnaissance Office (and presumably the Departments of State and Commerce).[34]

An apparently more restricted entity is the National HUMINT Committee, whose membership is probably restricted to Intelligence Community representatives and deals with more sensitive operational matters than does the board. The committee's origins go back to 1970, when it was first proposed by DIA director Gen. Donald Bennett as a means of providing a national-level forum to coordinate both overt and clandestine human source collection. Objections from the CIA's Directorate of Plans prevented its immediate creation, in part because the directorate wanted to minimize the number of individuals with access to information concerning clandestine sources. As a result, DCI Richard Helms established an ad hoc task force to study the problem of human source collection. After a year of study, the task force recommended the establishment of a USIB committee on a one-year trial basis. In June 1974, the committee attained permanent status as the Human Sources Committee, and in 1975 it became the Human Resources Committee.[35]

The committee's functions were specified by DCID 3/7 of October 12, 1982. They included the following:

> to examine problems and consider possible improvements in collection and procedures for dissemination of intelligence obtained by human resources and to provide recommendations to the DCI related thereto;
>
> to encourage and promote collection activities and coordination among human resources collection agencies concerning the allocation of effort and responsibility for the satisfaction of foreign intelligence needs.[36]

Through its Assessments Subcommittee, the HRC conducted community-wide assessments of human source reporting in individual countries. In 1976 and 1977, the subcommittees of the HRC included those for Collection Program Evaluation;

Research and Development; Organization, Training, and Advisory; Planning and Programming; and Guidance and Requirements.[37]

The guidelines establishing the committee specifically avoided giving it responsibility for reviewing the operational details or internal management of the individual departments or agencies. Departments and agencies were authorized to withhold "sensitive" information from the committee and to report directly to the DCI.[38]

As of 1975, the HRC had "only just begun to expand community influence over human collection," issuing a general guidance document called the Current Intelligence Reporting List (CIRL). The military made some use of the document, but the CIA's Directorate of Operations instructed CIA stations that the list was provided only for reference and did not constitute collection requirements for CIA operations.[39]

During 1977, the committee provided the U.S. Ambassador in Iran with a short prioritized list of items of national intelligence interest. The list was developed by the HRC with the advice of the National Intelligence Officer for the Near East and South Asia. The chairman of the HRC, in his cover letter, expressed his hope that the list would "be of some use . . . as a coordinated interagency expression of the most important information Washington needs."[40]

During the 1970s, the now-defunct Intelligence Community Staff began to issue the National Human Intelligence Collection Plan. The plan included an advisory for HUMINT collectors, such as Foreign Service officers, who were outside the NFIP. Apparently, it included a variety of subplans for specific subject areas. Thus, in 1988 there were National HUMINT Collection Plans for Space, for Soviet Naval Forces, for Soviet Strategic Forces, and for Soviet S&T. The National Human Intelligence Collection Plan's effect was limited by being only one of several guidance documents levied on human source collectors.[41]

Several initiatives were launched in the 1990s and post-9/11 to improve coordination of clandestine collection. In 1992, a National HUMINT Requirements Tasking Center (NHRTC) was established within the CIA's Directorate of Operations to allocate tasks among the collection agencies. At the time, DCI Robert Gates described the center as "an integrated interagency mechanism for tasking human intelligence requirements to that part of the community that has the best chance of acquiring the information at least cost and risk."[42]

The center—which consists of representatives from the DIA, the State Department, and the CIA, and a staff of about twelve drawn from the military and three CIA directorates (Intelligence, Operations, and Science and Technology)—has three key areas of responsibility:

- identifying information needs from policymakers, the military, science and technology centers, law enforcement, and analysts;
- establishing collection priorities for collection and reporting;
- tasking requirements to the most suitable collector and assessing their capability to respond to these requirements.[43]

In accordance with NHRTC guidance, a 1993 State Department cable requested information from various embassies about "host government laws and policies regarding in encryption." The information was expected to be a "key input" to a National Security Council study concerning U.S. policy on commercial encryption. Key topics included reaction to the "Clipper Chip" proposal, general policy on public encryption, and economic and trade issues.[44]

The principal products of the center are the National HUMINT Collection Directives (NHCDs), which define the requirements for HUMINT collection and tasking. They attempt to focus on the succeeding two-year period, although many are periodically updated. As of late 1997, there were more than one hundred current NHCDs on countries and transnational issues. Issues covered in the directives included support to military operations, weapons of mass destruction, advanced conventional weapons, and counterterrorism.[45]

Recent directives that have appeared on various websites, as a result of the Wikileaks document release of 2010, include those focusing on the United Nations, Bulgaria, Paraguay, the Palestinian issues, Romania, and the African Sahel region. The directive concerning the United Nations requested, from State Department officers, detailed biographic information about foreign nations' UN representatives and specified a number of priority issues concerning the UN—including near-term issues such as Iran and North Korea, continuing issues such as UN Security Council reform and the Middle East peace process, and UN General Assembly tactics and voting blocs.[46]

The NHCD on Palestinian issues requested information on the Palestinian-Israeli peace process, Palestinian leadership and governance, Palestinian internal security and control, and terrorism and Islamic activism. In addition, the directive requested information on Palestinian social development and infrastructure; the plans, policies, and actions of the Israeli government; and telecommunications systems.[47]

If the subject of an NHCD requires more detailed treatment, which may occur with technical subjects such as proliferation, Intelligence Community analysts write a Collection Support Brief (CSB), which is appended to the directive.[48]

NHRTC guidance is binding on the clandestine and overt HUMINT collections components of the National Clandestine Service and DIA Directorate of Human Intelligence. It was advisory with respect to collection elements outside the Intelligence Community, such as the Foreign Commercial Service of the Department of Commerce and Department of State embassy reporting. Thus, the State Department officers ignored portions of the United Nations NCHD requesting them to gather personal and technical information—including cell-phone and frequent-flier numbers—about other nation's diplomats.[49]

As noted in Chapter 2, the NHRTC as well as the Community HUMINT Coordination Center are managed by the Deputy Director of the NCS for Community HUMINT. The coordination center is responsible for de-confliction and coordination of the HUMINT activities of the NCS, the DIA, the FBI, the military service counterintelligence components, and the unified commands.[50]

MANAGING COVERT ACTION

Management of U.S. covert action programs involves procedures and review groups within the CIA and NSC. To initiate a covert action, a Presidential Finding is required by the Hughes-Ryan Amendment to the Foreign Assistance Act of 1961. Under that and subsequent regulations, the finding must state that the President has determined that the "operation in a foreign country . . . is important to the national security of the United States" and then described the scope (the country or countries that are the target) of the operation and what the operation entails. Findings must also specify each U.S. government entity that will participate in any significant way in the program's implementation and whether any third party will participate in the program in a significant way; findings may not authorize violation of the Constitution or any U.S. statute.[51] Figure 19.5 shows one of the findings signed in support of the attempt to establish contact with Iranian "moderates."

Since 1991, under Title V of the National Security Act, Presidential Findings must be in writing and may not confer retroactive authorization for covert activities—except in emergencies, when oral findings may be used for up to twenty-four hours.[52]

Findings are initially prepared within the CIA's National Clandestine Service, either as a result of a director initiative or in response to requests from the CIA Director, who in turn may be responding to a DNI or presidential request. In 1986, an article in the CIA's *Studies in Intelligence* reported that before a proposed finding left the Directorate of Operations (now the National Clandestine Service), it was reviewed by the Covert Action Planning Group (CAPG), composed of the Associate Deputy Director for the directorate, senior staff chiefs, and those individuals who had a substantive responsibility for the finding and its eventual implementation. If approved by the CAPG, the finding was sent on to the top echelon of CIA management for review and recommendations and then to the Director of the CIA (and then to the DCI).[53]

Under the Reagan administration, if the proposed finding was approved by the DCI, it would go to the Planning and Coordination Group (PCG) of the NSC, which consisted of senior representatives of the State Department, Defense Department, and NSC. If the PCG supported the finding, it sent a favorable recommendation to the National Security Planning Group (NSPG). Approval of the NSPG then resulted in a Presidential Finding. NSDD 159, of January 18, 1985, "Covert Action Policy Approval and Coordination Procedures," specified that all intelligence findings be written and circulated among the eight senior members of the NSPG before being put into effect.[54]

George W. Bush's first National Security Presidential Directive, signed on February 13, 2001, "Organization of the National Security Council System," continued the existence of the NSC Principals Committee from the Clinton administration (which had continued it from the George H.W. Bush administration) "to be the interagency forum for consideration of policy issues affecting national security"—including covert

FIGURE 19.5 Presidential Finding on Iran

Finding Pursuant to Section 662 of

The Foreign Assistance Act of 1961

As Amended, Concerning Operations

Undertaken by the Central Intelligence

Agency in Foreign Countries, Other Than

Those Intended Solely for the Purpose

of Intelligence Collection

I hereby find that the following operation in a foreign country (including all support necessary to such operation) is important to the national security of the United States, and due to its extreme sensitivity and security risks, I determine it is essential to limit prior notice, and direct the Director of Central Intelligence to refrain from reporting this Finding to the Congress as provided in Section 501 of the National Security Act of 1947, as amended, until I otherwise direct.

SCOPE   DESCRIPTION

Iran   Assist selected friendly foreign liaison services, third countries and third parties which have established relationships with Iranian elements, groups, and individuals sympathetic to U.S. Government interests and which do not conduct or support terrorist actions directed against U.S. persons, property or interests, for the purpose of: (1) establishing a more moderate government in Iran, (2) obtaining from them significant intelligence not otherwise obtainable, to determine the current Iranian Government's intentions with respect to its neighbors and with respect to terrorist acts, and (3) furthering the release of the American hostages held in Beirut and preventing additional terrorist acts by these groups. Provide funds, intelligence, counter-intelligence, training, guidance and communications and other necessary assistance to these elements, groups, individuals, liaison services and third countries in support of these activities.

The USG will act to facilitate efforts by third parties and third countries to establish contact with moderate elements within and outside the Government of Iran by providing these elements with arms, equipment and related materiel in order to enhance the credibility of these elements in their effort to achieve a more pro-U.S. government in Iran by demonstrating their ability to obtain requisite resources to defend their country against Iraq and intervention by the Soviet Union. This support will be discontinued if the U.S. Government learns that these elements have abandoned their goals of moderating their government and appropriated the material for purposes other than that provided by this finding.

The White House
Washington, D.C.
Date January 17, 1986

action. The regular membership consisted of the Secretary of State, the Secretary of Defense, the Secretary of the Treasury, the President's chief of staff, and the Assistant to the President for National Security Affairs, who served as the chair.[55]

Presidential Policy Directive-1, "Organization of the National Security Council System," of February 13, 2009, directed that the Principals Committee "continue to be the senior interagency forum for consideration of policy issues affecting national security." The directive also stipulated that the committee would be chaired by the National Security Advisor, while its other members would include the Secretary of State, the Secretary of the Treasury, the Secretary of Defense, the Attorney General, the Secretary of Energy, the Secretary of Homeland Security, the Director of the Office of Management and Budget, the U.S. Representative to the UN, the Chief of Staff to the President, the Director of National Intelligence, and the Chairman of the Joint Chiefs of Staff.[56]

MANAGING INFORMATION ACCESS

The basic means of managing or controlling access to intelligence information are delineated in the classification system, which defines different levels of sensitivity and restricts access to those who have been cleared at that level and have a "need to know." Classification as well as dissemination are the results of guidance issued in the form of executive orders, National Security Council Intelligence Directives, Director of Central Intelligence Directives, Intelligence Community Directives, and guidance from heads of agencies such as the NRO, NSA, and ONI.

The best-known classifications are those used to restrict access to a wide range of national security information: Confidential, Secret, and Top Secret. Confidential information, as defined in the most recent executive order on "Classified National Security Information," is "information, the unauthorized disclosure of which reasonably could be expected to cause damage to the national security that the original classification authority is able to identify or describe." Secret information differs from Confidential information in that the expected damage would be "serious." In the case of Top Secret information, the damage would be "exceptionally grave."[57]

In theory, at least, access for an individual with clearances at a certain level is further restricted to the information the individual needs to know in order to perform his or her job. In some cases, the need-to-know principle is implemented by compartmentalizing certain sets of data—such as that concerning specific operations or individuals. Thus, the Army Intelligence and Security Command's offensive counterintelligence operations have been designated by a special code word used to restrict access to information about those operations. Similar operations conducted by the Air Force Office of Special Investigations have been designated SEVEN DOORS.[58]

In addition to specifying the traditional Confidential, Secret, and Top Secret classifications, the executive order on national security information allows the Director of National Intelligence to established Special Access Programs with respect to intelligence sources, methods, and activities. The executive order directs that the number of programs be kept "at an absolute minimum" and specifies that such programs can be created only if "the vulnerability of, or threat to, specific information is exceptional" and "the normal criteria for determining eligibility for access applicable to information classified at the same level are not deemed sufficient to protect the information from unauthorized disclosure."[59]

Intelligence Community special access programs have been known as Sensitive Compartmented Information (SCI). According to a 1984 report by the National Foreign Intelligence Board Security Committee,

> Sensitive Compartmented Information is data about sophisticated technical systems for collecting intelligence and information collected by those systems. The characteristics of the systems that necessitated the development of SCI programs are (a) that compared to conventional intelligence activities employing human sources, many more people must know sensitive information in order to develop, build and operate the systems and to analyze the material they collect; (b) that they generally produce large quantities of accurate, detailed intelligence, which is needed and relied upon by senior planners and policymakers, and which, by its nature is extremely fragile, in that it reveals the characteristics of the systems that collect it; and (c) that they are extremely vulnerable to adversary countermeasures, i.e., denial and deception.[60]

The systems that generate such SCI are overhead imaging, signals intelligence, measurement and intelligence systems, submarines involved in Special Navy reconnaissance activities, and ground stations involved in the interception of foreign signals. In addition, as noted by the NFIB, information about many of the systems that produce SCI falls into the SCI category. And despite the NFIB's 1984 report, at least some human intelligence data are now considered SCI.[61]

The first public hint of the existence of such a category occurred during the Senate hearing on the Gulf of Tonkin Resolution in 1964, when Senate Foreign Relations Committee Chairman William Fulbright inquired into the source of a report that North Vietnamese patrol boats were about to attack the USS *Turner Joy* on the night of August 4, 1964. Defense Secretary Robert McNamara, Fulbright, and Senators Frank Lausche and Albert Gore engaged in the following colloquy:

MCNAMARA: We have some problems because the [committee] staff has not been cleared for certain intelligence.

LAUSCHE: I do not understand that. The members of the staff are not cleared?

FULBRIGHT: All of those who have worked on this matter, but he is talking of a special classification of intelligence communications. . . .

GORE: Mr. Chairman, could we know what particular classification that is? I had not heard of this super classification.

MCNAMARA: Clearance is *above Top Secret* for the particular information on the situation [emphasis added].[62]

The "above Top Secret" category dealt with communications or signals intelligence (rather than intelligence communications), and McNamara revealed that it was called Special Intelligence (SI)—which by that time was one of several categories of SCI.

The institutionalization of such categories and clearances, particularly SI, can be traced to the successful interception and decryption of Axis signals during World War II by the United States and the United Kingdom. The machine by which the United States was able to decipher Japanese diplomatic messages was designated PURPLE, while the intelligence produced was designated MAGIC. A "Top List" identified those who were authorized to have access to MAGIC intelligence, a list that included President Roosevelt; the Secretaries of State, War, and the Navy; and the Directors of Military and Naval Intelligence—but not the commander of U.S. Naval Forces at Pearl Harbor, Admiral Husband Kimmel.[63]

The British also instituted a code word system to guard the fact that they were able to decrypt German and Italian military communications. The most sensitive military material was originally designated PEARL, ZYMOTIC, SWELL, and SIDAR. The British settled on three codewords—ULTRA, PEARL, and THUMB—to indicate material of special sensitivity. Eventually, PEARL and THUMB were combined into a single code word—PINUP.[64]

In addition to intercepting Japanese diplomatic communications, the United States spent considerable effort in intercepting and trying to decipher Japanese military communications. The United States employed several code words to represent the product of such activity. DEXTER was the code word for intercepts of the highest-level traffic—for example, Admiral Yamomoto's travel plans. CORRAL indicated less sensitive intercepts. RABID was used to indicate Traffic Analysis intelligence. With the signing of the BRUSA Communications Intelligence Agreement in May 1943, which standardized signals intelligence procedures between the United States and Britain, ULTRA was made a prefix to each classification, so that the code words became ULTRA DEXTER, ULTRA CORRAL, and ULTRA RABID.[65]

Until late 2005, the most common clearances within the SCI category were Special Intelligence (SI), GAMMA (G), TALENT—KEYHOLE (TK), and BYEMAN (B). As McNamara indicated, the SI category concerns communications intelligence. Just as there were different ULTRA levels (for the United States), there were different compartments of the SI category corresponding to different levels of sensitivity. UMBRA was the successor to a long line of code words, including DINAR and TRINE, that designated the most sensitive SI material. Less sensitive was the SPOKE compartment, which, in earlier years, might contain information from intercepts of PLO communications. Least sensitive was the information in the MORAY compartment.[66]

To express these differing levels of sensitivity, a page containing only UMBRA SCI would be stamped TOP SECRET UMBRA; a page containing only SPOKE SCI would be stamped SECRET SPOKE; and a page containing only MORAY SCI would be stamped SECRET MORAY. Although the use of the Top Secret and Secret prefixes may appear to imply that UMBRA, SPOKE, and MORAY were simply "need-to-know" compartments of those conventional classifications, such a conclusion is inconsistent with, among other things, the fact that greater personnel and physical security measures were taken than for a plain Top Secret document.[67]

In 1998, the Director of Central Intelligence decided that the code words UMBRA, SPOKE, and MORAY were no longer classified—although the information they protected certainly was. Then, as a result of a decision by the National SIGINT Committee in May 1999, the code words UMBRA, SPOKE, and MORAY were eliminated altogether. Information that used to be classified as TOP SECRET UMBRA would be classified as TOP SECRET COMINT, while SECRET SPOKE or SECRET MORAY items would become SECRET COMINT.[68]

At one time there were DELTA compartments—including DACE, DICE, and DENT—within UMBRA for intercepts relating to Soviet military operations, such as the location of Soviet submarines or aircraft operations.[69]

Another UMBRA compartment that survived the elimination of UMBRA—one used by NSA for particularly sensitive COMINT—is GAMMA (G). Until 1969, GAMMA was a designator reserved exclusively for intercepts of Soviet communications. That year, NSA received instructions to use the same methods and procedures to monitor the communications of U.S. antiwar leaders. At one point, there were at least twenty GAMMA subcompartments, including GILT, GOAT, GULT, GANT, GUPY, GABE, GYRO, and GOUT—each of which referred to a specific operation or method. As noted in Chapter 8, GAMMA GUPY referred to the interception of radio-telephone conversations being conducted by Soviet leaders as they were driven around Moscow in their limousines. GAMMA GOUT referred to the material obtained by interception of South Vietnamese government communications.[70]

In addition to GAMMA two other SIGINT designations survived the May 1999 National SIGINT Committee eliminations—VRK and ECI. The VRK—Very Restricted Knowledge—designation was established in November 1974 by the Director of the NSA "to limit access to uniquely sensitive SIGINT activities and programs." ECI—for Exceptionally Controlled Information—has been described in a DOD document as a subcompartment of COMINT and in an NRO document as "an NSA administrative COMINT flag."[71]

An additional set of code words that have been attached to SIGINT documents are those indicating that the SIGINT was obtained from a Third Party to the UK-SUA Agreement. DRUID has been used to indicate a Third Party intercept, while code words that identify particular parties have included JAEGER (Austria), ISHTAR (Japan), SETTEE (Korea), DYNAMO (Denmark), RICHTER (Germany), and DIKTER (Norway).[72]

Another portion of the SCI-universe was designated TALENT-KEYHOLE (TK), which originated with the desire to restrict access first to U-2 imagery (TALENT) and then to satellite imagery and ELINT (KEYHOLE). For many years, there were three compartments within the TK category—RUFF, ZARF, and CHESS. RUFF pertained to information produced by imaging satellites (with the exception of the

ARGON KH-5 mapping satellite, whose product was designated DAFF). ZARF indicated ELINT obtained by satellite, while CHESS has been used to designate certain aerial imagery (such as that produced by SR-71 and U-2 aircraft). Thus, the 1986 final report of the DCI Mobile Missile Task Force Intelligence Requirements and Analysis Working Group was classified TOP SECRET RUFF ZARF UMBRA. In May 1999, ZARF was abolished as a code word. As a result, satellite-produced ELINT data are designated simply as TALENT-KEYHOLE information.[73]

For almost forty-five years, access to information about satellite and certain aerial intelligence systems was controlled via the BYEMAN Control System (BCS), with clearances for information being granted on a system-by-system basis and each system being designated by a specific code word. Table 19.2 lists the code words for various SIGINT satellites as well as their initial year of operation. Table 19.3 provides similar information for imagery satellites and aircraft.[74]

Individual systems still have their own code names. However, as a result of the 1993 BYEMAN Compartmentation Restructure Study, a single major compartment was established with access to specific programs on a need-to-know basis. Then in early 2005, in a memo to the Director of Central Intelligence, the director of NRO requested that the BCS be retired because "it has become an impediment to . . . initiatives to encourage greater sharing of the NRO's capabilities and resources." That request was approved, along with the NRO director's plan to "transfer virtually all BYEMAN information into the Talent-Keyhole (TK) system where it will be available to TK-briefed personnel with a need-to-know."[75]

Also approved was the NRO director's plan to establish the RESERVE Control System (RSV) "to protect a very small body of information related to research and development of breakthrough technologies and specific vulnerabilities in order to glean the maximum lead-time for development and acquisition." RESERVE compartment information would be converted to TK "at the earliest reasonable time to facilitate interagency collaboration and product utility."[76]

In the 1990s, two new clearances that appeared to be widely held in the SCI world were established. SPECTRE* concerned intelligence relating to terrorist activities. (Since that time it is clear that a number of new code words have been established with respect to intelligence concerning terrorist activities.) The other is LOMA, which apparently denotes foreign instrumentation and signature intelligence (FISINT).[77]

A 1985 document indicated a number of additional SCI code words used by the CIA, NSA, and Navy. Included were CS, PM, VER, SNCP, and M. PM and VER may correspond to two Navy (and possibly NSA) programs—PANGRAM and VERDANT. SNCP referred to the Special Navy Control Program, which employed

---

*This spelling suggests rather strongly that SPECTRE was based on the mythical organization that first appeared in the James Bond novel *Thunderball* (1961): the Special Executive for Counter-espionage, Terrorism, Revenge, and Extortion.

TABLE 19.2   SIGINT Satellite Code Words

CODE WORD	MISSION	INITIAL OPERATION
DYNO	ELINT	1960
POPPY	ELINT	1962
CANYON	COMINT	1968
RHYOLITE AQUACADE	TELINT/COMINT	1970
JUMPSEAT	COMINT	1971
PARCAE	ELINT	1977
CHALET VORTEX MERCURY	COMINT/TELINT	1975
MAGNUM ORION	TELINT/COMINT	1985
TRUMPET	COMINT	1993

submarines to collect intelligence in or near the territorial waters of the Soviet Union, as discussed in Chapter 8. M also represented a Navy SCI system—MEDITATE—that concerned information about IVY BELLS–type operations. Subsequently, the terms "Naval Activities Support Program (NASP)" and "DNI's Special Access Program (DSAP)" appear to have replaced SNCP and MEDITATE, respectively. In the 1970s the Navy also established the JENNIFER compartment for information concerning Project AZORIAN—the effort to raise a Soviet nuclear submarine that had sunk in the Pacific Ocean.[78]

Code words used to restrict access to documents pertaining to covert action have included VEIL (during the 1980s) and PEARL. It was an order classified TOP SECRET PEARL that authorized the CIA to operate "freely and fully" in Afghanistan in the aftermath of the terrorist attacks of September 11, 2001. Code words associated with the targeted killings of al-Qaeda members include SYLVAN and MAGNOLIA.[79]

Along with code words indicating compartments for SCI, there are designators used as dissemination controls for intelligence information. Some designators stipulate "Dissemination and Extraction of Information Controlled by Originator"(ORCON), or that information is not releasable to foreign nationals (NOFORN). A 1995 Director of Central Intelligence Directive explained that NOFORN might be used on intelligence that, "if released to foreign governments or nationals, could jeopardize intelligence sources or methods, or when it would

TABLE 19.3   Overhead Imagery System Code Words

CODE WORD	MISSION	INITIAL OPERATION
AQUATONE CHALICE IDEALIST	Imagery	1956
CORONA	Search	1960
ARGON	Mapping	1961
GAMBIT	Close look	1963
LANYARD	Close look	1963
QUILL	Radar imagery	1964
OXCART	Aerial Imagery	1968
EARNING	Aerial Imagery	1968
HEXAGON	Search	1971
KENNAN CRYSTAL	Real-time EO	1976
INDIGO LACROSSE ONYX	Radar imagery	1988

not be in the best interest of the United States." When one NOFORN document, the 1977 CIA study *Foreign Intelligence and Security Services: Israel,* became public after its seizure from the U.S. embassy in Tehran, it caused acute embarrassment to both the Israeli and U.S. governments because it alleged that Israeli intelligence had blackmailed, bugged, wiretapped, and offered bribes to U.S. government employees in an effort to gain sensitive information. An Israeli spokesman denounced the allegations as "ridiculous."[80]

Other dissemination controls indicate which particular country (designated by a trigraph) or countries are eligible to receive certain items of intelligence. Thus, Top Secret intelligence releasable only to Canada and the United Kingdom would be designated TOP SECRET//CAN GBR.[81]

Access to intelligence information also involves policies concerning personnel security as well as physical security—particularly with regard to Sensitive Compartmented Information.

Traditionally, a more stringent background investigation was required to gain access to SCI than was required to gain access to Top Secret information. The logic was that whereas denial of a Top Secret clearance required the presence of a well-defined character or personality defect that posed a threat to national security, "no risk is tolerable where SCI is involved and individuals who have been granted Top Secret clearances may be denied approval for access to SCI." National Security Directive 63, of October 21, 1993, established the practice of single-scope background investigations, which allow the same minimum standards for Top Secret and SCI background investigations. The directive does not prohibit more stringent requirements for access to SCI, however. Thus, an SCI screening interview might delve into an individual's family, financial, sexual, drug, criminal, political, travel, mental health, and physical histories.[82]

ICD 704, of October 1, 2008, "Personnel Security Standards and Procedures Governing Eligibility for Access to Sensitive Compartmented Information and Other Controlled Access Program Information," provides the DNI's guidance on the subject. It delegates to the heads of Intelligence Community elements the authority to grant access to SCI in accordance with the directive. The directive states general policy, personnel security standards, exceptions to those standards, and the responsibilities of assorted officials. An Intelligence Community Policy Guidance document, issued on October 2 of the same year, concerned denial or revocation of access to SCI—and includes a specification of the documents and information that an individual will be supplied with if access is denied or revoked.[83]

ICD 705, issued in May 2010, focuses on the facilities that house SCI. It states DNI policy with regard to the facilities—including that "all SCI must be processed, stored, used or discussed in an accredited SCIF [Sensitive Compartmented Information Facility]—and that "all SCIFs shall be accredited prior to being used for the processing, storage, use, or discussion of SCI." More detailed guidance is supplied in Intelligence Community Standard Number 705–1 ("Physical and Technical Security Standards for Sensitive Compartmented Information Facilities") and Number 705–2 ("Standards for the Accreditation and Reciprocal Use of Sensitive Compartmented Information)—both of which were issued in September 2010.[84]

Standard 705–1 covers authority, purpose, applicability, reciprocal use, risk management, SCIF planning and design, physical and technical security standards, waivers, operations and management, and roles and responsibilities. The section on technical security standards covers perimeter security, access control systems, intrusion detection, unclassified telecommunications systems, and portable electronic devices.[85]

Notes

1. DCID 1/13, "Coordination of Collection and Exploitation of Imagery Intelligence," February 2, 1973, *Declassified Documents Reference System (DDRS)* 1980–132D; DCID 1/13, "Committee on Imagery Requirements and Exploitation," July 1, 1967, *DDRS* 1980–132B; U.S. Congress Senate Select Committee to Study Governmental Operations with Respect to Intelligence Activities, *Final Report, Book I: Foreign and Military Intelligence* (Washington, D.C.: U.S. Government Printing Office, 1976), p. 85.

2. Roland S. Inlow, "An Appraisal of the Morison Espionage Trial," *First Principles* 11, 4 (May 1986): 1–5.

3. CINPACFLT Instruction S3822.1E, PACOM Imagery Reconnaissance Procedures and Responsibilities, July 5, 1983, p. 1; HQ EUCOM Directive No. 40–4, "Exploitation and Dissemination of Time-Sensitive Imagery," November 4, 1983, p. 1.

4. DCID 2/9, "Management of National Imagery Intelligence," June 1, 1992.

5. Jeffrey T. Richelson, *America's Secret Eyes in Space: The US Keyhole Spy Satellite Program* (New York: Harper & Row, 1990), pp. 252–256. On the directorate's other functions, see Gene Reich, "Source Directorate Expands," *Pathfinder*, May–June 2006, pp. 9–10.

6. Walter Pincus, "Space Imagery Overhaul Aims at Better Data and Easier Access," *Washington Post*, January 20, 1998, p. A7.

7. National Security Agency, *NSA Transition Briefing Book* (Fort George G. Meade: NSA, 1980), not paginated; National Security Agency/Central Security Service, *NSA/CSS Manual 22–1* (Fort Meade, Md.: NSA, 1986), p. 1.

8. Department of Justice, *Report on CIA-Related Electronic Surveillance Activities* (Washington, D.C.: Department of Justice, 1976), pp. 77–79.

9. Private information.

10. George A. Brownell, *The Origins and Development of the National Security Agency* (Laguna Hills, Calif.: Aegean Park Press, 1981), p. 3.

11. James Bamford, *The Puzzle Palace: A Report on NSA, America's Most Secret Agency* (Boston: Houghton Mifflin, 1982), p. 50; Department of Justice, *Report on CIA-Related Electronic Surveillance Activities*, p. 91; DCID 6/1, "Communications Intelligence Committee," October 21, 1958, *DDRS* 1980–130C; DCID 6/2, "Electronic Intelligence Committee," October 21, 1958, *DDRS*, 1980–130D; DCID 6/1, "SIGINT Committee," May 1, 1962, *DDRS* 1980–131D.

12. Department of the Army, Office of the Deputy Chief of Staff for Intelligence, *Annual Historical Review, 1 October 1992 to 30 September 1993*, n.d., p. 4-4.

13. U.S. Congress, Senate Select Committee to Study Governmental Operations with Respect to Intelligence Activities, *Final Report, Book I, Foreign and Military Intelligence*, p. 85.

14. Naval Intelligence Command, *Naval Intelligence Command (NAVINTCOM) History for CY-1972*, August 1, 1973, p. 20.

15. Department of the Army, *Office of the Assistant Chief of Staff for Intelligence Annual Historical Review, 1 October 1984–30 September 1985*, p. 2–30; Department of the Army, Office of the Deputy Chief of Staff for Intelligence, *Annual Historical Review, 1 October 1990–30 September 1991*, p. 4–34; Lois G. Brown, "National SIGINT Committee," *NSA Newsletter*, February 1997, p. 2; Department of the Army, *Office of the Assistant Chief of Staff for Intelligence Annual Historical Review, 1 October 1984–30 September 1985*, p. 2–30; Department of the Army, Office of the Deputy Chief of Staff for Intelligence, *Annual Historical Review, 1 October 1990–30 September 1991*, p. 4-34; Brown, "National SIGINT Committee," p. 2.

16. Brown, "National SIGINT Committee"; Naval Intelligence Command, *Naval Intelligence Command (NAVINTCOM) History for CY-1972*, p. 19.

17. Michael V. Hayden, Director, DIRgram-417, "Evolving Role of the National SIGINT Committee," April 18, 2005.

18. Department of Justice, *Report on CIA-Related Electronic Surveillance Activities*, pp. 101–103.

19. Ibid., p. 103.

20. U.S. Congress, Senate Select Committee to Study Governmental Activities with Respect to Intelligence Activities, *Final Report, Book I, Foreign and Military Intelligence*, pp. 85–86; U.S. Congress, House Permanent Select Committee on Intelligence, *Annual Report* (Washington, D.C.: U.S. Government Printing Office, 1978), p. 55; Stephen J. Flanagan, "The Coordination of National Intelligence," in *Public Policy and Political Institutions: United States Defense and Foreign Policy—Policy Coordination and Integration*, ed. Duncan Clarke (Greenwich, Conn: JAI, 1985), p. 177.

21. National Security Agency, *NSA Transition Briefing Book*, not paginated.

22. See Jeffrey T. Richelson, *American Espionage and the Soviet Target* (New York: Morrow, 1987), pp. 120–126.

23. Bamford, *The Puzzle Palace*, pp. 184–184, 216–231; U.S. Congress, House Committee on Armed Services, *Inquiry into the U.S.S. Pueblo and EC-121 Plane Incidents* (Washington, D.C.: U.S. Government Printing Office, 1969); "Radar Detector Aboard SR-71 Alerted Plane to Missile Attack," *New York Times*, August 29, 1983, p. 3.

24. U.S. Congress, Senate Select Committee to Study Governmental Operations with Respect to Intelligence Activities, *Final Report, Book I: Foreign and Military Intelligence*, p. 335; Sherry Sontag and Christopher Drew with Annette Lawrence Drew, *Blind Man's Bluff: The Untold Story of American Submarine Espionage* (New York: Public Affairs, 1998), p. 83.

25. U.S. Congress, House Committee on Appropriations, *Department of Defense Appropriations for 1994, Part 1* (Washington, D.C.: U.S. Government Printing Office, 1993), p. 37; Col. Thomas G. Shepherd, chief, Reconnaissance Programs Division, J-3, Memorandum for the Record: "Conversation Between Colonel Earnest R. Harden (USAF Ret.) and Colonel Thomas G. Shepherd, OJCS/JRC, 11 August 1977," August 12, 1977.

26. Joint Chiefs of Staff, JCS Publication 4, *Organization and Functions of the Joint Chiefs of Staff* (Washington, D.C.: U.S. Government Printing Office, 1985), pp. III-3–28 to III-3–29.

27. Charles P. Wilson, *Strategic Reconnaissance in the Middle East* (Washington, D.C.: Washington Institute for Near East Policy, 1997), pp. 13–14; Chairman of the Joint Chiefs of Staff Instruction, CJCSI 3141.01D, "Management and Review of Campaign and Contingency Plans," April 24, 2008, p. B-2.

28. Department of Defense Inspector General, Report No. 97–031, *Evaluation Report on Measurement and Signature Intelligence*, p. 2, "An Introduction to MASINT," www.nmia.org/masint.htm; Intelligence Community Directive 300, "Management, Integration, and Oversight of Intelligence and Covert Action," October 3, 2006.

29. ICD 304, "Human Intelligence," March 6, 2008 (Amended July 9, 2009), p. 2.

30. Ibid., p. 1.

31. Ibid., p. 3.

32. Ibid., p. 4.

33. Ibid., pp. 3 n. 3, 4.

34. Central Intelligence Agency, "Statement to Employees by Director of Central Intelligence Agency General Michael V. Hayden on the First Meeting of the HUMINT Enterprise Board of Governors," March 8, 2007, www.cia.gov; U.S. Congress, Senate Select Committee on Intelligence, "Questions for the Record, Ambassador Philip S. Goldberg, Nominee to Be Assistant Secretary for Intelligence and Research at the Department of State," 2009, p. 5.

35. U.S. Congress, Senate Select Committee to Study Governmental Operations with Respect to Intelligence Activities, *Final Report, Book I, Foreign and Military Intelligence*, p. 85 n. 42.

36. DCID 3/7, "Human Resources Committee," October 12, 1982.

37. U.S. Congress, Senate Select Committee to Study Governmental Operations with Respect to Intelligence Activities, *Final Report, Book I, Foreign and Military Intelligence*, pp. 86–87; Department of the Army, Office of the Assistant Chief of Staff for Intelligence, *Annual Historical Review, 1 October 1976–30 September 1977*, n.d., pp. 28–34.

38. U.S. Congress, Senate Select Committee to Study Governmental Operations with Respect to Intelligence Activities, *Final Report, Book I, Foreign and Military Intelligence*, p. 86.

39. Ibid.

40. Scott Armstrong, "Intelligence Experts Had Early Doubts About Shah's Stability," *Washington Post*, February 2, 1982, pp. 1, 9.

41. Flanagan, "The Coordination of National Intelligence," p. 177; Navy Operational Intelligence Center, *Command History for CY 1987*, May 20, 1988, p. 7.

42. Remarks by Robert M. Gates, Director of Central Intelligence, to Association of Former Intelligence Officers, Boston, November 14, 1992, p. 5.

43. Teresa M. Jones, "The National HUMINT Requirements Tasking Center," *Communiqué*, October–November 1997, pp. 11–12.

44. Department of State, Subject: (U) Encryption Technologies, July 2, 1993.

45. Jones, "The National HUMINT Requirements Tasking Center."

46. State Department, "Reporting and Collection Needs: The United Nations," July 31, 2009, available at www.nytimes.com.

47. State Department, "Reporting and Collection Needs: Palestinian Issues," October 31, 2008, www.cryptome.org.

48. Jones, "The National HUMINT Requirements Tasking Center."

49. U.S. Congress, House Permanent Select Committee on Intelligence, *IC 21: Intelligence Community in the 21st Century* (Washington, D.C.: U.S. Government Printing Office, 1996), p. 194 n.; Ken Dilanian, "Data-seeking cables ignored, officials say," *Los Angeles Times*, December 3, 2010, p. A8; Mark Mazzetti, "Blurring Line Between Spy and Diplomat," *New York Times*, November 29, 2010, pp. A1, A11.

50. Office of the Director of National Intelligence, ODNI Press Release No. 3–05, "Establishment of the National Clandestine Service (NCS)," October 13, 2005; Information provided by CIA Public Affairs Office.

51. U.S. Congress, House Select Committee to Investigate Covert Arms Transactions with Iran and Senate Select Committee on Secret Military Assistance to Iran and the Nicaraguan Opposition, *Report of the Congressional Committees Investigating the Iran-Contra Affair with Supplemental, Minority, and Additional Views* (Washington, D.C.: U.S. Government Printing Office, 1987), pp. 376–377; Caspar Weinberger, Memorandum to the Secretary of the Army, Subject: DOD Support [to CIA Special] Activities, June 13, 1983, p. 1; U.S. Congress, Senate Select Committee on Intelligence, *U.S. Actions Regarding Iranian and Other Arms Transfers to the Bosnian Army, 1994–1995*, 1996, p. 3.

52. U.S. Congress, Senate Select Committee on Intelligence, *U.S. Actions Regarding Iranian and Other Arms Transfers to the Bosnian Army, 1994–1995*, p. 3.

53. William G. Hinsleigh, "Covert Action: An Update," *Studies in Intelligence*, Spring 1986.

54. Ibid.; NSDD 159, "Covert Action Approval and Coordination Procedures," January 18, 1985; NSDD 266, "Implementation of the Recommendations of the President's Special Review Board," March 31, 1987 p. 7.

55. George W. Bush, National Security Presidential Directive-1 (NSPD-1), "Organization of the National Security Council System," February 13, 2001.

56. Barack Obama, Presidential Policy Directive-1, Subject: Organization of the National Security Council, February 13, 2009. The size and composition of the committee suggests that some smaller subcommittee would actually sit with regard to covert action issues.

57. Barack Obama, Executive Order 13526 of December 29, 2009, "Classified National Security Information," *Federal Register* 75, 2 (January 5, 2010): 707–731 at 707–708.

58. *Documents from the U.S. Espionage Den (52): U.S.S.R., the Aggressive East* (Tehran: Muslim Students Following the Line of the Imam, n.d.), pp. 46–94; Army Regulation 381–47, "U.S. Army Offensive Counterintelligence Operations," May 15, 1982, p. B-1.

59. Barack Obama, Executive Order 13526 of December 29, 2009, "Classified National Security Information," p. 722.

60. NFIB Security Committee, "Sensitive Compartmented Information: Characteristics and Security Requirements," June 1984, p. 1.

61. Air Force Directorate of Security Forces, "Guidelines for CAPCO Markings," May 30, 2006.

62. Quoted in David Wise, *The Politics of Lying: Governmental Deception, Secrecy, and Power* (New York: Viking, 1973), p. 86.

63. Ronald Lewin, *The American Magic: Codes, Ciphers and the Defeat of Japan* (New York: Farrar, Straus & Giroux, 1982), p. 17; Anthony Cave Brown, *The Last Hero* (New York: Times Books, 1982), p. 183.

64. Bamford, *The Puzzle Palace*, p. 314; Nigel West, *MI6: British Secret Intelligence Service Operations, 1909–1945* (London: Weidenfeld and Nicolson, 1983), p. 163; Cave Brown, *The Last Hero*, p. 182; David Martin, *Wilderness of Mirrors* (New York: Harper & Row, 1980), p. 15.

65. Bamford, *The Puzzle Palace*, p. 314.

66. Wise, *The Politics of Lying*, p. 83; Jack Anderson, "Syrians Strive to Out Arafat as PLO Chief," *Washington Post*, November 10, 1982, p. D22; Bob Woodward, "ACDA Aide Faulted on Security," *Washington Post*, November 4, 1986, pp. A1, A16; National Intelligence Council, *National Intelligence Daily (Cable)*, December 13, 1983.

67. Bamford, *The Puzzle Palace*, p. 120.

68. "Director of Central Intelligence Declassification Decisions," May 18, 1998; SSO USAF, Subject: Elimination of COMINT and TK Codewords," October 22, 1999; SSO DIA, Subject: Implementation Guidance for Elimination of Codewords," October 22, 1999.

69. Bob Woodward, "Messages of Activists Intercepted," *Washington Post*, October 13, 1975, pp. 1, 14.

70. Ibid.; Seymour Hersh, *The Price of Power: Kissinger in the Nixon White House* (New York: Summit, 1983), p. 183.

71. Department of Defense Inspector General, IR-96–03, *Final Report on the Verification Inspection of the National Security Agency*, February 13, 1996, p. 13; SSO DIA, Subject: Implementation Guidance for Elimination of Codewords; Office of the Under Secretary of Defense for Intelligence, *Classification and Control Marking Implementation Manual*, April 1, 2008, p. 15; National Reconnaissance Office, *National Reconnaissance Office Review and Redaction Guide for Automatic Declassification of 25-Year-Old Information, Version 1*, 2006, p. 119.

72. Seymour Hersh, *"The Target Is Destroyed":What Really Happened to Flight 007 and What America Knew About It* (New York: Random House, 1986), p. 4; private information.

73. James Ott, "Espionage Trial Highlights CIA Problems," *Aviation Week & Space Technology*, November 27, 1978, pp. 21–22; Gregory A. Fossedal, "U.S. Said to Be Unable to Verify Missile Ban," *Washington Times*, November 18, 1987, p. A6; Dale Van Atta, "The Death of the State Secret," *New Republic*, February 18, 1985, pp. 20–23; SSO DIA, Subject: Implementation Guideline for Elimination of Codewords; SSO USAF, Subject: Elimination of COMINT and TK Codewords.

74. William E. Burrows, *Deep Black: Space Espionage and National Security* (New York: Random House, 1986), p. 23; Bob Woodward, *Veil: The Secret Wars of the CIA, 1981–1987* (New York: Simon & Schuster, 1987), pp. 221–224; private information.

75. Admiral David Jeremiah et al., *Report to the Director National Reconnaissance Office: Defining the Future of the NRO for the 21st Century, Final Report*, August 26, 1996, p. 171; Peter B. Teets, Memorandum for Director of Central Intelligence, Subject: Retirement of the BYEMAN Control System, January 4, 2005.

76. Teets, Memorandum for Director of Central Intelligence, Subject; Retirement of the BYEMAN Control System, January 4, 2005.

77. U.S. Strategic Command, *Organization and Functions Manual*, August 17, 1992, p. 61; private information.

78. HQ USAF, ACS, I, INOI 205–4, "Designation of Special Security Officer (SSO), TK Control Officer (TCO), Gamma Control Officer (GCO), and Bravo Control Officer (BCO)," March 15, 1985, p. 2; private information; Norman Polmar and Michael White, *Project AZORIAN: The CIA and the Raising of the K-129* (Annapolis, Md.: Naval Institute Press, 2010), pp. 59, 63.

79. Bob Woodward, *Bush at War* (New York: Simon & Schuster, 2002), p. 101; Bob Woodward, *Obama's War* (New York: Simon & Schuster 2010), p. 6.

80. Office of the Under Secretary of Defense for Intelligence, *Department of Defense Classification and Control Markings Implementation Manual*, p. 33; Director of Central Intelligence Directive 1/7, "Security Controls on the Dissemination of Intelligence Information," April 12, 1995, p. 3; Scott Armstrong, "Israelis Have Spied on U.S., Secret Papers Show," *Washington Post*, February 1, 1982, pp. A1, A18; "Israel Calls Report on CIA Findings Ridiculous," *Washington Post*, February 3, 1982, p. 10.

81. Stephen A. Cambone, Memorandum, Subject: Security Classification Marking Instructions, September 27, 2004, with attachment: "Security Classification Marking Instructions."

82. NFIB Security Committee, "Sensitive Compartmented Information," p. 3; National Security Directive 63, "Single Scope Background Investigations," October 21, 1991; U.S. Strategic Command, USSTRATCOM Administrative Instruction 321–28, *Sensitive Compartmented Information (SCI) Personnel Security Operating Policy and Procedures*, June 30, 1992, pp. 25–27.

83. Intelligence Community Directive Number 704, "Personnel Security Standards and Procedures Governing Eligibility for Access to Sensitive Compartmented Information and Other Controlled Access Program Information," October 1, 2008; Intelligence Community Policy Guidance Number 704.3, "Denial or Revocation of Access to Sensitive Compartmented Information, Other Controlled Access Program Information, and Appeals Processes, October 2, 2008.

84. Intelligence Community Directive Number 705, "Sensitive Compartmented Information Facilities," May 26, 2010; Intelligence Community Standard Number 705–1, "Physical

and Technical Security Standards for Sensitive Compartmented Information Facilities," September 17, 2010; Intelligence Community Standard Number 705–2, "Standards for the Accreditation and Reciprocal Use of Sensitive Compartmented Information," September 17, 2010.

85. Intelligence Community Standard Number 705–1, "Physical and Technical Security Standards for Sensitive Compartmented Information Facilities."

20

U.S. INTELLIGENCE IN THE TWENTY-FIRST CENTURY

While the end of the Cold War produced a shift both in U.S. intelligence priorities and in the architecture of U.S. intelligence collection operations—as exemplified by the National Security Agency's closure of major European ground stations—the terrorist attacks of September 11, 2001, served as the catalyst for even more drastic changes.

The major organizational change, of course, was the elimination of the position of Director of Central Intelligence and the creation of a Director of National Intelligence. While the creation of the post of DNI was a change internal to the Intelligence Community, probably the more significant changes that had to be faced were external ones—some resulting from U.S. government decisions, others from the action of foreign states or groups, and still others from changes in technologies, particularly communications technologies.

The terrorist attacks produced several U.S. responses—including a more extensive (in terms of scope, resources, and methods) effort against terrorism, and particularly al-Qaeda—with much of the effort actually or ostensibly covert. The attacks also resulted in the major U.S. combat operation in Afghanistan that continues to this day. And they undoubtedly helped push President George W. Bush further along the path of toppling Saddam Hussein by whatever means were necessary—although historians will certainly debate just how influential the 9/11 factor was in comparison to other considerations.

In addition, the DNI has had to deal with the nuclear programs of the two remaining members of the Axis of Evil—the regimes ruling Iran and North Korea. While Kim Jong-Il's regime has already detonated two devices, Iran is clearly making an intensive effort to allow for the incorporation of nuclear weapons in its arsenal.

Naturally, one topic of discussion has been how creation of the DNI position has helped solve assorted problems that plagued the Intelligence Community prior to 9/11—from information sharing between foreign intelligence agencies (e.g., CIA and NSA) to the "wall" between domestic and foreign intelligence. Thus, in April

2010, the Bipartisan Policy Center, a Washington think-tank, sponsored a series of panels on intelligence reform, one of which asked "What Are the Future Challenges for the Director of National Intelligence?" Among those participating was former DNI Admiral Mike McConnell, who suggested enhancing the DNI's powers further and establishing a Department of Intelligence that the DNI would head.[1]

But before greater power is given to the DNI or other decisions are made about Intelligence Community reorganization, it might be useful to examine the very concept of the Intelligence Community, some dramatic changes in the world in recent years, and the extent to which there is intelligence activity outside the Intelligence Community.

WHAT IS THE INTELLIGENCE COMMUNITY?

The answer to the question "What is the Intelligence Community" is one that can be found in the frequently-asked-questions sections of various Intelligence Community organizations' websites, or in executive orders on intelligence. Despite whatever minor variations in wording might exist, the fundamental answer is the same: The Intelligence Community consists of the Office of the DNI plus sixteen additional organizations: the Central Intelligence Agency; the Defense Intelligence Agency; the Bureau of Intelligence and Research; the National Reconnaissance Office; the National Geospatial-Intelligence Agency; the National Security Agency; one intelligence element each from the Treasury, Homeland Security, Justice, and Energy departments; an intelligence element from the Drug Enforcement Administration; and the intelligence elements from the five armed services (Army, Navy, Air Force, Marines, Coast Guard).

The fact that the Intelligence Community comprises seventeen different organizations has prompted many individuals to wonder about the need for so many separate organizations that seem to be doing the same thing. Some have called for a simpler community or decentralization; others, for more authority on the part of the DNI to make the different organizations "work together."[2] But the Intelligence Community is actually much more complex than this debate might imply—and that complexity may have significant implications for how the community should be organized.

Indeed, as noted in Chapter 17, the Office of the DNI actually contains within it several organizations with very different functions. Consider, for example, the National Intelligence Council, the National Counterterrorism Center, and the National Counterproliferation Center. These organizations do more than simply assist the DNI in managing the effort of the other sixteen organizations: They produce their own products. Each could exist outside the DNI's office.

A closer look at some of the ostensibly single intelligence elements that make up the Intelligence Community, particularly the DIA and military services intelligence organizations, produces comparable results. In addition to DIA's directorates, DIA has a number of centers that are subordinate to its Directorate of Analysis. These centers are the National Center for Medical Intelligence (NCMI), the Underground Facilities Analysis Center (UFAC), and the Missile and Space Intelligence Center (MSIC). The directorate is also responsible for the National Media Exploitation Center (NMEC).

Similarly, the Air Force's intelligence apparatus is far more complex than would appear to be the case from counting it as one member of the Intelligence Community. The issue is not that there is a deputy chief of staff for intelligence, surveillance, and reconnaissance as well as the Air Force Intelligence, Surveillance, and Reconnaissance Agency but, rather, that within the latter one finds both the National Air and Space Intelligence Center (NASIC) and the Air Force Technical Applications Center (AFTAC). And the Army's intelligence establishment comprises not only a deputy chief of staff as well as a major collection agency, the Intelligence and Security Command (INSCOM), but also a major analytical center, the National Ground Intelligence Center (NGIC), which is subordinate to INSCOM.

Many of these centers—particularly those in DIA and the military services—had long histories during which they were not part of their current parent organization. In some cases, this outcome reflects the evolution of military intelligence—in which technical intelligence organizations, such as the earlier versions of NASIC and NGIC, grew out of materiel and ordnance procurement organizations rather than out of the service intelligence organizations.

In some cases, two additional factors set the centers apart from their parent organizations—geographic location and culture. For example, NCMI is located at Ft. Detrick, Maryland, and MSIC is headquartered in Huntsville, Alabama, where it began as the Special Security Office of the Army Ballistic Missile Agency—not at DIA headquarters at Bolling Air Force Base, Washington. NGIC's home is Charlottesville, Virginia, a substantial distance from INSCOM's Northern Virginia's headquarters. NASIC headquarters is at the same base, Wright-Patterson AFB in Ohio, as its earlier incarnations—such as the Foreign Technology Division of the Air Force Systems Command. The Air Force Technical Applications Center has been at the same location for decades, Patrick AFB in Florida, rather than in the Pentagon where the Air Force's intelligence chief is to be found or in Texas where the AFISR Agency has its headquarters. And it would not be surprising if there were significant cultural differences between those organizations and their parent organizations as a consequence of their histories, their specialities, and their geographic separation.

Such differences are arguably of no great importance, especially given modern communications capabilities. And the difference between being labeled a center and being labeled a directorate could be considered simply a matter of semantics or internal public relations (though the term *center* sounds more prestigious). But what is truly relevant to the question of intelligence organization is the extent to which some of the centers are simply residing within other organizations rather than being an integral part of the organization. For example, when the CIA's Directorate of Intelligence produces a study of the Iranian nuclear program or missile development in China, it will likely rely, in part, on the raw intelligence that the other two key components of the agency—the National Clandestine Service and the Directorate of Science and Technology—have obtained.

In contrast, INSCOM headquarters does not produce products that integrate the production of NGIC, and the AFISR Agency headquarters does not produce finished intelligence that builds on the work of NASIC. The agency's core activities comprise a variety of collection operations—SIGINT, HUMINT, and MASINT—that do not produce finished intelligence. NASIC's product is usually the end of the line for the AFISR Agency's finished intelligence product—at least within that agency.

The most dramatic case is AFTAC. At one time it was completely separate from the traditional Air Force intelligence structure—a recognition that it was truly a national collection agency, responsible for operating the U.S. Atomic Energy Detection System. Since then it has become an organization "administratively supported" by the Air Intelligence Agency (AIA) and is now a component of AIA's successor. But AFTAC's product is not integrated into its parent agency's product. Its key relationships are with the Joint Atomic Energy Intelligence Committee, the Energy Department intelligence organizations, the CIA, the DIA, and other organizations involved in nuclear intelligence.

Such cases raise the possibility that at least some of these centers might be removed from their parent organizations and have a more independent and productive existence, whether as parts of the Department of Defense or as national agencies. In this connection, there are several key questions that need to be answered with regard to such centers: (1) Is the center's work integrated into the agency's larger effort, and if so, to what extent? (2) Who are its primary consumers? (3) How diverse is its customer base, and what is the distribution of effort among its customers? (4) Is its current subordinate status hindering its ability to work for key customers?

CHANGING TARGETS AND TECHNOLOGIES

China may currently be considered a more urgent target than Russia—but there is a certain similarity in the approaches to monitoring today's China and yesterday's Soviet Union. Both are large nations, with an extensive array of military facilities and test sites. And much of what the United States wants to monitor can still be accomplished through its array of reconnaissance and surveillance assets—from space systems to undersea intelligence collectors.

Even though nations with much smaller and covert nuclear programs represent a greater challenge, from an intelligence standpoint they are similar in some respects to large nation states with overt programs. The terrorist target is, as has often been noted, more elusive and far less susceptible to technical collection than traditional targets such as Chinese strategic weapons programs—at least, remote technical collection.* An additional consideration has to do with the shifting locations of terrorist activities of primary concern.

---

*Nevertheless, it is far easier to retask an imagery satellite or to move a SIGINT satellite to cover a new area than it is to establish human sources where there were none previously or to get an emplaced sensor near a target.

Thus, Afghanistan—which somewhat fell off the list of significant collection targets after the Soviet departure and became a more important target in the late 1990s—emerged as a primary target after 9/11. And very recently the significance of Yemen as a target has grown dramatically.

Indeed, Yemen could be the poster-child for the variability of nations important to the U.S. Intelligence Community. Such dramatic shifts in targets call for dramatic changes in expertise—requiring that the Intelligence Community, particularly its analytical elements, have greater access to outside experts in universities or to private contractors than it did during the Cold War, as well as an infusion of outside help in country experts and linguists.

Changing technologies can be both a problem and a potential solution. They may also have an impact on judgments concerning Intelligence Community management and direction. The dramatic changes in communication technology have been well reported—with regard to communication devices (cell-phones, Blackberry devices, personal computers), the method of transmission (fiber optic cables), and the quantum leap in the volume of communication traffic. Clearly these changes have challenged and stressed the U.S. SIGINT effort.

But, as suggested above, there are also ways in which technology has aided the U.S. intelligence effort. One is the ability to produce relatively low-cost collection systems—including the satellites being developed by the Pentagon's Operationally Responsive Space Office as well as numerous UAVs, which are smaller and cheaper than the better-known Predators and Reapers. In addition to flying those UAVs, the Air Force has in its arsenal the RQ-11B Ravena "back-packable" UAV (with color electro-optical and infrared cameras), which has been used in Afghanistan and Iraq.[3]

Equally important are the improvements being made in dissemination technologies as well as the ability to transform, merge, and exploit data gathered by collection systems—including data gathered by collection systems from different disciplines.

These technological advances are particularly important given the extent of U.S. combat operations in Afghanistan and Iraq over the last decade. When the priority of intelligence support to military operations was raised during the Clinton administration, with the signing of Presidential Decision Directive–35, there was no apparent need for the increase in priority. But to the extent that the United States remains engaged in either major combat operations or significant counterterrorist operations conducted by U.S. special forces and special mission units (Delta Force or the Naval Special Warfare Development Group), the ability to conduct extensive intelligence, surveillance, and reconnaissance operations and quickly deliver the information gathered to those on the front lines will remain of major importance.

In addition to changing technologies making such support more extensive, cheaper, and less classified, they also raise the question of how much of that effort needs to be provided by the Intelligence Community (and managed by the DNI or by DIA) in contrast to the organizations conducting the military operations or other intelligence organizations outside of the Intelligence Community. Certainly, the Intelligence Community has played a significant role, such as NRO and CIA assistance with the location of IEDs or the NGA's provision of "tool kits" for analyzing data or research and development work on processing and analytical techniques—and this significant role will continue into the future. But the availability of low-cost collection systems allows direct procurement by operational organizations, which may be the best judge of exactly what capabilities will work for them. In addition, there are a multitude of intelligence organizations outside the Intelligence Community that can be of assistance.

OUTSIDE THE INTELLIGENCE COMMUNITY

It is misleading not only to conceive of the Intelligence Community as consisting of seventeen organizations but also to equate the Intelligence Community with the overall extent of U.S. government intelligence activities. In some cases the additional intelligence capabilities come from organizations dedicated to intelligence activities; in other cases an organization's contribution to the intelligence effort may be a secondary or tertiary activity.

As noted in Chapter 6, two of the Intelligence Community's elements, the DEA's Office of National Security Intelligence and the Treasury Department's Office of Intelligence and Analysis, are components of larger intelligence organizations—the DEA's Intelligence Division and the Treasury's Office of Terrorism and Financial Intelligence, which are not elements of the Intelligence Community. A number of intelligence organizations in executive departments also fall outside of the Intelligence Community. For example, in addition to its DEA-based narcotics intelligence effort, the Justice Department operates the National Drug Intelligence Center in Pennsylvania, and the Department of Transportation also operates an Office of Intelligence, Security, and Emergency Response.

Many of the various agencies that were absorbed into the Department of Homeland Security (DHS) had intelligence units when they were absorbed, and they still operate those units. Specifically, a Congressional Research Service study of the Homeland Security Intelligence Enterprise identified five intelligence organizations operated by department components other than the one that is formally part of the Intelligence Community. Thus, Customs and Border Protection, Immigration and Customs Enforcement, Citizenship and Immigration Services, the Transportation Security Administration, and the Secret Service all contain intelligence units. Hence the need to establish a Homeland Security Intelligence Council. The DHS Intelligence organization chart is shown as Figure 20.1.[4]

In the past, some intelligence activity, such as that conducted by border or immigration units had no significant national security component (other than that pertaining to the occasional, and usually unproductive, Soviet illegal). Today, by contrast, the intelligence activities of the Homeland Security components involved in border security or immigration law enforcement can help avert a terrorist attack, and intelligence provided by the CIA, NSA, or other agencies can allow Homeland Security enforcement agencies to apprehend individuals planning an attack.[5]

In the Department of Defense and military services one can find numerous examples of intelligence organizations, or organizations that perform some intelligence activities, that are not part of the Intelligence Community. In a key sense, what the Operationally Responsive Space Office does is what the NRO does; it designs space systems to produce intelligence—but without Intelligence Community membership. Likewise, if the X-37B spaceplane were to engage in overhead collection, the office that operates it—the Air Force Rapid Capabilities Office—would become another example of an organization outside the Intelligence Community involved in intelligence activities. And, as noted in Chapter 4, the non-member Naval Criminal Investigative Service, rather than the Office of Naval Intelligence, is responsible for the Navy's HUMINT program. Nor is the NCIS the only Navy HUMINT collector. The Navy Expeditionary Intelligence Command, which reports to the Navy Expeditionary Combat Command, operates Navy Human Intelligence Teams, Expeditionary Intelligence Support Elements, and Maritime Intercept Operations/Intelligence Exploitation Teams. In the Air Force, counterintelligence is the responsibility of the Air Force Office of Special Investigations.[6]

The Joint Intelligence Operations Centers of the Combatant Commands—from the Africa Command to the Strategic Command—are also not members. Although their civilian employees now work for DIA and their budgets are provided through the National or Military Intelligence Programs, the organizations are not included in the definition of the Intelligence Community and do not send representatives to National Intelligence Board meetings.

Furthermore, each combatant command has component commands—such as the Army Special Operations Command (subordinate to the U.S. Special Operations Command) and the Air Force Space Command (subordinate to the U.S. Strategic Command)—that operate their own intelligence directorates. And in the field there are thousands of intelligence personnel in the field, attached to brigades, battalions, or squadrons. Thus, according to the Army's deputy chief of staff for intelligence, as of December 2009 over 16,000 individuals were employed by INSCOM, and the Army had another 38,000 individuals involved in intelligence activities (about 5,000 in joint DOD organizations and 33,000 with theater forces, special operations forces, and other units).[7] As noted earlier, the intelligence components of combat brigades—whether in Bosnia or Iraq—have either produced intelligence reports or applied analytical techniques to assist operations, including the hunt for Saddam Hussein.

One can also find a number of organizations that, from time to time, contribute to the U.S. intelligence effort—including the Federal Research Division (FRD) of the Library of Congress and the U.S. Geological Survey. FRD was created in 1948 as the Air Research Division, with responsibility for using the resources of the Library of Congress to identify targets in the Soviet Union. Although it no longer has an exclusive relationship with DIA and does not focus solely on intelligence work, some of its research contributes to the intelligence effort; examples include its 1984 study on Soviet denial and deception and its co-sponsorship (with the NIC) of a 2001 conference on the outlook for North Korea.[8]

FIGURE 20.1 DHS Intelligence

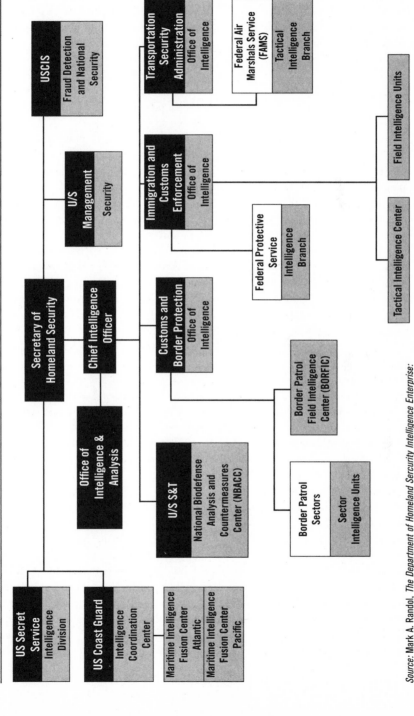

Source: Mark A. Randol, *The Department of Homeland Security Intelligence Enterprise: Operational Overview and Oversight Challenges for Congress,* March 19, 2010.

The USGS, at least as of December 1992, had a military geology project. Two years earlier it had signed a memorandum of agreement with the Air Force Technical Applications Center to specify its contribution to the nuclear detonation monitoring effort. More recently, it became a contributing organization to the DIA Underground Facilities Analysis Center.[9]

In addition, it would not be surprising to discover that the National Center for Medical Intelligence, particularly its infectious disease component, had an agreement with the Centers for Disease Control and Prevention (CDCP) to provide assistance when one or the other requested such help. Thus, not only has the NCMI produced assessments of disease in Haiti but so has the CDC—which, in December 2010, reported on the consequences of an outbreak of cholera in that nation.[10]

Also, as detailed in Chapters 9 and 10, considerable technical collection activities are conducted by organizations outside of the Intelligence Community. A significant number of platforms that gather MASINT—from DSP in space to SOSUS under the ocean—do not "belong" to members of the Intelligence Community. Similarly, the surveillance of space is carried out by a multitude of organizations that are not part of the Intelligence Community.

Given the degree to which intelligence activities permeate the U.S. government and its operations, both at home and overseas, careful thought must be given to the question of how intelligence operations are to be managed to produce optimal results. Perhaps some intelligence activities conducted by organizations outside the Intelligence Community should be moved within the community. Thus, if AFTAC were transformed into a "National Technical Applications Center," it might absorb some of the MASINT activities presently conducted by organizations outside the Intelligence Community. But in many instances, organic intelligence units can perform their limited missions without significant guidance and are likely to have a better sense than someone from the DNI's office as to what their parent organizations need in the way of intelligence support. And, clearly, unless the DNI is a computer, he or she cannot possibly manage all significant U.S. intelligence activities. Indeed, the idea that an intelligence czar could do so, or that all such activities could reside in the Intelligence Community, is misleading.

FINAL THOUGHTS

The confluence of world events and technological developments has had a significant impact on the organization of U.S. intelligence as well as on its activities and capabilities. Assessing the role and authority of the DNI requires going beyond the traditional view of equating "U.S. Intelligence" with the "U.S. Intelligence Community"—and asking not only what the DNI should do but also what the DNI should *not* do. Answering the *should not* part will be a key complement to answering the *should* part if the DNI's job is to be a manageable and productive one.

Notes

1. "Panel Discussion: What Are the Future Challenges for the Director of National Intelligence?," Bipartisan Policy Center—State of Intelligence Reform Conference, April 6, 2010, p. 4, available at www.dni.gov. Also see Richard A. Best Jr., Congressional Research Service, *Intelligence Reform After Five Years: The Role of the Director of National Intelligence (DNI)*, June 22, 2010.

2. See, for example, Doyle McManus, "How to connect the intelligence dots," *Los Angeles Times*, January 10, 2010, p. A28; Luis Garicano and Richard A. Posner, "What Our Spies Can Learn from Toyota," *Wall Street Journal*, January 13, 2010, p. A23; David Ignatius, "How about a leaner and meaner intelligence system?," www.washingtonpost.com, July 21, 2010; and Richard A. Posner, "What Our Intelligence Agencies Could Learn from Silicon Valley," *Wall Street Journal*, May 28, 2010, p. A17.

3. U.S. Air Force, Fact Sheet, "RQ-11B Raven," www.af.mil/information/factsheets, accessed December 16, 2010.

4. Mark A. Randol, Congressional Research Service, *The Department of Homeland Security Intelligence Enterprise: Operational Overview and Oversight Challenges for Congress*, March 19, 2010.

5. Richard A. Best Jr., Congressional Research Service, *Securing America's Borders: The Role of the Intelligence Community*, December 7, 2010.

6. "Navy Expeditionary Intelligence Command," www.necc.navy.mil/neic.htm, accessed November 30, 2007; Robert E. Jordon, "Navy Expeditionary Command Adds First Tactical Intelligence Unit," *Naval Intelligence Professionals Quarterly*, Spring 2008 p. 27; Office of the Chief of Naval Operations, OPNAV Instruction 3501.382, Subj: Required Operational Capabilities and Projected Operational Environment for Navy Expeditionary Intelligence Command Forces, March 1, 2010; U.S. Air Force, Fact Sheet, "Air Force Office of Special Investigations," November 22, 2010.

7. Deputy Chief of Staff, G-2, *A Strategy to Rebalance the Army MI Force*, December 15, 2009, www.dami.army.pentagon.mil.

8. Jeffrey Richelson, *American Espionage and the Soviet Target* (New York: William Morrow, 1987), pp. 252–253; Defense Intelligence Agency, *Defense Intelligence Agency Review and Analysis of the General Intelligence Career Development Program (ICDP) Annual Status Report for FY 1980 and FY 1981*, 1983, p. III-12; Federal Research Division, *Federal Research Division*, n.d.; Library of Congress, Regulation 214–10, "Functions and Organization of the Federal Research Division, Research Services," May 10, 1985; National Intelligence Council and Federal Research Division, *North Korea's Engagement: Perspectives, Outlook, and Implications: Conference Report*, May 2001.

9. United States Geological Survey, "The USGS Military Geology Project," December 1992; "Memorandum of Agreement Between the Air Force Technical Applications Center and the United States Geological Survey," April 6, 1990; Mark Esterbrook, "'Unearthing' the Truth in Defense of Our Nation," *Pathfinder* (January–February 2005): 19–21.

10. Rong-Gon Lin II, "Cholera now throughout Haiti, U.S. says," *Los Angeles Times*, December 9, 2010, p. A3.

ACRONYMS

AABL	Advanced Atmospheric Burst Locator
AARS	Advanced Airborne Reconnaissance System
ABM	Anti-Ballistic Missile
ABMA	Army Ballistic Missile Agency
ACC	Air Combat Command
ACIC	Army Counterintelligence Center
ACINT	Acoustic Intelligence
ACIS	Arms Control Intelligence Staff
ACOUSTINT	Acoustic Intelligence
ADONIS	AMOS Daylight Near-Infrared Imaging System
ADSN	AFTAC Distributed Sensor Network
AEC	Atomic Energy Commission
AEDS	U.S. Atomic Energy Detection System
AEOS	Advanced Electro-Optical System
AFAR	Azores Fixed Acoustic Range
AFIA	Air Force Intelligence Agency
AFIC	Air Force Intelligence Command
AFIS	Air Force Intelligence Service
AFISA	Air Force Intelligence Support Agency
AFISRA	Air Force Intelligence, Surveillance, and Reconnaissance Agency
AFMIC	Armed Forces Medical Intelligence Center
AFOSI	Air Force Office of Special Investigations
AFRICOM	Africa Command
AFSA	Armed Forces Security Agency
AFSAC	Air Force Special Activities Center
AFSC	Air Force Systems Command
AFSG	Air Force Security Group
AFSSS	Air Force Space Surveillance System
AFTAC	Air Force Technical Applications Center
AGER	Auxiliary General–Environmental Research

AGTR	Auxiliary General–Technical Research
AIA	Army Intelligence Agency
	Air Intelligence Agency
AID	Agency for International Development
AIO	Australian Imagery Organization
ALCOR	ARPA Lincoln C-Band Observable Radar
AMOS	Air Force Maui Optical System
AMSIC	Army Missile and Space Intelligence Center
AOMC	Army Ordnance Missile Command
AQAP	Al-Qaeda of the Arabian Peninsula
ARL	Airborne Reconnaissance Low
ARPA	Advanced Research Projects Agency
ARS	Advanced Reconnaissance System
ARSP	Advanced Reconnaissance Support Program
ASA	U.S. Army Security Agency
ASARS	Advanced Synthetic Aperture Radar System
ASAT	Anti-Satellite
ASDI	Assistant Secretary of Defense for Intelligence
ASIP	Advanced Signals Intelligence Platform
ASN	AFTAC Seismic Network
ATIC	Air Technical Intelligence Center
BBC	British Broadcasting Corporation
BCS	BYEMAN Control System
BGIO	Bundeswehr Geoinformation Office
BMDS	Ballistic Missile Defense System
BMEWS	Ballistic Missile Early Warning System
BND	Bundesnachrichtendienst (Federal Intelligence Service) (Germany)
C^3I	Command, Control, Communications, and Intelligence
C^4ISR	Command, Control, Communications, Computers, Intelligence, Surveillance, and Reconnaissance
CAMS	COMIREX Automated Management System
CAOC	Combined Air Operations Center
CAPG	Covert Action Planning Group
CCP	Consolidated Cryptologic Program
CCPC	Critical Collection Problems Committee
CCSCC	Counterintelligence and Security Countermeasures Committee
CDCP	Centers for Disease Control and Prevention
CENTCOM	Central Command
CERP	Combined Economic Reporting Program
CFJIC	Canadian Forces Joint Imagery Center
CGICC	Coast Guard Intelligence Coordination Center
CI	Counterintelligence
CIA	Central Intelligence Agency

CIC	Counterintelligence Center
CIFA	Counterintelligence Field Activity
CIFC	Combined Intelligence and Fusion Center
CIG	Central Intelligence Group
CINC	Commander-in-Chief
CIO	Central Imagery Office
CIPC	Critical Intelligence Problems Committee
CIRVIS	Communications Instructions for Reporting Vital Intelligence Sightings
CITO	Clandestine Information Technology Office
CMO	Central MASINT Office
CNC	Crime and Narcotics Center
	Counternarcotics Committee
COMINT	Communications Intelligence
COMIREX	Committee on Imagery Requirements and Exploitation
COMOR	Committee on Overhead Requirements
COMSEC	Communications Security
CONUS	Continental United States
COS	Chief of Station
CPC	Counterproliferation Center
CPD	Counterproliferation Division
CPSU	Communist Party of the Soviet Union
CRITIC	Critical Intelligence Communications
CRS	Congressional Research Service
CSB	Collection Support Brief
CSE	Communications Security Establishment (Canada)
CSIS	Canadian Security Intelligence Service
CSO	Center for Special Operations
CSS	Central Security Service
CTBT	Comprehensive Test Ban Treaty
CTIC	Counterterrorism Intelligence Center
CTPT	Counterterrorism Pursuit Teams
CTC	Counterterrorism Center
DARP	Defense Airborne Reconnaissance Program
DARPA	Defense Advanced Research Projects Agency
DAS	Defense Attaché System
DCCC	Defense Collection Coordination Center
DCGS	Distributed Common Ground System
DCGS-A	Distributed Common Ground System-Army
DCHC	Defense Counterintelligence and Human Intelligence Center
DCI	Director of Central Intelligence
DCID	Director of Central Intelligence Directive
DCP	Defense Cryptologic Program

DCSI	Deputy Chief of Staff, Intelligence
DDCI	Deputy Director of Central Intelligence
DDMS	Deputy Director for Military Support
DDNI	Deputy Director of National Intelligence
DDNS	Deputy Director for National Support
DEA	Drug Enforcement Administration
DEFSMAC	Defense Special Missile and Astronautics Center
	Defense Special Missile and Aerospace Center
DGSE	Directorate General for External Security (France)
DHS	Defense HUMINT Service
	Department of Homeland Security
DI	Directorate of Intelligence
DIA	Defense Intelligence Agency
DIAC	Defense Intelligence Analysis Center
DIATP	DIA Tactical Program
DICP	Defense Intelligence Counterdrug Program
DID	*Defense Intelligence Digest*
DIE	Defense Intelligence Estimate
DIFAR	Directional Low-Frequency Analysis and Recording
DIGO	Defence Imagery and Geospatial Organisation
DIOCC	Defense Intelligence Operations Coordination Center
DIRD	Defense Intelligence Reference Document
DISTP	Defense Intelligence Special Technologies Program
DJIOC	Defense Joint Intelligence Operations Center
DIRNSA	Director, National Security Agency
DITS	Digital Imagery Transmission System
DITSUM	*Defense Intelligence Terrorism Summary*
DMA	Defense Mapping Agency
DMS	Daily MASINT Summary
DMSP	Defense Meteorological Satellite Program
DNI	Director of National Intelligence
DNRO	Director, National Reconnaissance Office
DOD	Department of Defense
DSAP	DNI's Special Access Program
DSCS	Defense Satellite Communication Systems
DSD	Defence Signals Directorate (Australia)
DSP	Defense Support Program
DSRP	Defense Space Reconnaissance Program
DST	Directorate for Territorial Surveillance (France)
DTM	Decision-Type Memoranda
EAL	*Economic Alert List*
ECI	Exceptionally Controlled Information
EIC	Economic Intelligence Committee

ECS	Enhanced CRYSTAL System
EIW	*Economic Intelligence Weekly*
ELF	Extremely Low Frequency
ELINT	Electronic Intelligence
EMP	Electromagnetic Pulse
EPA	Environmental Protection Agency
EPIC	El Paso Intelligence Center
ERS	Expeditionary Reconnaissance Squadron
ESC	Electronic Security Command
ESMC	Eastern Space and Missile Center
EUCOM	European Command
EUCOMSITS	EUCOM Secondary Imagery Transmission System
EUDAC	European Defense Analysis Center
EXCOM	Executive Committee
FARC	Revolutionary Armed Forces of Columbia
FASTC	Foreign Aerospace Science and Technology Center
FBI	Federal Bureau of Investigation
FBIS	Foreign Broadcast Information Service
FCA	U.S. Army Foreign Counterintelligence Activity
FCIP	Foreign Counterintelligence Program
FDS	Fixed Distributed System
FEMA	Federal Emergency Management Agency
FICEURLANT	Fleet Intelligence Center, Europe and Atlantic
FICPAC	Fleet Intelligence Center Pacific
FIG	Field Intelligence Group
FINCEN	Financial Crimes Enforcement Network
FIPC	Foreign Intelligence Priorities Committee
FISINT	Foreign Instrumentation Signals Intelligence
FIST	Fleet Imagery Support Terminal
FLTSATCOM	Fleet Satellite Communications System
FMP	Foreign Materiel Program
FORSCOM	Forces Command
FOSIC	Fleet Ocean Surveillance Information Center
FRB	Foreign Resources Branch
FRD	Federal Research Division
FSB	Federal Security Service (Russia)
FSS	Fixed Surveillance System
FSTC	Foreign Science and Technology Center
FTAC	Farragut Technical Analysis Center
FTC	Foreign Technology Center
FTD	Foreign Technology Division
GBS	Global Broadcast System
GCHQ	Government Communications Headquarters (United Kingdom)

GDIP	General Defense Intelligence Program
GEODSS	Ground-Based Electro-Optical Deep Space Surveillance
GEOINT	Geospatial Intelligence
GFU	Ground Filter Unit
GID	General Intelligence Directorate (Jordan)
GIUK	Greenland-Iceland-United Kingdom
GMAIC	Guided Missile and Astronautics Intelligence Committee
GNAT	General Atomics
GPS	Global Positioning System
GRAB	Galactic Radiation and Background
GRU	Glavnoye Upravelinye Razevatelnoye—Chief Intelligence Directorate, General Staff (Russia/Soviet Union)
GTSN	Global Telemetered Seismic Network
GWOT	Global War on Terrorism
HAX	Haystack Auxiliary radar
HCS	HUMINT Control System
HF	High Frequency
HITRAC	Homeland Infrastructure Threat and Risk Analysis Center
HRC	Human Resources Committee
HSE	HUMINT Support Element
HSI	Hyperspectral Imagery
HUMINT	Human Intelligence
HUSIR	Haystack Ultra-Wideband Satellite Imaging Radar
IAEA	International Atomic Energy Agency
ICBM	Intercontinental Ballistic Missile
ICD	Intelligence Community Directive
ICE	Intelligence Collection Equipment
ICON	Image Communications and Operations Node
ICPG	Intelligence Community Policy Guidance
ICPM	Intelligence Community Policy Memorandum
IDC	Interagency Defector Committee
IED	Improvised Explosive Device
IHC	Information Handling Committee
IMINT	Imagery Intelligence
IMS	International Monitoring System
INC	Iraqi National Congress
INF	Intermediate Range Nuclear Forces
INFOSEC	Information Security
INMARSAT	International Maritime Satellite
INR	Bureau of Intelligence and Research
INSCOM	U.S. Army Intelligence and Security Command
INTELSAT	International Satellite
IPAC	Intelligence Center, Pacific

IPC	Intelligence Producers Council
IRC	Intelligence Requirement Committee
IRTPA	Intelligence Reform and Terrorism Prevention Act
ISA	Intelligence Support Activity
ISDAF	Integrated Sensor Data Analysis Facility
ISI	Inter-Services Intelligence
IUSS	Integrated Undersea Surveillance System
JAC	Joint Analysis Center
	Joint Intelligence Operations Center–Europe Analytical Center
JAEIC	Joint Atomic Energy Intelligence Center
JCS	Joint Chiefs of Staff
JICC	Joint Intelligence Community Council
JICCENT	Joint Intelligence Center, Central
JICPAC	Joint Intelligence Center Pacific
JIOC	Joint Intelligence Operations Center
JMIS	Joint Intelligence Centers/Joint Analysis Center
	Military Intelligence Program
JRAAC	Joint Research Analysis and Assessment Center
JRC	Joint Reconnaissance Center
JSOC	Joint Special Operations Command
JSpOC	Joint Space Operations Command
JTC-I	Joint Transformation Command–Intelligence
KGB	Committee for State Security (USSR)
LAKAM	Scientific Liaison Bureau (Israel)
LANTFLT	Atlantic Fleet
LATS	Large Aperture Tracking System
LAVR	Large Area Vulnerability Report
LEGAT	Legal Attaché
LNI	Library of National Intelligence
LSSC	Lincoln Space Surveillance Complex
MAD	Magnetic Anomaly Detector
MAGTF	Marine Air-Ground Task Force
MARFORLANT	Marine Corps Forces Atlantic
MASINT	Measurement and Signature Intelligence
MCE	MASINT Community Executive
MCIA	Marine Corps Intelligence Activity
MCIC	Marine Corps Intelligence Center
MIA	Military Intelligence Agency
MIB	Military Intelligence Brigade
MID	*Military Intelligence Digest*
MIFC, Atlantic	Maritime Intelligence Fusion Center, Atlantic
MIP	Military Intelligence Program
MIRA	Medium-Wave Infrared Array

MiTEx	Micro-Satellite Technology Experiment
MMW	Millimeter Wave
MOIS	Ministry of Intelligence and Security (Iran)
MOSS	Moron Optical Space Surveillance
MOTIF	Maui Optical Tracking and Identification Facility
MPAC	Medical and Psychological Analysis Center
MRBM	Medium-Range Ballistic Missile
MSI	Multispectral Imagery
MSIDS	MAGTF Secondary Imagery Dissemination System
MSIC	Missile and Space Intelligence Center
MSX	Midcourse Space Experiment
MTAC	NCIS Multiple Threat Alert Center
MTI	Moving Target Indicator
MTS	Multi-Spectral Targeting System
NA	Northern Alliance
NAIC	National Air Intelligence Center
NALT	Northern Alliance Liaison Team
NAS	Naval Air Station
NASA	National Aeronautics and Space Administration
NASP	Naval Activities Support Program
NATO	North Atlantic Treaty Organization
NAVMIC	Naval Maritime Intelligence Center
NAVSPASUR	Naval Space Surveillance System
NBACC	National Biodefense Analysis and Countermeasures Center
NCB	National Collection Branch
NCIS	Naval Criminal Investigative Service
NCIX	National Counterintelligence Executive
NCMI	National Center for Medical Intelligence
NCPC	National Counterproliferation Center
NCS	National Clandestine Service
NCTC	National Counterterrorism Center
NDS	NUDET Detection System
NED	National Endowment for Democracy
NEIS	National Emitter Intelligence Subcommittee
NETWARCOM	Naval Network Warfare Command
NEWSS	National Emitter, Weapons, and Space Subcommittee
NFAC	National Foreign Assessment Center
NFIB	National Foreign Intelligence Board
NFIP	National Foreign Intelligence Program
NGA	National Geospatial-Intelligence Agency
NGIC	National Ground Intelligence Center
NGO	Non-Governmental Organization
NHCD	National HUMINT Collection Directive
NHM	National HUMINT Manager

NIA	National Intelligence Authority
	National Imagery Agency
	Naval Intelligence Activity
NIB	National Intelligence Board
NIC	Naval Intelligence Command
	National Intelligence Council
NIC-C	National Intelligence Coordination Center
NICM	NIC Memorandum
NID	*National Intelligence Digest*
NIE	National Intelligence Estimate
NIIC	Narcotics Intelligence Issues Committee
NIMA	National Imagery and Mapping Agency
NIO	National Intelligence Officer
NIOC	Naval Information Operations Command
NIOD	Naval Information Operations Detachment
NIP	National Intelligence Program
NIPB	National Intelligence Production Board
NMD	National Monitoring Directorate (Iraq)
NMEC	National Media Exploitation Center
NMIC	National Maritime Intelligence Center
NNSA	National Nuclear Security Administration
NOA	Notice of Arrival
NOC	Non-Official Cover
NOFORN	Not Releasable to Foreign Nationals
NOIC	Navy Operational Intelligence Center
	Nimitz Operational Intelligence Center
NOL	NCTC Online
NOPF	Naval Ocean Processing Facility
NORAD	North American Aerospace Defense Command
NORTHCOM	Northern Command
NPIC	National Photographic Interpretation Center
NRD	National Resources Division
NRO	National Reconnaissance Office
NROC	National Resettlement Operations Center
NRP	National Reconnaissance Program
NSA	National Security Agency
NSC	National Security Council
NSCID	National Security Council Intelligence Directive
NSD	National Security Directive
NSDD	National Security Decision Directive
NSGC	Naval Security Group Command
NSO	Nevada Site Office
NSOC	National Security Operations Center

NSPD	National Security Presidential Directive
NSPG	National Security Planning Group
NSR	National Security Review
NSRL	National SIGINT Requirements List
NSSD	National Security Study Directives
NTIC	Naval Technical Intelligence Center
NTOC	NSA/CSS Threat Operations Center
NUDET	Nuclear Detonation
OACMI	Office of the Assistant Chief of Staff for Missile Intelligence
OBST	Operations Base Stuttgart
OCMC	Overhead Collection Management Center
OD&E	Office of Development and Engineering
OFAC	Office of Foreign Assets Control
OFCO	Offensive Counterintelligence Operations
OIA	Office of Intelligence and Analysis
OIR	Office of Intelligence Resources
OIS	Office of Intelligence Support
OMB	Office of Management and Budget
ONE	Office of National Estimates
ONI	Office of Naval Intelligence
ONIR	Overhead Non-Imaging Infrared
ONSI	Office of National Security Intelligence
OPIR	Overhead Persistent Infrared
ORCON	Originator Controlled
ORS	Operationally Responsive Space
ORTT	Office of Resources, Trade and Technology
OSA	Office of Systems Applications
OSC	Open Sources Committee; Open Source Center
OSD	Office of the Secretary of Defense
OSI	Office of Scientific Intelligence
OSINT	Open Source Intelligence
OSO	Office of SIGINT Operations
OSS	Office of Strategic Services
OTA	Office of Terrorism Analysis
OTC	Office of Technical Collection
OTFI	Office of Terrorism and Financial Intelligence
OTI	Office of Transnational Issues
OTS	Office of Technical Service
OTSTI	Office of Transnational Security and Technology Issues
OWTP	Office of Weapons, Technology, and Proliferation
PACFAST	Forward Area Support Team, Pacific
PACOM	Pacific Command
PAMIFC	Pacific Maritime Intelligence Fusion Center

PARCS	Perimeter Acquisition Radar Characterization System
PCB	Planning and Coordination Group
PD	Presidential Directive
PDB	*President's Daily Brief*
PDD	Presidential Decision Directive
PFLP-GC	Popular Front for the Liberation of Palestine—General Command
PIBS	Presidential Intelligence Briefing System
PKK	Kurdish Worker's Party
PNIO	Priority National Intelligence Objectives
POW	Prisoner of War
PRC	People's Republic of China
PRD	Presidential Review Directive
PRM	Presidential Review Memoranda
RADEC	Radiation Detection
RASA	Radionuclide Aerosol Sampler/Analyzer
RAW	Research and Analysis Wing (India)
RDI	Remodeling Defense Intelligence
RDT&E	Research, Development, Test, and Evaluation
ROD	Reconnaissance Operations Division
RPV	Remote Piloted Vehicle
RRS	Remote Relay System
RSV	RESERVE Control System
RSVC	Reconnaissance Satellite Vulnerability Computer program
RV	Re-entry vehicle
SABER	Surface Branch for Evaluation and Reporting
SAC	Strategic Air Command
SALT	Strategic Arms Limitation Treaty
SATRAN	Satellite Reconnaissance Advanced Notice
SBIRS	Space-Based Infrared System
SBSS	Space-Based Surveillance System
SCE	Service Cryptologic Element
SCI	Sensitive Compartmented Information
SFIP	Special Field Intelligence Programs
SFS	Seismic Field Subsystem
SCI	Sensitive Compartmented Information
SCS	Special Collection Service
SDI	Strategic Defense Initiative
SDIE	Special Defense Intelligence Estimate
SDS	Satellite Data System
SEIB	Senior Executive Intelligence Brief
SI	Special Intelligence
SIGINT	Signals Intelligence

SIPRI	Stockholm International Peace Research Institute
SIRVES	SIGINT Requirements Validation and Evaluation Subcommittee
SNIE	Special National Intelligence Estimate
SOCM	Sense of the Community Memo
SOFAR	Sound Fixing and Ranging
SOI	Space Object Identification
SORS	SIGINT Overhead Reconnaissance Subcommittee
SOSUS	Sound Surveillance System
SOUTHCOM	Southern Command
SPACECOM	U.S. Space Command
SPEAR	Strike Project and Anti-air Warfare Research Division
SRO	Sensitive Reconnaissance Operations
SSA	Space Situational Awareness
SSC	Space Surveillance Center
SSN	Space Surveillance Network
SST	Strategic Support Team
SSTS	Space Surveillance and Tracking System
STRATCOM	Strategic Command
SVR	Foreign Intelligence Service (Russia)
	Satellite Vulnerability Report
SWB	Summary of World Broadcasts
SWIFT	Society for Worldwide Interbank Financial Telecommunications
SWINT	Safe Window Intelligence
SWORD	Submarine Warfare Operations Research Division
SWS	Space Warning Squadron
SYERS	SENIOR YEAR Electro-Optical Reconnaissance System
TAD	Terrorism Analysis Division
TCP	Tactical Cryptologic Program
TDRSS	Tracking and Data Relay Satellite System
TELINT	Telemetry Intelligence
TIARA	Tactical Intelligence and Related Activities
TIDE	Terrorist Identities Datamart Environment
TK	Talent Keyhole
TPED	Tasking, Processing, Exploitation, and Dissemination
TRADEX	Target Resolution and Discrimination Experiment
TRANSCOM	Transportation Command
TSD	Technical Services Division
TTIC	Technology Transfer Intelligence Committee
TWD	Terrorism Warning Division
UAV	Unmanned Aerial Vehicle
UCP	Unified Command Plan
UCS	Unified Cryptologic System
UFAC	Underground Facilities Analysis Center

UFO	UHF Follow-On
UGS	Unattended Ground Sensor
UMS	Unattended MASINT Sensors
UN	United Nations
USACOM	U.S. Atlantic Command
USAFE	United States Air Forces Europe
USD(I)	Under Secretary of Defense for Intelligence
USIB	United States Intelligence Board
USJFCOM	U.S. Joint Forces Command
USLANTCOM	U.S. Atlantic Command
USSID	U.S. Signals Intelligence Directive
USSOCOM	U.S. Special Operations Command
VHF	Very High Frequency
VRK	Very Restricted Knowledge
WINPAC	Weapons Intelligence, Nonproliferation, and Arms Control Center
WMD	Weapons of Mass Destruction
WSSAG	Weapons and Space Systems Advisory Group
WSSIC	Weapons and Space Systems Intelligence Committee

INDEX